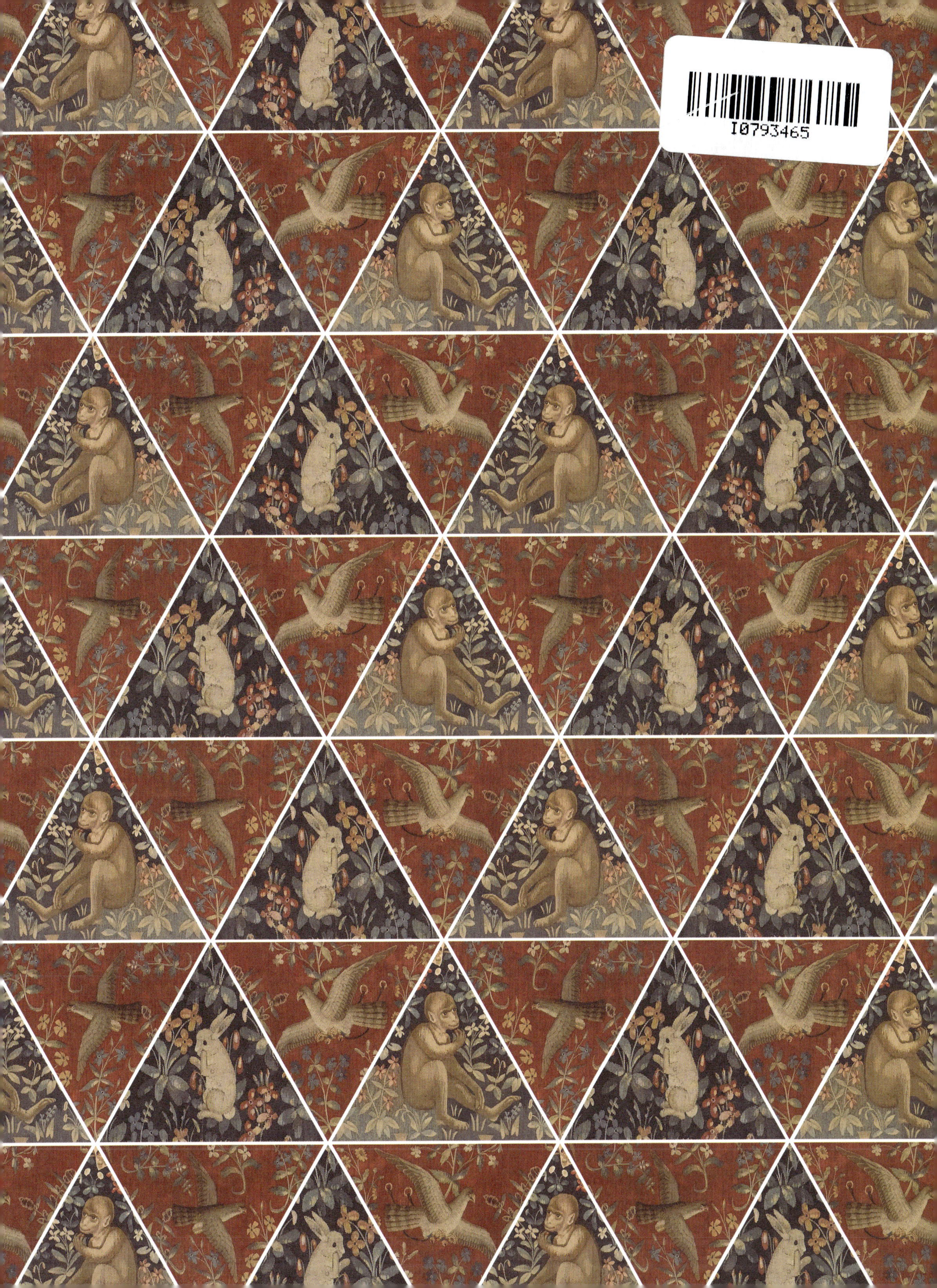

FROM MINOR TO MAJOR

The Minor Arts in Medieval Art History

THE INDEX OF CHRISTIAN ART

Occasional Papers · XIV

FROM MINOR TO MAJOR

The Minor Arts in Medieval Art History

EDITED BY COLUM HOURIHANE

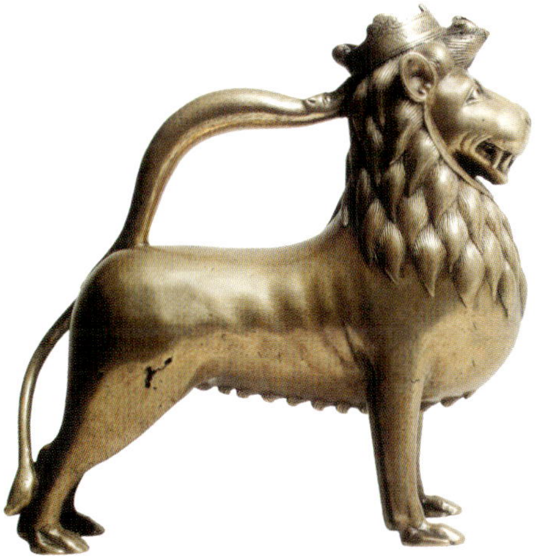

INDEX OF CHRISTIAN ART
DEPARTMENT OF ART AND ARCHÆOLOGY
PRINCETON UNIVERSITY
in association with
PENN STATE UNIVERSITY PRESS

MM·XII

In the Nation's Service
and in the Service of all Nations

DISTRIBUTED BY
PENNSYLVANIA STATE UNIVERSITY PRESS
820 NORTH UNIVERSITY DRIVE, USB 1, SUITE C
UNIVERSITY PARK, PENNSYLVANIA 16802

ISBN 978-0-9837537-1-1

*

BOOKS PUBLISHED BY THE INDEX OF CHRISTIAN ART
PRINCETON UNIVERSITY
ARE PRINTED ON ACID-FREE PAPER AND MEET THE
REQUIREMENTS FOR PERMANENCE AND
DURABILITY OF ♾ ANSI/NISO Z39.48-1992
(PERMANENCE OF PAPER)

CONTENTS

PREFACE

THE INDEX OF CHRISTIAN ART celebrates the ninety-fifth anniversary of its foundation this year. It continues to play an important role in medieval art-historical studies, and, with the advent of computerization, it has found a new audience and is more widely used than ever before. It is particularly rewarding to see how the Index is now being used in the classroom as well as in the private study throughout the world. It has not changed its mission, however, and it continues to support and direct iconographical research in the medieval world as it never did before.

It was with excitement that we interrupted our recent series of conferences devoted to the major stylistic movements of the Middle Ages to look instead at the minor arts. Whether we wish to admit it or not, the medieval arts have been divided into a primary and secondary division since man first began to look at art and it is also not unexpected that much of our research and attention has been devoted to the former. In looking at this subject we have attempted to cover all the media represented in the Index itself, which treats all with an equal importance. Much dissension still exists as to what constitutes the minor arts, and over the two days of this conference we discussed such factors as size, preciousness, value, workmanship, etc., in an effort to understand why these arts are sometimes overlooked.* We aimed to look at why such arts were relegated to a minor role both in our studies and in terms of popular appreciation. We saw how some of these arts were now being more fully integrated into general studies and what means were used to achieve this. It was a particularly stimulating two days and if it accomplished nothing more it made us aware of the need to evaluate all, and not just what has traditionally been deemed most important in terms of scale or research.

All of the authors attempted to meet the needs of the conference. All were asked to deal specifically with particular media and to give a historiographical perspective as to why they felt their subjects have been considered minor in the past, and what, if anything, has been undertaken to correct that. It was interesting to see so many scholars refusing to believe that their fields of study were anything but the most pivotal and important in the field of medieval art history! Many of the authors made their arguments through case studies justifying their important

* The conference was organized by The Index of Christian Art and held on the 17th and 18th of March in 2011.

status alongside a history of their field. New research has always been the interest of the Index and it is good to see so many of the authors answering that need.

Organizing and running an Index conference involves many people and I would like to thank everybody who contributed in any way towards making it an enjoyable and scholarly event. Our sessions were impeccably moderated by Naomi Kline, Giles Constable, and Michael Curschmann and my thanks go to them. Once again I am particularly grateful to the Council of the Humanities in Princeton University for their generous support and in particular to Gideon Rosen and Carol Rigolot.

I wish to thank all of my colleagues in the Index of Christian Art who gave sage advice and practical help. As usual, we were fortunate to have the assistance of Michelle Horgan from the Conference and Events Services in Princeton University as well as the support of Marilyn Hansen from Visual Resources, Department of Art and Archaeology, and my thanks go to both.

The book that you now see before you results from the magisterial eye and scholarly overview of Mark Argetsinger, who has been responsible for copy-editing, designing, indexing, and steering this volume from paper to print. It gives me great pleasure to acknowledge his help and to thank him for all his invaluable work.

—COLUM HOURIHANE
Director, Index of Christian Art

NOTES ON THE CONTRIBUTORS

David S. Areford is Associate Professor of Art History at the University of Massachusetts, Boston. A specialist in late medieval European devotional art, much of his research has been focused on early printmaking. His research and teaching interests include the reception of images in terms of the visual, physical, emotional, psychological, and spatial dynamics of the viewing experience, as well as the role of the body, gender, and sexuality in contemporary visual culture. He was a co-curator of the exhibition *Origins of European Printmaking: Fifteenth-Century Woodcuts and Their Public* (National Gallery of Art, Washington, D.C., and Germanisches Nationalmuseum, Nuremberg, Germany, 2005–2006) and curator of the exhibition *Queer Eye* (Harbor Art Gallery, University of Massachusetts, Boston, 2006). He has been the recipient of a Fulbright Fellowship for research in Germany, as well as Postdoctoral Curatorial Fellowship at the National Gallery of Art in Washington, D.C. He is currently a director on the board of the International Center of Medieval Art. He is the author of the book *The Viewer and the Printed Image in Late Medieval Europe* (2010). His essay "Multiplying the Sacred: The Fifteenth-Century Woodcut as Reproduction, Surrogate, Simulation," was published in *The Woodcut in Fifteenth-Century Europe*, edited by Peter Parshall (2009). He is the co-editor (with Nina A. Rowe) of *Excavating the Medieval Image: Manuscripts, Artists, Audiences* (2004), and co-author (with Peter Parshall, Rainer Schoch, Peter Schmidt, and Richard Field) of *Origins of European Printmaking: Fifteenth-Century Woodcuts and Their Public* (2005). His next book project is preliminarily titled *Embracing Vision: The Maulbronn Altarpiece and Late Medieval Piety*.

Brigitte Bedos-Rezak is Professor in the History Department at The Institute of Fine Arts, New York University, and one of the foremost experts on medieval seals. She received her Ph.D. from the École Nationale des Chartes (Sorbonne) in 1977. After graduating she became the curator of the Seal Department at the Archives Nationales in Paris. She joined the History Department at SUNY, Stony Brook, in 1985 and stayed there for two years before becoming a visiting Associate Professor in the History Department at the University of Maryland, College Park. It was in 2002 that she assumed her current post. Throughout her distinguished career she has received many awards and honors. She has been a visiting professor at the École des Hautes Études en Sciences Sociales (1995) and the École Nationale des Chartes (2001). She was also a member of the Institute for Advanced Study in Princeton in 1996–1997. She has numerous books and articles to her credit. Amongst her publications are *Form and Order in Medieval France: Studies in Social and Quantitative Sigillography* (1993); *Corpus des sceaux français du Moyen Âge*, tome 1er: *Les sceaux de villes* (1980); *La châtellenie de Montmorency des origines à 1368* (1980); and *When Ego was Imago: Signs of Identity in the Middle Ages* (2010).

Frédérick Billiet is Professor of Music in the University of Paris-Sorbonne. A specialist in medieval music, he is also director of Misericordia International, an association that encourages researches on medieval choir-stalls. He is also founder and director of an online inventory of medieval stalls (1300–1600) known as *Musicastallis*. He is joint manager of the publication series entitled *Profane Arts in the Middle Ages* (Brepols) and the author of numerous articles and publications. Amongst these are *Concert imaginaire dans les stalles de la cathédrale d'Amiens*, with Gilbert Lefeuvre (1982); *Rock à la clé, guide théorique* (1989); *De la pub pour Mozart* (1991); *Les stalles de la Cathédrale de Rouen: histoire et iconographie*, co-authored with Elaine C. Block and the with the assistance of Sylvie Bethmont-Gallerand (2003); *Bible de bois du Moyen Age: Bible et liturgie dans les stalles médiévales*, co-edited with Jean-Michel Matz (2003); and *Profane Images in Marginal Arts of the Middle Ages: Proceedings of the VI Biennial Colloquium, Misericordia International, organized by and presided over by Malcolm Jones, University of Sheffield, 18–21 July 2003*, edited by Elaine C. Block with the assistance of Frédéric Billiet, Sylvie Bethmont-Gallerand, and Paul Hardwick (2009). His most recent publication is *De l'interprétation du patrimoine musical à l'historiographie*, co-authored with Barbara Haggh (2011).

Paul Binski is Professor of the History of Medieval Art in the University of Cambridge where he has been since 1996. A specialist in the Gothic medieval arts of Western Europe, many of his publications and much of his research has focused on England. An expert on manuscript studies, he has also published widely on panel and wall painting, sculpture, architecture, and patronage. A Fellow of the British Academy since 2007, he is also a corresponding member of the Medieval Academy since 2008. He was Slade Professor at Oxford University for 2006–2007 and is also a Fellow of Caius College and a Syndic of the Fitzwilliam Museum. He has lectured widely and has delivered the British Academy Aspects of Art Lecture in 2001 as well as the Paul Mellon Lectures for 2002–2003 held at the National Gallery, London, under the auspices of the Paul Mellon Center for Studies in British Art, Yale University. Amongst his many publications are *The Painted Chamber at Westminster* (1986); *Westminster Abbey and the Plantagenets* (1995); and *Becket's Crown: Art and Imagination in Gothic England 1170–1300* (2004). He has also co-edited *The Westminster Retable: History, Technique, Conservation* (2009). His most recent publication is *Western Illuminated Manuscripts: A Catalogue of the Collection in Cambridge University Library* (2011).

John Cherry is Keeper Emeritus of Medieval and Modern Europe in the British Museum, a post he held from 1964 until his retirement in 2002. During his career he specialized in medieval archaeology and art and wrote many articles on medieval jewelry, seals and seal matrices, metal, and leatherwork. His first article on medieval jewelry, in 1969, was on the white-enamelled Dunstable Swan Jewel. He is currently a member of the Treasure Valuation Committee, which values items of gold and silver that are to be acquired by British museums. Amongst his many publications are "Leather" in *English Medieval Industries: Craftsmen, Techniques, Products*, edited by John Blair and Nigel Ramsay (1991); *Medieval Goldsmiths* (1992); and "Containers for Agnus Dei" in *Through a Glass Brightly: Studies in Byzantine and Medieval Art and Archaeology Presented to David Buckton*, edited by Chris Entwistle (2003). His latest work is *The Holy Thorn Reliquary* (2010), a study of the remarkable piece of white-enamelled goldsmith's work commissioned by the Duc de Berry around 1400.

Michael W. Cothren is Professor of Art History at Swarthmore College and an authority on Gothic art and architecture, with a particular expertise in stained glass, especially the stained glass of France and the glazing programs of the abbey of Saint-Denis and cathedrals of Beauvais and Rouen. He received his B.A. from Vanderbilt University and his M.A. and Ph.D. from Columbia University. He is also the consultative curator of medieval stained glass at the Glencairn Museum in Bryn Athyn, Pennsylvania, and is currently writing a catalogue of that collection for the international Corpus Vitrearum project. A more recent research interest is the fetish carvers of the Zuni Pueblo in New Mexico. From this work, he is in the process of developing a new course on Native American art. Amongst his many publications are *Art: A Brief History* (2009) and *Art History* (2011), both co-authored with Marilyn Stokstad; *Picturing the Celestial City: The Medieval Stained Glass of Beauvais Cathedral* (2006); and "The Recollection of the Past is the Promise of the Future: The Medieval Heritage of Philadelphia's Sacred Windows" in *Stained Glass in Catholic Philadelphia*, edited by Jean M. Fransworth, Carmen R. Croce, and Joseph E. Chorpenning (2002).

Thomas E. Dale received his Ph.D. in 1990 from Johns Hopkins University for a study on "The Crypt of the Basilica Patriarcale at Aquileia: Its Place in the Art and History of the Upper Adriatic," under the supervision of William Tronzo. He taught at Columbia University (1990–1999) before moving to his current position as Chair of the Department of Art History at the University of Wisconsin, Madison. He has received many awards and honors throughout his career. He was a member of the School of Historical Studies at the Institute for Advanced Study, Princeton, between

1997–1998. He contributed to and also edited, with John Mitchell, *Shaping Sacred Space and Institutional Identity in Romanesque Mural Painting: Essays in Honour of Otto Demus* (2004). He has also published *Relics, Prayer, and Politics in Medieval Venetia: Romanesque Painting in the Crypt of Aquileia Cathedral* (1997), and is currently working on a volume tentatively titled *Romanesque Corporealities: Sculpture, Emodiment, the Senses and Religious Experience in as Western Europe, c. 1050–1215.*

Sharon E. J. Gerstel is Professor of Byzantine Art and Archaeology at the University of California, Los Angeles, where she has been since 2005. An energetic scholar who is both an archaeologist and art historian, her work has focused on the relationship of ritual and art. As an archaeologist she has been involved in many excavations in Greece, both as a field director and as a ceramics specialist. She is also a member of the Governing Board of the Byzantine Studies Association of North America. Her comprehensive study of the medieval village of Panakton appeared in *Hesperia* in 2003; other archaeological publications of hers have appeared also in *Hesperia* as well as in several edited volumes. She has lectured widely on both sides of the Atlantic and has edited several volumes, including *A Lost Art Rediscovered: The Architectural Ceramics of Byzantium*, co-edited with J. Lauffenburger (2001); *Thresholds of the Sacred: Art Historical, Archaeological, Liturgical, and Theological Views on Religious Screens, East and West* (2007); and *Approaching the Holy Mountain: Art and Liturgy at St. Catherine's Monastery in the Sinai*, co-edited with Robert S. Nelson (2010). Her first book, *Beholding the Sacred Mysteries*, was published as a CAA monograph in 1999. She is currently editing the papers of the 2009 Dumbarton Oaks Symposium that she chaired, *Morea: The Land and its People in the Aftermath of the Fourth Crusade.* Her current book project, *Landscapes of the Village: The Devotional Life and Setting of the Late Byzantine Peasant*, is under contract with Cambridge University Press.

Cynthia Hahn is Professor of Art History at Hunter College and The Graduate Center in New York. She received her Ph.D. from the Johns Hopkins University in 1982 as well as her M.A. from the University of Chicago. She has previously held teaching positions at Florida State University where she was Gulnar K. Bosch Professor of Art History, the University of Chicago, the University of Delaware, and the University of Michigan. Her work has appeared in *Art History*, *Art Bulletin*, *Gesta*, *Speculum*, and many other journals and collections. Her books include a study on the Hannover manuscript of the lives of Saints Kilian and Margaret, *Passio Kiliani, Ps. Theotimus, Passio Margaretae, Orationes: vollständige Faksimile-Ausgabe im Originalformat des Codex MS. I 189 aus dem Besitz der Niedersächsischen Landesbibliothek Hannover*, with commentary by Cynthia Hahn, introduction, transcription, and translation by Hans Immel (1988); and *Portrayed on the Heart: Narrative Effect in Pictorial Lives of the Saints from the Tenth through the Thirteenth Century* (2001). She has served on the boards of the ICMA, CASVA, and CAA online reviews, where she has also been an editor. Her current projects include a book-length essay on reliquaries from early Christianity to the sack of 1204.

Harald Wolter-von dem Knesebeck has been Director of the Institute of the History of Art and Archaeology at the University of Bonn since 2010. Before that he was Professor of Art History at the Institute of the History of Art at the University of Bonn, where he had a particular focus on the arts of the medieval and Byzantine worlds. He received his Ph.D. in 1998 in art history from the University of Göttingen for a study entitled *Der Elisabethpsalter in Cividale del Friuli. Buchmalerei für den Thüringer Landgrafenhof zu Beginn des 13. Jahrhunderts* (*The Psalter of Saint Elisabeth: Book Illumination Made for the Court of the Thuringian Landgraves at the Beginning of the 13th Century*), which was subsequently published in Denkmäler deutscher Kunst, hg. vom Deutschen Verein für Kunstwissenschaft, in 2001. After that he received his Habilitation in the history of art at the University of Kassel in 2006 for a study entitled *Bilder für wirt, wirtin und gast. Studien zur profanen Wandmalerei von 1200 bis 1500.* Much of his research has focused on profane and Christian art and iconography, medieval manuscript illumination, and wall paintings, especially in Germany and Italy, as well as goldsmiths' works and bronze castings. One of his most recent publications is *Das Mainzer Evangeliar. Strahlende Bilder-Worte in Gold* (2007).

JOS KOLDEWEIJ is Professor in Medieval Art History at the Radboud University, Nijmegen, where he has been since 1993. He studied art history at Utrecht University, where he also received his Ph.D. in 1985 for a study entitled "Der gude sente Servas. Sint Servatius en de Servatiana: een onderzoek naar de beeldvorming rond een heilige in de Middeleeuwen." He has curated several exhibitions in the Noordbrabants Museum at 's-Hertogenbosch, amongst which are *Zilver uit 's-Hertogenbosch* (1985) and *In Buscoducis* (1990). In 2001 he was guest curator for the exhibition *Jheronimus Bosch* in Museum Boijmans Van Beuningen, Rotterdam, and in 2006/2007 for the exhibition *Faith & Fortune: Medieval Badges from Flanders*, in Bruges, which was held at the Bruggemuseum, Gruuthuse. Much of his research has focused on religious and profane pilgrim badges from the late Middle Ages, but other areas of interest include late medieval art in general, art and devotion, and the applied arts, mainly in north-western Europe. Amongst his many publications are "Pilgrim Badges Painted in Manuscripts: A North Netherlandish Example" in *Masters and Miniatures: Proceedings of the Congress on Medieval Manuscript Illumination in the Northern Netherlands, Utrecht, 10–13 December 1989*, edited by Koert van der Horst and Johann-Christian Klamt (1991).

WELLEDA MULLER received her Ph.D. in art history in 2009, *magna cum laude*, at the University of Burgundy under the direction of Daniel Russo for a study entitled "The Art of the *Huchiers*, Restricted to Liturgical Furniture of the Choir in 15–16th Century Burgundy, Flanders and the Rhine-Meuse." She is currently a researcher in the department of Patrimoines et Langages Musicaux at the University of Paris-Sorbonne. She also teaches medieval studies at the University of Burgundy (Dijon), where she is a junior lecturer in Medieval Art History. She teaches art history as well at the Université pour Tous of Puisaye-Forterre, and art history and the philosophy of art at the École Normale Catholique Blomet in Paris. She is secretary to the association Misericordia International, as well as editor of the database *Musicastallis*, and general editor to the publication series *Profane Arts of the Middle Ages* (Brepols). Her own areas of research include the profane arts, the relationships between the Middle Ages and the Renaissance, liturgical furniture, choir-stalls, rood screens, altars, and the arts of the Grand Duchy of Burgundy.

ALAN M. STAHL is curator of numismatics at Princeton University where he has been since 2004. Prior to moving to Princeton, he was curator of Medieval Coins and Medals at The American Numismatic Society (1980–2000). A renowned scholar, he has also taught at Rutgers University (1977–1978), Università di Venezia (1987–1988), University of Michigan, Ann Arbor (2000–2001), Rice University (2001–2002), and the University of Notre Dame (2002). He received his Ph.D. in history from the University of Pennsylvania in 1977. Co-Director of The Michael of Rhodes Project at The Dibner Institute for the History of Science and Technology at MIT from 2002, he has also received many awards and honors, amongst which are a John Simon Guggenheim Foundation Fellowship in 2008 and The Royal Numismatic Society Medal in 2010. Amongst his many publications are *The Merovingian Coinage of the Region of Metz* (1982); *The Venetian Tornesello: A Medieval Colonial Coinage* (1985); *The Medal in America*, editor (1988); *The Documents of Angelo de Cartura and Donato Fontanella: Venetian Notaries in Fourteenth-Century Crete*, editor (2000); *The Book of Michael of Rhodes*, edited with Pamela O. Long and David McGee, 3 vols. (2009); and *Money on Paper: Bank Notes and Related Graphic Arts from the Collections of Vsevolod Onyshkevych and Princeton University* (2010). He is currently working on a monograph entitled *The Nexus of Wealth and Power in Medieval Venice*.

ALICIA WALKER is Assistant Professor of Medieval Art at Bryn Mawr College. Her primary fields of research include cross-cultural artistic interaction in the medieval world from the ninth to thirteenth centuries and gender issues in the art and material culture of Byzantium. Her first monograph, *The Emperor and the World: Exotic Elements and the Imaging of Byzantine Imperial Power*, is currently in press. She is co-editor (with Amanda Luyster) of the essay collection *Negotiating the Secular in Medieval Art: Christian, Islamic, Buddhist* (2009), and is currently co-editing (with Heather Grossman) a special issue of the journal *Medieval Encounters*, entitled

Mechanisms of Exchange: Transmission, Scale, and Interaction in the Arts and Architecture of the Medieval Mediterranean (to appear in 2012). She has published essays on topics relating to medieval inter-cultural artistic transmission, the role of women in Byzantine art and culture, and the function and meaning of early Byzantine marriage jewelry. Her work has appeared in journals including *Muqarnas*, *Gesta*, *Ars Orientalis*, *The Art Bulletin*, and *The Medieval History Journal.*

Laura Weigert is Associate Professor in Art History at Rutgers University in New Jersey. She received her Ph.D. from Northwestern University. She also studied at the University of Tübingen and the École des Hautes Études en Sciences Sociales, Paris. She has taught at the University of Nantes and the École Nationale des Ponts et Chaussées and was Associate Professor of Art History and Humanities at Reed College before joining the Rutgers faculty in September 2006. An expert on Northern Renaissance art, her research focuses on the interaction between visual images and their architectural and ritual settings in the fifteenth and sixteenth centuries and includes the study of manuscript illumination, prints, panel painting, and textiles. Amongst her many publications are *Weaving Sacred Stories: French Choir Tapestries and the Performance of Clerical Identity* (2004); "'Vellum Templi': Painted Cloths of the Passion and the Making of the Lenten Ritual in Reims" in *Studies in Iconography* (2003); and "La Tenture de choeur de la vie de saint Etienne dans la cathédrale d'Auxerre" in *Histoire de Saint Etienne: La Tenture de Choeur de la Cathedrale d'Auxerre*, co-edited with Micheline Durand (2000). She is currently working on a project, "Images in Action: The Theatricality of Franco-Flemish Art," which hopes to explore the complex relationship between large-scale visual imagery and theatrical performance in late medieval France and Flanders.

Kim W. Woods is Senior Lecturer in the Open University in Great Britain. In October 1980 she began a two year M.Phil. course in fifteenth-century art at the Courtauld Institute, University of London, and her doctoral thesis, entitled "Netherlandish Carved Wooden Altarpieces of the 15th and early 16th Centuries in Britain," was submitted eight years later in 1988. The main focus of her research is fifteenth- and sixteenth-century Netherlandish sculpture, and she has published widely in the subject. She is currently working on a study of alabaster sculpture in the Netherlands in the early fifteenth century, and much of her study has focused on the work of the anonymous alabaster carver known as the Master of Rimini. She has contributed to the exhibition catalogue *Gothic Glory: Art in England c. 1400–1547* (2003). A Fellow of the Society of Antiquaries, she has lectured widely. Amongst her publications are *Making Renaissance Art* (2006); *Imported Images* (2007); *Viewing Renaissance Art* (2007), which she co-edited with C. M. Richardson and A. Lymberopoulou; and *Renaissance Art Reconsidered: An Anthology of Sources*, (2007), which she co-edited with Carol M. Richardson and Michael W. Franklin.

INTRODUCTION

OF COURSE it would be good to examine the minor arts at any time, but now seems a particularly propitious time to do so. Medieval art-historical study has changed over the last twenty or so years and it is time to re-evaluate where we are. Although there have been a number of essays on individual media, which are referenced in the various essays in this collection, no single study of the minor *vis-à-vis* the major arts has been published for well over thirty years.[1] Many of the authors in this volume highlight the fact that no such division as minor and major existed in the medieval arts. Others accept a division between major and minor and then stress the primary nature of their own material; a third group accepts that such a division existed in earlier research but maintains that it is no longer valid. It is clearly a contentious issue that is not going to be resolved within the covers of this collection. It is beneficial, however, to see how such a division was first created and, furthermore, to look at what the future holds for fields that might have been somewhat tangential in the past. Although such a division existed in earlier medieval research, I believe that it has been slightly eroded over time in certain media. In our more holistic modern approach to study, we have integrated some areas of research that were not included in the past, but it is clear that some neglected media still exist. Naturally, the lessening of the major-minor divisions has happened with the advent of greater information and we can see how the medieval mind did not work with such rigid divisions. Modern study has had a far more realistic approach and the hard edges of old-fashioned connoisseurship have been justifiably softened.

It is usually Vasari who is credited as the first to formally assert the primary nature of architecture, painting, and sculpture in his *Lives of the Most Eminent Painters, Sculptors, and Architects*, which was first published in 1568.[2] Vasari's belief was that these "primary" media resulted from intelligence and genius, whereas the other media required a lower level of thought and skill to produce. Even though this division was initially applied to Italian art, it was not long before it gained more widespread currency. The other arts, such as ivory carving, glass, enamels, and goldsmiths' work, were lumped together into a secondary group. This secondary group took on pejorative associations, especially in the eighteenth and nineteenth centuries, as being more artisanal in nature rather than the work of genius. Other labels have been used over time to describe these arts—we have spoken of them as decorative, applied, ornamental, luxury, sumptuous, or even as the mechanical arts. Some of these labels may go some way towards defining these arts in terms of purpose rather than status, but they are still tinged with the implication of being less than primary. The whole story is not clear-cut, as many of these essays will show. For example, Alicia Walker, in her fine study on decorative art in Byzantium, has shown how the field has benefitted from such marginalization, as it was later championed by the Arts and Crafts Movement. She shows how the ornamental, functional, and material aspects of these works should be seen as the basis for insightful interpretations.

There are certain underlying principles that are common to most of these essays, which have been used to explain these arts' minor standing in art-historical

1. One of the most recent examinations, which unfortunately has not been published, was a conference session organized by The International Center of Medieval Art and held at the College Art Association Conference in 2007. This was organized by Brigitte Buettner of Smith College and titled *The Coming of Age of Medieval "Minor" Arts.* The literature on the minor arts of the Byzantine world is far more impressive and many studies have been undertaken on different media, most of which are referenced in essays in this volume.

2. Giorgio Vasari, *Lives of the Most Eminent Painters, Sculptors, and Architects.* Abridged from the translation by Gaston DuC. De-Vere. Edited with an introduction by Robert N. Linscott (New York, 1959).

appreciation. These include the pivotal concepts of size, preciousness, materiality, portability, production, function, and uniqueness, or lack of it, that all came into play when the minor arts were first designated as such. All or some of these factors have been seen as playing significant roles in why the minor arts have been so classified. Is importance related to the size, or workmanship, or genius of a work of art? Some authors have questioned the use of decoration, the function or purpose of these works, their fabric or materiality, or the lack of the creators' names as distinguishing elements that define the minor arts. Paul Binski, in his encyclopaedic survey of the arts of painting, highlights our need, as well as the need of the medieval viewer, to look at these works in terms of the sentiments evoked by their workmanship and scale—their *magnificentia*—rather than looking in terms of minor or major. This is a theme that is repeated throughout this collection and is worthy of further exploration. It is also clear from the historiographical analyses that accompany these essays that the museum world played a pivotal role in leading the viewer as well as the historian along a pre-determined path as to how such works should be viewed and appreciated—all of which has changed in the last twenty or so years.

There are many who now see no justification in even looking at the term minor, as they believe that it is no longer valid, and of course this is explored in this collection of essays. There are others who have written about sub-fields within their own divisions and shown that even within sculpture or painting there is a further hierarchy of major arts that have not been universally examined. Are manuscript paintings or frescoes viewed as less in stature than panel painting? Is wooden sculpture or that in bone on a hierarchically lower footing than stone figures carved in the round? Paul Binski raises the issue of works that are multi-media—part sculpture and part painting—and what relegates them to one field or the other. Does it depend on which artist had the greater input or which part of the work is larger in scale, or does it depend on what we call the work—a carving, or a book, or an ivory? Do criteria other than those proposed by Vasari come into play? Do we, for example, look at the impact a work has on us before we relegate it to a division? What are the points of intersection between the major and the minor? Tom Dale is the first author to point out that such designations as major or minor can change over time. In his historiographical review he shows how wall paintings and manuscript studies have changed status, due largely to their state of preservation and their more thorough documentation. While agreeing that the terms were once valid, there is also the recurring wish in most of these essays to now abolish these divisions and to adopt a more holistic approach. Minor in this volume is used to refer not just to individual media outside of architecture, sculpture, and painting, but also to those areas of medieval studies that have been neglected, such as the secular arts, which are dealt with in this collection by Harald Wolter-von dem Knesebeck. Of course these are minor not in terms of scale or media, but by virtue of their being understudied and neglected. They have been relegated to a backwater when compared to the sacred arts of the Middle Ages and the question is posed as to why this happened. It is clear that a historiographical assessment is critical to see how or why the various arts came to be classified as minor in the first place, and this is beautifully demonstrated in Sharon Gerstel and Thomas Dale's articles. They trace the subtle vagaries of time and connoisseurship, especially in the nineteenth century, that have led to some of the media being seen as minor. All of these essays will make us more aware of the need to abandon such divisions and to incorporate as much data as we can into our studies to fully understand the medieval world.

The opening essay by Paul Binksi offers an insightful and succinct introduction to the whole subject of minor versus major, with Paul looking at different criteria before focusing on a case study with which he is more than familiar, the Westminster Retable. This work forms a perfect *exemplum* with which to study the whole nature of minor. He examines it from such different perspectives as collaboration in terms of Anglo-French origins, iconography, and material, and under such concepts as invention, patronage, makers, responsibility, design, and taste. It is a finely paced holistic approach. Very little is excluded in Paul's study of the relationship between wall painting in the northern and southern worlds. His whole approach aims to look at the points of intersection between what is considered minor and major, and northern and southern. Manuscript painting, for example, may be minor in scale but is considered major in other areas and certainly in the amount of research that has been undertaken.

The second essay in this collection looks at color in terms of minor or major. Needless to say, this novel approach traverses the boundaries of both divisions. In his essay, Thomas Dale does not categorize but seeks to build bridges between different media—through the use of color in particular. Tom believes that wall paintings have been accepted as major by virtue of their sheer scale but they have also occasionally been assimilated into the minor arts. His paper attempts to transcend such categorization and to look at the works from a new perspective, that of devotional function. He sees the ways these works were reproduced as having a major influence in their categorization. He shows how the huge focus on tracing iconographic sources for these works—in resources such as the Index of Christian Art—has influenced their categorization. The meaning of these works comes not from their placement within a category but from understanding their purpose and how they worked with other media and objects. His study is devoted to looking at how the use of color led to them being seen spiritually and how this was also used to complement smaller-scale works that were restricted to the more privileged, but which also need to be seen from a holistic perspective. The use of color, although essential to understanding the meaning of a work, can also be contradictory in its use and symbolism, as the author clearly points out. This is an essay that attempts to break down the traditional approach and shows how a more neutral stance using the study of color can yield significant results.

Although primarily a Byzantine scholar, the third contributor to this collection, Sharon Gerstel, also covers Western material in her fine essay on the use of tiles. This really is a holistic study of this much-neglected field, with Sharon looking at Byzantine tiles, and ceramic tiles in wall facings and pavements in the late medieval West as well as in Seljuk and Ottoman Anatolia. Ceramic pavements in the West have also been isolated and only occasionally studied, and neither their form nor their iconography has been related to other media. Is it because they were seen as mass produced, simply decorative, and of minor importance? This insightful essay examines the historiography of the subject and looks at the technical details from an analytical perspective. The benchmark study looks at the iconography and purpose of tiles and makes the reader aware of just how important these were in both the East and West.

Harald Wolter-von dem Knesebeck looks at the equally under-studied field of secular arts and wonders if indeed the terms minor and major are still valid today. He also speculates as to whether a division existed between the secular and the sacred in the Middle Ages. Throughout this essay it is clear that he wants to replace such a division with a more unified approach and to do so he looks at a few case studies, including the Ebstorf *Mappa Mundi* and the sculptural program of the Naumburg choir. In both cases he shows that secular and sacred worked in tandem and to classify them as major or minor is misleading. He sees them as parts of one unified program whose reception and appreciation were the same. How do we distinguish the manner in which these works were viewed in the Middle Ages? He argues that it is well near impossible and that we have to see all as part of the same thing. He looks at similar iconography—in the form of Henry the Lion's lion and lions depicted in *aquamanilia*—and tries to distinguish how they were viewed and received. He argues that their reception was not separated in the medieval mind by virtue of one being a major work and the other minor, but rather in regard to their intended use and message. This encyclopaedic essay makes us think as to how works of art were received and viewed in the Middle Ages and his conclusion is that there was no such division as major or minor.

Sculpture has traditionally been viewed as a major art but certainly one of its subsets, alabaster, has not had the same premier status in recent times. In a beautifully crafted essay, Kim Woods looks at the historiography of this medium and charts its rise and fall—from its being a high-value and precious commodity to its more popular and undervalued usage. In many ways this is an essay that charts the reverse trend of many of the other essays in this volume, as alabaster shifted from major to minor in appreciation. Kim highlights the relationship of the medium to marble and its use not only in England but throughout Europe, where it is best known in such works as altarpieces and tombs. She shows how it went from being used by royalty and the elite to its debasement later on when production methods changed. It goes from large-scale usage to being found in small-scale devotional objects of a more provincial nature. Even though she points out that it is a historiographical study, her essay is far more in that it beautifully interweaves case studies with the narrative to make a finely rounded examination of the fate of this medium.

It is unfortunate that the two other studies on sculpture in this collection highlight an equal neglect of their subject. These are by Frédéric Billiet and Welleda Muller, both of which look at the misericord and its neglected status. These fascinating carvings deserve better than the press they have received and they have never entered the mainstream of medieval iconography. Welleda points out that they are small in size and difficult to locate and view but that should not negate their importance. They have been ignored by art historians and seen as lying outside of the mainstream iconographical repertoire of the Middle Ages. That still does not make them minor and she points out the means by which scholars have fought back to improve their reputation. Not least amongst these means are the efforts undertaken by the Index of Christian Art, which recently electronically catalogued the image and record collection of Elaine Block, one of the foremost scholars in the field. These are now available online and have attracted considerable interest, which hopefully will lead to increased research. Welleda's essay looks at the historiography, structure, and iconography of these works with a particular interest on the last and its profane subjects. Frédéric Billiet continues the focus on these carvings with an essay on their value as sources for the study of medieval music. He looks at the instruments represented on these small carvings, on how music was played and performed, and shows in an insightful study just how valuable these neglected sources can be.

Despite the fact that we all like to think of medieval metalwork as a primary area of research, it is also clear that there are many subsets within this field that still have not entered into the mainstream area of study, and amongst these are five areas that are dealt with in this collection: jewelry, seals, enamels, pilgrim badges, and coins. We were fortunate in having Brigitte Bedos-Rezak address the minor role of seals at the event, as I can think of no one more steeped in their study to deal with the subject. Even though over fifty-thousand seal dies and two- to three-million impressions have survived from Medieval Europe, it is surprising to see them still relegated to a minor form that has never been fully integrated (with few exceptions) into the mainstream of art-historical research. Brigitte sees this as the result of an antiquarian approach that first developed in the sixteenth century and persisted until recent times. They were seen as formulaic and stereotypical in character, technique, and design, and as such stood little chance. It was only those few exemplary ones that made it into art-historical literature. Their minor status resulted from the way they were studied rather than their inherent value, and she argues their true meaning was obscured until recently. They were traditionally seen as support to art as being a species of *disegno* and to history as being items of physical data, but with new approaches in art history drawing from phenomenology, history, and anthropology we are discovering their true value. They are entering the realm of a major art form.

John Cherry's essay looks at English jewelry and the history of its collecting. He traces how its study was very much influenced by such pivotal figures as Joan Evans and Sir Augustus Wollaston Franks, who brought into play their own set of beliefs. The study of Western jewelry has now assumed a life of its own that unfortunately still lags a little behind research into Byzantine jewelry. No Eastern museum exhibition or catalogue would be complete without a sizeable tract on jewelry, unlike a parallel example from the Western world. John shows how literary studies, the history of dress, and the amuletic qualities of jewelry all influenced its study, but how these have now been extended by research into ownership, the way it is worn, theories of design, and even sociological and psychological factors. It is clear from his paced study that research into jewelry is destined to increase and that it will become far more integrated into the mainstream of art-historical research in the future.

Cynthia Hahn's paper is closely related to John's in that it looks at medieval enamels and their marginalization from the core of medieval studies. Like John, she restates that small in size does not mean minor. It is the scale of these works that first engages Cynthia in what she calls a series of random thoughts on the field of enamelwork. Like Alicia Walker in the next essay, she also notes the pivotal role that the museum curator had in fashioning the public perception that surrounds these works, as they are largely the remit of museum scholarship. She expands on other issues in attempting to paint a holistic picture of the minor status of these works and looks at such factors as technique, patronage, and production. She shows how valued enamel was as a medium and how it was used by privileged patrons in search of the best. Despite the perceived mass production of enamels in the thirteenth century and onwards, Cynthia points out how they are not simply mindless replications. She wonders if indeed their production in terms of numbers caused them to be seen as minor. Did their success kill them off as a major art? Like a number of other authors in this volume, she concludes with the issue of reception and how importance and beauty of the highest status can be embedded in works as small as these. It is an essay that resonates beautifully with a number of other studies here and shows our need to understand just how these works came to be outside the pale.

Although presented at another Index conference, the study by Alicia Walker on Byzantine decorative arts is included in this collection by virtue of its suitability to the overall theme of the collection. Alicia begins by saying that the term "decorative arts" is no longer valid, especially within Byzantine art history. Its disappearance she believes is due to the new approaches and methodologies that have developed in the field in the last thirty or so years. Interestingly, she believes that its marginalization before that benefited it and the very qualities that set it apart led directly to new and innovative interpretative approaches. In a finely structured essay, Alicia presents a historiographical analysis of the subject and neatly explains the unusual title of her essay. Her study focuses on the use of ornamentation in the decorated arts of the Byzantine world and it is on this linchpin that she sees both their initial marginalization and also the current renewed interest in them. Her belief that the museum world was responsible for the shift away from separation is studied in the second part of her essay, where she also looks at such concepts as function versus display, production, and portability. Two further essays on aspects of metalworking highlight a similar story of art-historical neglect. The first of these, by Jos Koldeweij, is on pilgrim souvenirs and secular badges, and, despite the volume of publications on them which he details, Jos is still prepared to acknowledge that they are a minor art. From his careful analysis of the works it is clear, however, that there is no reason why they should be marginalized. They were first documented as works in the mid-nineteenth century in England, and in France soon after that. Like enamels in the previous essay, it is clear that huge numbers have survived, but unlike those works, it is apparent that badges cut across all levels of society or cultures as Jos refers to them. Their value comes not from their size, material, or number but from their iconography, which is finely detailed in this survey essay. The iconography is similar in badges from the upper and lower levels of society and, like misericords, it also focuses heavily on the profane. My belief is that they have been marginalized from art-historical studies by virtue of their being seen largely as archaeological finds and as such are deemed the remit of another field. This historiographical essay details the level of research underway that must over time increase their profile and lead to them becoming a mainstream subject of study. The second essay to deal with mass-produced works is by Alan Stahl, one of the foremost experts on coinage, whose benchmark essay brings the reader through a general survey of coinage of all periods and geographies across medieval Europe. Alan points out that there is nothing smaller in scale than the coin and nothing in greater currency or more formulaic, and he is clear that art was of secondary importance when it came to establishing the monetary value of these works. Yet it is surprising that art historians of the medieval period have not studied them more. While similar to seals, they were in far greater currency and must have been used to define identity as well as establish value. While Alan is understandably cautious about defining these coins as major or minor, it is clear that his essay will provide much that will be of use to the art historian and hopefully encourage all to look again at what has been much neglected.

No study of the minor arts could be complete without looking at glass, prints, and tapestries—three fields that have all changed status over the last twenty or so years. These are the arts that have fought back and much is due to the three authors whose essays are included here. It seems unusual to define stained or painted glass as a minor art, but its status as such really resulted from our avoidance of it in terms of research and to a certain extent to the approaches taken by those who actually did study it. In what Michael Cothren has called a "personal reflection," we can see just how the subject of stained glass remained slightly moribund up until recently. In many ways it was not unique in this aspect, as many other subjects suffered the same Modernist approach that he details so finely in his essay. The same could be said of sculpture or wall paintings, but it is the sheer scale of these windows that makes this all the more unbelievable. Using a historiographical framework for the first half of his study, Michael shows how the fundamentals of this approach prevented its complete understanding. He shows how the emphasis on glass was on spirituality and its role in supporting the broader architectural framework. Windows were seen as part of the interior decoration and the emphasis was on style, iconography, and structure. He and many of his colleagues have moved this study into a broader Postmodernist framework with an emphasis on reception and viewing. They have used the existing research and impressively added to the way it is studied; the benefits are clear. Lest there be any doubt, the second part of Michael's essay uses case studies to highlight these new Postmodernist approaches and shows how far the study of glass has progressed. Wisely or cautiously, he does not define the medium in terms of minor or major status, but it is clear from the pioneering research in the field what changes have taken place.

The study of tapestry is similar in its marginalization from the mainstream of art-historical research, as Laura Weigert points out in her fine essay. She opens her study by showing how valued tapestries are in popular appeal—major in the modern perception of the Middle Ages, but definitely minor in the art-historical purview. She believes that current art-historical models are inadequate for understanding the medium, and it is here that she proposes a new methodology in a case study. This looks at the works in terms of portability, spatiality, and materiality—all of which point to reception, a recurring factor in the minor versus major discussion. She justifiably points out how tapestries were highly valued in the Middle Ages and explains the historiography of their decline in the subsequent periods as the result of a number of factors, not least of which are the facts that they were considered Renaissance rather than medieval and were believed to have been made by women. Laura's essay resonates beautifully with other studies in this collection, and who can disagree with her wish to have them considered a major art form?

Even if manuscripts have always been considered a major art, their successors, prints, have been less than favored in art-historical values. David Areford beautifully shows the problems surrounding these experimental, multimedia, devotional works and how such factors have always placed them on the margins of art history. This is a situation that is changing thanks to the likes of David and his colleagues who are slowly making us more aware of this medium that seems to have fallen in the cracks between the manuscript proper and printed books. The very title of his essay indicates, with the word "trouble," that prints have never been an easy subject to deal with, as they resist categorization. They have usually been seen as transitional between the manuscript and the printed book; they emulate and yet they are independent (they are works in themselves and yet they sometimes depend on a bigger context or medium for meaning); their purpose is varied and yet their meaning is intrinsic. David highlights how such issues influenced their reception, not only at the time they were made but also in modern art-historical research. This fascinating essay on the origins of prints and their relationship with other media also looks at their purpose, reception, value, and engagement with the viewer. Like tapestries, prints were first produced at the end of the medieval period and may traditionally have been perceived as transitional—an unfair categorization that has done them no favors. It is rewarding to see that their press has improved in the last few years and that they have gained an independence that they previously did not have.

Whatever we do, it is clear that we are still going to categorize and prioritize, but hopefully we will learn to be as inclusive as possible in our conscious reassessment of the largely artificial divisions of major and minor.

FROM MINOR TO MAJOR

The Minor Arts in Medieval Art History

PAUL BINSKI

London, Paris, Assisi, Rome around 1300: Questioning Art Hierarchies

WE CONFRONT, first, a paradox: that while the concept of major and minor arts did not explicitly ruffle the minds of medieval commentators, the arts were still frequently considered in the Middle Ages from an hierarchical perspective. The nature of human agency and ethos ensured that many narratives of art concerned large acts by patrons possessed of great minds. The character of actions counted for more than the character or standing of single objects or "media." This tended to favor generous behavior on the grand scale. Thus "Wonders"—beginning with the Wonders of the Ancient World, or *theamata*, "sights"—were on the whole large, technically astonishing things produced by, or for, remarkable people. In Latin literature, wonder is experienced especially at that which is either very complex, possessing boundless variety (of which more presently), or at that which is very big. Hence the association of the words *miror* and *magnitudo* in ancient and medieval discussion of the Wonders of the World, the nature of great sea monsters, or the art patronage of the Popes in Rome, as in the *Liber pontificalis*.[1] If God himself appears as some sort of artificer, it is as a dividers-wielding architect or *conditor* (as in the Moralised Bibles or the Holkham Bible Picture Book), not as a goldsmith: saints or monks, not God, were workers in gold.[2] Hierarchy too mattered formally as well as socially and metaphysically. Rhetoric provided Latin writers with a familiar hierarchy of style within which to operate, the *genera dicendi* or high, middle, and low style.[3] Roman encyclopædists such as Pliny the Elder (*Historiae naturalis*, XXXIII–XXXVII) conveyed a firm sense of the hierarchy of the materials used to make art, which may explain the ordering of descriptions of first bronze, then marble, statuary in the *mirabilia* writing about Rome by the so-called Master Gregorius in the decades around 1200.[4] To the treasure-minded embodiments of sacral kingship, such ranks were a sort of default position; so, in 1245, King Henry III of England wrote to his keeper of the works:

> The King to Edward of Westminster, greeting. Since we recall that you told us that it would be rather more splendid to make the two leopards which are to be on either side of our throne at Westminster of bronze instead of cutting them out of marble, we command you to have them made of metal as you said, and to have the steps before the throne made of cut stone.[5]

We have literally to look harder for greatness in small things. But we will find it. That the small could occasion lofty feelings, a sort of wonder, is evident from that passage in Gerald of Wales's late twelfth-century

1. P. Binski, "Reflections on the 'Wonderful height and Size' of Gothic Great Churches and the Medieval Sublime," in *Magnificence and the Sublime in Medieval Aesthetics*, ed. C. S. Jaeger (New York, 2010), 129–56.

2. On which issue, see J. B. Friedman, "The Architect's Compass in Creation Miniatures of the Later Middle Ages," *Traditio* 30 (1974), 419–29; for a critique, see K. H. Tachau, "God's Compass and *Vana Curiositas*: Scientific Study in the Old French *Bible Moralisée*," *Art Bulletin* 80/1 (1998), 7–33; and "What has Gothic to do with Scholasticism?" in *Gothic Art & Thought in the Later Medieval Period*, ed. C. Hourihane, Index of Christian Art Occasional Papers XII (Princeton, N.J., 2011), 14–34, esp. 30–33; for the Holkham Bible, see M. P. Brown, *The Holkham Bible Picture Book* (London, 2007), at 2–3 no. 3, and fol. 2.

3. D. Kelly, "Topical Invention in Medieval French Literature," in *Medieval Eloquence: Studies in the Theory and Practice of Medieval Rhetoric*, ed. J. J. Murphy (Berkeley, Calif., 1978), 231–51, at 236.

4. *Master Gregorius, The Marvels of Rome*, trans. John Osborne, Mediaeval Sources in Translation, 31 (Toronto, 1987).

5. Cited in *The History of the King's Works: The Middle Ages*, ed. H. M. Colvin, vol. I (London, 1963), 102.

Topography of Ireland in which he describes the Gospels of Kildare:

> If you look at them carelessly and casually and not too closely, you may judge them to be mere daubs rather than careful compositions. You will see nothing subtle where everything is subtle. But if you take the trouble to look very closely, and penetrate with your eyes to the secrets of the artistry, you will notice such intricacies, so delicate and subtle, so close together and well-knitted, so involved and bound together, and so fresh still in their colourings that you will not hesitate to declare that all these things must have been the result of the work not of men, but of angels.[6]

The object is the fractal-like art of something like the Book of Kells, but the sentiment is Horatian, for as Horace says, "a poem is like a painting: the closer you stand to this one the more it will impress you, whereas you have to stand a good distance from that one." We know a modern version of this: C. W. Bynum's distinction, drawn in her essay on "Wonder," between *admiratio*—standing back in wonder—and *imitatio*—stepping forward to study, peer at, and assimilate.[7] Small things, though not at first sight associated with conventional ideas of *magnificentia*, can undoubtedly occasion large sentiments and high language. They are especially likely to occasion feelings of the uncanny, for the aesthetics of the very small—what we might call "nano-aesthetics"—in goldsmiths' work (Fig. 1), ivory carving, or book illumination, are the product of extraordinary skill, and provoke in us a special form of fascination that does not immediately accord with the aesthetics of magnification that are presently provoking a revival of interest.[8]

If we concede immediately, as we should, that the precious arts could claim important artistic successes and the larger arts equally monumental failures, we are still left with the complex human realities of artistic training and the artist's relationship with the media, practicalities that cannot readily submit to formulaic notions of rhetorical or material hierarchy, because they have to be assessed by inference from specific cases. Pedantry about scale as such is useless. Vasari popularized the hierarchy of architects, painters, and sculptors, but Vasari had been trained in goldsmiths' work. No art historian needs reminding that Brunelleschi too had been trained young as a goldsmith, but went on to build a great dome; the supposed "author" of the great octagon at Ely (begun in 1322), the monk Alan of Walsingham, was also reputedly a goldsmith by training, who "with the skill of an architect" measured out *illa artificiosa structura lignea novi campanilis, summo ac mirabili mentis ingenio imaginata.*[9] But the *ingenium* in this case was more likely not that of Alan the sacrist, but of the carpenters and architects employed under him: a goldsmith had command of such heroic work not because he was the very embodiment of *ingenium* or invention, but rather of practical wisdom, of prudence in the handling of money and men, and of attention to detail in art and administration. Hence our observation that saints and monks (St. Eligius, St. Dunstan, Matthew Paris) were goldsmiths or metalworkers: such art embodied prudential virtue, a licit worldliness. The example of the subtle reprobate architect Dedalus, on the other hand—*vir ingeniosissimus sed execrabilis*, in the words of one post-medieval wit—had taught the monastic world that a deficiency of prudence and an excess of *ingenium* could be dangerous.[10] Invention—a key Renaissance concept—was of theoretical importance in the visual

6. T. A. Heslop, "Late Twelfth-century Writing about Art, and Aesthetic Relativity," in *Medieval Art: Recent Perspectives. A Memorial Tribute to C. R. Dodwell*, ed. Gale R. Owen-Crocker and T. Graham (Manchester, 1998), 129–141, at 132.

7. C. W. Bynum, "Wonder," in *Metamorphosis and Identity* (New York, 2001), 37–75, at 42–43, 51–53.

8. See the studies in Jaeger, *Magnificence* (as in note 1). For the magnificence of book illumination, see A. S. Cohen, "Magnificence in Miniature: The Case of Early Medieval Manuscripts," in Jaeger, *Magnificence* (as in note 1), 79–101, esp. 84–5.

9. H. Wharton, *Anglia Sacra* (London, 1691), vol. 1, 643–44.

10. For Matthew Paris, see *Gesta abbatum monasterii Sancti Albani*, Rolls Series 28, ed. H. T. Riley (London, 1867–69), vol. 1, 394–95: *Vir quidem eloquens et famosus, innumeris virtutibus plenus … inerat ei tanta subtilitas in auro et argento caeteroque metallo, in sculpendo et in picturis depingendo ut nullum post se in Latino orbe creditur reliquisse secundum.* For the critique of skill, see X. Muratova, "Vir quidem fallax et falisidicus, sed artifex praeelectus. Remarques sur l'image sociale et littéraire de l'artiste au moyen âge," in *Artistes, Artisans et production artistique au Moyen Âge*, ed. X. Barral i Altet, vol. 1 (Paris, 1986), 53–72. The wit I have in mind is Francis Bacon, *De sapientia veterum liber* (London, 1609), sigs. D10^r–11^v.

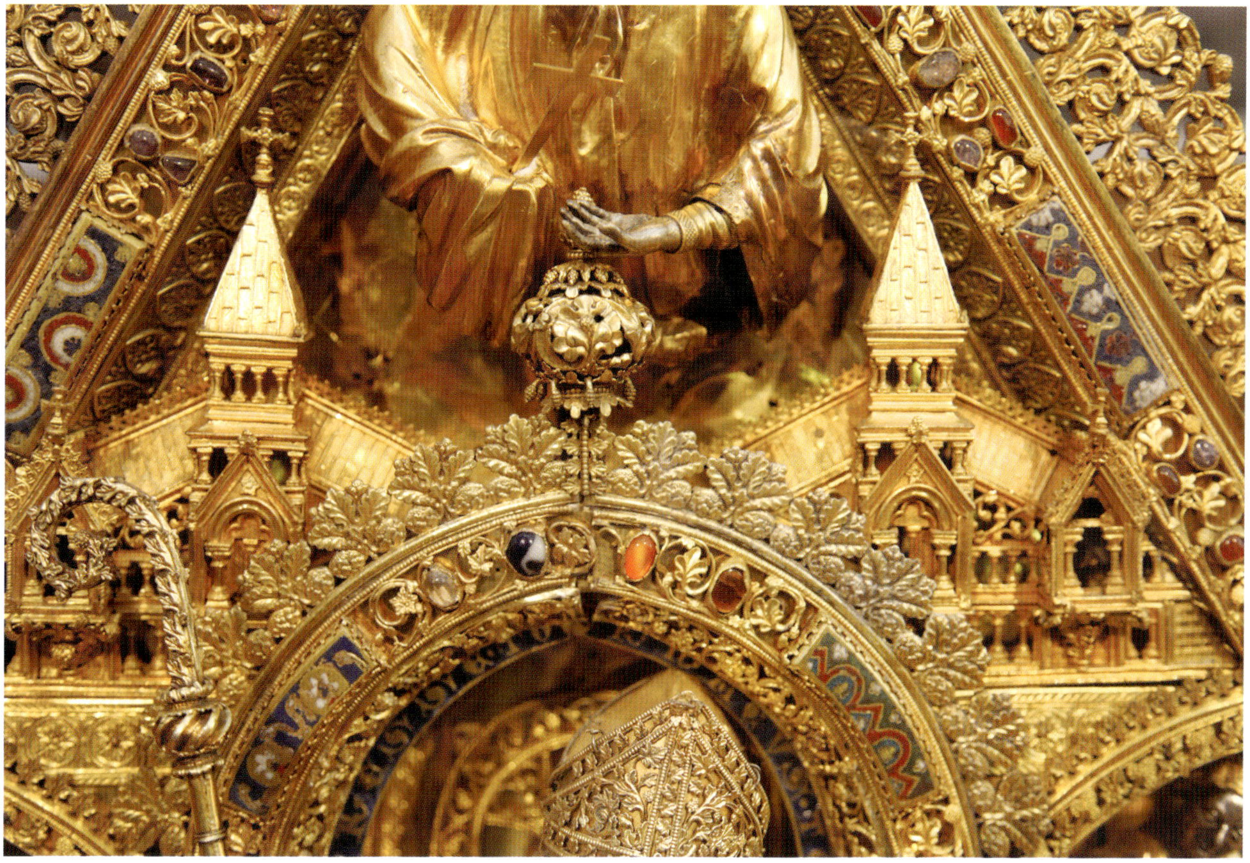

FIGURE 1. Tournai Cathedral, shrine of St. Eleutherius, *c.* 1247 (photo: author).

arts in the Middle Ages before the thirteenth century, essential as it may have been for the verbal arts, in part because under the Christian dispensation of "creation" it carried with it moral and metaphysical danger. Its meaning was more often material, governing, for instance, the finding of relics, or the provision by patrons for artists of the materials to be worked.

What tipped the balance was the self-evident splendor and technical accomplishments of the great Gothic churches, built by men commemorated explicitly by the giant labyrinths of Amiens and Reims, monuments to Dedalus himself.[11] These men were now, theoretically at least, *auctores*, and their social rise as ambitious savants, men of reason, was accompanied by a coercive rhetoric of theory-driven professionalism. This might suggest that only architecture, and so the major arts, "possessed" true invention. But the reality was more complex. Literary invention mattered in medieval art not least because it pertained to narrative, and it figured in the crafting of things as well as words.[12] Nor was invention the sole preserve of either large or small arts: in the practical cases that follow, all of which concern innovation, we encounter a much-less-stable sense of hierarchy and cause and effect than art history, conventionally understood, might lead us to expect. As well as all being high-status, each case is "mixed" in regard to medium or style-identity. The cases challenge the disciplinary tendency to split the media up from

11. P. Binski "'Working by Words alone': The Architect, Scholasticism and Rhetoric in Thirteenth-century France," in *Rhetoric Beyond Words: Delight and Persuasion in the Arts of the Middle Ages*, ed. M. Carruthers (Cambridge, 2010), 14–51.

12. Kelly, "Topical Invention" (as in note 3); see also A. A. Jordan, *Visualizing Kingship in the Windows of the Sainte-Chapelle*, Publications of the International Centre of Medieval Art, 5 (Turnhout, 2002).

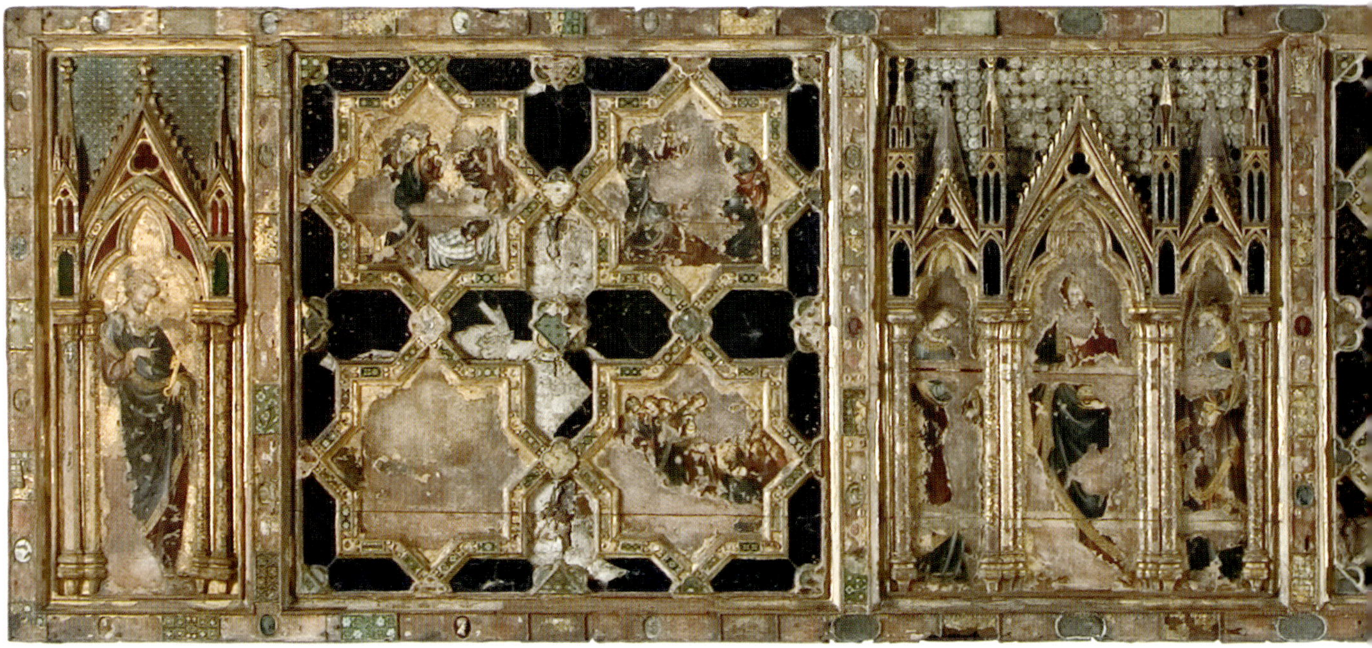

FIGURE 2. Westminster Abbey, Westminster Retable, general view of front (photo: Hamilton Kerr Institute).

one another in a way contrary to much in medieval aesthetics that, on the contrary, placed particular emphasis on mixture and *varietas* as sources of aesthetic pleasure and invention. And, importantly, they suggest that relations, as well as differences, between media of different scale had a hand in provoking innovation at the practical level. The issue of invention leads us to treat great and small alike with scepticism, and to look harder instead at the middle, at the zone of co-operation between the arts.[13]

I. *London and Paris: Panel Painting*

How true of some medieval art are those words of Gaston Bachelard: "Thus the miniscule, a narrow gate, opens up an entire world. The details of a thing can be the sign of a new world which, like all worlds, contains the attributes of greatness. Miniature is one of the refuges of greatness."[14] So I want to begin with a work that is well known to me and that yet may suggest some fresh ideas: the great altarpiece now in the museum of Westminster Abbey known as the Westminster Retable (Fig. 2). The findings of a long program of investigative conservation of this extraordinary panel painting have recently been published.[15] It is a sort of gateway both iconographically and imaginatively; it opens up a world of astonishing artistic and technical excellence generally lost to us; and it contains the attributes of greatness. Yet it is neither large nor small: at 3.3 meters wide, it is as wide as any major painted altarpiece of the period, but it is painted in way that occasions *imitatio*, close looking, by its very design. Witness at its very center the little globe, a world in a grain of sand, teeming with life, nurtured in the hand of the blessing Savior. In a sense, it lies in the "middle," neither wholly monumental nor wholly miniaturist. In

13. For this theme, see the essays in *The Mindful Hand: Inquiry and Invention from the Late Renaissance to Early Industrialisation*, ed. L. Roberts, S. Scaffer, and P. Dear (Amsterdam, 2007).

14. G. Bachelard, *The Poetics of Space*, trans. M. Jolas (Boston, Mass., 1994), 155.

15. For what follows, see the contributions in *The Westminster Retable: History, Technique, Conservation*, ed. P. Binski and A. Massing (Turnhout, 2009).

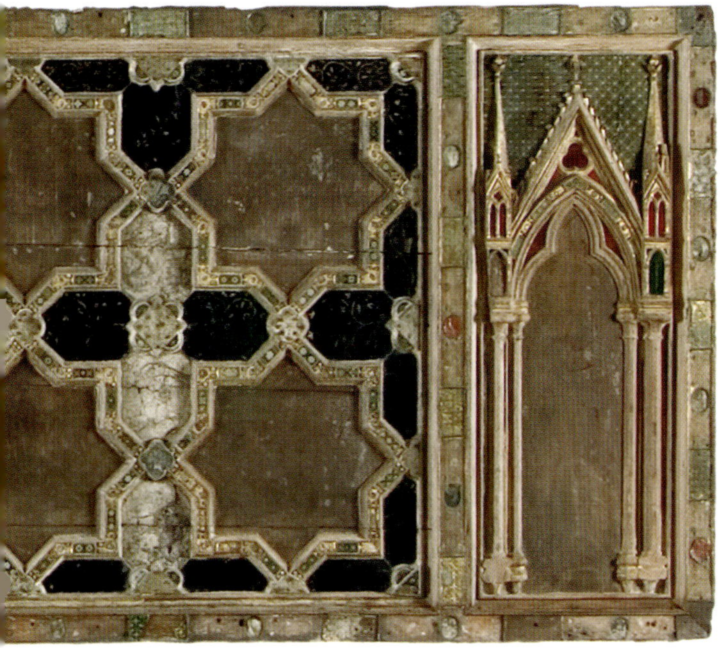

this regard, its remarkable combination of media and effects—micro-architecture, oil-gilded glass, painted enamels, and false gemstones, together with the most subtle paintwork—place it in a space between, but also connecting, the art forms. It provides a model for the notion that the middling arts were among the major engines of invention.

Because it is totally undocumented, the Westminster Retable stretches our inferential powers to their limit. In sum, the findings of the collaborative work of art historians, archaeologists, experts in the "minor" arts, scientists, and dendrochronologists were these:

(1) the Retable was designed under very close French (probably Parisian) supervision but made at Westminster for its high altar dedicated to St. Peter;

(2) the Retable's oak can be dated to 1235–1270, which almost certainly indicates the period of use;

(3) its joinery reveals a radical revision to its width, by means of which the two outer panels eventually showing St. Peter and St. Paul were added at an early stage in manufacture; this cannot have happened other than at a time when the high altar environment was still in the hands of workmen, as it was in the period 1259–1269;

(4) the earliest documentable commissioning date for the Retable (i.e., the opening for furnishing of the church's east end) is 1259, giving us a window for its execution of 1259–1269.

The collective conclusion was that, relative to the dates proposed for it by art historians between 1260 and 1300, this astonishing painting in linseed oil is "early" and hence in the vanguard of innovation. Three issues therefore arise immediately: the role of collaboration of media, the issue of the originating agency of the conception, and the relationship of panel painting to book illumination.

First, collaboration: the Retable is an instance of courtly eclecticism in its selection of techniques and borrowing of forms that, in 1260, had little currency in England. Thematically the Retable displays (or better, displayed, since it is much damaged) the Abbey's patron saints, Peter (Fig. 3) and Paul, eight of Christ's miracles in medallions (Figs. 4, 5), and Christ as Savior of the World (Fig. 6) with St. Mary and St. John. Standing on the medieval high altar, it "fronted" the shrine of St. Edward the Confessor immediately behind it. This will have been one factor in the unusual choice of Miracles of Christ as the sole narrative component of the panel. Its borrowing will, first, have taken into account the metalwork language of the shrine, including its numerous cameos and gemstones. All the metalwork effects on the Retable are transposed into paste, glass, and paint in an extraordinary technical alchemy (Fig. 7, compare Fig. 1), an "inventive" counterpart perhaps to the religious themes of transformation and miraculous renewal depicted in the paintings. But the red, blue, green, and clear glass of French manufacture used to surround the compartments and enhance the micro-architecture will have been derived from, or sanctioned by, other sources. Such "glass" altarpieces were not unique in northern France, since a similar if simpler pair was commissioned in 1324 by Mahaut of Artois.[16] But the major model was certainly the Sainte-Chapelle (Fig. 8), that shiny, bejewelled, and enamelled

16. Binski and Massing, *The Westminster Retable* (as in note 15), 113–15.

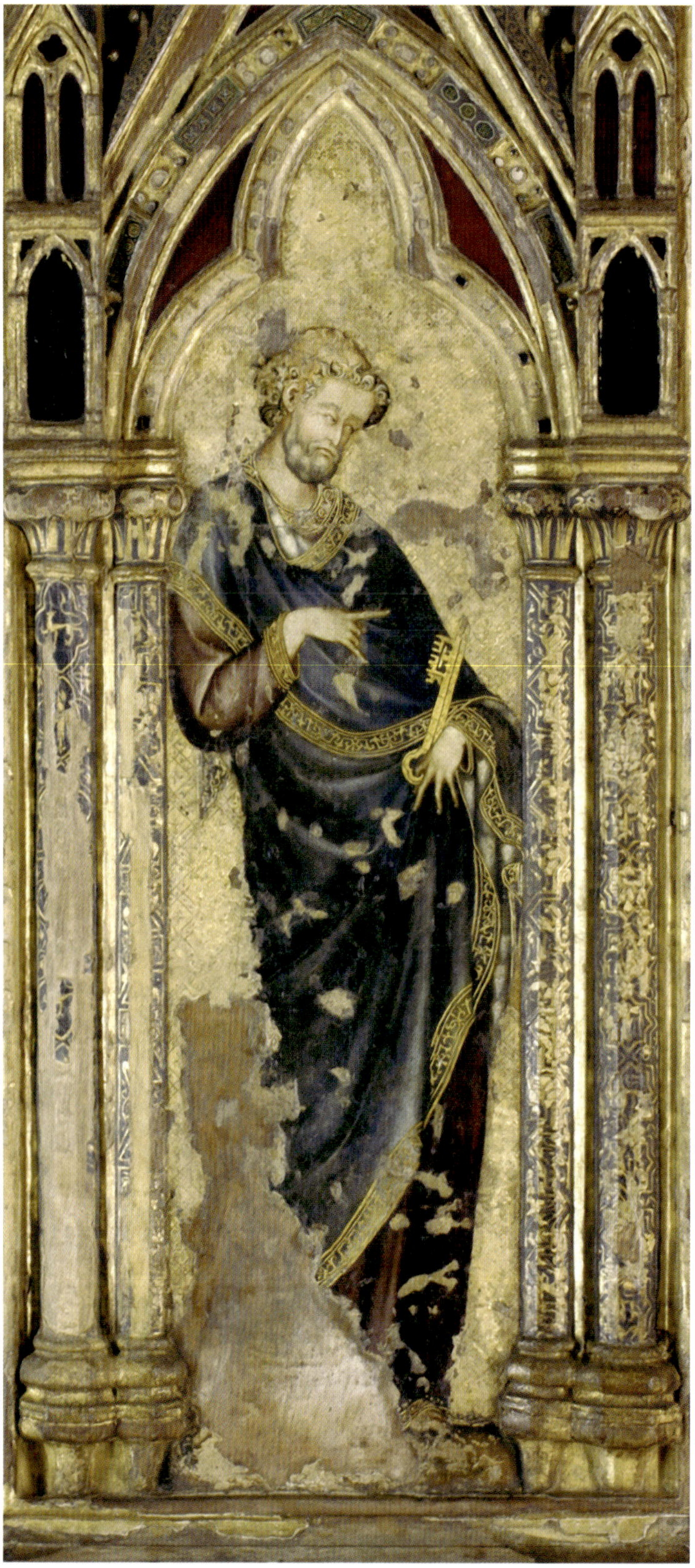

FIGURE 3. Westminster Abbey, Westminster Retable, St. Peter (photo: Hamilton Kerr Institute).

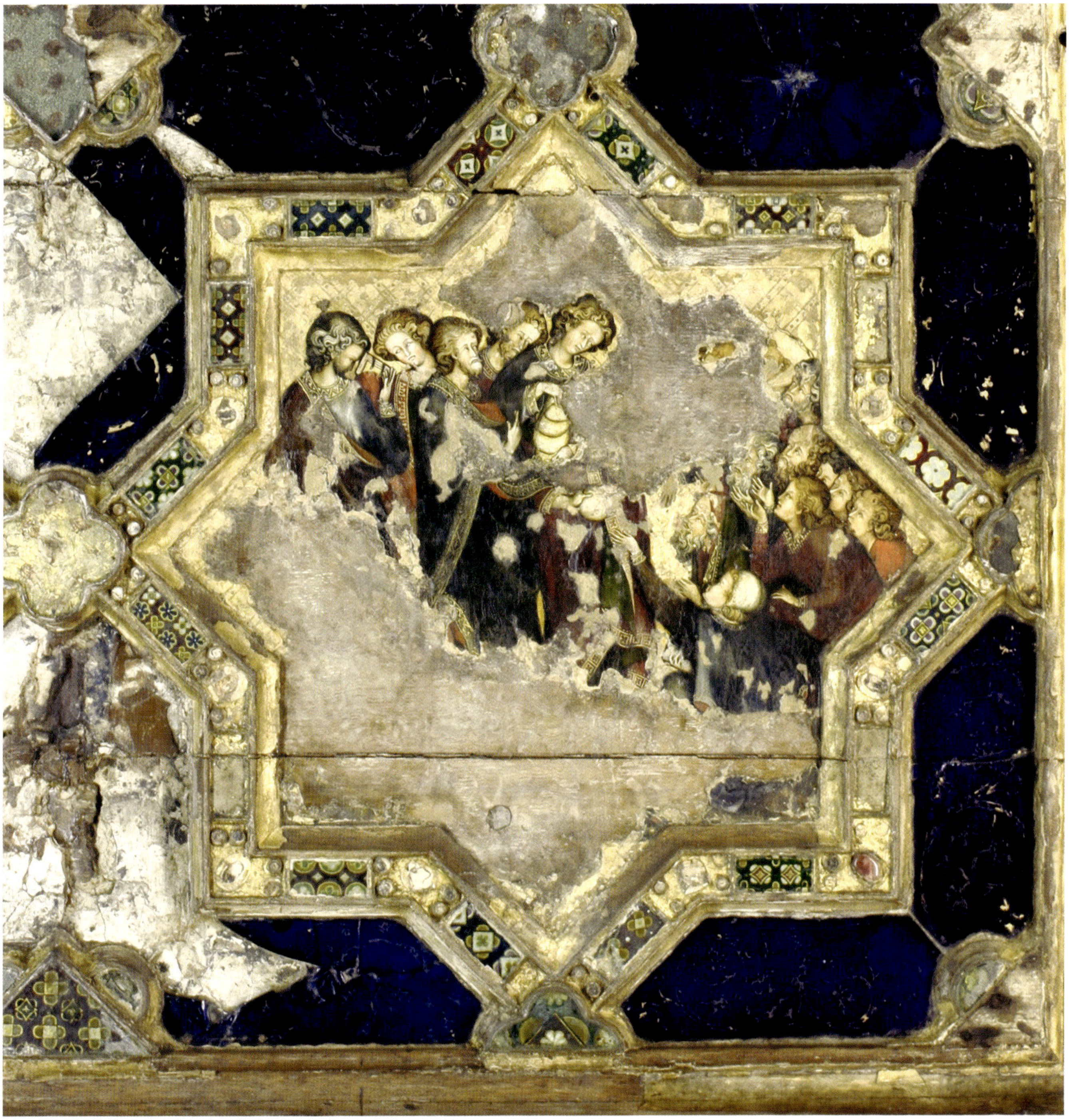

FIGURE 4. Westminster Abbey, Westminster Retable, Feeding of the Five Thousand (photo: Hamilton Kerr Institute).

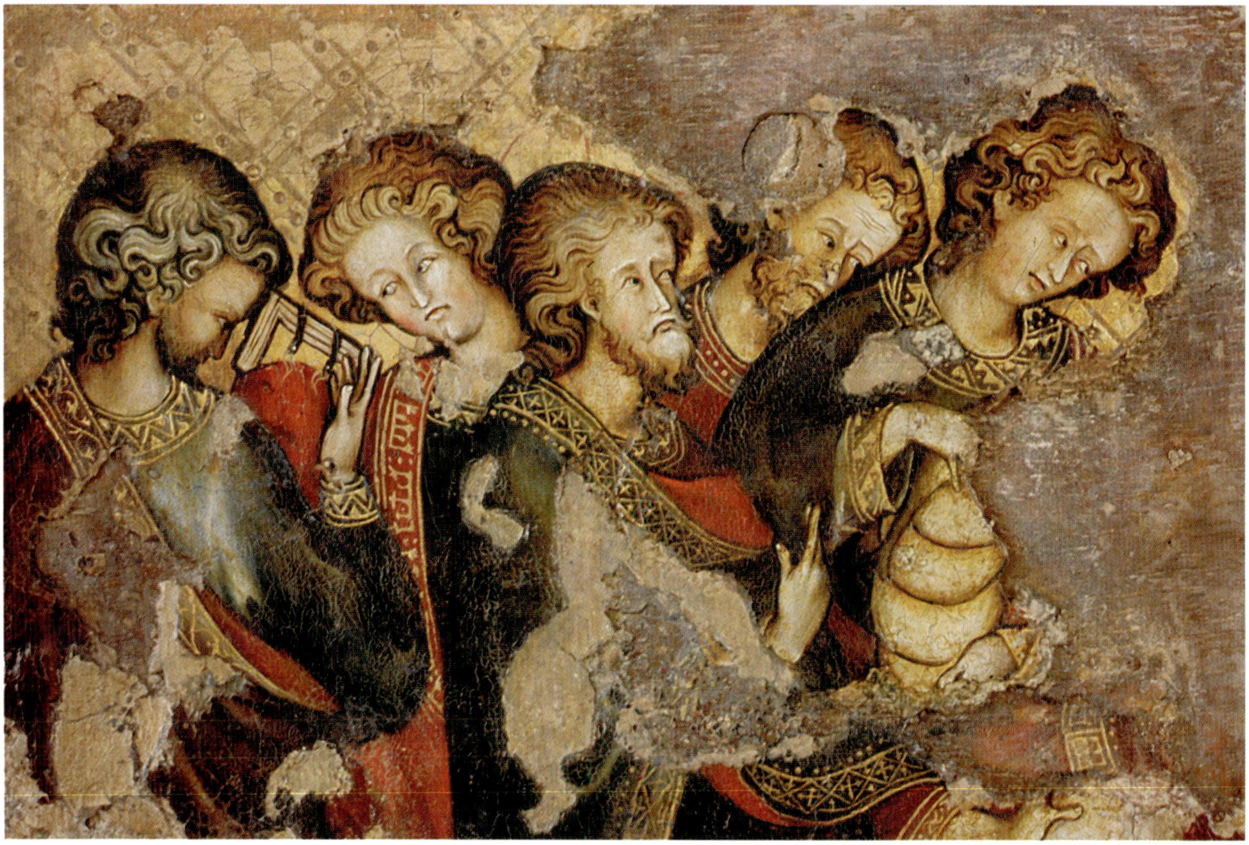

FIGURE 5. Westminster Abbey, Westminster Retable, detail of Feeding of the Five Thousand (photo: Hamilton Kerr Institute).

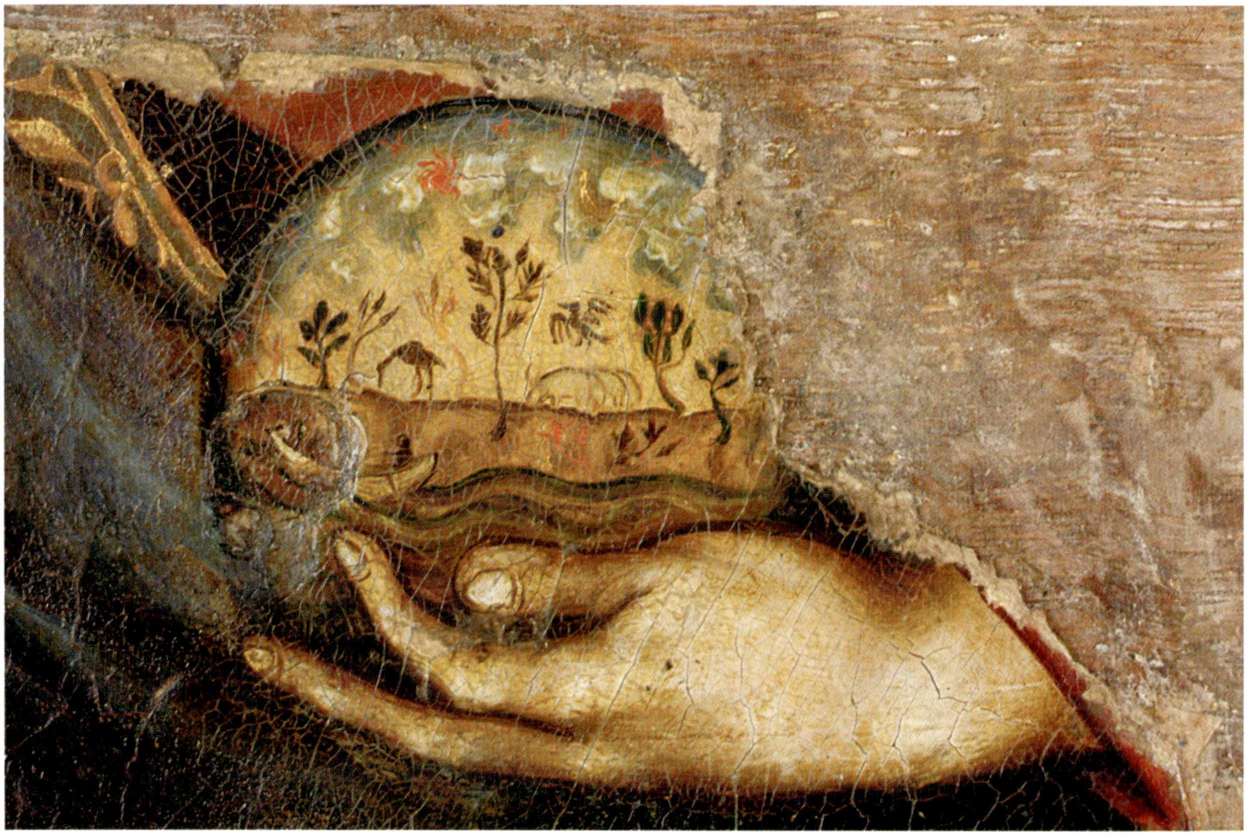

FIGURE 6. Westminster Abbey, Westminster Retable, detail of Christ as Savior of the World (photo: Hamilton Kerr Institute).

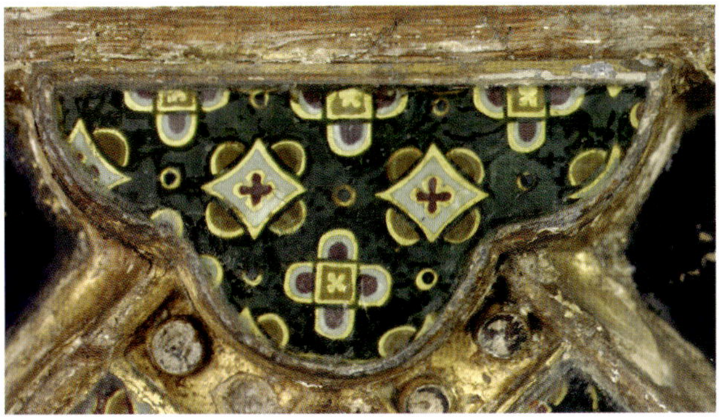

FIGURE 7. Westminster Abbey, Westminster Retable, painted enamel (photo: Hamilton Kerr Institute).

instance of the neo-Dionysianism largely complete by 1248 and, like Saint-Denis and Notre-Dame, known to Henry III by about 1260. From it and its reliquaries alone, the Retable borrowed its micro-architecture, its patterns of enamels and jewels, its eight-pointed medallions, and its glazed work, to say nothing of its elegant figure style. This style depended upon the sort of painting we see in the medallions showing the martyrdom of the saints, Parisian saints especially, in the dado arcade of the chapel, a style in turn almost certainly reflecting, in the very process of its execution, on the new idiom of figurative sculpture of the Apostles introduced alongside them in the 1240s. Such effects were not those proper to, or possible in, the giant spaces of the cathedrals—they were instead the concentrated, affordable idiom of the middling chapel-sized space and of its furnishings. Accordingly, Henry III allowed them to flood into his (public) state bedroom in the Palace of Westminster by the 1260s.

Choice and selection according to pleasure create mixture: but (our second issue) who sanctioned and articulated this? Henry III, as we saw earlier, took artistic advice from his keepers of the works, of whom the most favored was Edward of Westminster, who we note came from a family of goldsmiths, and who

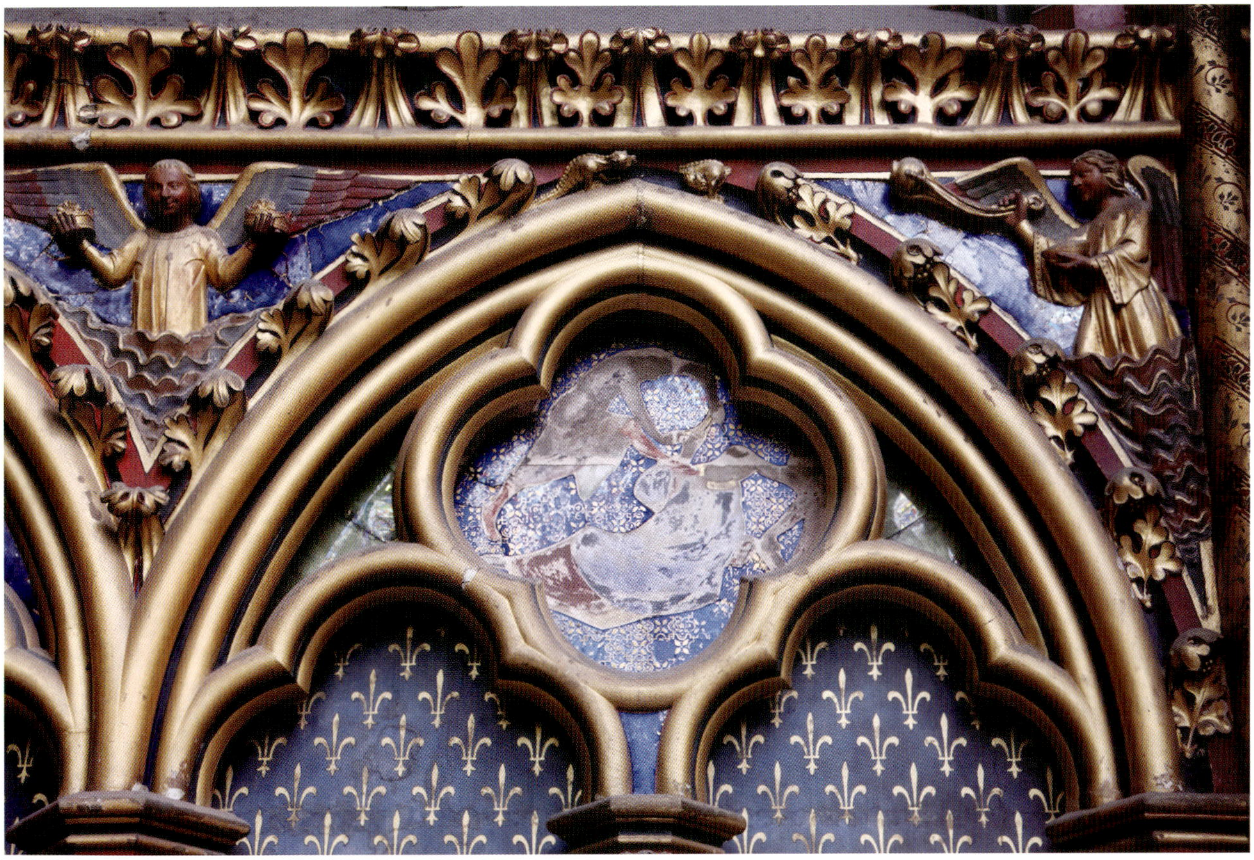

FIGURE 8. Paris, Sainte-Chapelle, wall arcade (photo: author).

was evidently a prudent judge.[17] The mixed "formula" of the Retable is however French in character. The style of its micro-architecture, the little aedicules or portals (Fig. 2), is mid-thirteenth-century Picard or Parisian. Its metalwork-like finish and ornament suggest the input of a French-trained goldsmith familiar with the type of micro-architecture found on French cathedral portals such as Amiens or Notre-Dame.[18] A document from 1249 in which Henry III commissions a new chalice for Westminster Abbey shows us how the process might have worked: Henry, requiring that Christ's body should be placed in the chalice (*cuppa*), which he obtained from Elias le Evesk' the Jew, orders Edward of Westminster that the chalice in question should be adorned in the fashion explained to Edward by John the Frenchman (*Francigena*) and then passed to the Abbot of Westminster.[19] John is more likely to have been a northern Frenchman rather than from Limoges. But what matters is the chain of command. The idiom is sanctioned by Henry and his keeper but formed by the French goldsmith. This seems to give the goldsmith ultimate responsibility in regard to invention. Something like this could have happened with the Retable. We are reminded of the 1272 contract for the micro-architectural shrine of St. Gertrude of Nivelles made "according to the drawing (*pourtrature*) that Master Jakenez d'Anchin, the goldsmith, has made."[20] Presumably this man drew in the prominent ogee arch on the Nivelles shrine's terminal elevation: the ogee arch seems to have originated in the supple manipulation of gold, and certainly in the sphere of metalwork. The ogee's future as an inventive form, a seed, in the plastic arts and architecture was to be immense.[21] Again, it is characteristic of the finest enamelled objects that the patterns of the enamels—in the case of the Retable of Rheno-Mosan type (Figs. 1, 7)—should never repeat and should show an inexhaustible resourcefulness: such patterns are the ultimate expression of protean *varietas.* No pattern on the Retable recurs, and there are hundreds of patterns.

So goldsmiths were still important, and their proper sphere of invention was small things of great formal potential, a kind of artistic insemination. To repeat, invention is as much the preserve of the small-to-middling as of the huge, since the greatest projects in scale are as likely to have been taken up by technical as by aesthetic innovation; certainly this is the case in France before about 1240. And yet an object like the Retable can only be understood as a form of obeisance to architecture itself: its micro-architecture thematizes the tabernacle and the portal and spiritual "liminality" by almost literal reference to actual portal architecture. Westminster Abbey, as rebuilt from 1245, possessed a particularly inventive architect in Henry of Reyns, whose knowledge of Reims Cathedral and the Sainte-Chapelle is evident, and whose manipulation of smaller-scale architectural forms is by all accounts almost revolutionary. If Henry III pointed for personal reasons to France for his works at Westminster, his architect namesake will have done the legwork, the sheer study, and opened the sluices of "influence." There are numerous signs of this detailed practical engagement with northern France at Henry's Westminster court in the period 1240–1250, the years of Henry of Reyns's ascendancy.[22] The period of the rebuilding of the Abbey, 1245–1269, also seems to witness the end, administratively speaking, of the dominion of the goldsmith-clerk at the English court, and the ascendancy of

17. Colvin, *King's Works* (as in note 5), 101–4; R. K. Lancaster, "Artists, Suppliers and Clerks: The Human Factors in the Art Patronage of King Henry III," *Journal of the Warburg and Courtauld Institutes* 35 (1972), 81–107.

18. See the analysis by Christopher Wilson, in Binski and Massing, *The Westminster Retable* (as in note 15), 79–96.

19. *Calendar of the Close Rolls*, 1247–51, 343.

20. C. Donnay-Rocmans, "La Châsse de Sainte Gertrude à Nivelles," *Gazette des Beaux-arts*, sér. 6, 58 (1961), 185–202; H. D. Bork, "Le contrat de la châsse. Texte et transcription," in *Un trésor gothique. La châsse de Nivelles*, Exhib. Cat. (Paris, 1996), 79–81.

21. C. Wilson, *The Gothic Cathedral: Architecture of the Great Church* (London 1990), 193; P. Crossley, "Salem and the Ogee Arch," in *Architektur und Monumentalskulptur des 12.–14. Jahrhunderts. Produktion und Rezeption. Festschrift für Peter Kurmann zum 65. Geburtstag*, ed. S. Gasser, C. Freigang, and B. Boerner (Bern, 2006), 321–42.

22. P. Binski, *Westminster Abbey and the Plantagenets: Kingship and the Representation of Power 1200–1400* (New Haven and London, 1995), 13–29, 33–43; and *Becket's Crown: Art and Imagination in Gothic England, 1170–1300* (New Haven and London, 2004), 236–47.

the architects themselves.[23] There were possible precedents: a case has been made for an impresario-like role for William of Sens in regard to the glazing as well as the building of the east choir at Canterbury from 1174; elsewhere, by the fourteenth century it was possible to hand over the building and furnishing of a collegiate church entirely to an architect, as in the case of Jean de Lobres at the Augustinian church of Toulouse after 1316.[24]

At this point, however, courtly eclecticism draws us into a causal labyrinth. A goldsmith, in turn in touch with, or even chosen by, a royal architect, will have given exact instructions to joiners and painters to produce the details of the Retable before us. So did the goldsmith in question think the whole thing through, or did true invention lie elsewhere, with the architects? Yet it cannot be said in response to this that the painters were passive in such a process. The choice of idiom on the Retable—a shrine-like framing aesthetic for oil paintings—reveals above all a form of pictorial intelligence. The fundamental decision was to have a painted altarpiece with images of a particular intellectual depth, and this creates a *prima-facie* case for imagining that whoever selected the themes, treatment, and idiom was not a goldsmith but a picture-maker who will have set out the subjects, their connections, and relative scale, as well as the character of their context, i.e., he provided a kind of thematic *ordinatio*.

The Retable exposes a quite fundamental principle in our discussion of minor and major: that in certain commissions, selection and mixture, serving the ends of pictorial intelligence and pleasure, will tend to overthrow or confuse the agency of hierarchies implicit in invention. This confusion, far from being damaging, in fact creates a productive friction or mediating catalytic effect that hugely stimulates invention as a mode of practical and manual, quite as much as intellectual, engagement. To argue about relative hierarchy of art forms or agency in such cases as if they could be "pinpointed" is to miss the point that under exceptional circumstances exceptional things happen, including a setting aside of authorial sovereignty. Context is not all, but it is important.

What, thirdly, of the illuminators? This is a problem made by art history. The "early" date for the Retable of *c.* 1259–1269 is based on an unprecedented level of investigation and triangulated thinking. But it does not accord with the usual criteria of style evolution in the pictorial arts. The earliest commentators on it, E. E. Viollet-le-Duc and W. R. Lethaby, were untroubled by an early date and the possibility of an actual French origin for the Retable. The difficulty started to arise in the 1960s when Continental European scholars such as Gerhard Schmidt, and later Peter Klein, saw in the Retable either an immediate anticipation of, or even a response to, later thirteenth-century French styles of book illumination of the sort associated with the so-called Honoré manuscripts not dated before the later 1280s and 1290s.[25] That the visual analogy, in general, works is not in dispute. The problem is that the hard archaeological evidence suggests not the dependence, but the priority, of the panel painting. This disrupts decisively the settled notion that Honoré represented a vanguard and not, as may now appear, a rear guard of styles that had formed in the Paris–London region as early as 1260. That the Retable's architecture fits into the Parisian or north French context of the 1250s, say, is established beyond doubt. But what, actually, lay behind its pictorial style? Only the Douce Apocalypse in Oxford (Bodleian Library Ms. Douce 180), made probably before 1270 for Edward I or Eleanor of Castile, matches it point for point in many details, and the script and format of that book seem to be English. The style of this book cannot be imagined without knowledge of northern or north-eastern French painting and sculpture, and panel and wall painters at Westminster were working in this style not long after 1263. The Parisian Royal Psalters dating before 1270 made for Louis IX

23. Colvin, *King's Works* (as in note 5), 161–89.

24. M. H. Caviness, "Canterbury Cathedral Clerestory: The Glazing Progamme in Relation to the Campaigns of Construction," *Medieval Art and Architecture at Canterbury before 1220*, British Archaeological Association Conference Transactions, v (1982), 46–55; M. Durliat, "Les attributions de l'architecte à Toulouse au début du XIVe siècle," *Pallas* 11 (1962), 205–12, at 210.

25. For a summary discussion, see Binski and Massing, *The Westminster Retable* (as in note 15), 12–14, 35–40.

and his circle are idiomatically much less close, even if they resemble the Retable in many details and essentials. The one French royal masterpiece, about which more will soon be known as a result of recent research, is the painted ensemble of medallions in the Sainte-Chapelle in Paris, whose importance was recognized not just by Robert Branner but by Henry III, and which belonged to the single most likely ensemble to have influenced the Retable.

The point, of course, is the nature of our *comparanda* and the hierarchies implicit in them. We are told that the illuminated manuscript record is more reliable because it is more complete. Illuminated manuscripts now form a huge, authoritative, and prestigious industry of study. In the 1960s Robert Branner worked from architecture and sculpture to the history of Parisian book painting in the reign of St. Louis, via the small painted medallions in the Sainte-Chapelle, presumably complete by 1248 (Fig. 8).[26] The largely lost but copied wall paintings in the chapel were the crucible of the so-called "broad-fold style" that had appeared earlier still in sculpture. Yet the murals were even then ruins, and all the related French panel paintings are lost. And there was a more substantial hurdle in the form of the authoritative voice of Erwin Panofsky. In 1953 Panofsky justified his handing of the palm of innovation in the International Gothic style to an illuminator, Jean Pucelle (d. 1334), in these terms:

> we must not forget that … the tradition of fresco painting was somewhat weakened and a tradition of panel painting practically nonexistent in France at the beginning of the fourteenth century … Thus book illumination had a head start over panel painting, which by comparison tended to remain somewhat retardataire.[27]

We will overlook the identification of wall painting with fresco painting, since fresco was not used in the Gothic north, where oil techniques were normal in wall and panel painting. The key problem is the weak evidential base for the assumed hierarchy of cause and effect, in which manuscripts are necessarily in touch and ahead of other media more stunted in their development, a position that may, simply, be as often wrong as it is right. The difficulties with this stance were being sensed over a generation ago: to an extent it was itself a reaction to the demotion of illumination to a minor art in favor of wall and panel painting. But the Westminster Retable seems to subvert it entirely, by pointing to the existence of lost court panel and wall paintings produced in the "inventive" mixed context of the public ensemble, not the more private sphere of book art.

II. *Assisi, Rome, and Paris: Wall Painting*

The basilica of S. Francesco at Assisi is a larger and, in terms of technical *varietas*, more simply decorated church than the Sainte-Chapelle or Westminster Abbey: but for other reasons it may justly be seen as another instance where mixture and invention went hand in hand. After its completion, the first act of decoration, in the Upper Church at least, was the introduction not of mosaic (which was planned) or fresco, but northern-European-type stained glass. This translucent and radiant medium was soon to be joined by the matte effects of fresco, but via an "oil interlude" formed by the workshop of the so-called "Northern Master" at Assisi (Figs. 9, 10), at work about ten years after the Westminster Retable had been installed on its altar—let us say the late 1270s.[28] This exceedingly mixed and ambivalent cooperative of Gothic-influenced (or, in virtue of their oil technique, actually Gothic) painters and central Italian collaborators in effect introduced Gothic painted detailing into the Italian pictorial *milieu*. Once again, selection and mixture (of training, of technique, and of style) are preconditions for invention under unusual circumstances.

26. R. Branner, "The Painted Medallions in the Sainte-Chapelle in Paris," *Transactions of the American Philosophical Society*, N.S., 58 (1968), 1–42; *Manuscript Painting in Paris during the Reign of Saint Louis: A Study of Styles* (Berkeley, Calif., 1977). I must note the new work being done on the medallions and their context by my Ph.D. student Ms. Emily Guerry.

27. E. Panofsky, *Early Netherlandish Painting: Its Origin and Character* (Cambridge, Mass., 1953), vol. 1: 28.

28. For a full discussion of the question, and for what follows, see P. Binski, "How Northern was the Northern Master at Assisi?" *Proceedings of the British Academy* 117 (2002), 73–138.

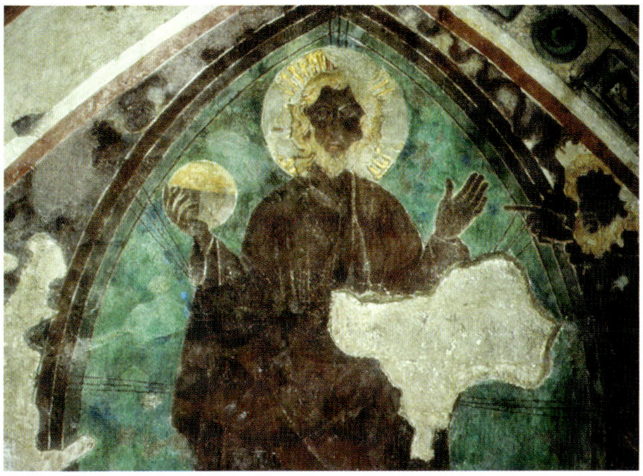

FIGURE 9. Assisi, S. Francesco, Upper Church, right transept, detail of Transfiguration of Christ (photo: author).

The likelihood is that the patron who first sponsored the Northern Master's work in the right transept of the basilica was Pope Nicholas III Orsini (1277–1280): the Orsini arms occur in Cimabue's great crossing murals of the Evangelists, which are pretty well contiguous with the work of the Northern Master in the upper parts of the transept, and which further the same fundamental message of all the murals in this part of the church, namely, the universality of the mission to the World of the Franciscan order. The "homeland"—to use Hans Belting's word *heimat*—of the very curious amalgam of styles associated with the Northern Master has been utterly obscure. But in the face of such obviously exceptional (and unrepeated) art, do we actually need a "homeland?" Since Marchini wrote on

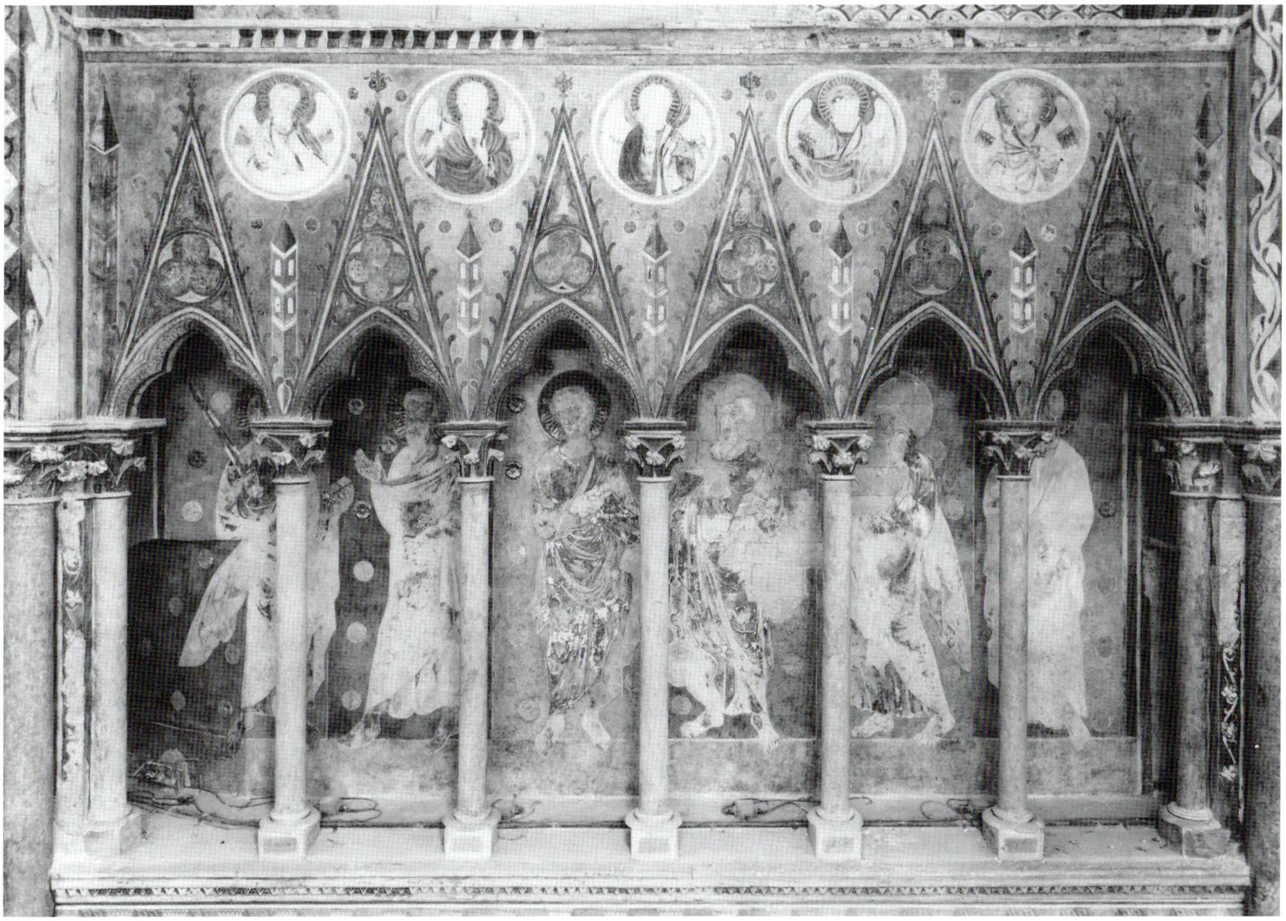

FIGURE 10. Assisi, S. Francesco, Upper Church, right transept, triforium with Apostles and angels (photo: Kunsthistorisches Institut Florenz).

the stained glass, a settled tendency developed, in Italian writing at least, to think of the Northern Master as English in origin. This was based on an, not necessarily helpful, analogy between the Northern Master's transfiguration iconography (Fig. 9) and English manuscript sources, and on an equally tendentious identification of this style or group of styles with the Westminster Retable, with which identification Belting persisted in his study of the Upper Church. Here cautions are necessary. As in the Northern Master's Transfiguration picture at Assisi, God the Father appears with his Son in the murals at Gurk in Carinthia, as well as in the Munich Psalter circle of books illuminated in England around 1200. For reasons already given, the Westminster Retable is as much French as English work.

The Northern Master's art was not an expatriated court art, following from earlier English illuminations and panels. All the signs are that he was *sui generis* because the idioms produced under him were a product of the very specific aesthetic ambitions and outlook of the early patrons of the basilica. Stained glass of an almost wholly conventional northern type was being introduced into the church's equally northern traceried windows from around 1270, perhaps earlier. We might expect this under a French-dominated papacy. But where would papal patrons in Umbria around 1270 have looked for practical ideas about glazing and decorating a major church? Clearly they would have looked northwards, but not necessarily as far as Paris, since there were prestigious centers of innovation nearer Italy itself. Key to this are two specific features of the Northern Master's handling of the right transept decoration. First, exceptionally for an Italian project, the intention in the transept was to create a triforium *ordinatio* containing standing figures beneath sharply detailed canopies with, above them, bust-length figures, here angels, in tondos (Fig. 10). The source for this conceit is specific: the nave triforium glazing of the cathedral of Strasbourg underway in the 1260s and 1270s (Fig. 11). This provides the only exact compositional analogy for the Assisi scheme at the right (i.e., prior) date. That this was the source is confirmed by the actual detailing of those sharp painted canopies at Assisi, whose faces combine trefoil and quatrefoil tracery in a way absolutely characteristic of the stained glass, architectural drawings, and actual fabric of Strasbourg produced by the late 1270s (Fig. 12). That Assisi was drawing on the Upper Rhine, and Alsace-Lorraine specifically, is confirmed by the transfer into wall paintings of just these motifs in the nave pier murals of the cathedral at Metz (Fig. 13), which again has to be understood as a borrowing from architectural thinking of the 1270s in the Upper Rhine. To understand the "range" of the Northern Master we have to abandon manuscript illumination, even panel painting, and turn to the altogether larger *ordinatio* of architecture and stained glass around 1270. The preference for stained glass will have been the immediate cause of this orientation to Alsace-Lorraine, but that some Assisi connections to this area were older is suggested by the names of the bell founders who made the bells for the campanile of the basilica around the time of its structural completion in 1239: Bartholomaeus Pisanus and his (Lorraine-born?) son Lotharingio.[29] Mixture of this degree of complexity and depth is the product of a particular set of circumstances: not, in this case, the court ethos and relic-cult of Louis IX, but the "global" evangelizing of the Franciscan Order itself—a large "homeland" indeed. That an experiment was at work here is evident from the end of the tale—the presumed expulsion of the Northern Master and his assistants around 1280 and the triumphant assertion by Cimabue of Italian "order" and "Roman arguments."

This returns us finally to the problem already touched on by Panofsky in regard to Jean Pucelle: not what Italy gained from the north, but what the north gained from Italy. Here I really do intend to speculate, but I hope within reason. The position established by Panofsky was that, although Pucelle owed much to Sienese painting on the larger scale, French fourteenth-century book illumination surpassed panel and wall painting as the chief agent of innovation: "This whole development, then, set in with Jean Pucelle."[30] But was this really so? According to the *Journaux du Trésor de Philippe le*

29. R. Brooke, *The Image of St Francis: Responses to Sainthood in the Thirteenth Century* (Cambridge, 2006), 60.

30. Panofsky, *Early Netherlandish Painting* (as in note 27), 29; K. Morand, *Jean Pucelle* (Oxford, 1962).

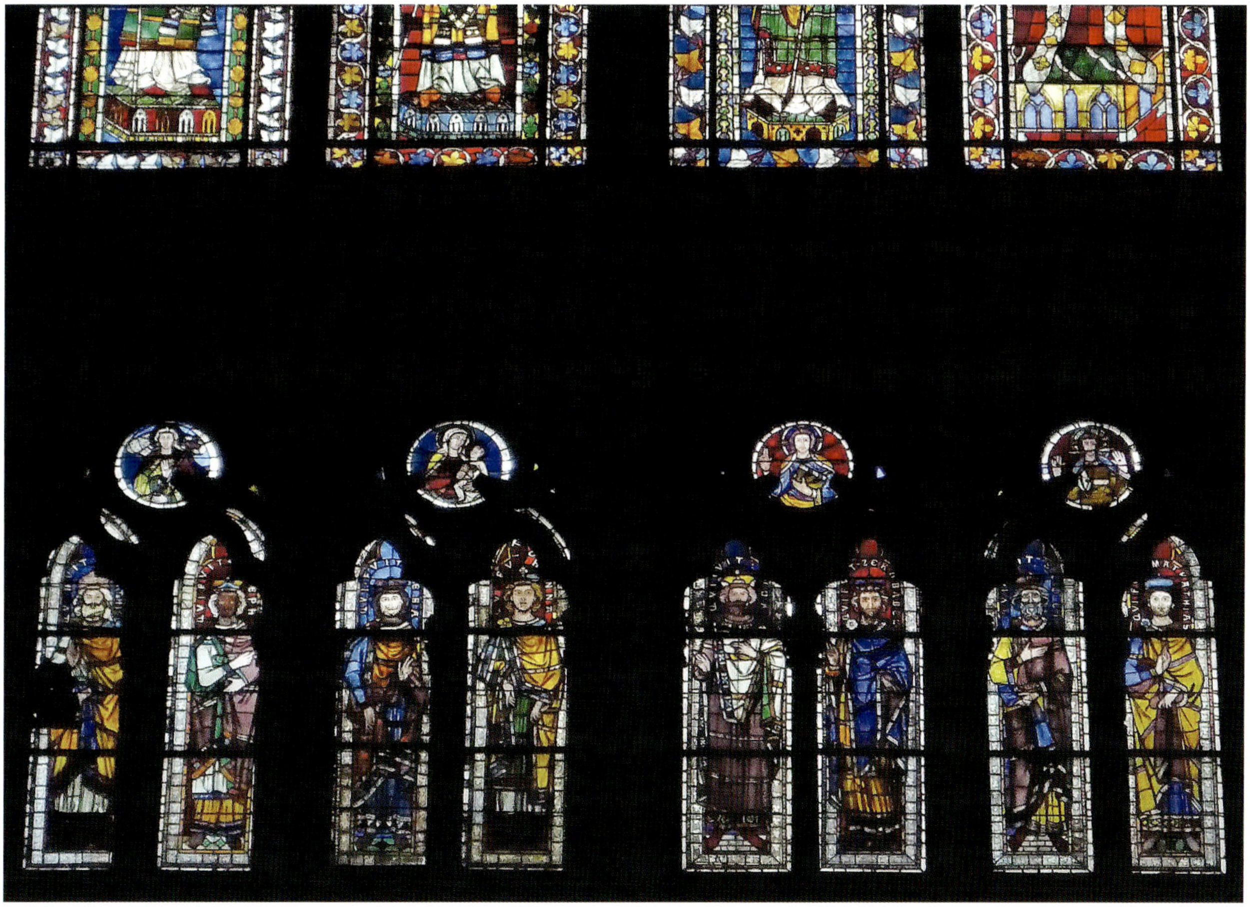

FIGURE 11. Strasbourg Cathedral, nave triforium glazing (photo: author).

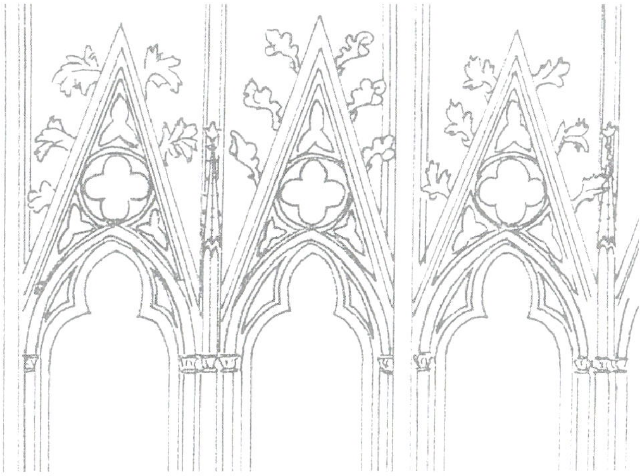

FIGURE 12. Strasbourg Cathedral, triforium arcading in north-west tower, from Riss D (after Wortmann).

Bel under the year 1298, Master Stephen of Auxerre, painter, was sent to Rome on certain royal business, and paid 100 Parisian *livres* for his trouble.[31] Other documented work by Stephen was for the Counts of Artois at Hesdin, where he was paid for decorating the chapel in 1295, a commission close to the French royal circle. What was the "royal business?" Was Etienne sent to Rome as a painter to purchase, or to deliver, artworks? Was Etienne sent to Rome to gain experience or training in Italian painting? Was Etienne sent to Rome to tempt Italian painters into French royal employment with a cash inducement? I think the last case is the

31. P. Binski, "Art-historical Reflections of the Fall of the Colonna, 1297," in *Rome Across Time and Space: Cultural Transmission and the Exchange of Ideas, c. 500–1400*, ed. C. Bolgia, R. McKitterick, and J. Osborne (Cambridge, 2011), 278–290.

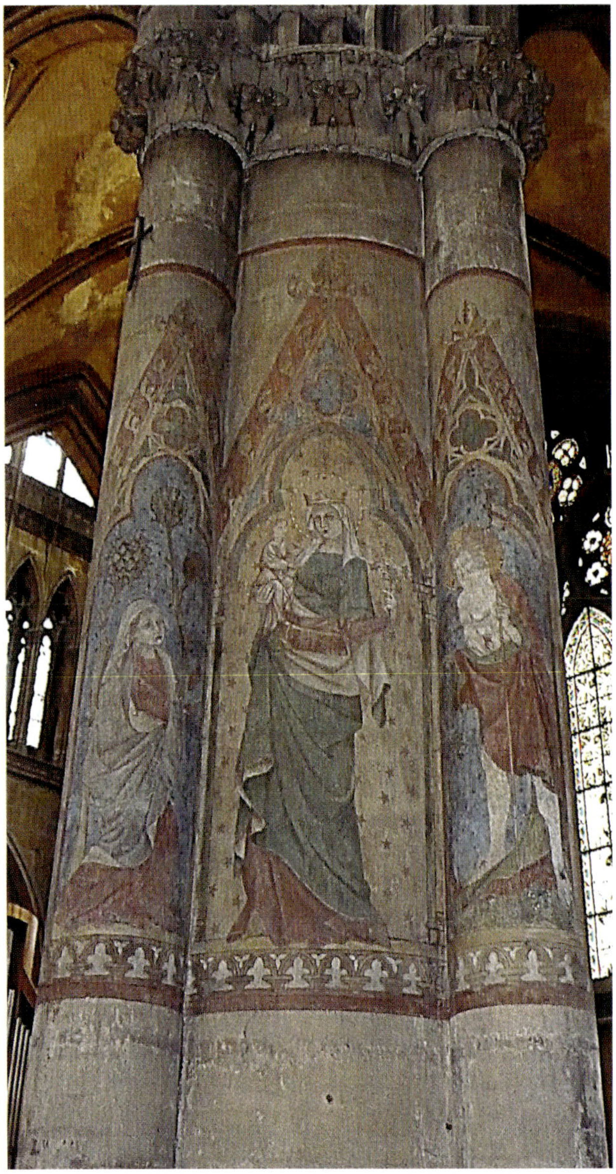

FIGURE 13. Metz Cathedral, nave pier, mural (photo: author).

most likely for reasons I will give shortly, but we note that speculative instances of this sort smoke out the tendentious nature of much art-historical discussion.

My reasoning is as follows. First, from 1304/5 through to 1323 we know from documentary sources that the senior French royal painters included men from the Italian Rusuti family working certainly at Poitiers and probably in Paris. This is notable because, second, the Rusuti were employed in the 1290s at the Roman basilica of Sta. Maria Maggiore, whose exterior façade mosaic, showing Christ in Majesty with angels, patrons, and saints, is signed PHILIPP[US] RVSVTI FECIT HOC O[P]VS (Fig. 14). The Rusuti joined the prestigious array of artists employed to decorate the exterior and interior of the Roman basilica by Pope Nicholas IV (1288–1292), the pope whose patronage may have enabled the completion of the frescoes of the Upper Church of S. Francesco at Assisi. Sta. Maria Maggiore matters especially because it was a church of the powerful Colonna family: Nicholas IV, whose kneeling image appears in the apse mosaic, did much to promote the Colonna, and they him. The Colonna, moreover, sponsored not only the Rusuti but also Iacopo Torriti, author of Sta. Maria Maggiore's great apse mosaic and of frescoes at Assisi.

The point of this is simple: the Colonna controlled some of the most important fresco and mosaic artists of the day and may have had a substantial say as patrons not only at Sta. Maria Maggiore but also at Assisi.[32] But on 3 May 1297, Stefano Colonna hijacked a consignment of papal gold heading for Rome. In return, Pope Boniface VIII, in a fury, deposed and excommunicated the Colonna cardinals, razed the family's fortresses, and seized their lands. Some Colonna family members sought refuge at the court of Philippe IV, whose final attack on Boniface was to follow. The patronage of this family in Rome and its environs in effect collapsed.

This is the first reason for thinking that the timing of Etienne's visit to Rome early the next year, 1298, may be explicable by a search for talent formerly controlled by the Colonna, which may have opened the way to the new arts of Rome and Assisi. The second point about timing is that in August 1297 Boniface had canonized Louis IX of France. These two very different

32. On which, see Brooke, *Image of St Francis* (as in note 29), 378–453; and, in addition, the pair of papers by D. Cooper and J. Robson, "'A great sumptuousness of paintings': Frescos and Franciscan Poverty at Assisi in 1288 and 1312"; and P. Binski, "The Patronage and Date of the Legend of St. Francis in the Upper Church of S. Francesco at Assisi," *Burlington Magazine* CLI (2009), 656–62 and 663–65.

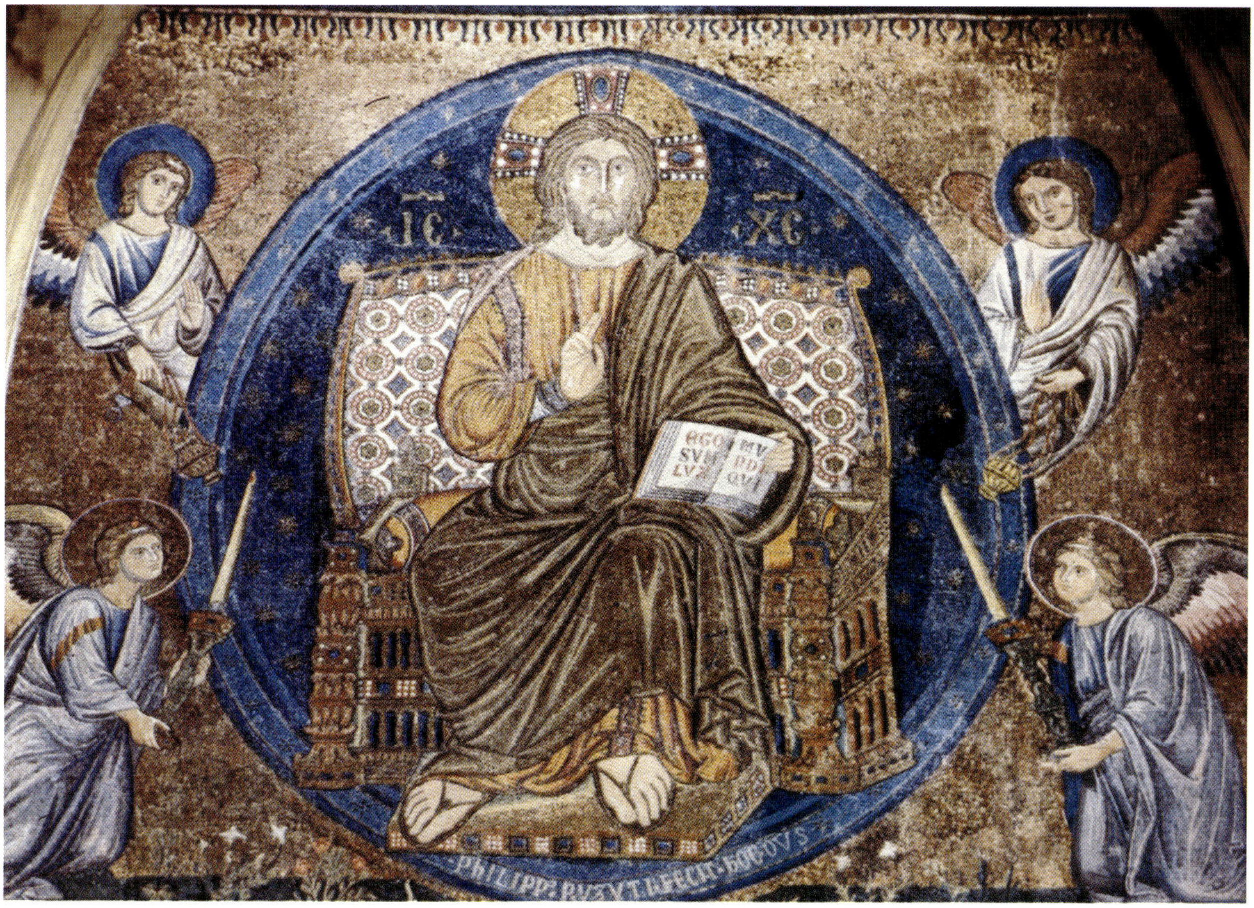

FIGURE 14. Rome, Sta. Maria Maggiore, detail of west façade exterior mosaic (photo: author).

events, the fall of the Colonna and the canonization of Louis, seem to me to be related in a way that advises us about the role of art media in these very elevated circles, namely that they are actors in a larger and more important plot. For Louis's hagiographers conceived of Louis as a very "Franciscan" saint. We note the strong Franciscan and Dominican presences amongst those conducting the canonization inquiry and composing the liturgical and hagiographical material that followed it: Guillaume de Saint-Pathus was a Franciscan. What did the earliest French picture cycles about St. Louis in the "mendicant mode" look like? Were they Italianate? We might guess as much from the rendering by Jean Pucelle himself of the Life of St. Louis in the famous Hours of Jeanne d'Evreux. If so, had Philippe IV, in promoting the cult of Louis, turned in 1297–1298 to the most spectacular picture cycle about a Franciscan, that about St. Francis himself at Assisi, and had he ordered Etienne to go to Rome to pick up people who could do the same for St. Louis, but in Paris?

If something like this happened, the Pucellian "revolution"—in any case Tuscan in inspiration—will not necessarily have been the thing that lent impetus to Panofsky's grand unfolding of International Gothic and Netherlandish art. The illuminators only played a part, quite possibly a secondary role, in this essentially formalistic narrative. This unfolding may not take into account sufficiently the role of major and minor arts within more far-reaching and powerful movements of religion, politics, and ideas that forced things together in unexpected and unrepeatable ways. Before Pucelle, I think, there came the Romans, and their role was ideological—to convey, via the dramatic narrative power of fresco in the manner of Giotto and his colleagues, the

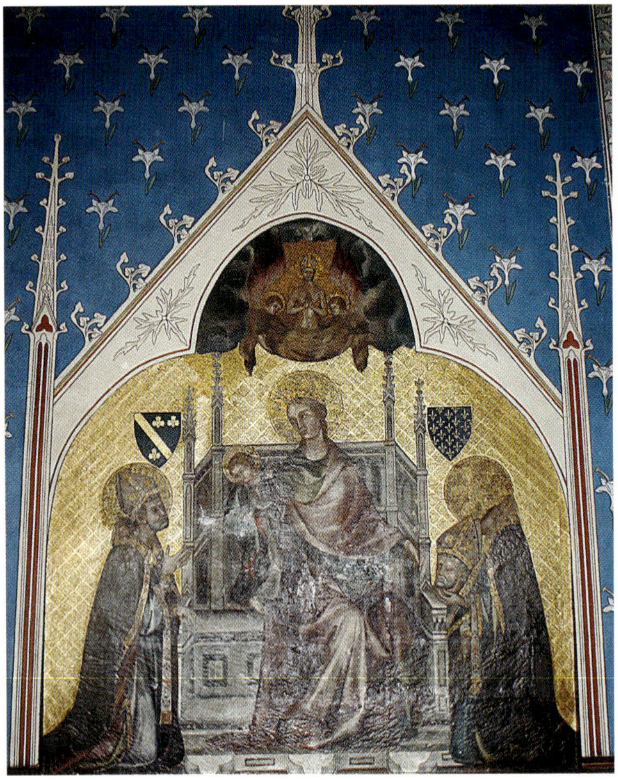

FIGURE 15. Paris, Notre-Dame, east chapel, mural over site of the tomb of Bishop Simon Matifas de Bucy (d. 1304) (photo: Emily Guerry).

standing of the cult of Louis IX. Again, I am suggesting that focussing on the art of manuscript illumination may mislead us. At the east end of Notre-Dame in Paris to this day is a tomb wall painting that accompanied the marble effigy of Simon Matifas de Bucy, Bishop of Paris in just these critical years 1290–1304. In style, the image, albeit much retouched, is "Pucellian;" in format, with the Virgin Mary approached by kneeling saints, it is unquestionably Roman (Fig. 15).[33] It represents a meeting-place, a synthesis. I suggest that this is a fragment of a much larger and vastly more influential culture of larger-scale painting in Paris, which fell under Italian influence no later than 1300. Pucelle as illuminator, like Honoré, I venture to suggest, forms a rear guard. The real work went on elsewhere.

III. *Conjuncture*

To reiterate: in these instances, the search for certain forms of invention leads us to treat the idea of great and small arts alike with scepticism, and to look harder instead at their relations, their points of intersection in projects that were well-funded, short-lived, not overly large, and, perhaps above all, that served vivid larger objectives: at Westminster, the celebration of the cult of St. Edward as the model for the Plantagenets; at Assisi, the promotion of St. Francis within the evangelical mission of the Franciscans; at Paris, the development of the cult of St. Louis and the prestige of the Capetians. All these "projects" were foyers, meeting-places, marked by eclecticism, by selection and unique re-mixture, and not always by obvious causal hierarchies in the media. In each case the outcome was a kind of paradigmatic shift in idiom of the sort that has interested developmental art history. It should be stated clearly that this is not a "rule" about the arts, but a context-dependent, contingent truth. We might seek an analogy to it in the verbal arts through the idea of *conjointure* as explored by Chretien de Troyes amongst others: namely the Horatian notion of *coniunctura*, the recombination of parts by original arrangement that accordingly changes perception of the matter at hand, or *matière*, in topical invention.[34]

If the balance has shifted at all in this essay, it has therefore been somewhat towards the major arts, but more importantly towards the operational context of the media towards a sociable "center" favoring not the giant corporate project of the "age of the cathedrals," but the smaller and more richly funded collaborative project better suited to the complex, and in many ways more challenging, social, cultural, and economic cli-

33. For the context, see M. T. Davis, "Splendor and Peril: The Cathedral of Paris, 1290–1350," *Art Bulletin* 80 (1998), 34–66; see J.-M. Guillouët and G. Kazerouni, "Le tombeau de Simon Matifas de Bucy: Une nouvelle peinture médiévale à Notre-Dame de Paris," *Revue de l'Art* 159 (2008), 35–44; see also J. Adhémar, "Les tombeaux de la collection Gaignières. Dessins d'archéologie du XVIIe siècle," *Gazette des beaux-arts* 84 (1974), 1–192, at 87, no. 455.

34. Kelly, "Topical Invention" (as in note 3), 243; see, again, the essays in Roberts, Scaffer, and Dear, *The Mindful Hand* (as in note 13); and, notably, P. H. Smith, "In a Sixteenth-century Goldsmith's Workshop," at 33–37.

mate of the centuries after 1300. If a notion of authorial sovereignty was being created anywhere in Gothic art at this time, it was within the circles of the great church architects whose professional standing as *auctores* was being re-theorized in the academic schools in the thirteenth century. But authorial prestige—indeed the prestige of an entire large-scale aesthetic system such as that of Parisian Rayonnant architecture—did not necessarily guarantee continued powers of invention. It may not be a coincidence that the increasing aesthetic sterility and academic character of French Rayonnant towards 1300 coincided closely with the period when the largest claims, intellectually speaking, were being made for its human producers. The more rational, the more simple, the more absolute the system, the greater was the risk of its creative neutering.

Finally, how aloof actually were the major arts from their smaller counterparts? Architecture, the greatest art technically, whose authors were esteemed highest as *auctores*, was scarcely ever an entirely closed system, granted that it had technical responsibilities like no other. The manner of working stones in the French way, *opere Francigeno*, noted *c.* 1280 by the chronicler Burchard von Hall at the new Gothic church at Wimpfen im Thal in one of the most famous passages about French Gothic art, was connected in his mind (rightly or wrongly) with windows and columns modeled on goldsmiths' work (*ad instar anaglifi*), provoking much wonder in the people. The astonishing Grail Temple in Albrecht's *Der Jüngere Titurel* written in the same years is also such as to bring to mind the mixed aesthetic of *kleinkunst.*[35] A body of opinion in Germany at least saw no harm in relating the largest and the smallest. Was this weak view of hierarchy what ultimately provoked Filarete's sense of the barbaric? Filarete, we recall, stated in the 1460s that with the ruin of Italy the barbarians introduced new customs and rites; since no "great buildings" were built, knowledge was lost, so when anyone wanted to build he had to have recourse to goldsmiths, painters, or (mere) masons; so the goldsmiths "built their buildings like tabernacles and thuribles" because these forms seemed beautiful in their own work. These customs came especially from across the mountains, "from the Germans and the French."[36] This technical babble, this disregard of the high style (and hence of the human capacity for greatness), was an affront to the Albertian sense of decorum. But can we necessarily say that, as an account of some forms of Gothic practice, Filarete was wholly wrong, however unsympathetic his purpose?

35. For Wimpfen im Thal, see *Cronica ecclesiae Wimpinensis auct. Burcardo de Hallis et Dythero de Helmestat*, ed. Heinrich Boehmer, in MGH SS 30, pt. 1 (Hannover, 1896), 659–77, at 666; R. Branner, *St Louis and the Court Style in Gothic Architecture* (London, 1965), 1; H. Klotz, *Der Ostbau der Stiftskirche zu Wimpfen im Tal. Zum Frühwerk des Erwin von Steinbach* (Berlin, 1967). For *Titurel*, see A. Timmermann, "Architectural Vision in Albrecht von Scharfenberg's *Jüngerer Titurel*" in *Architecture and Language: Constructing Identity in European Architecture c. 1000–c. 1650*, ed. Georgia Clarke and Paul Crossley (Cambridge, 2000), 58–71.

36. J. R. Spencer, trans., *Filarete's Treatise on Architecture* (New Haven and London, 1965), vol. 1, 176 (Book XIII, fol. 100^{v}).

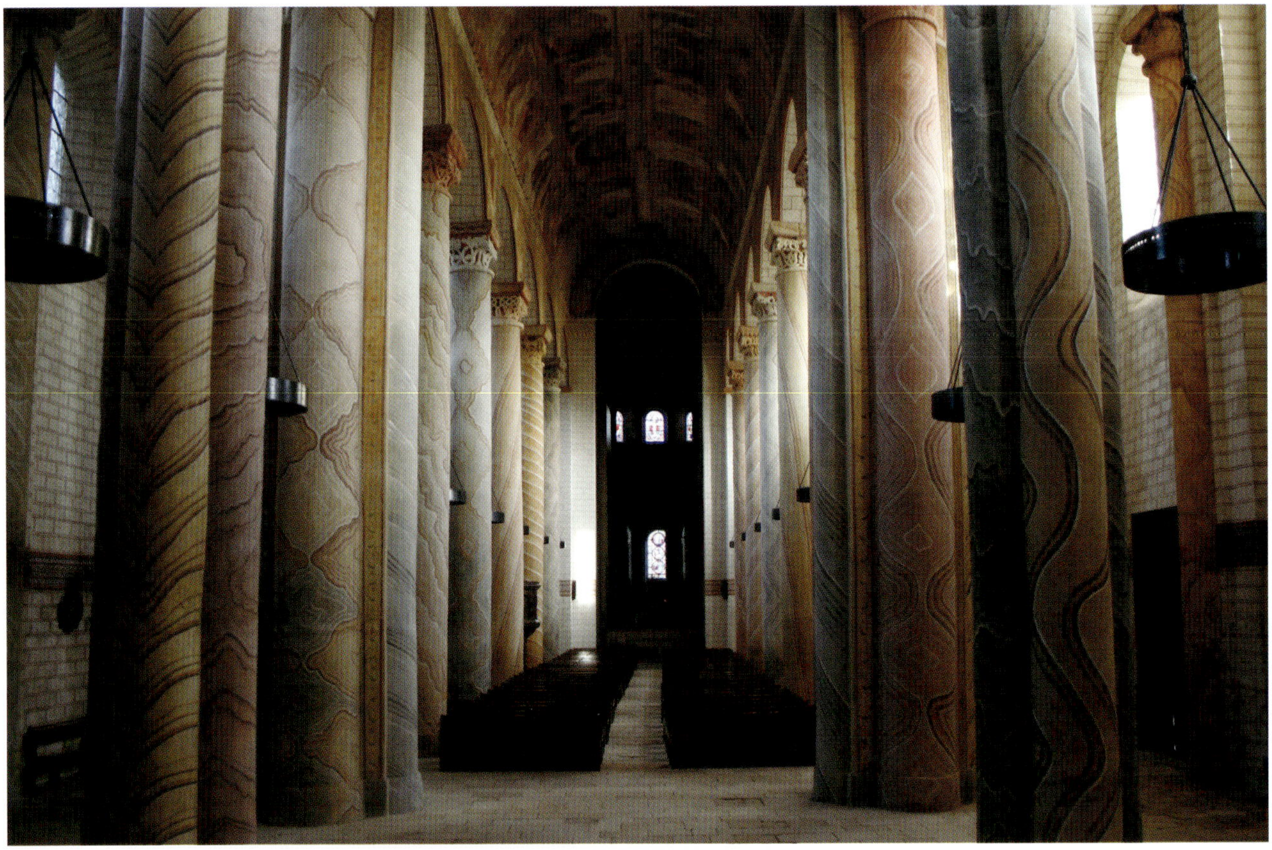

FIGURE 1. Saint-Savin-sur-Gartempe, nave towards the east (photo: author).

THOMAS E. DALE

Transcending the Major/Minor Divide: Romanesque Mural Painting, Color, and Spiritual Seeing

ROMANESQUE mural painting—which once encompassed all or most of the expansive wall surfaces of church interiors throughout Europe in the eleventh to thirteenth centuries with complex programs of sacred imagery executed in often brilliant colors—is usually understood as a "major" art by virtue of its scale. And the better preserved examples, such as the interior of the Benedictine Abbey of Saint-Savin-sur-Gartempe (Poitou), continue to attract considerable scholarly attention and even popular acclaim (Fig. 1).[1] It is also true, however, that this monumental medium has at times been assimilated to a minor art by the assumptions of much modern historiography and also by the technique of reproduction, which mediated often fragmentary or badly damaged programs of imagery. This paper seeks to transcend the traditional major/minor divide by emphasizing the essential devotional functions of mural painting as part of a seamless colorscape that encompassed both the major and minor arts—liturgical vessels in precious metal adorned with radiant gems, and the brightly painted pages of illuminated service books, as well as larger-scale polychrome sculpted capitals and wall paintings.

We gain a better impression of this polychrome effect in the original decoration of Saint-Savin-sur-Gartempe, which was preserved almost intact beneath whitewash until it was uncovered in the early nineteenth century. The program includes a cycle of the Apocalypse and Last Judgement in the west porch, a cycle of the Passion and Easter in the tribune, and a Genesis cycle in the nave, the *Passio* of the patron saint, Savinus, in the crypt, and fragments of painted decoration in the ambulatory and radiating chapels. The columns and capitals of the nave were also painted. Although much has been written about color in illuminated manuscripts,[2] and there is a growing literature on the rediscovered polychrome on ivories, stone and wood sculpture, the role played by color on the vast interior wall surfaces has been largely neglected due to the greatly diminished state of surviving examples, often faded, abraded, fragmented, or re-painted in the nineteenth century. Furthermore, as far as modern historiography is concerned, when it comes to painting, the major and minor arts have changed places. Though technically a minor art in scale, manuscript illumination has gained greater prominence due to its excellent state of preservation, its association with prestigious patrons, and perhaps most important its close proximity with texts.[3] Indeed, our logo-centric modes of interpreting medieval art have favored manuscript illumination as the leading medium for medieval visual imagery throughout the Middle Ages.

I will argue here that mural painting was essential to the experience of sacred space, physically surrounding the viewers with sacred images and immersing them in a brilliant colorscape that served to engage the senses

1. Delia Viola Kottmann, *Die romanischen Wandmalereien von Saint-Savin-sur-Gartempe*. Deutsches Historische Institut (Paris, 2007).

2. E.g., A. Petzold, "'Of the Significance of Colours': The Iconography of Colour in Romanesque and Early Gothic Book Illumination," in C. Hourihane, ed., *Image & Belief: Studies in Celebration of the Eightieth Anniversary of the Index of Christian Art* (Princeton, N.J., 1999); E. S. Bolman."*De coloribus*: The Meanings of Color in Beatus Manuscripts" *Gesta* 38, no. 1 (1999), 22–34.

3. The primacy of text illustration was promoted in particular by K. Weitzmann whose method of picture criticism was based on critical methods of textual study. See his *Illustrations in Roll and Codex: A Study of the Origin and Method of Text Illustration*, Studies in Manuscript Illumination (Princeton, N.J., 1947; 2nd ed. 1970); and M.-L. Dolezal, "Manuscript Studies in the Twentieth Century: Kurt Weitzmann Reconsidered," *Byzantine and Modern Greek Studies* 22 (1998), 216–63.

as part of the devotional practice. As Otto Demus so perceptively observed, "Romanesque mural paintings are not individual pictures, but parts of a veil of color drawn over the entire interior of the church."[4] Demus insisted on the need to imagine the original completeness of now fragmentary cycles in order to understand their unification of the experience of interior space but also their broader programmatic functions. His concept of a "veil of color," however, might also be understood as an apt metaphor for the fundamental, revelatory role of color. As Michel Pastoureau has shown, the period of the Romanesque, beginning in the late eleventh century, marked a crucial threshold in the acceptance of color as integral to the operation of sight, both in the realm of social rank and identification with the development of heraldry, and in the realm of the church, where it was widely accepted as having the potential to lead to a higher spiritual vision, beyond the realm of the senses.[5]

Before presenting the fruit of preliminary research on this topic, I will briefly suggest three ways in which the medium has been transformed from a major into a minor art in modern historiography, thus diminishing its role as a spatial medium for contemplation: (1) the antiquarian project of copying mural painting in the form of small-scale drawings and watercolors, and collecting actual fragments starting in the seventeenth century; (2) the formalist interpretations of Romanesque in the early decades of the twentieth century as precursor to modern abstraction, and (3) the search for iconographic sources that dominated much of the twentieth century.

One can trace the seeds of the miniaturization and fragmentation of Romanesque mural painting to the antiquarian enterprise of the later sixteenth and seventeenth centuries in Italy. In the wake of the Counter-Reformation, the reawakening of interest in the origins of the Christian church in Rome encouraged the careful documentation, and in some instances, the collection of medieval Christian antiquities including mural painting. Cassiano del Pozzo, for example, created a "paper museum" comprising a series of watercolors and drawings he had commissioned to document both ancient Roman and Christian antiquities in Rome; his documentation of medieval churches was intended to support a larger project of the Barberini family to restore them to their former grandeur.[6] We see, for example, how the still-extant paintings of *c.* 1100 in the oratory of Santa Pudenziana (Fig. 2) were presented as a collection of individual panels, rendered faithfully in terms of subject matter and inscriptions, but in a modern style, and divorced from a larger architectural or narrative context.[7]

This antiquarian exercise was repeated on a larger scale in the course of the nineteenth and early twentieth centuries when painted copies were made of mural paintings to record their original state and aid in their restoration. Among the earliest of such projects in Europe was that initiated by Ludovic Vitet, the first Inspecteur Général des Monuments Historiques and then President of the Commission of the Monuments Historiques up to 1848.[8] Vitet and the celebrated literary figure Prosper Mérimée, who rediscovered the murals of Saint-Savin-sur-Gartempe, sought to reverse the French taste for whitewashed church interiors that had prevailed during the eighteenth century by making detailed watercolor copies to record recently recovered medieval murals in their original state and furnish models for their restoration.[9] These copies served in turn as the basis for color lithographs that illustrated publications of mural painting around the turn of the twentieth century. Although the original project was rooted in the desire to conserve and restore the ensemble of medieval church decoration, the plates re-

4. O. Demus, *Romanesque Mural Painting* (New York, 1970).

5. M. Pastoureau, "L'Église et la couleur, des origines à la Réforme," *Bibliothèque de l'École des chartes* 147 (1989), 203–230.

6. J. Osborne and A. Claridge, *Early Christian and Medieval Antiquities in The Paper Museum of Cassiano dal Pozzo,* Series A: Antiquities and Architecture, Part II (London, 1996), vol. I, 43–52.

7. *Ibid.*, 308–17, pls. 143–147

8. F. Bercé, "La Commission des Monuments Historiques et la protection des peintures murales sous la monarchie de juillet," in *"De fresque en aquarelle": Relevés d'artistes sur la peinture murale romane*, Exhib. Cat. (Paris and Saint-Savin-sur-Gartempe, 1994), 19–21.

9. P. Mérimée, *Notice sur les peintures de l'église de Saint-Savin* (Paris, 1845), new ed. as "L'Église de Saint-Savin et ses peintures murales," in *Études sur les arts du Moyen Âge, Oeuvres complètes de Prosper Mérimée* (Paris, 1891; rpt. Paris, 1967), 55–149.

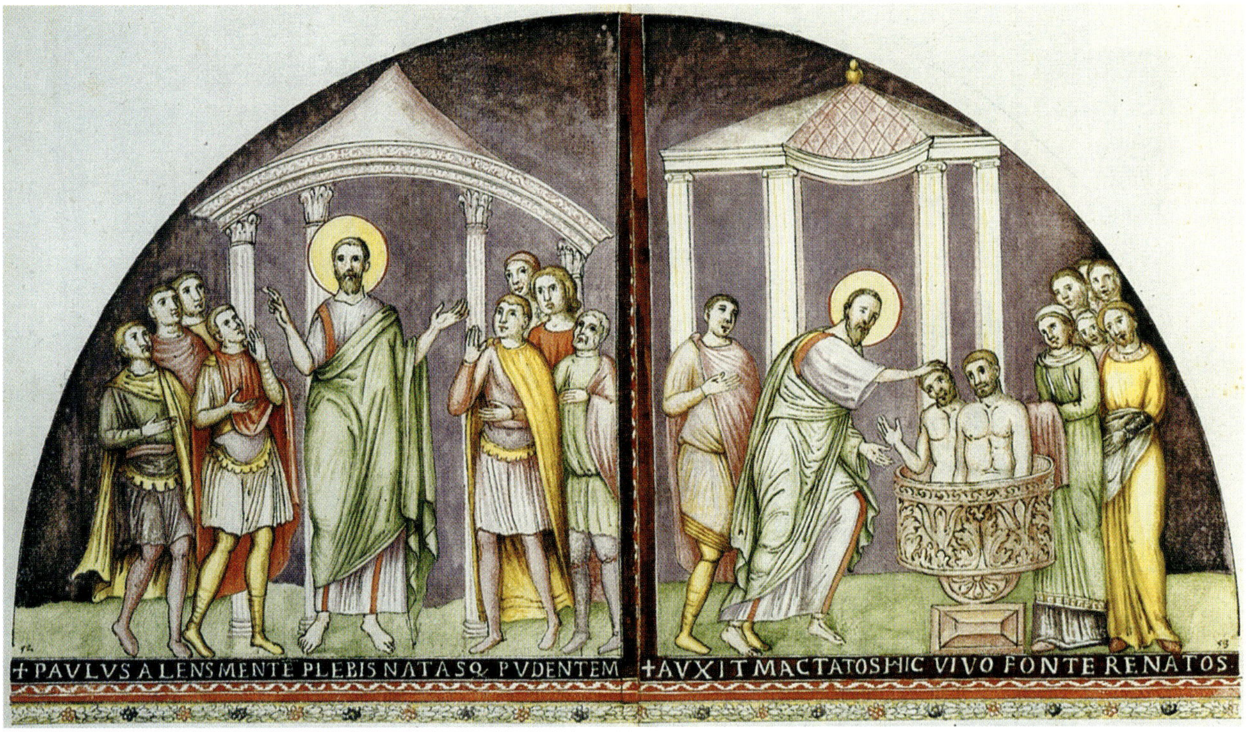

FIGURE 2. Antonio Ecclissi, watercolor copy of frescoes depicting Paul baptizing and preaching to the sons of Pudens, Oratory of the Madonna, Santa Pudenziana, Rome, from the Paper Museum of Cassiano del Pozzo (photo: after J. Osborne and A. Claridge, *Early Christian and Medieval Antiquities* in *The Paper Museum of Cassiano dal Pozzo*, Series A: Antiquities and Architecture, Part II [London, 1996]).

produced in publications later in the century presented an assemblage of details—individual scenes, figures, and selected ornamental motifs that illustrate the brilliant palette and distinctive regional styles. We see this beautifully illustrated in the color plates showing Saint-Savin-sur-Gartempe, and Saint-Martin at Nohant-Vicq in an 1889 publication, *La peinture decorative en France* (Fig. 3).[10] This publication inspired, in turn, a series of publications on Catalan Romanesque painting, starting in 1907, including a comparable series of lithographic reproductions based on watercolor copies commissioned by the Junta de Museos between 1907 and 1920.[11] A little later, sets of colored lithographs based on watercolors were being used to illustrate texts on comparative ornament such as Alexander Speltz's *Coloured Ornament of All Historical Styles*, published in 1914–1915 (Fig. 4).[12] The composition of these plates shows that Romanesque painting was valued for its two-dimensional, decorative quality, understood as parallel to the relative abstraction and decorative use of color in contemporary art. It may further be suggested that these fragmented displays of monumental mural painting contributed in part to its collectibility, especially as it became common in certain regions to remove the best-preserved fragments of paintings to museums. This is how the Metropolitan Museum of

10. P. Gélis-Didot and H. Laffillée, *La Peinture Décorative en France du XI au XVI siècle* (Paris, 1889; 3rd ed. Paris, 1907).

11. J. Camps i Sòria, "Còpia i publicació de les pintures," in *Puig i Cadafalch i la collecció de pintura romànica del MNAC*, ed. J. Camps i Sòria (Barcelona, 2001), 15–19; M. Guardia, J. Camps i Sòria, and I. Lorés, *El descubrimiento de la pintura mural románica catalana. La colección de reproducciones del MNAC* (Barcelona, 1993), 11–36.

12. A. Speltz, *The Coloured Ornament of all Historical Styles, with Coloured Plates from Own Paintings in Water Colours*, Part II: *Middle Ages*, 3 vols. (Leipzig, 1914–1915).

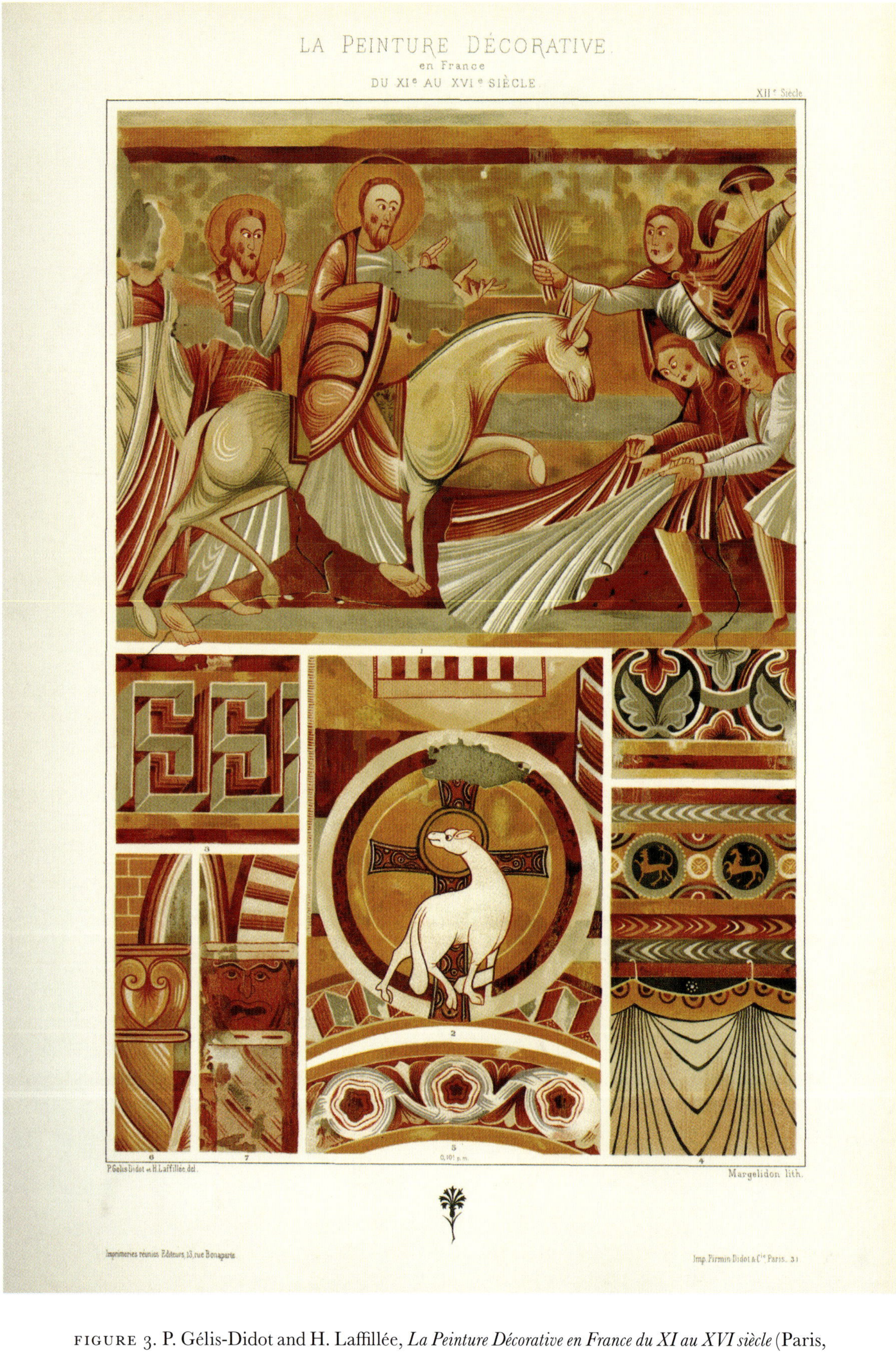

FIGURE 3. P. Gélis-Didot and H. Laffillée, *La Peinture Décorative en France du XI au XVI siècle* (Paris, 1889; 3rd ed. Paris, 1907), pl. 11, Priory of Saint-Martin at Vicq (photo: Kohler Art Library, University of Wisconsin, Madison).

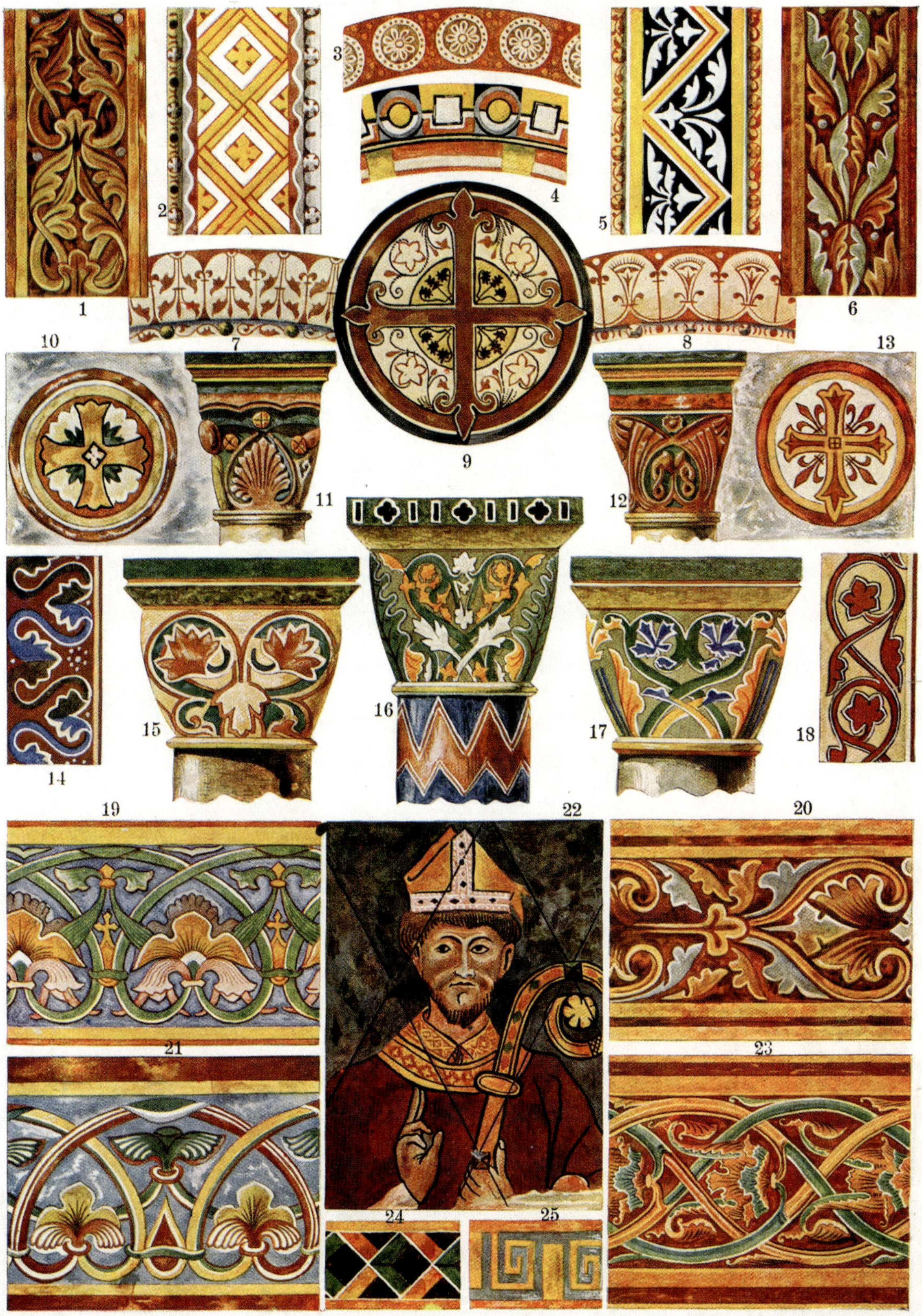

FIGURE 4. A. Speltz, *The Coloured Ornament of All Historical Styles*, Part II: Middle Ages, 3 vols. (Leipzig, 1914–1915), French Romanesque Mural Painting (photo: Kohler Art Library, University of Wisconsin, Madison).

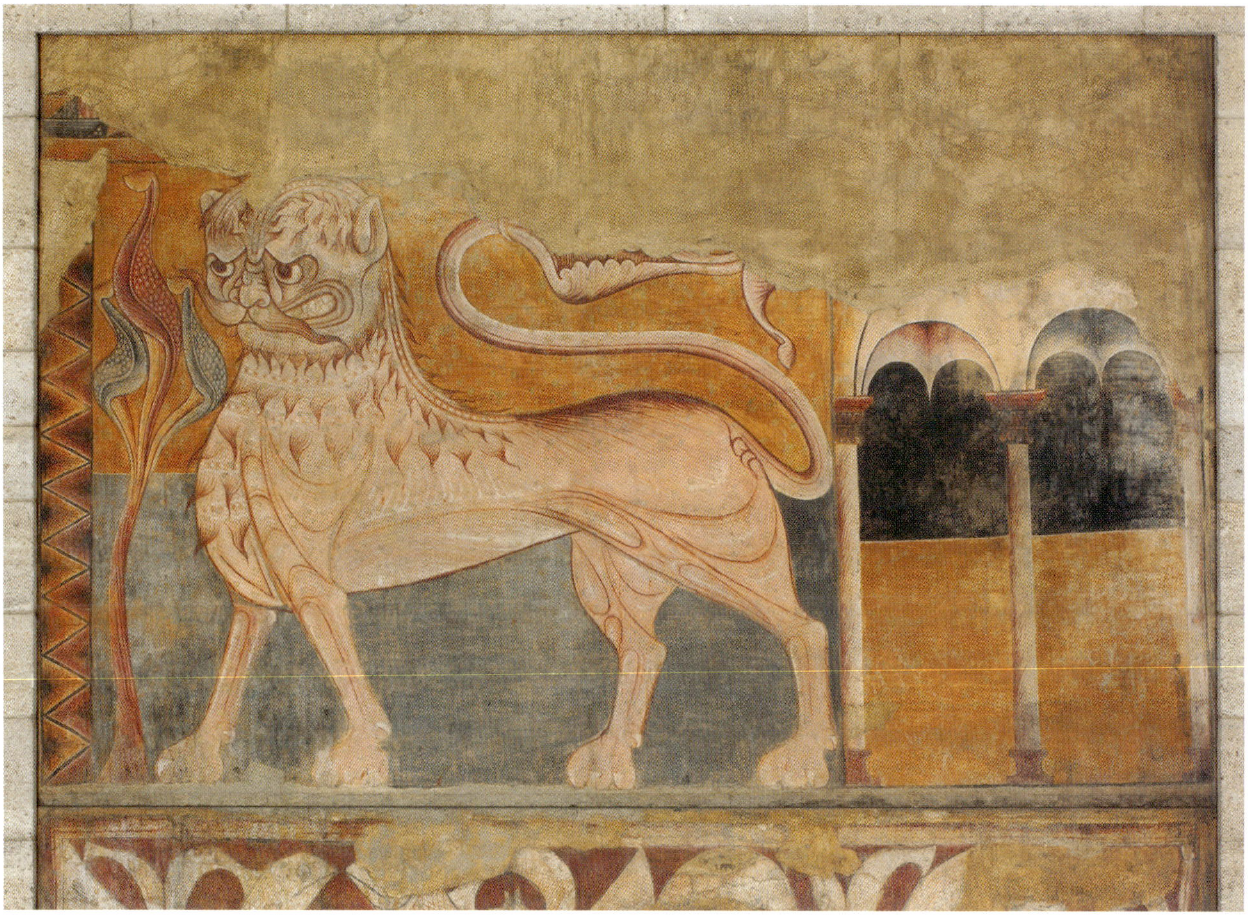

FIGURE 5. Lion passant, fresco, remounted on canvas, after 1200, from Chapter House of S. Pedro de Arlanza, New York, The Cloisters, The Metropolitan Museum of Art, New York, acc. no. 31.38.1ab (photo: The Metropolitan Museum of Art / Art Resource, N.Y.).

Art in New York, for example, obtained the fragments depicting a majestic lion (Fig. 5) and the dragon passant from the chapter house of Arlanza, as well as nine panels of animals, hunting scenes, and narratives from the life of Christ originating in the hermitage of San Baudelio de Berlanga in Soria.[13] The neatly framed fragments function in a way similar to the initials cut from illuminated manuscripts as works of art worthy of collecting apart from their original texts.[14]

The antiquarian exercise of collecting and reproducing Romanesque mural painting in fragmented views also made accessible and drew attention to the bright

13. For San Pedro de Arlanza (The Cloisters Collection, Metropolitan Museum of Art, 31.38.1ab; 31.38.2ab), see Demus, *Romanesque Mural Painting*, 487, fig. 35; and W. Cahn, "The Frescoes of San Pedro de Arlanza," in *The Cloisters: Studies in Honor of the Fiftieth Anniversary*, ed. E. C. Park and M. B. Shepard (New York, 1992), 87–109. For San Baudelio de Berlanga (The Cloisters Collection, The Metropolitan Museum of Art, 59.97.1–6, 59.196, 61.219, 61.248), see Demus, *Romanesque Mural Painting*, 481–82; J. D. Dodds, "Wall Paintings: Hermitage of San Baudelio de Berlanga (Soria)," in *The Art of Medieval Spain, A.D. 500–1200*. ed. J. D. Dodds, B. F. Reilly, J. W. Williams, *et al.*, Exhib. Cat. (New York, 1993), 223–228; M. Guardia, "Relire les espaces liturgiques à travers la peinture murale : Le programme iconographique de San Baudelio de Berlanga (Soria)," *Les Cahiers de Saint-Michel de Cuxa* 34 (2003), 79–97.

14. R. Weick, "*Folia fugitiva*: The Pursuit of the Illuminated Manuscript Leaf," *Journal of the Walters Art Gallery* 54 (1996), 233–54.

colors and formal language of mural painting that had particular appeal to modern painters and formalist art criticism. The French scholar Henri Focillon, a medievalist who also wrote about early twentieth-century art, affirms in 1938 that "respect for the wall dominates. Bright or dark, empty or subdivided into bands ... the ground imposes upon us the idea of a limit and of a stability. They do not seek to create a fictive space...."[15] Paul-Henri Michel writing in 1949 pushed the resemblance between Romanesque and modern painting more explicitly: "an affinity exists between Romanesque painting and that of our own day, in its most characteristic and essential manifestation. This affinity is particularly notable in the deliberate intention of surface-painting without attempting an illusion of depth, and the desire to escape from the world of appearances...."[16] The larger context for this formalist view of the Romanesque was the shift away from perspectival space in the art of the post-Impressionists—in the Fauves painters such as Matisse, and in the Nabis painters such as Bonnard, Denis, and Vuillard who pursued large-scale mural decoration and screens between the 1890s and 1930s.[17]

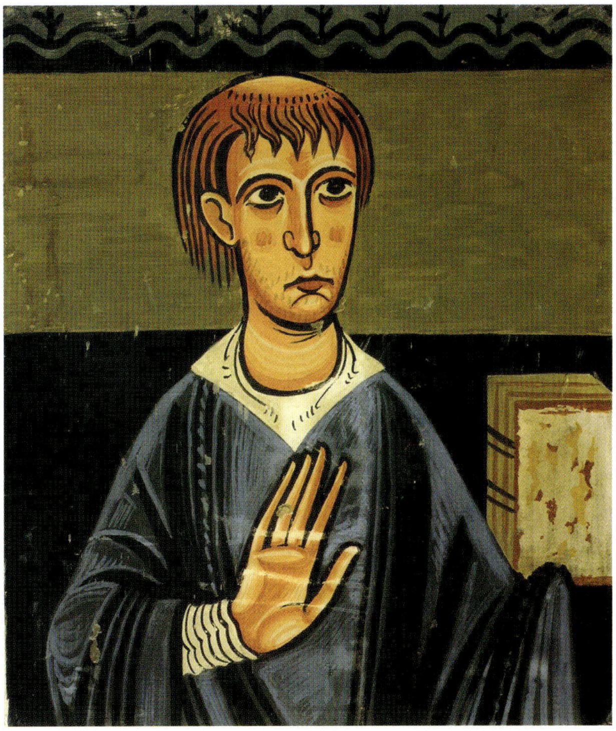

FIGURE 6. Joan Vallhonrat, Reproduction of deacon from apse of Sta. Maria d'Aneu, tempera on paper, 1909, Museu Nacional d'Art de Catalunya, Barcelona, acc. no. 63872 (photo: copyright MNAC, Barcelona).

The idea of escaping the world of appearances to recover an originary "primitive" art also inspired French and Spanish modernist painters to emulate certain aspects of Catalan Romanesque painting, newly rediscovered at the end of the nineteenth century.[18] Shortly after 1900, many Romanesque mural paintings were uncovered in Catalonia, carefully documented, and, in order to save them from being sold out of the country, most of the best murals were cut into sections and removed to museums, including the Museu d'Art i Arqueologia (Museum of Art and Archaeology) at the Ciutadella de l'Arsenal in Barcelona, which opened in 1915, the predecessor of the Museu d'Art de Catalunya (Museum of Catalan Art), which opened in 1934 in the Palacio Nacional on Montjuïc.[19] The apse of Santa Maria d'Aneu, for example, which was acquired by the museum between 1919 and 1923, had already been fully documented in 1909 by a series of black-and-white photographs, a large-scale watercolor reproduction by Joan Vallhonrat, and a detail of the deacon (Fig. 6); the copies were displayed in the museum shortly after they were made. Joan Miró admitted to being inspired by the language of the Romanesque murals that he saw

15. H. Focillon, *Peintures romanes des églises de France* (Paris, 1938; 2nd ed. 1950), 16.

16. P.-H. Michel, *Romanesque Wall Paintings in France*, trans. J. Evans (London, 1950), 26.

17. G. L. Groom *et al.*, *Beyond the Easel: Decorative Painting by Bonnard, Vuillard, Denis, and Roussel, 1890–1930* (New Haven and Chicago, 2001). These artists were treated by H. Focillon in *Le peinture aux XIX et XX siècles du réalisme à nos jours* (Paris, 1928). For Focillon's engagement with formalism in modern painting of his time, see C. Brien and A. Thomine, *La vie des formes: Henri Focillon et les arts*, Exhib. Cat. (Paris and Lyon, 2004).

18. See the useful overview by M. Castiñeiras, "The Legacy of Romanesque Art: The Vision of Modernity," in *Romanesque Art in the MNAC Collections*, ed. M. Castiñeiras and J. Camps i Sòria with J. Duran-Porta (Barcelona, 2008), 205–213.

19. M. Pagès, "La resposta: compra i trasllat de les pintures al Museu," *Puig i Cadafalch i la collecció de pintura romànica del MNAC*, 25–31.

in the museum as a child; from Romanesque painting he developed his own immersive color fields, a sense for brilliant luminosity and certain symbolic details, such as the disembodied eyes that appear in his Head of Catalan Peasant and Catalan landscape paintings of the 1920s.[20] The eyes on the wings of the seraphim in the apse of Santa Maria d'Aneu, for example, offered a specific source for the motif of the disembodied eye. Francis Picabia, who visited the museum at the Ciutadella in 1927, made a series of works that alluded to themes of motifs in the Romanesque apse compositions of Santa Mara d'Aneu and Sant Climint de Taüll.[21] Finally, Pablo Picasso, who was born in Barcelona and began his artistic career there, saw the Romanesque paintings in the newly opened Museum of Catalan Art at Montjuïc as "an invaluable lesson for the moderns."[22]

A third way in which modern historiography has diminished the distinctive spatial and coloristic impact of mural painting is through the obsession with tracing iconographic sources. Particularly influential in France was Émile Mâle's iconographical research, which emphasized the role of manuscript illumination as sources for both monumental painting and sculpture.[23] In America, Charles Rufus Morey furthered iconographic research by creating the Index of Christian Art at Princeton in 1917.[24] He was also instrumental in bringing Kurt Weitzmann to Princeton in 1935 to work in the Index, which he considered the "research cell for the Department."[25] This undoubtedly contributed to Weitzmann's highly influential theory of "picture criticism," which he developed to classify biblical iconography in all media as part of larger recensions or families related to key manuscripts thought to reflect lost archetypes in papyrus rotuli.[26] The application of this theory to mural painting is illustrated by George Henderson's analysis of the Old Testament cycle on the vault of Saint-Savin-sur-Gartempe; comparing the Genesis scenes with Carolingian and Anglo-Saxon Bible manuscript illumination, he concludes that "the designer of the Saint-Savin Genesis cycle did not as a rule rely on scripture and his own imagination, but on earlier pictorial models."[27] Tracing a presumed late antique archetype, Henderson ignores the innovative disposition of narrative on the vault and the impact of the specific spatial organization of the church.

As Ernst Kitzinger has persuasively argued, manuscripts only rarely can be proven to have served as sources for mural decoration, and this occurs under special circumstances.[28] Thus, the replication of both the style and iconography of Cotton Genesis manuscript in the atrium mosaics of San Marco in Venice may have been intended to reinforce Venice's connection with an Early Christian past at a time when Venice was reasserting its connection to the homeland of its patron saint in Alexandria. As Kitzinger argues,

20. See B. Rose, "Miró Finds his Vocation as an Artist," in *Depression and the Spiritual in Modern Art: Homage to Miró*, ed. J. J. Schildkraut and A. Otero (Chichester and New York, 1996), 172–185, esp. 173–175; and X. Barral i Altet, "Joan Miró i l'art romànic català," *Revista de Catalunya* 87 (1994), 90–103.

21. Castiñeiras, "The Legacy of Romanesque Art" (as in note 18), 207–208.

22. *Ibid.*, 210, citing a press release by C. Capdevila in the Barcelona newspaper, *La Publicitat.*

23. É. Mâle, *L'art religieux du XIIIe siècle en France* (Paris, 1899); *idem*, *L'art religieux de la fin du moyen âge en France: Étude sur l'iconographie du moyen âge et sur ses sources d'inspiration* (Paris, 1908); *idem*, *L'art religieux du XIIe siècle en France: Étude sur les origines de l'iconographie du moyen âge* (Paris, 1922).

24. C. Hourihane, "'They stand on his shoulders': Morey, Iconography and the Index of Christian Art," in *Insights and Interpretations: Studies in the Celebration of the Eighty-fifth Anniversary of the Index of Christian Art*, ed. C. Hourihane (Princeton, N.J., 2002), 3–16.

25. K. Weitzmann, "The Contribution of the Princeton University Department of Art and Archaeology to the Study of Byzantine Art," in *Byzantium at Princeton: Byzantine Art and Archaeology at Princeton University*, ed. S. Ćurčić and A. St. Clair (Princeton, N.J., 1986), 11–30, esp. 14.

26. Weitzmann, *Illustrations in Roll and Codex*; and Dolezal, "Manuscript Studies in the Twentieth Century: Kurt Weitzmann Reconsidered" (as in note 3).

27. G. Henderson, "The Sources of the Genesis Cycle at Saint-Savin-sur-Gartempe," *Journal of the British Archeological Association* 26 (1963), 11–26. A similar approach was taken by I. Yoshikawa, *L'Apocaylypse de Saint-Savin* (Paris, 1939).

28. E. Kitzinger, "The Role of Miniature Painting in Mural Decoration," in *The Place of Book Illumination in Medieval Art*, ed. K. Weitzmann (Princeton, N.J., 1975), 99–142; rpt. in E. Kitzinger, *Studies Late Antique Byzantine and Medieval Western Art* (London, 2002), 448–97.

mosaicists and mural painters more often relied upon pictorial guides, drawings designed specifically to transfer ideas within a workshop that could be applied in more than one location. He uses this concept to explain iconographic resemblances among the mosaics of Monreale and Palermo.[29] A similar process must also have been used in a workshop responsible for both painted decoration in mosaics in the Upper Adriatic. The figures of John the Evangelist, Paul, Philip, and Bartholomew at Aquileia (Fig. 7) replicate the style and iconography of their counterparts in the north apse mosaic of San Giusto at Trieste (Fig. 8).[30] The Aquileia crypt also draws on the mosaics of San Marco in Venice as models for Saint Nicholas and the group of grieving women in the Crucifixion.[31]

Since the late 1960s, the study of Romanesque mural painting has been transformed in ways that have helped restore its monumental presence and broader programmatic meaning. Otto Demus laid the foundation for a more holistic interpretation, arguing that "Romanesque mural paintings were, and are, integral components of three-dimensional works of art.... The walls echoed the text of the liturgy in pictorial terms; to the congregation they were both shelter and a means to sanctity. The pictures were more than decoration or instruction; they were models of spiritual behavior."[32] This thoughtful engagement of the spatial and ritual aspects of Romanesque painting surely reflects Demus's own engagement with the concept of icons in space as a focus for individual and collective devotion in Byzantine Church decoration some twenty-five years earlier.[33] Taking up Demus's lead, much scholarship over the past fifty years has explored the ways in which entire programs of mural paintings were designed to fashion sacred space in relationship to ritual and institutional life.[34] Much has also been said of the didactic and mnemonic functions of mural painting, especially the nave cycles that present biblical and hagiographic history. What remains largely unexplored is the ways in which the color and form of Romanesque painting—the two crucial aspects of vision according to twelfth-century theories—complement the subject matter to offer a concrete starting point for contemplation. In the remainder of this paper, I would like to suggest how the selection and disposition of color

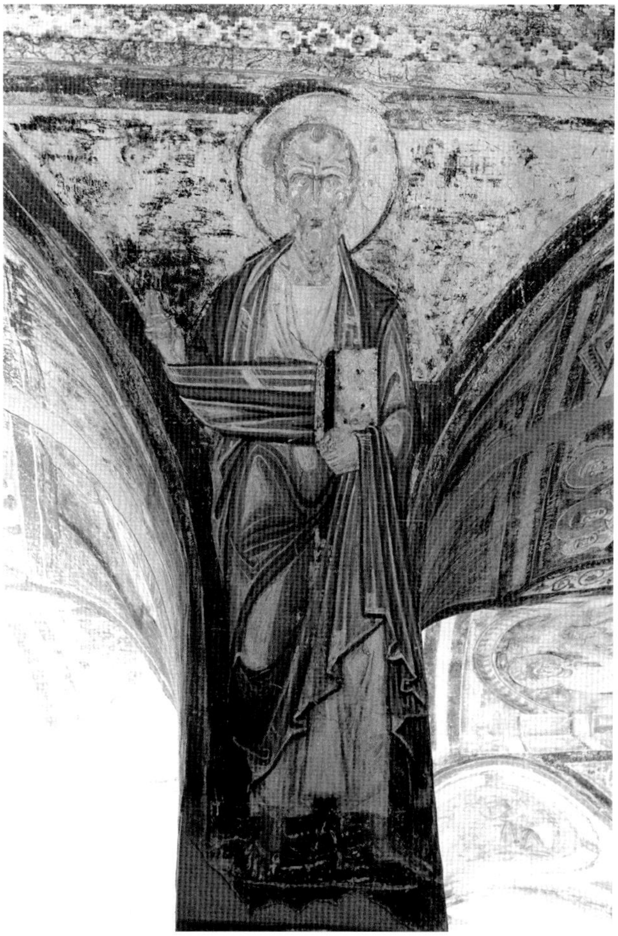

FIGURE 7. Saint John the Evangelist, fresco, crypt of Basilica Patriarcale Aquileia, *c.* 1180 (photo: author).

29. *Ibid.*, esp. 458–66.

30. T. Dale, *Relics, Prayer, and Politics in Medieval Venetia: Romanesque Painting in the Crypt of Aquileia Cathedral* (Princeton, N.J., 1997), 30–31.

31. D. dalla Barba Brusin and G. Lorenzoni, *L'arte del patriarcato di Aquileia dal secolo IX al secolo XIII* (Padua, 1968), 59–67; Dale, *Relics, Prayer, and Politics* (as in note 30), 30.

32. Demus, *Romanesque Mural Painting* (as in note 4), 7.

33. O. Demus, *Byzantine Mosaic Decoration: Aspects of Monumental Art in Byzantium* (London, 1948; rpt. 1976).

34. T. Dale, "Introduction" in *Shaping Sacred Space and Institutional Identity in Romanesque Mural Painting: Essays in Honour of Otto Demus*, ed. T. Dale with J. Mitchell (London, 2004), 1–34.

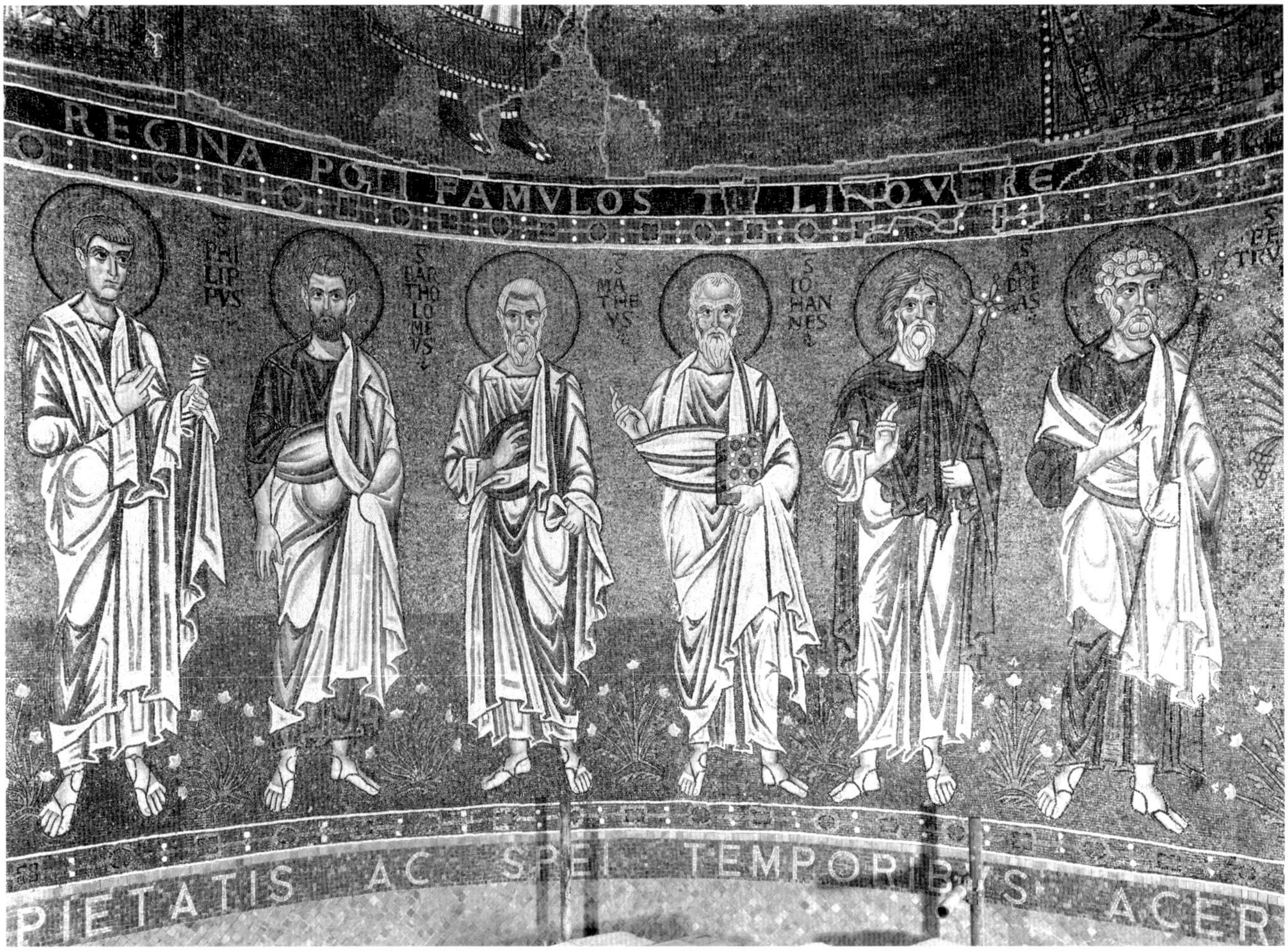

FIGURE 8. North Apse Mosaic of S. Giusto, Trieste, twelfth century (photo: Dumbarton Oaks, Image Collections and Fieldwork Archives, Washington, D.C.).

in large-scale mural paintings help structure the individual devotional and communal ritual processes that foster spiritual seeing, complementing the smaller-scale objects that were the purview of a much more limited and privileged audience.[35]

Before turning to an analysis of individual case studies, it will be helpful to summarize briefly the conclusions of recent research on color in medieval culture. As the path-breaking research of John Gage, Michel Pastoureau, and others have emphasized, color was perceived and understood throughout the Middle Ages not primarily in terms of hue but rather in terms of value on a scale ranging from white to black, with red occupying a midpoint between the two.[36] Brightness was associated with white, yellow, and gold, darkness with black, purple, and blue at the opposite end of

35. For the concept of "spiritual seeing," see H. L. Kessler, *Spiritual Seeing: Picturing God's Invisibility in Medieval Art* (Philadelphia, Pa., 2000); and *idem*, *Seeing Medieval Art* (Peterborough, Ontario, 2004), 165–179.

36. J. Gage, *Color and Culture: Practice and Meaning from Antiquity to Abstraction* (Berkeley, Calif., 1993), 34–35; M. Pastoureau, "L'Église et la couleur, des origines à la Réforme," *Bibliothèque de l'École des chartes* 147 (1989), 219–20; M. Pastoureau, *Blue: The History of a Color* (Princeton, N.J., 2001), 14–16; S. Fayet, "Le regard scientifique sur les couleurs à travers quelques encyclopédistes latins du XIIe siècle," *Bibliothèque de l'École des chartes* 150 (1992), 51–70, esp. 51, 57–59.

the scale. Color symbolism was interpreted largely in terms of the associative values of materials, including precious metals and gemstones;[37] particular emphasis was placed on those mentioned in the description of the Heavenly Jerusalem in the Book of Revelation. In lapidaries and commentaries on the Revelation up to the twelfth century, sapphire blue, for example, is associated with heaven and heavenly contemplation;[38] red sardonyx with fire and blood, and thus with martyrdom and the Passion of Christ.[39] But as Andreas Petzold has emphasized the meaning of colors was unstable, often contradictory, and individual context is crucial to interpretation.[40]

Beyond its iconographic use, color was associated in the twelfth century with the physiology of sight. According to William of Saint-Thierry, "the air and the spirit (of sight) mix easily with the colors of the things seen. The spirit that goes out from the crystalline humor and is changed, quickly changes the crystalline. When the mind which is in the lobe of the brain senses this change, it discerns exterior things by their colors; through colors it understands the shape, quantity, and motion of bodies.... Likewise the exterior air carries the changes in visible colors and the spirit brings the same change into the mind."[41] William of Conches further reinforces the role played by color in defining the surface of the object seen in his *De philosophia mundi.* He affirms that "the eye is round so that it can turn this way and that, but its surface is a plane, so that it can more readily receive the forms and colours of things, shining forth and flashing or twinkling out the humors so that it may be penetrated by the spirit of vision."[42] Following the dominant theory of extramission, he argues that seeing occurs when the eye sends out a fiery spirit in the presence of a luminous body, and the spirit encounters an obstacle. The visual information about the form and color on the planar surface of this object is then communicated back through the eye and when it reaches the cell of the imagination or *phantasia*, seeing occurs.

As Michel Pastoureau has shown, this understanding of how the eye worked affected how color was displayed and worn.[43] In a world in which most people wore undyed fabrics, color was a privilege for ecclesiastics and aristocrats, but it was also regulated such that colors were presented in layers rather than juxtaposed on a single plane.[44] Thus in the celebrated enamel portrait of Geoffrey Plantagenet (Fig. 9), one of the earliest surviving displays of heraldry, we see the Plantagenet emblem of the gold rampant lion set against an azur or blue field, and his clothes appropriately layered with a pale blue chlamys worn over a green tunic and pale blue undergarment exposed over the legs.[45] Each color establishes a plane that coincides with a distinct distance from the eye that carries one back from the gold lions on the shield to the gold backdrop. We see how this approach to color translates into a planar system of vision that is also applied, at times, to manuscript

37. J. Gage, "Color in Western Art: An Issue?" *Art Bulletin* 72 (December 1990): 518–41, esp. 534; C. Meier, *Gemma Spiritalis, Methode und Gebrauch der Edelsteinallegorese vom frühen Christentum bis ins 18. Jahrhundert* (Munich, 1977), 142–236

38. Meier, *Gemma Spiritalis* (as in note 37), 157–161.

39. *Ibid.*, 182, n. 216, 190, n. 239, 195.

40. Petzold, "On the Significance of Colours" (as in note 2).

41. William of Saint-Thierry, *De natura corporis et anime*, I, ed. Migne, *PL* 180: 705D: *Aer enim et spiritus facile visarum rerum se commiscent coloribus. Spiritus atuem crystalleidon exiens, mutationemque sibi deferens, cito eam mutat. Quam mutationem cum mens senserit que in cerebri ventriculo est, res exteriores coloribus discernit, per colores quoque formam corporis, quantitatem atque motum intelligit ... Similter aer exterior visibilis colorum fert mutationes, et spiritu eandem menti infert mutationem.* Cited in Fayet, "Le regard scientifique des couleurs," 54–55. Translated by B. McGinn, *Three Treatises on Man: A Cistercian Anthropology* (Kalamazoo, Mich., 1977), 119–120.

42. William of Conches, *De philosophia mundi*, Bk. IV, Ch. 25, *De oculis*, ed. Migne, *PL* 172: 95D–96A: *Oculus ergo est quaedam orbiculata substantia et clara, sed in superficie aliquantulum plana, ex tribus humoribus, et septem tunicis constans. Orbiculata est, ut huc et illuc verti possit: in superficie plana, ut melius formas rerum et colores in se possit recipere, lucens et coruscans ex humoribus, ut a visuali spiritu possit penetrari.* See F. Curta, "Colour Perception, Dyestuffs, and Colour Terms in Twelfth-Century French Literature," *Medium Aevum* 73 (2004), 42–65; and Fayet, "Le regard scientifique des couleurs," 53–54.

43. Pastoureau, "L'Église et la couleur" (as in note 36), esp. 214

44. Pastoureau, "L'Église et la couleur" (as in note 36), 214; and Pastoureau, "L'image héraldique" in *Recherches et documents du Centre Thomas More* 11 (1984), 85–92.

45. Le Mans, Musée de Tessé, inv. No. 23-1; *Enamels of Limoges 1100–1350*, ed. B. Drake Boehm, E. Taburet-Delahaye, *et al.*, Exhib. Cat. (New York, 1996), no. 15, 98–101.

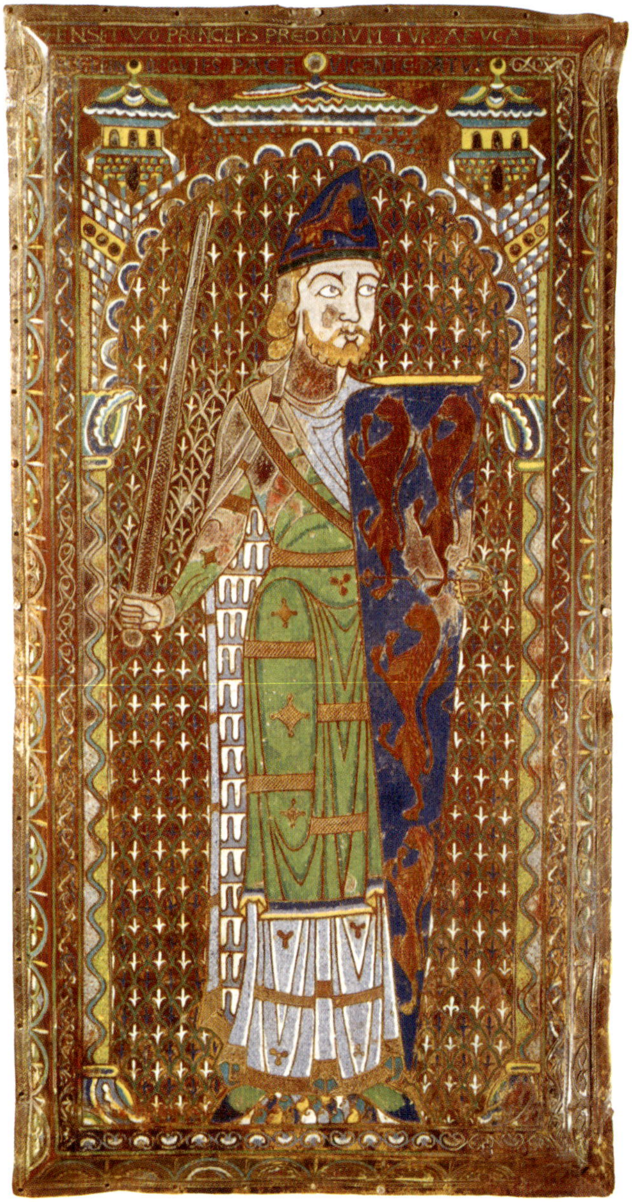

FIGURE 9. Geoffrey Plantagenet, Count of Anjou, Limoges enamel tomb cover from Lemans Cathedral, 1151–1160, now in Musée Tessé, Lemans (photo: Giraudon / Art Resource, N.Y.).

illumination and wall painting. In the Bury Bible (Fig. 10), and in a ceiling painting from the crypt of the Basilica Patriarcale at Aquileia (Fig. 11), we see a comparable system of nested color fields. In the English manuscript, a deep blue field frames a green one; at Aquileia, a residual illusionism dictates that green is used for the main, framing field and ground for the figures, the inner blue one serving as the inner or distant field set behind the figures. In both cases, this device is conventionally understood as offering a two-dimensional foil for the figures. In her study of perspective in medieval painting, for example, Miriam Bunim describes the Romanesque "background" as a "non-representative, two-dimensional, vertical surface" and further affirms that "the picture plane remained a positive and active pictorial surface which had solidified into a decorative vertical backdrop acting as a foil for the figure."[46] In light of what has just been said regarding the understanding of vision in twelfth-century thought, it may be suggested that the nested color fields represent different planes as the means of defining distinct spaces—in this case a simple distinction between foreground and background planes. This twelfth-century perspective system, often using equally bright colors, contrasts with earlier Ottonian and Carolingian painting in which there is often a coloristic shift from warm to dark.

The importance of color in medieval thought, particularly during the Romanesque period, goes beyond the physical sense of sight, for vision and the colors that made seeing possible were understood further as vehicles for a higher level of seeing that translated the terrestrial sanctuary into a vision of the celestial one. Writing early in the twelfth century, Theophilus assures painters that "by setting the ceiling panels and walls (of the church) with a variety of kinds of work and a variety of pigments, they have shown the beholders something of the likeness of the Paradise of God."[47] The belief in the capacity for sight, along with the other senses, to aid the faithful in reaching a more perfect spiritual vision of God was part of an increasingly material or embodied spirituality, that extended from real presence in the Eucharist to concrete visions based on new interpretations of sensual imagery of the Song of

46. M. Bunim, *Space in Medieval Painting and the Forerunners of Perspective* (New York, 1940; rpt, New York, 1970), 97.

47. Theophilus, *On Divers Arts*, trans. J. G. Hawthorne and C. S. Smith (Chicago, Ill., 1963; rpt. New York, 1979), Bk. III, prologue, 79; cited and discussed by Kessler, *Spiritual Seeing*, (as in note 35), 42.

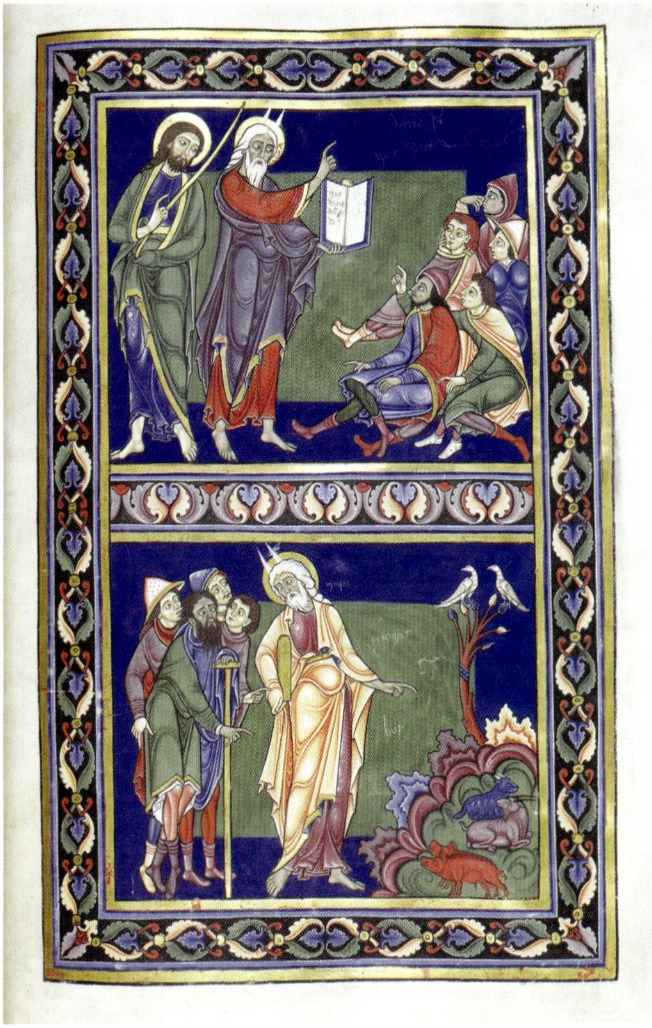

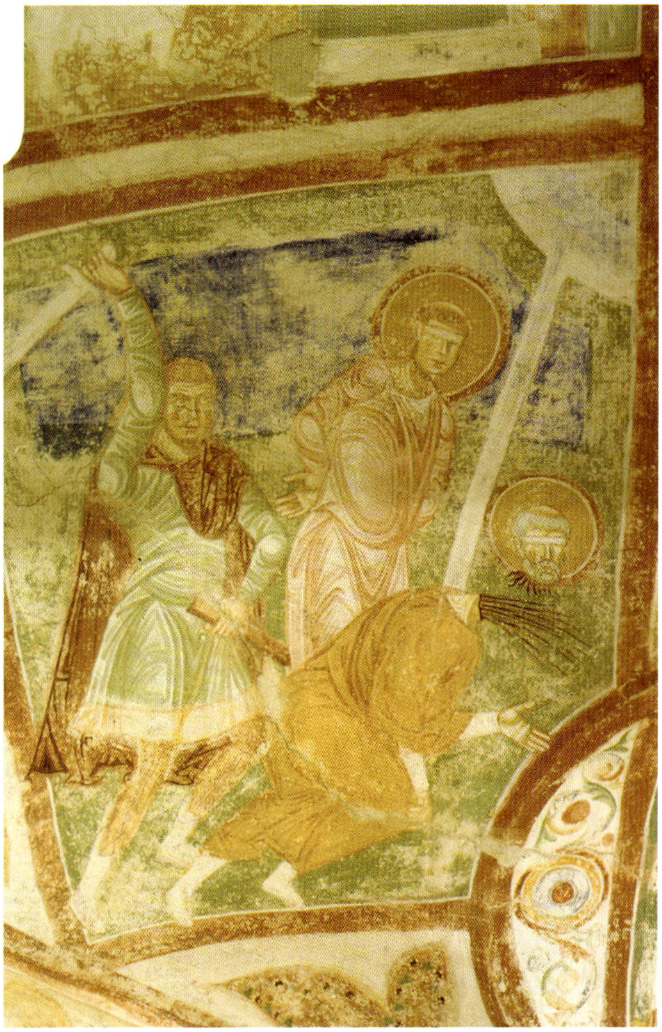

FIGURE 10. Deuteronomy Frontispiece, Bury Bible, Cambridge, Corpus Christi College Ms. 2, fol. 94^{r} (photo: Master and Fellows of Corpus Christi College, Cambridge).

FIGURE 11. Decapitation of Saints Hermagoras and Fortunatus, fresco, crypt of Basilica Patriarcale, Aquileia (photo: author).

Songs and commentaries on the Celestial Hierarchies of Dionysius the pseudo-Areopagite. Leaving aside the asceticism of Bernard of Clairvaux and his followers, for most theologians of the period of the Romanesque, the capacity to behold God with corporeal eyes was predicated on the Incarnation and the ability to use all of the physical senses to perceive the traces of the invisible Trinity in the sacraments or visible signs of the created world. It is thus in the context of a *Treatise on the Sacraments* that Hugh of Saint Victor pursues his theory of vision.[48] Hugh argues that whatever has not been taken in by corporeal seeing will not remain in the soul because it cannot be comprehended by thought. In order to bridge the gap between corporeal and spiritual seeing, Hugh posits three distinctive forms of vision. The eye of the flesh takes in images from the outside

48. Hugh of Saint Victor, *De sacramentis Christiane fidei*, 1.10.2, *Quid sit fides*, Migne, *PL* 176: 327C–331B; trans. by R. J. Deferrari as *Hugh of Saint Victor, on the Sacraments of the Christian Faith* (*De sacramentis*) (Cambridge, Mass., 1951), 165–67.

world, the eye of reason allows him to see the reality that is in his soul, and the eye of contemplation, ultimately inaccessible until the end of time, is what grants access to God. Hugh's confidence in being able to behold the Trinity in fleshly form is reflected in the new visual imagery of the Trinity, which is illustrated in an early twelfth-century sacramentary as counterpart to the canon of the Mass:[49] The Crucified Christ, projected forward towards the priestly viewer as he reads aloud the *Te igitur* prayer, drips blood into a chalice, thus connecting the historical body of Christ with the eucharistic body. This creates a ladder of images that leads the viewer from the chalice and the sense of taste, to the body of Christ held on the cross, evoking touch as well as sight, and thence to behold God the Father who holds the arms of the cross; the dove of the Holy Spirit hovers midway between the Father and the Son to suggest its mediating power in this process of spiritual enlightenment, that lies beyond the physical senses.

Modern formalist analysis, as we have seen, erroneously described Romanesque mural painting as flat or decorative, even an escape from reality. It may be argued, however, that Romanesque painting is actually more akin to the contemporaneous relief sculpture, with which it originally shared its brilliant polychrome and planar structure. Programs of mural painting throughout Western Europe seem to thematize their own role in stimulating the senses as a bridge to a transcendent vision in a number of ways: through the common convention of articulating the wall surface with a monochrome veil at the lowest level, through the architectonic structuring of the surface in a series of planes, through the use of certain symbolic colors as the backdrop for figural elements, and sometimes through the simulation of radiant materials or their actual incorporation. In the apse of the early twelfth-century Cluniac priory of Berzé-la-Ville (Fig. 12), for example, the lowest zone is articulated as an illusionistic curtain, behind which appear busts of saints, quite literally unveiled to embody the interceding presence of Cluniac saints whose names were read as part of liturgical prayer.[50] At the next level, a real arcade frames light from windows, linking the architecture of the church with the heavenly Jerusalem above, represented by the Wise Virgins bearing lamps, and by the fictive pearls, sapphires, cabochons, and other gems embedded within the frames of the arches. In the conch, Christ emerges from the mandorla of light, projecting forward into viewer space, set against a dark blue heavenly sky studded with stars, which were originally inset with glass to catch natural or flickering candle light.[51]

As I have argued elsewhere, the convention of the curtain is a particularly significant element in Romanesque mural painting that calls attention to the revelatory function of color.[52] Both the curtain itself and the contrast of monochrome and polychrome resonate with Pauline exegesis. The curtain alludes to the veil of the Hebrew temple, which, St. Paul argues in II Corinthians, is opened by the coming of Christ, who makes the God of Moses visible in the flesh. The contrast of monochrome and color relates to a passage from Paul's epistle to the Hebrews (10:1), in which he contrasts the Jewish law as a shadow of things to come with the true image of the Incarnate God. From the Carolingian period onward, the pictorial metaphor was made more explicit by contrasting the *lineamenta* or outlines of the Old Testament image with the image

49. H. L. Kessler, "Turning a Blind Eye: Medieval Art and the Dynamics of Contemplation," in *The Mind's Eye: Art and Theological Argument in the Middle Ages*, ed. J. F. Hamburger and A.-M. Bouché (Princeton, N.J., 2006), 413–439, esp. 432–433, fig. 19. On the iconography of this image of the Trinity, see F. Buchheim, *Der Gnadenstuhl. Darstellung der Dreifaltigkeit* (Würzburg: Echter Verlag, 1984), 16–18. A. von Perger attributed the miniature to Ireland, but it is now accepted as West German or Belgian in origins, following the opinion of A. Stix, ed., *Katalog der Sammlung Albertina*, (Vienna, 1933), IV, p. 3.

50. On Berzé-la-Ville, see Demus, *Romanesque Mural Painting* (as in note 4), 416–417; Focillon (as in note 15), 52–54; E. Palazzo, "L'iconographie des fresques de Berzé-la-Ville dans le contexte de la réforme grégorienne et de la liturgie clunisienne," *Cahiers de Saint-Michel de Cuxa* 19 (1988), 169–186; D. Russo, "Espace peint, espace symbolique, construction ecclésiologique: Les peintures de Berzé-la-Ville (Chapelle-des-Moines)," in *Revue Mabillon* 11 (2000), 57–87; E. Lapina, "The Mural Paintings of Berzé-la-Ville in the Context of the First Crusade and the Reconquista," *Journal of Medieval History* 31, no. 4 (2005), 309–326.

51. H. L. Kessler, *Seeing Medieval Art* (as in note 35), 30.

52. Dale, *Relics, Prayer, and Politics* (as in note 30), 73–76.

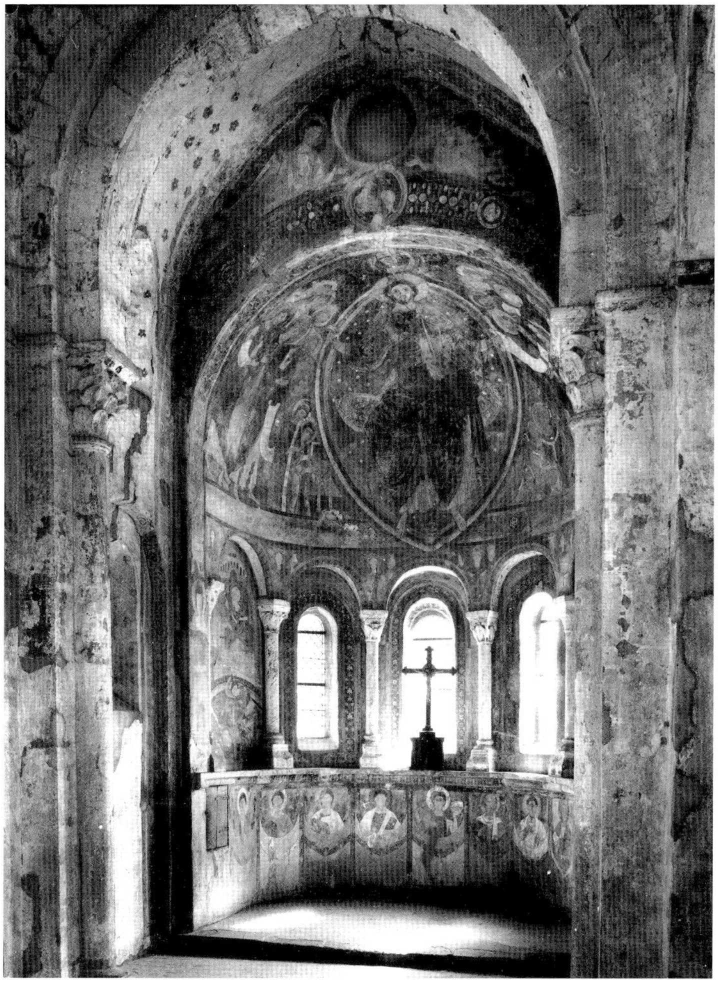

FIGURE 12. Apse fresco with Christ in Majesty, Berzé-la-Ville, Cluniac Priory, early twelfth century (photo: copyright Photothèque Zodiaque).

of truth "painted in colors" in the New Testament, as Alcuin describes it.[53]

We can see how color potentially complements the subject matter of wall painting to structure a pathway for spiritual contemplation in two Catalan apse compositions that present Old Testament visions of the temple sanctuary as types for both the present sanctuary of the Christian Church and the future heavenly one. Though fragmentary, the apse of San Pere de Burgal (Fig. 13), attributed to the circle of the Master of Pedret in the province of Lérida, is particularly instructive in its appeal to the senses through color and program.[54]

53. Alcuin, *Expositio in Epistolam Pauli ad Hebraeos*, ed. Migne, *PL* 114:660; *Dale, Relics, Prayer and Politics* (as in note 30), 76.

54. Demus, *Romanesque Mural Painting* (as in note 4), 477; J. Sureda, *La pintura románica a Catalunya* (Madrid, 1981), no. 12, 282–83; J. Ainaud de Lasarte, *Catalan Painting: The Fascination of Romanesque* (Geneva, 1990), 73, 74–75; J. A. Adell Gisbert and M. Guitart, "La reproducció de les pintures murals de l'església del monestir de Sant Pere del Burgal (La Guingueta d'Àneu, Pallars Sobirà)" in *Boî, Burgal, Pedret, Taüll: Imitació o interpretació contemporània de la pintura mural romànica catalana. i taula rodona* (Barcelona, 2000); M. Pagès i Paretas, "Noblesse et patronage: El Burgal et Mur: La peinture murale en Catalogne aux XIe et XIIe siècles," in *L'aristocratie, les arts et l'architecture à l'époque romane: actes des XXXVIIe Journées romanes de Cuxa, 8–15 juillet 2004* = *Cahiers de Saint-Michel de Cuxa* 36 (2005), 185–194.

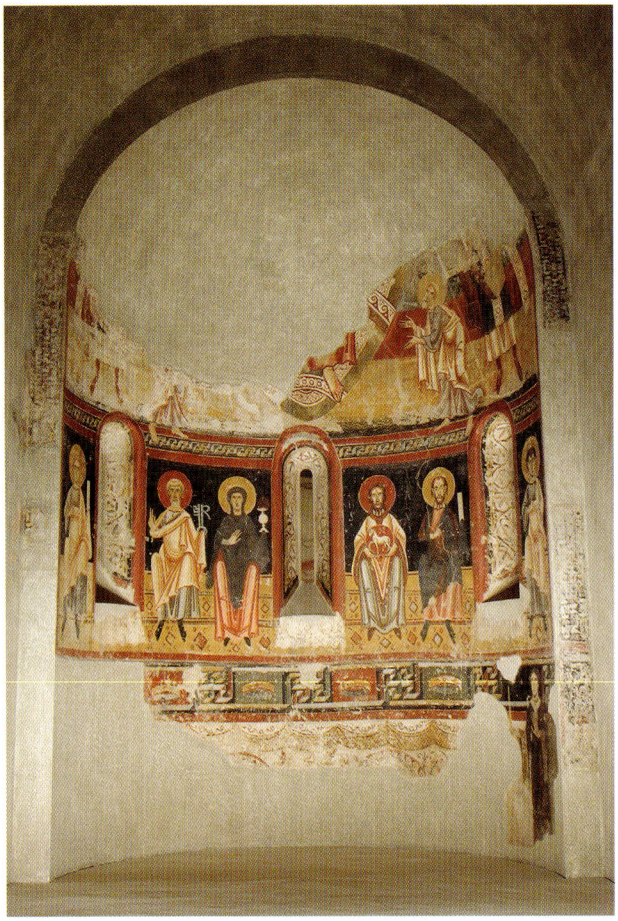

FIGURE 13. Circle of Master of Pedret, Apse Fresco with Christ and Majesty, Isaiah and Ezekiel, and saints, S. Pere de Burgal, *c.* 1095–1120, now in Museu Nacional d'Art de Catalunya, Barcelona, acc. no. 113138 (photo: copyright MNAC, Barcelona).

The lowest zone is articulated as an undulating curtain, adorned with monochrome designs, barely preserved, including medallions and foliate patterns. Standing in front of the curtain, as if projecting forward from the wall plane is a female donor, usually identified as Countess Llúcia de Pallars, who faces the interior of the apse towards the altar, holding a votive candle that overlaps a dark blue panel in the meander border, as if to call attention to the theme of light and illumination.[55] In the next zone, we see a golden synthronon studded with gems upon which are seated apostles and saints, including John the Baptist with the Lamb of God and the Virgin Mary holding a flaming chalice; both these central figures allude to the Eucharist and participation in the body of Christ through the sense of taste. The radiance of gold and gems clearly evokes the heavenly Jerusalem as described in Revelation and thus the theme of illumination, but it is juxtaposed with a dark blue field behind them, which might be understood as the evening sky, or, as I will argue later, the enigmatic darkness of heaven. In the upper zone of the conch proper, the prophets Isaiah and Ezekiel,[56] who deliberately overlap the painted border, behold a heavenly theophany of Christ enthroned between the archangels Gabriel and Michael. Both prophets stand partly on the undulating green landscape with small plants alluding to the celestial Paradise. A golden band may again refer to celestial light, a band of red to the fire of the spirit or the blood of Christ; again, the blue suggests the darkness of the heavens around the figure of Christ.

Elizabeth Bolman has shown how the color bands in the Beatus Commentaries on the Apocalypse serve mnemonic functions related to the key descriptive words in the text: the description of darkness, for example, is translated in many of the Beatus manuscripts as black, purple, or dark blue.[57] While the dark blue of the Catalan apses may likewise be associated with the apocalyptic sky, it may also be related to a tradition rooted

55. The fragmentary inscription reads, (LUC)IA CONMITESA, and on this basis Joan Ainuad identified her as the Countess Llúcia of Pallars, wife of Count Artau I of Pallars. She ruled in his stead following his death, from 1081 to 1090. See Ainaud de Lasarte, *Art romànic, Guia* (Barcelona, 1973), 79–83; and Pagès i Paretas, "Noblesse et Patronage" (as in note 54). Castiñeiras argues that the donor portrait is a posthumous, commemorative image, and that the program of decoration dates to the period in which the monastery was returned to the jurisdiction of the Counts of Pallar Sobirà, during the reign of her son Artau II, Count of Pallars (1090–1124). See Castiñeiras "The Legacy of Romanesque Art" (as in note 18), 66.

56. The identity of the two prophets is based on fragmentary inscriptions. Both appear here appropriately as the authors/beholders of significant theophanies in the Bible. A similar pairing places Ezekiel opposite Jeremiah in the apse fresco of San Vincenzo at Galliano in Lombardy. See Demus, *Romanesque Mural Painting* (as in note 4), 291; M. Beretta, "Le pitture murali della navata di San Vincenzo a Galliano," *Arte Lombarda* 144 (2005), 5–15.

57. Bolman, "De coloribus" (as in note 2), esp. 26.

in the spiritual aesthetics of Dionysius the pseudo-Areopagite widely known in the twelfth century through the Latin commentaries of John Scot Eriugena and Hugh of Saint Victor.[58] John Gage has suggested that the dark sapphire blue glass used in Romanesque and Early Gothic stained glass, such as Suger's anagogical windows at Saint-Denis, represents not so much divine radiance as a paradoxical luminous darkness—the "incomprehensible and inaccessible light" of the dwelling place of God.[59] Thus in elaborating on Dionysian negative symbolism, Eriugena claims that light of the sun becomes brighter the closer it approaches earth, for it is only by mixing with the substantial vapors of the material world that it can be apprehend by material senses. The light of the distant heavens by contrast was a form of darkness, an "incomprehensible and inaccessible light."

According to Gage, this is what Suger had in mind in using dark sapphire glass as a vehicle for complex allegories simultaneously veiling and revealing the nature of God.[60] Similarly it may be suggested that the juxtaposition of golden yellow field with dark blue sky seeks to show simultaneously the positive metaphor of radiance and the negative image of an "inaccessible light" that can only be perceived ultimately through what it is not. The red band that echoes the color of Christ's robe may be associated both with fire, as it appears in the apocalypse commentaries and lapidaries, and with blood, evoking the Incarnate Christ.[61]

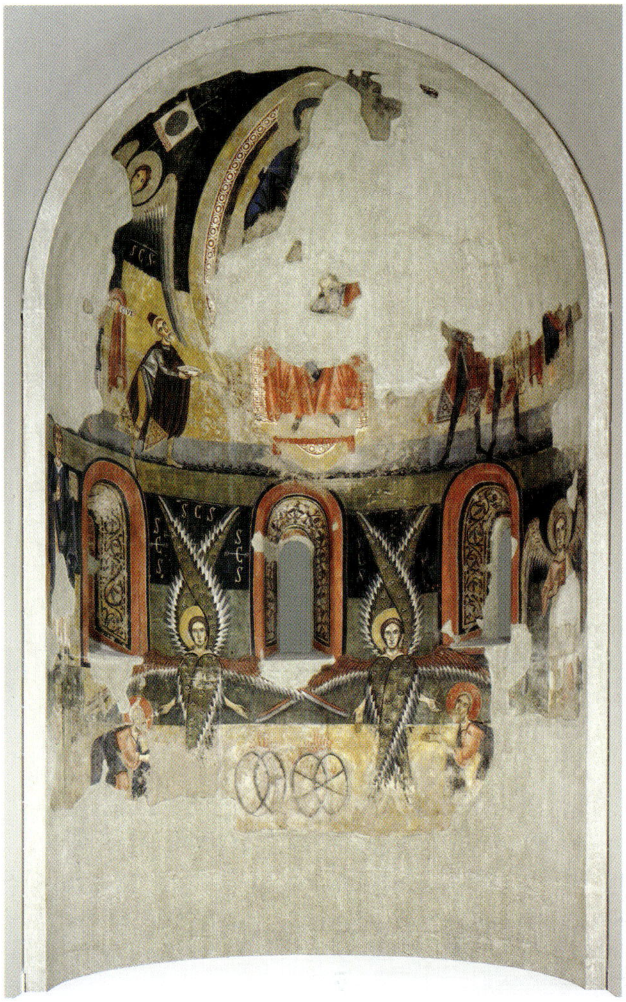

FIGURE 14. Circle of the Master of Pedret, Apse fresco with Epiphany and the Purification of Isaiah's Lips, *c.* 1100, now in Museu Nacional d'Art de Catalunya, Barcelona, acc. no. 15874 (photo: copyright MNAC, Barcelona).

This interpretation gains some credence if we analyze the iconographic program of the apse. The inclusion of Isaiah and a second prophet as direct witnesses to the divine vision of Christ enthroned within the aureole of light here is particularly significant, because it reinforces a belief in the power of visual images as a means of reaching a higher vision. Isaiah appears in a second apse composition with Elijah or Ezekiel in the apse painting from the Augustinian canonry of Santa Maria d'Aneu (Fig. 14; see also Fig. 6), now in

58. For the reception of Dionysius in the Middle Ages, see P. Rorem, *Pseudo-Dionysius: A Commentary on the Texts and an Introduction to their Influence* (Oxford, 1993),73–82; and *Die Dionysius-Rezeption im Mittelalter*, ed. T. Boiadjiev, G. Kapriev, and A. Speer (Turnhout, 2000); and G. A. Zinn, "Suger, Theology, and the Pseudo-Dionysian Tradition," in *Abbot Suger and Saint-Denis: A Symposium*, ed. P. L. Gerson (New York, 1986), 33–40.

59. J. Gage, *Color and Culture* (as in note 36), 70–73.

60. J. Gage, "Gothic Stained Glass: Two Aspects of a Dionysian Aesthetic," *Art History* 5 (1982), 36–58, esp. 42–46. The meaning of the sapphire glass in relation to the subject matter of the windows is carried further by H. L. Kessler, "The Function of *Vitrum Vestitum* and the Use of *Materia Saphirorum* in Suger's St.-Denis," in Kessler, *Spiritual Seeing* (as in note 35), 190–205.

61. Meier, *Gemma Spiritalis* (as in note 37), 146–150.

the Museum of Catalan Art in Barcelona (*c.* 1100).[62] In the apse we find a clear demonstration of the pathway from mundane, corporeal vision to a transcendent heavenly vision of the Godhead through color, relief, and iconography. Although the socle painting no longer survives, we can certainly imagine that it originally was adorned with a simple curtain or veil in monochrome. On the apse wall above is a vision combining elements of Isaiah 6:6, Ezekiel 1, and Ezekiel 10. Two seraphim prepare the way for a purified speech and purified vision, holding burning coals in tongs to the tongues of two prophets, who may be identified as Isaiah and Elijah or Ezekiel.[63] Between them lie chariot wheels ablaze with red fire. The connection with the senses of seeing and hearing is made in Isaiah's prophecy of the vision of the Almighty enthroned in Chapter 6: "I saw the Lord, high and exalted, seated on a throne; and the train of his robe filled the temple. Above him were seraphim, each with six wings.... And they were calling to one another: 'Holy, holy, holy is the Lord Almighty; the whole earth is full of his glory.'" This text, incorporated into the eucharistic liturgy as the *Sanctus*, is alluded to in the inscription above the two seraphim. The act of purification relates to Isaiah's admission that he is unworthy of the vision because "I am a man of unclean lips, and I live among a people of unclean lips, and my eyes have seen the King, the Lord Almighty." One of the seraphs then flies to him with a live coal in his hand to place on Isaiah's lips.

What we see in the apse is the "purification of the lips" that allows the prophet to speak truly of God to those who hear, then, up above in the conch, the purified vision, face to face with the Godhead enthroned in a radiant aureole of light. Relatively rare in Romanesque mural painting, the purification of Isaiah's lips also appears in the sanctuary of the parish church of Nohant-Vicq, where, as Hahn and Kupfer have suggested, it offers an intermediary towards the purified vision of Christ in Majesty in the conch, and, further, an analogy for the viewer's experience of the holy vision.[64] In the apse of Santa Maria d'Aneu, the second prophet figure may be identified as Ezekiel who had his own mystical vision of the Godhead, mediated by tetramorphs, and by fiery cherubim. Between the tetramorphs in Ezekiel's vision, there are wheels within wheels that sparkled like topaz (Ezekiel 1:15–21). Finally, Ezekiel refers to the vision of God in the vault above the cherubim in the form of a figure like a man seated on a lapus lazuli throne, surrounded by light, a vision that inspired the Christ in majesty enthroned within a mandorla in the conch, and perhaps the juxtaposition of light and dark colored bands.

Although these biblical texts offer the primary basis for the image, the emphasis on the mediation of cherubim and seraphim and the appeal to the physical senses here through light and color suggests a connection with the increasingly somatic modes of contemplation fostered in mystical writings. Particularly instructive for our purposes is the treatise on the Six Wings (*Tractatus de sex alis cherubim*), which combines a first part by Hugh of Saint Victor, and a second part once attributed to Alan of Lille, but now thought to have been composed by the Victorine, Clement of Llanthony.[65] Drawing inspiration from the Neoplatonic theology of Dionysius the pseudo-Areopagite, who described the role of the celestial hierarchy of angels, and of physical light in leading one to a more perfect vision of God, *De sex alis* focuses on a physical picture or diagram of the sera-

62. Demus, *Romanesque Mural Painting*, 477; de Lasarte, *Catalan painting* 71–72; Sureda, *La pintura romànica a Catalunya*, no. 11, 281–282; M. Pagès Paretas, "L'eglésia de Santa Maria d'Àneu i les seves pintures," *Lambard: Estudis d'art medieval* 11 (1999), 65–77.

63. The inclusion of Isaiah is based on the biblical account of the purification of his lips, but the second prophet's identity has been disputed. Demus, *Romanesque Mural Painting* (as in note 4), 477, assumes that Elijah is shown, as does Castiñeiras (as in note 18), 68, on the basis of inscription ("ELHIA"), but Sureda (as in note 54), 281, identifies the figure as Ezekiel, who would relate more directly to the representation of cherubim and seraphim as mediators of the vision in the apse.

64. See C. Hahn, "Purification, Sacred Action, and the Vision of God: Viewing Medieval Narratives," in *Reading Ancient and Medieval Art*, ed. H. L. Kessler, special issue of *Word & Image* 5 (1989), 71–84, esp. 73–75; and M. Kupfer, *Romanesque Wall Painting in Central France: The Politics of Narrative* (New Haven, Conn., 1993), 139–145.

65. *De sex alis cherubim*, ed. Migne, *PL* 210: 267A–280C; trans. by S. Chase, *Angelic Spirituality: Medieval Perspectives on the Ways of Angels* (New York, 2002), 121–145.

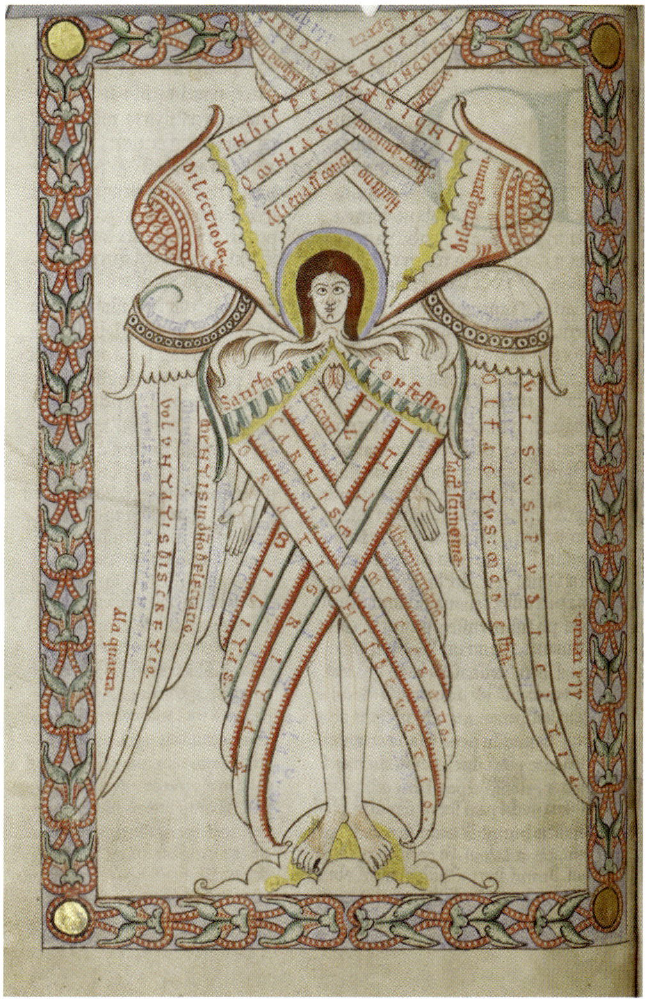

FIGURE 15. Memory Diagram of Seraph, *Tractatus de sex alis cherubim*, Sawley Abbey, *c.* 1200, Cambridge, Corpus Christi College Ms. 66, p. 100 (photo: Master and Fellows of Corpus Christi College, Cambridge).

phim as the basis for expounding on a journey towards God, a version of which is shown in a manuscript from Sawley Abbey, dated around 1200 (Fig. 15). The author argues that "the two seraphim are the two testaments, and the seraphim, which means burning, so beautifully represented in divine scripture, symbolize those men and women who are illuminated by understanding and afterward are made to burn brightly with love.... First God illuminates the mind as to his desires, then God restores the mind by setting it aflame. Thus our mind burns as the Seraphim bring burning into being, just as it is said elsewhere that whatever illuminates enlightens."[66] The writer goes on to identify each wing with a stage on a journey of contemplation culminating in the love of God. Seeing and the other senses are implicated in the third wing, which entails the purification of all the senses in preparation for the purification of the mind—a parallel to the purification of the speech and sight of the two prophets in the apse.

Mary Carruthers argues that the drawing accompanying the text served as a mnemonic aid for the process of meditation presented in the text,[67] and I would ask if the mural paintings might have functioned in a similar fashion. Such a complex viewing of the apse composition as a form of Dionysian anagogical vehicle for contemplation of the divine vision may seem at first surprising, as we are used to associating that kind of imagery with the more intimate images of illuminated manuscripts.

In conclusion, I would argue that mural painting worked in concert with sculpture, smaller-scale devotional objects including statuettes and panel paintings, vestments and liturgical books, which shared the luminosity and polychrome. It was for the larger congregation what books were for a more privileged and limited audience—the priest-celebrant or monk who had access to these intimate works. That wall paintings acted as objects of meditation in conjunction with other media has been documented by Eric Palazzo.[68] For example, Andrew of Fleury, writing around 1041, records how Abbot Gauzlin of Saint-Benoît-sur-Loire made use of a series of different images portable and monumental. According to this account, the abbot, sensing his own imminent death, descended to the crypt of Chatillon and prostrated himself before a wooden Sedes Sapientiae behind the altar, a crucifix, possibly in metalwork, and an apse painting of the enthroned judge "as if he

66. Chase, *Angelic Spirituality* (as in note 65), 127.

67. M. Carruthers, "Moving Images in the Mind's Eye," in *The Mind's Eye* (as in note 49), 287–305, esp. 297–298.

68. E. Palazzo, "Les pratiques liturgiques et dévotionnelles et le décor monumental dans les églises du Moyen Âge," in *L'emplacement et la fonction des images dans la peinture murale du Moyen-Âge, Cahiers du Centre International d'art Mural*, 2 (Saint-Savin-sur-Gartempe, 1993), 45–56.

were already appearing before the tribunal of the stern judge ..." [69] A second example focuses on a late twelfth-century mural painting at Prüfening Abbey. In the *Liber de miraculis sanctæ Dei Genetricis*, the monk Boto, writes of a dream he had in which the Virgin appeared to him through the vehicle of a wall painting: "this work of the Mother of God, which was made to decorate the church, was so welcome that the Mother of God herself saw to it to show this through her presence." [70] What this last example forcefully suggests is that the image in colors on the wall impressed itself with such force on the memory and imagination of the viewer, joining real with fictive space, that it had the capacity to inspire dreams and vision, as well as serving as a focus for contemplation.

As Eric Palazzo has recently proposed, it was also in the context of the ritual moment that the sacred images, vestments, and ritual objects, including the service books on the altar, activated the senses in a powerful way as the means of generating sacred space.[71] Extending this argument, I would suggest that mural painting played a particularly prominent role in fashioning the sacred space of meditation and imagining the faithful to be at one with God, for mural painting physically embraces the actual space of the apse that offers a simulacrum of the Holy of Holies, and an image of the celestial sanctuary embodied by the majestic vision of Christ. It also simulates and provides a model of the ritual movement that contributes a kinetic dimension to the production of sacred space.[72] Particularly in the sanctuary, painting not only conveyed through its color and iconography a celestial vision to the eyes, its texts proclaimed to the ears the cherubic hymn of the liturgy, angels swinging censers evoked the sweet smells of heaven, and the images of burning coals as well as the wafer-like Lamb of God carried by the Baptist, the senses of taste and touch that were so central to the Eucharist celebrated in the space of the apse. Within the brilliant colorscape of the sanctuary, distinctions of scale, between major and minor, are transcended as each work contributes to the stimulation of the senses as part of individual and collective devotional experience.

69. *Vita Gauzlini abbatis Floriacensis monasterii*, ch. 73, ed. R. H. Bautier and G. Labory, André de Fleury, *Vie de Gauzlin, abbé de Fleury*, Sources d'histoire médiévale publiées par l'Institut de Recherche et d'Histoire des Textes , 2 (Paris, 1969), 144–145: *Jamque sese sentiens ad christum vocari, in criptam Dei genetricis se deferri precepit, in qua idea ipsius matris Domini ex ligno honestissimae arae supereminet insculpta, cum ipsius nostri Redemptoris humane assumptionis forma, quo ac si jam positus ante tribunal districti judicis, humile prostratus, se suosque quos usque in ultimum diem, Deo disponente, gubernaverat, sub obtentu orationis Jesu Christo commendat.*

70. Boto of Prüfening, *Liber de miraculis sanctae Mariae Dei Genetricis,* cited in H. Stein, *Die romanischen Wandmalereien in der Klosterkirche Prüfening,* Studien und Quellen zur Kunstgeschichte Regensburgs, I (Regensburg, 1987), 9: *Et quam gratum et acceptam fuerit hoc opus Dei genetrici, quod ad ornatum domus eius fiebat, ipsa gloriosa virgo per suam praesentiam ostendere dignata est. Nam nocturno tempore, quando cursus s. Mariae in capella cantabatur, dormitanti mihi visa est gloriosa virgo ibidem deambulare et picturam diligenter considerare et alacri vultu conventui gratias agere pro impenso tantae venerationis obsequio.*

71. E. Palazzo, "Art, Liturgy, and the Five Senses in the Early Middle Ages," *Viator* 41 (2010), 25–56.

72. In current humanities discussions, encompassing history, art history, anthropology, and geography, it is common to distinguish space from place, considering space as being generated by movement and ritual, experienced by the senses, place as having a fixed, concrete existence. See, e.g., M. de Certeau, *The Practice of Everday Life* (Berkeley, Calif., 1984), 91–110, who speaks of space as "practiced place" animated and given meaning by the people who move through them; Y.-F. Tuan, *Space and Place: The Perspective of Experience* (Minneapolis, Minn., 1977; 3rd ed. 2003), esp. 12, where the role of experience and the senses in sacred space is emphasized; and A. Lidov, "Hierotopy: The Creation of Sacred Spaces as a Form of Creativity and Subject of Cultural History," in *Hierotopy: Spatial Icons and Image-Paradigms in Byzantine Culture* (Moscow, 2009, in Russian), 11–38, English summary, 307–311; and *Hierotopy: The Creation of Sacred Spaces in Byzantium and Medieval Russia* (Moscow, 2006). Lidov has coined the term "hierotopy" to describe the dynamic qualities and multi-sensory practices of sacred space in the Eastern Orthodox realm. See also S. Hamilton and A. Spicer, "Defining the Holy: The Delineation of Sacred Space," in *Defining the Holy: Sacred Space in Medieval and Early Modern Europe* (Aldershot, 2005), 1–47.

SHARON E. J. GERSTEL

Facing Architecture: Views on Ceramic Revetments and Paving Tiles in Byzantium, Anatolia, and the Medieval West

IN 1893, two fragments of Byzantine polychrome tiles were discovered in the course of excavations for a railway line in Haydarpaşa, on the Asian side of İstanbul. Sold to the İstanbul Archaeological Museum in 1894, they were first published in 1910 by Jean Ebersolt as sherds from a glazed bowl.[1] This misidentification is understandable; only one other group of Byzantine architectural ceramics had come to light when Ebersolt published his museum catalogue. These tiles, discovered in 1907–1908 by the Russian Archaeological Institute during the course of work in the venerable basilica of St. John Stoudios, were only fully published in 1954.[2] Since then, architectural ceramics have been revealed in excavations at a number of sites in İstanbul and as chance discoveries within the city; yet others have circulated, without provenance, on the art market.[3] These brightly glazed architectural ceramics, which were associated with the most important decorative programs of the Middle Byzantine period, have yet to take their place within scholarly discussions about the luxury arts in medieval Byzantium. These arts, which include works of enamel, glass, inlaid sculpture, and *opus sectile*, are characterized, like the tiles, by ornate patterning and radiant polychromy.

Because of the timing of their initial discovery and their very fragmentary condition, Byzantine tiles have never been included in popular publications on European decorative tiles.[4] The relatively obscure position of Byzantine architectural ceramics stands in sharp contrast to the fame of white-bodied tiles produced in Ottoman İznik, and to the popularity of others that were used for pavements and wall facings in Gothic buildings in Western Europe. New discoveries, however, urge us to reconsider the importance of Byzantine architectural ceramics and their place within discussions of monumental decoration in their own culture and more broadly within the history of tile making.

Although the focus of this paper is primarily on Byzantine tiles, the discussion also concerns the use of ceramic tiles as wall facings and components of pavements in religious constructions in the late medieval West and in Seljuk and Ottoman Anatolia. The study of tiles in these areas, each the subject of a different field of art-historical scholarship, has taken different

I thank Colum Hourihane for his invitation to participate in the stimulating conference "From Minor to Major" and for his invitation to expand the scope of the presented paper, which has resulted in hours of joyous discoveries. This paper was written while I was in residence at the Institute for Advanced Study through the generous support of The Andrew W. Mellon Foundation and the Fund for Historical Studies.

1. J. Ebersolt, *Catalogue des poteries byzantines et anatoliennes du Musée de Constantinople* (Constantinople, 1910), 39, nos. 151, 152.

2. Preliminary reports on work at the Stoudios church, primarily on the *opus sectile* pavement, can be found the *Izviestiia Russkago arkheologicheskago instituta v Konstantinopoli* 14 (1909), 136–55. On the tiles, see E. S. Ettinghausen, "Byzantine Tiles from the Basilica in the Topkapu Sarayi and Saint John of Stoudios," *Cahiers archéologiques* 7 (1954), 79–88.

3. On the findspots of Byzantine tiles, see M. Mundell Mango, "Polychrome Tiles Found at Istanbul: Typology, Chronology, and Function," in S. Gerstel and J. Lauffenburger, *A Lost Art Rediscovered: The Architectural Ceramics of Byzantium* (University Park, Pa., 2001), 12–41.

4. See, for example, *1000 Tiles: 2000 Years of Decorative Ceramics*, ed. G. Lang (London, 2004); T. Herbert and K. Huggins, *The Decorative Tile in Architecture and Interiors* (London, 1995; repr. London, 2000); H. Van Lemmen and J. Malam, *Fired Earth: 1000 Years of Tiles in Europe* (Somerset, 1991).

trajectories based on the preservation of the materials, the value of monumental ceramic plaques as a decorative medium, and the relationship of ornament and figural design within each culture. Thus, architectural tiling within mosques has been seen as a major decorative contribution of the Ottoman Turks; Seljuk tiles, primarily known through excavation, have received less notice. Ceramic pavements in the medieval West have been considered as an integral part of the Gothic aesthetic, although, because of their fragmentary preservation and primarily ornamental design, they have been less studied than works of sculpture and stained glass. Tiling in Byzantium has received considerably less attention in modern scholarship. Clearly, architectural tiles, which were associated with significant architectural constructions in both East and West, were an important and valued decorative feature. Our misperception of tiles as a "minor art" derives more from the biases of art historians than from a full and inclusive understanding of the history of art.

In December 1911, "in response to many inquiries," the Metropolitan Museum of Art published a pamphlet describing the classification systems employed by its library to catalogue both photographs and books. Acknowledging "the growing importance of crafts in the modern world, and their recognized place in ancient and medieval times...," the library paid close attention to the Minor Arts, which were divided into subcategories by country, period, and material.[5] The authors' reference to the "importance of crafts," undoubtedly acknowledged the influence of the Arts and Crafts movement, which, in valorizing the medieval guild system, had embraced artistic media that had languished for centuries, including the fabrication of architectural tiles for pavements and wall facings. The critic Richard Redgrave had already mapped out the difference between modern and medieval approaches to the manufacture of crafts in his "Supplementary Report on Design" written in 1851 in response to the Exhibition of the Works of Industry of all Nations:

> The ornament of past ages was chiefly the offspring of handicraft labour, that of the present age is of the engine and the machine. This great difference in the mode of production causes a like difference in the results. In old times the artist was at once designer, ornamentist, and craftsman, and to him was indifferent the use of the pencil or the brush, of the hammer, the chisel, or the punch: his hand and his mind wrought together, not only in the design, but in every stage of its completion, and thus there entered a portion of that mind into every minute detail, and into every stage of finish, and many a beautiful after-thought was embodied by the hand of the 'cunning artificer,' many a grace added to the work by his mastery and skill. He worked, not to produce a rigid sameness, but as Nature works:—she produces nothing exactly similar to its fellow, in every turn of every stage of growth, in every flower, and in every leaf, adding a changing grace, a differing beauty; so he varied his labours with every feeling of his overflowing mind. But this is not possible with the stamp, the mould, the press, and the die, the ornamental agents of our days: after the type or model is made, all the products are rigidly the same, whence arises a sickening monotony, a tiresome sameness, unknown in the works of nature and peculiar to these artificial works of man: the varying mind has no share in their production, and man himself becomes only the servant of the machine. Moreover, the old ornamentist worked generally from feelings of piety, from love of his labours, or from the desire of fame, motives hardly known to the artist of this class in our days, at least in this country.[6]

In England, where the Arts and Crafts Movement had begun, an interest in architectural tiles was inspired both by the Gothic Revival Movement, which began in the 1840s, and by the lure of the "Orient," which captured the imagination of travelers and collectors at the same time. Owen Jones, who published *The Grammar of Ornament* in 1856, embodied the spirit of this movement, with his curiosity in the design history of England and its place within the ornamental grammar of world cultures.[7] Within this "chromolithographed compendium of nineteen styles of historic and world

5. E. A. Pennell and L. E. Wallace, *The Metropolitan Museum of Art: Classification Systems used in the Library* (New York, 1911), 18.

6. R. Redgrave, "Supplementary Report on Design," in *Exhibition of the Works of Industry of all Nations, 1851. Reports to the Juries on the Subjects of the Thirty Classes into which the Exhibition was Divided* (London, 1852), 710.

7. O. Jones, *The Grammar of Ornament* (London, 1856).

ornament,"[8] Jones included examples from Byzantium, the Islamic world, and the Medieval West, fitting them into a history of visual culture that unfolded through the careful ordering of one hundred colored plates.[9] The lavish illustrations were accompanied by short discussions of the ornamental aesthetic of each culture, some written by Jones, and others by collaborators who were known architects or designers. The assessment of each culture's contribution to the development of world ornament depended on the authors' knowledge of the field that, in some cases, was rudimentary. The architect John B. Waring's discussion within the *Grammar* reveals the near absence of information on Byzantine ornament in the mid-nineteenth century:

> The vagueness with which writers on Art have treated the Byzantine and Romanesque styles of Architecture, even to within the last few years, has extended itself also to their concomitant decoration. This vagueness has arisen chiefly from the want of examples to which the writer could refer; nor was it until the publication of Herr Salzenberg's great work on Sta. Sofia at Constantinople, that we could obtain any complete and definite idea of what constituted pure Byzantine ornament.[10]

An entire plate within the *Grammar* was devoted to examples of Gothic encaustic tiles, which were seen as part of the integral, polychrome appearance of the building interior in the medieval West (Fig. 1).[11] According to Jones:

> The attempt to reproduce in our time a building of the thirteenth century must be vain indeed. Whitewashed walls, with stained glass and encaustic tiles, cannot alone sustain the effect which was arrived at when every moulding had its colour best adapted to develope its form, and when, from the floor to the roof, not an inch of space but had its appropriate decoration; an effect which must have been glorious beyond conception. So glorious a point, indeed, had the style reached that it was exhausted by the effort,—the light burnt out; not only architecture, but all the decorative arts which accompanied it, immediately began to decline,—a decline which never stops till the style dies out.[12]

Jones includes a discussion of Islamic tiles, though primarily under the category of Persian art. In some ways, the absence of Ottoman tiles from his design history is surprising. An interest in these ceramics, however, would be picked up by his contemporaries, who were inspired both by their bright coloration and by their practical use as architectural facings.

Gothic Tiles

The Gothic Revival produced an enormous interest in the materials that had once adorned churches and luxury buildings in England. The discovery of medieval tiles in excavations across England stimulated preservationists and architects to copy the venerable models for new constructions.[13] An account of the excavation of medieval tiles during the restoration of Lichfield Cathedral (1857–1861) demonstrates the process of using the fragmented and abraded originals as models for nineteenth-century copies:

> On the soil under the surface being disturbed, fragments of tile work were discovered here and there all over the building. A very clever workman, one John Hamlet, collected these fragments and made out several patterns of tiles, which in early days had plainly formed

8. J. Kresten Jespersen, "Originality and Jones' *The Grammar of Ornament* of 1856," *Journal of Design History* 21.2 (2008), 143.

9. On Owen Jones and Islamic tilework, see M. Darby, *The Islamic Perspective: An Aspect of British Architecture and Design in the 19th Century* (London, 1983).

10. Jones, *Grammar* (as in note 7), 50. Together with M. Digby Wyatt, Waring had already published The *Byzantine and Romanesque Court in the Crystal Palace* (London, 1854), in which he stated: "From the sixth to the tenth centuries, during which period the Greeks were indeed "arbitri elegantiarum," numerous works of ornamental art, such as richly woven and embroidered stuffs, wood and ivory carvings, ornaments in the base and precious metals, enriched with damascene work, and enamels, illuminated manuscripts, and paintings on panel, were carried by traders, and bought by the clergy and others, throughout Europe..." (p. 15). His discussion of Byzantine ornament, which identified polychromy as a defining element, focused on mosaics, particularly in Italy.

11. Although the tiles are dated to the 13th and 14th centuries, they are not individually identified by the author.

12. Jones, *Grammar* (as in note 7), 103.

13. Medieval kilns and tiles were excavated at Malvern Priory, Worcestershire, for example, as early as 1833. H. Eginton, "Kiln for Ancient Church Tiles, found near Malvern," *Gentleman's Magazine* 103.2 (1833), 162.

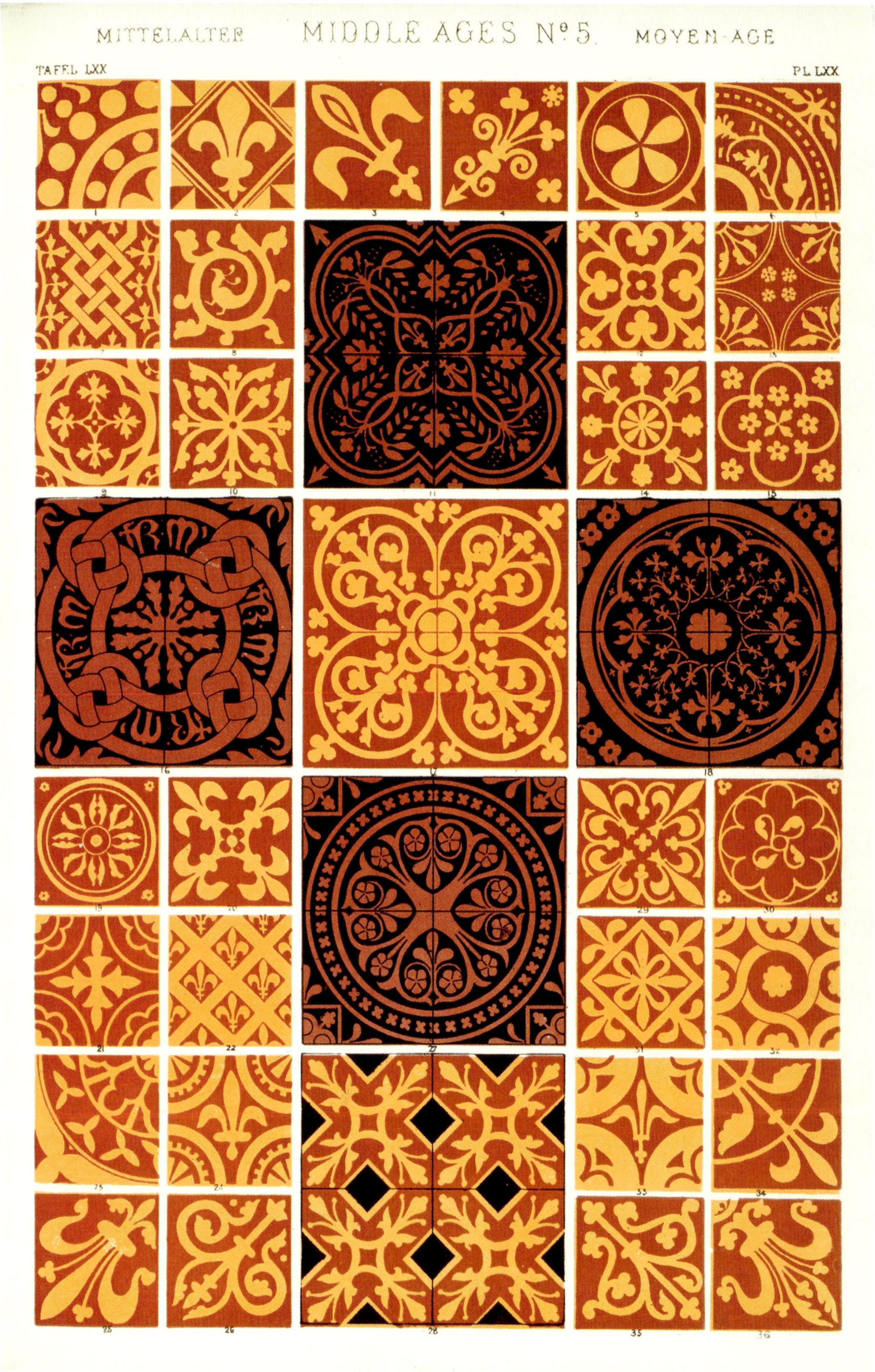

FIGURE 1. "Middle Ages No. 5," after Owen Jones, *The Grammar of Ornament.*

> part of the pavement. These patterns were drawn out in colours and placed in the hands of Messrs. Minton; and the beautiful floor in the center Choir Aisle between the Stalls is composed in the main of tiles made after the patterns thus happily brought to light and reproduced.[14]

The rapid building of church buildings in the mid-nineteenth century gave rise to discussions about the internal appearance of Gothic buildings, including their overall polychromy. The production of tiles that were faithful to the Gothic aesthetic was advocated by such designers and architects as A. W. N. Pugin and George Gilbert Scott.[15] Ceramic works for both large scale and domestic commissions were produced by companies including Minton (and its successors) and Maw & Co.[16] Similar relationships of architects/restorers and tile manufacturers are also attested in France, where Eugène Viollet-le-Duc collaborated with the Boulenger Tile Factory, which was established in Auneuil near Beauvais in 1848.[17]

The use of lead-glazed tiles for the pavements of Gothic buildings began at the end of the twelfth century in France, Germany, and a century later in England and Ireland.[18] Less frequently, the tiles were set vertically as wall facings (Fig. 2).[19] The tiles were produced by craftsmen who established tileries on land belonging to the patron, often sharing facilities with those who produced roof tiles; in the case of Cistercian monasteries, the labor may have fallen to lay brethren.[20] The ceramic medium was manipulated to produce different effects. Monochrome tiles assumed a number of colors based on the composition of the glaze. The most common decorative practice, popular from the mid-thirteenth to the sixteenth centuries, was to inlay white kaolinite clay into a darker clay matrix, creating a two-color effect. Ranging from very simple inlay to complex patterns formed from two-color inlay, such tiles had both ornamental and, less frequently, figural decoration (Fig. 3).[21] The upper surfaces of the tiles

14. F. Crewe, J. H., and J. Parker, *Annals of the Diocese of Lichfield, Past and Present: Being a Supplement to the Lichfield Church Calendar, 1859* (Newcastle, 1859). Cited in Herbert and Huggins, *The Decorative Tile* (as in note 4), 81.

15. A. Pugin, *The True Principles of Pointed or Christian Architecture* (London, 1841), 26; G. G. Scott, *A Plea for the Faithful Restoration of our Ancient Churches* (Oxford, 1850), 32. On Pugin, see R. Hill, *God's Architect: Pugin & the Building of Romantic Britain* (New Haven, Conn., 2009).

16. J. Jones, *Minton: The First Two Hundred Years of Design & Production* (Shrewsbury, 1993); Maw & Co., *Pattern Book for Geometrical and Roman Mosaics Encaustic Tile Pavements and Enamelled Wall Decorations* (London, 1850). On the Maw family, see Herbert and Huggins, *The Decorative Tile* (as in note 4), 51–57.

17. Herbert and Huggins, *The Decorative Tile* (as in note 4), 80–81.

18. The bibliography on Gothic tiles in England is extensive. See E. S. Eames, *Catalogue of Medieval Lead-Glazed Earthernware Tiles in the Department of Medieval and Later Antiquities, British Museum*, 2 vols. (London, 1980); J. Stopford, *Monastic Mosaics: Medieval Tile Pavements from Great Northern Abbeys* (York, 1991); J. Stopford, *Medieval Floor Tiles of Northern England—Patterns and Purpose: Production between the 13th and 16th Centuries* (Oxford, 2005). For Ireland, see E. S. Eames and T. Fanning, *Irish Medieval Tiles: Decorated Medieval Paving Tiles in Ireland with an Inventory of Sites and Designs and a Visual Index* (Dublin, 1988). For France, see E. C. Norton, "Les Carreaux de pavage en France au moyen âge," *Revue de l'art* 63 (1984), 59–72; M. Carette and D. Deroeux, *Carreaux de pavement médiévaux de Flandre et d'Artois (XIIIe–XIVe siècles)* (Arras, 1985). For Germany, see E. Landgraf, *Ornamentierte Bodenfliesen des Mittelalters in Süd- und Westdeutschland, 1150–1550* (Stuttgart, 1993), and U. Schwitalla, *Varietas pavimentorum—Die mittelalterlichen ornamentierten Bodenfliesen der Zisterzienserabtei Bebenhausen* (Tübingen, 1998).

19. This may be the case for a set of tiles divided between the British Museum and the Victoria and Albert Museum that have been associated with the parish church of Tring, Hertfordshire. These rectangular, earthernware tiles were covered with a white slip that was incised through with apocryphal scenes from the Infancy of Christ. See Eames, *Catalogue* (as in note 18), 1, 56–61. The tile facings at Great Malvern, decorated with architectural and heraldic designs, inscriptions and dates, were produced *c.* 1453–1548 and originally decorated the curved wall of the apse behind the altar and the altar screen. Decorated with coats of arms, the tile wall has been seen as a memorial to the founders of the Priory. See A. Darracott, *Great Malvern Priory: Rebuilding of the Quire in the 15th Century* (Maidenhead, Berkshire, 2005); Eames, *Catalogue* (as in note 18), 236–39.

20. For a list of tile kilns found in England, see Eames, *Catalogue* (as in note 18), 1, 23–32; *eadem*, *English Tilers* (Toronto, 1992), 4.

21. The most famous examples of two-color inlaid tiles with figural decoration were found at Chertsey Abbey, Surrey, *c.* 1250 and *c.* 1260s–1280s, where they may have decorated a royal chapel. The tiles represent episodes from the life of Richard the Lionheart, and the Romance of Tristan and Isolde. Most recently, see E. Morrison and A. D. Hedeman, *Imagining the Past in France: History in Manuscript Painting, 1250–1500* (Los Angeles, Calif., 2010), cat. no. 54 (with collected bibliography). See also Eames, *Catalogue* (as in note 18), 1, 10–11, 141–71.

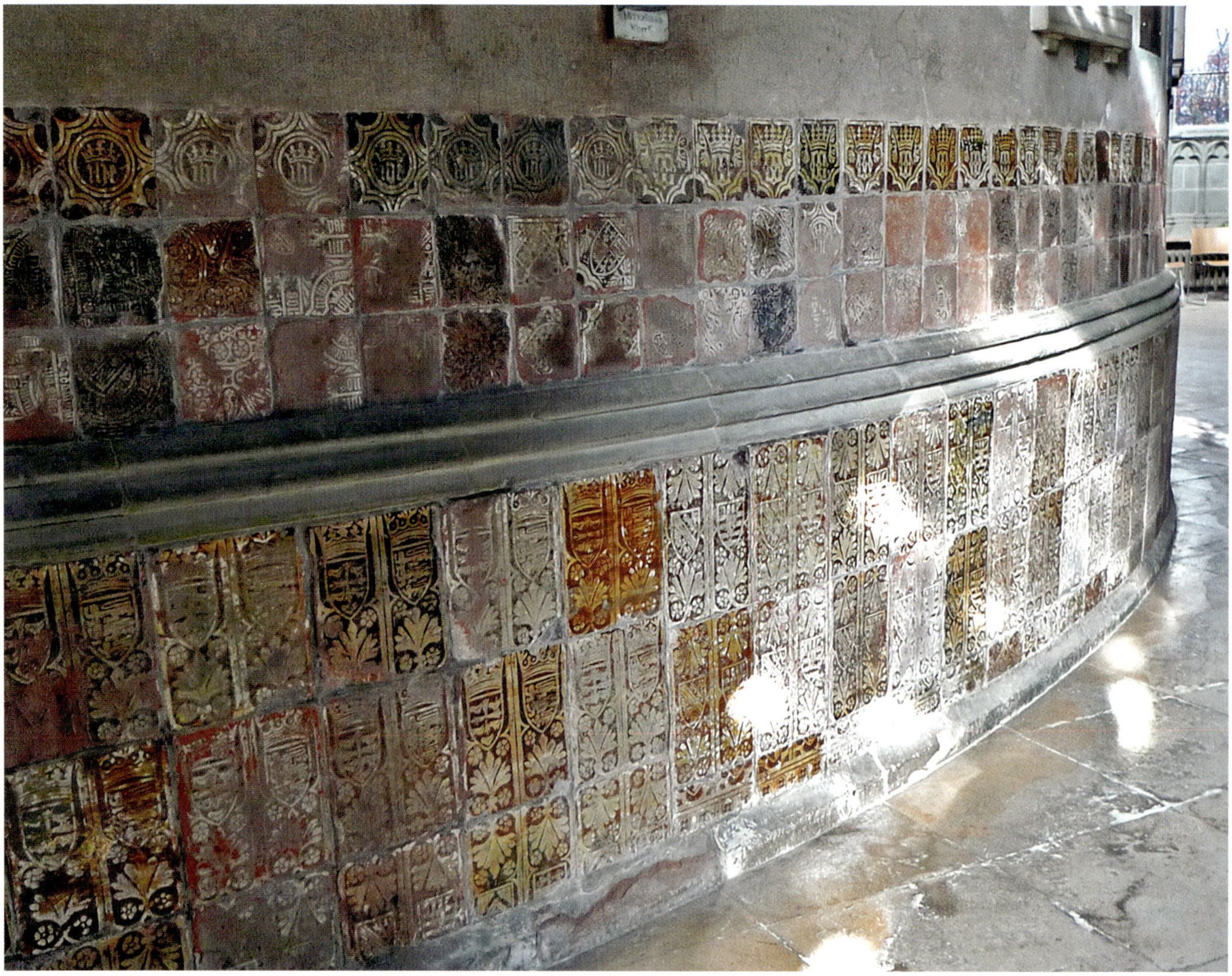

FIGURE 2. Wall of apse, Great Malvern Priory, Malvern, Worcestershire, England (photo: A. Fletcher).

could also be stamped or incised with a stylus, creating a line-impressed pattern. Conversely, moulded reliefs and counter-reliefs could raise the surface of the tile and provide a subtle sculptural component. Tiles created in these ways were often trimmed into shapes and installed as floor mosaics, a practice that originated in France, where stone paving slabs inlaid with a resinous mastic composition imitated Italian *opus sectile*. More frequently, however, square plaques were canted, creating repeated diamond or chevron patterns that were enlivened by the juxtaposition of color and decoration. These patterns were often transected and bordered by bands of opposing color.

Tile finds in Gothic churches in England have been especially well documented, although their contribution to the overall, integral appearance of the church interior has yet to be fully understood. Their lively decoration was highly desirable and was linked, through their patterns, with stained glass and perhaps with other media employed in church decoration and liturgical celebration, such as metalwork.[22] The relative ease with which they could be installed and maintained also

22. H. Zakin, *French Cistercian Grisaille Glass* (New York, 1979), 120–25.

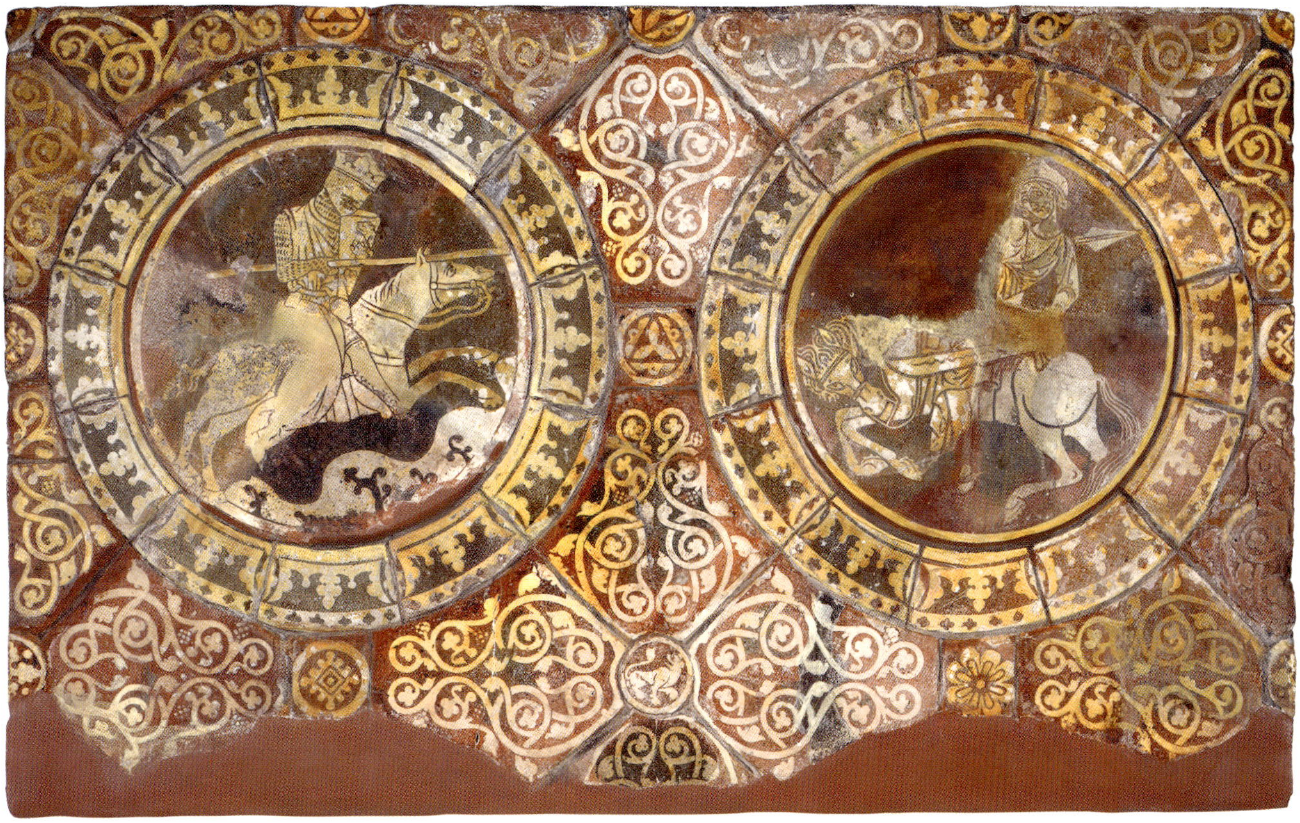

FIGURE 3. Richard I the Lion Heart fighting Sultan Saladin I, Chertsey Abbey, Surrey, England, *c.* 1250–1260. (photo: © The Trustees of the British Museum / Art Resource, N.Y.).

recommended their use in ecclesiastical contexts. And, compared to actual *opus sectile*, which required a ready supply of colored marbles, tiling offered a comparable effect at a greatly reduced price. Their frequent association with monasteries, however, suggests that there was something more at play in selecting this type of material for the paving of the church floor. Responding to scholarly discussions concerning the patterning and arrangement of Cosmatesque and *opus sectile* pavements in Italy and Byzantium,[23] Richard Foster and Jenny Stopford have recently suggested that mosaic pavements in tile (the so-called Plain Mosaics) may have also expressed the relationship between man and the cosmos through the repetition of geometric shapes.[24] Their flexible decoration and installation opened up a number of options for installing patterns and narrative scenes in innovative and meaningful ways. Patterns could be altered to highlight discrete spaces of the building, such as the choir, or to form long visual axes that mirrored processional routes and guided the eye to areas of spiritual import. Indeed, the tile mosaics may have played a role in the staging of liturgical ceremony, particularly the highlighting of liturgically significant stations through the installation of roundels

23. On this subject, particularly within the context of Cistercian monasteries, see E. S. Eames and G. K. Beulah, "The Thirteenth-Century Tile Mosaic Pavements in the Yorkshire Cistercian Houses," *Cîteaux in de Nederlanden* 7 (1956), 264–77; M. Cothren, "Cistercian Tile Mosaic Pavements in Yorkshire: Context and Sources," in *Studies in Cistercian Art and Architecture*, ed. M. P. Lillich, I (Kalamazoo, Mich., 1982), 112–29.

24. R. Foster, *Patterns of Thought: The Hidden Meaning of the Great Pavement of Westminster Abbey* (London, 1991); Stopford, *Medieval Floor Tiles* (as in note 18), 15–18.

or the division of pavements into colored lanes that may have guided processions or passages.[25] Stopford has suggested, provocatively, that "[the] divisions of the paving into lanes in the aisles may have been a practical decision in a building devoted to ceremonial activities which, much of the time, would have been performed in near darkness."[26] The contrast of light and dark effects, in additional to considerations of polychromy (most evident in daylight), urges a reconsideration of the perception of patterns in darkened buildings, when the eye would perceive colors as contrasts of black and white.

Tiles in Seljuk and Ottoman Anatolia

From the end of the twelfth to the beginning of the fourteenth century, tiles were produced in the region of Konya for the Seljuk Turks.[27] Although influenced by tile production in the town of Kashan in central Iran and ceramic works from Raqqa on the Euphrates, the Anatolian tiles have a unified color palette and style of decoration that identify them as the product of local workshops. The Seljuk tiles, which were cut into star and cruciform shapes and installed as mosaics, are largely associated with the decoration of palaces, such as the Kubad Abad summer residence on the shore of Lake Beyşehir in Central Anatolia.[28] Many of the tiles have figural decoration illustrating scenes of court life, such as drinking parties and hunting. Yet others are decorated with fantastic animals, including sphynxes, sirens, griffons, and double-headed eagles. The frequent representation of peacocks and the Tree of Life also suggests that a number of the tile compositions may have manifested notions of paradise and eternal life; similarly, the representation of dragons may be related to Seljuk views on cosmology.[29] A small number of tiles are ornamented with calligraphy or with scrolling tendrils. Similar tile finds have been reported at a palace at Antalya, at the Huand Hatun Bath in Kayseri, and elsewhere, suggesting that a consistent form of tile decoration was used for the decoration of elite monuments in Seljuk Anatolia.[30]

The production of tiles in Anatolia, however, is best displayed in large-scale commissions produced for the Ottoman sultans by workshops in İstanbul and in the town of İznik;[31] the latter were most active from the early sixteenth century and were closely associated with the ruler, his family, and high-ranking officials.[32] Although tiles were used to adorn particular areas of Ottoman buildings, such as the *mihrab* or portals, the İznik workshops also produced sets of tiles that were intended to cover entire wall surfaces, creating lush patterns based on nature and on geometric patterns. The prayer hall in the mosque of the Grand Vizier Rüstem Paşa (d. 1561) is covered in tiles produced in İznik, from the ground level to the level of the second gallery, and then again in the spandrels below the central dome (Fig. 4). Adhering to the innovative architectural frame designed by Sinan, the tiles cover engaged piers, flat wall surfaces, and faceted columns, creating a rich texture of design that also reflected light and sound. Calligraphic tiles were seamlessly woven into the overall decorative scheme; the tapered and curved letterforms played off of the shapes of curling stems and, through the repetition of forms, created the impression that word and nature were one. The eternally blooming spaces, created

25. Such ideas have also explained the placement of *opus sectile* panels or colored marble bands in Byzantine church pavements. See, for example, G. Majeska, "Notes on the Archeology of St. Sophia at Constantinople: The Green Marble Bands on the Floor," *Dumbarton Oaks Papers* 32 (1978), 299–308.

26. Stopford, *Medieval Floor Tiles* (as in note 18), 18.

27. M. Meinecke, *Fayencedekorationen seldschukischer Sakralbauten in Kleinasien* (Tübingen, 1976).

28. The palace was built by ʿAla al-Din Kaykubad (A.D. 1219–37). The tile decoration of a group of sarcophagoi in the türbe of Kiliç Arslan (1156-92) in Konya presents the rare opportunity to see tile facings used in a burial context.

29. G. Oney, "Kubadabad Ceramics," in *The Art of Iran and Anatolia from the 11th to the 13th Century A.D.*, ed. W. Watson (London, 1974), 68–84.

30. R. Arik and O. Arik, *Tiles: Treasures of Anatolian Soil, Tiles of the Seljuk and Beylik Periods* (Istanbul, 2008).

31. For tiles produced in İstanbul, see G. Necipoğlu, "From International Timurid to Ottoman: A Change of Taste in Sixteenth-Century Ceramic Tiles," *Muqarnas* 7 (1990), 136–70.

32. The bibliography in İznik tiles is extensive. See N. Atasoy and J. Raby, *İznik: The Pottery of Ottoman Turkey*, ed. Y. Petsopoulos (London, 1989); W. B. Denny, *İznik: The Artistry of Ottoman Ceramics* (London, 2005).

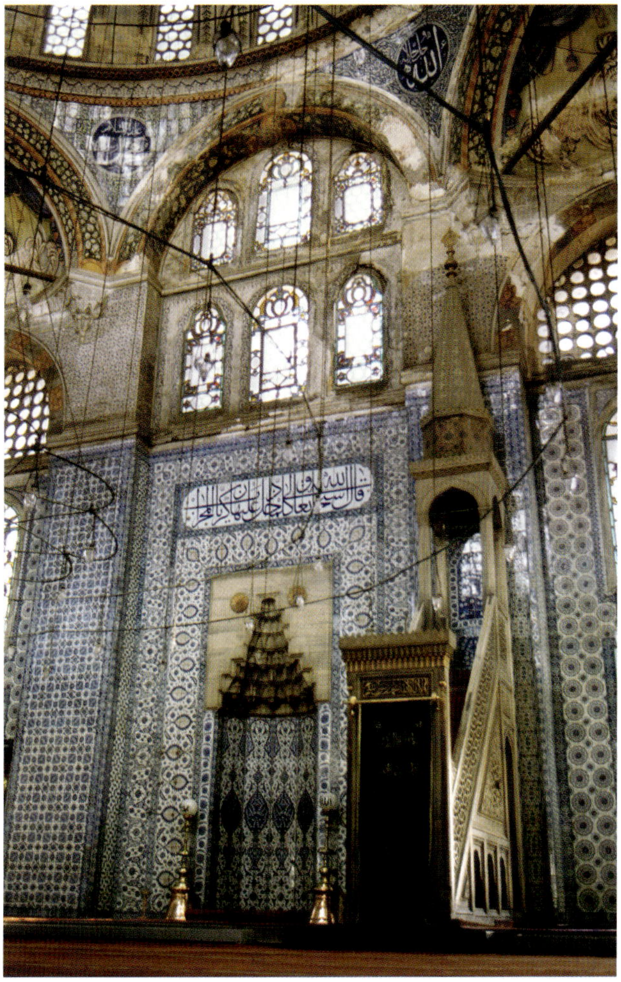

FIGURE 4. View of *mihrab*, Rustem Paşa Çamii, İstanbul, Turkey (photo: Vanni / Art Resource, N.Y.).

by the durable and highly reflective surfaces of tiles, were glazed in a color palette that was characteristic of the İznik workshop: turquoise, sage green, purple, and, depending on the date of production, "sealing wax red."[33] Metallic oxides—manganese, cobalt, and copper—were used to create the wide range of colors associated with İznik tile productions. To these were added chromium and antimony, which produced rich yellows and greens, and iron oxide, which yielded the famous deep red color. These bright colors stood out against the white background of the ceramic plaque, a bright white created through the overall application of a thin layer of slip. The same color schemes and decorative patterns found on tiles also marked a wide range of ceramic vessels, which were produced for use in the Ottoman court, as well as for export.[34]

Ottoman tiles are well known because of their preservation, nearly intact, in a large number of buildings. They also caught the attention of Western European visitors who included İstanbul as a stopping point on the Grand Tour. As signifiers of the exotic Orient, tiled walls served as the background for photographs and paintings. Jean-Léon Gérôme's *The Snake Charmer*, perhaps the best known Orientalist painting to capture the ceramic medium, stages its subject against a tiled wall from the Topkapı Sarayı. The tiles were known to the artist through a photograph he had purchased from the Abdullah Frères of Constantinople (Figs. 5 and 6).[35] In the late nineteenth century, the enthusiastic collection of İznik wares—often attributed to Persia, Rhodes, and Damascus—introduced polychrome ceramic vessels and tiles to the broader public in England, France, and elsewhere.[36] Excited by the design potential of ceramic wall facings and their association with the exotic, a number of artists and architects incorporated İznik-style tiles into building commissions. William

33. Changes in color palette assist in dating vessels and tiles produced by the İznik workshop.

34. For exportation of Ottoman tiles to Europe, see the early works of F. Sarre, "Der Import orientalischer Keramik nach Italien im Mittelalter und in der Renaissance," *Forschungen und Fortschritte* 9 (1933), 423–24; *idem*, "Die Fayencen von Nicaea und ihr Export nach dem Abendland," *Pantheon* 24 (1939), 341–45. More recently, see F. Yenişehirlioğlu, "Ottoman Ceramics in European Contexts," *Muqarnas* 21 (2004), 373–82; M. V. Fontana, "Islamic Influence on the Production of Ceramics in Venice and Padua," in *Venice and the Islamic World, 828–179*, ed. S. Carboni (New York and New Haven, 2006), 280–93.

35. K. Jacobson, *Odalisques and Arabesques: Orientalist Photography 1839–1925* (London, 2007), 69–70.

36. See *Discovering Islamic Art: Scholars, Collectors and Collections, 1850–1950*, ed. S. Vernoit (London, 2000); L. Komaroff, "Exhibiting the Middle East: Collections and Perceptions of Islamic Art," *Ars Orientalis* 30 (2000), 1–8; D. Roxburgh, "Au Bonheaur des Amateurs: Collecting and Exhibiting Islamic Art, ca. 1880–1910," *Art Orientalis* 30 (2000), 9–38; F. Hitzel, "French Tiles Produced for the Islamic World at the End of the 19th Century," in *Thirteenth International Congress of Turkish Art*, ed. G. Dávid and I. Gerelyes (Budapest, 2009), 323–30. On "Rhodian wares," see F. Hitzel and M. Jacotin, *Iznik: L'aventure d'une collection. Les*

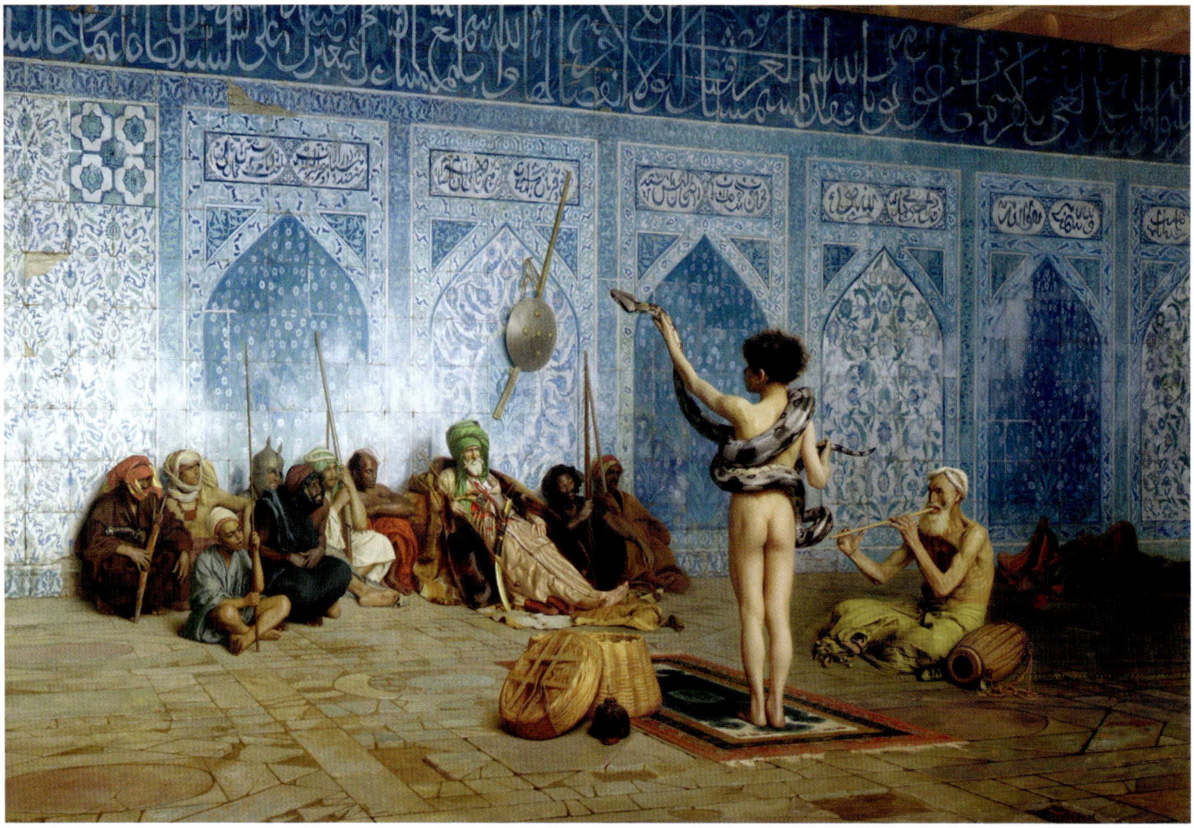

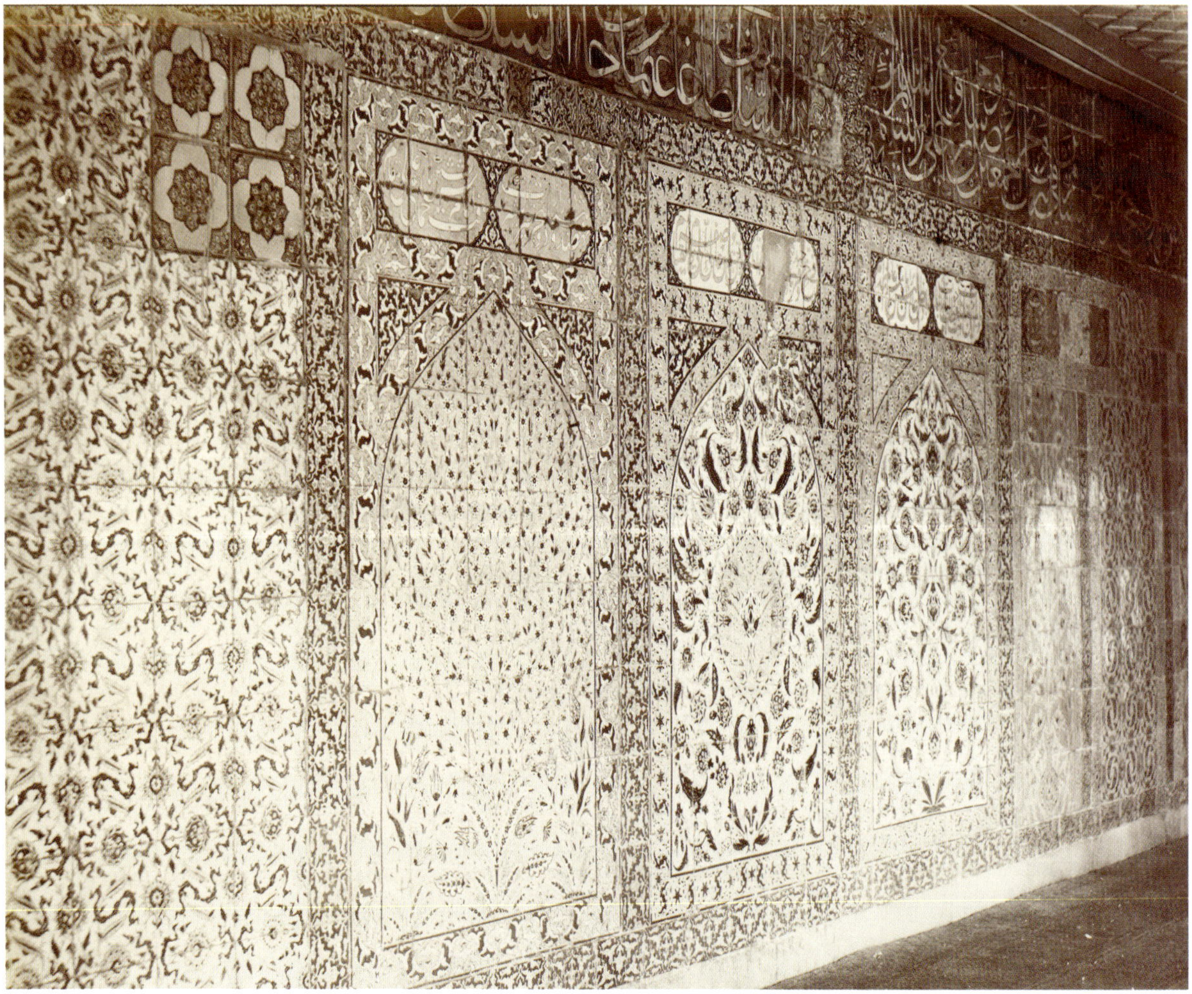

FIGURE 5 (*opposite*). Jean Leon Gerome (1824–1904), *The Snake Charmer*, *c.* 1870, oil on canvas, Sterling & Francine Clark Art Institute, Williamstown, Mass. (photo: © Sterling & Francine Clark Art Institute, Williamstown, Mass. / The Bridgeman Art Library International).

FIGURE 6 (*opposite*). Abdullah Frères (1850–1890), "Interior Harem Wall, Topkapi Saray, Istanbul," *c.* 1860s, Ken and Jenny Jacobson Orientalist Photography Collection, Research Library, The Getty Research Institute (acc. no. 2008.R.3).

de Morgan (1839–1917), the best known ceramic artist of his period, drew inspiration for his tile designs from works on display in the South Kensington Museum (renamed as the Victoria and Albert Museum in 1899), to produce such commissions as the Arab Hall in Leighton House, once the Kensington home of the President of the Royal Academy and now a museum.[37]

Byzantine Tiles

Byzantine architectural ceramics had not yet been discovered when Jones compiled his *Grammar.* Nor were they known when Albert Racinet published his *L'Ornement Polychrome* in 1869 (published in English as *Polychromatic Ornament* in 1877), which introduced objects and buildings from France as the source for a study modeled on Jones's *Grammar.*[38] Nor were they included in Helmuth Bossert's *Ornamentwerk* of 1924, a compendium based on collections in Germany.[39] It is the unfortunate circumstance regarding the timing of their discovery that has, in part, led to their marginalization in modern scholarship on architectural ceramics. Ironically, Bossert, Chair of the Department of Near Eastern Archaeology at İstanbul University, directed the excavation of the Topkapı Sarayı Basilica in 1937, a church that revealed a large number of Byzantine tiles in investigations of the eastern end of the building.[40] Had the Topkapı tiles been excavated only a decade and a half earlier, they might have taken their place as a critical source for the history of Byzantine ornament.[41]

Since the initial discovery of Byzantine tile fragments at Haydarpaşa in 1893, tiles intended for architectural revetment have been found at a large number of sites in İstanbul and its suburbs; their important role as a decorative medium can no longer be questioned.[42] The majority are associated with churches of extremely high status, that is, imperial commissions or constructions associated with court patronage.[43] Unfortunately, the tiles have been recovered in fairly small quantities

céramiques ottomanes du musée national de la Renaissance—Château d'Écouen (Paris, 2005).

37. For this commission, carried out from 1877–1881, de Morgan repaired and filled in tile panels that had been purchased by Frederic Leighton in Damascus. M. Greenwood, *The Designs of William de Morgan* (Somerset, 1989); W. Gaunt and M. D. E. Clayton-Stamm, *William de Morgan: Pre-Raphaelite Ceramics* (Greenwich, Conn., 1971).

38. Racinet included a plate of western medieval "tiles and glazed facings" in his *Polychromatic Ornament,* published in French in 1872 and in English in 1877 (pl. XLVI). The tiles derive from churches and museums in France, including the Saint-Omer and Laon Cathedrals, the Cluny Museum, and the Louvre. The author also provides notes on the installation of the tiles, what he calls "the combinations adopted to secure economy in the manufacture of the tiles."

39. H. Bossert, *Das Ornamentwerk: Eine Sammlung angewandter Schmuckformen fast aller Zeiten und Völker* (Berlin, 1937).

40. On the excavations, see A. Oğan, "Les fouilles de Topkapi Saray. Enterprises en 1937 par la société d'histoire Turque," *Türk Tarih Kurumu Belleten* 4 (1940), 317–35; A. M. Schneider, "Grabung im Hof des Topkapı Sarayı," *Jahrbuch des deutschen Archäologischen Instituts* 4 (1939), 179–82; E. Mamboury, "Deuxième cour du Sérail (1937)," *Byzantion* 13 (1938), 305–6; E. Sgalitzer (Ettinghausen), "Die byzantinische Baukeramik" (unpublished *license* thesis, İstanbul University, 1941); E. Mamboury, "Les fouilles Byzantine à Istanbul et ses environs et les trouvailles archéologiques faites au cours de constructions au de travaux officials et privés depuis 1936 ," *Byzantion* 21 (1951), 426–27.

41. Curved and straight tiles decorated with at least 40 distinct patterns were founds in the excavations. See E. S. Ettinghausen, "Topkapı Sarayı Basilica," in Gerstel and Lauffenburger, *A Lost Art Rediscovered* (as in note 3), 208–24. I am deeply indebted to Elizabeth Ettinghausen for sharing this material with me.

42. See Gerstel and Lauffenburger, *A Lost Art Rediscovered* (as in note 3), 171–229. Polychrome tiles found at the western end of the Yenikapı metro construction site in Istanbul in 10th- or 11th-century levels have yet to be published.

43. See, for example, the church of the Virgin Panachrantos, built by Constantine Lips, and the Myrelaion, constructed by Romanos I Lekapenos. Gerstel and Lauffenburger, *A Lost Art Rediscovered* (as in note 3), 189–95; 197–99 (with earlier bibliography).

in excavated buildings; others have been found, decontextualized, in archaeological fill, suggesting that they had been moved from their original location. The evidence provided by archaeological context suggests that tiles were used to decorate buildings in Constantinople from the end of the ninth to the end of the eleventh century. The tiles intended as wall facings are generally thin (0.5–0.8 cm). They are both curved and flat in profile, suggesting their application as cornice facings or as decorative highlights on church furnishings, such as screens, frames, and ciboria. Formed from kaolin-rich clay, the white-bodied facing tiles are very different from the red-bodied terracotta examples used for pavements in Middle and Late Byzantium. Tiles intended to support weight are substantially thicker and foreshadow, in decoration and the encaustic technique, Gothic floor tiles.[44] Although Middle Byzantine tile pavements are not well known, one paving tile fragment from the area of Nicomedia (modern-day İzmit), now in a private collection, is glazed deep green; a fish of opposing color is inlaid into a hollowed-out cavity in the terracotta matrix (Fig. 7).[45] The technique of manufacture is very similar to that used to produce Gothic encaustic tiles. The Byzantine paving tile is 1.8 cm thick and has traces of mortar on the reverse and on its sides.[46]

A Latin inventory is the sole document to give a name to the Byzantine architectural ceramics—*tiles of Nikomedia*. The inventory was compiled in May 1192 by a trained appraiser who listed the buildings and furnishings of a palace complex. The text also described their state of preservation, which was, in most cases, decaying. According to the inventory, within the Church of Christ, one of two churches in the complex, the walls "from the center of the church towards the west, are encrusted with Nikomedian tiles."[47] A copy of the inventory from 1202 offers a slightly fuller description, stating: "the revetment of the gamma-shaped spaces on the western side are of Nikomedian tiles, as is the cornice."[48] Understood within the architectural framework of a cross-in-square church, tiles faced the walls of the western bays of the nave. The inventory also demonstrates that the tiles were highly valued since they were appraised together with works of marble, *opus sectile*, gilded wood, and mosaic. Throughout the inventory, the appraiser is very specific in his terminology. He refers, for example, to "Bithynian" and "Sangarian" marble, terms that not only identified the site of the quarry, but also referred to the quality and color of the stone. In a similar fashion, the term "tiles of Nikomedia" suggests not only a site of manufacture, but denotes a distinctive style of decoration and, perhaps, a quality of design.

Anatolia was blessed with kaolin-rich clay, which was used by both the Nicomedia workshop in the Byzantine period and the İznik workshop in the Ottoman.[49] This

44. Glazed terracotta paving tiles found in Bithynia were uniformly 1.8 cm thick. Plain terracotta paving tiles from a 14th-century church in Panakton, Boeotia, were 4 cm thick and measured 47 × 40 cm. The coarse, reddish-yellow fabric had large stone inclusions and the tiles were set into a thick bed of mortar. See S. Gerstel *et al.*, "A Late Medieval Settlement at Panakton," *Hesperia* 72.2 (2003), 178.

45. The tile, which measures 18.0 × 9.0 cm, is in a private collection in London and has not been previously published. One of a set of 31 that includes a chevron tile border, the tile was found in building construction in İzmit *c.* 1960.

46. Tiles used for wall facing in Byzantine churches flake off the wall without any adhesive stucco on the reverse side. Only two tiles recovered from the Church of the Virgin Panachrantos at the Lips Monastery could be matched with their plaster backing. See Gerstel and Lauffenburger, *A Lost Art Rediscovered* (as in note 3), cat. nos. VI.3, VI.14.

47. For the inventory of the Botaineiates *oikos*, see F. Miklosich and J. Müller, ed., *Acta et diplomata graeca medii aevi sacra et profana*, III (Vienna, 1865), X; C. Imperiale, ed., *Codice diplomatico della Repubblica di Genova, Fonti per la storia d'Italia* 89 (1942), 68.14–17. For a translation of the text into English, see M. Angold, "Appendix," in *The Byzantine Aristocracy, IX to XIII Centuries*, ed. M. Angold, BAR International Series 221 (Oxford, 1984), 255, 263 n. 1; C. Mango, *The Art of the Byzantine Empire: 312–1453, Sources and Documents* (Englewood Cliffs, N.J., 1972), 239–40; R. B. Mason and M. Mundell Mango, "Glazed 'Tiles of Nicomedia' in Bithynia, Constantinople, and Elsewhere," in *Constantinople and its Hinterland*, ed. C. Mango and G. Dagron (Aldershot, 1995), 313–31; Gerstel and Lauffenburger, *A Lost Art Rediscovered* (as in note 3), 230. The relevant phrase is: "a medio templo versus occidentem indutis testis de Nicomedia."

48. The inventory is dated 13 October 1202. For the text, see Miklosich and Müller, *Acta et diplomata* (as in note 47), 55. For a translation of the text into English, see Angold, "Appendix" (as in note 47), 259, 263 n.4.

49. The clay sources for these workshops have yet to be localized, although scholars have identified clay beds near the village

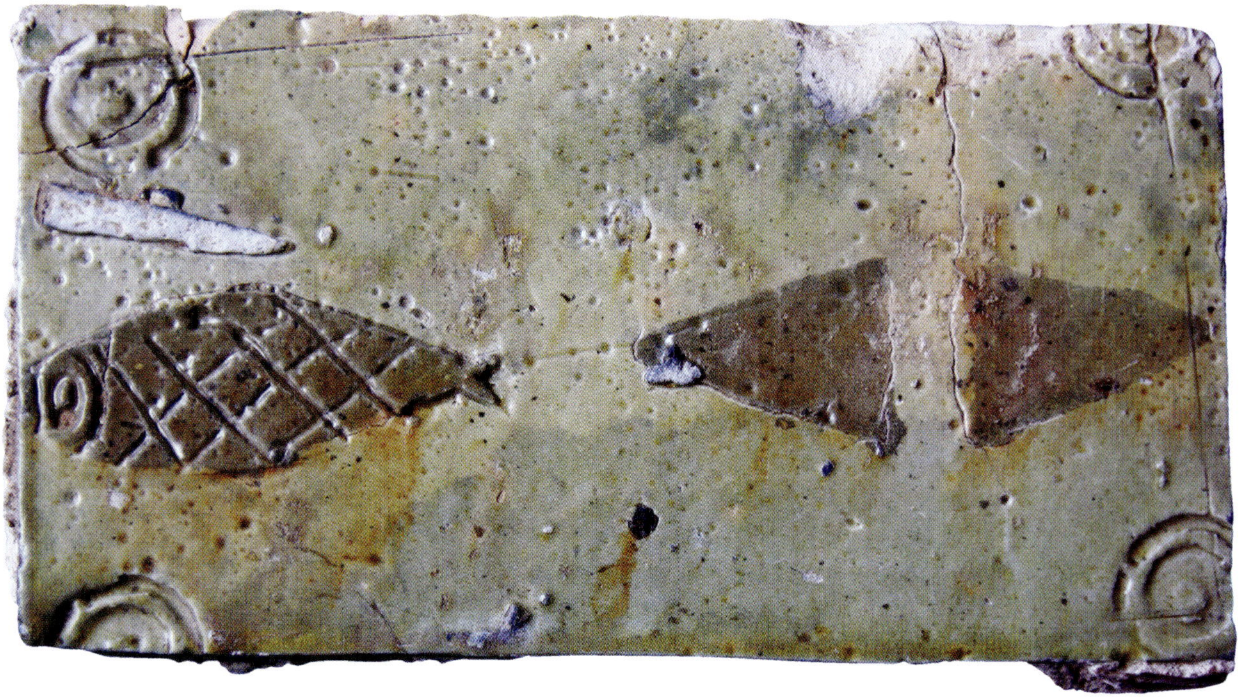

FIGURE 7. Byzantine "encaustic" paving tile, from İzmit, private collection, London (photo: author).

clay, when mixed with silica, was easily shaped, bonded well with lead glazes, and was extremely durable when fired. It also was highly prized for its white color, which allowed brightly glazed patterns outlined in black line to project from the background. The Byzantine glazes are limited in their palette: green produced by copper oxides, amber produced by iron oxides, and deep purple or brown that resulted from a mixing of manganese and iron oxides.[50] The coloration of the tiles is reminiscent, in many ways, of the contrasting polychrome and white ground of inlaid marbles, which were very popular in Middle-Byzantine churches at precisely the same period, both for wall facings and pavements.[51]

Nicomedia (modern-day İzmit) lay approximately 52 nautical miles from Constantinople; tiles and ceramic vessels produced in the Bithynian center could

---

of Arnavutköy on the Bosporos compatible in chemical profile. A *firman* connected to Ottoman kiln production at the Tekfur Sarayı "was sent to the *mutasarrif* of the *Sançak* of Kocaeli, and to the *kadı* of Lefke, ordering 2,000 *vukiye* of clay to be transported from a spot called Karacalar in the village of Verdlü near Lefke to the landing station at Karamürsel." See J. Raby, "The Making of an İznik Pot," in Raby and Atasoy, *İznik* (as in note 32), 51. Kocaeli is in the region of Nicomedia/İzmit. The term "Lefke" also may indicate a region with kaolin-rich (i.e., white-colored) soil. For a chemical analysis of some Byzantine tile fragments and white ware sherds, see Mason and Mundell Mango, "Glazed 'Tiles'" (as in note 47), 328–31; C. Vogt, A. Bouquillon, M. Dubus, and G. Querré, "Glazed Wall Tiles of Constantinople: Physical and Chemical Characterization, Manufacturing and Decorative Processes," in *Materials Analysis of Byzantine Pottery*, ed. H. Maguire (Washington, D.C., 1997), 51–66. Seismic activity in the region of İzmit in 1999 provided the opportunity for geologists to analyze the mineral composition of soils in the region, which revealed numerous deposits of kaolin in the vicinity of the city. As far as I know, none of the clay beds in the city or its surrounds has yet been identified as the source of clay for the Nicomedia workshop.

50. A blue glaze produced by cobalt oxide is found on tiles excavated at the Hospital of Sampson, but on only one tile linked to the Nicomedia workshop. See Gerstel and Lauffenburger, *A Lost Art Rediscovered* (as in note 3), 258. For the use of cobalt oxide, see J. A. Lauffenburger and J. L. Williams, "Byzantine Tiles in the Walters Art Gallery and Dumbarton Oaks Collections: A Comparison of Technique," in *Materials Analysis of Byzantine Pottery* (as in note 49), 71.

51. The most famous example of Middle Byzantine inlaid marble work is a plaque representing St. Eudokia, which was found in investigations of the church of the Virgin Panachrantos, dedicated by Constantine Lips in 907. See S. Gerstel, "Saint

have been easily sent by ship to the City and beyond. The production and exportation of Nicomedian tiles appears to have ceased following the City's conquest by the Seljuk Turks in 1087, re-conquest by the Byzantines, and subsequent capture by Crusading knights. The Nicomedian tile industry never recovered following the Constantinople's destruction, a condition revealed in a letter sent in 1097 by Stephen, count of Chartres, to his wife Adele, in which he describes the City as "desolatam a Turcis." The Botaneiates inventories of 1192 and 1202 describe a church that was decorated at least one hundred years earlier. It is clear, however, that the tile revetment remained intact in the church through the beginning of the thirteenth century, and this demonstrates that such tiles were visible to both the Crusaders who took up residence in Constantinople and, perhaps, as well to the Turks, who may have seen them still in place in buildings in Bithynia.[52] The effects of such exposure have yet to be fully assessed.

Tiles produced by the Nicomedia workshop are today found in a substantial private collection in London.[53] The tiles are stylistically and chemically identical, as proven by neutron activation analysis (NAA), to a large collection of tiles divided between the Walters Art Museum and the Musée du Louvre. The London tiles derive from a single building that was in ruins in the early 1960s; the structure has since been destroyed by agricultural cultivation of the surrounding fields. In 1961, however, investigations revealed more than three thousand fragments in deposition along the north wall. Since the south wall of the church and its decoration had tumbled down the adjacent slope, the material under consideration constitutes the tile facing of a single wall. The tiles are unlike anything that has been published to date. An evaluation of these tiles suggests that the decoration was much more extensive and integral to the building's interior program than has been previously imagined, and forces reconsideration of other monuments that were once decorated with tiles.

Seventeen ceramic plaques are painted with figures of saints; these were made by the same painters who were responsible for the ceramic icons today in Baltimore and Paris.[54] The work is of extremely high quality and provides an excellent example of figural painting of the tenth century, a period that is not otherwise well represented in monumental art in Constantinople. The vast majority of the tiles, however, is decorated with ornamental patterns. Among the represented shapes are half colonettes, approximately 35 cm high, formed from bisecting tall cylinders produced on a wheel. The collection has more than thirty shafts, which were created in segments that would have been stacked on top of one another and fixed to the wall surface. Shaft segments with bulbous centers are decorated with figures of Christ, the Virgin Mary, and a military saint framed within a guilloche band (Fig. 8).[55] Numerous capitals and bases covered in a wide variety of patterns match the designs on the shafts: faux marble (or porphyry), chevron, sawtooth frieze, scrolling tendrils, etc.[56] The collection also has dozens of flat plaques, measuring

---

Eudokia and the Imperial Household of Leo VI," *The Art Bulletin* 79 (1997), 699–707 (with collected bibliography). A short synopsis of Middle Byzantine inlaid sculpture is provided by J.-P. Sodini in "La sculpture médio-byzantine: Le marbe en ersatz et tel qu'en lui-même," in *Constantinople and its Hinterland: Papers from the Twenty-seventh Spring Symposium of Byzantine Studies, Oxford, April 1993*, ed. C. Mango and G. Dagron (Aldershot, 1995), 289–311. For pavements with inlaid patterns, see U. Peschlow, "Zum byzantinischen opus sectile-Boden," in *Beiträge zur Altertumskunde Kleinasiense, Festschrift für Kurt Bittel*, ed. R. M. Boehmer and H. Hauptmann (Mainz, 1983), 435–47.

52. The potential survival of tiles in the apse cornice of the church of the Dormition, Nicaea, a church that was destroyed in 1922 and is known only from photographs, suggests that Byzantine tiles may have been visible in the main center of Ottoman tile production. Gerstel and Lauffenburger, *A Lost Art Rediscovered* (as in note 3), 236–37.

53. S. E. Gerstel, "The Nikomedia Workshop: New Evidence on Byzantine Tiles," *The Walters Art Journal* 66/67 (2011), 5–53.

54. S. E. Gerstel, "Ceramic Icons from Medieval Constantinople," in Gerstel and Lauffenburger, *A Lost Art Rediscovered* (as in note 3), 42–65.

55. In a previous publication these were identified as column capitals. It now appears that they were placed at the center of stacked shafts. See Gerstel, "The Nikomedia Workshop" (as in note 53), cat. nos. 18, 19, 20.

56. S. E. Gerstel, "New 'Tiles of Nicomedia' and Architectural Polychromy in Medieval Byzantium," in *Anathēmata Eortika: Studies in Honor of Thomas F. Mathews*, ed. J. Alchermes, H. Evans, T. Thomas (Mainz, 2009), 173–80.

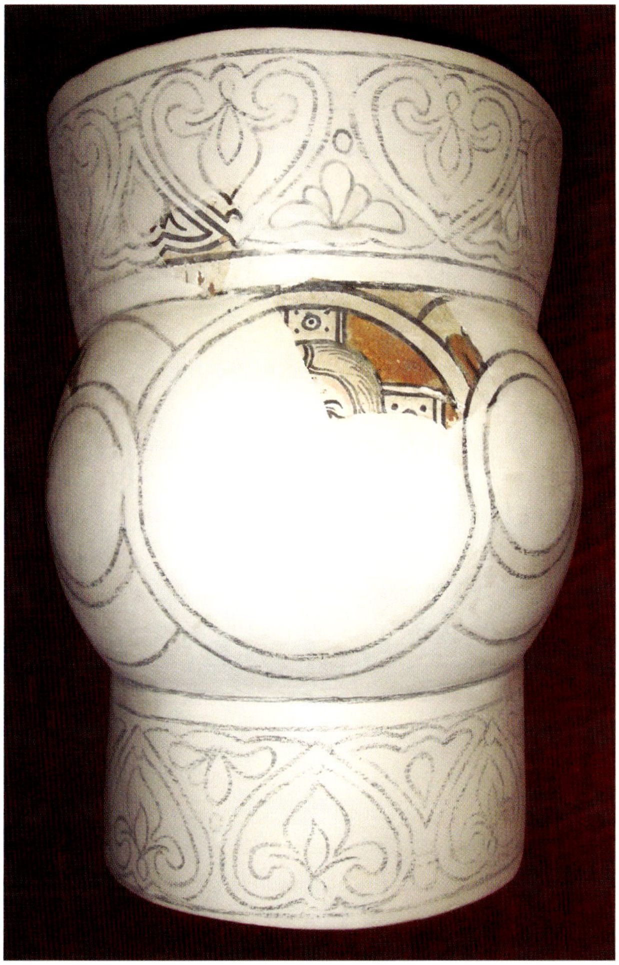

FIGURE 8. Column shaft with image of Christ, from Nicomedia chapel, private collection, London (photo: author).

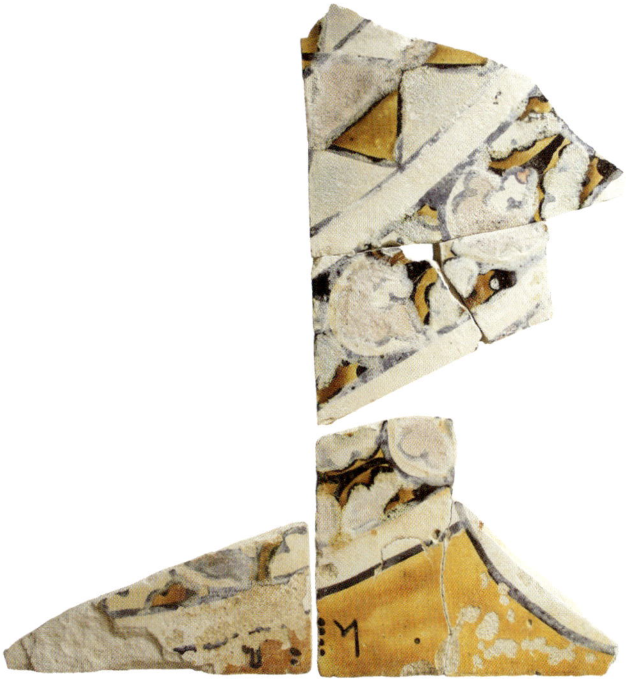

FIGURE 9. Flat plaque with Greek letters to facilitate installation, from Nicomedia chapel, private collection, London (photo: author).

between 28–32 cm, that were installed in pairs or as sets and others that were created from joining multiple tiles to form a single composition. Several sets of nine tiles, roughly 90 cm square when assembled, are decorated with a quincunx formed of intersecting triangles that enclose a foliate pattern.[57] These tiles have Greek letters or symbols painted at the edge of each tile in order to facilitate installation (Fig. 9).

The reconstruction of these tiles provides a new view of the polychrome interior of at least several churches in the region of Nicomedia, and perhaps even beyond. Colonettes formed of stacked shafts lined the lateral walls of the church. These ordered the interior space of the building according to decorative pattern, starting from the base of the ceramic colonette, which rested on the pavement, and terminating in the capital, which probably rose to a cornice that divided the vertical wall from the curved springing of the vault. Flat plaques of matching or complementary design would have been placed between the colonettes. At the center of four of the colonettes is a medallion enclosing a cross. Glazed green, the cross imitates actual examples of metal crosses that were affixed to columns (Fig. 10). The crosses and the bulbous sections of four colonette shafts must have been set at eye level, perhaps drawing attention to an icon, whether ceramic or painted, that covered the intervening wall surface.

The effects of such a profusely colorful and patterned interior must have been striking. Dulled after years of burial in the acidic soil of Bithynia, one can hardly appreciate the shock of the tiles' polychromy (Fig. 11).

57. Gerstel, "The Nikomedia Workshop" (as in note 53), cat. no. 54.

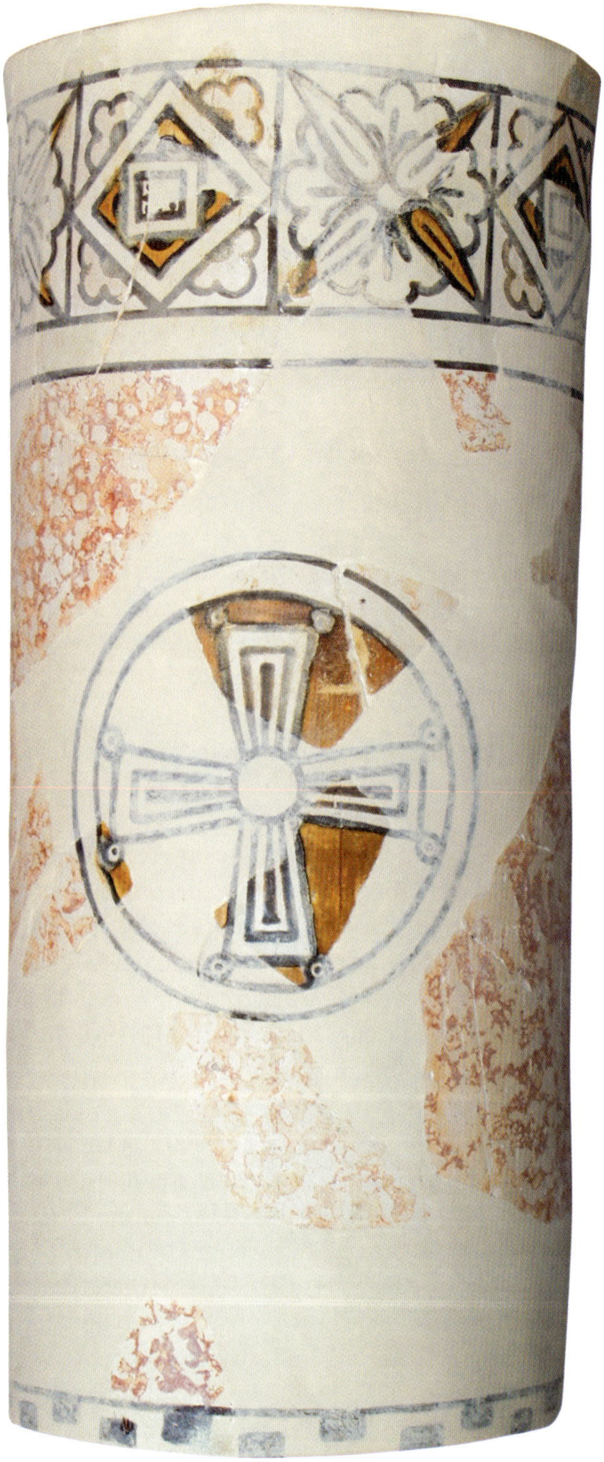

FIGURE 10. Column shaft with "porphyry" decoration and "inset cross," from Nicomedia chapel, private collection, London (photo: author).

FIGURE 11 (*opposite*). Archangel Gabriel flanked by painted columns, Karanlik kilise, Cappadocia, Turkey (photo: V. Kalas).

FIGURE 12 (*opposite*). *Maqsura* Dome, Great Mosque at Córdoba, Spain (photo: Erich Lessing / Art Resource, N.Y.).

Dominated by amber and emerald green, the colors were meant to evoke the visual effects of more precious materials such as gold and enamel, materials that could never have been used to cover great expanses of the wall surface. One must turn to contemporary churches in Cappadocia, which are decorated with the same patterns on colonettes and imitate tile work in the decoration of walls, screens, arches, and vaults (Fig. 12). Within the tiled church, seemingly discordant patterns, both geometric and derived from the natural world, were harmonized by a common glaze palette. The unusual use of a sponge technique to produce the effect of porphyry also imitated a precious material that was associated with high-class construction; it would have been nearly impossible to obtain porphyry for the decoration of a church in Bithynia at this time (Fig. 10).

The lustrous glazed surface also had several practical effects. When diffused on the glazed surface, the flickering candlelight within the building would have assumed a mystical quality. The used of glazed tiles as wall facings also enhanced acoustical resonance; the chanted liturgy would have reflected from the nonporous surface of the plaques that covered the walls flanking both the celebrant and the faithful, enclosing the community in a virtual sound box. One wonders, considering the acoustical properties of the tiled surface, whether the decision to face the western walls of the Botaneiates church with tiles was based on acoustics, in addition to design; the tiles would have reflected sound that issued from the eastern part of the church back to the center of the building.

If this is indeed an accurate understanding of the tile finds in and near Nicomedia, then tiles covered large expanses of the wall surface of buildings already in tenth-century Byzantium, that is, centuries before the İznik workshops produced their vast tile programs at the behest of the Ottoman sultans. Their use as wall facings, rather than as coverings for cornices, suggests

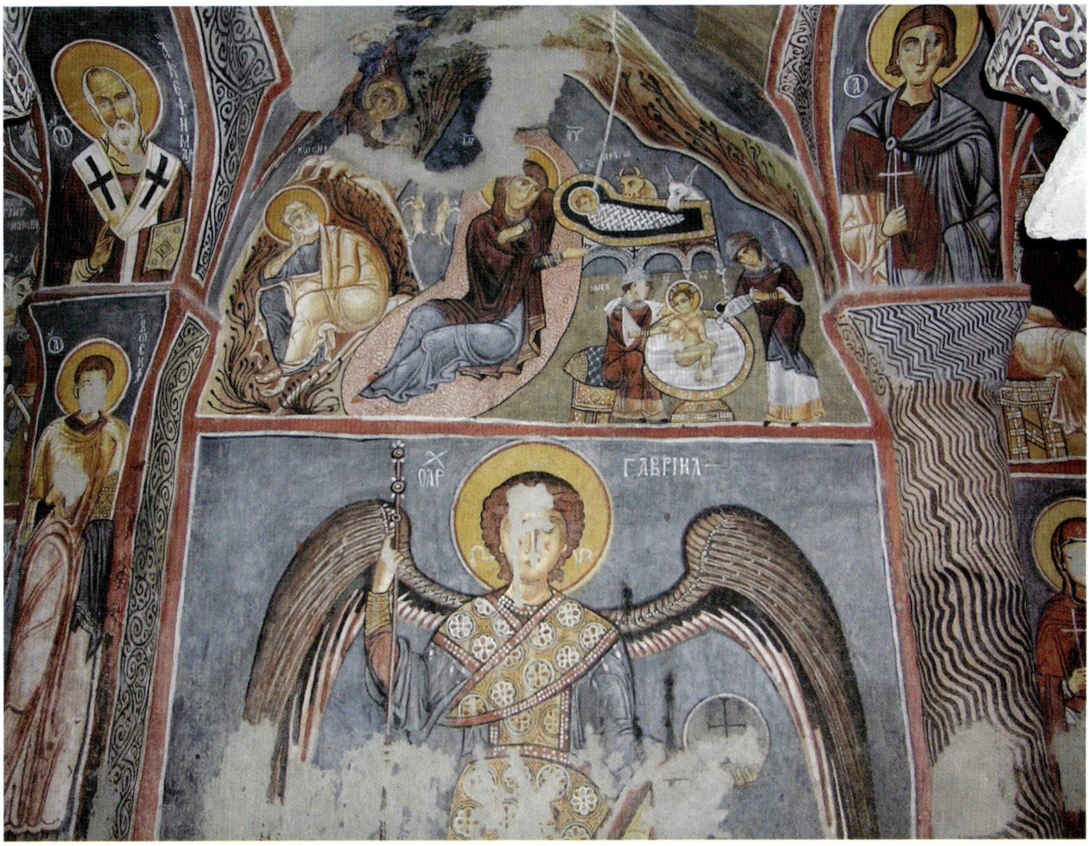
ΓΑΒΡΙΗΛ

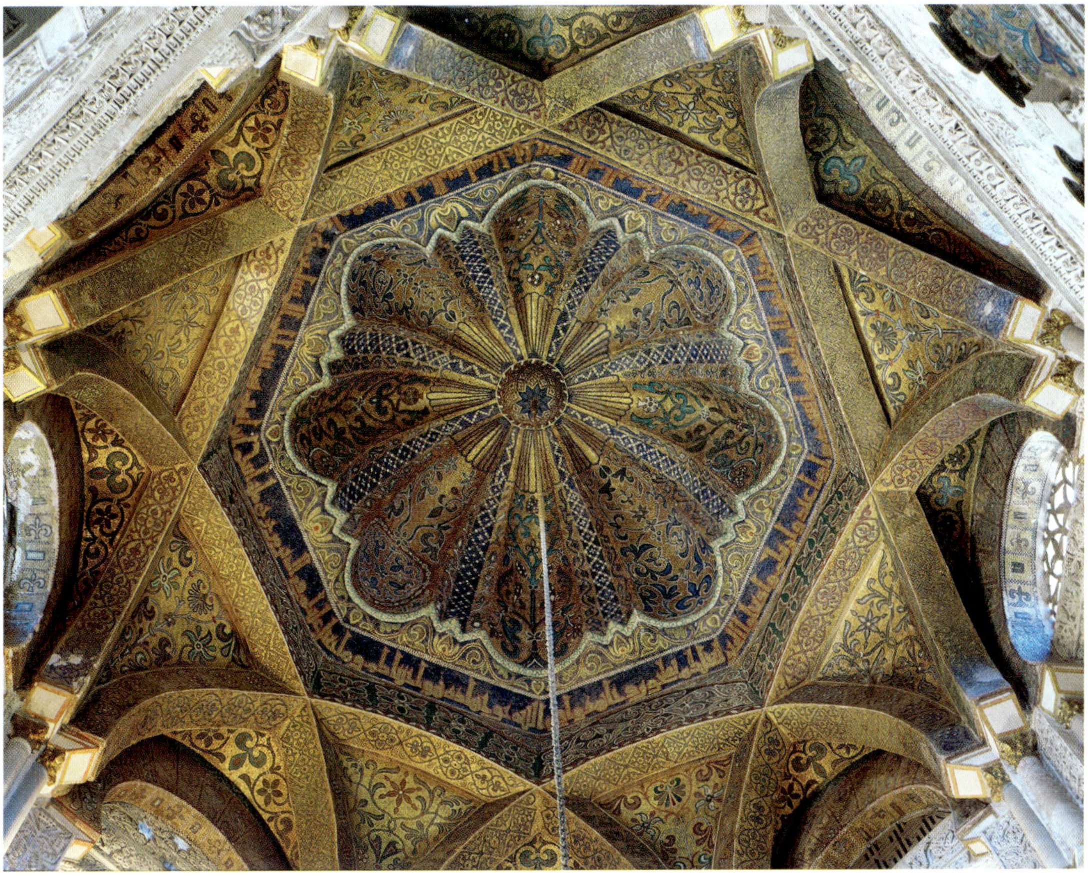

that they may have had an influence on the overall use of tiles for wall coverings in later buildings in Anatolia.[58]

The tile industry in Ottoman Turkey was, of course, centered in the city of İznik less than 85 kilometers from İzmit, Byzantine Nicomedia. As in Ottoman constructions, Byzantine tiles framed meaningful designs, contrasted patterns, and created an acoustically resonant chamber. The difference, of course, is the patterns that each workshop employed, as both cultures negotiated between ornamental roots in the Mediterranean and the Near East, and the color palette, which not only witnessed the availability and cost of certain types of glazes at certain periods, but also reflected the desired effect of the program. "Sealing wax red" is absent from Byzantine tiles, though it is the signature color of the İznik workshop. The use of gold leaf on Byzantine tiles is not, as far as I am aware, found on Ottoman tiles. Both Byzantine and Ottoman tiles respond to patterns in other media. In Byzantium, tiles evoked the coloration of enamels and painted icons, they imitated marble or porphyry, they used motifs derived from inlaid stonework and *opus sectile*. Part of the so-called Macedonian renaissance, they fit within the polychrome aesthetic that characterizes works of the period. Ottoman tiles, too, share their patterns with those on textiles, metalwork, and other precious materials. In both cultures, the glazed ceramics proclaim luxury, in the quality of their design, their luminous colors, and their unique imitative properties. In both cultures, tile workshops also produced vessels which, in their own time, were esteemed for the beauty of their decoration, closely linking the tile decoration of high-status monuments to tablewares used in the domestic sphere.[59]

Tiles Across Borders

In 970/1 the Caliph al-Hakam II enlarged the Great Mosque of Córdoba, adding a new *mihrab* chamber and triple-domed *maqsura*. As part of the new decoration, the dome of the *maqsura* was covered with mosaics. These have often been seen as the efforts of Byzantine craftsmen who were summoned, at the behest of the Caliph, to work on the building.[60] Less noticed is the narrow ceramic cornice that girds the base of the dome. The banding of the dome was complicated and required craftsmen to shape tiles that would fit the unusual foliate profile. The cornice is composed of forty half-cylindrical tiles decorated with a continuous series of imbrications enclosing palmettes (Fig. 12).[61] The tiles are white-bodied and the design is painted in green, purple (manganese), and amber colored glazes, similar to the palette of Byzantine tiles. While the mosaics were certainly executed by Byzantines, it remains an open question whether the tiles were made by a workshop from the East or by local ceramicists. One fact is indisputable: the coupling of mosaics and tiles was common in Byzantine churches in Constantinople. Moreover, the patterns on the Córdoba tiles strongly resemble the decoration of tiles excavated by Bossert at the Topkapı Sarayı Basilica.[62] The glaze colors, too, are identical to those used by Byzantine workshops.

The existence of Byzantine tiles in an Islamic mosque raises interesting questions about the use of a common medium in radically different contexts. Not only were Byzantine-style tiles found at Córdoba, but, conversely, Seljuk and Ottoman tiles found their place in Orthodox churches.

Long after the Nicomedia workshop ceased to produce tiles, Orthodox congregations continued to be interested in ceramic plaques as wall facings. At the

58. Considering the large number of tiles in the Walters Art Museum, R. B. Mason and M. Mundell Mango posited "the possibility of a decoration on a much broader scale, comparable to Roman/Byzantine *opus sectile* wall revetments in marble, glass or fresco imitation, on the one hand, or of Ottoman tile revetments, on the other." Mason and Mundell Mango, "Glazed 'Tiles of Nicomedia'" (as in note 47), 321.

59. For Byzantine polychrome tablewares, see, most recently, G. D. R. Sanders, "Byzantine Polychrome Pottery," in *Mosaic: Festchrift for A. H. S. Megaw*, ed. J. Herrin, M. Mullett, and C. Otten-Froux (London, 2001), 89–104.

60. Ibn 'Idhari al-Marrakushi, *Kitab al-Bayan al-Mughrib* (Leiden, 1948–50), 392.

61. E. S. Ettinghausen, "The Great Mosque at Córdoba," in Gerstel and Lauffenburger, *A Lost Art Rediscovered* (as in note 3), 239–41 (with collected bibliography).

62. Gerstel and Lauffenburger, *A Lost Art Rediscovered* (as in note 3), cat. nos. XII.5–XII.7).

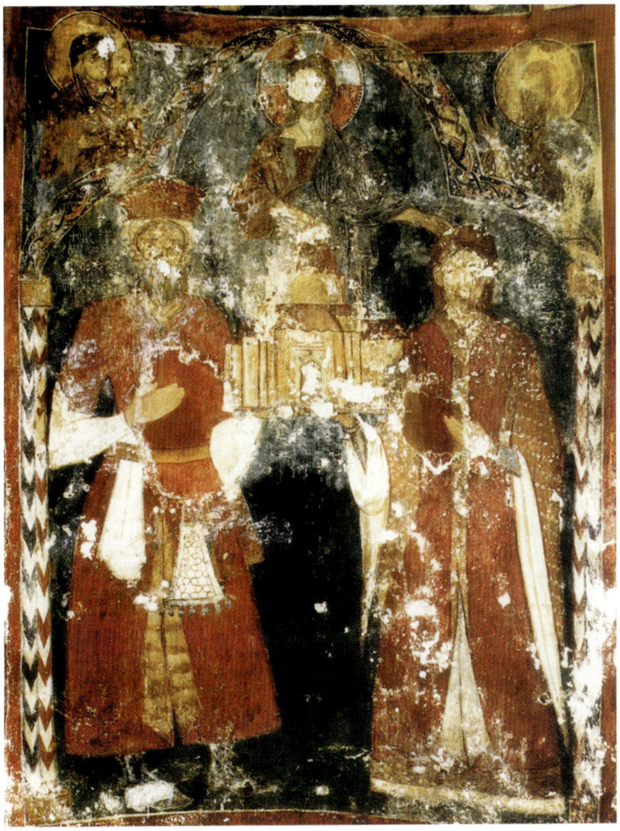

FIGURE 13. *Logothetes* Nikolaos Bardoanes and his wife, Eudokia Strevlou, Church of St. Nicholas, Phountoukli, Rhodes (photo: I. Christoforaki, with permission of the Fourth Ephoreia of Byzantine Antiquities, Rhodes).

end of the fifteenth century, dazzling tiles created by Seljuk workshops in the Konya region of Anatolia embellished a small church on Rhodes, though as painted replicas. St. Nikolaos at Phountoukli is best known for the elaborate portraits of its builder, the *pansebastos kyr* and *logothetes* Nikolaos Bardoanes and his wife, Eudokia Strevlou (Fig. 13). Their children, memorialized in an adjacent portrait, had recently died of the plague and it was their commemoration that occasioned the construction of the church in 1498.[63] The exalted title of the father and the expensive, fur-lined garments and jewelry worn by members of the family, demonstrate that the church patrons were of very high social status. Because the Bardoanes name is unattested in the island's records, some scholars have suggested that Nikolaos was a refugee from the coast of Asia Minor. If so, he was a refugee with means or wished to present himself as such.

The decoration of the tetraconch church is fairly standard. Yet, the Orthodox imagery is supported in the dado zone and framed in the three portals by painted ornament that evokes the appearance of Seljuk tiles. Such tiles, trimmed into cruciform and octagonal star patterns that were pieced together, covered the dado zones of Seljuk palaces, kiosks, and luxury baths. At Phountoukli, the cruciform and star pattern is also found in the dado zone, but here inside the sanctuary and in association with the church's most important icons, including that of its patron saint (Fig. 14). The patterns here mediated the faithful's experience of the icon program, conjuring notions of passage through the complex interaction of the pattern's components.[64]

There is precedent for the use of Seljuk tiles in a Byzantine building. In the twelfth century, Nikolaos Mesarites described the decoration of the staircase of the Mouchroutas reception hall in the Great Palace, the work of a "Persian (i.e., Seljuk) hand," as "colored blue, deep red, green and purple by means of a medley of cut, painted tiles of cruciform shape." [65] It is noteworthy that Mesarites focused on the interstitial cruciform shapes within the pattern for the dominant design element in Seljuk wall decoration was the eight-pointed star, a shape that was most often found in palaces, kiosks, and luxury baths. Forms that were associated

63. M. Acheimastou-Potamianou, "Οι *τοιχογραφίες της οικογενείας Βαρδοάνη στον Άγιο Νικόλαο στα Φουντουκί της Ρόδου*," Θωράκιον· *Αφιέρωμα στη μνήμη του Παύλου Λαζαρίδη*, ed. L. Kypraiou (Athens, 2004), 247–62; A. Semoglou, "Contribution à l'étude du portrait funéraire dans le monde byzantine (14ᵉ–16ᵉ siècle)," *Zograf* 24 (1995), 6–7; A.-M. Talbot, "The Death and Commemoration of Byzantine Children," in *Becoming Byzantine: Children and Childhood in Byzantium*, ed. A. Papaconstantinou and A.-M. Talbot (Washington, D.C., 2009), 304.

64. R. Bozer, "Forms of Seljuk Tile Panels, Observations on the Designs of Wall Coverings and Some Processes After Glazing," in Arik and Arik, *Tiles* (as in note 30), 191–207; O. Grabar, *The Mediation of Ornament* (Princeton, N.J., 1992), 151

65. For the text, see Nikolaos Mesarites, *Die Palastrevolution des Johannes Komnenos*, ed. A. Heisenberg (Würzburg, 1907), §§ 27–29. For an English translation, see C. Mango, *The Art of the Byzantine Empire* (as in note 47), 229. See also P. Magdalino, "Manuel Komnenos and the Great Palace," *Byzantine and Modern Greek*

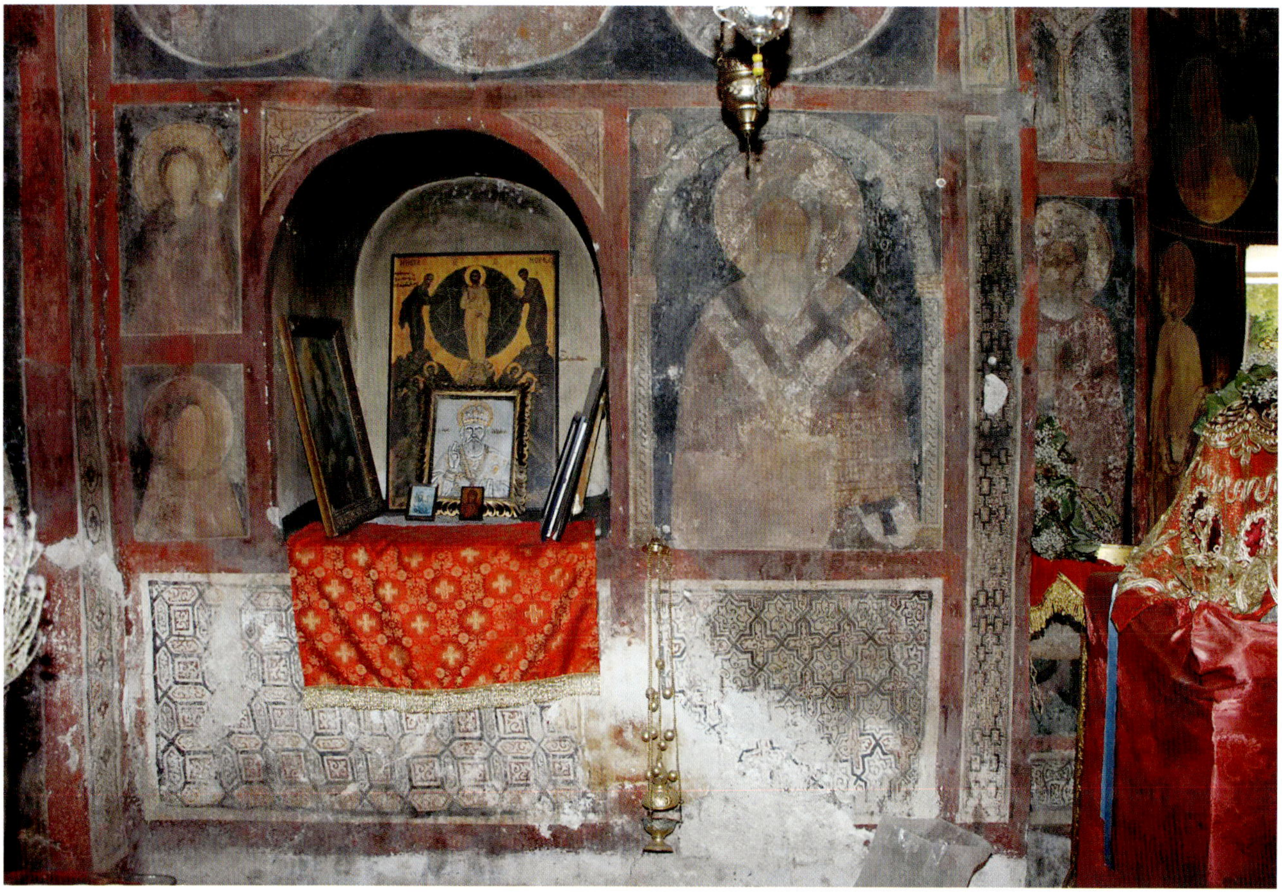

FIGURE 14. South Wall of Sanctuary. Church of St. Nicholas, Phountoukli, Rhodes (photo: I. Christoforaki. With permission of the Fourth Ephoreia of Byzantine Antiquities, Rhodes).

with Seljuk palace decoration were thus transferred to the Byzantine palace, along with the prestige of their original context. Scholars have viewed the decoration of the Mouchroutas Hall as a one-off, but the Phountoukli decoration provides another case of the use of Seljuk-style tilework, though, importantly, in an ecclesiastical setting and in decoration done by Orthodox rather than "Persian" hands.

The similarity of the Rhodian paintings to tiles excavated in the region of Konya and described above is startling, both in the imitation of their cut patterns and in their appropriation of their painted designs. The Phountoukli works are decorated with scrolls that find parallels in a group of Seljuk tiles that were found stacked in a workshop excavated in the Kubad Abad palace; the tiles have been dated to the end of the thirteenth and early fourteenth century.[66]

In buildings where Seljuk tiles have survived or have been reconstructed archaeologically, such as the Kubad Abad palace, the ceramic revetments cover the lowest register of the wall surface. At Phountoukli, the dado zone is less than one meter tall; the cruciform shapes in

Studies 4 (1978), 101–15; L.-A. Hunt, "Comnenian Aristocratic Palace Decoration: Descriptions and Islamic Connections," in *The Byzantine Aristocracy* (as in note 47), 138–70, esp. 141–42; N. Asutay-Effenberger, "Muchrutas. Der seldschukische Schaupavillon im Grossen Palast von Konstantinopel," *Byzantion* 74/2 (2004), 313–29; R. Arik, "Tiles in Anatolian Seljuk Palace Architecture," in Arik and Arik, *Tiles* (as in note 30), 239–41.

66. On tiles decorated with foliate ornament, see Arik and Arik, *Tiles* (as in note 30), 345–55, 397.

the church sanctuary are thickly outlined so that they project from the plane, suggesting that within the Byzantine context, the ornamental pattern of cruciforms and stars could be subtly Christianized by emphasizing one design component over another.[67] Other patterns within the church also find parallels within Seljuk buildings; the piecework octagons of the south door and sanctuary, created from trapezoidal shapes and squares, is a tile pattern found in the Buruciye Madrasa in Silvas, an elaborate structure built by the Ilkhanid official Muzaffer Burucirdi in 1271.[68]

The painted tiles on Rhodes imitated Seljuk tiles on the mainland, ones that may have been familiar to this church's high-class patron.[69] The representation of Seljuk tiles in this church provides material evidence for the thriving micro-economy of the late fifteenth-century Eastern Mediterranean, where islands off the coast of Turkey traded with settlements on the shore and further inland, as well as with each other. Preserved treaties attest that commercial interactions between the coast and mainland were protected even in times of war or political strife.[70] If, indeed, the *logothetes* Nikolaos Bardoanes was a refugee from Asia Minor, then he may have been the motivating force in the unusual inclusion of tiles—an art form that was both familiar and one that denoted status—in his children's burial church. Seen within the history of Anatolian tile production, the Rhodian church follows a tradition of church decoration that had already been long established in Byzantium.

Ottoman tiles, too, found a place in Orthodox churches, both as markers of status but also for their artistry. In the middle of the seventeenth century the monastery of the Virgin Panachrantos on the Cycladic island of Andros received a gift of more than one hundred İznik tiles from the ecumenical patriarch in İstanbul.[71] The tiles were fitted shortly thereafter into the lower register of the church's iconostasis, covering pre-existing frescoes (Fig. 15).[72] Colored in the characteristic turquoise blue, green, and red glaze palette of the İznik workshop, the tiles complement, through their radiant polychromy, a program that is otherwise devoted to icons of devotional and ritual significance that were reveted in silver.

The decision to display the tiles on the most sacred threshold of the church, the border between the nave and sanctuary, acknowledged the prestige of the gift and manifested the close connection of the monastery to the head of the Orthodox Church, Dionysios III, a native of the island.[73] In 1683 the monastery was elevated to *autocephalous* status; its removal from the jurisdiction of the local metropolitan and its placement under the direct administration of the patriarch was visually asserted in the exhibition of works that linked the island monastery to distant İstanbul. Given their prominent and potentially meaningful display, it hardly seems to have mattered that the tiles were a hodgepodge. The individual plaques, which date from the fourteenth to the sixteenth century, appear to have been assembled from stock stored in the warehouses of İstanbul and İznik. They were then shipped as an assemblage, to be pieced together and given new meaning.

Although the inclusion of İznik tiles in a church program appears to be unique, this was not the only occasion in which Ottoman ceramics appeared in an Orthodox context. Six monasteries on Mount Athos were also the recipients of İznik tiles and vessels, an indication of the desirability of the colorful products of the Bithynian workshop.[74] In the Great Lavra, İznik tiles cover the wall surface immediately below an image of signal importance to the community, the celebration

67. Bozer, "Forms of Seljuk Tile," in Arik and Arik, *Tiles* (as in note 30), 191–207.

68. Arik and Arik, *Tiles* (as in note 30), fig. 90.

69. The painter of the church may have been aware of similar patterns on ceramic vessels and textiles (including carpets and silks) that were imported to Rhodes from the Turkish coast.

70. Z. N. Tsirpanlis, "*Φιλικὲς σχέσεις τῶν Ἱπποτῶν τῆς Ῥόδου μὲ τοὺς Τούρκους κατὰ τὸν 15ον αἰ*," *Byzantinische Forschungen* 3 (1968), 197.

71. The main source on the tiles in this church is K. Korre-Zographou, *Τα Κεραμεικά Iznik της Μονής Παναχράντου Ἄνδρου* (Athens, 2004). The narthex of the church is also decorated with İznik tiles.

72. A date of 1644 on one of the paintings covered by the plaques provides a *terminus post quem* for the installation.

73. The patriarch's gift may have reflected lingering familial ties to the island.

74. J. Carswell, "Pottery and Tiles on Mount Athos," *Art Orientalis* 6 (1966), 77–90.

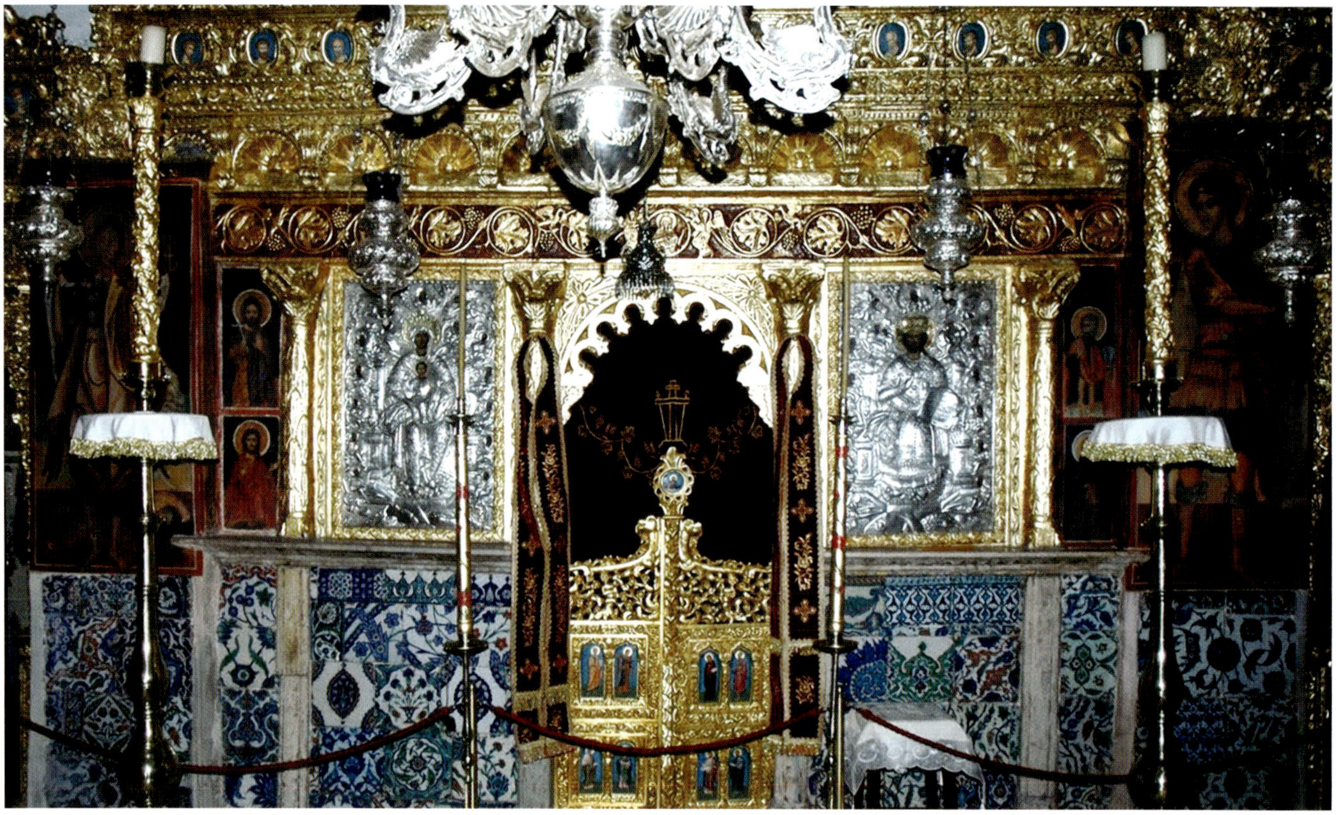

FIGURE 15. Iconostasis with İznik Tiles, Church of the Virgin Panachrantos, Andros (photo: author).

of the Triumph of Orthodoxy following the termination of Iconoclasm in 843, an event that was recalled in the Church calendar on the first Sunday of Lent. Other tiles frame the openings of the icon screens and are inscribed in Greek. The juxtaposition of the most Ottoman of crafts with the most Orthodox of subjects and locations seems jarring to the modern viewer, but hardly would have registered with the Lavra monks who, after all, resided in Ottoman territory.

Far from being a rarity, the use of ceramics, or an interest in ceramics as an important decorative medium, can be traced back in time to a moment in which tiles, made by Byzantine workshops, were considered an integral part of the most lavish constructions. Tiles, when placed in these ecclesiastical contexts, raise important issues. They witness, because of their portability, networks that transgress boundaries modern scholars have erected between the medieval and early modern periods, between regions and cultures, and between minor and monumental arts. The colorful ceramics also document the extensive trade of materials and luxury objects that crossed the Mediterranean in the late medieval and early modern period, and suggest something, as well, about the peregrinations of monks, emissaries of the patriarch, and merchants. The display of tiles, whether actual or fictive, was not only an aesthetic choice but one that was pregnant with meaning, The placement of İznik tiles on the icon screen is a material manifestation of important relationships at a time and in a place where Byzantium, with its cultural center in Constantinople, was preserved in the memory of the Orthodox, whose spiritual center was İstanbul. It is possible, too, in the case of the "Seljuk" tiles that were painted in Rhodes, that the tiles also conjured memories—memories of a lost homeland and subsequent displacement. The tiles were not only signs of prestige, but were quintessentially Anatolian.

The decoration of churches on Rhodes, Andros, and

Athos reveals both a practical and aesthetic appreciation of a medium that was durable, luminous, colorful, and luxurious. The decision to display these decorative plaques or their imitations on an icon screen or on the walls of a church also reveals something about the meaning of ornament and demonstrates how the same signs and forms could be deployed in radically different ways based on responses to economic, political, and cultural changes. Seljuk and Ottoman tiles were painted with abstract vegetation, a subject that suited the aniconic demands of mosque decoration and was symbolically interpreted, in that context, as a reference to paradise and the inexhaustible creativity of God. The motifs painted on the tiles also fit within the cosmological view of the Orthodox monk and the faithful, who viewed the interior of the church as a type of paradise, a theological space described in the flowery language of ekphrastic texts as a garden. Placed on the icon screen, the tiles form an integral part of a larger ornamental program of vegetation that manifests notions of the world to come: the carved epistyle covered with a vine scroll, the columns with their foliate capitals, and the wooden doors at the center of the screen, which eternally bloom with flowers. Ornament, read as a longing for return to the lost state of paradise, dominates the threshold program, just as the icons sited in the intercolumnar spaces, through proper devotions, were the vehicles of that return through active prayer.

Tiles used for pavements and facing in the East and West demonstrate a concern for the decoration of the building interior that is both practical and artistic. The interactions between the cultures that produced the tiles—ones that occupied lands at different times or traded with each other over long distances—urges us to consider the use of this decorative medium across borders that have been erected by scholars since the nineteenth century, if not earlier, and to consider their common functional qualities and ornamental significance. Byzantine tiles, even if decorated with icons, form part of a long Anatolian tradition. Western medieval tiles imitate, in their placement and design, pavements from lands further east. The examination of this durable medium suggests that architectural tiles were not only cheap works that lay underfoot or facing walls, but that they were deeply embedded in the minds of those who viewed them. Durable, economical, polychromatic, unfading, cool to the touch, reflective of sound … one of the least appreciated of media today may have been one of the most valued in the past.

HARALD WOLTER-VON DEM KNESEBECK

Secular Arts: Their Order and Importance

WRITING on a subject as vast and heterogeneous as the "Secular Arts," as a sub-division of the "Minor Arts," is a potentially risky undertaking. The discourse on terminology alone could fill an entire paper. Instead, I shall give a personal and subjective introduction to the topic and discuss how it has been studied to date, in order to identify and describe its problems and possibilities. As a term, the word "minor" is always used pejoratively, since it is derived from *minor*, the comparative of the Latin word *parvus*, or little/small. Of course, it can also imply "lesser" in a more judgmental way. The application of this term to art is not a medieval creation. It can be mainly understood from the point of view of the nineteenth- and twentieth-century art business and as a normative-idealistic art term from whence it derives. The term "secular arts," too, is a modern concept, as distinct from the "profane arts," or *artes profanae*, which ultimately goes back to antiquity. The concept of "profane" is understood in this context to mean outside of or in front of the holy district, while the term "secular" or "of the world" sets itself off from the spiritual-religious sphere.[1] These are modern ideas and are similar to the distinction between minor and major arts.

How much sense does it make to distinguish secular from sacred? In art-historical research of the nineteenth and early twentieth centuries this separation was usually very strict, but that was when the discipline centered mainly on religious art. Its dominance in the field of study, especially in the minor arts of the Middle Ages, usually resulted from unequal fortunes of tradition. For example, Johann Michael Fritz stated in his standard work on the art of Gothic goldsmithing that the ratios between profane and religious works seem to have exactly reversed themselves in today's tradition. In the Middle Ages, the production of the profane works that have become so rare today, constituted the majority. Only church treasuries, however, offered protection from obsolescence and being melted down for those objects made of desirable and precious materials.[2] The same is found when delicate textile works such as bags that were made for profane use are examined. Very frequently these survive thanks to their being used as reliquaries. Interestingly, research in textiles—an understudied area of the "minor arts"—is currently booming even in the "secular arts."

Nowadays, there are hardly any strict hierarchies between the art genres, nor is there a clear distinction between sacred and secular, even though both of these also existed in the Middle Ages in one form or another. This paper hopes to look at the complex interaction between the various categories of "secular" and "sacred" that are still not easy to understand at first sight. It was Alicia Walker and Amanda Luyster who recently discussed this concept in a corporeal simile in their volume *Negotiating Secular and Sacred in Medieval Art*: "Rather than performing dissections of secular and sacred organs from the anatomies of objects and buildings, scholars today allow worldly and spiritual features that were conjoined by their makers to work together as a single body."[3] It is this "working together" that I should like to examine in relation to a number of works that lie on the boundaries between secular and sacred. This, I hope, will also paint a clearer picture of "order and importance" in the secular arts of the Middle Ages. In addition, I would like to show how the areas shunted

1. See A. Cutler, "Sacred and Profane: The Locus of the Political in Middle Byzantine Art," in *Arte profana e arte sacra a Bisanzio*, ed. A. Iacobini, E. Zanini (Rome, 1995), 315–338, esp. 317.

2. J. M. Fritz: *Goldschmiedekunst der Gotik in Mitteleuropa* (Munich, 1982), 33, 67–68.

3. A. Walker, A. Luyster, "Introduction—Mapping the Heavens and Treading the Earth: Negotiating Secular and Sacred in Medieval Art," in *Negotiating Secular and Sacred in Medieval Art*, ed. A. Walker and A. Luyster (Aldershot, 2009), 1–16, esp. 8.

off into the "minor arts" both contributed to and were influenced by essential developments in medieval art —developments that formerly would have been linked only to the "major arts." To undertake this task requires that a number of essential questions be asked regarding function and context that lend modern art history a promising methodology for approaching this highly dynamic research area of the secular arts.

The Ebstorf World Map

The first work I should like to examine is the Ebstorf World Map (Fig. 1), which was made in Northern Germany around 1300.[4] It is a strange combination of a wall painting and book art, as well as devotional object and teaching aid. At a height of around 3.6 meters, or 11.8 feet, it is the largest world image of its kind. However, it was not painted on a wall, but on thirty parchment sheets sewn together so that it could be rolled up on two rods like an old school map. Yet it approaches the category of a book in its voluminous captions. According to the latest count, there are approximately fifteen hundred Latin texts compared to eight hundred pictorial elements. Among the latter are depictions of cities and buildings, one hundred sixty bodies of water, sixty animals, as well as forty-five human and mythical beings. The world is orientated towards the east on this map in that East along with Paradise is found at the top. All geometrically fixed points on this map are defined Christologically. The center of the world is Jerusalem, which is shown as the eternal or golden city with an image of the risen Christ. Christ himself is literally "written in" as the sufferer of the world: his head appears as a Vera Icon at the top, on the edge of the world. His hands and feet with the stigmata are found in the north, south, and west. God reveals himself in the world he created. The world itself, however, is finite and needs to be redeemed. God only will remain with those who approach him and thus find their way into Paradise, which is depicted in the east with the fall from grace, very close to Christ's face.

There is a camel directly next to the image of the Heavenly Jerusalem in the center of the map, and both are similar in size. It is one of a number of animals integrated into the map, all of which are closely linked to the captions. Thus, the map virtually incorporates a bestiary, a topic so popular in the High Middle Ages, and organizes it topographically. As well as these animals there are the monsters from Africa's extremities next to Christ's hands in the outer reaches of the world and, in the north, there are the Amazons and the man-eating Gog and Magog peoples. Europe is the continent of cities. Consequently, it is in comparison staid, and is organized along the rivers as main traffic arteries, which had, of course, positive connotations. Europe lacks almost all figurative elements and only two lions catch our attention. The one on the crenellations of Rome was inspired by the supposed lion-shaped footprint of the city. The other one depicts the famous lion's statue of Henry the Lion in Braunschweig (Brunswick) (Fig. 2). Braunschweig was one of two big cities of the Duchy of Braunschweig-Lüneburg, where the Ebstorf monastery was located, and whence this world map originated. Its purpose, however, is unknown, but it may possibly have been a teaching aid or a devotional image. A prayer before the Vera Icon, which forms Christ's head at the top of the map, promises absolution. Categorizing the map as either profane or sacred is, at any rate, just as useless as its pejorative or

4. For the Ebstorf world map, see H. Kugler, *Die Ebstorfer Weltkarte. Kommentierte Neuausgabe in zwei Bänden*, vols. 1–2 (Berlin, 2007); see also the review of this edition: J. Wilke, *Göttingische Gelehrte Anzeigen* 260 (2008), 177–189, and a virtual edition on the world wide web: http://weblab.uni-lueneburg.de/kulturinformatik/projekte/ebskart/content/start.html. For the controversy about the date of the Ebstorf world map, see now A. Wolf, "The Ebstorf Mappamundi and Gervase of Tilbury: The Controversy Revisited," in *Imago Mundi* 64 (2012), Part 1: 1–27. For the following, see especially H. Wolter-von dem Knesebeck, "Neue Formen der Bildung und neue Bildformen im Vorfeld der Ebstorfer Weltkarte in Sachsen," *Kloster und Bildung im Mittelalter, Ebstorfer Kolloquium 2004*, Studien zur Germania Sacra 28; Veröffentlichungen des Max-Planck-Instituts für Geschichte 218, ed. N. Kruppa and J. Wilke (Göttingen, 2006) 231–261; H. Wolter-von dem Knesebeck, "Neue Formen des Sehens und das mittelalterliche Weltbild. Die Ebstorfer Weltkarte," in *Modernisierung des Sehens. Sehweisen zwischen Künsten und Medien*, ed. M. Bruhn and K.-U. Hemken (Bielefeld, 2008), 68–80.

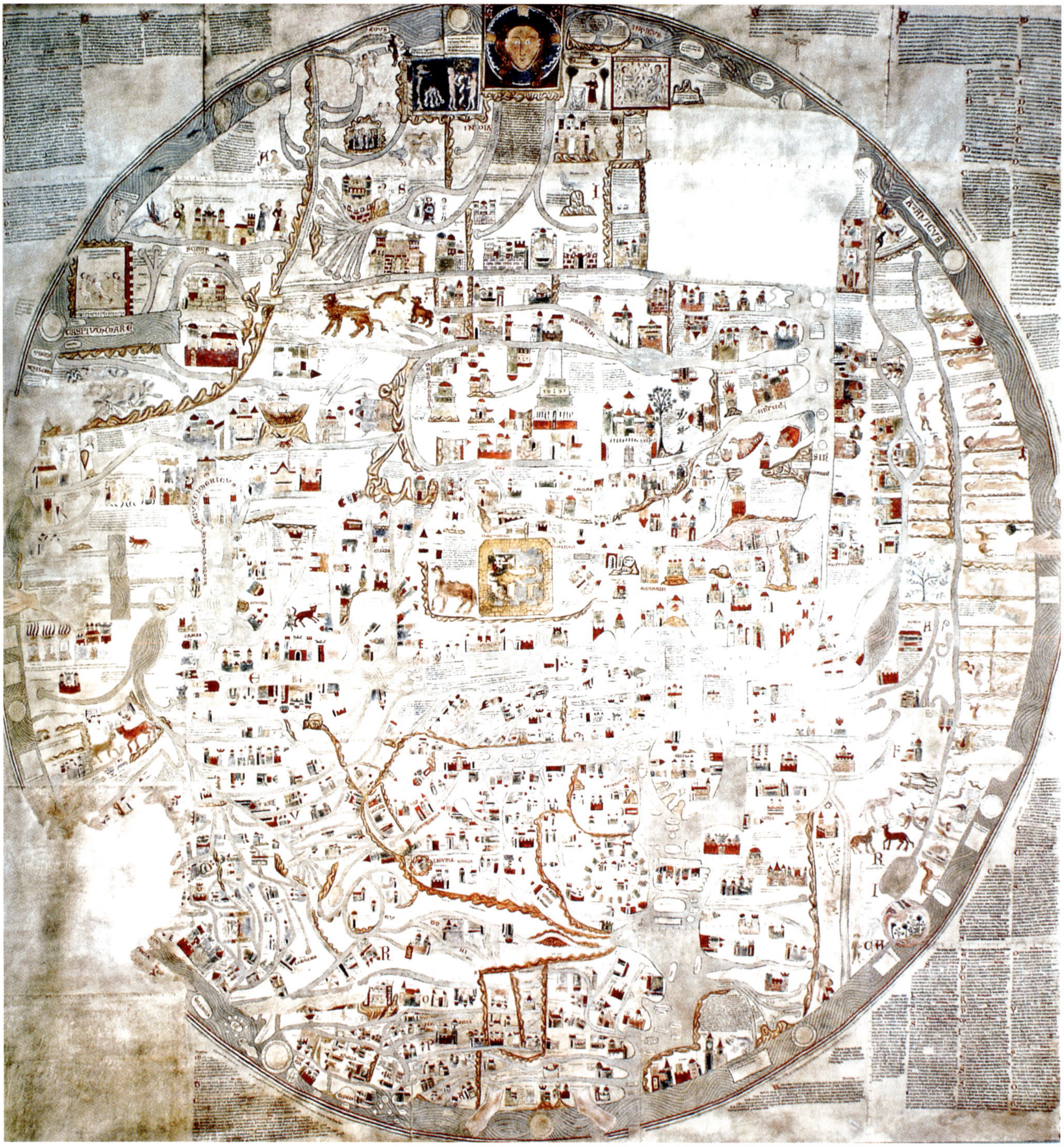

FIGURE 1. Ebstorf World Map, *c.* 1300, northern Germany (modern copy of the 1943 destroyed original).

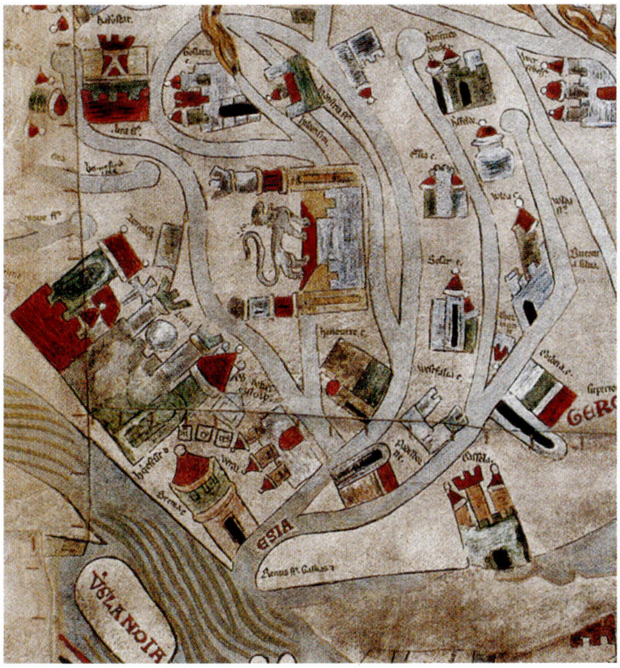

FIGURE 2. Ebstorf World Map, *c.* 1300, northern Germany (modern copy of the 1943 destroyed original), detail showing Lüneburg and Braunschweig with Henry the Lion's Lion Statue.

enhancing categorization as it being one of the minor or major arts.

Looking at the map in terms of its reception is more useful. The diversity of the world it shows can be confusing, especially for the curious, since the only fixed point is the representation of Christ. In the Middle Ages, curiosity or *curiositas*, was a vice according to St. Augustine.[5] It was only Christ who lent meaning to the world, and thus to secular things. And yet, the relationship with the world is an open one. It ranges from its acceptance as a kind of book that can lead humans to God as their creator, all the way to a withdrawal from the world that is as complete as possible. But the world is always thought of as finite, deficient, and needing redemption. This is what the Hereford Map—the second preserved large medieval world map—shows.[6] It is sealed with the word "MORS" or "death," and, in its depiction of the Last Judgment, it points out its temporality.

The Naumburg West Choir

It was this view of the world that made it possible for the repertoire of profane and peripheral arts, which could be called "minor," to enter into the major arts in the Middle Ages. I should like to illustrate this with a sculptural ensemble that could easily be understood as a prime example of the major arts—the famous founders' statues of the Naumburg West Choir (Figs. 3 and 4), dating from around 1240.[7] In several of the founders' statues, the non-ideal, pathognomonic expressions of their faces and postures have always had a striking effect (Fig. 4). These expressions cannot be linked to founders' images on tombstones, such as the contemporary tomb of Henry the Lion in Braunschweig, which were becoming popular at this time.[8] Instead, at Naumburg, standards were used that were first tested on masks made by the Reims workshop (Fig. 5).[9] These masks had been relocated to parts of the cathedral in Reims that were very high up and barely visible, a marginal position in which they could easily be understood as representative of the minor arts.

I believe that these are explained by the fact that the founders' statues in the West Choir of Naumburg Cathedral are part of a Judgment scene. In order to

5. See K. Krüger, "Einleitung," in *Curiositas. Welterfahrung und ästhetische Neugierde in Mittelalter und früher Neuzeit*, ed. K. Krüger (Göttingen, 2002), 7–18.

6. See P. D. A. Harvey, *The Hereford World Map* (London, 2010); S. D. Westrem, *The Hereford Map: A Transcription and Translation of the Legends with a Commentary* (Turnhout, 2001).

7. See several contributions in *Meisterwerke mittelalterlicher Skulptur. Die Berliner Gipsabgußsammlung*, ed. H. Krohm (Berlin, 1996). The sculptures will be the center of the first major exhibition on the Naumburg Master taking place 2011 in Naumburg. See my article in the catalogue of this exhibition: "Zum Bildprogramm des Naumburger Westchores Ein eschatologischer Rahmen für Lettner, Stifterfiguren und die Glasmalerei," in *Der Naumburger Meister. Bildhauer und Architekt im Europa der Kathedralen*, ed. H. Krohm and H. Kunde (Petersberg, 2011), 1158–1168.

8. See K. Niehr, *Die mitteldeutsche Skulptur der ersten Hälfte des 13. Jahrhunderts* (Artefact 3), ed. T. Buddensieg, F. Neumeyer, and M. Warnke (Berlin, 1992), 141–145, 175–181.

9. See W. Sauerländer, "Die Naumburger Stifterfiguren. Rückblick und Fragen," in *Die Zeit der Staufer. Geschichte—Kunst—Kultur, Supplement*, Katalog der Ausstellung Stuttgart 5, ed. R. Haussherr and C. Väterlein (Stuttgart, 1979), 169–245, esp. 231–234.

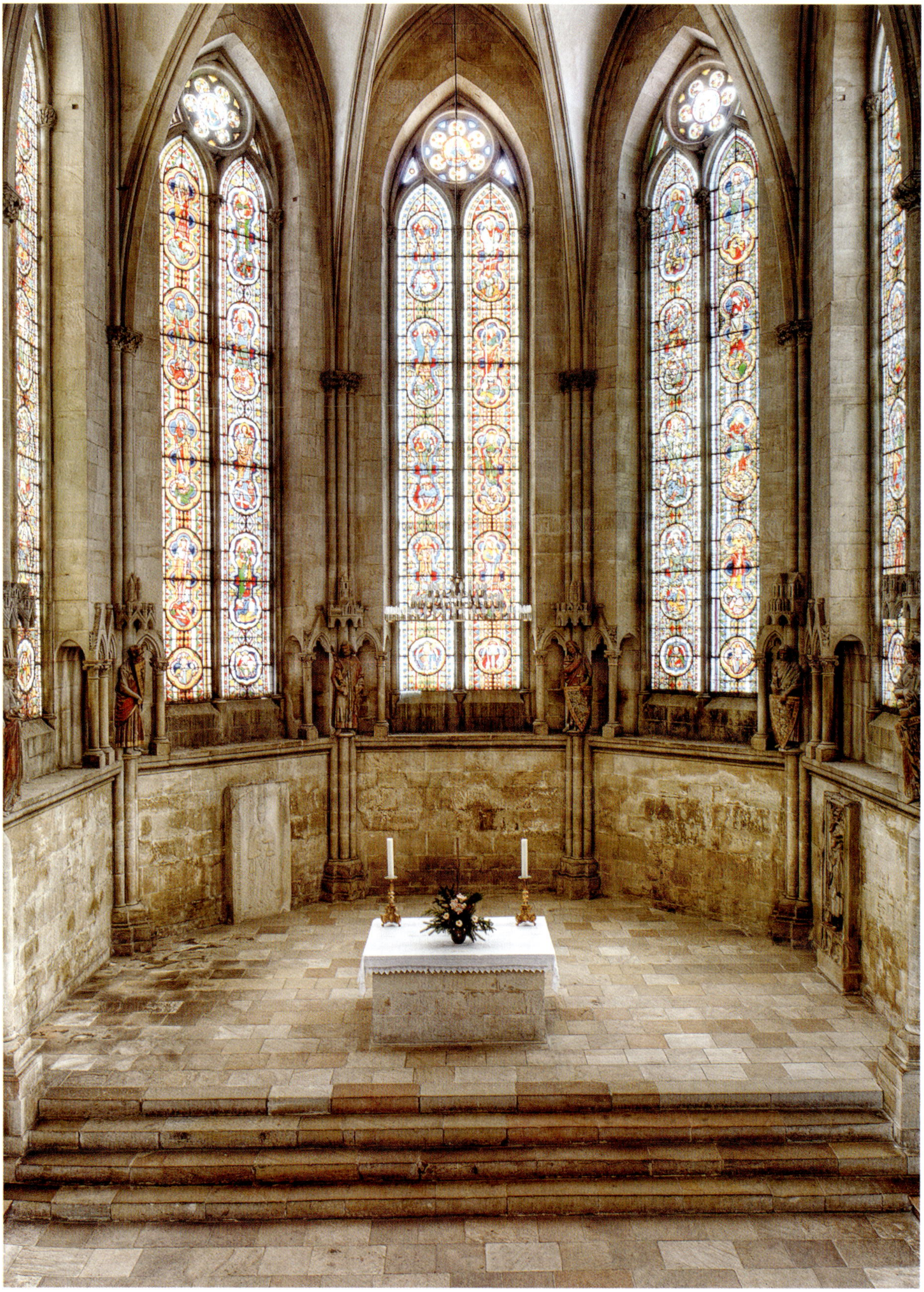

FIGURE 3. Naumburg Cathedral, west choir, *c.* 1240–1250.

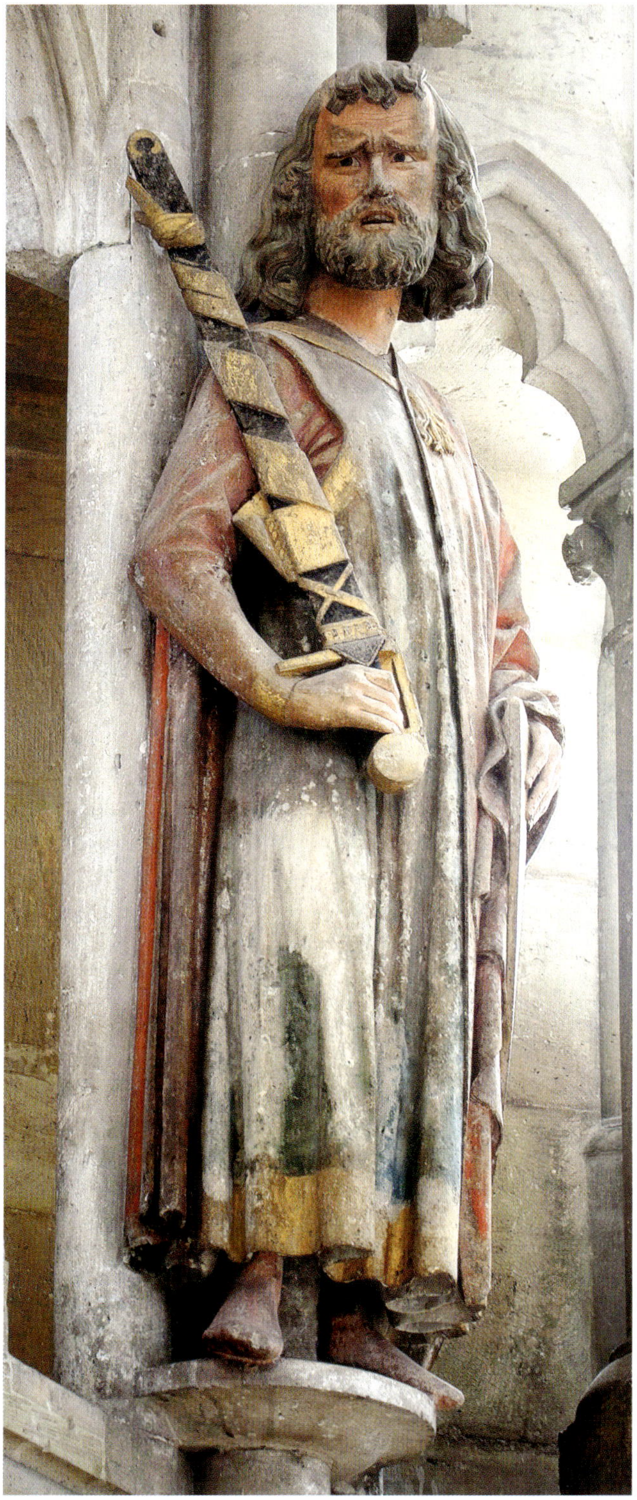

FIGURE 4. Naumburg Cathedral, west choir, founder statue of Sizzo, *c.* 1240–1250.

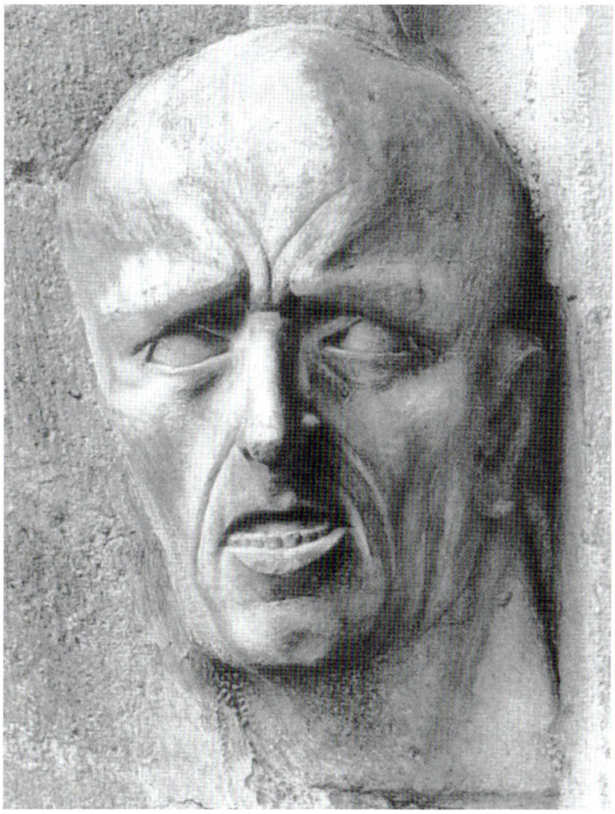

FIGURE 5. Reims Cathedral, exterior, upper parts of the choir, mask, before 1225.

recognize this it is necessary, however, to turn the hierarchies of minor and major arts, and consequently the values of art genres at Naumburg's West Choir, upside-down. What defined the overall program of the West Choir was possibly not so much the conspicuous sculptures, but rather the little-known paintings. Christ as the Judge of the World in the tympanum of the rood screen is found on the central axis of the choir, and above the entrance to the West Choir the Judge of the World was most likely repeated in a lost *deësis* in the *couronnement* of the choir's glass windows. The glass windows in the West Choir gathered the saints as co-chairs of the Judgment.[10] The founders'

10. See E. Schubert, "Zum ikonographischen Programm der Farbverglasung im Westchor des Naumburger Doms," in *Deutsche Glasmalerei des Mittelalters. Bildprogramm, Auftraggeber, Werkstätten*, Deutsche Glasmalerei des Mittelalters 2, ed. R. Becksmann (Berlin, 1992), 43–52.

statues directly below the glass windows on the walls of the choir represent humanity needing redemption, whose fate is at stake in the Judgment. Thus, they link to the "real people" below in the choir. Their need for redemption is reflected in their facial expressions and gestures that are characterized by the Reims mask style. This adoption from the peripheral areas of Reims Cathedral thus emphasized a statement that was dear to those in power in Naumburg. A document, sealing a general prayer fraternization between the clergy and potential founders and dating from 1249, identifies the names of the founders' statues.[11] The West Choir was supposed to be an example of the first Naumburg founders for potential future founders. In the context of a world judgment, however, it is their pathognomonics that show that even worldly sinners can find redemption through their donations.

Henry the Lion's Braunschweig Lion Statue and Aquamanilia

Further links between large works of sculpture and those from the minor arts can also be seen in another seminal work of high medieval sculpture—Henry the Lion's lion (Fig. 6). This is already known from the Ebstorf Map (Fig. 2) and dates to about 1166.[12] It stood on a high pedestal in the Braunschweig Castle square between Henry's Dankwarderode Castle and his burial church. There, it served as a personal monument to Henry and was adorned with the "lion" moniker, a fact that was always understood as such. This lion is an example of the importance of the secular arts and the development of the major arts in a court context; in Braunschweig it is also an early example that was used to establish residency. In this context, Braunschweig is a successor to Charlemagne's imperial palace in Aachen, whose antique and Carolingian bronzes have been well studied, as has been the Braunschweig lion.

This has not been the case for such medieval small bronzes as *aquamanilia* (Figs. 7 and 8). They are mostly animal shaped, and rarely depict human forms; together with a bowl they were used for handwashing.[13] For a long time, they were merely catalogued and attributed to different regions and workshops, and it was only in recent years that questions have been posed regarding their imagery and its meaning and their position within medieval art history generally. This was initiated by two important exhibitions—one of them in New York, and the other in Hildesheim, Germany.[14] *Aquamanilia* are discussed here for several reasons, but primarily because of the formal links suggested by the small lion-shaped items with such a prime example of the major arts as the Braunschweig lion. They are also particularly interesting in that they were used both in the sacral area in the priest's handwashing during Mass, as well as for washing hands in a secular context during meals at courts. Their use was thus common to both the secular as well as the sacral spheres. It seems that *aquamanilia* in the shape of horsemen were the only ones restricted to the area of the profane.

It is their imagery that is really still unclear, both as to its origins and meaning. Amongst the *ornamenta ecclesiae*, such as chalice, paten, and crucifix, it is the animal figures that are unusual. Then as today, lion-shaped *aquamanilia* are most frequently found, and they consist of about one third of all those surviving.[15] The

11. See *Urkundenbuch des Hochstifts Naumburg*, Part 2, (1207–1304), ed. H. K. Schulze, auf den Grundlagen der Vorarbeiten von F. Rosenfeld und W. Möllenberg bearbeitet von H. Patze und J. Dolle (Cologne, Weimar, Vienna, 2000), s. 258, Nr. 236.

12. See P. Seiler, "Der Braunschweiger Burglöwe. Spurensicherung auf der Suche nach den künstlerischen Vorbildern," in *Heinrich der Löwe und seine Zeit. Herrschaft und Repräsentation der Welfen 1125–1235*, Katalog der Ausstellung Braunschweig 2, ed. J. Luckhardt and F. Niehoff (Munich, 1995), 244–255.

13. See O. von Falke and E. Meyer, *Romanische Leuchter und Gefäße, Gießgefäße der Gotik*, Bronzegeräte des Mittelalters 1 (Berlin, 1935; reprint Berlin, 1983); M. Hütt, *"Quem lavat unda foris....". Aquamanilien. Gebrauch und Form* (Mainz, 1993); *Lions, Dragons, & Other Beasts: Aquamanilia of the Middle Ages, Vessels for Church and Table*, Exhib. Cat., New York, 2006, ed. P. Barnet and P. Dandridge (New Haven and London, 2006). See my review in *Sehepunkte* 8 (2008), Nr. 4: http://www.sehepunkte.de/2008/04/12358.html; and my article "Zur Inszenierung und Bedeutung von Aquamanilien," in *Bild & Bestie. Hildesheimer Bronzen der Stauferzeit*, Exhib. Cat., Hildesheim, 2008, ed. M. Brandt (Regensburg, 2008), 217–228.

14. *Lions, Dragons, & Other Beasts* (as in note 13); *Bild & Bestie* (as in note 13).

15. Cf. O. von Falke and E. Meyer, "Romanische Leuchter und Gefäße" (as in note 13).

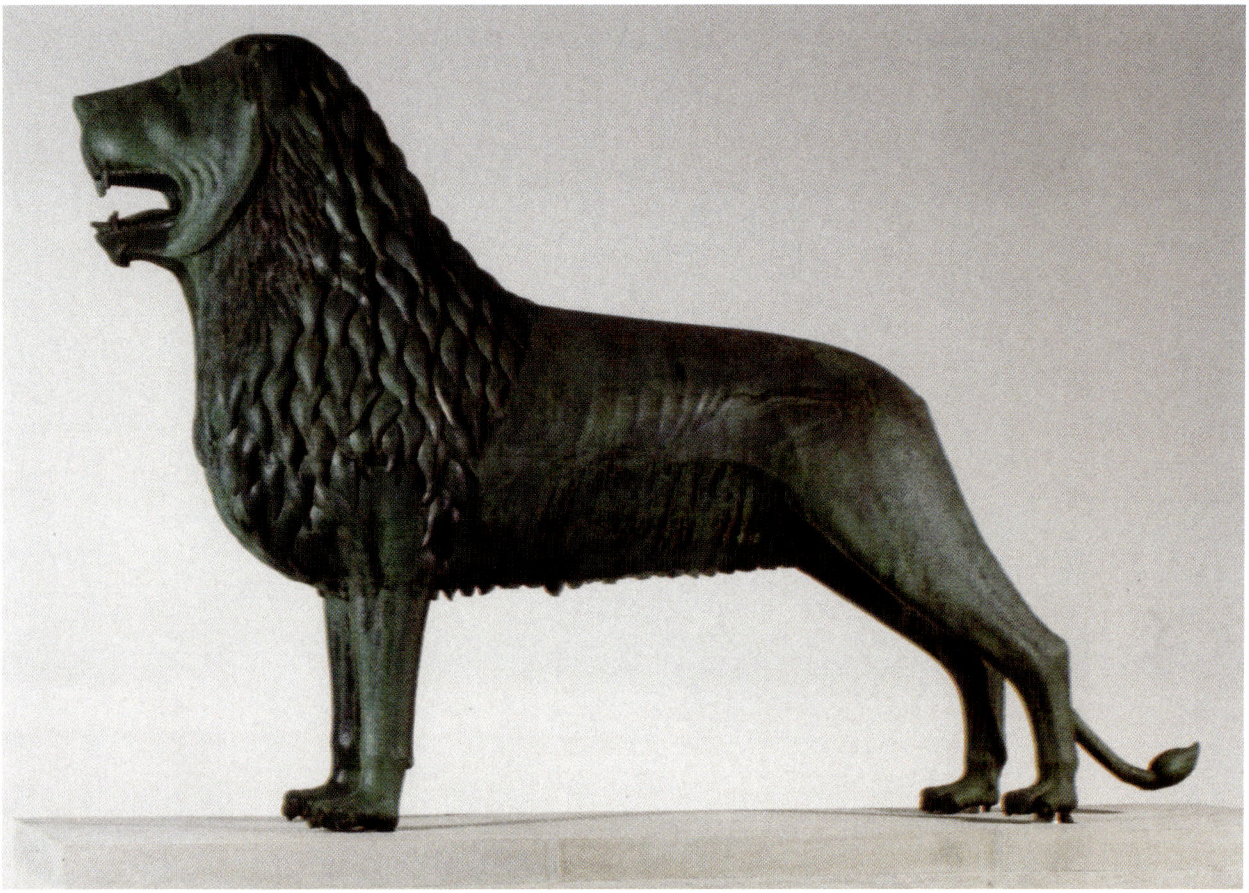

FIGURE 6. Braunschweig, Herzog Anton Ulrich Museum, Henry the Lion's Lion Statue, formerly in front of the Burg Dankwarderode at Braunschweig, *c.* 1166.

lion is followed by the horse-shaped *aquamanilia* (horses and occasionally unicorns, mostly carrying a rider), then by such winged beings as dragons, griffins, and birds. Dogs, stags, or rams, as well as mythical beasts including centaurs and mermaids are relatively rare. Another special case is "Aristotle Ridden by Phyllis." [16] In general, human-form *aquamanilia* including heads, upper torsos, or, even more unique, the full body, are amongst the exceptions. The fact that images of God, the angels, and saints are missing links *aquamanilia* to medieval floors, which have recently been discussed by Thomas Weigel.[17] It is clear that a medieval hierarchy between the locations of such images, from the apsis at the top to the floor underneath, exists. But what was the problem posed by the human hand in respect to its function as a user of *aquamanilia*?

In a pioneering article in 1993, Michael Hütt attempted to define the content of this genre of the minor arts more precisely, and he started with the examples I used initially in this paper in his linking of *aquamanilia* and Henry the Lion's lion statue (Fig. 6).[18] For Hütt *aquamanilia* are "small sculptures serving the self-representation of their users," while satisfying their need "to create a relationship to societal ideals." [19] In this

16. *Lions, Dragons, & Other Beasts* (as in note 13), 136–141, Cat. Nr. 19.

17. T. Weigel, *Schmuckfußböden des 12. Jahrhunderts aus inkrustiertem Estrichgips*, Studien zur internationalen Architektur- und Kunstgeschichte, Vol. 67 (Petersberg, 2009).

18. Hütt, "Aquamanilien" (as in note 13), 65–72.

19. *Ibid.*, 223.

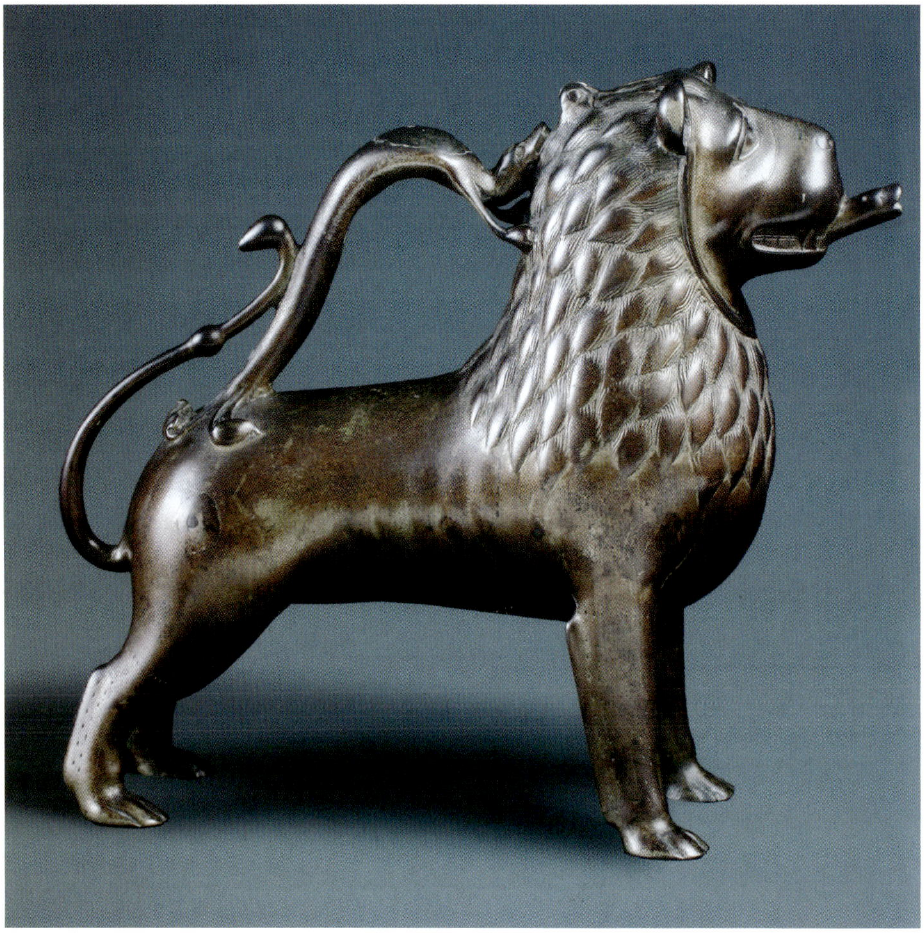

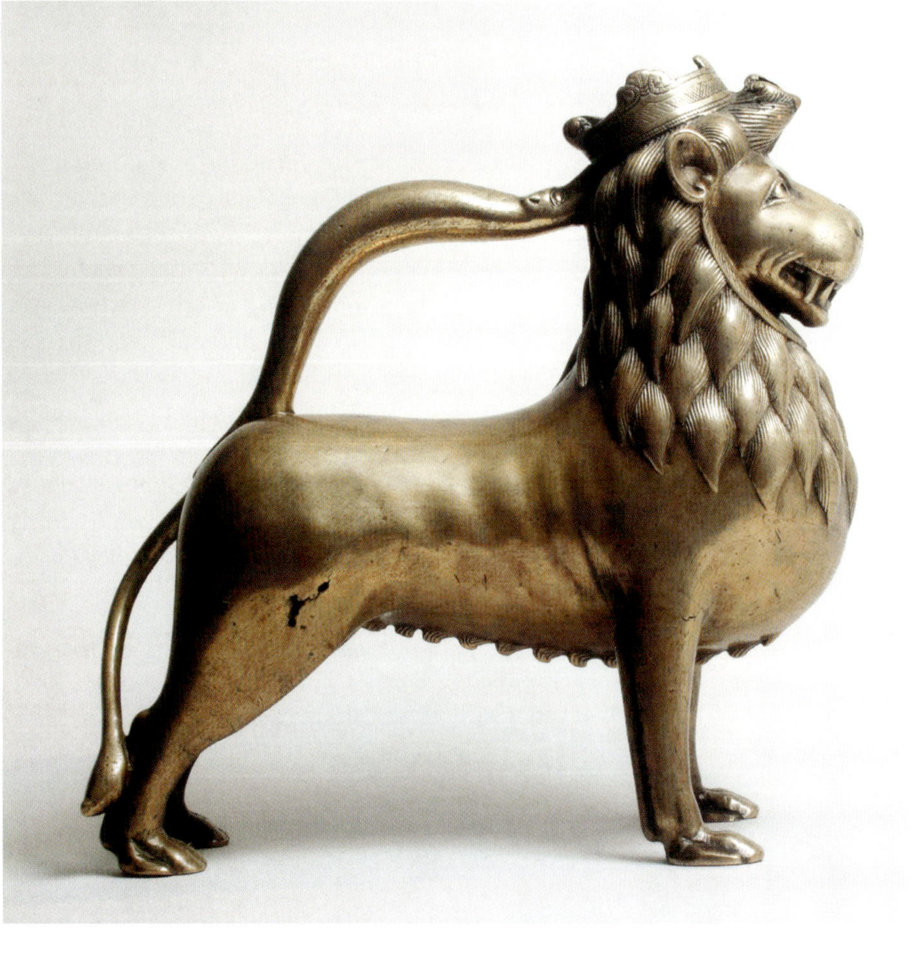

FIGURE 7 (*opposite*). Halberstadt Cathedral Treasury, lion *aquamanile*, Hildesheim, *c.* 1220–1230, Inv.-Nr. 321.

FIGURE 8 (*opposite*). Hildesheim Cathedral Treasury, lion *aquamanile*, Hildesheim, *c.* 1220–1230, Inv.-Nr. 2006-1 (Stiftung Niedersachsen / Ernst von Siemens Kunststiftung).

context, Hütt also referred to related depictions of lions and horsemen, frequently found as *aquamanilia*, to those found on seals and coats of arms. In doing so, he mentioned two areas to which recent research in art history and history generally has been paying more attention and that are usually also categorized as minor arts.[20] Seals and coats of arms were—as personal representations—of paramount importance to the individuals ordering them. This is why seals are amongst the best of the goldsmiths' work. This clearly shows that for the Middle Ages the pejorative connotation inherent in the term "minor arts" is actually out of place.

In his interpretation of *aquamanilia* as personal images and representations of their owners, Hütt has, however, overlooked an essential fact. The typical lion *aquamanilia* (Figs. 7 and 8) always show a lion that does not act freely and this is unlike those on seals and coats of arms or, for that matter, the Braunschweig lion statue (Fig. 6). Instead, it is an animal that has been pressed into service. This is shown by the stream of water during handwashing, which in many lion *aquamanilia* represents the lion in a servile or subjugated position. The importance of the stream of water in the design of the *aquamanile* is demonstrated by the high-quality lion example—probably from Hildesheim (dating to *c.* 1220–1230)—now in Halberstadt Cathedral Treasury (Fig. 7).[21] The dynamic tension of this small sculpture is focused on emphasizing the stream of water that shoots forth from the clearly emphasized spout in its mouth. This is similar to the effect that dragons have when they appear as handles on medieval lion *aquamanilia*. The dragons smoothly push off from the lion's lower back towards the front in order to attack the lion at the back of its head at exactly the place where the stream of water exits the spout in the front. Thus, not only does the dragon provide the compositional reason for the stream of water, but it also adds to the narrative embellishment of the *aquamanilia*. A closely related lion in Hildesheim Cathedral Treasury (Fig. 8) shows this in an impressive way. Here the stream gushes forth from a spout formed of hairs at the dragon head's height, above the lion's forehead, forcing the lion's crown into a precariously skewed position.[22]

This narrative embellishment becomes even clearer when Samson serves as a handle and also attacks the back of the lion's head.[23] But a dragon can also take the place of the lion, and an unnamed hero can take that of Samson.[24] Not infrequently, lions and dragons regurgitate their most recent victims and these are used to form the spout. On the dragon, this is indicated by the hands of a figure that has otherwise disappeared. Such a merging of attacker and attacked can assume acrobatic proportions. This is the case of the dragon at the Hermitage in Saint Petersburg, which has already half swallowed the head of a nobleman so that his face is no longer visible.[25] And yet, this intrepid person is pulling the ears at the back of the monster's head, whereupon the monster ejects two streams of water from its maw. However, the only way for them to flow past the half-eaten man is through the latter's ample head of hair. The lion from Hildesheim Cathedral Museum (Fig. 8) is even more obvious in that the strands of hair and the stream of water heighten each other's effect. And, finally, the old humpback who in the later Middle Ages has the spout on his belly seems to mock these wild struggles.[26] It is clearly a medieval

20. See B. Bedos-Rezak's contribution in this volume.

21. U. Mende, "Löwen-Aquamanile." in *Bild & Bestie* (as in note 13), 378–379, Cat. Nr. 52.

22. U. Mende, "Löwen-Aquamanile," in *Bild & Bestie* (as in note 13), 374–377, Cat. Nr. 51.

23. O. von Falke and E. Meyer, "Romanische Leuchter und Gefäße" (as in note 13), figs. 329, 330.

24. O. von Falke and E. Meyer, "Romanische Leuchter und Gefäße" (as in note 13), fig. 246; U. Mende, "Drachen-Aquamanile," in *Bild & Bestie* (as in note 13), 349–353, Cat. Nr. 43.

25. O. von Falke and E. Meyer, "Romanische Leuchter und Gefäße" (as in note 13), fig. 251; U. Mende, "Drachen-Aquamanile," in *Bild & Bestie* (as in note 13), 354–357, Cat. Nr. 44.

26. O. von Falke and E. Meyer, "Romanische Leuchter und Gefäße" (as in note 13), fig. 285; U. Mende, "Aquamanile in Gestalt eines Buckligen," in *Bild & Bestie* (as in note 13), 298–300, Cat. Nr. 25.

resumption of the old motif of the goose strangler, as when we see him he seems to be squirting water from a small snake.

Thus, the central act of the *aquamanilia* is a violent attack on a strong animal that causes it to spit water. This illustrates the universal principle of struggle and makes its point by using the lion, the king of animals. During the act of pouring, the role of the victor over the strong one is transferred to the person pouring, whose hands conceal most of the dragon or Samson, depending on what subject is used. Thus the pourer became part of the subject matter and, in some sense, a participant in the constant struggle in the world. This understanding of the objects' use obviously eliminated the need to depict any holy persons in the iconographical repertoire of *aquamanilia*.

The use of struggle, persecution, and force as the major themes in *aquamanilia* must have been understood as representing the lives of everyday people in a fleeting and imperfect world. Such subject matter is well suited to *aquamanilia*, since they are actually hybrids lying somewhere between living beings and round-bellied vessels. They are without a core and appear lifelike in the sense of filling and ejecting—similar to gargoyles or wellheads—but also remaining deficient.

But how did such deficient beings find their way into liturgy and court ritual? In the liturgical context, it is the priest who elevates himself from worldly pollution by washing his hands with water from the *aquamanile* so that he can face God during Mass cleansed. And in the courtly sphere, a parallel rite is provided in the realm of hospitality, which is entered into by washing one's hands with water from an *aquamanile*. This brought the visitor from the part of the world that is described as the adventurous forest in courtly novels. Thus, *aquamanilia* allow travelers to go from a worldly threshold into a special place removed from the earthly limits, be it sacred or secular. The imagery of the *aquamanilia*, then, represents an image of the world. In the ritual, it indicates a boundary by showing the transient world—in a quasi apotropaic way—in the place where it is left behind, and where its threatening components can be destroyed by the act of putting it to use.

Based on such uses, it seems to me that there is a strong correlation between *aquamanilia* and architectural sculpture, which entered its critical developmental phase in the early twelfth century at exactly the same time as the former's appearance and distribution. This is more than obvious when such themes as Atlantes figures complaining of their load, or lion statues supporting Italian porticos, or bronze doors with lions for door pulls are examined. These are all found on church portals, a critical spatial boundary between the outside world and the sacral space. It is specifically at these spatial boundaries that the use of sculpture was concentrated at that time, as well as in the choir at the rood screen and barriers. *Aquamanilia*—as well as the Reims masks (Fig. 5)—deserve more attention than they currently receive. They need to be examined for their expressiveness, as well as for their narrative content.

To extend this even further, *aquamanilia* as well as large carvings can be seen as part of an expanded type of imagery in all areas of high medieval culture. It is the *aquamanilia* in particular that show how important "minor arts" can frequently be left out of the bigger picture, especially when they can caste such significant light on other areas. *Aquamanilia* as such are an indispensable part of the history of table culture, of conversation at the table. Aristotle and Phyllis have to be remembered and especially their links to such early modern devices as table games, or again, as lavabos for the courtly table.

Profane Wall Paintings

The reference to hospitality enables me to refer briefly to secular wall paintings.[27] My past research on this subject developed out of a wish to examine and un-

27. See H. Wolter-von dem Knesebeck, *Bilder für 'wirt,' 'wirtin' und 'gast.' Studien zur profanen Wandmalerei* (Denkmäler Deutscher Kunst, Deutscher Verein für Kunstwissenschaft), ed. R. Becksmann (forthcoming), and H. Wolter-von dem Knesebeck, "'Hûsêre' and the 'Topography of Contrasts' in 15th Century Mural Paintings from Tyrol and Trentino," in *Out of the Stream: Studies in Medieval and Renaissance Mural Painting*, ed. L. Urbano Afonso and V. Serrão (Cambridge, 2007), 22–41. The example I have selected for this purpose is from the area that Michael Curschmann, at Princeton, has dedicated so many essential con-

derstand any possible iconographical links that existed in wall paintings found castles as well as in burghers' houses.

Secular wall paintings in the Middle Ages have a dual relationship to the house.[28] The house is both the subject and the object of the paintings. In terms of the first relationship, the individual paintings acquire an additional significance. The interrelationship of paintings in a given room is an important part of the statements made by them, as indeed is their connection to doors, windows, and fireplaces. The decoration of a particular room is developed from this, i.e., its topographical features. On the other hand, the house is also a favorite theme of secular wall paintings, in that they frequently show house-related values. These values are organized around the master and lady of the house.[29] They are concerned with their relationship to each other, the family, the servants, and the outside world. The "outside world" arrives at the house in the guise of a guest.[30] The framework surrounding the visit of the guest, which is also reflected in the wall paintings, is the "house honor," adumbrated in the Middle High German concept *Hûsêre.*[31] In the Middle Ages it meant not only hospitality, but also a well-ordered and administered house; in the late Middle Ages it came to mean the lady of the house herself.

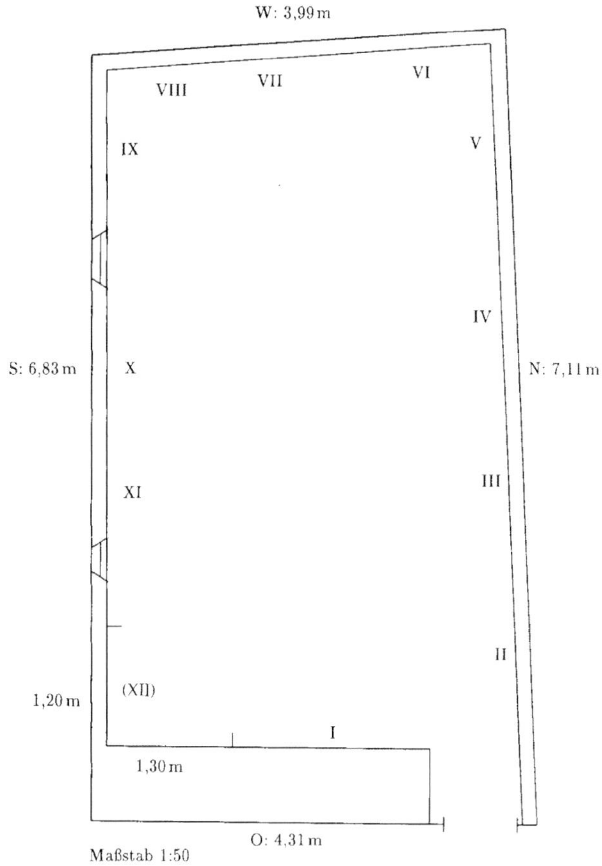

FIGURE 9. South Tyrol, Rodenegg Castle, plan of the Iwein cycle, *c.* 1210–1220 (according to Szklenar 1996).

Understood in this way, the house and its dual relationship with secular wall paintings formed the nucleus of my earlier research, and I was able to illustrate this relationship using numerous examples. Among the earliest extant examples of secular wall paintings are the Iwein (Ywain) cycles in Rodenegg Castle in South Tyrol (Figs. 9–12) and in Schmalkalden in Thuringia, both of which date to the first half of the thirteenth

tributions to, in which he was able to show, among other things, that vernacular literature and its images go quasi hand in hand, especially in the illuminated manuscripts, and represent a similarity in level between the means of communication.

28. For the House, see *Lexikon des Mittelalters*, vol. 4, 1960–1971, *s.v.* "Haus, -formen" (K. Bedal, H. Hinz, G. Köbler, H. Ehrhardt, G. Vismara, D. Anex-Cabanis, H. Hellenkemper, H. Gaube), and *ibid.*, 2176–2179, *s.v.* "Herr, Herrschaft" (D. Willoweit); *Historisches Wörterbuch der Philosophie*, vol. 3, 1007–1022, *s.v.* "Haus" (G. Bien, H. Rabe), esp. 1007 (G. Bien); *Theologische Realenzyklopädie*, vol. 14, 472–492, *s.v.* "Haus," esp. 474 ff. (G. Lanczkowski); *Home and Homelessness in the Medieval and Renaissance World*, ed. N. Howe (Notre Dame, Ind., 2004).

29. For "wirt" and "wirtin" in late medieval vernacular economical writing, see T. Ehlert, "Die Rolle von 'Hausherr' und 'Hausfrau' in der spätmittelalterlichen volkssprachlichen Ökonomik," in *Haushalt und Familie in Mittelalter und früher Neuzeit. Vorträge eines interdisziplinären Symposions vom 6.–9. Juni 1990 an der Rheinischen Friedrich-Wilhelms-Universität Bonn*, ed. T. Ehlert (Sigmaringen, 1991), 153–166.

30. For the guest in the Middle Age, see J. Bumke, *Höfische Kultur. Literatur und Gesellschaft im hohen Mittelalter* (Munich, 1986), 240–341; *Feste und Feiern im Mittelalter. Paderborner Symposion des Mediävistenverbandes*, ed. D. Altenburg, J. Jarnut, and H. Hugo (Sigmaringen, 1991).

31. Cf. M. Dallapiazza, *Minne, hûsêre und das ehlich leben. Zur Konstitution bürgerlicher Lebensmuster in spätmittelalterlichen und frühhumanistischen Didaktiken*, Europäische Hochschulschriften, Reihe I: Deutsche Sprache und Literatur, 455 (Frankfurt am Main, Bern, 1981).

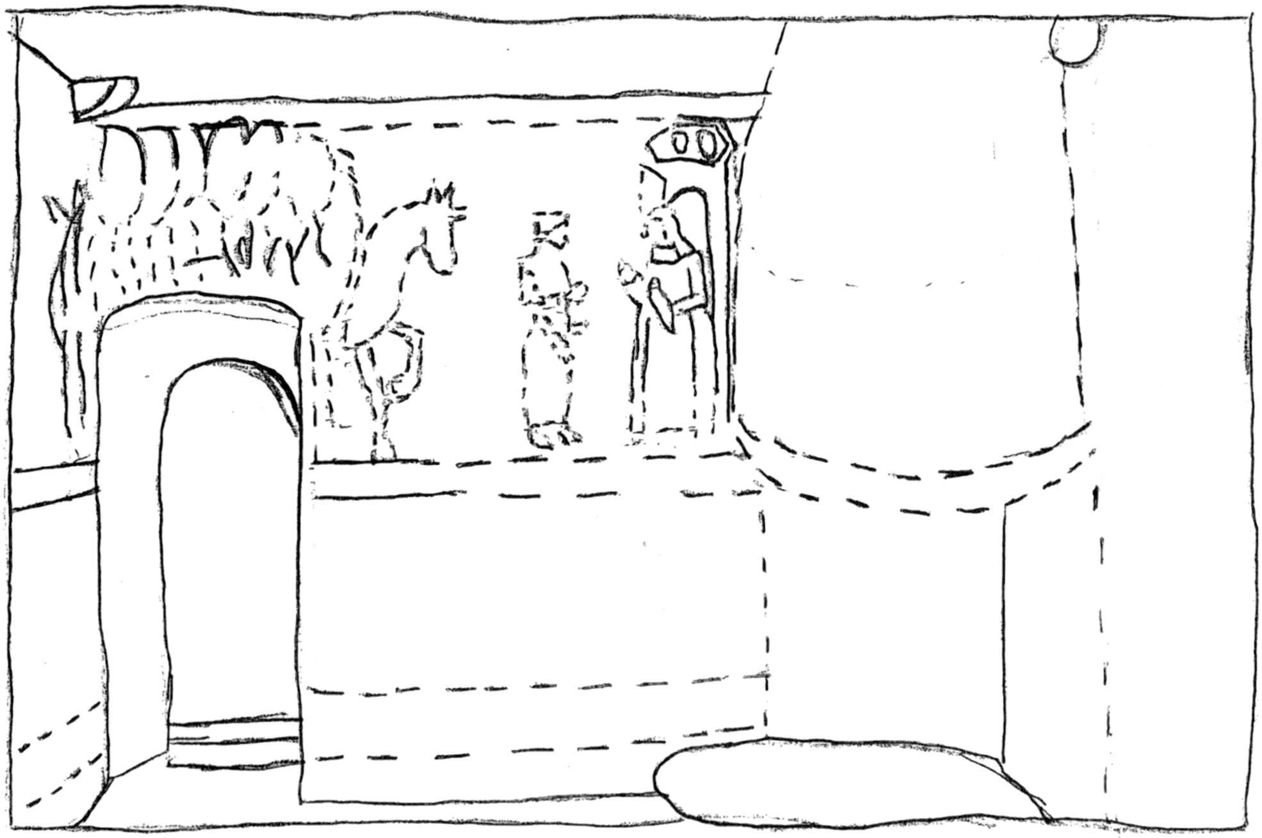

FIGURE 10. South Tyrol, Rodenegg Castle, east wall, Iwein cycle, Iwein and the host castle in the wilderness, *c.* 1210–1220 (reconstruction by the author).

century.[32] This first cycle is particularly well suited to illustrate the nucleus of my thesis.

Little attention has been paid to the first or opening scene, which is in a poor state of preservation (Figs. 10–11). This is the only scene in the entire room to which an entire wall has been devoted. It shows Iwein in front of the host castle in the wilderness, where he receives exemplary hospitality.[33] The lord of the castle, his host, represents this and appears in the ideal guise of a falconer. The image of Iwein is no longer preserved.

32. For Rodenegg and Schmalkalden, see A. M. Bonnet, *Rodenegg und Schmalkalden. Untersuchungen zur Illustration einer ritterlich-höfischen Erzählung und zur Entstehung profaner Epenillustration in den ersten Jahrzehnten des 13. Jahrhunderts*, Tuduv-Studien, Reihe Kunstgeschichte, 22 (Munich, 1986); J. Rushing, Jr., *Images of Adventure: Ywain in the Visual Arts* (Philadelphia, Pa., 1995), 30–132; V. Schupp and H. Szklenar, *Ywain auf Schloss Rodenegg. Eine Bildergeschichte nach dem "Iwein" Hartmanns von Aue* (Sigmaringen, 1996). For Rodenegg, also see M. Curschmann, "'Der aventiure bilde nemen': The Intellectual and Social Environment of the Iwein Murals at Rodenegg Castle," in *Chrétien de Troyes and the German Middle Ages*, ed. M. Jones and R. A. Wisbey (Cambridge, 1993), 219–227; H. Stampfer, *Schloß Rodenegg. Geschichte und Kunst* (Bozen, 1998); M. Curschmann, *Vom Wandel im bildlichen Umgang mit literarischen Gegenständen: Rodenegg, Wildenstein und das Flaarsche Haus in Stein am Rhein*, Wolfgang Stammler Gastprofessur für Germanische Philologie, Vorträge 6 (Freiburg/Switzerland, 1997); M. Curschmann, "Volkssprache und Bildsprache," in *Literatur und Wandmalerei I: Erscheinungsformen höfischer Kultur und ihre Träger im Mittelalter*, ed. E. Lutz, J. Thali, and R. Wetzel (Tübingen, 2002), 9–46, esp. 24–25.; J. Nössing and M. Hörmann, "Rodenegg," in *Pustertal*, Tiroler Burgenbuch 9, ed. M. Hörmann-Weingartner (Innsbruck, 2003), 8–42.

33. See Hartmann von Aue, *Iwein*, v. 279–397, 975–979; Hartmann von Aue, *Iwein. Eine Erzählung*, ed. G. Benecke and K. Lachmann, 2 vol. (Berlin, 1968); Hartmann von Aue, *Iwein. Aus dem Mittelhochdeutschen übertragen*, ed. M. Wehrli (Zurich, 1988).

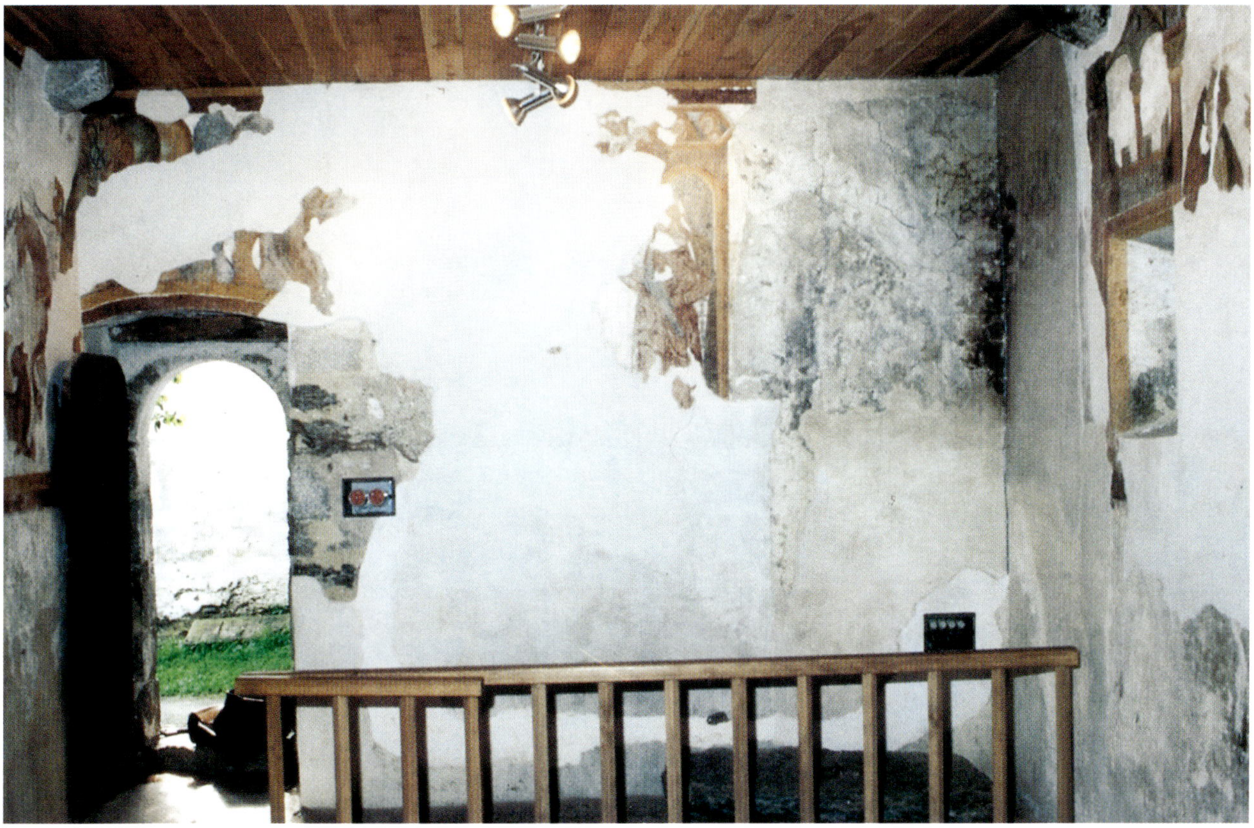

FIGURE 11. South Tyrol, Rodenegg Castle, east wall, Iwein cycle, Iwein and the host castle in the wilderness, *c.* 1210–1220, actual condition.

This castle in the wilderness was clearly something with which the lords of Burg Rodenegg identified, as it too is found in the wilderness of the Alps, on a steep crag some two hundred metres above a mountain stream. This also explains why the scene is placed between the door to the left and the (now destroyed) fireplace to the right.[34] The fireplace, like no other element in the room, stands for the house, which according to pre-modern legal concepts was nothing other than a walled fireplace.[35] The door is the only one in the room and it leads directly to the courtyard and ultimately to the wilderness outside. So it is surrounded by the adventurous forest into which Iwein makes his way so that he can overcome the Lord of the Magic Well. This can be seen on the adjacent longitudinal wall (Fig. 9).

On the narrow west wall (Fig. 12), which is directly opposite to the wall with the first scene of the cycle (Figs. 10–11), it is possible to see the inhospitable castle of the defeated lord, who dies in the arms of his wife (Fig. 13). This castle will become, over the course of time with its new master Iwein, a "house honor," as it will become part of Arthurian court culture.[36] This

34. For the fireplace at Rodenegg, see H. Stampfer, *Rodenegg* (as in note 32), 34; J. Nössing and M. Hörmann, "Rodenegg" (as in note 32), 40.

35. For fireplaces in the Middle Age, see H. Gebelein, "Das Element Feuer in Haushalt und Familie," in *Haushalt und Familie* (as in note 29), 137–150; R. Schmidt-Wiegand and U. Schowe, *Deutsche Rechtsregeln und Rechtssprichwörter* (Munich, 1996), 105, 166.

36. See Hartmann von Aue, *Iwein*, v. 2653 ff.; Hartmann von Aue, *Iwein. Eine Erzählung*, ed. G. Benecke and K. Lachmann, 2 vols. (Berlin, 1968); Hartmann von Aue, *Iwein. Aus dem Mittelhochdeutschen übertragen*, ed. M. Wehrli (Zurich, 1988).

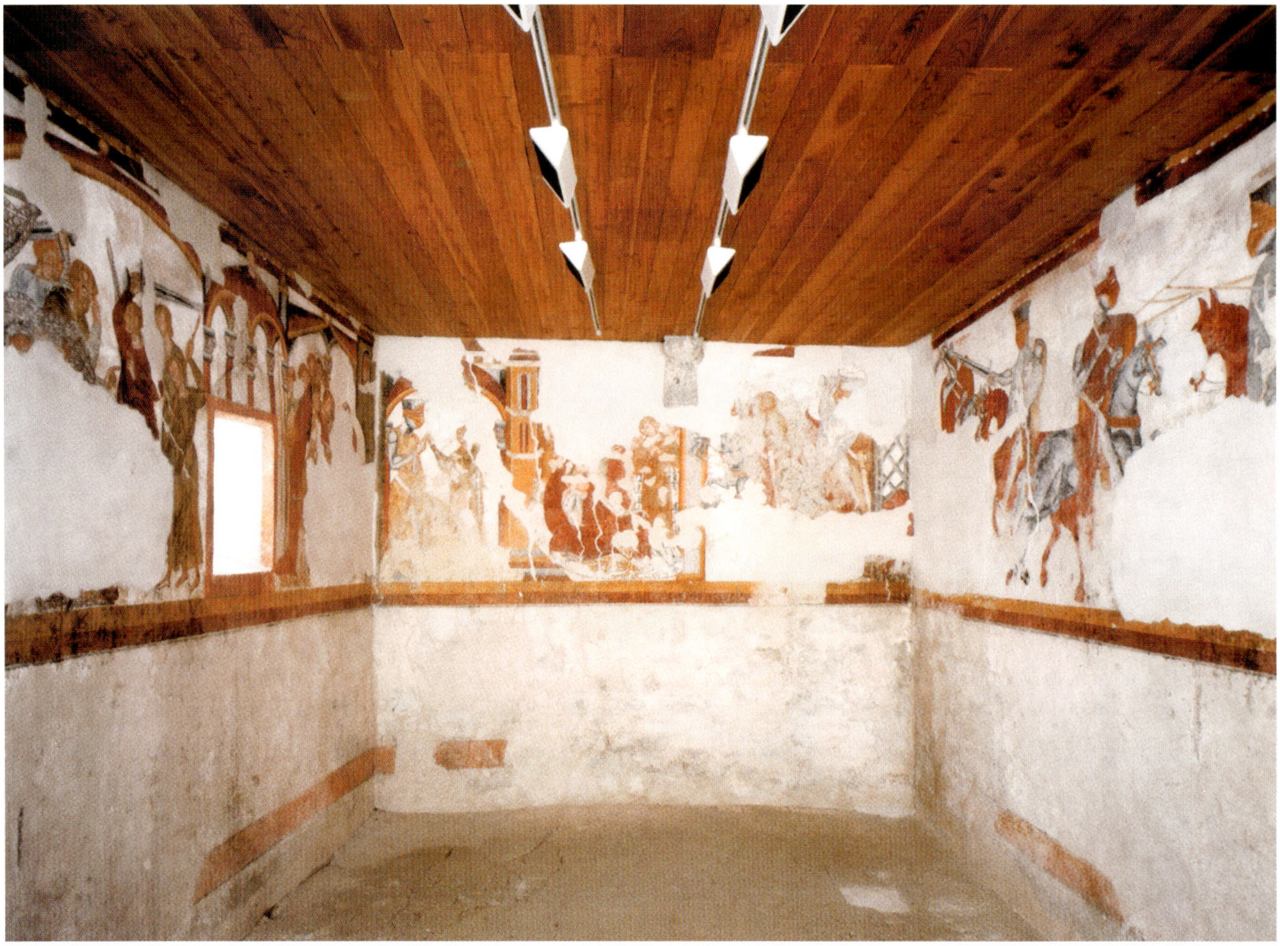

FIGURE 12. South Tyrol, Rodenegg Castle, west wall, Iwein cycle, *c.* 1210–1220.

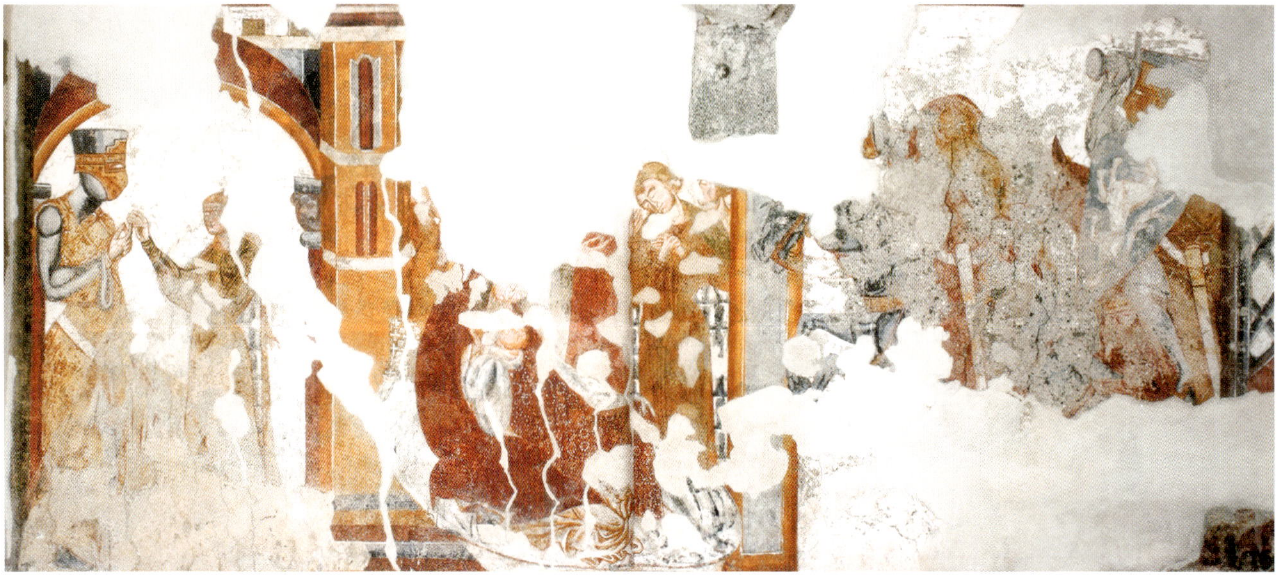

FIGURE 13. South Tyrol, Rodenegg Castle, detail of west wall, Iwein cycle, *c.* 1210–1220: Iwein trapped by the falling gate; death of Ascalon; Lunete giving Ywain the ring.

painting then is the first example of an antithetical allocation of representations in secular wall painting, which might be described as a topography of contrasts. In such wall painting, images from large pictorial repertoires, which are connected to each other by certain elements, are juxtaposed in rooms in such a way that they refer to a common substantive linking-element in a forcefully positive or negative way. This linking-element in Rodenegg is the "house honor." Here, the idealized and welcoming castle on the east entrance wall is contrasted with the inhospitable castle of the Lord of the Magic Well on the west wall.

Outlook

In this short introduction to what is clearly a much larger program, I hope that I have assigned inherent values to some of the very diverse groups of medieval objects that are still classified and disrespected as "secular" or "minor." Their values are based to a certain extent on their importance in the larger developmental picture, but are also the result of their independent existence from such developments. This has to be seen both as being posited by a discipline such as art history and also as a resistance to the mainstreams of traditional art history in general. This shows what great potential there is for thematic research as well as for the advancement of theory in art history.

KIM WOODS

The Fortunes of Art in Alabaster: A Historiographical Analysis

ALABASTER forms a rather special case in the debate about major or minor works of art. As a material rather than a genre, whether works of art in alabaster have been designated major or minor depends partly on the view taken of the material, and in part on what kind of works of art were produced and where. Alabaster is often associated first and foremost with English alabaster sculpture, which has always been studied in isolation and has hardly figured in the overall canon of fifteenth-century European sculpture. In fact, the material was relatively widely used in northern Europe, and its critical fortunes will be discussed in several different contexts here, not just England; however, the status of *English* sculpture in alabaster has been arguably the most problematic and this will be explored later in the paper.

A Brief Bibliographic Survey

The fortunes of art in alabaster have been examined in relation to England in two recent articles in the *Journal of the History of Collections*: the first on the rediscovery and collecting of English alabasters by William Anderson in 2004 and the second on the alabaster collector and scholar Walter Hildburgh by Catherine Oakes in 2006.[1] The authors explain that the widespread loss of English sculpture in alabaster during the Reformation meant that as late as the nineteenth century there was considerable confusion about what an English alabaster actually looked like. They chart the rediscovery in the eighteenth and nineteenth centuries of alabaster carvings concealed in English churches and the gradual realization that some of the alabaster sculptures on the Continent hitherto categorized as Continental were in fact English exports. Key landmarks in the rediscovery of English alabasters were the 1890 publication of William St. John Hope's article on alabaster St. John's heads;[2] his seminal 1890 publication on the early working of alabaster;[3] the Society of Antiquaries' exhibition of English Medieval alabaster work in 1910; and the collecting of and scholarship on English alabasters by Edward Prior, Philip Nelson, and Walter Hildburgh from the turn of the twentieth century.

Both Anderson and Oakes raised important questions about the value and interpretation of alabaster sculpture, but only English alabaster *altarpieces*, not tombs, which also have an equivocal status in the major/minor debate. With the exception of Nigel Ramsey's exemplary essay in the *English Medieval Industries* volume of 1991, studies of English alabaster have tended to remain divided along genre lines.[4] The iconographic work on altarpieces has been dominated by Francis Cheetham, while chronology was tackled firstly by Prior, who grouped alabasters into four main

1. W. Anderson, "Re-discovery, Collecting and Display of English Medieval Alabasters," *Journal of the History of Collections* 16/1 (2004), 47–58; Catherine Oakes, "Dr Hildburgh and the English Medieval Alabaster," *Journal of the History of Collections* 18/1 (2006), 71–83.

2. W. St. John Hope, "On the Sculptured Alabaster Tablets called Saint John's Heads," *Archaeologia* 52 (1890), 669–708.

3. W. St. John Hope, "On the Early Working of Alabaster in England" *Archaeological Journal* 61 (1904), 220–240, reprinted in the 1910 Society of Antiquaries exhibition catalogue *English Medieval Alabaster Work*, 10–14

4. N. Ramsay, "Alabaster," in J. Blair and N. Ramsay, eds., *English Medieval Industries: Craftsmen, Techniques, Products* (London, 1991), 29–40. For another review of the arguments surrounding Nottingham as a center of the alabaster industry, see C. C. Coombs, "Walter Hilton & Nicholas Hill, 'alabastermen' from Nottingham," in *East Midland Historian* 7 (1997), 25–28.

periods, and more recently by Linda Rollason.[5] The principal survey of alabaster tombs remains the one by Arthur Gardner, though there have also been many more recent articles.[6] Recent work has addressed the location and *oeuvre* of the Prentice and Sutton workshop documented to have carved the Lowick tomb of 1418–1419 and still operating in 1443.[7] The tomb of Sir Edmund (d. 1418) and Lady Joan de Thorpe (d. 1415) in the church of Ashwellthorpe, Norfolk, is usually attributed to Prentice and Sutton, for example (Fig. 1; *c.* 1418).[8]

The only attempt to place English alabaster *altarpieces* alongside European alabaster traditions was in an exhibition of English and Mechelen alabasters in Brussels in 1967.[9] Michael Wustrack and more recently Aleksandra Lipińska have since taken up the study of sixteenth-century Mechelen alabasters.[10]

German alabasters received close attention from the 1920s by Georg Swarzenski to the present day by Norbert Jopek.[11] Interest has concentrated primarily on the anonymous early-fifteenth-century alabaster carver named the Master of Rimini after his most famous work, an alabaster altarpiece from Santa Maria delle Grazie just outside Rimini and now in the Liebieghaus in Germany. Many other alabaster sculptures survive by him (Fig. 2). He has never been considered minor, and at the time of writing an exhibition of his work in the Liebieghaus, Frankfurt, is at planning stage. Nothing extensive has been published on either Netherlandish or Spanish alabaster sculpture as a genre beyond occasional articles, despite the fact that Spain had large alabaster reserves and important traditions of alabaster sculpture.[12]

Several questions arise out of this often strong field

5. F. Cheetham, *English Medieval Alabasters with a Catalogue of the Collection in the Victoria and Albert Museum* (London, 1984, new ed.: Woodbridge, 2005); *The Alabaster Images of Medieval England* (Woodbridge, 2003); *Unearthed: Nottingham's Medieval Alabasters* (Nottingham, 2004). For chronology, see E. S. Prior's essay "The Sculpture of Alabaster Tables," in *Illustrated Catalogue of the Exhibition of English Medieval Alabaster Work* (London, 1913), 16–50, and L. Rollason, "English Alabasters in the Fifteenth Century," in D. Williams, ed., *England in the Fifteenth Century, Proceedings of the 1986 Harlaxton Symposium* (Woodbridge, 1987), 245–254.

6. A. Gardner, *Alabaster Tombs of the Pre-Reformation Period in England* (Cambridge, 1940). For the most recent consideration of alabaster tombs, see N. Saul, *English Church Monuments in the Middle Ages* (Oxford, 2009), 66–71, and *passim*, and J. Crease, "'Not commonly reputed or taken for a saincte': The Output of a Northern Workshop in the Late 14th and Early 15th Centuries," in S. Badham and S. Osterwijk, eds., *Monumental Industry: The Production of Tomb Monuments in England and Wales in the Long 14th Century* (Donington, 2010), 114–135.

7. For the Lowick and Bisham Abbey tombs, see S. Badham and S. Osterwijk, "English Tomb Contracts of the Long 14th Century" in ed. S. Badham and S. Osterwijk, *Monumental Industry: The Production of Tomb Monuments in England and Wales in the Long 14th Century* (Donington, 2010), docs. IV–VI, 217–235. See also J. Bayliss, "An Indenture for Two Alabaster Effigies," *Church Monuments* 16 (2001), 22–29. The 1443 document records that Robert Sutton, Thomas Sutton, and John Chaloner were sued by client Sir Thomas Cumberworth for using defective alabaster; see P. Lindley, *Gothic to Renaissance, Essays on Sculpture in England* (Stamford, 1995), p. 26. For attributions to Sutton and Prentice, see C. Ryde, "Chellaston Standing Angels with Shields at Aston-on-Trent: Their Wider Distribution, 1400–1450," *Derbyshire Archaeological Journal* 113 (1993), 69–90.

8. For Ashwellthorpe, see T. A. Heslop, "The Alabaster Tomb at Ashwellthorpe, Norfolk: Its Workmanship, Cost and Location," in P. Binski and E. New, eds., *Patrons and Professionals*, Harlaxton Medieval Studies XXII (Donington, 2012, forthcoming).

9. G. Derveaux-Van Ussel, *Exposition de Sculptures anglaises et malinoises d'Albâtre*, Exhib. Cat. (Brussels: Musées royaux d'Art et d'Histoire, 1967).

10. M. K. Wustrack, *Die Mechelner Alabaster: Manufaktur des 16 und frühen 17 Jahrhunderts* (Frankfurt and Bern, 1982); A. Lipińska, *Wewnętrzne Światło. Południowoniderlandzka rzeźba alabastrowa w Europie Środkowo-Wschodniej* [*Inner Light: Southern Netherlandish Alabaster Sculpture in Central and Eastern Europe*], *Wydawnictwo Uniwersytetu Wrocławskiego* (Wroclaw, 2007).

11. G. Swarzenski, "Deutsche Alabasterplastik des 15. Jahrhunderts," *Städel Jahrbuch* 1, (1921), 167–213; and "Der Kölner Meister bei Ghiberti," *Vorträge der Bibliothek Warburg* 6, 1926/7 (Leipzig/Berlin, 1930), 21–42. W. Paatz, "Stammbaum der gotischen Alabasterskulptur 1316–1442," *Kunstgeschichtliche Studien für Hans Kauffmann* (Berlin, 1956), 127–135; and "Prologomena zu einer Geschichte der deutschen spätgotischen Skulpturen im 15 Jahrhundert," *Abhandlungen der Heidelberger Akademie der Wissenschaften, Philosophisch-Historische Klasse* (1956), Part 2. A. Legner, "Der Alabaster Altar aus Rimini," in *Städel Jahrbuch*, N.F. 2 (1969), 101–68; N. Jopek, *Studien zur Deutschen Alabasterplastik des 15. Jahrhunderts* (Worms, 1988); and "Kalvarienberg," in H. Meller, I. Mundt, and E. H. Schmuhl, eds., *Der Heilige Schatz im Dom zu Halberstadt* (Regensburg, 2008), 350–53.

12. These issues will be discussed in K. W. Woods, *Cut in Alabaster: An Aspect of European Sculpture c. 1330 – c. 1530* (Turnhout, forthcoming).

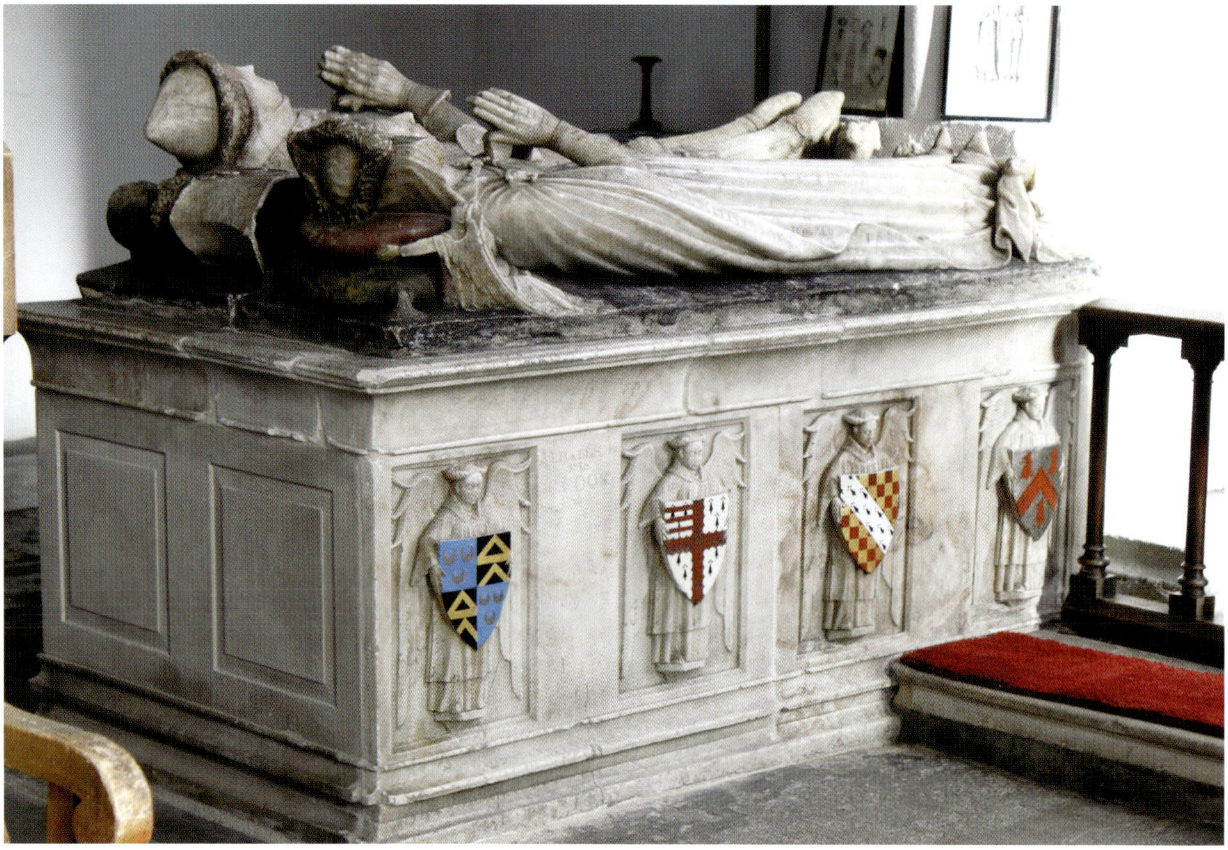

FIGURE 1. Prentice and Sutton, tomb of Sir Edmund (d. 1418) and Lady Joan de Thorpe (d. 1415), Ashwellthorpe church, Norfolk.

of scholarship: the choice and prestige of alabaster as against marble; the status of sculpture in alabaster; and the relative reputation of English alabasters in comparison with their Continental counterparts. It is these that this essay sets out to address.

Alabaster—A Major or a Minor Material?

The dominance of Italian marble in high-status European sculpture was noted by Nicholas Penny in 1993 in his book *The Materials Of Sculpture*: "So closely identified is white marble with European art, so easily taken for granted as the chief material for the most serious sculpture."[13] Marble was the material used in both ancient Roman and Italian Renaissance sculpture, which together served as the dominant models for Europe from the Renaissance onwards. Its use was ratified through the well-known first century Roman text, Pliny's *Natural History*, in which Book 36 begins with a long section on the quarrying and transportation of marble and elite marble sculptors such as Phidias and Praxiteles.[14] Vasari introduces Italian marble as the key material of Renaissance sculpture in his technical introduction to both the 1550 and 1568 versions of his widely read *Lives of the Artists*.[15] Vasari seems not to have heard of alabaster at all, though he described the

13. N. Penny, *The Materials of Sculpture* (New Haven and London, 1993), 35.

14. Pliny, *Natural History*, ed. D. E. Eichholtz, vol. x (Cambridge, Mass., 1962), 5–47. Pliny very briefly mentioned what he called onyx marble or alabastrite in connection with plaster-making and preserving unguents, but he was referring to Egyptian alabaster, which is chemically distinct from European alabaster.

15. Now published as the separate volume *Vasari on Technique*, ed. by G. Baldwin Brown, translated by L. S. Macklehose (New York, 1960).

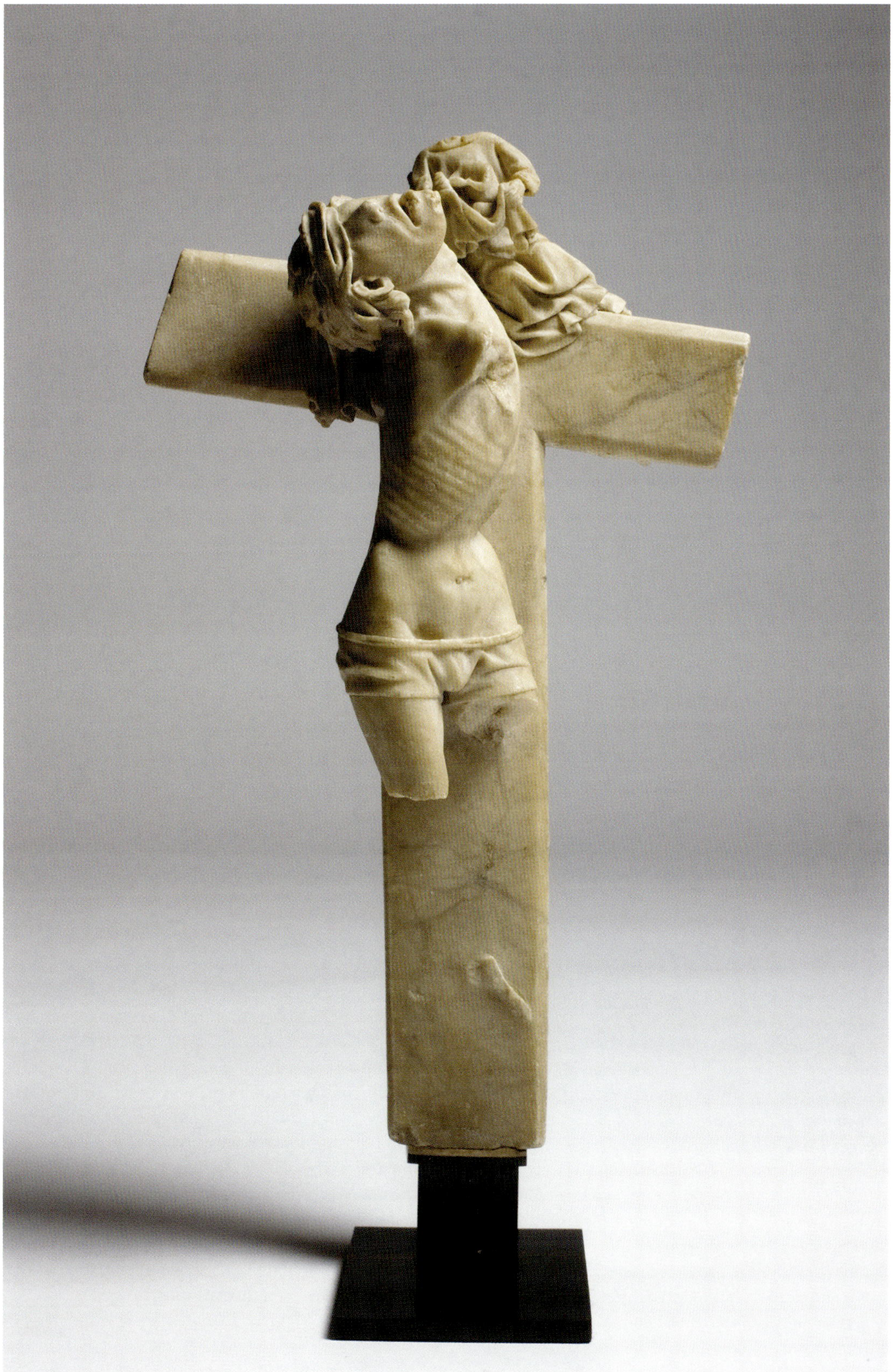

FIGURE 2. Master of Rimini, *The Good Thief*, *c.* 1430, private collection.

use of "transparent marbles" for window panes, almost certainly alabaster.[16] The situation in northern Europe was radically different, however. From the turn of the fourteenth century, Italian marble was sometimes exported to northern Europe, notably to make French royal tombs (see below). Nevertheless, "marble" in the north generally meant the black limestone that could be polished, known as touchstone, Purbeck marble, Tournai or Mosan marble. The white equivalent was usually alabaster.

According to Vasari, all the "moderns" used marble "not only in Italy, but in France, England, Spain and Portugal."[17] At the peak of Vasari's writing career in the 1550s and 1560s, several northern European courts in fact employed Netherlandish craftsman working in alabaster for exactly the same Renaissance purposes for which marble was employed by Italians further south. Far from being superseded by imported Italian marble, alabaster was in great demand in the sixteenth century, whether for tombs by Cornelis Floris, such as the tomb of Frederik I of Denmark in Schleswig Cathedral *c.* 1551–1555;[18] for palace decoration by Willem van den Broecke, like the alabaster reliefs made for the Schwerin Palace of Johann Albrecht I of Mecklenburg-Schwerin in the 1560s;[19] or for altarpieces. The passion altarpiece made by Jean Mone for the Palace Chapel in Brussels 1536–1541 and now in Brussels Cathedral anticipates this sort of northern Renaissance alabaster carving (Fig. 3). There is little suggestion in these prestige commissions that alabaster was in any way an inferior substitute for marble, despite its apparently less secure claim to antique prestige status. It does not seem to have been until the turn of the seventeenth century that marble can be said to have begun to take precedence over alabaster in these northern territories and the term "marble" to signify increasingly antique or Italian Renaissance "marbles;" even then, alabaster continued to be used.[20]

In northern Europe, alabaster had always been an elite material. In his *Book of Minerals*, possibly dating from around 1260, the influential Dominican scholar Albertus Magnus said of alabaster that "because of its marvellous power it is placed among precious stones."[21] This power was as a preservative, whether as vessels for aromatic unguents or as tombs for dead bodies, which indeed came to be one of the primary uses of alabaster. According to Albertus, it was because of their gleam that "marbles are more noble than other stones...," and he singled out alabaster for particular comment.[22] In contrast to Pliny and Vasari, alabaster is clearly distinguished from marble and, if anything, more highly praised.

Northern documents dating from the fourteenth century reveal frequent mistakes in distinguishing marble and alabaster. Visually, this is perfectly justifiable as the two stones are indeed sometimes quite hard to tell

16. *Ibid.*, 43. 17. *Ibid.*, 47.

18. A. Huysmans, J. Van Damme, C. Van de Velde, C. Van Mulders, *Cornelis Floris 1514–1575. Beeldhouwer, architect ontwerper* (Brussels, 1996), 81–3.

19. A. Jolly, "Philip Brandin, ein niederländischer Bildhauer des 16. Jahrhunderts im Dienst der Herzöge von Mecklenburg," *Oud Holland* 113 (1999), 13–34. Among other Northern Renaissance works in alabaster are Conrad Meit's *Judith* and his Brussels Cathedral *Virgin and Child* (the busts of Margaret and Philibert by Conrad Meit in Margaret of Austria's library were marble, however); Jean Mone's tomb of Guillaume de Croy for the Celestine church, Heverle, now in the Capuchin church, Enghien 1525–8/9 and his 1533 Halle altarpiece; Guyot de Beaugrant's alabaster chimneypiece for the Franc of Bruges 1529–31; Cornelis Floris's tombs of Frederik I (Cathedral Schleswig *c.* 1551–5), Jan van Merode and Anna van Gistel (Sint-Dimfnakerk Geel 1553–4), Albrecht of Brandenburg (Königsberg cathedral 1568–70), Herluf Trolle and wife (Herlufsholm, Denmark 1568), the Schauenberg tombs (Cologne Cathedral 1556–61) and Christiaan III (Roskilde Cathedral 1568–75); Willem van den Broeck, also known as Paludanus, carved Old Testament alabaster reliefs for the Augsburg Dominican church (1560) and alabaster reliefs dated 1563 for Schwerin Castle. Philip von Hessen, Langraf of Kassel commissioned an alabaster room in his palace from Cambrai carver Elias Godfroy completed in 1559. Ulrich III, ruler of Mecklenburg-Güstrow (1527–1603), also commissioned alabaster memorials for himself and his two wives from Philip Brandin for Güstrow Cathedral 1583–99. 16th-century alabaster reliefs traditionally known as Mechelen alabasters were exported to Central Europe in some quantities: J. Kriegseisen and A. Lipińska, eds., *Matter of Light and Flesh*, Exhib. Cat. (Gdańsk: Muzeum Narodowe, 2011).

20. Thanks to Leon Lock for discussing this with me. Aleksandra Lipińska is currently exploring this transition.

21. Albertus Magnus, *Book of Minerals*, translated by D. Wyckoff (Oxford, 1967), 107.

22. *Ibid.*, 45–6.

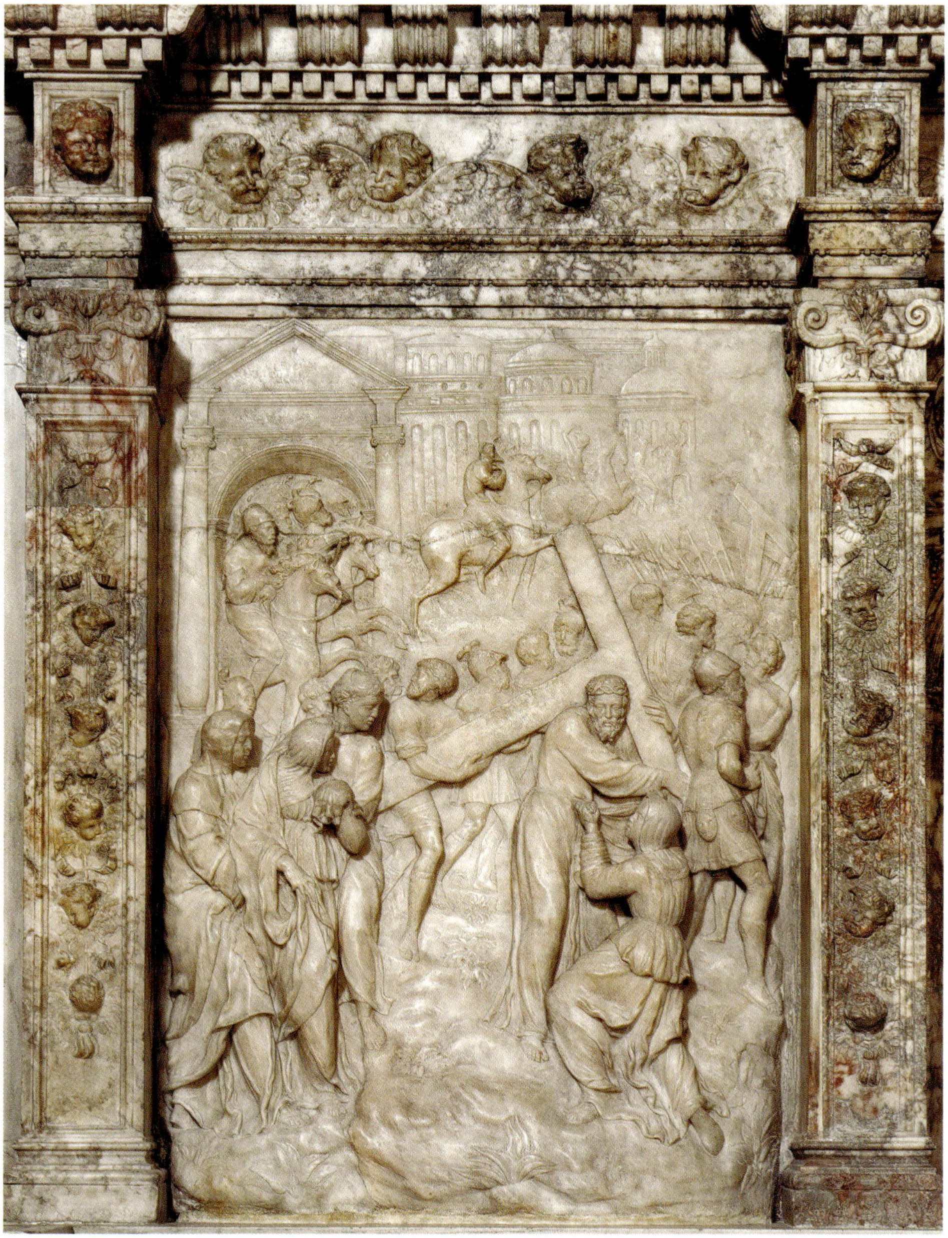

FIGURE 3.
Jean Mone, *Christ Carrying the Cross*, detail from Passion altarpiece, 1536–1541, now in Brussels Cathedral (photo: copyright IRPA-KIK, Brussels).

apart, and mistakes are made to this day. But imported Italian marble was very much more expensive than alabaster, hence clear boundaries might be expected between the two materials for this reason alone, whereas the boundaries are in fact porous. In 1392, the sculptor Claus Sluter is recorded to have purchased an alabaster stone in Paris from Genoese merchant Cristoffle de le Mer for 400 francs "pour fair un ymaige pour sa sepulture" (to make the effigy) for the tomb of Philip the Bold at the Chartreuse de Champmol near Dijon.[23] Recent restoration has revealed the effigy of Philip to have been made not of alabaster but of marble, which

23. C. Dehaisnes, *Documents et Extraits divers concernant l'Histoire de l'Art dans la Flandre, l'Artois et le Hainaut avant le XVe Siècle* (Lille, 1886), 695, 705, 719, and R. Prochno, *Die Karthause von Champmol: Grablege der burgundischen Herzöge, 1364–1477* (Berlin, 2002), 263.

certainly helps to explain the exorbitant price paid for the stone, nearly twice the amount the abbey of Fécamp later paid in 1414 for a tomb-size block of English alabaster.[24] The substitution of cheaper alabaster for marble might be understandable, but here it is the other way round. The apparent conflation of marble and alabaster suggests there is no real hierarchy of materials here and that alabaster and marble were equivalents, despite the disparity in cost and despite very obvious differences in workability and vulnerability.

There *is* a clear hierarchy of materials at the Augustinian church of St. Nicholas of Tolentino at Brou in south-east France, founded by Margaret of Austria, Regent of the Netherlands, but it is not the hierarchy that might be expected. The tombs commissioned from Conrad Meit in 1526 combine upper, formal effigies of Margaret and her husband Philibert in marble (Fig. 4) with less formal, lower effigies in alabaster together with the alabaster effigy of Margaret of Bourbon, mother of Philibert (Fig. 5). This might appear to indicate that the more important material had been reserved for the more important effigies.

In fact, the final decision to use a combination of marble and alabaster seems to have been made for entirely practical reasons. The contract specifies alabaster for the effigy of Margaret of Bourbon "a cause que ladite sepulture est en lieu remote qui ne se peut dampniffier comme les autres" (because the said tomb is in a peripheral location where it will not get damaged like the others).[25] This was no mere pretext, for in 1535 Margaret's executors proposed making railings to protect the tombs from damage.[26] Alabaster is considerably more vulnerable to damage than the harder marble and the lower alabaster effigies of Philibert and Margaret were indeed more protected than the upper effigies.

In his history and description of Brou written in 1767, Père Pacifique Rousselet, an Augustinian monk at Brou, made an impressive attempt to distinguish between alabaster and marble, no doubt using original documents kept at the monastery. He did not always get it right—like many other sources he described the tomb of Margaret of Bourbon as Carrara marble—but he was remarkably even-handed in his appraisal of the two materials. He described the alabaster of Margaret of Austria's lower image as "très fin et très poli."[27] By contrast, his predecessor prior Raphael de la Vièrge, writing around the turn of the eighteenth century, is mildly dismissive of the alabaster, and hastens to add "mais (and that 'but' is crucial one) les principales figures sont de beau marbre blanc de la dernière perfection."[28] Here there is arguably a sense that marble holds greater prestige in the writer's mind, but it is not true of the tombs or of Brou, where alabaster, not marble, was the visible signifier of status and dynasty.

Alabaster had been decided upon as the material for the tombs by 1510.[29] When in 1509 the initial designer, Jean Perréal, had first spoken of introducing into his tomb design elements that he had learned in Italy, there was no suggestion that this also implied the use of Italian marble. On the contrary, he was fully supportive of

24. S. Jugie, "La restauration des tombeaux des ducs de Bourgogne au musée des Beaux-Arts de Dijon," *Revue du Louvre et des Musées de France* 55/3 (2005), 7. Prochno, *Karthause* (as at note 23), 263, also suggested the block was to make the effigy, while believing the material to be alabaster. The tomb-sized alabaster block for the Abbot of Fécamp in Normandy purchased at Chellaston in 1414 cost only 200 écus including transportation, though, since an écu was worth slightly more than a franc, the gap is a little smaller than it appears. J. Bilson, "A French Purchase of English Alabaster in 1414," *Archaeological Journal* 64, (1907), 32–37. The Norman-French document is transcribed and translated in full in *A History of Chellaston* (Chellaston, 1988), 32, and W. Stevenson, "Art Sculpture in Alabaster, Preserved in France, Considered in its Relationship to the Nottingham School of Alabasterers," *Transactions of the Thoroton Society* XI (1907), 92–96.

25. G. Troescher, *Conrat Meit von Worms: ein Rheinischer Bildhauer der Renaissance* (Freiburg-im-Breslau, 1927), 64; "dampniffier" is an obsolete verb meaning to damage.

26. M. Bruchet, *Marguerite d'Autriche, Duchesse de Savoie* (Lille, 1927), 255, doc. 180.

27. P. Rousselet, *Histoire et Description de l'Église royale de Brou*, (Paris, 1767), 49.

28. Père Raphaël de la Vièrge Marie, *Description historique de la belle église et du couvent royal de Brou*, Bibliothèque d'émulation de l'Ain, Bourg-en-Bresse, 75 (transcript Bibliothèque Dijon, 37; my thanks to the library at Brou for making a photocopy of this transcript available to me).

29. Bruchet, *Marguerite* (as in note 26), 195, doc. 20.

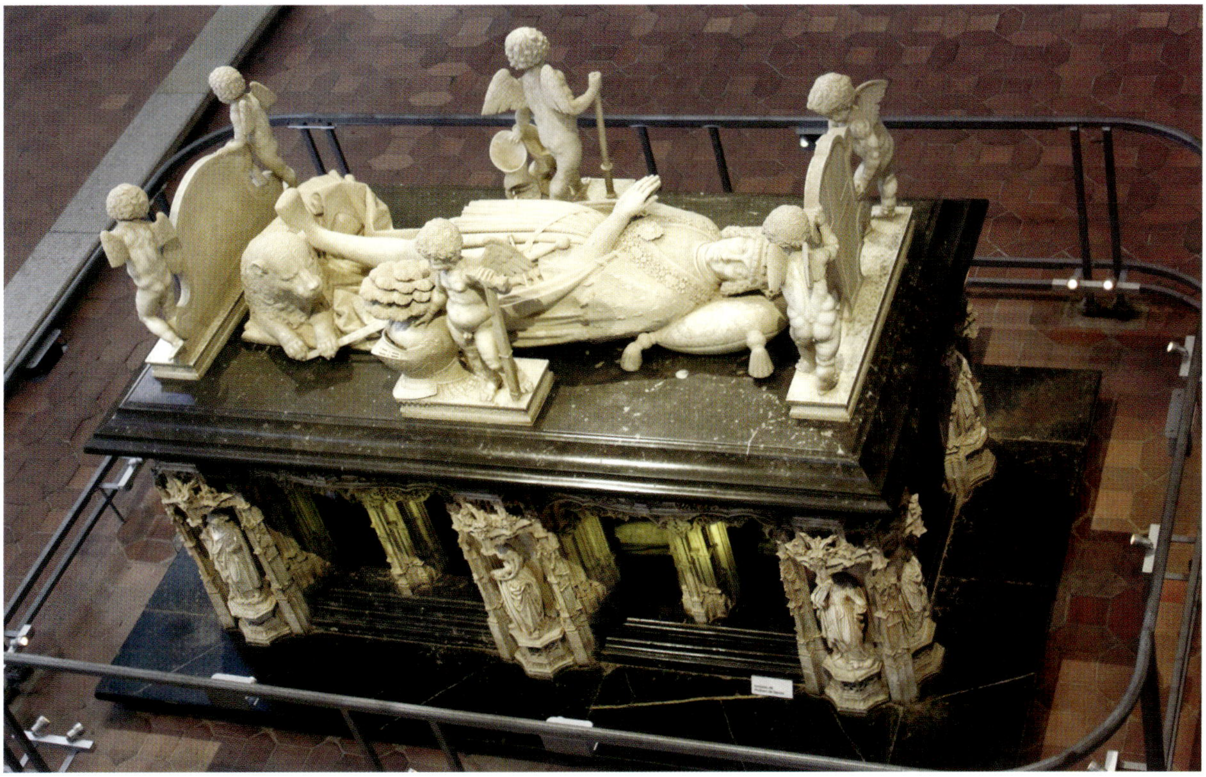

FIGURE 4. Conrad Meit, tomb of Philibert of Savoy, Brou, 1526–1531.

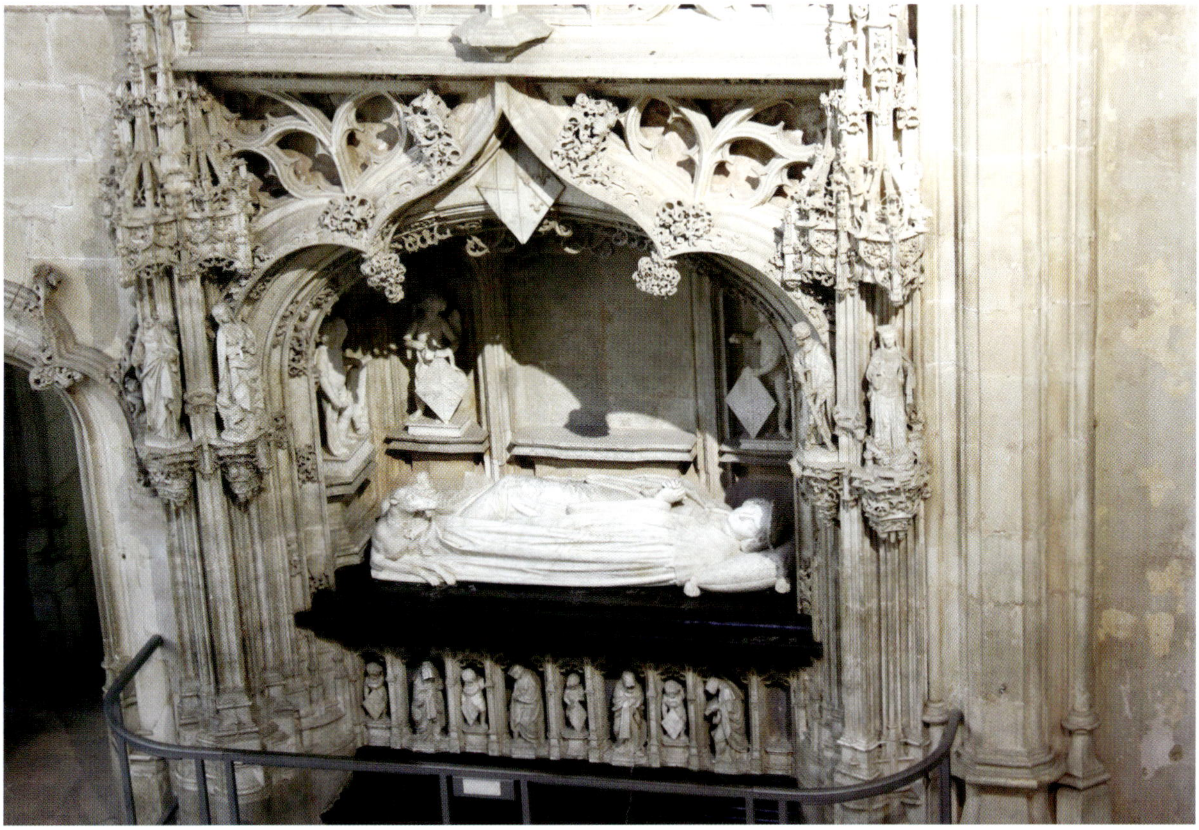

FIGURE 5. Conrad Meit, tomb of Margaret of Bourbon, Brou, 1526–1531.

Jean Lemaire's efforts to secure good supplies of local alabaster.[30] Perréal knew Italy and he knew the French tradition of marble tombs, and in January 1511, he did express a slight preference for marble: "car, sans mentir, ce sera oeuvre perpétuelle et de princesse" (because it is not lying to say that this would be an enduring work worthy of a princess).[31] He did not prevail, however.

A mandate of 1510 specified that the tombs should follow the example of the dukes and counts of Burgundy in the use of black "marble" of Liège and "marbre blanc qu'on dit albastre."[32] The use of these materials is restricted to those parts of the church of greatest spiritual and, above all, temporal significance. No alabaster is to be found to the west of the choir screen nor on the screen itself. Alabaster statues are or were to be found east of the screen in Margaret's own chapel, on the high altar and in the Montacute and Gorravod chapels. Alabaster wall cladding is to be found only in Margaret's own chapel and the ground floor of her oratory (Fig. 6), and even here not in the upper floor, which would not be seen except by her. Alabaster cladding is not found elsewhere, not even in the choir. The polychromatic contrast of black "marble" and white alabaster is to be found in all three tombs and in Margaret's own chapel (Fig. 7), where a black marble bench runs along the alabaster-clad north wall and the base of the alabaster altarpiece is also black, but it is not found anywhere else, not even in the choir.

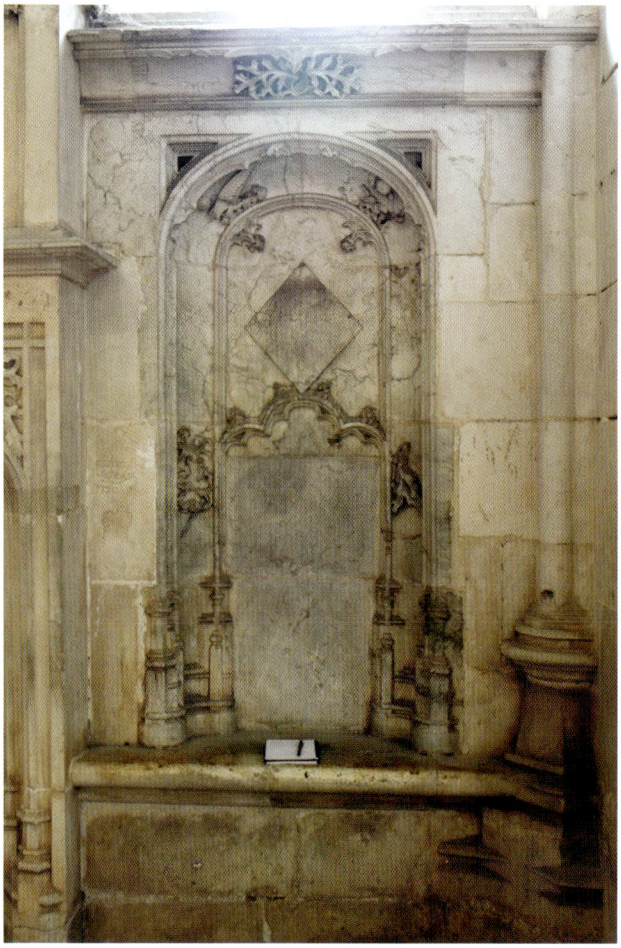

FIGURE 6. Oratory of Margaret of Austria, Brou.

The introduction of a Renaissance approach into northern Europe did not necessarily imply the demise of alabaster in favor of Italian marble. Where this did happen it was arguably as much because of the triumph of Italian craft practices in northern European courts as for its reflected prestige of the antique and the Italian Renaissance. In Spain, high-status effigies in Aragon had traditionally been made of alabaster, of which this area of Spain had copious supplies. Alabaster was also a favored material for tombs in Castile during the fifteenth century, for example the tomb of John II of Castile at the Carthusian monastery of Miraflores (1486–1493) and of Alvaro de Luna in Toledo Cathedral (commissioned 1489).

The use of marble for the tomb of Archbishop Diego Hurtado de Mendoza in Seville Cathedral (1508–1510), that of the Infante Juan in Santo Tomás, Avila (1512–1513), and that of Ferdinand and Isabella in Granada Cathedral (1514–1517) may be accounted for by the employment of an Italian sculptor, Domenico Fancelli, whose prestige was such that he was permitted to produce the tombs in Italy with all the associated transport costs, using what was for him his local

30. Bruchet, *Marguerite* (as in note 26), 193, doc. 11.

31. Bruchet, *Marguerite* (as in note 26), 202, doc. 40, and 203, doc. 41. Given the problems that had been encountered in obtaining satisfactory alabaster to that point, it may be a mistake to read too much into Perréal's statement: in a further letter of 1 December he appears to be defending local alabaster as against imported marble; Bruchet, *Marguerite* (as in note 26), doc. 63.

32. Bruchet, *Marguerite* (as in note 26), 365.

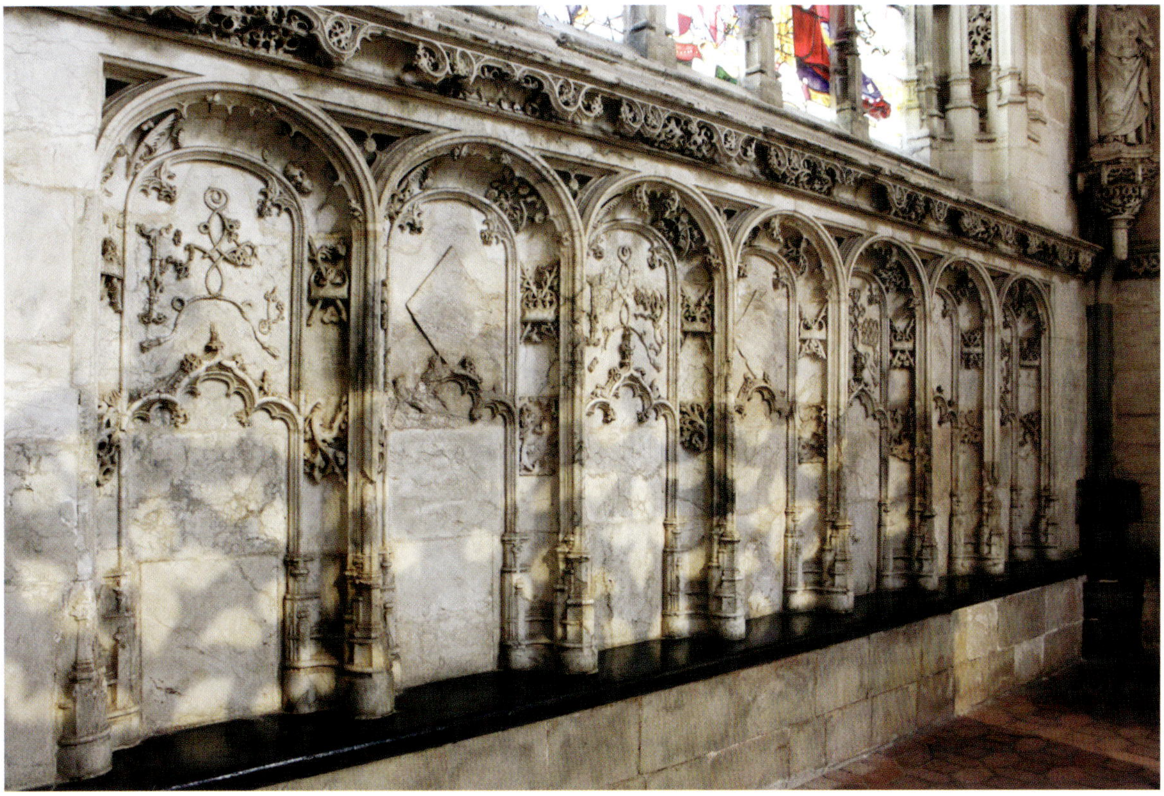

FIGURE 7. Chapel of Margaret of Austria, Brou.

and customary material, marble.[33] Marble also had the practical advantage of coming in effigy-sized blocks, whereas alabaster effigies in Spain are almost invariable made of more than one block. For craft practice and for patrons alike, marble must have been enticing as a means of avoiding a join at the knees.

Alabaster Sculpture—Major or Minor?

The alabaster tombs at the Chartreuse de Champmol and Miraflores and the tombs and altarpiece at Brou are clearly classifiable as "major:" large-scale sculpture made for elite clients for prestigious architectural settings. In England also, alabaster began as an elite material used for the most exclusive sculpture.

The key period in England was the reign of Edward III. The stone and alabaster tomb of his murdered father Edward II (d. 1327) is on the north side of the choir in what used to be St. Peter's Abbey and is now the Cathedral, Gloucester (Fig. 8). The date of the tomb is uncertain and depends partly on the chronology of building work in the south transept and choir and partly on who might have placed the commission; it may, however, date from the 1330s.[34] It has long since been remarked that the use of alabaster and (imitation) Purbeck marble appear to imitate the marble and black polished limestone characteristic of French royal tombs.[35] The small angels to either side of the deceased king's head resemble that of Philip of France, son of Louis VIII (d. 1235; originally in the Abbey of

33. A. Cloulas, "La sculpture funéraire dans l'Espagne de la Renaissance I: Le mécénat royal," *Gazette des Beaux-Arts* 118 (1991), 61–78; P. Lenaghan, *The Arrival of the Italian Renaissance in Spain: The Tombs by Domenico Fancelli and Bartolomé Ordóñez*. Ph.D. Diss. (New York, New York University, 1993).

34. D. Wellander, *The History, Art and Architecture of Gloucester Cathedral* (Stroud, 1991), 146–9. The choir was rebuilt 1337–1355.

35. Ed. J. Alexander and P. Binski, *Age of Chivalry: Art in Plantagenet England 1200–1400*, Exhib. Cat. (London, 1987), 416–7, cat. 497.

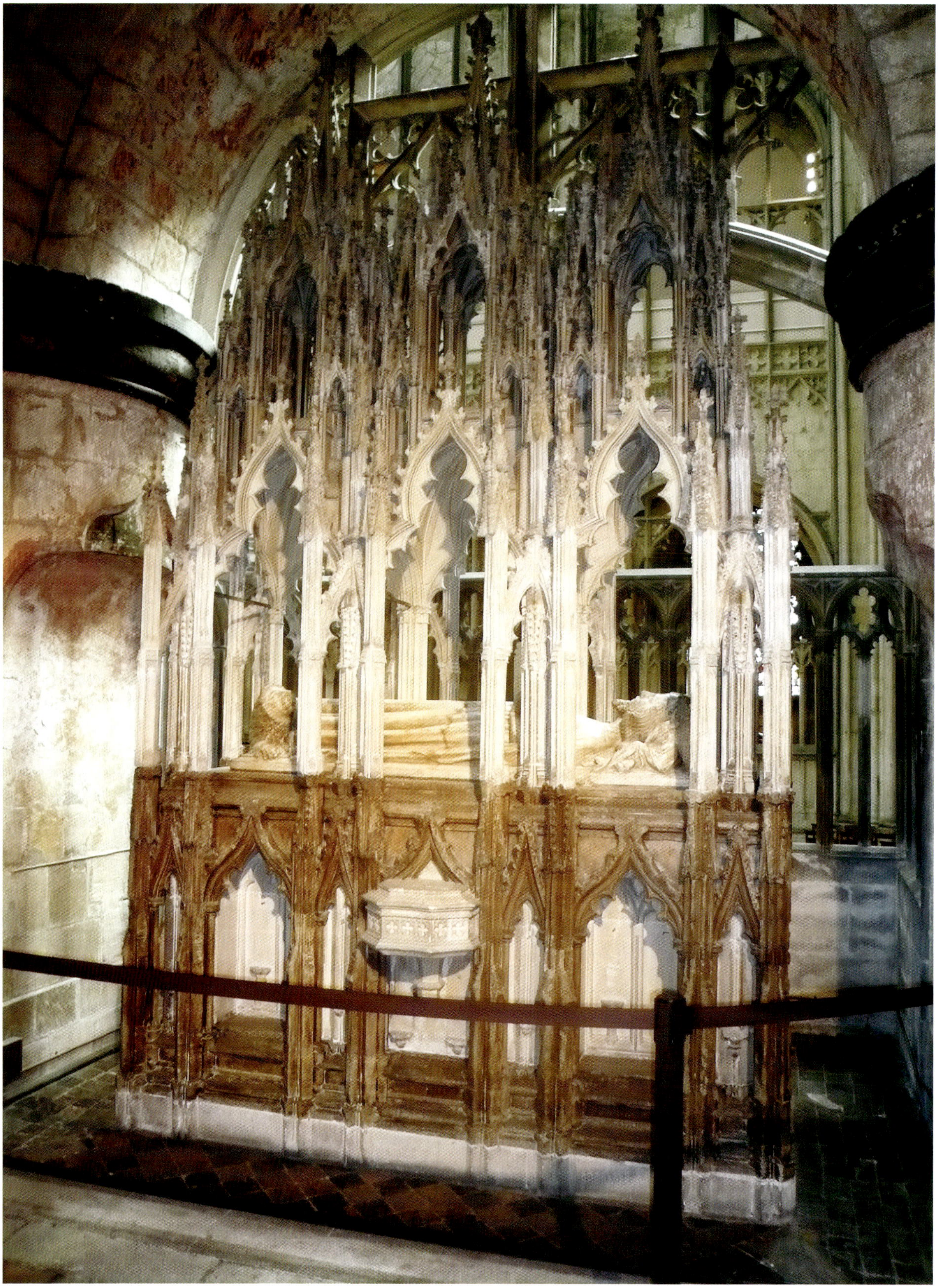

FIGURE 8. Tomb of Edward II, Gloucester Cathedral, 1330s?

Royaumont, now St.-Denis), but had been used before in England in the tombs of Edmund Crouchback (d. 1296) and his wife Aveline, Countess of Lancaster (d. 1274) in Westminster Abbey. Equally it is acknowledged that the distinctive stone tracery of Edward's tomb differentiates it from the roof-like canopies of some French tombs such as that of Enguerrand de Coucy (d. 1312) in the abbey of Longpont.[36] Indeed it has sometimes been seen as the model for the Avignon tomb of Pope John XXII.[37]

Who was behind the tomb is a matter of dispute: Morganstern believes it to be Edward's widow Isabella of France in which case the French connotations are simply a matter of heritage style. It is by no means clear why Isabella should have wished to draw such attention to the man whose murder she was responsible for, however, or why she, rather than her son and Edward's heir, might have taken charge of the commission.[38] Ormrod opted for the monks of Gloucester, who certainly had much to gain financially from visitors, but who would not normally expect to undertake a royal tomb, let alone one as innovative as this one.[39] Others, including Julian Luxford, have taken the view that the tomb was a royal commission for which Edward III himself was responsible, even though, puzzlingly, there is no surviving documentation to prove it.[40] Given that recent conservation has made it clear that the traceried tomb encompasses an earlier, simpler tomb, it is unlikely that the more elaborate tomb was undertaken immediately after Edward's funeral.[41] The possibility must be considered that Edward III did indeed oversee his father's tomb during the 1330s, when he was nurturing a claim to the French throne. In this case, arguably there could be a political message in this distinctively English variation on a French-style royal tomb. The use of alabaster appears not a "passably good substitute for a marble effigy," as it was recently described, but a definitively English equivalent.[42] That alabaster should be seen as an attribute of royalty is suggested by the tomb of Edward's and subsequently Richard II's trusted knight Guy Bryan at Tewkesbury Abbey, which had a very similar open traceried canopy but canopy and tomb alike were made of stone, avoiding a breach of decorum.[43]

Were the use of alabaster restricted to Edward II's tomb, there would be no argument to be made, but this is not so. On the contrary, there seems a strong case for proposing alabaster as a kind of cultural signifier for Edward III and his close associates. The French-style tomb formula was adapted in the alabaster tombs of Edward's widow Isabella, commissioned before her death in 1358 for the Franciscan church in Newgate, in the canopied tomb of Edward's brother John of Eltham (d. 1337) at Westminster and of his son Prince William of Hatfield in York Minster (d. 1346).[44] The fact that the 1367 Westminster tomb of Edward's own wife, Philippa of Hainaut, is also of alabaster and not of marble, despite the employment of Franco-Flemish

36. J. Gardner, *The Tomb and the Tiara: Curial Tomb Sculpture in Rome and Avignon in the Later Middle Ages* (Oxford, 1992), pl. 166.

37. *Ibid.*, 140, where Francis Bond is first credited with suggesting the idea.

38. See A. McGee Morganstern, *Gothic Tombs of Kinship in France, the Low Countries and England* (University Park, Pa., 2000), chapter 5.

39. W. Ormrod, "The Personal Religion of Edward III," *Speculum* 64 (1989), 870.

40. J. Luxford, *The Art and Architecture of English Benedictine Monasteries 1300–1540: A Patronage History* (Woodbridge, 2005), pp. 157–166; see too Paul Crossley in Alexander and Binski, *Age of Chivalry* (as in note 35), p. 72.

41. C. Heighway and R. Bryant, *The Tomb of Edward II: A Royal Monument in Gloucester Cathedral* (Stonehouse, 2007).

42. F. Cannan, "'If Marble will not serve': Medieval English Alabaster Sculpture, from Quarry to Object of Devotion" in P. Williamson ed., *Object of Devotion: Medieval English Alabaster Sculpture from the Victoria and Albert Museum* (Alexandria, Va., 2010), p. 24.

43. C. A. Stothard, *The Monumental Effigies of Great Britain* (new ed.: London, 1876), 133.

44. For Isabella, see F. D. Blackley, "The Tomb of Isabella of France, Wife of Edward II of England," *Bulletin of the International Society for the Study of Church Monuments* 8 (1983), 161–164; for John of Eltham, see F. Sandford, *A Genealogical History of the Kings of England* (London, 1677), and available on-line (16/04/2011) at: http://www.britishmuseum.org/research/search_the_collection_database/search_object_details.aspx?objectid=1632260&partid=1&searchText=john+of+eltham&fromADBC=ad&toADBC=ad&numpages=10&images=on&orig=%2fresearch%2fsearch_the_collection_database.aspx&currentPage=1. See also P. Binski, *Westminster Abbey and the Plantagenets: Kingship and the Representation of Power 1200–1400* (London and New Haven, 1995), 176–179.

craftsman, Jean de Liège, testifies to the association between alabaster and the English royal family.[45] The tomb of Edward's son John of Gaunt in Old St. Paul's, begun in both his and his father's lifetime in 1374, was also alabaster, again with a substantial canopy.[46] Edward's own bronze tomb was presumably the decision of Richard II.

Royal use of alabaster was not restricted to tombs. In 1367, Edward also commissioned a large alabaster altarpiece for the refurbished thirteenth century Chapel of St. George at Windsor Castle for the high price of £166.13*s* 4*d*, or 300 marks, more than the £133.6*s* 8*d* paid to Jean de Liège for making Philippa's tomb, and it required ten carts each pulled by eight horses to carry it from Nottingham to Windsor.[47] This must have been a massive work quite unlike the average alabaster altarpiece existing today, and the choice of alabaster as opposed to, say, painting or metalwork is curious. Indeed, the chapel did contain a copper gilt altarpiece of St. George to the north of the high altar.[48] When viewed in conjunction with all the alabaster tombs, the choice of materials for the high altarpiece seems highly significant. It must have been dismantled when Henry VII transformed this oldest part of the chapel into his Lady Chapel, and it is now difficult to reconstruct what it might have looked like.

The altarpiece was a late aspect of the building project at Windsor, which Nigel Saul sees as an attempt to establish it as a kind of new Camelot.[49] The Chapel of St. George was a royal collegiate institution serving the Order of the Garter, and the annual three-day celebrations of the feast of St. George took place in the chapel. Each day culminated with the knights kneeling in pairs before the altar to make financial offerings while the choir sung the *Te Deum*, and the alabaster altarpiece would have constituted a performative staging for these ceremonies.[50] Around the same time, Edward commissioned a large carved wooden altarpiece thought to be for the Chapel in his own private apartments.[51] The choice of materials was clearly dictated by the function of the space to be decorated. Unsurprisingly, alabaster was subsequently a popular choice for high-status tombs including those of Knights of the Garter. Thomas Beauchamp, third Earl of Warwick (d. 1371; Fig. 9) was one of the original Knights of the Garter of 1348, for example. Alabaster altarpieces were also diffused to a much wider public.

It is this wider public with which *small-scale* alabasters have often been associated and rightly so, for documents make it quite clear that the clientele owning small devotional alabaster carvings from the fourteenth century certainly included the gentry, whether in England or on the Continent. This does not mean that privately-owned alabasters constituted a so-called "minor" art reproduced by rote like pipe-clay statues, however, for the social range of ownership also extended to the most exclusive elite. The private chapel of Queen Isabella, mother of Edward III, contained an alabaster Virgin and a St. Stephen, for example.[52] Margaret of Austria kept a small alabaster statue of the Virgin in

45. G. Scott, *Gleanings from Westminster Abbey* (Oxford and London, 1863), 64–5 and 169–70; Binski, *Westminster Abbey* (as in note 44), 176–180. Older sources sometimes described this tomb as marble. The services of Jean of Liège were presumably secured as a goodwill gesture during the nine years of peace between England and France 1360–69. It was presumably for this tomb that Philippa arranged delivery of six carts of alabaster from Tutbury in 1362: *Calendar of Patent Rolls Edward III, 1361–4* (London, 1891–1916), 232.

46. *John of Gaunt's Register*, ed. S. Armitage-Smith, vol. 2, Camden Society, third series 21 (1911), 212–3, no. 13944; W. Dugdale, *The History of St Paul's Cathedral* (London, 1818), 60–61. John of Gaunt was Lord of Tutbury where the alabaster quarries were.

47. W. St. John Hope, *Windsor Castle, An Architectural History*, I, (London, 1913), 201; St. John Hope, *Early Working* (as in note 3), 2.

48. St. John Hope, *Windsor* (as in note 47), II, note 11, and M. Bond, *The Inventories of St George's Chapel, Windsor Castle, 1384–1667* (Windsor, 1947), appendix B.

49. Ed. N. Saul, *St George's Chapel Windsor in the 14th Century* (Woodbridge, 2005), 2.

50. H. E. L. Collins, *The Order of the Garter 1348–1461: Chivalry and Politics in Late Medieval England* (Oxford, 2000), p. 198.

51. C. Wilson, "The Royal Lodgings of Edward III at Windsor Castle: Form, Function and Representation," in L. Keen and E. Scarff, eds., *Windsor: Medieval Archaeology, Art, and Architecture of the Thames Valley*, British Archaeological Association Conference Transactions 25 (2002), 38–39.

52. F. Palgrave, *The Antient Kalendars and Inventories of the Treasury of His Majesty's Exchequer*, III (London, 1836), 245. These are listed as movable items, so presumably were small-scale rather than architectural fixtures.

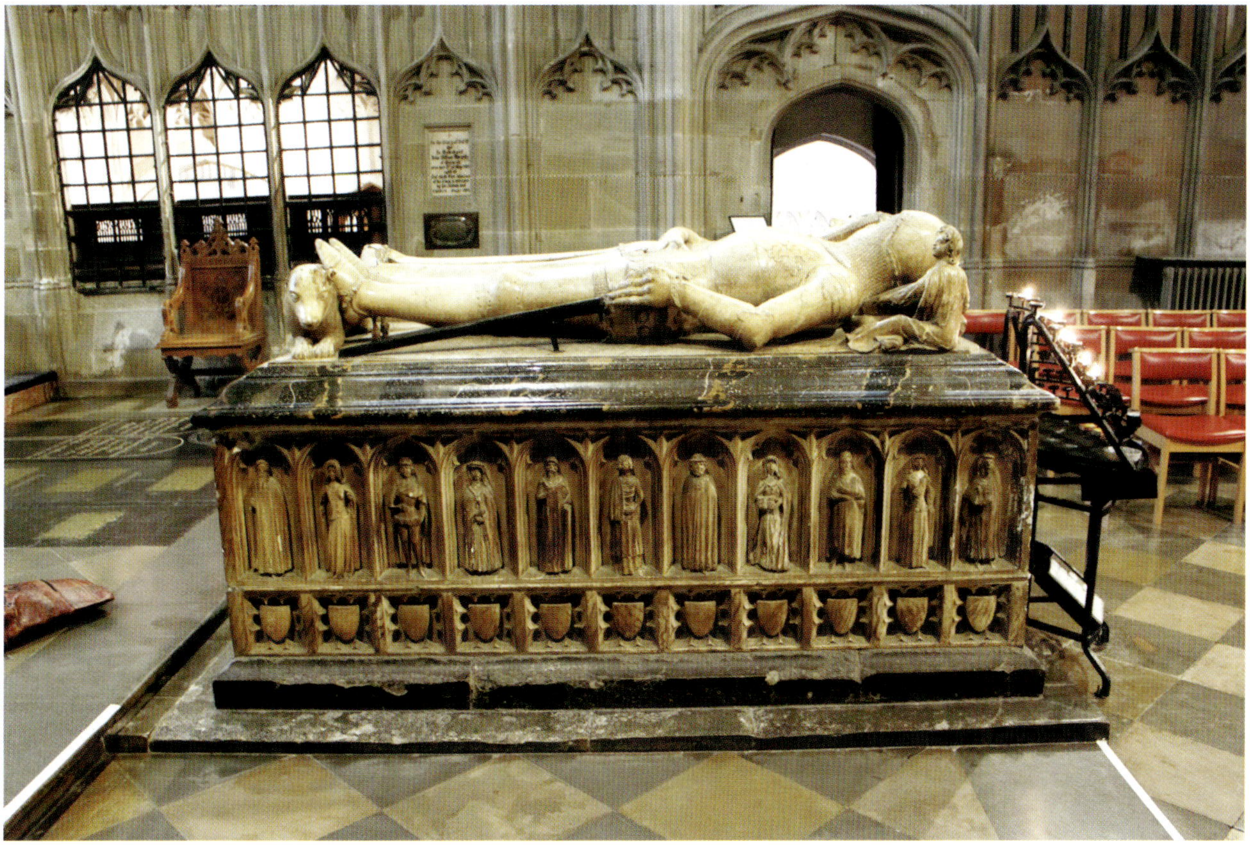

FIGURE 9. Tomb of Sir Thomas Beauchamp, Third Earl of Warwick (d. 1371), St. Mary's, Warwick.

her library and an alabaster *Pietá* in her petit cabinet, of which the latter at least was likely to have been an older work.[53] The alabaster St. Margaret also listed in her collection is almost certainly the one known to have been carved for her by Michel Colombe.[54]

Nor was Margaret the only collector to own alabasters. The 1598 Fickler inventory of the Habsburg Munich collection included alabaster tableware, statues, portrait medallions, and both classicizing and devotional reliefs.[55] Tableware occupying Table 19 appears to have been particularly highly prized, perhaps because of its reputation for detecting poison in food as well as for its aesthetic properties.[56] Table 20 included an alabaster statue of Lucretia and a memento mori, while classicizing alabaster reliefs were also to be found on Table 21.[57] Among the artifacts at Table 13 were five little devotional reliefs which, judging by their lunettes, columns, and tiny statues on top, seem to have been Renaissance works.[58] The collection also contains several small alabaster portrait medallions of members of the Habsburg family, the material presumably selected for its capacity for fine detail.[59]

53. J. Finot, *Inventaire Sommaire des Archives Départementales antérieurs à 1790, Nord, archives civiles, sér. B, Chambre des Comptes de Lille, nos. 3390–3665*, vol. 8 (Lille, 1895), 208 and 236; M. le Glay, *Correspondance de l'Empereur Maximilien Ier et de Marguerite d'Autriche, sa fille, gouvernante des Pays-Bas de 1507 à 1519*, vol. 2 (Paris, 1839), 478. The *Pietà* was an extremely popular subject for alabaster sculpture at the very beginning of the 15th century.

54. W. Stechow, *Northern Renaissance Art 1400–1600: Sources and Documents* (Englewood Cliffs, N.J., 1966), 150.

55. Ed. P. Diemer *et al.*, *Johann Baptist Fickler: Das Inventar der Münchner herzoglichen Kunstkammer von 1598*, 3 vols. (Munich, 2004).

56. Diemer *Johann Fickler* 1 (as in note 55), 417 and footnote.

57. *Ibid.*, 425–444.

58. *Ibid.*, 111–2.

59. *Ibid.*, 218–227.

The famous inventory of Schloss Ambras made in 1596, was arranged by material. Most of the items in the alabaster section (section 10) were tableware,[60] and the fact that items in alabaster that would now qualify as sculpture are mostly found elsewhere in the collection arguably suggests greater discrimination between art and artifacts here.[61] In the Chapel of St. Nicholas, there was an alabaster crucifix with statues of the three Maries, described as "zerbrochens," or broken: the evidently still treasured remains of an alabaster altarpiece perhaps very much earlier in date.[62]

From the fourteenth century, alabasters, whether tombs, altarpieces, or items in private collections, were most certainly *not* seen as minor but as highly sought after works of art associated with royalty that spread in a trickle-down effect to other elite branches of society. The rising cult of the antique in Habsburg Kunstkammers or among pioneering collectors like Thomas Howard, Earl of Arundel (d. 1646) in England, meant that from the seventeenth century onwards marble took on the new aura of antique "marbles" and alabaster was arguably relegated to an increasingly "minor" status.[63]

Pugin and Alabaster

The prestige of alabaster did not vanish overnight, but by the nineteenth century so forgotten was the material in England that in his architectural treatise *The Present State of Ecclesiastical Architecture in England*, 1841–1842, the neo-Gothic architect A. W. N. Pugin argued in favor of its revival:

> it is to be hoped that the use of this beautiful material, which was constantly used by the Catholic artists in their more elaborate works, will be generally revived. It is admirably adapted for the finest style of carving, easily worked, exceedingly durable, and capable of receiving a high polish. The best quarries are at Tutbury in Staffordshire; but at present they remain quite neglected, being only casually worked, when materials for plaster are required. Blocks of a sufficient size for sepulchral effigies might be easily procured, and at a moderate cost. Many of the most beautiful ancient monuments were worked in alabaster; also reredoses of altars, and generally images.[64]

Pugin did in fact revive the use of alabaster in the Convent of Mercy in Nottingham (1845–1848) and in the altar and reredos of the hospital chapel of St. John's in Alton (1841–1842), this last at the wish of his patron the sixteenth Earl of Shrewsbury, whom he quotes as saying "you must get the altar worked in alabaster. All the old men used it."[65] As the Earl's home Alton Towers is in the heart of the Midlands and alabaster country, it is quite possible that it was he who first thought of using alabaster, though it is also feasible that it was Pugin who put the idea into his head. By the 1840s alabaster quarrying had evidently all but died out. Pugin complained "your lordship has no idea of the trouble I have had to get it in pieces large enough for the purpose. It pays the people so much better to blast it and sell it for plaster that they could scarcely be prevailed upon to let us have what we wanted."[66]

At St. John's, Alton, despite reviving a distinctively English material, Pugin stuck to his usual Continental models. The angels on the side altar made by Thomas Roddis are modeled on a small carved cupboard door probably originally made in Utrecht *c.* 1480 and now in Oscott College in Birmingham, for example (Figs. 10–11); the St. John the Baptist on the altar frontal was taken from a late Gothic statue from Leuven in St. Chad's, Pugin's Roman Catholic Cathedral in Birmingham.[67] Bizarrely, the reredos contains late Gothic

60. H. Zimmerman, ed., *Jahrbuch der Kunsthistorische Sammlungen des Allerhöchsten Kaisershauses* 7 (1999), ccxcv–vi.

61. Alabaster is also represented in the stone cabinet, where again artifacts such as a little alabaster bowl are listed alongside a gilded alabaster statue of St. George, for example, or a Saint Anna in a black case. *Ibid.*, cclxxvi.

62. *Ibid.*, cclxv.

63. D. Kurtz, *The Reception of Classical Art in Britain: An Oxford Story of Plaster Casts from the Antique* (Oxford, 2000).

64. A.W.N. Pugin, *The Present State of Ecclesiastical Architecture in England, and Some Remarks Relative to Ecclesiastical Architecture and Decoration* (Leominster, 2004), 88.

65. M. Belcher, *The Collected Letters of A. W. N. Pugin*, vol. 1 (Oxford, 2001), 329.

66. *Ibid.*, 275–6.

67. K. W. Woods, *Imported Images: Netherlandish Late Gothic Sculpture in England c. 1400–c. 1550* (Donington, 2007), 276–8.

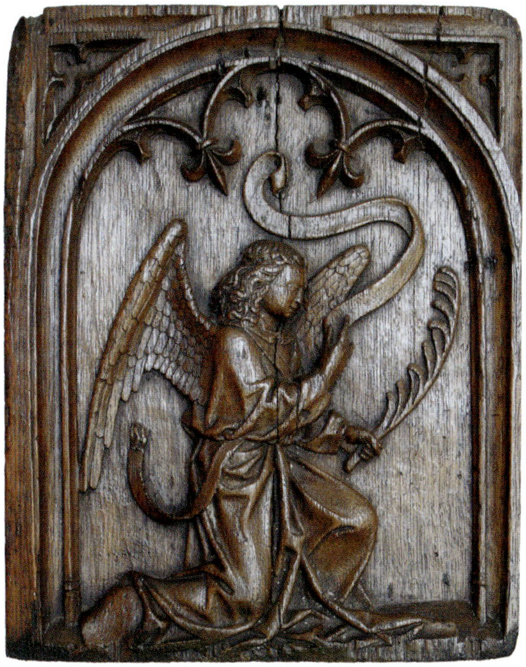

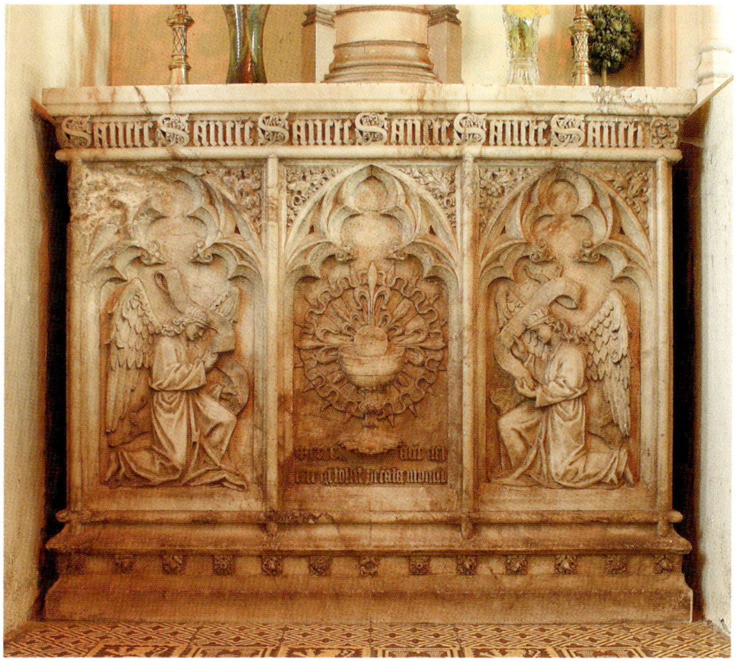

FIGURE 10 (*left*). *Angel of the Annunciation*, Utrecht, *c.* 1480, now in Oscott College, Birmingham (photo: Malcolm Daisley Photography).

FIGURE 11 (*right*). Thomas Roddis, side altar, St. John's Alton (1841–1842) (photo: Malcolm Daisley Photography).

statues painted to resemble alabaster but actually made of wood, and again Continental in style.

It seems unlikely that in all his travels Pugin had never seen an English alabaster relief, though of course given the rudimentary knowledge of English alabasters at the time he may not have recognized it as such. He had certainly visited Long Melford in Suffolk, where an alabaster relief of the *Nativity* had been discovered in 1790, and he did a lot of work in Nottingham, near which the Flawford alabaster figures had been discovered in the eighteenth century.[68] He actually owned three alabaster statues of saints and a St. George on horseback, but they are described in his sale catalogue as fourteenth-century French.[69]

Pugin's brief revival of alabaster was part of his wider campaign to revive pre-Reformation, Catholic art. It did not imply renewed interest in English alabaster carving. Pugin was not alone in giving priority to Continental alabasters: it seems to have happened ever since.

English Alabasters from Major to Minor

The transition of alabaster sculpture from an elite material used to produce elite items to one serving an ever widening clientele arguably also signals the transition from major to minor, not because the genres of art in alabaster changed but because the commercial methods of production and apparent absence of creative invention and intellectual exertion failed to satisfy the Renaissance criteria of high art. Partly because of the ready availability of the material, this is something that

68. *A. W.N. Pugin and the Pugin Family*, ed., A. Wedgwood (London, 1985), diary, 7 March 1840 and sketchbook p. 290; for the Long Melford relief, see Anderson *Rediscovery* (as in note 1), 48 and 50.

69. Sotheby's 1853, 12th of December, lot 47 and lot 78.

has particularly affected English alabaster carving. The random survival of English alabasters appears more representative of the lower rather than the elite end of the patronage spectrum, and this too has affected their reputation in relation to the canon. Ironically it was Hildburgh, himself a champion of alabasters as folk art, who pointed this out:

> there are but few which can be claimed as fine examples of craftsmanship, and fewer still which can stand comparison with the best English sculpture of the 14th and 15th centuries carried out another materials. Yet we can hardly doubt that alabaster-work was then being turned out more carefully executed … than the finest of the tables were accustomed to look upon as typical.[70]

The trickle-down effect from the highest elite to less prestigious popular patronage may be traced in other fields. To cite just one, in 1390 Jacques de Baerze of Dendermonde was contracted to produce two carved wooden altarpieces for Duke Philip the Bold of Burgundy and the Netherlands for his newly founded Chartreuse de Champmol near Dijon for the price of 400 francs.[71] The dukes of Burgundy do not ever seem to have commissioned carved altarpieces again, any more than the English royal family appears to have commissioned an alabaster altarpiece after Windsor, but Netherlandish carved altarpieces, like English alabasters, attained extraordinary levels of popularity in the export market. Until scholars began to take this altarpiece industry more seriously from the 1970s onwards, they suffered much the same fate as English alabasters in being dubbed repetitive, second-rate commercial art.[72]

The 1987 exhibition catalogue the *Age of Chivalry* deftly identified a further status problem for English alabaster: its apparently provincial character. I quote: "The English alabaster industry, a small scale, low price enterprise based near the alabaster quarries in the North Midlands (although the stone's exploitation had begun in London, in the second quarter of the 14th century), cannot really be compared in importance with the leading luxury goods industries of the continent."[73]

The fact that English alabasters were clearly exported to a number of European countries including France, Spain, Italy, and Scandinavia is nevertheless an argument for indeed comparing them with some Continental exports such as Netherlandish carved wooden altarpieces and Continental alabasters. The development of separate traceried canopies and pedestals that Prior used as dating criteria may conceivably have been adopted for ease of export as well as to give a competitive market edge. The same might be said for the unusually ambitious depth of carving and illusion of space in the Society of Antiquaries of London St. Catherine in prison (Fig. 12), for example, for Netherlandish carved altarpieces competed for a very similar market and conventionally had elaborate tracery, and stage-like scenes that created both real depth and the illusion of still greater depth.

Specialization in theory implies ultimate mastery of a material; in the case of English alabasters at least it has more often been seen as something that, in the words of Phillip Lindley, "tends to hinder stylistic innovation."[74] Margaret Whinney declared of the alabaster tomb specialists of the early sixteenth century:

70. W. L. Hildburgh, "A Group of Panels of English Alabaster," *The Burlington Magazine* 46/267 (1925), 307–317 (p. 308).

71. C. Monget, *La Chartreuse de Dijon*, vol. 1 (Montreuil-sur-Mer, 1898), 201.

72. Scholars Lynn Jacobs and Ria de Boodt in particular have succeeded in putting scholarship on a sensible footing: L. F. Jacobs, "The Commissioning of Early Netherlandish Carved Altarpieces: Some Documentary Evidence," in *A Tribute to Robert A. Koch: Studies in the Northern Renaissance*, ed. G. T Clark *et al.* (Princeton, N.J., 1994), pp. 83–111; L. F. Jacobs, *Early Netherlandish Carved Altarpieces, 1380–1550: Medieval Tastes and Mass Marketing* (Cambridge, 1998); R. de Boodt, *Retabelkasten, ornematiek en beeldsnijwerk. Onderzoek naar de mate van formele standaardisatie in de Antwerpse retabelproductie van de zestiende eeuw*, unpublished dissertation (Brussels: Vrije Universiteit, 4 vols., 2004); R. de Boodt and U. Schäfer, *Vlaamse Retabels: een internationale reis langs laatmiddeleeuws beeldsnijwerk* (Leuven, 2007). See also K. W. Woods, *Netherlandish Carved Wooden Altarpieces of the 15th and Early 16th Centuries in Britain*, unpublished Ph.D. thesis (Courtauld Institute, University of London, 1988).

73. Alexander and Binski, *Age of Chivalry* (as in note 35), 54.

74. P. Lindley *Gothic to Renaissance, Essays on Sculpture in England* (Stamford, 1995), 28.

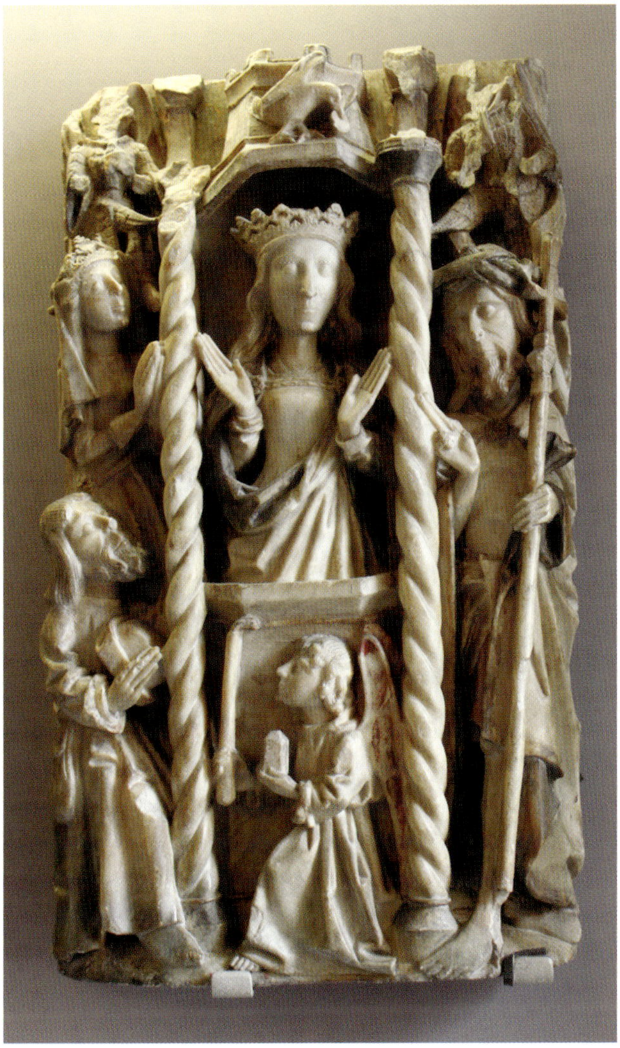

FIGURE 12. *St. Catherine in Prison, c.* 1480, Society of Antiquaries, London (by permission of the Society of Antiquaries of London).

"it was hardly a case of dominant artists, but rather of better trained craftsmen," which assigns English alabaster tombs at least to the status of minor in a single sentence.[75] This does not appear to do justice to examples like the tomb of Judge William Rudhall (d. 1530; Fig. 13) in Ross-on-Wye, which even offers a little iconographic novelty in the Christ child descending from God the Father to the Annunciate Virgin on an outstretched wing.

Continental alabasters have generally fared better than English alabasters, although produced through very much the same commercial specialization and for a similar range of clients. The carvers in the Master of Rimini group avoid production by rote, however, and show that specialization can on the contrary be a means to increased refinement.

An additional problem is that English alabasters at least have been subjected to a biological cycle of growth, flowering, and decay. Given the difficulties of dating English alabasters, to impose a cycle of decadence is a risky strategy in itself. The alabaster altarpiece of St. James given by John Goodyear (Gudguer) to Santiago da Compostella in 1456 is one of the few surviving dated examples (Fig. 14). As the only known English alabaster altarpiece of this subject, the designs are likely to be original rather than reproduced by rote. Lawrence Stone comments, however, that the "empty, expressionless faces, heavy hands, and awkward gestures are evidence of an art form in decay."[76] Arguably, what it is more likely to show is the patron's limited purchasing power: as a rector on the Isle of Wight he presumably had neither the money to command a top carver nor the possibility of supervising his commission closely. Clientele and quality of output varies in many artistic media, including painting, but nobody would dream of designating painting minor because some of its exponents were weak.

Rather than challenging the alleged popular character of English alabasters, Hildburgh made a virtue out of it: alabaster was in fact "the most perfect expression in representational art of the English character and temperament of its time...."[77] The quintessentially English character of alabasters is also asserted by Nicolas Pevsner in his 1955 Reith lectures "The Englishness of English Art." He associated the "long, lean, thin faced" figures in alabaster carving with the verticality of English perpendicular architecture.[78] The

75. M. Whinney, *Sculpture in Britain 1530–1830* (Harmondsworth 1964, 2nd ed., 1988), 43.

76. L. Stone, *Sculpture in Britain: The Middle Ages* (Harmondsworth, 1955), 203.

77. Oakes, "Dr Hildburgh" (as in note 1), 79.

78. N. Pevsner, *The Englishness of English Art* (Birkenhead, 1956), 94.

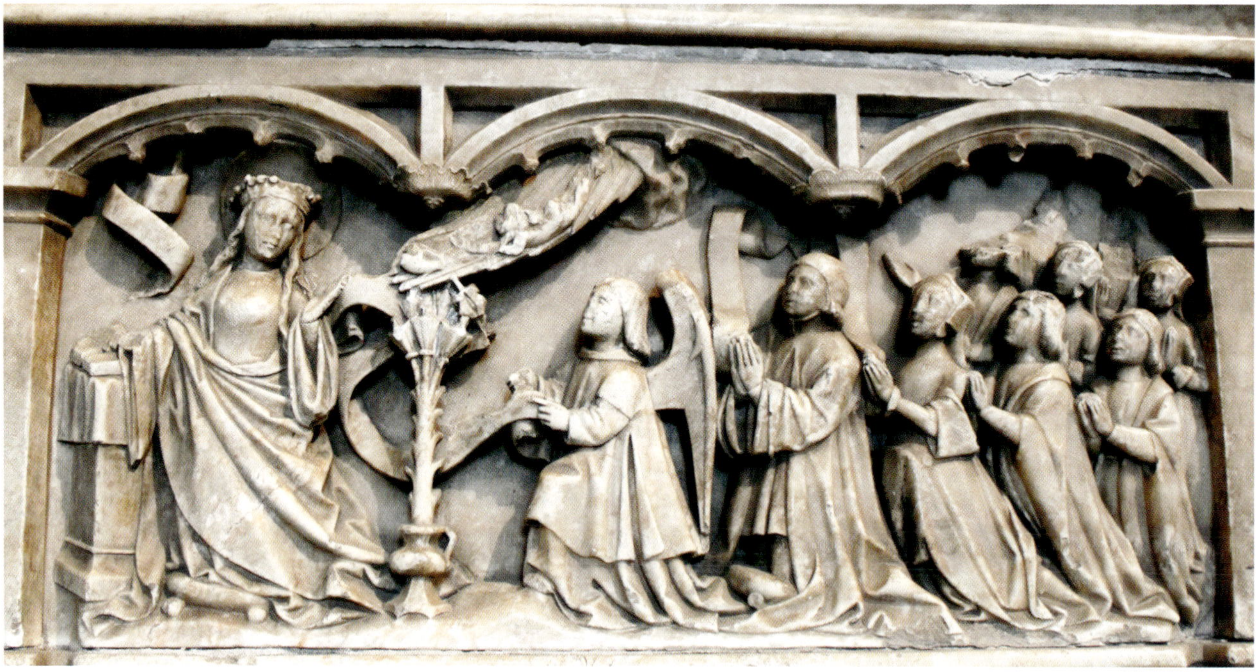

FIGURE 13. Tomb of Judge William Rudhall (d. 1530), Ross-on-Wye church.

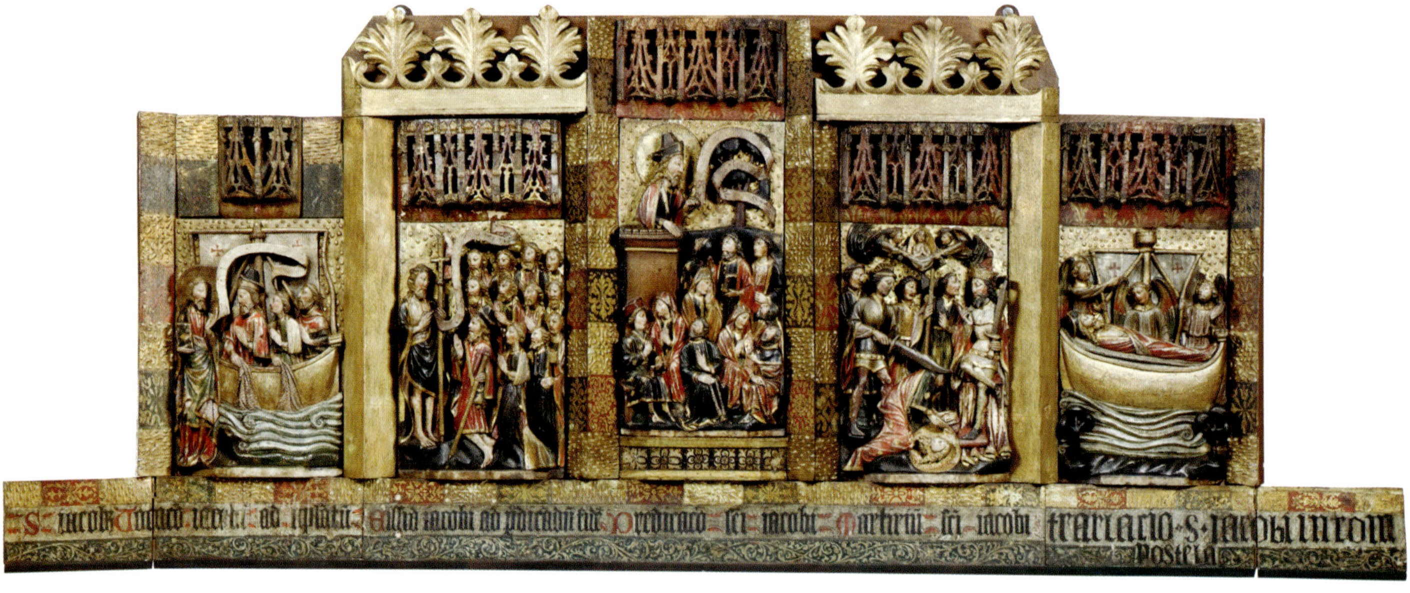

FIGURE 14. Altarpiece of St. James, 1456, Cathedral of Santiago da Compostella (photo: copyright Museo de la Catedral de Santiago de Compostela).

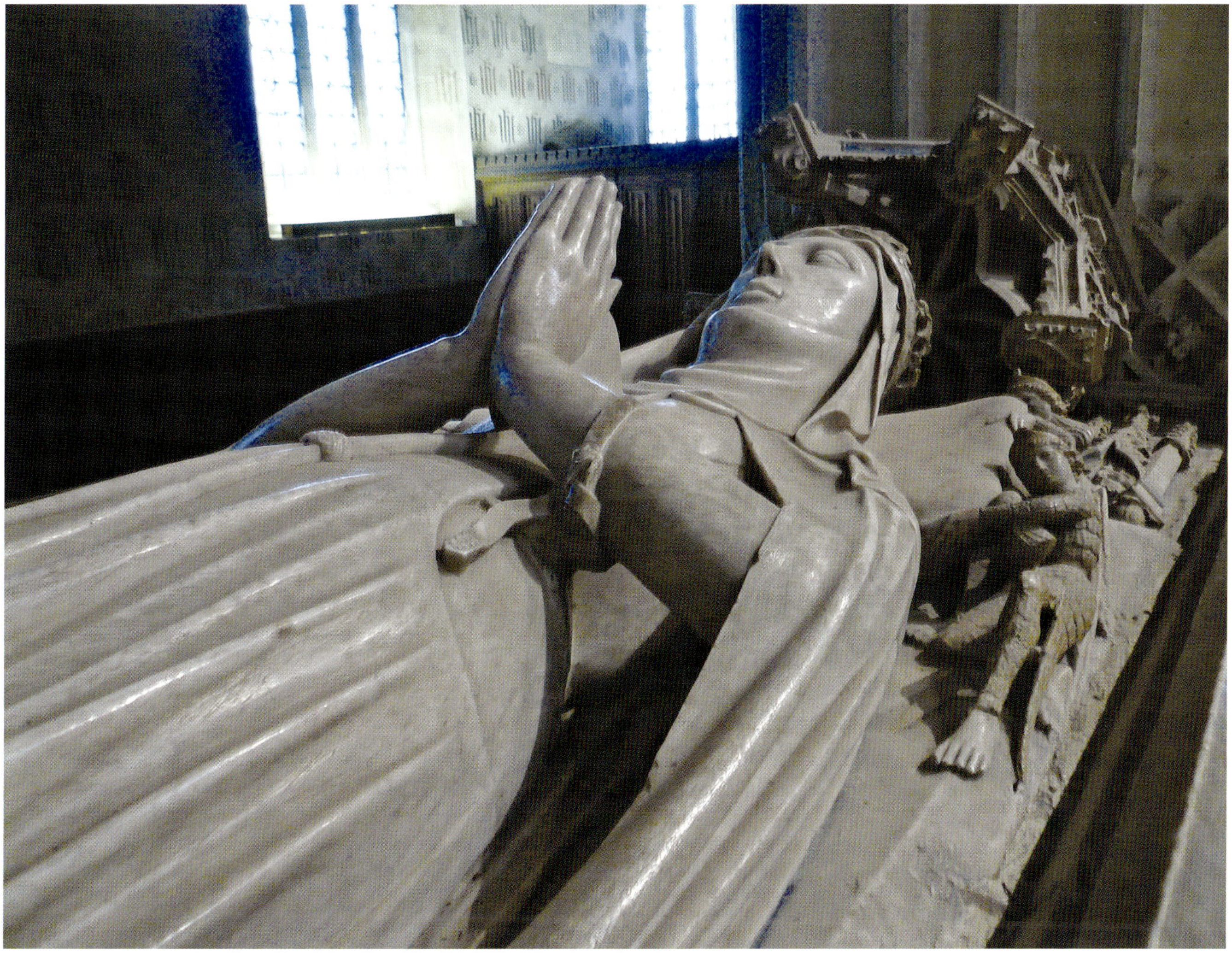

FIGURE 15. Tomb of Alice de la Pole, Duchess of Suffolk, *c.* 1470–1475, St. Mary's, Ewelme.

2011 three-part BBC television series *Romancing the Stone* on English sculpture included the Ewelme tomb of Alice Chaucer (*c.* 1470–1475; Fig. 15) and alabaster altarpiece panels as unapologetic aspects of English sculptural tradition. There is only a limited sense as yet, however, that English alabasters are being integrated into the canon of European sculpture as they so clearly were in their own day. The traveling exhibition of English alabasters from the Victoria and Albert Museum 2010–2012 might conceivably constitute a beginning.[79]

Enough has been said to show that alabaster and alabaster carving were very far from being simply the folk art that Hildburgh held it to be. A better model is to be found in William Morris, that great opponent of the principles of major and minor, who claimed that the fine arts when separated off from the broad craft tradition "become nothing but dull adjuncts to unmeaning pomp, or ingenious toys for a few rich and idle men."[80] The richness of the study of alabaster carving is surely that it is neither major nor minor, but covers

79. Ed. P. Williamson, *Object of Devotion* (as in note 42).
80. William Morris, "Innate Socialism," in A. Briggs, ed., *William Morris: Selected Writings and Designs* (Harmondsworth, 1977), p. 85.

sculpture ranging from small-scale devotional items to royal commissions, and the widest possible audience from rulers to parishioners. That is surely something worthy of scholarly attention.

Acknowledgements

The author would like to thank Benoît-Henri Papounaud and Margali Briat-Philippe of Brou, Christina Ceulemans, Julia Dudkiewicz of the Society of Antiquaries, Sam Fogg, Sandy Heslop, Colum Hourihane, Chris Jeens of Gloucester Cathedral, Annick Lapotre, Leon Lock, Rocio Sanchez Amereijas and the Cathedral of Santiago da Compostella, Paul Williamson.

LAURA WEIGERT

The Art of Tapestry: Neither Minor nor Decorative

WHO SAYS tapestry is a minor art? The producers of the Harry Potter movies did not, when they prominently displayed the Lady and the Unicorn tapestry set on the walls of the Gryffindor Common Room (Fig. 1). Nor did the excited public and reviewers of the 2002 show at the Metropolitan Museum of Art, *Tapestry in the Renaissance: Art and Magnificence.*[1] With ticket sales for the first five Harry Potter films amounting to 4.5 billion dollars and a record number of visitors attending the Met exhibition, tapestry is clearly at the center of mainstream movie and highbrow museum cultures.[2] It seems that more than any other medium, the general public associates the Middle Ages with tapestry, even when the object in question is technically an embroidery, like the so-called Bayeux tapestry. Tapestries have become the symbol of the wealth of lords and ladies; provide vibrant depictions of the battles of knights; and evoke the charm and mystery of courtly ladies. In contrast, art historians have marginalized tapestry within their account of the Middle Ages.

Focusing on the tapestry set of the Lady and the Unicorn and that of the Story of Troy, a panel from which was one of the highlights of the Metropolitan Museum's tapestry exhibition (Fig. 2), this article explores the disjunction between the neglect of the medium in art history and its renown in the popular perception of the Middle Ages. I will suggest that the anachronism of art history's attribution of value parallels the anachronism of its models of interpretation. My goal is not simply to remind us of how important tapestry was from the fourteenth to the sixteenth century but to elucidate how the current models of art history are inadequate for our understanding and appreciation of this medium, and finally to offer an interpretive framework through which to evaluate and discuss tapestries in historically viable terms.

The Reception of Tapestry in History & Art History

From the emergence of the tapestry industry at the end of the fourteenth century in Arras and Paris, tapestry had the same kind of popular and elite appeal that we see in the recent enthusiasm for the medium. For instance, the woven story of Gideon's victory over the Mideonites, commissioned by Philip the Good, was the most expensive artistic project financed by the Burgundian or French courts in the fifteenth century: the tapestry set measured about five and a half meters in height; together its eight sections stretched to 98 meters.[3] They cost 8,960 gold crowns to produce.[4] The series was displayed in the banquet hall at each chapter meeting of the Order of the Golden Fleece, in The Hague, St. Omer, and Brussels. It was also displayed for other occasions: in Paris, following the coronation of Louis XI in Reims; during the wedding of Charles the Bold and Margaret of York in Bruges; in Trier at the meeting of Charles the Bold and Emperor Friedrich III; and in Brussels at Charles V's ceremonial abdication of his rule; it disappeared in 1794 en route to Vienna.[5] The public for this tapestry set was large and diverse. Following the coronation of Louis XI in 1461, Philip the Good had the walls of the Hotel d'Artois in Paris covered with the Gideon tapestries.[6] What might be considered the first temporary art exhibition

1. The Metropolitan Museum of Art, New York, 14 March–19 June 2002.
2. http://www.the-numbers.com/movies/series/HarryPotter.php; Metropolitan Museum of Art (exhibition documentation).
3. Jeffrey Chipps Smith, "Portable Propaganda-Tapestries as Princely Metaphors at the Courts of Philip the Good and Charles the Bold," *Art Journal* 48 (1989), 123–129.
4. *Ibid.*, 123.
5. *Ibid.*, 124–126.
6. Georges Chastellain, *Oeuvres*, ed. Baron Kervyn de Lettenhove, 8 vols. (Brussels, 1863–66), vol. 3, pp. 93–94; Jacques Duclercq, *Mémoires sur le règne de Philippe le Bon (1448–1467)*, ed. J. A. C. Buchon, in *Choix de chroniques et mémoires sur l'histoire de France* (Paris, 1838), 159–160.

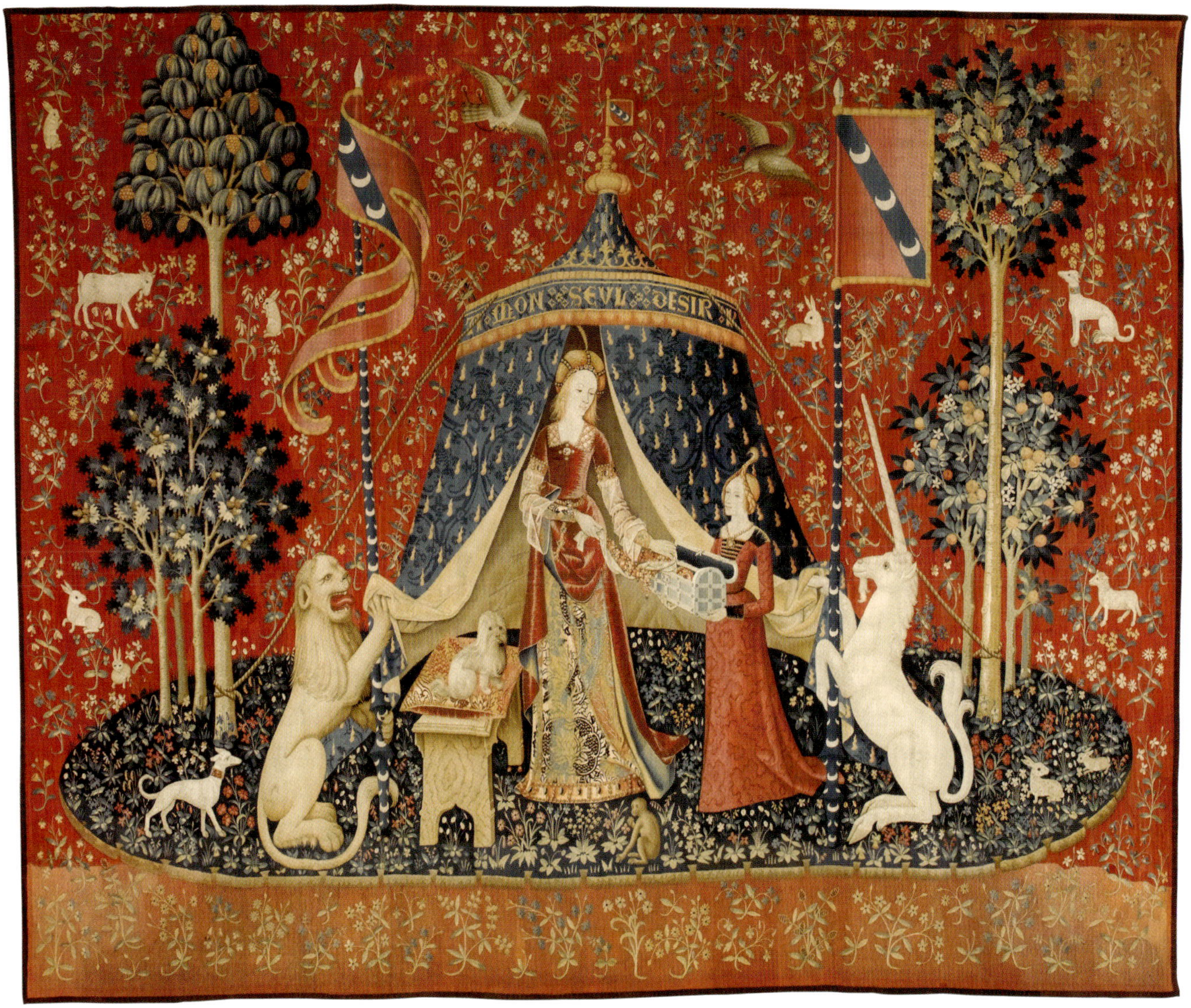

FIGURE 1. "A Mon Seul Désir" (from the series Lady and the Unicorn), tapestry, wool, 3.77 × 4.73 meters, Paris, Museum of the Middle Ages (Photo: RMN / Art Resource)

was open to the public for over a month. During that time the tapestries were visible to lucky Parisians who processed before them day and night, when torches arranged around the walls probably provided artificial lighting. This tapestry exhibition received rave reviews. According to the contemporary chronicler, Georges Chastellain, the Gideon tapestry was "the richest on the earth at this time and richer than all the others of the world in the past." He concludes that the experience of seeing it was something that the Parisians "were able neither to recover from nor to get enough of."[7]

Woven sets depicting the Trojan War stories of Troy, no less modest in scale, were also enormously popular.[8] They are listed, for instance, in the collections of

7. Chastellain, *Oeuvres*, 94.

8. J.-P. Asselberghs, "Les Tapisseries tournaisiennes de la guerre de Troie," *Revue Belge d'Archéologie et d'Histoire de l'Art* 39 (1970), 93–182; S. McKendrick, "The *Great History of Troy*: A Reassessment of the Development of a Secular Theme in Late Medieval Art," *Journal of the Warburg and Courtauld Institutes* 54

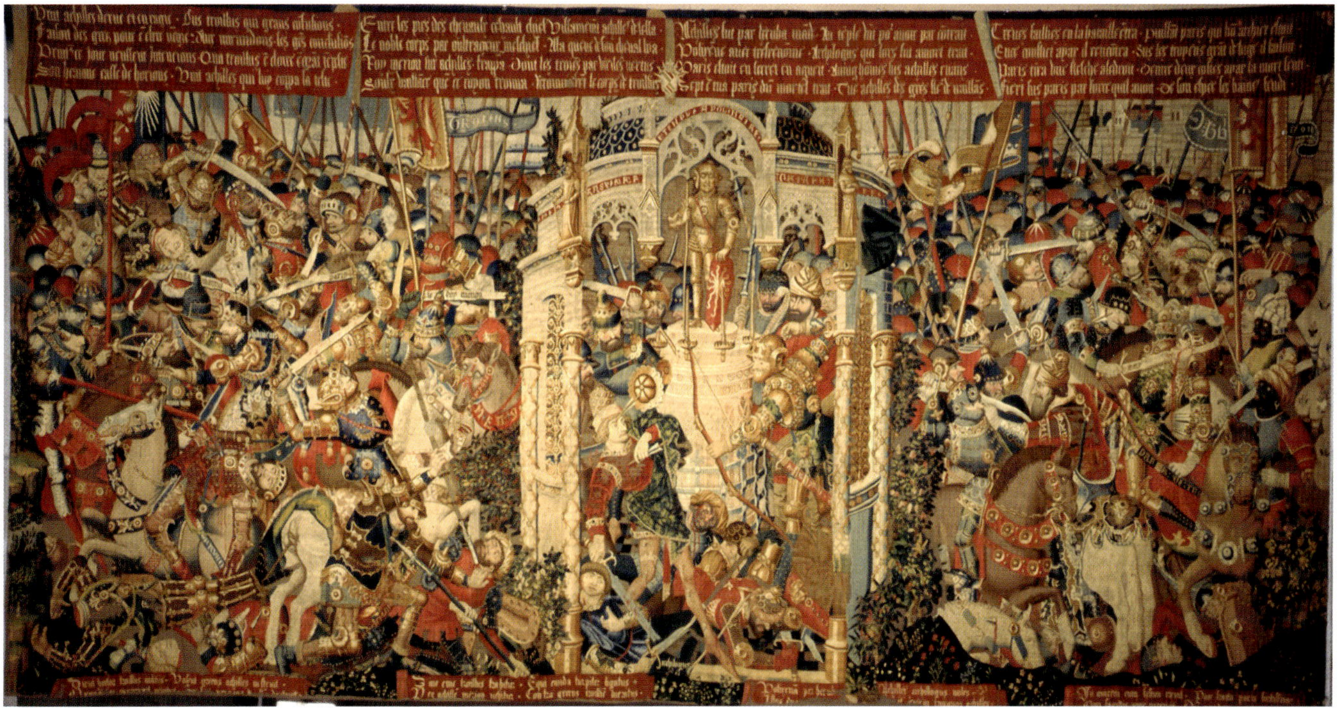

FIGURE 2. The Death of Achilles (from the Trojan War Series), tapestry, wool and silk, *c.* 1475, 4.81 × 9.42 meters, Zamora, Cathedral Museum (photo: Cuauhtli Gutierrez).

Louis, Duke of Anjou, Charles, Duke of Berry, Charles VIII and Louis XII, kings of France; the set woven for Charles the Bold, Duke of Burgundy, was duplicated six times for other European courts.[9] No accounts survive of the contemporary reaction to the Lady and the Unicorn tapestries, but they generated an enormous excitement beginning at their rediscovery in 1844. George Sand was one of the most vocal advocates of their artistic value. In an article published in *L'Illustration* in 1847, she describes the eight tapestries she saw in the chateau of Boussac in the following terms: "these tapestries attest to incredible skill of production and great art: from the folds, the texture, and the shimmer of the fabrics, the style what we call today the 'chic' of the cut of the clothing, to the glitter of the reflection off the stones to the transparency of the cloth, all of this is rendered with a skill and attention to detail that has not been diminished by the devastation of time and neglect."[10]

In contrast to the importance accorded the medium through the late Middle Ages and at the discovery of individual examples in the nineteenth century, early art-historical writing devalued tapestry. The narrative about art's history that emerged with the foundation of the discipline placed tapestry at its margins. This narrative is indebted to Vasari, whose *Lives* focused on the

(1991), 43–82; A. Rapp Buri and M. Stucky Schürer, *Burgundische Tapisserien* (Munich: Hirmer, 2001), 313–325; T. P. Campbell *et al.*, *Tapestry in the Renaissance: Art and Magnificence*, Exhib. Cat., New York: Metropolitan Museum of Art (New Haven, Conn.: Yale University Press, 2002), 55–64.

9. McKendrick, "*Great History of Troy*" (as in note 8), 44–59.

10. "Ces tapisseries attestent une grande habilité de fabrication et un grand gout mêlés à un grand savoir naïf chez l'artiste inconnu qui en a tracé le dessin et indiqué les couleurs. Le pli, le mat et les lustrés des étoffes, la manière, ce qu'on appellerait aujourd'hui le *chic* dans la coupe des vêtements, le brillant des agrafes de pierreries, et jusqu'à la transparence de la gaze, y sont rendus avec une conscience et facilité dont les outrages du temps et de l'abandon n'ont pu triompher," *L'Illustration, journal universel*, no. 227, vol. IX (3 July 1847), 275.

arte del disegno (painting, sculpture, and architecture).[11] Although tapestry was an important component of Vasari's artistic production and of several of the artists whose stories he tells, this component of their artistic practice is minimized in his description of their work. The rare tapestries that appear in the *Lives* are linked to the individual responsible for the preliminary sketch or cartoon; he mentions the weavers only in passing.[12] Art history has inherited this characterization of the past, by privileging painting, sculpture, and architecture and focusing on works of art for which the name of an artist has been preserved. So tapestries, which were the product of a collaborative effort between painters, draftsmen, and weavers, and for which we rarely have the names of their creators, fall outside of the professional interest of art historians.[13]

Most scholars of medieval art face this bias, yet certain kinds of medieval art have maintained their centrality in the discipline. Tapestry, on the other hand, has been marginalized for other reasons. First, the traditional designation of distinct fields within art history has played a role. Except for a few isolated cases, the tapestries that survive date to the fifteenth and sixteenth centuries, a period considered within the discipline to be Renaissance. Within scholarship on and teaching of Renaissance art history, there is still an emphasis on the individual artist as creator and on monographic studies of these artists. Moreover, given the emphasis in this field on the pursuit of spatial illusionism, or in the terms of the Northern Renaissance, the pursuit of realism, the medium seems out dated and medieval. The extensive survival of tapestries devoted to secular subject matter, however, fits uneasily into a narrative of medieval art, still focusing on religious subject matter. The assumption that women wove tapestries also has led to the marginalization of tapestry within the discipline of art history. In fact, the regulations of the guilds to which the weavers of tapestries belonged, from the fourteenth to the sixteenth century, forbade women from working in tapestry workshops. Nonetheless, tapestries are still gendered as feminine, thereby diminishing their worth as object of serious academic study.[14]

In contrast to this neglect within the discipline of art history, textiles occupy an important place within the most influential of the theoretical discussions of the decorative arts, exemplified in the work of Gottfried Semper and Alois Riegl. Riegl's interest lay primarily in the support textiles provided for ornament.[15] For Semper, the medium was central to his architectural theory.[16] In his *Bekleidungstheorie* (theory of dressing), he articulates the specific architectural use of textiles, stressing the original role of carpets to enclose and divide space, the activity that formed the conceptual basis of all architecture. In a second stage of his theory, Semper argued that the decoration on these tex-

11. G. Vasari, *The Lives of the Painters, Sculptors and Architects*, 4 vols., trans. W. Gaunt (London, 1963).

12. Two of Vasari's references to tapestries include more specific discussions of the medium of tapestry. His description of Salviati's designs underscores the way designs for tapestries must take the woven medium into account: "Ingenious inventions and varied compositions require the figures to stand out from each other, so that they may have relief and bright colouring with rich vestments." And Vasari praises the tapestries made for Leo X from Raphael's cartoons in the following manner: "The work is so marvellously executed that it excites the wonder of those who see it that such things as hair and beards and delicate flesh-colouring can be woven work. It is certainly a miracle rather than a production of human art, containing, as it does, water, buildings, animals, all so well done that they seem the work of the brush and not of the loom. It cost 70,000 crowns, and is still preserved in the papal chapel." However, his references to tapestry appear within his discussion of the careers of painters, such as Raphael and Salviati. Names of weavers appear occasionally: Book 3, 109 (Giulio Romano); Book 3, 304 (Bastiano San Gallo); Book 4, 63 (Salviati); when he mentions one of his own designs for tapestries, Vasari does not include the name of the weaver (Book 4, 282).

13. T. Campbell also makes this point: *Tapestries in the Renaissance*, 9–10.

14. R. de Lespinasse and F. Bonnardot, eds., *Les métiers et corporations de la ville de Paris, XIIIe siècle: Le Livre des Métiers d'Etienne Boileau* (*Histoire générale de Paris*) (Paris: Imprimerie Nationale, 1879), LXVII–LXVIII, 1–2, 102–107.

15. A. Riegl, *Problems of Style: Foundations for a History of Ornament*, trans. E. Kain (Princeton, N.J., 1992), 300–301. Riegl's publications on textiles are numerous. See, for instance, *Altorientalische Teppiche* (Leipzig, 1891).

16. G. Semper, *Style in the Technical and Tectonic Arts; or Practical Aesthetics*, trans. H. F. Mallgrave and M. Robinson, Vol. 1, "Textile Art: Considered in Itself and in Relation to Architecture" (Los Angeles, Calif., 2004), 103–465.

tiles was inseparable from the structure of the walls.[17] The structural and decorative elements were created simultaneously to form a whole; neither one could be altered without affecting the other.

Tapestries, however, never entered these discussions of textiles within the decorative arts. The absence is explained by the focus within these theoretical and historical discussions on ornament and on artifacts produced within "primitive," that is, non-European cultures. French and Flemish tapestries and the figural compositions they incorporated were, in contrast, central to Aby Warburg's concerns. He recognized tapestry as an essential remnant and document of ceremonial occasions in the past and, like Semper, acknowledged the architectural nature of tapestries, which contributed to what he called their *monumentale Bildkraft*, monumental pictorial power.[18]

The renewed interest in the work of Riegl, Semper, and Warburg within the field of art history, beginning in the 1990s, has paved the way for accepting textiles into the discipline as serious objects of inquiry. My discussion of the Lady and the Unicorn set and the Story of Troy set draws on some of the implications of these scholars' contribution to the study of textiles in order to outline the specific characteristics of the medium of tapestry. I will focus on three features of these tapestries: their portability, their spatiality, and their materiality. The articulation of how these features contribute to an audience's experience of tapestries has the potential to bring the medium into the center of the discipline of art history.

Toward a Method for Interpreting Tapestry: The Lady & the Unicorn

The extant scholarship on the Lady and the Unicorn series is, to a large extent, beholden to traditional art-historical approaches: stylistic analysis, patronage, and iconography. Scholars have attempted to identify the artist responsible for the six extant tapestries that comprise the set. A draftsman working in Paris in the 1480s and 90s, known as the Master of Anne of Brittany, has become the best candidate and is now repeated in discussions of the work as the designer of the tapestries.[19] The identity of the patron of the work also has been established: Jean IV le Viste, based on the presence of three crescents, which were identified as the arms of this family.[20] Finally, the gestures of the Lady, the objects she holds, and her interaction with her animal and human companions led A. F. Kendrick, textile conservator at the Victoria and Albert Museum, to identify the subject matter of the set as that of the five senses (Figs. 3–7).[21] Following Kendrick's proposal, which was widely accepted, numerous explanations have been provided for the meaning of the sixth tapestry (Fig. 1). Art-historical accounts thereby ascribe to the tapestries a design originating in the hand of a maker, a patron, and a descriptive meaning.

These three pieces of information provide plausible responses to what are important questions, concerning the production, patronage, and subject matter of any work of art. In this case, however, they have limited the interpretive possibilities of the object they attempt to explain. Locating the creative origin of the

17. H. F. Mallgrave, *Gottfried Semper: Architect of the Nineteenth Century* (New Haven, Conn., 1996), 293–94; Semper, *Style*, vol. 1, 123–130.

18. Among his articles that focus on tapestries, please see: "Peasants at Work in Burgundian Tapestries," in A. Warburg, *The Renewal of Pagan Antiquity: Contributions to the Cultural History of the European Renaissance*, trans. D. Britt (Los Angeles, Calif., 1999), 314–23. Warburg's student, Frances Yates, developed this interest in tapestries: *The Valois Tapestries* (London, 1959).

19. N. Reynaud, "Un peintre français cartonnier de tapisseries au XVe siècle: Henri de Vulcop," *Revue de l'Art* 22 (1973), 16; G. Souchal, "Un grand peintre français de la fin du XVe siècle: le Maître de la Chasse à la Licorne," *Revue de l'Art* 22 (1973), 40.

20. G. Souchal, "'Messeigneurs Les Vistes' et la 'Dame à la Licorne,'" *Bibliothèque de l'École des Chartes* 141 (1983), 209–267; J.-B. de Vaivre, "Messire Jehan le Viste, chevalier, seigneur d'Arcy et sa tenture au lion et à la licorne," *Bulletin Monumental* 142 (1984), 397–434; F. Joubert, *La tapisserie médiévale au Musée de Cluny* (Paris, 1987), 66–92; A. Erlande Brandenburg, *The Lady and the Unicorn Tapestries* (Paris, 1989) 67; Michele Monsour, "The Lady and the Unicorn," *Gazette des Beaux-Arts* 134 (1999), 238.

21. A. F. Kendrick, "Quelques remarques sur les tapisseries de la Dame à la Licorne au Musée de Cluny. Les ateliers de tapisserie en Angleterre," *Actes du Congrès d'Histoire de l'Art, Paris, 1921*, III (1924), 662–666.

tapestries in the hand of the Master of Anne of Brittany focuses attention on the figural groups, rather than on the fracture of the medium, the weaving process, and the pattern that comprises such a large part of its surface. Locating the impetus for the tapestry's making in Jean IV le Viste serves as a sufficient explanation for the presence of the armorial shields and banners, rather than prompting an inquiry into how unusual they are both in terms of their pervasiveness and their colors, or into the cases in which three crescents appear as the arms of fictional characters.[22] Locating the meaning of the tapestries in terms of their portrayal of the five senses assumes that the series is complete, and focuses almost exclusively on the actions of the principal figures and the textual sources upon which they might be based.[23] Moreover, this approach ignores the rest of the imagery depicted on its surface and fails to acknowledge the diverse ways in which a set of tapestries such as this one would have affected its audience.

While taking into account the specificity of the medium, I will argue that the Lady and the Unicorn tapestries can be understood in relation to a contemporary tradition of love.[24] The favorite site for amorous pursuits within this love tradition was the garden, referred to as a *locus amoenus*, a lovely place and a place for loving.[25] In this strange and fantastic world, an individual could depart from the familiar order and confines of daily life, and experience love. Medieval discussions of the garden as *locus amoenus* describe it as an enclosure, or as a whole cosmos.[26] Love, here, is not an activity that happens to take place in a garden, nor is it an internal subjective emotion. Rather, being surrounded by the garden represents the very state of love that manifests itself through the soul's encounter with the sensual world. Like the *locus amoenus*, the Lady and the Unicorn tapestries would have surrounded the viewer in a world of natural pleasure that both represents and incites the state of love.

First, the tapestries relied on their architectural properties to situate their viewers within a garden. The series recalls a time when the French royal and noble courts understood tapestries not as autonomous pictures but as ensembles that served an architectural function. Referred to as *chambres* (rooms), such sets of tapestries were destined for the parts of aristocratic dwellings to which the nobility retreated for relaxation, or for intimate gatherings.[27] The theme of love was the focus of numerous such *chambres*, referred to in inventories as a "room of the desires of love" or a "room of the Defense of Love," or simply as a "room of love."[28] To interpret the Lady and the Unicorn series as a *chambre* with all of its architectural implications, we must imagine the tapestries constituting the space they enclose. Hanging from the top of the walls, they would have softened the sharpness of the corners. The number of tapestries, at least six, would have, in turn, worked

22. M. Pastoureau, *Armorial des chevaliers de la Table Ronde* (Paris, 1983), 83.

23. Following this approach and focusing on the theme of the senses, scholars have produced nuanced interpretations of the tapestries' meaning in relation to contemporary discussions of the senses. See, for instance, J.-P. Boudet, "Jean Gerson et La Dame à la Licorne," in *Religion et société urbaine au Moyen âge. Études offertes à Jean-Louis Biget par ses anciens élèves* (Paris, 2000), 551–563; K. Gourlay, "La Dame à la Licorne: A Reinterpretation," *Gazette des Beaux-Arts* 130 (1997), 47–72; J.-P. Jourdan, "Le Sixième Sens et la théologie de l'amour (essai sur l'iconographie des tapisseries à sujets amoureux à la fin du Moyen Âge)," *Journal des Savants* (Jan.–June, 1996), 137–53.

24. For a longer discussion of the relationship between a tapestry set and the courtly love tradition, please see my "Chambres d'amour: Tapestries of Love and the Texturing of Space," *Oxford Art Journal* 31 (2008), 317–336.

25. J. V. Fleming, *The Roman de la Rose: A Study in Allegory and Iconography*, (Princeton, N.J., 1969), 69–70; D. Thoss, "Studien zum *Locus amoenus* im Mittelalter," *Wiener romanistische Arbeiten* 10, (Vienna, 1972); A. Chastel, "Les jardins et les fleurs," *Revue de l'Art* 51 (1981), 42–50; P. Watson, *The Garden of Love in Tuscan Art of the Early Renaissance* (Philadelphia, Pa., 1979); R. Smith Favis, *The Garden of Love in Fifteenth-Century Netherlandish and German Engravings: Some Studies in Secular Iconography in the Late Middle Ages and Early Renaissance* (Ph.D. Diss., University of Pennsylvania, 1974).

26. T. Comito, *The Idea of the Garden in the Renaissance* (New Brunswick, N.J.: Rutgers University Press, 1978), 90–93.

27. V. Gay, *Glossaire archéologique du Moyen Âge et de la Renaissance*, vol. 1 (Paris, 1887), 309–310; J. Labarte, *Inventaire du mobilier de Charles V, roi de France* (Paris, 1879), 362, note 1.

28. C. Dehaisnes, *Documents et extraits divers conçernant l'histoire de l'art dans le Flandre, l'Artois et le Hainaut avant le XVe siècle*, vol. 2 (Lille, 1886), 697; *Histoire générale de la tapisserie*, vol. 3 (Paris, 1880), 24; Dehaisnes, *Documents*, 844, 845; J. Guiffrey, *Histoire de la tapisserie depuis le Moyen Âge jusqu'à nos jours* (Tours, 1886), 40.

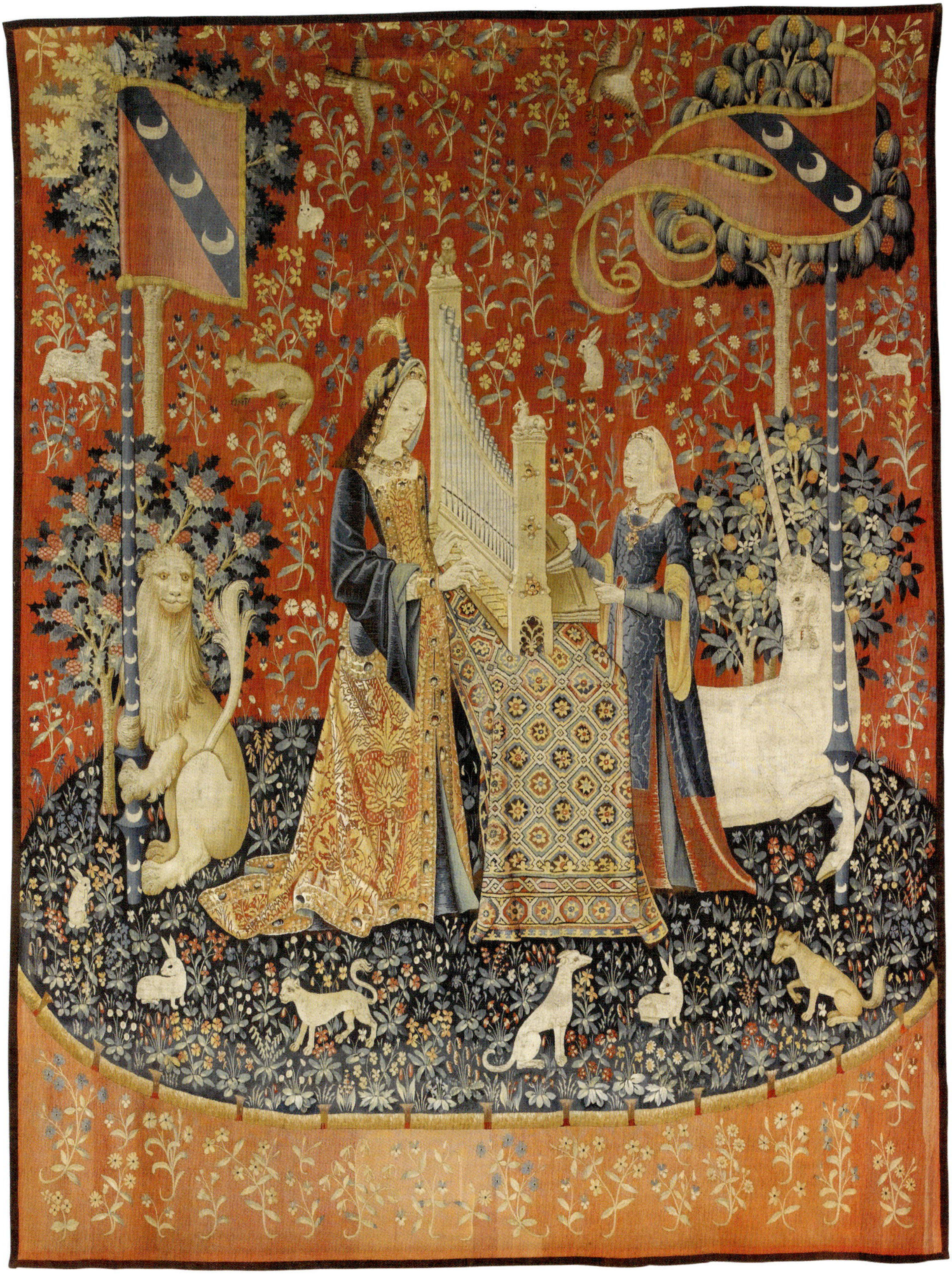

FIGURE 3. Lady with the Organ (from the series Lady and the Unicorn), tapestry, wool, 3.68 × 2.90 meters, Paris, Museum of the Middle Ages (photo: RMN / Art Resource).

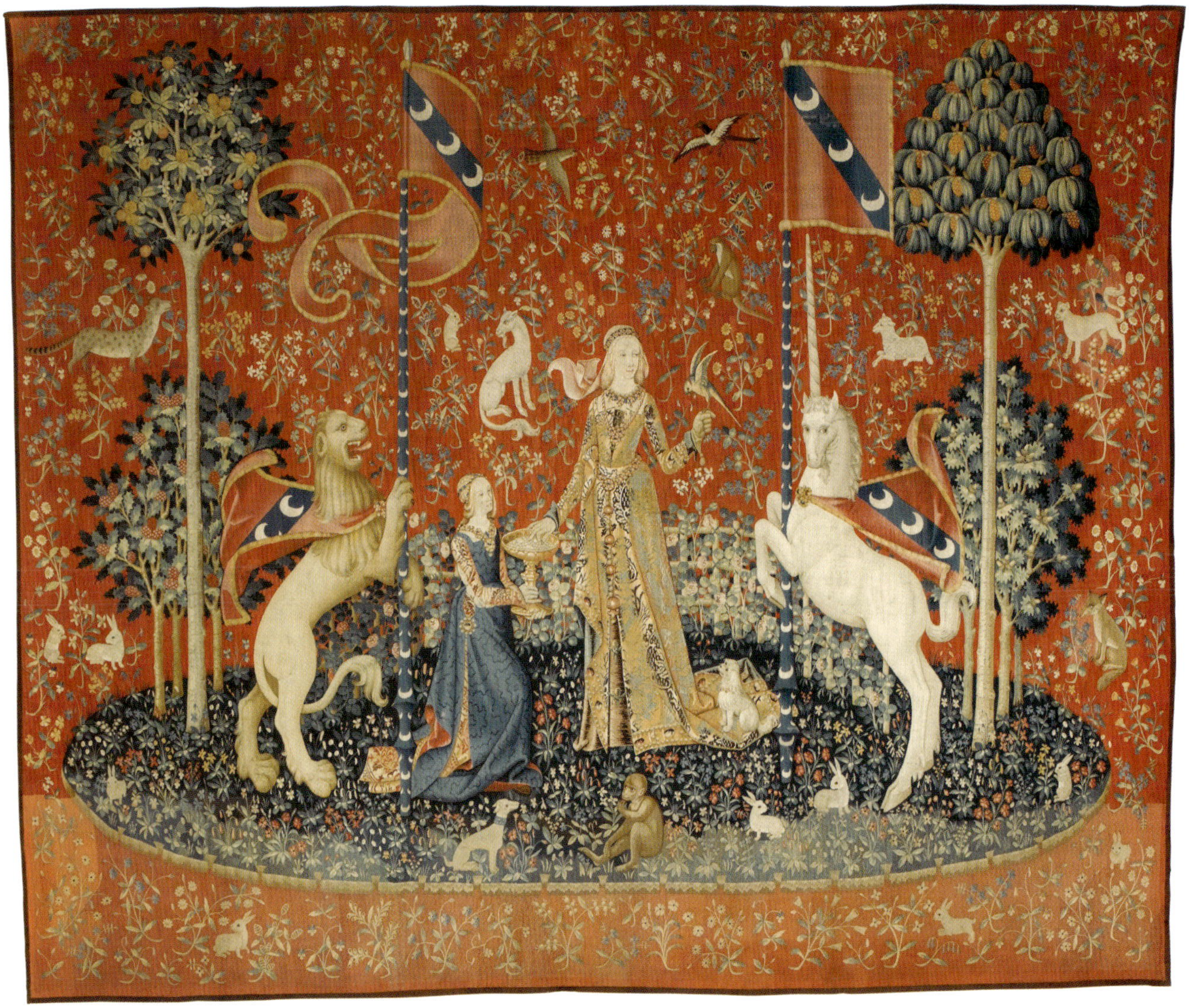

FIGURE 4. Lady with the Parrot (from the series Lady and the Unicorn), tapestry, wool, 3.77 × 4.66 meters, Paris, Museum of the Middle Ages (photo: RMN / Art Resource).

against the sensation that the views of the garden correspond with the existing walls of a room. Finally, no frame controlled these glimpses into the garden and no border limited the expanse of verdure, which encircled the viewer.

Second, the tapestries create an aesthetic that constantly shifts between an impression of surface pattern and of spatial illusionism. The human scale and volume of the figures suggest that the viewer might be able to inhabit their world (Fig. 1, Figs. 3–7). The blue-green semicircles create an island, which is inhabited by the two human figures and their animal companions. Within this delimited field the figures and objects conform to conventions of spatial illusionism. The flora and fauna placed along the red ground, however, create an expansive and repeated pattern spanning the woven panels. The junctures between this backdrop and the cues to an image of three-dimensionality on the island disrupt the spatial illusionism of the figures' environment. Even within the island itself the illusion

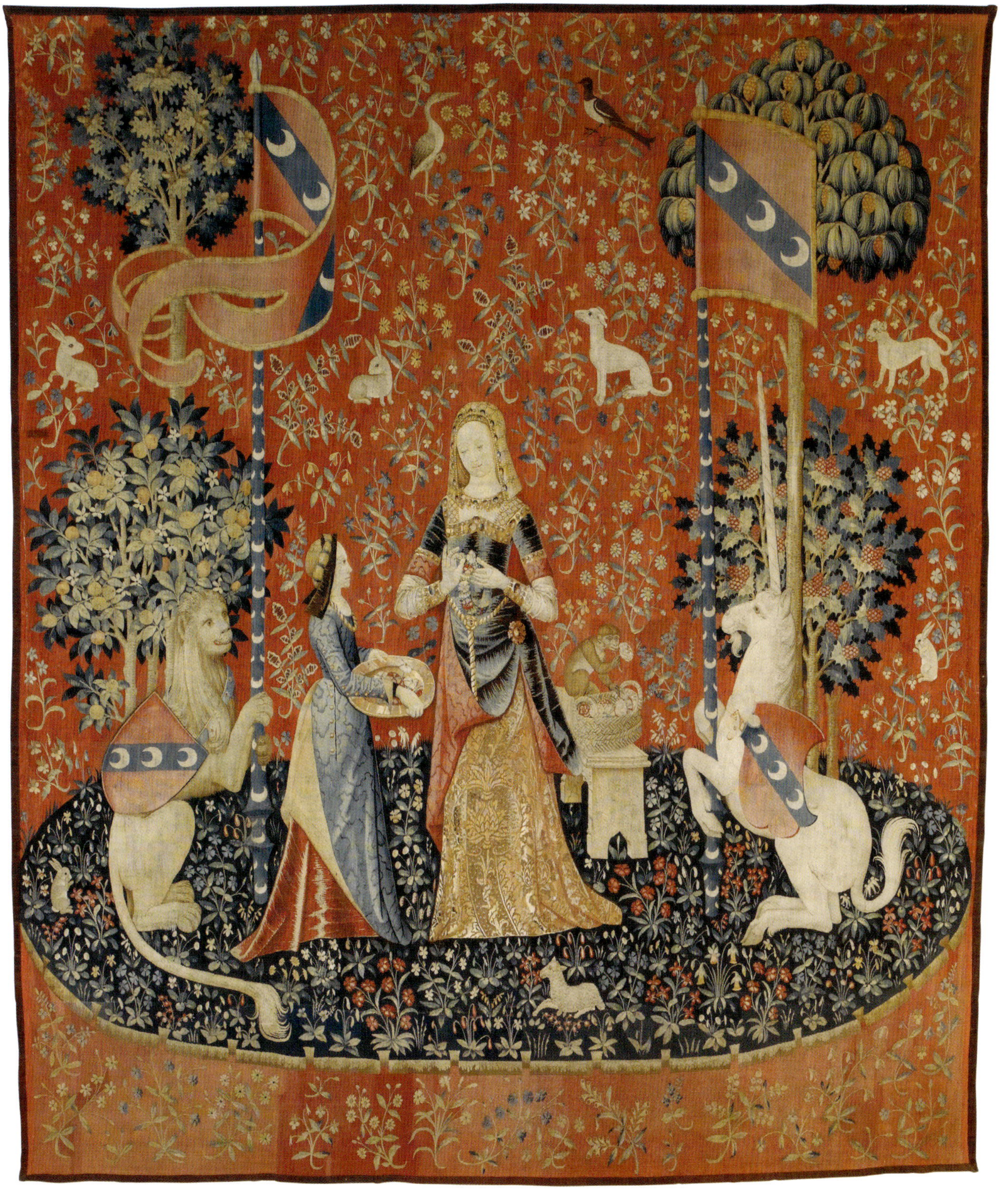

FIGURE 5. Lady with the Carnation (from the series Lady and the Unicorn), tapestry, wool, 3.68 × 3.22 meters, Paris, Museum of the Middle Ages (photo: RMN / Art Resource).

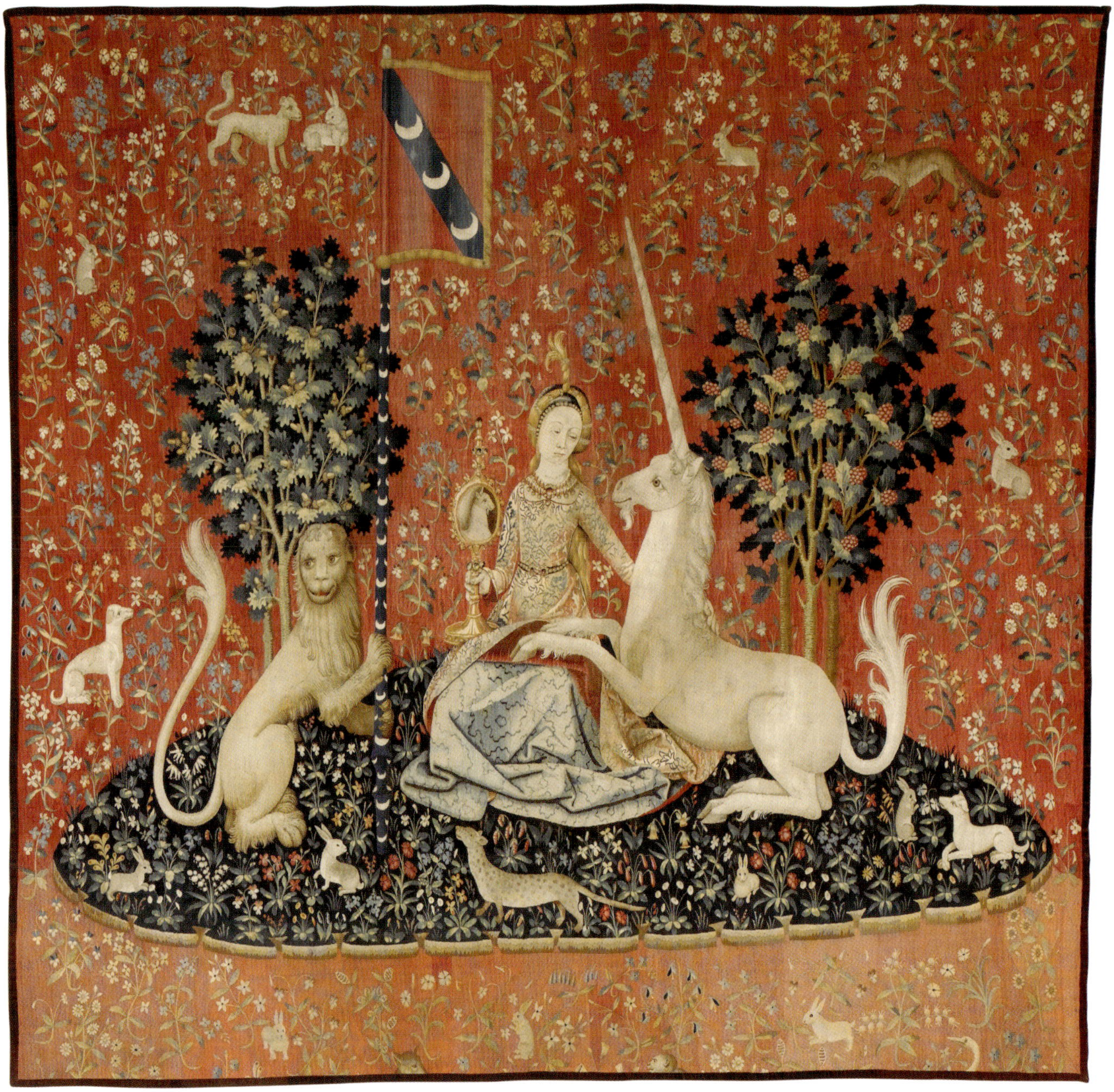

FIGURE 6. Lady with the Mirror (from the series Lady and the Unicorn), tapestry, wool, 3.12 × 3.30 meters, Paris, Museum of the Middle Ages (photo: RMN / Art Resource).

of space is called into question. The foreshortening of the portable organ and the carpet-covered table upon which it is set, for instance, in Figure 3, make these objects appear to recede into space. The Lady and her companion playing the organ stand on either side of the table, flanked by the lion and the unicorn placed before flowering and fruit-bearing trees. Above these trees emerges another pair of similar trees. That the trunks of the higher trees do not extend to the island serves to locate them visually within the realm of the

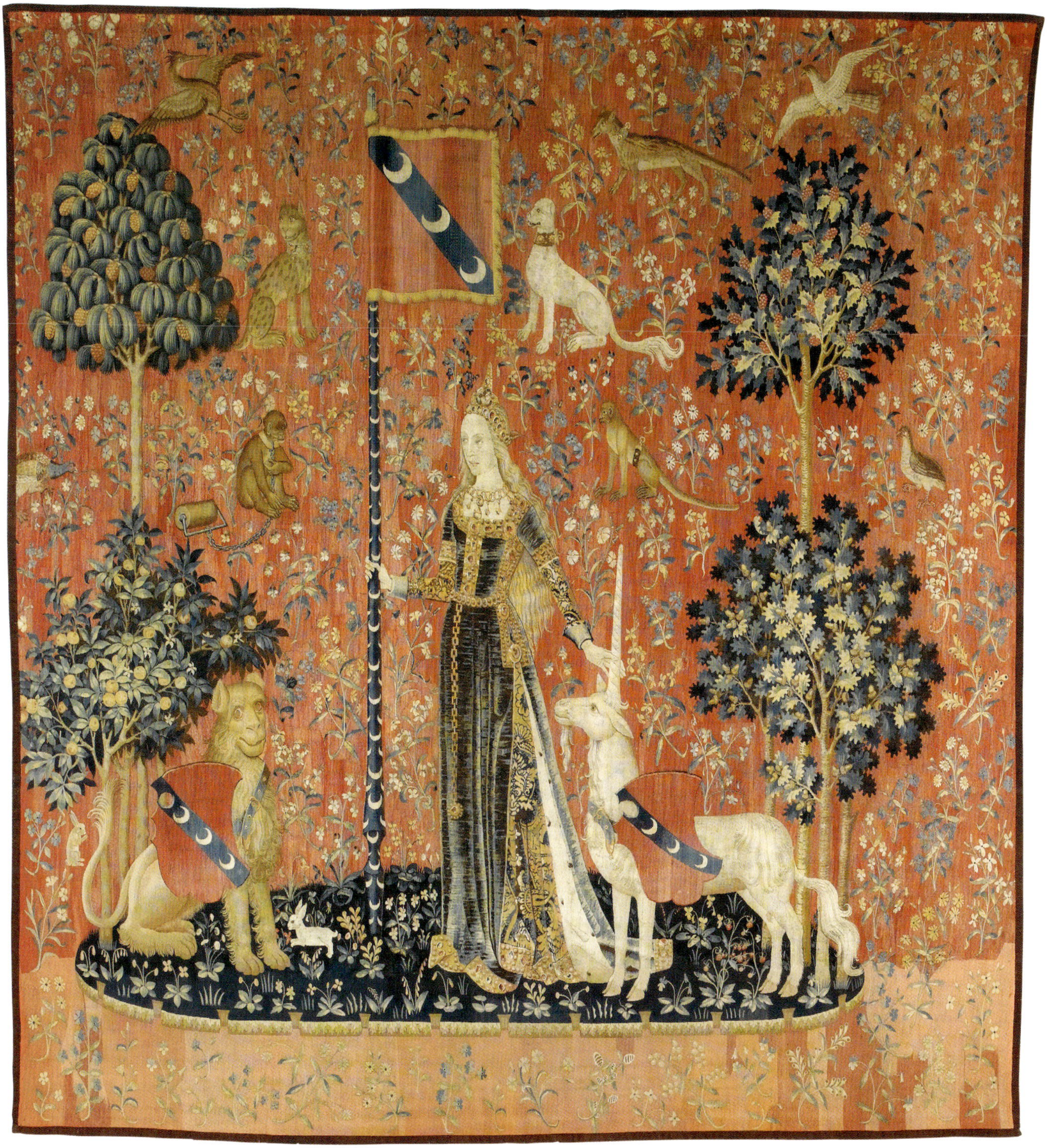

FIGURE 7. Lady and the Unicorn (from the series Lady and the Unicorn), tapestry, wool, 3.73 × 3.58 meters, Paris, Museum of the Middle Ages (photo: RMN / Art Resource).

backdrop. The similarity of the four trees creates a repetition that, in turn, asks us to question whether the three-dimensional space of the island is distinct from the patterned surface of the backdrop. Or, in Figure 4, we might wonder whether the Lady holds the parrot, or if she merely gestures to one of the animals that populate the realm of the backdrop and if the flowers and vines that appear behind her are extensions of the woven trellis or components of the floral backdrop. The tension between surface pattern and spatial illusionism denies the viewer the possibility of identifying with and inhabiting the world it represents.

The figures' striking lack of engagement with the viewer underscores the self-sufficiency of the depicted environment they inhabit. The lady's gaze is not directed outwards but toward the expanse of garden to her side. In each tapestry she and her companions intently pursue their discrete activities; they communicate with neither the figures in adjacent panels nor the viewer. Consequently, their gestures or positions do not indicate how the panels should be organized nor are their activities directed towards a specific point that the viewer might occupy. No spot affords a more complete or propitious view of the woven garden for the viewer.

Third, the materiality of the tapestry prompts an experience that is both visual and tactile. Its woven surface reminds viewers that these hangings physically surround and enclose them. The tapestries appeal to the viewer's body in two ways: using attention to surface pattern and texture to create awareness of the woven object's tactility and by creating a space, reminding viewers that they are bodies in space.

What emerges when we incorporate these three aspects of the medium into a reading of the Lady and the Unicorn series is a model of spectatorship that does not lead to the objectification of the female protagonist. As we have seen, the viewers can neither identify with the lady and her companions nor imagine themselves within the environment these figures create. Consequently, the tapestry set destabilizes conventional interpretations of the courtly love tradition, according to which the male subject objectivizes the courtly lady and recreates her in his image.[29] The figures invite the viewer to take part in the pleasures the woven garden offers, while denying that access. Moreover, the female figures resist appropriation by the male viewer through the indeterminacy of their gaze and their vacillation between three dimensionality and surface pattern; the garden prevents him from becoming its master. Finally, the focus on the luxurious fabrics worn by these women and on the tactility of the tapestries points to a kind of looking that integrates touch and inscribes the women's presence in the image.[30]

Toward a Method for Interpreting Tapestry: The Story of Troy

As in the case of the Lady and the Unicorn series, scholarship on the second example, the History of Troy series, has focused on questions of subject matter, patronage, and artistic design. The textual and pictorial evidence relating to these tapestries is, however, more complete. Consequently, the responses scholars have given to traditional art-historical questions are less hypothetical and more helpful in furthering our understanding of these tapestries. In terms of subject matter, the *tituli* incorporated into surviving tapestries, which appear in Latin on the bottom and in French at the top, allow us to identify individual events. Benoît de Ste.-Maure and Guido delle Colonne's transformations of Homer's story provide precise textual sources for the set.[31] Inventory records supply a list of individuals who

29. This dynamic is implicit in traditional interpretations of the courtly love literature. For an overview of recent critiques of this traditional approach, please see: E. J. Burns, S. Kay, R. Krueger, and H. Solterer, "Feminism and the Discipline of Old French Studies: Une bele disjointure," in H. Bloch and S. Nichols, eds., *Medievalism and the Modernist Temper* (Baltimore, Md., 1996), 225–266; E. J. Burns, "Courtly Love Who Needs It? Recent Feminist Work in the Medieval French Tradition," *Signs* 27 (2001), 24–7.

30. This feature of the tapestries would create a visual parallel to the role of fabrics and clothes in courtly love literature (E. J. Burns, "'Speculum of the courtly lady': Women, Love, and Clothes," *Journal of Medieval and Early Modern Studies* 29 (1999), 253.

31. M.-R. Jung, "La légende de Troie en France au moyen âge: analyse des versions françaises et bibliographie raisonnée des manuscrits," *Romanica Helvetica* 114 (Basel, 1996); Asselberghs, "Les Tapisseries" (as in note 8), 157–161; McKendrik, "The *Great History of Troy*" (as in note 8), 43; Rapp Buri and Stucky-Schürer, *Burgundische Tapisserien* (as in note 8), 313.

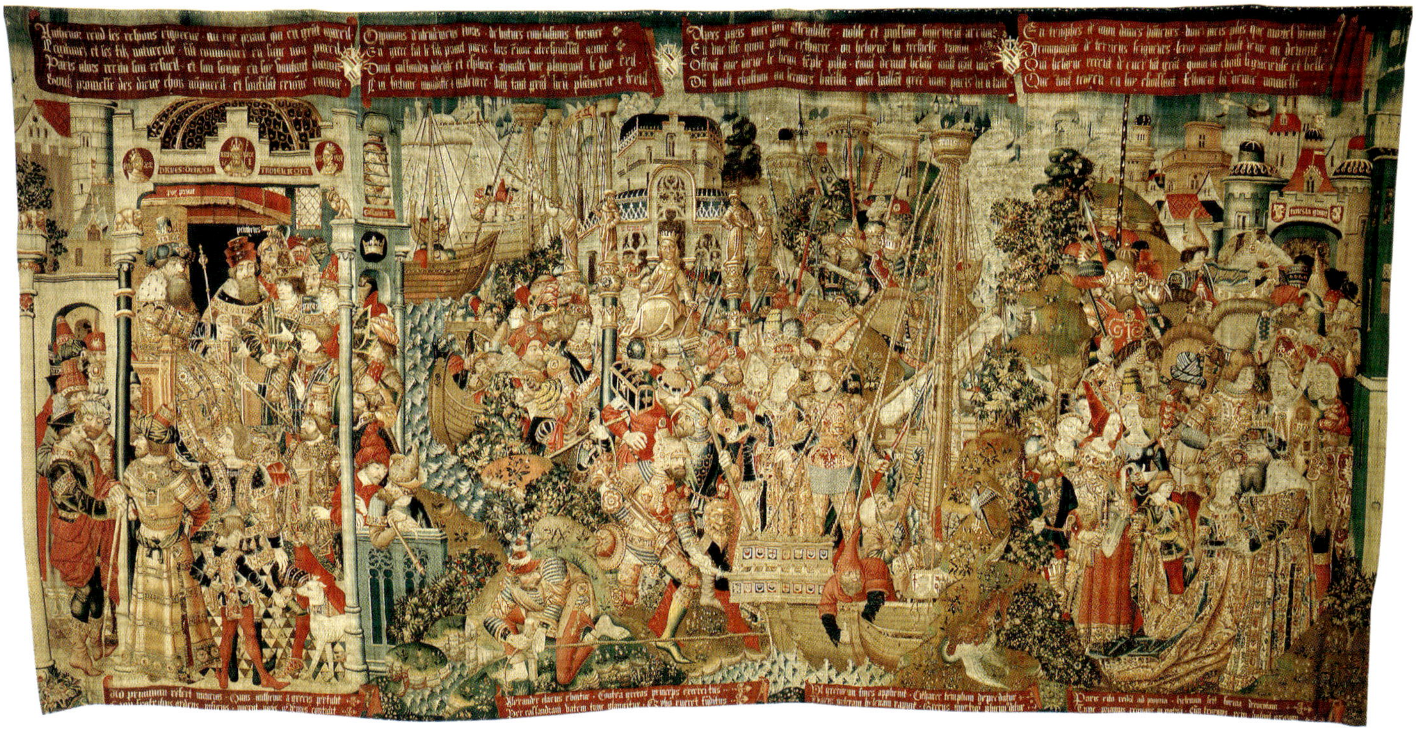

FIGURE 8. The Abduction of Helen (from the Trojan War Series), tapestry, wool and silk, *c.* 1475, 4.80 × 9.60 meters, Zamora, Cathedral Museum (photo: IRPA, Brussels, ©KIK-IRPA).

possessed tapestries of the story of Troy, even though it remains difficult to identify the patron who purchased or commissioned a set for which extant tapestries survive. Finally, the existence of preparatory drawings against which the corresponding hangings have been compared has advanced the discussion of these tapestries from a search for their original designer to the distinct ways in which the tapestries depart from the drawings (Figs. 10, 13).[32] These differences range from details, like the replacement of a male effigy for one of Minerva in the drawing and the addition of an author portrait in the panel featuring the Trojan horse (Figs. 12–13), or the general flattening of space that appears in the tapestries, in contrast to the drawings. This type of investigation has led to a focus on the specificity of tapestry and the role of the weavers in its creation.

We might go further, however, along this line of inquiry and take into account the other characteristics of the medium: spatial, tactile, and ceremonial. In so doing, I propose that the Troy tapestries can be understood as part of a contemporary tradition of battle performances, rather than being limited to the particular events they depict from the legend. Within the chronologic span of the production of the multiple woven versions of the History of Troy, battles were the subject matter of the stages erected along processional routes, of large-scale urban drama, and of the tournaments, which preceded and followed ceremonial occasions.[33] The tapestries prompt a similar experience of violence.

As in the textual versions of the Trojan War upon

32. Identifying the designer of the tapestries still remains the focus of certain scholars: Nicole Reynaud, "Un peintre français cartonnier de tapisseries au XVe siècle: Henri Vulcop," *Revue de l'Art* 22 (1973), 6–21 (cited in note 19) and, with a revised attribution: François Avril and Nicole Reynaud, *Les Manuscrits à peintures en France 1440–1520* (Paris, 1993), 64–66. For a discussion of these drawings or "petits patrons," please see: A. Rapp Buri and Monica Stucky-Schürer, *Burgundische Tapisserien* (as in note 8), 313–325.

33. No study has covered the range of battles that formed part of this variety of performance practices in the late Middle Ages. In the case of the battles that formed part of the story of the

which they drew, images of battle occupy most of the tapestries that comprised the eleven-piece set.[34] The first two tapestries provide a prelude to the war: one focuses on the Mission of Antenor, the other on Helen's abduction (Fig. 8). The first scene of battle, the Greek's capture of the Island of Tenedon, follows, after which the Greeks arrive in Troy in the fourth tapestry. The remaining panels focus on the assault of and victory over the city. Key events transpire in each one: Achilles and Hector negotiate and Hector prepares for battle in the sixth tapestry; the death of Achilles occurs in the eighth (Fig. 2, 9); and Penthesilea, queen of the Amazons, and her troops join the Trojan defense in the ninth (Fig. 11). The final tapestry depicts the Greeks' gift of the horse and the fall of Troy (Fig. 12). Each of the pieces surviving from what would have been several sets measures about five by nine and a half meters. The woven story as a whole would have spanned at least one hundred meters in length.[35]

The scale of the tapestries, their subject matter, and their description in inventories identify them in terms of their destination: *salles*, or banquet halls.[36] Inventories differentiate this type of tapestry from *chambres*, on the one hand, and *chapelles* (tapestries which formed part of the adornment of sites for private prayer and liturgical celebration), on the other. Like the *chambre* that the Lady and Unicorn tapestries evoke, the individual tapestries of the story of Troy were not seen as framed and discrete pictures; they would have covered and transformed the walls of the banquet hall. In the process, the tapestry set became architecture, surrounding the viewer with images of battle. The life-size figures often seem to spill over the edge of the woven fabric, unhampered by the barrier a border or frame would impose. Consequently, the boundaries between the space in which the woven action takes place and the one the viewer occupies are permeable.

The materiality of the tapestry, however, disallows the viewers' perception that they might potentially enter into this fray. For instance, the eighth tapestry (Figs. 2 and 9) confronts us initially with a sense of confusion, which gradually begins to make sense as we situate events both temporally and spatially and identify the relationships between what might initially appear to be a confusion of bodies. The *tituli* establish a preliminary division into three parts. We move from the battle characterized by Troilus's death, to the moment of Achilles' death, to another battle, this time focusing on the confrontation between Ajax and Darius. To move back to the first episode in this panel (Fig. 9): this, one of the numerous encounters between the Greeks and the Trojans, captures the movement and chaos of a battle through the profusion of overlapping figures engaged in exaggerated gestures and dynamic motions. The identifying tags and figural groupings serve to organize the section of the tapestry into discrete, although related, groups. Above on the left, Achilles is in the process of decapitating Troilus, whose body Achilles then carries around the walls of the city, as king Memnon confronts him.[37] These figures stand out from the mass

---

Trojan War, the heroes of this legendary material were featured in the stages of entry processions. Hector was particularly popular as one of the Nine Worthies, a common feature of such procession: P. Meyer, "Les Neufs Preux," *Bulletin de la Société des Anciens Textes Français* 9 (1883), 45–54; H. Schroeder, *Der Topos der Nine Worthies in Literatur und Bildender Kunst* (Göttingen, 1971). Although no performance records for large-scale dramatic versions of the Troy legend survive, an extensive tradition of manuscripts and printed versions of Jacques Milet's play script does: L. Durham, "Jacques Milet's 'Destruction de Troie la Grant': Reassessing French Theatre in the late Medieval Period" (Ph.D. Diss., University of Pittsburgh, 2009). Events from the Trojan War were performed at a banquet held in honor of Louis of Anjou in Avignon in 1382 and in 1389 in Paris, following the entry of Isabel of Bavaria into the city: G. Cohen, "Mystères réligieux et profanes en Avignon à la fin du XIVe siècle," *Neophilologus* XXXIV (1939), 310–313; J. Froissart, *Chroniques*, XIV, ed. J. Kervyn de Lettenhove (Brussels, 1872), 15–16; McKendrik, "*Great History of Troy*," (as in note 8), 77–78. For a general overview of tournaments, please see: D. Crouch, *Tournament* (London, 2005); R. C. Clephan, *The Mediaeval Tournament* (New York, 1995).

34. The drawings, surviving pieces, and references to sets in archival documents strongly support the argument that the original sets comprised eleven pieces: Rapp Buri and Stucky-Schürer, *Burgundische Tapisserien* (as in note 8), 313.

35. Rapp Buri and Stucky-Schürer, *Burgundische Tapisserien* (as in note 8), 314.

36. Weigert, "Chambres d'Amour" (as in note 24), 325.

37. James Harper correctly identifies Memnon, to whom the *titulus* (but not the name on his sword) mistakenly refers to as king

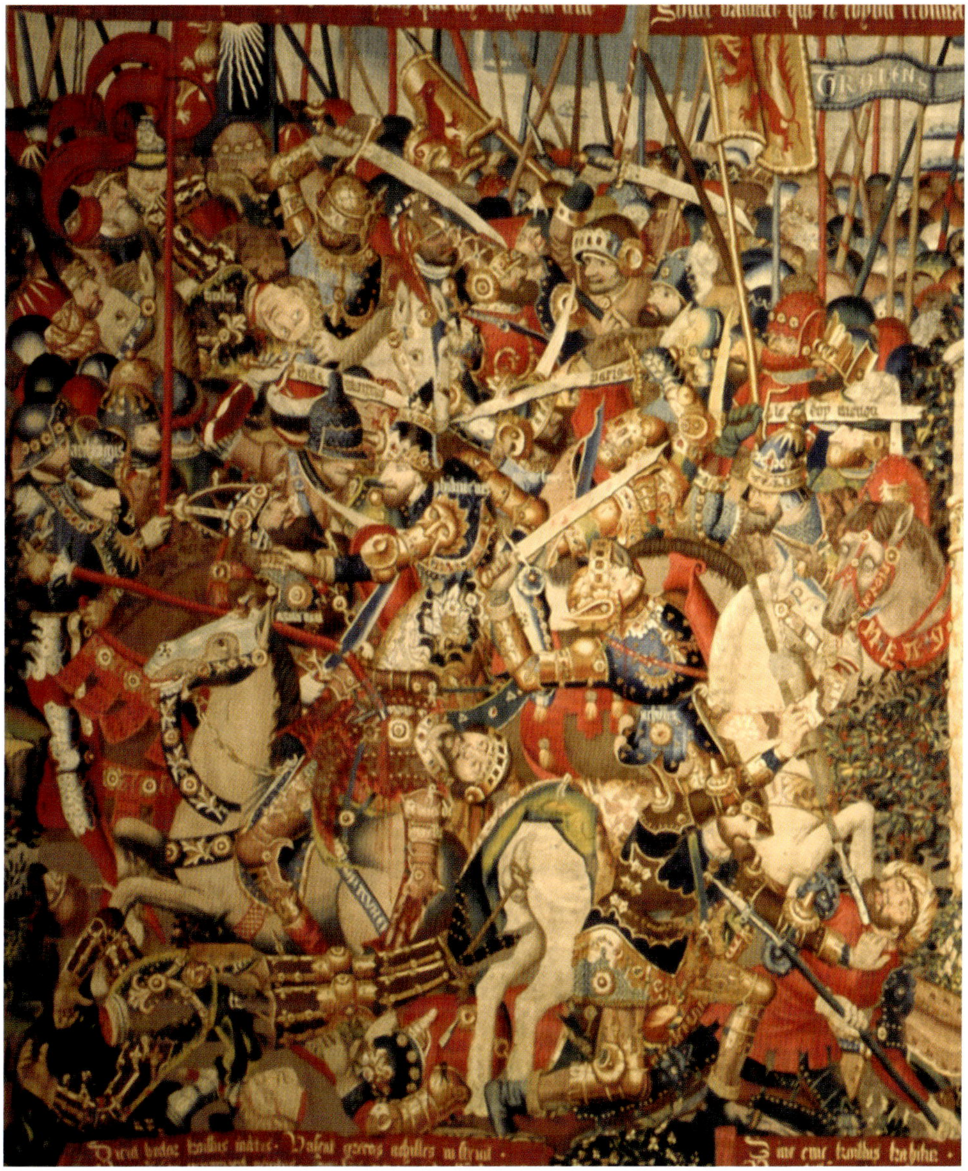

FIGURE 9. Achilles' Death, detail of the death of Troilus (from the Trojan War Series), tapestry, wool and silk, *c.* 1475, 4.81 × 9.42 meters, Zamora, Cathedral Museum (photo: Cuauhtli Gutierrez).

of bodies and armor around them. At the same time, we cannot attach all the limbs, weapons, and miscellaneous armor to a specific warrior and the junctures between a figure and those around it are often difficult to determine. Again and again the spatial distance separating the warriors along the plane of the battlefield is ambiguous and the juxtaposition of shapes creates a pattern. The constant vacillation between figures

Merion. "Turks as Trojans; Trojans as Turks: Visual Imagery of the Trojan War and the Politics of Cultural Identity in Fifteenth-century Europe," in *Postcolonial Approaches to the European Middle Ages: Translating Cultures*, ed. A. J. Kabir and D. Williams (Cambridge, 2005), 165 and 177, note 37.

situated and acting within space and surface pattern underscores the tactility of the woven image.

Finally, the occasions during which these woven battles were seen contributed to their effect on viewers. The story of Troy tapestries were reserved for the celebration of important and diverse occasions. Each banquet was a carefully choreographed event through which the power and wealth of the ruler was established and reiterated. To take just one case of the display of the story of Troy, the French king Louis XII had his set placed on the walls of the banquet hall at the Castle of Blois, when Philip the Handsome and Joanna of Castile came to visit in 1501.[38] It is likely that this tapestry set was based on the same preparatory drawings now in Paris and that the ninth hanging, now in the Victoria and Albert Museum comes from the set belonging to Louis XII (Fig. 11).[39] My point here is more general: the subject matter was carefully chosen and directed at this particular audience and the meaning of the tapestry was inflected by this occasion. Jeffrey Chipps Smith has argued persuasively that the History of Gideon tapestries were instrumental in positioning Philip the Good as a new Gideon, whose victory over the infidels in his proclaimed Crusade against the Turks, would mirror Gideon's victory over the Mideonites.[40] In line with this argument, the tapestries of the story of Troy prompted the ruler and his allies, that is Louis XII and Philip the Handsome, to identify with the victor in the woven story.

Yet if we take into account the specificity of the medium that I have just outlined, this process of identification is much more complex. Given the particular players in this banquet scenario, they both could trace their lineage back to the Trojans, or alternately to the Greeks.[41] To further complicate things, James Harper has recently argued that the Turkish garb of some of the vanquished Trojans establishes an alternate lineage in which the Turks descend from the Trojans, thereby promoting an ideology of the inevitability of Turkish defeat through Crusade.[42] Which of the warriors with whom the audience was meant to identify remained ambiguous. And if we move beyond a discussion of subject matter, the process of identification becomes even more complex and interesting. The materiality of the tapestry emphasized in the attention to surface pattern denies the viewer's identification with the woven figures; its spatial disposition prevents viewers from achieving an overview of the story as a whole. Unlike visual technologies from linear perspective, to the camera, to simulated warfare, the tapestries do not situate viewers as masters over an event or situate them on the side of the victor.[43] Nor do they promote the

38. Jules Guiffrey cites the description of this occasion included in T. Godefroy, *Cérémonial François*, vol. 2 (Paris, 1649), 731: "Et pour parler de l'accoustrement du chasteau de Blois, la grande salle par où entrèrent lesdits Archiduc et Archiduchesse estoit fort grande et estoit tendue d'une tapisserie de la *Destruction de Troye*, et pareillement une chapelle qui estoit au bout de ladite salle," J. J. Guiffrey, *Tapisserie Française*, vol. 1 of *Histoire Générale de la Tapisserie*, ed. E. Müntz (Paris, 1878), 67; McKendrik, "*Great History of Troy*" (as in note 8), 55.

39. The panel was acquired by the Victoria and Albert Museum in June 1887 and can be traced back to the Château de Bayard, near Grenoble: G. Wingfield Digby, assisted by W. Hefford, *Victoria and Albert Museum. The Tapestry Collection: Medieval and Renaissance* (London, 1980), 17; J. Guiffrey, "La Guerre de Troie. A propos de dessins récemment acquis par le Louvre," *Revue de l'Art Ancien et Moderne* 5 (1899), 506–509. The medallion at the top of the panel is the device of Charles VIII. On the ownership of the panel, please see J. P. Asselberghs, "Charles VIII's Trojan War Tapestry," *Victoria and Albert Museum Yearbook* 1 (1969), 82–83; G. Souchal, "Charles VIII et la tenture de la guerre de Troie," *Revue Belge d'Archéologie et d'Histoire de l'Art* 39 (1970), 185–189. Asselberghs dates it to 1489–93, "Les Tapisseries" (as in note 8), 177; Rapp Buri and Stucky-Schürer date this panel to the late 1480s early 1490s.

40. Chipps Smith, "Portable Propaganda"(as in note 3), 124.

41. For the role of the Troy legend in the construction of French royal ideology, please see: E. Morrison, "Illuminations of the *Roman de Troie* and French Royal Dynastic Ambition (1260–1340)" (Ph.D. Diss., Cornell University, 2002), 46–57; "Linking Ancient Troy and Medieval France: Illuminations of an Early Copy of the *Roman de Troie*," *Medieval Manuscripts, Their Makers and Users. A Special Issue of Viator in Honor of Richard and Mary Rouse* (Turnhout, 2011).

42. James Harper, "Turks as Trojans"(as in note 37), 159–166.

43. V. Groebner, *Defaced: The Visual Culture of Violence in the Late Middle Ages* (New York, 2004); J. Butler, "Introduction to the Paperback," and "Torture and the Ethics of Photography: Thinking with Sontag," in *Frames of War: When is Life Grievable?* (London, 2010), ix–xxx, 63–100.

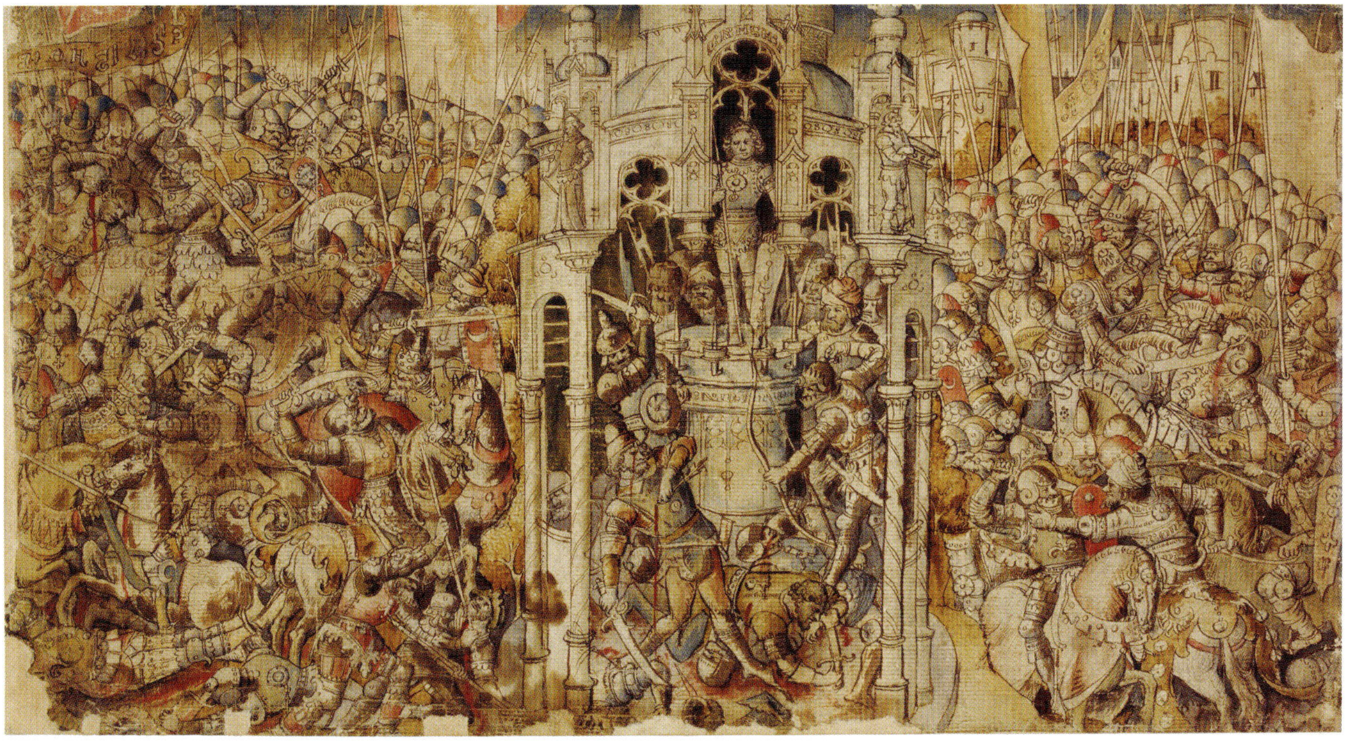

FIGURE 10. The Death of Achilles (drawing corresponding with tapestry no. 8 from the Trojan War Series), pen and ink with watercolor on paper, *c.* 1465, 30 × 57.5 cm, Paris, Louvre Museum, Département des Arts graphiques R.F. 2144 (photo: RMN / Art Resource).

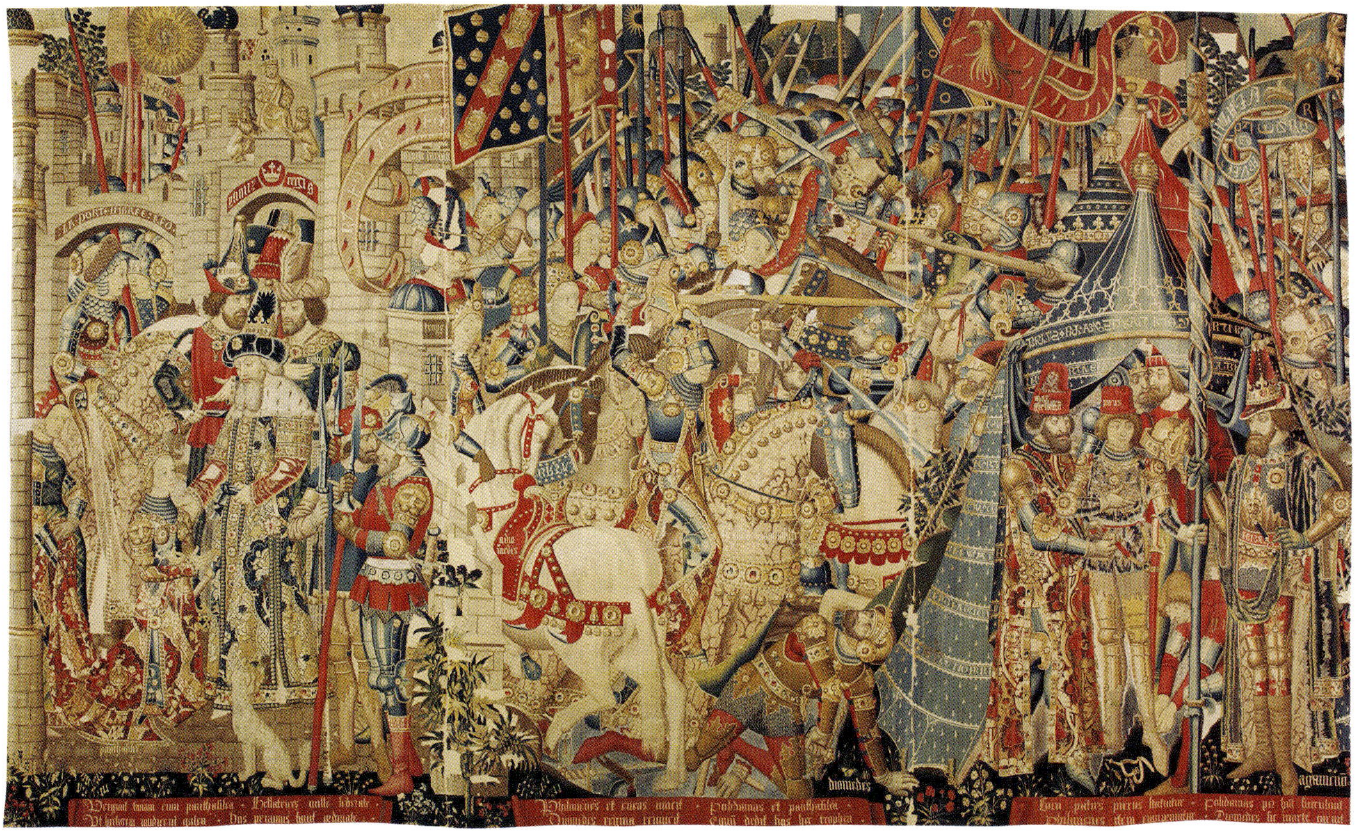

FIGURE 11. Penthesilia Enters the Battle (from the Trojan War Series), tapestry, wool and silk, late 1480s or early 1490s, 4.16 × 7.37 meters, London, Victoria and Albert Museum (photo: Victoria and Albert Museum, London).

illusion that their fictive world corresponds with that of the viewer. Rather than promoting actual battles, they might represent an alternate form of violence, one that does not solicit imitation. Like the other battle performances of their time, they might have encouraged a non-destructive participation in violence.

To conclude, these brief discussions of the Lady and the Unicorn and Story of Troy tapestries suggest how art history might learn from tapestry. It might recognize the insufficiency of methods of connoisseurship, patronage studies, and certain models of iconography. It might do away with an artificial separation between medieval and Renaissance and appreciate the continuity evidenced in art produced in the fifteenth and sixteenth centuries with what came before. Finally, it might revise its account of spectatorship. Rather than promoting the idea of an intellectualized, disembodied, and exclusively visual experience of the image, these tapestry sets signal their physical impact on the viewer's body. Within this phenomenological account, the image maintains its presence as fabricated object and resists being appropriated by the gaze of viewers into a narrative that fulfils and promotes their mastery over others as objects of desire or destruction.

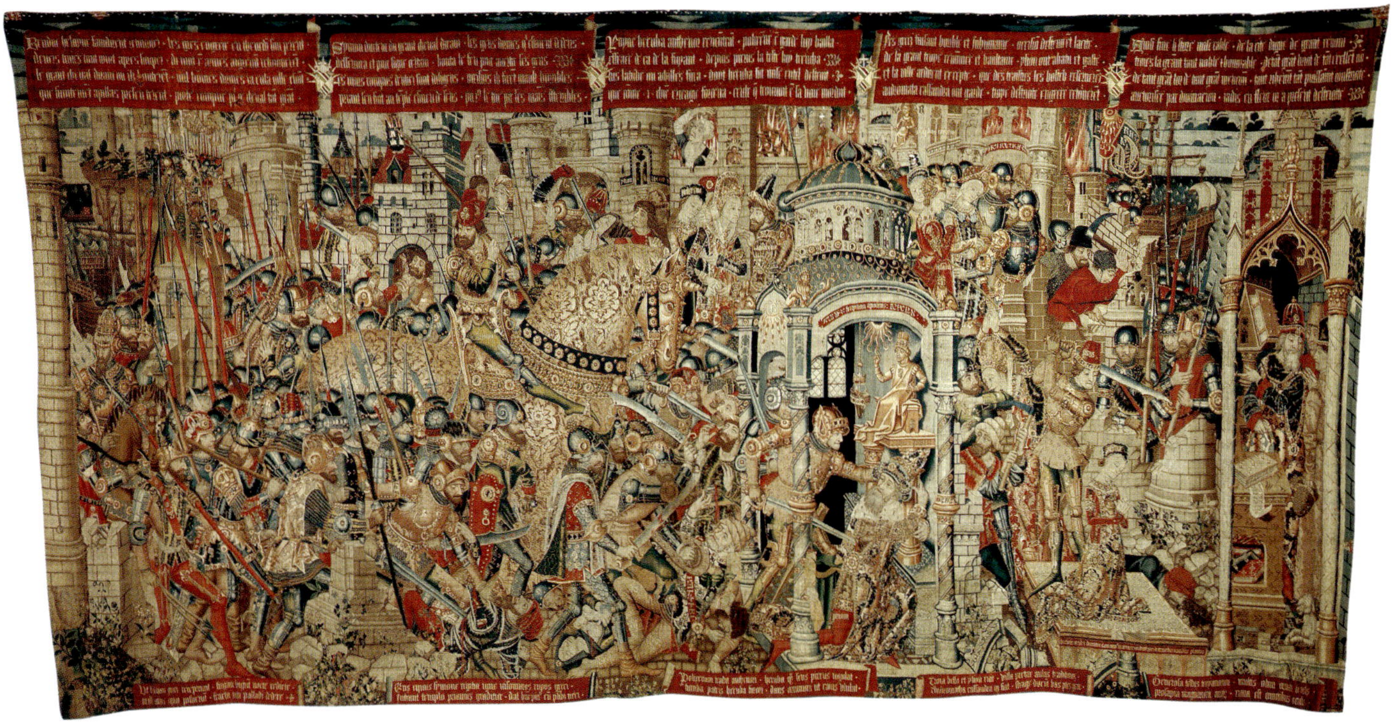

FIGURE 12. The Fall of Troy (from the Trojan War Series), tapestry, wool and silk, *c.* 1475, 4.81 × 9.42 meters, Zamora, Cathedral Museum (photo: IRPA, Brussels, ©KIK-IRPA).

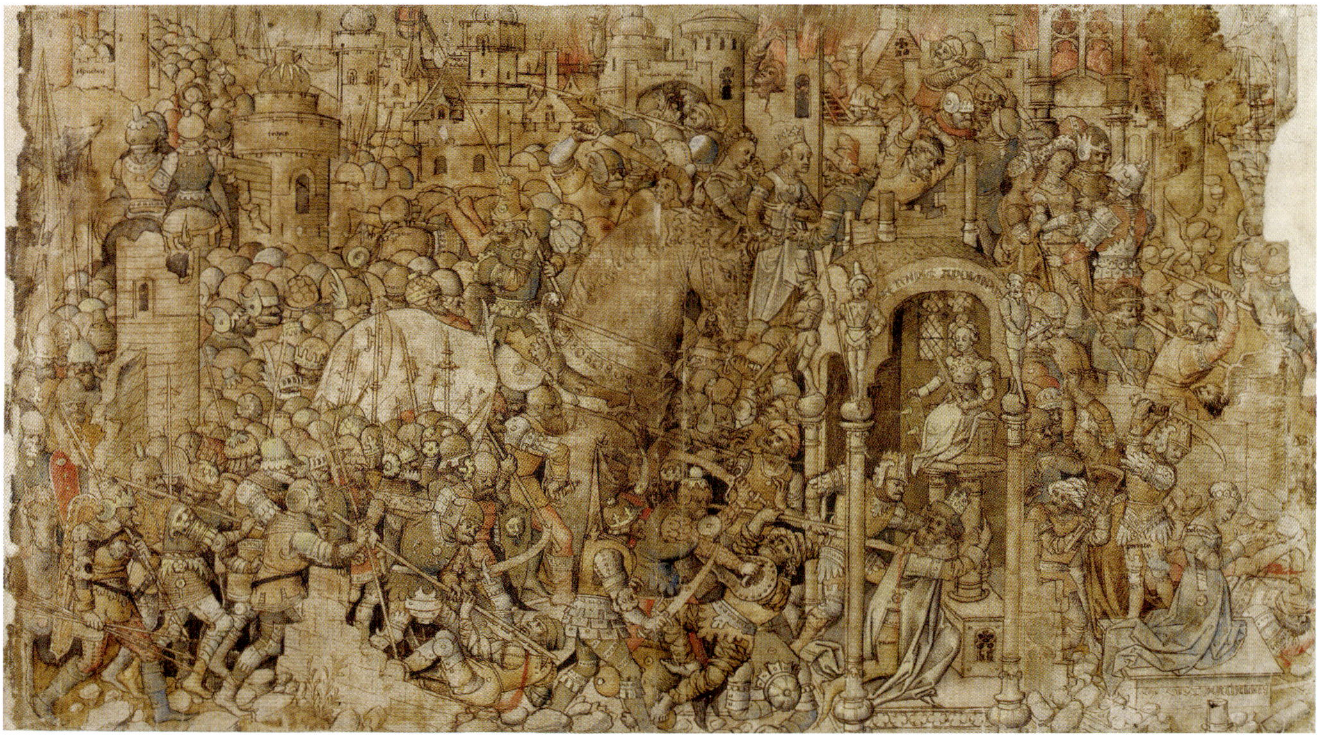

FIGURE 13. The Fall of Troy (drawing corresponding with tapestry no. 11 from the Trojan War Series), pen and ink with watercolor on paper, *c.* 1465, 30 × 57.5 cm, Paris, Louvre Museum, Département des Arts graphiques R.F. 2144 (photo: RMN / Art Resource).

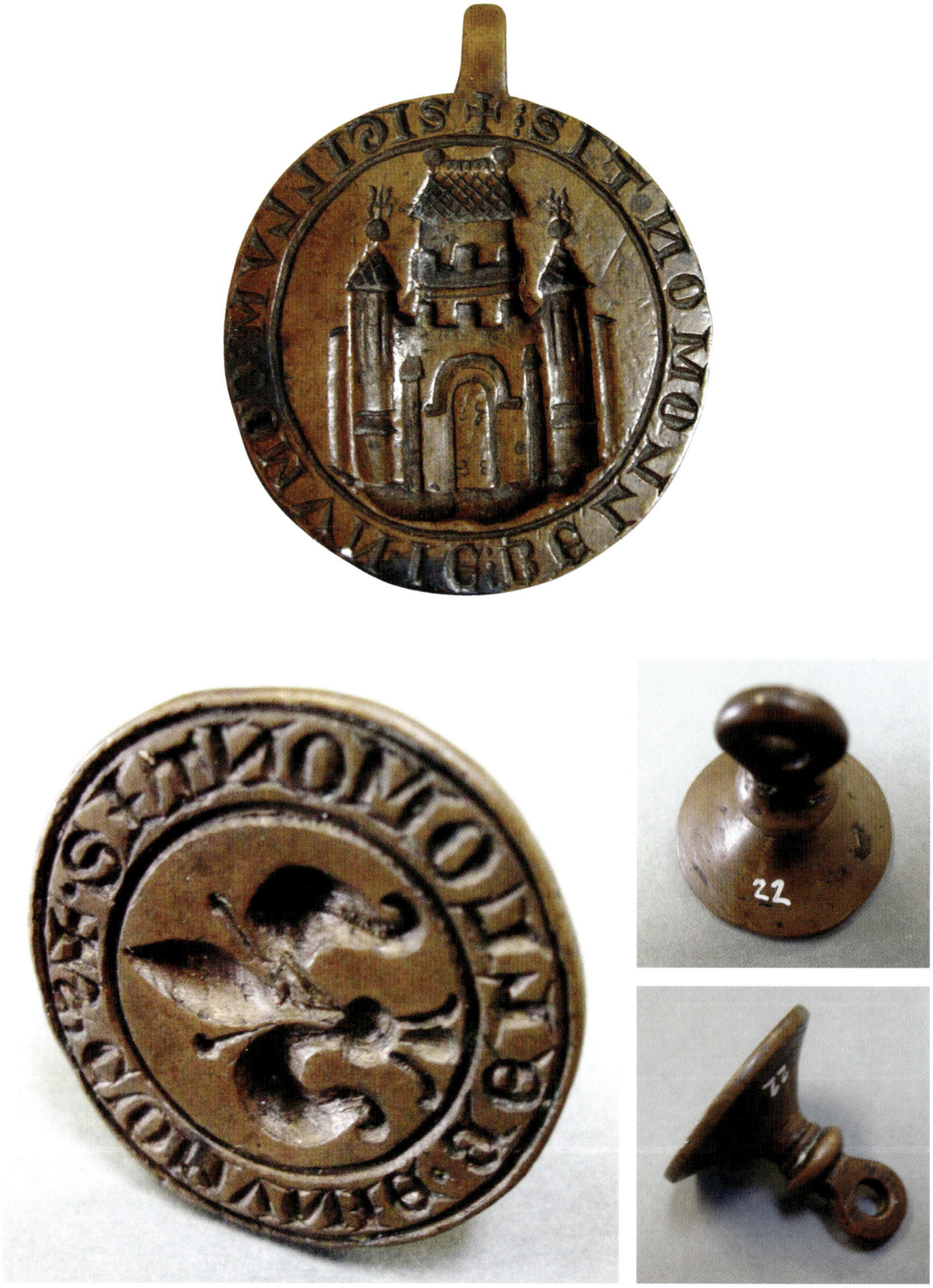

FIGURE 1. City seal of Beaumont; matrix, late twelfth or early thirteenth century, Paris, Archives nationales, Collection de sceaux-matrices, 840; Various views of the counter-seal of the city seal of Beaumont, Paris, Archives nationales, Collection de sceaux-matrices, 22.

BRIGITTE BEDOS-REZAK

Outcast: Seals of the Medieval West and Their Epistemological Frameworks (Twelfth to Twenty-first Century)

SOME 50,000 seal dies (Fig. 1) and about two to three million seal impressions (Fig. 2) have come down to us from medieval western Europe;[1] of these seals, the very few that have found their ways into art-historical studies tend to be thematically and technically significant (Fig. 3). Truth be told, the vast corpus of medieval seals has escaped the attention of art historians and, it should be noted, of most historians as well. The aesthetic mediocrity of their vast majority (Fig. 4) and their formulaic and stereotypical character (Fig. 5)

1. Scholars who attempted to estimate the number of extant seal matrices and seal impressions in western Europe have emphasized the difficulty in reaching firm conclusions: M. Pastoureau, *Les sceaux* (Turnhout, 1981), 43, 46–47; M. Fabre, *Sceau médiéval. Analyse d'une practique culturelle* (Paris, 2001), 225–27.

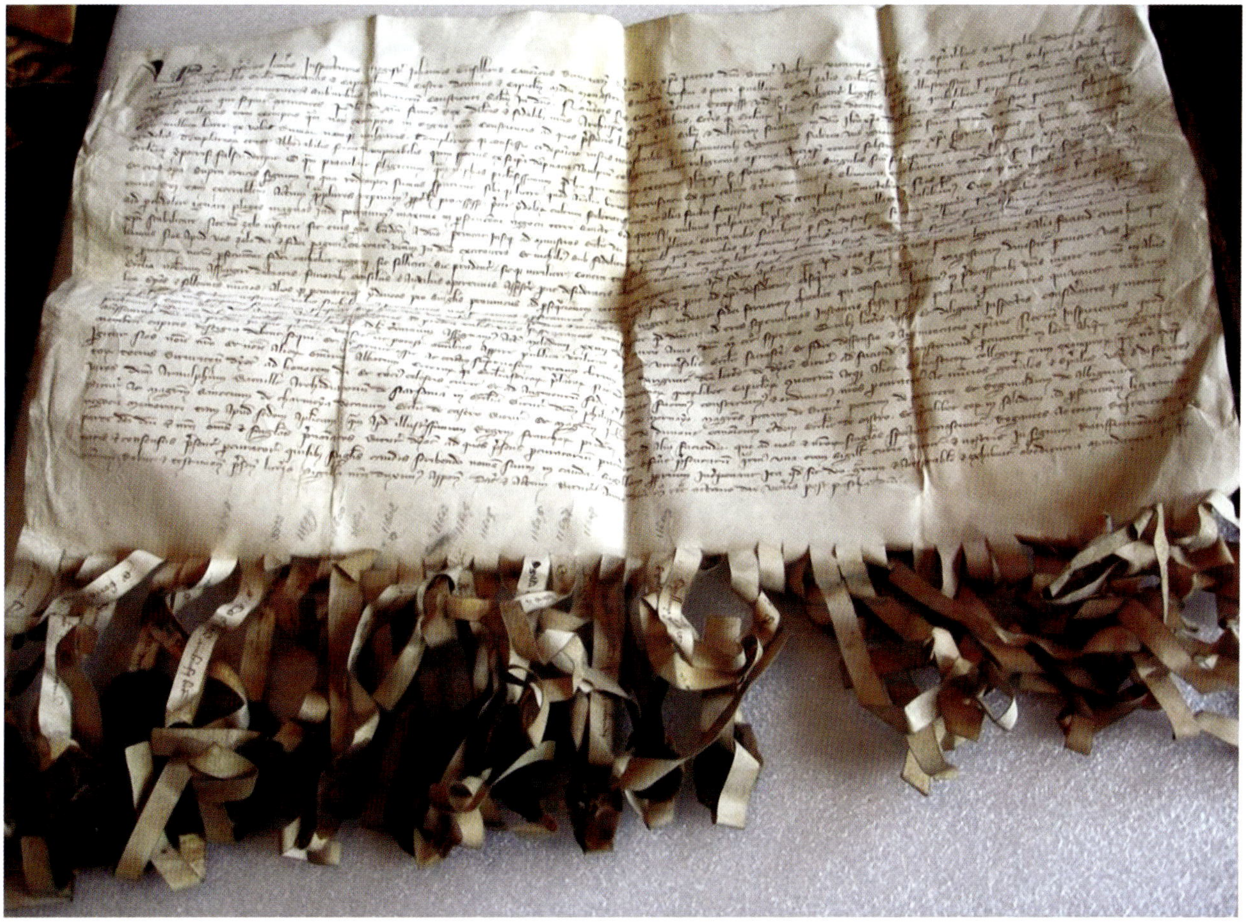

FIGURE 2. Paris, Archives nationales, J 414B no. 108; 1308.

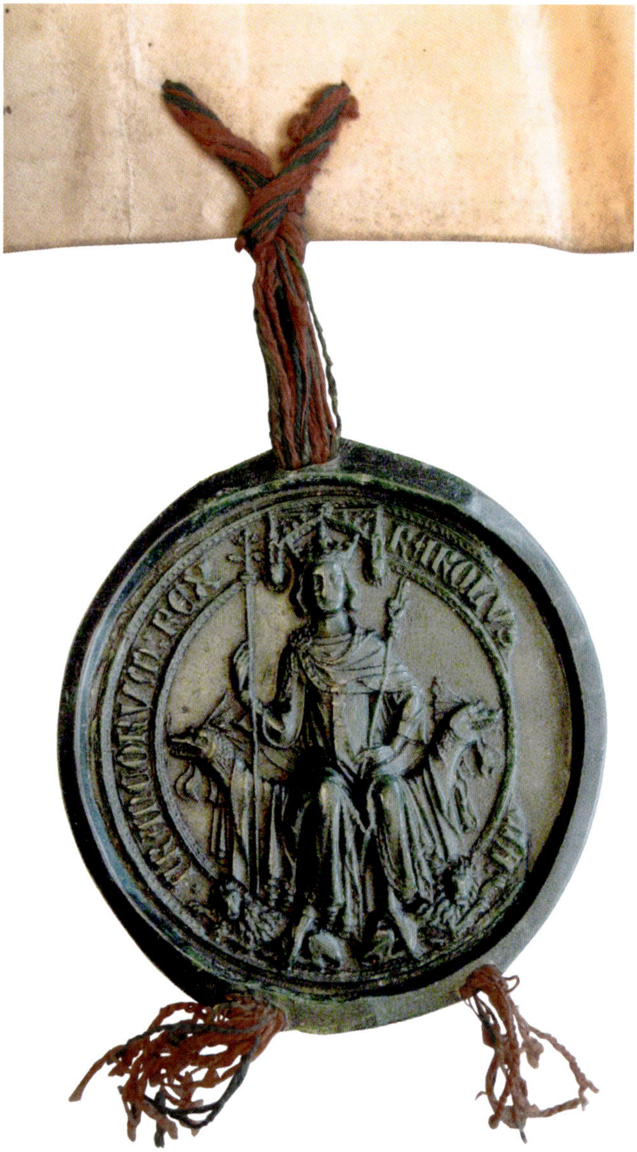

FIGURE 3. Paris, Archives nationales, J 354; seal of Charles V, king of France, appended to a charter of July 1364.

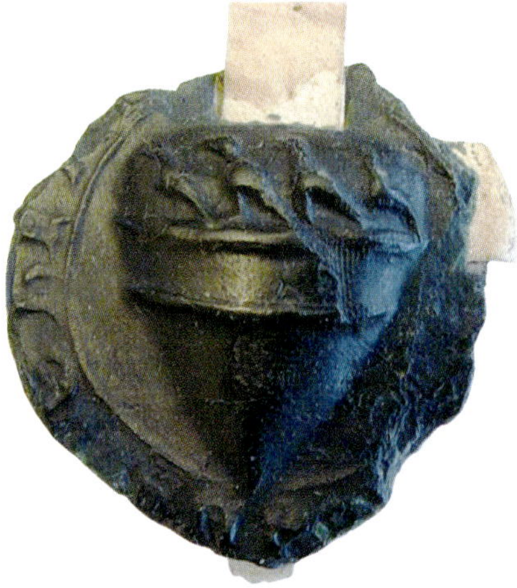

FIGURE 4. Paris, Archives nationales, L 809 no. 38; seal of Guillaume de Berchères, knight, appended to a charter of March 1239.

bar seals from any "grand" history of style. Though design, technique, module, and material, largely account for the traditional classification of seals among the minor arts, a further explanation is nevertheless warranted to account for the under-exploitation of so rich a corpus of objects and images, many of which are artful if even hardly artworks.

Medieval seals entered the world of scholarship in the sixteenth century, as humanists and antiquarians undertook to situate themselves *vis-à-vis* past cultures, defining discontinuities and enunciating paradigms that would soon crystallize into epistemological patterns. In the first part of this essay, therefore, I propose to examine the treatment seals have received between the sixteenth and the twentieth century. I will then contrast this earlier analytical viewpoint with both the medieval and the current interpretations of seals, hoping thereby to highlight the ways in which the material and intellectual consideration of seals from the sixteenth century until fairly recently has obscured the original functional, medial, and reproductive dimensions of seals. Traditional scholarly treatment substantially diverted seals from the operative loci they had occupied in medieval times, rendering them anachronistic with respect to their own historical significance even as they were being enlisted to support and guarantee the foundational disciplinary epistemologies of art and history. Within these disciplines, seals provided a scaffolding upon which to construct the noble nature of art as *disegno*, and of history as truth. Thus deployed, seals were instrumental in the presentation of art and history as intellectual practices mediated by technique: Hence the relegation of seals to their status as a mere handmaid of intellectual creativity, to the minor arts, and to the auxiliary sciences of diplomatics and

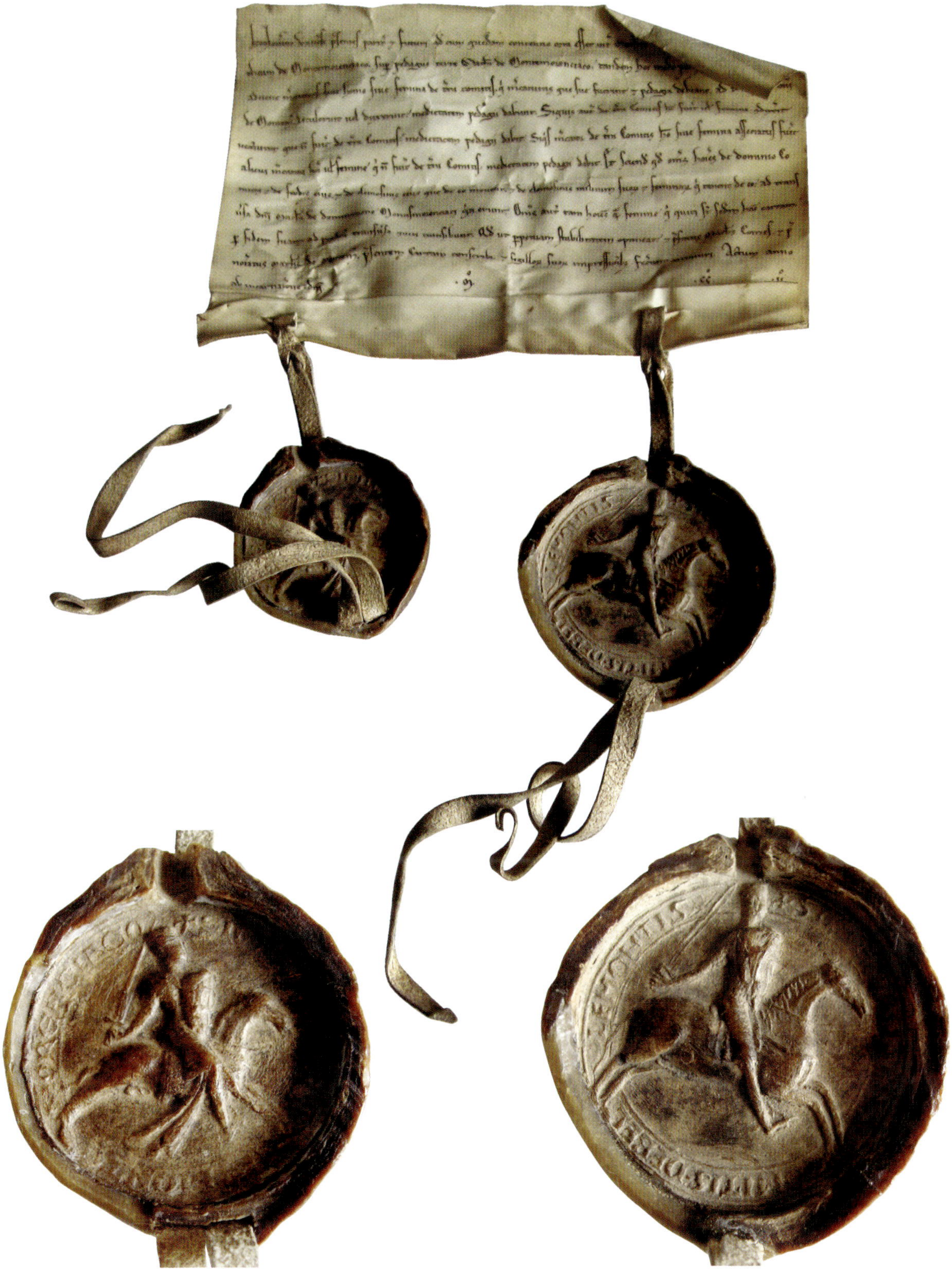

FIGURE 5. Charter of 1207, authorized by the seals of Matthew, lord of Montmorency (*detail, bottom left*), and Matthew, count of Beaumont (*detail, bottom right*), Paris, Archives nationales, J 168 no. 11.

sigillography. In their imposed subservience, these categories of knowledge reveal the full implication of their demotion, since they involve nothing less than the heuristic role of disfiguration in figuring the past. In conclusion, therefore, I will consider those medieval seal features being retrieved by current research, in order to reflect upon the meaning and consequences of the earlier silence about them. I am not of course suggesting that recent scholarship can rectify the historical record without introducing some new distortions of its own; for I acknowledge our contingent position as viewing subjects. I do, however, submit that recent approaches in art history have helped significantly to bridge the cleavage between fine and minor arts by adopting a multi-pronged method derived from phenomenology, history, and anthropology, thus allowing medieval objects a wider range for the expression of their hermeneutical potential, shifting their modal focus from art to act, from aesthetic to agency, and from hierarchical divisions to lateral associations.

Antiquarian Methods

Sixteenth-century humanists altered temporality of artifacts from the past, by removing them from the ordinary world and placing them in a spatial framework where questions of physical appearance came to assume a central position. For having been exiled from the present and cut off from mundane experience, the past now needed to be seen.[2] In their quest to gain access to a desired tangibility and visibility of ancient times, antiquarians gathered seals, engraved gems, coins, and medals. Their eagerness for collection was not limited to original items, but included copies, which they exchanged and circulated among themselves. Using this specific material, their goal was to create a universe of mental images that would enable their visual apprehension of historical figures. Thus, the French antiquarian Nicolas-Claude Peiresc (1580–1637) asserted that "seals are uncorrupted witnesses of Antiquity, and that they give legitimate portraits of princes."[3] With this view, he obtained several impressions of the seals of the Carolingian Charles the Bald (d. 877), and of Hugh Capet (d. 987), the first Capetian king to ascend the French throne—this latter seal, parenthetically, is no longer extant and is now accessible only by reference to drawings of the Ancien regime (Fig. 6).[4] These seals were attached to charters then in the archives of the abbey of St.-Maur-des-Fossés. Peiresc also went to the abbey of St. Denis, and, unaware that it was a medieval forgery, secured an aftercast of the seal of Offa, king of Mercia (d. 796), which he proudly sent to Sir Robert Cotton in England. Peiresc's biographer, Gassendi, reports with praise that his subject had casts made of the royal seals preserved in the monastic archives of Saint-Denis, Saint-Germain-des-Prés, Saint-Maur, and many others. Peiresc had at his disposal several techniques of Italian origin for molding seals and other glyptic and numismatic objects. He was adamant in his insistence on the exactitude of the molding process.[5] Nevertheless, he and many of his contemporaries also resorted to drawings, which being amenable to publication, became the primary means by which seals were reproduced, studied, and circulated.

As early as 1591, Francis Tate, the secretary of the first English Society of Antiquaries presented a paper, supported by drawings, on the history of English heraldic seals.[6] The extensive collecting of seals and sealed

2. D. Woolf, *The Social Circulation of the Past: English Historical Culture, 1500–1730* (Oxford, 2003), 183–85

3. P. Burke, "Images as Evidence in Seventeenth-Century Europe," *Journal of the History of Ideas* 64 (2003), 273–96, at 285; O. Guyotjeannin, "Nouveaux témoins du sceau perdu de Hugues Capet," *Bulletin de la Société nationale des Antiquaires de France*, 1993, 122–35, at 127.

4. Guyotjeannin, "Nouveaux témoins" (as in note 3).

5. I. Villela-Petit, "Les techniques de moulage des sceaux du XVe au XIXe siècle," *Bibliothèque de l'Ecole des chartes* 152 (1994), 511–20, at 513–14; L. de Laborde, "Préface," in L. Douët d'Arcq, *Collection de sceaux*, 3 vols (Paris 1863–1868), vol. 1, 10, gives the text of a seventeenth-century recipe for molding seals: "Pour tirer des empreintes des vieux seaux qui se trouvent apposez aux plus anciennes chartes des abbayes sans rien endanmager les originaux;" Y. Conry, "Peiresc et l'ordre des 'portraits' dans les investigations sur les vivants au XVIIe siècle," in *Peiresc ou la passion de connaître* (Paris, 1990), 111–38, at 135–38. Gassendi's remark is reported in Jean Mabillon, *De re diplomatica libri VI*, 2 vols. (Naples, 1789), 2:139.

6. P. D. A. Harvey and A. McGuinness, *A Guide to British Medieval Seals* (London, 1996), 22.

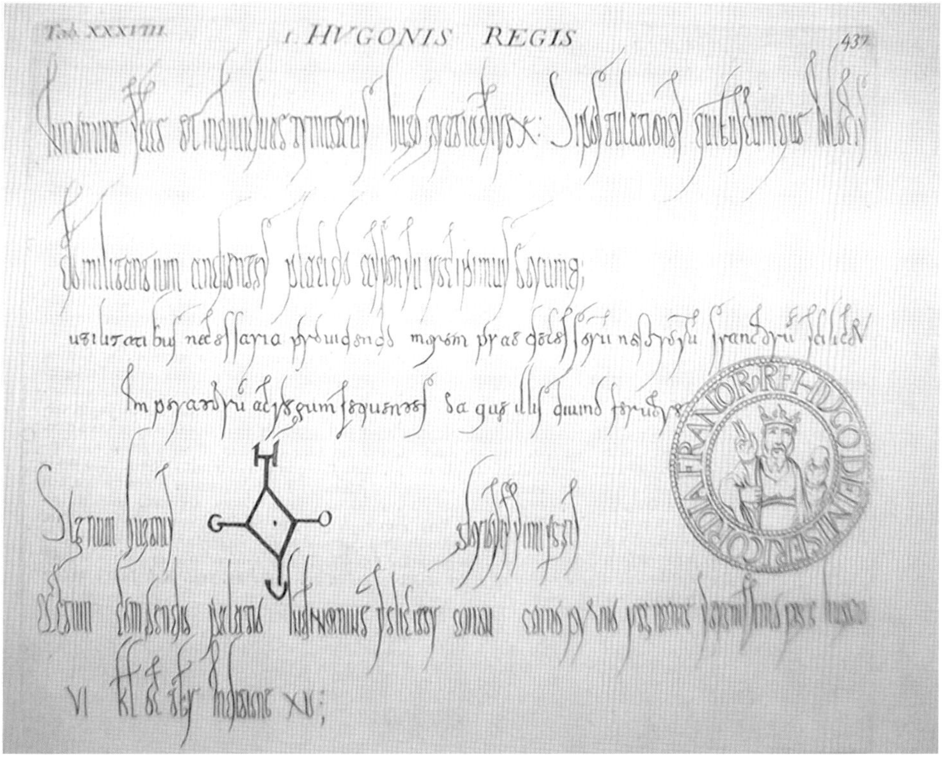

FIGURE 6. Seal of Hugh Capet, king of France (d. 996), from Mabillon, *De Re Diplomatica* (1681).

documents that were drawn and transcribed in England during the sixteenth and seventeenth centuries was primarily prompted by the "pedigree craze," an intense moment in British history when heralds diligently scrutinized all documentation, and seals in particular, which were submitted to them by families eager to prove the nobility of their lineage.[7] Thus, Sir Christopher Hatton's *Book of Seals* originated in part from the work of the herald William Dugdale (1605–1686), who had been specifically charged with the gathering and copying of seals.[8] In the letters he sent out in the process of collecting this material, Dugdale requested copies of items that were the most historical and especially beautiful (Fig. 7).[9] His research produced yet another publication, *The Antiquities of Warwickshire*, in 1656.[10] In this work, however, the seals, though individually carefully drawn, had become independent roundels, entirely separated from their original charters and, furthermore, re-contextualized among images of stained glass or funerary slabs, all being deployed in support of genealogical history.[11]

In Flanders, genealogical history focused on the ruling princes. Charles van Riedwijck (1580–1656), alderman of Brussels, carefully drew up a catalogue of the seals and sealed charters of medieval Brabant (eleventh–fifteenth centuries). This manuscript catalogue,

7. Woolf, *Social Circulation* (as in note 2), 99–101, 105–14.

8. *Sir Christopher Hatton's Book of Seals*, ed. L. C. Loyd and D. M. Stenton (Oxford, 1950), xxiii; the original manuscript is in the Northamptonshire Record Office, Ms. Finch Hatton 170. One of the notebooks in which Dugdale consigned drawings and notes about seals is housed in Oxford's Bodleian Library, Ms. Dugdale 17

9. *Hatton's Book of Seals* (as in note 8), xxviii.

10. See above at note 8.

11. Woolf, *The Social Circulation of the Past* (as in note 2), 135, where are given the facsimiles of pages from the *The Antiquities of Warwickshire*, which are devoted to the genealogy, seals, and tombs of the Shirley family.

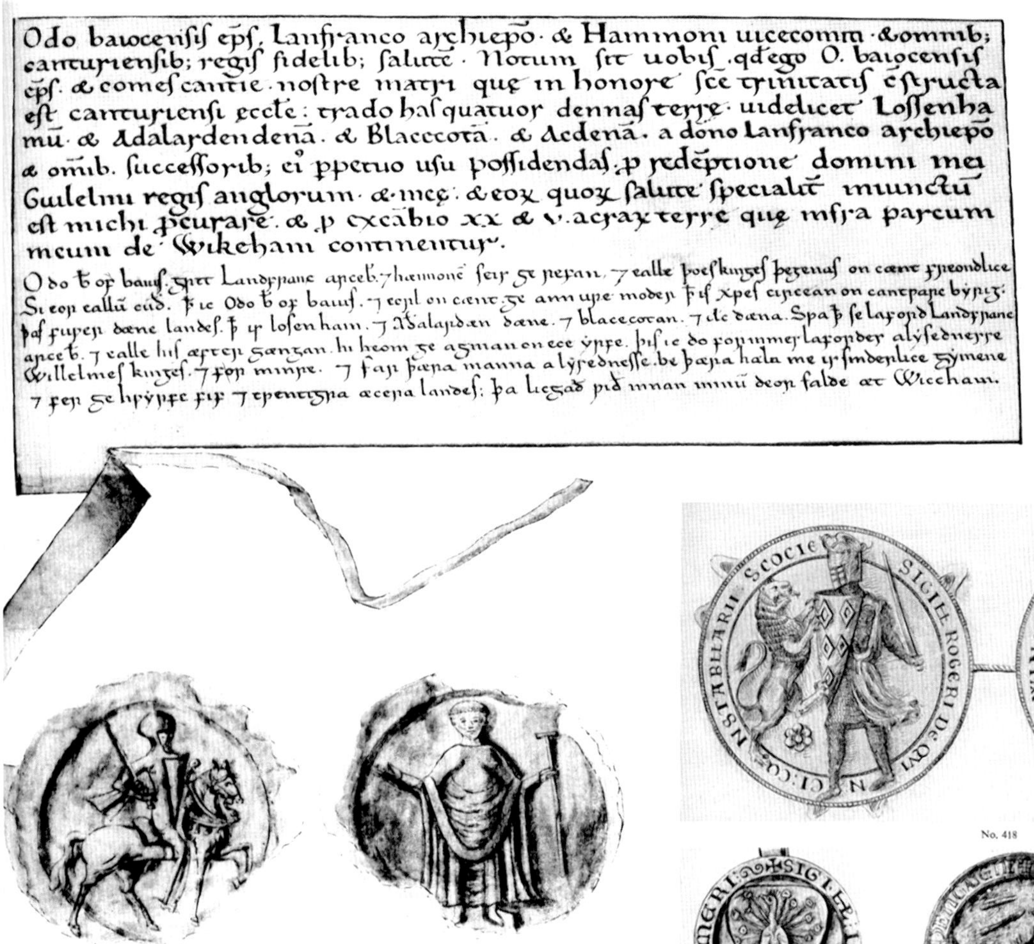

Odo baiocensis eps. Lanfranco archiepo. & Hammoni uicecomiti & omnib; canturiensib; regis fidelib; salutē. Notum sit uobis, qđ ego O. baiocensis eps. & comes cantię. nostre matri quę in honore scē trinitatis cōstructa est canturiensi ecclē: trado has quatuor dennas terre. uidelicet Lossenham. & Adalardendenā. & Blaccecotā. & Acdenā. a dono Lanfranco archiepō & omib. successorib; ei' ppetuo usu possidendas. p redēptione domini mei Gulelmi regis anglorum. & meę. & eox quox salutē specialit̄ iniunctū est michi pcurare. & p excābio xx & v. acrax terre quę infra parcum meum de Wikeham continentur.

Odo b of baius. gret Landfranc arceb. 7 hæmonē scir gerefan. 7 ealle þoes kinges þegenas on cænt freondlice. Si eow eallū cud. þ ic Odo b of baius. 7 eorl on cænt ge ann ure moder þis xpes circean on cantpare byrig. þas fuper dæne landes. þ is losenham. 7 Adalardæn dæne. 7 blaccecotan. 7 ac dæna. Spa þ se lafond Landfranc arceb. 7 ealle his æfter gangan hi heom ge agnian on ece yrfe. þis ic do for mines laforder alysednesse Willelmes kinges. 7 for minre. 7 fair þæra manna alysednesse. be þæra hala me is sindenlice gymene 7 fer ge hrypfe fif 7 tpentigra æcera landes: þa liegað wið innan minū deor falde æt Wiccham.

FIGURE 7. Seals from *Sir Christopher Hatton's Book of Seals* (seventeenth century). (*Above*): Charter in the name of, and sealed by, Odo, bishop of Bayeux, addressed to Lanfranc, archbishop of Canterbury (late eleventh century). Odo's seal is known only by this drawing. (*Right*): Plate III.

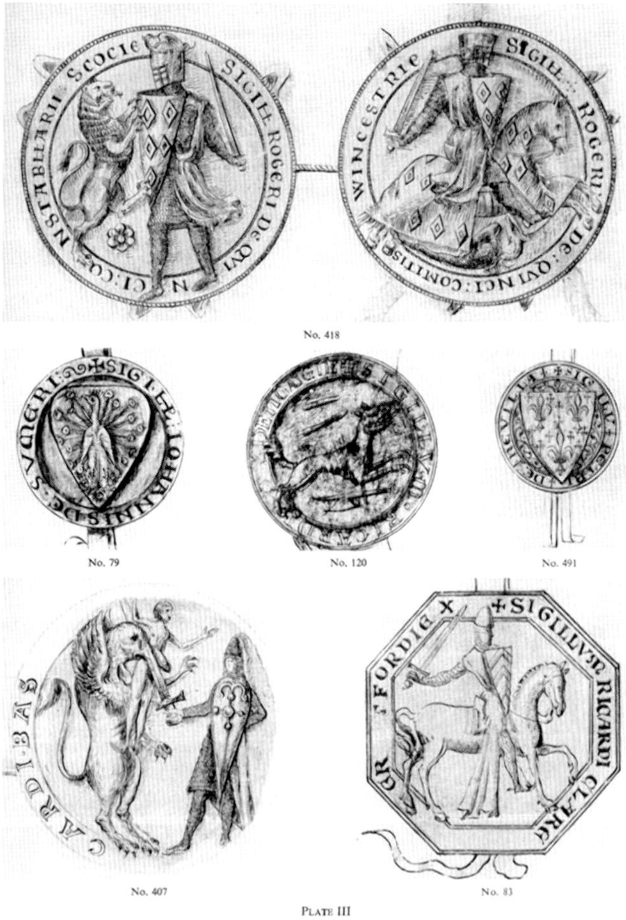

which remained unpublished, has only recently been discovered among the collections of the Bibliothèque royale in Brussels.[12] Van Riedwijck, however, communicated the results of his research on Brabant seals to Christopher Butkins, who published them in 1642 as part of his own *Trophées de Brabant* (Fig. 8).[13] During the same period, Olivier Vredius (1596–1652), notary public and mayor of Bruges, conducted sustained research in local monastic archives (Saint-Peter of Gand, Saint-Vaast of Arras), which lead to the publication in 1639 of the *Sigilla comitum Flandriae et inscriptiones diplomatum*,[14] a corpus of 301 items cataloguing and illustrating the seals of the counts and countesses of Flanders from the tenth to the seventeenth century (Fig. 9).[15] Dedicated to the king of Spain, then also the count of Flanders, the volume opens with a dedication that eloquently articulates the import medieval seals had in the learned culture of early seventeenth-century Northern Europe:

> According to Suetonius, Emperor Augustus first sealed his diplomas with the figure of a sphinx, then with the effigy of Alexander the Great and finally, with his own image. Carolingians, who were themselves great emperors, imitated this usage. O, Philip, your very own ancestors, the counts of Flanders, stem from this Carolingian stock. Contemplate those waxes with which they signed their diplomas. Use these waxes to decorate the walls of your palace, just as ancient Romans decorated their houses with wax portraits. These images which I found on the seals, I had them engraved on copper, so as to secure their survival and I have published these

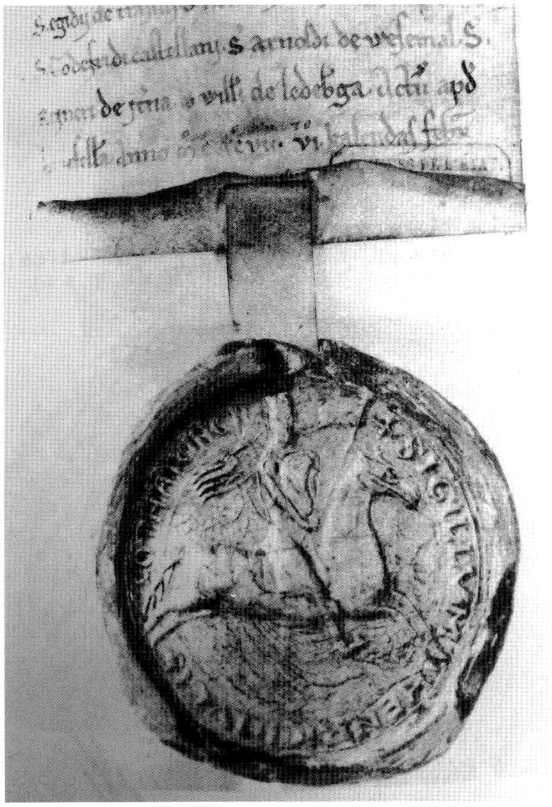

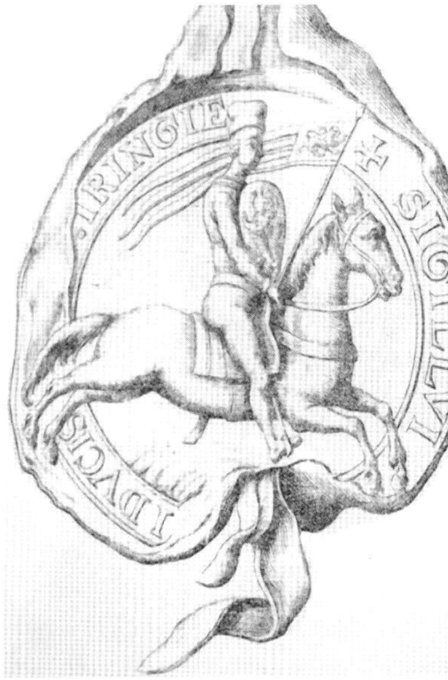

FIGURE 8. Seals of Henry, duke of Lotharingia and of Brabant (1165–1235). (*Above*): Henry's seal appended to a charter of January 1197, Gand, Archives de l'Etat, Abbaye de Ninove, Fonds de Smets, 78. (*Below*): Drawing of Henry's seal, from Butkins, *Trophées de Brabant* (1642).

12. The circumstances of this important discovery are related by C.-G. Dallemagne, "Le manuscrit de l'écuyer Charles van Riedwijck," *Annales de la Société royale de Bruxelles* 46 (1942–1943), 27–98, pls. I–XIII, at 32.

13. In the "Avis au lecteur," with which he prefaced the *Trophées*, Butkens described the documents communicated by van Riedwijck whose generosity and knowledge he acknowledged with gratitude, Dallemagne, "Le manuscrit" (as in note 12), 30, 33.

14. O. Vredius, *Sigilla comitum Flandriae et inscriptiones diplomatum ab iis editorum cum expositione* (Bruges 1639).

15. M. Hoc, "Olivier Vredius," in *Bibliotheca Belgica: Bibliographie générale des Pays Bas*, founded by F. van der Haeghen, ed. M.-Th. Lenger, vol. v, Brussels, 1964, notices nos. 340–50, pp. 788–805, at notice 340, p. 791. Notice 344 at p. 798 is devoted to the first edition, in Latin, of the *Sigilla comitum Flandriae*. This text appeared in Flemish in 1640 (notice 345, p. 799), and in French in 1641 (notice 346, p. 800).

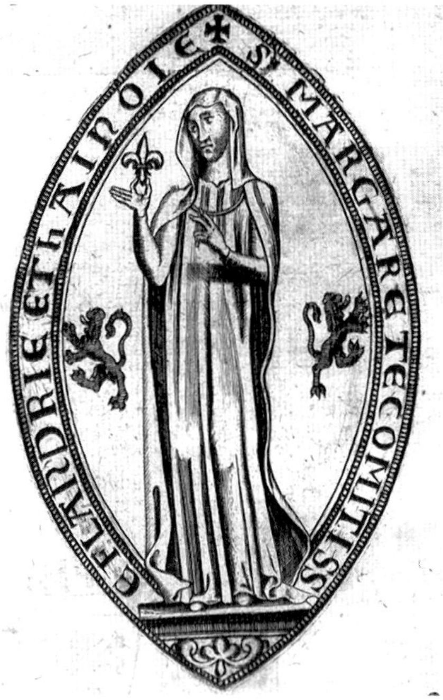

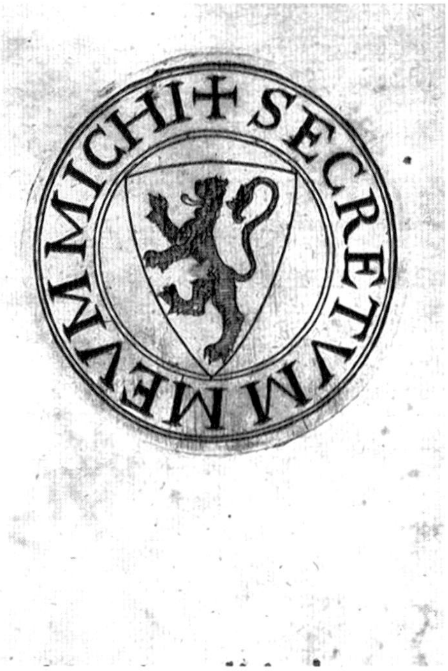

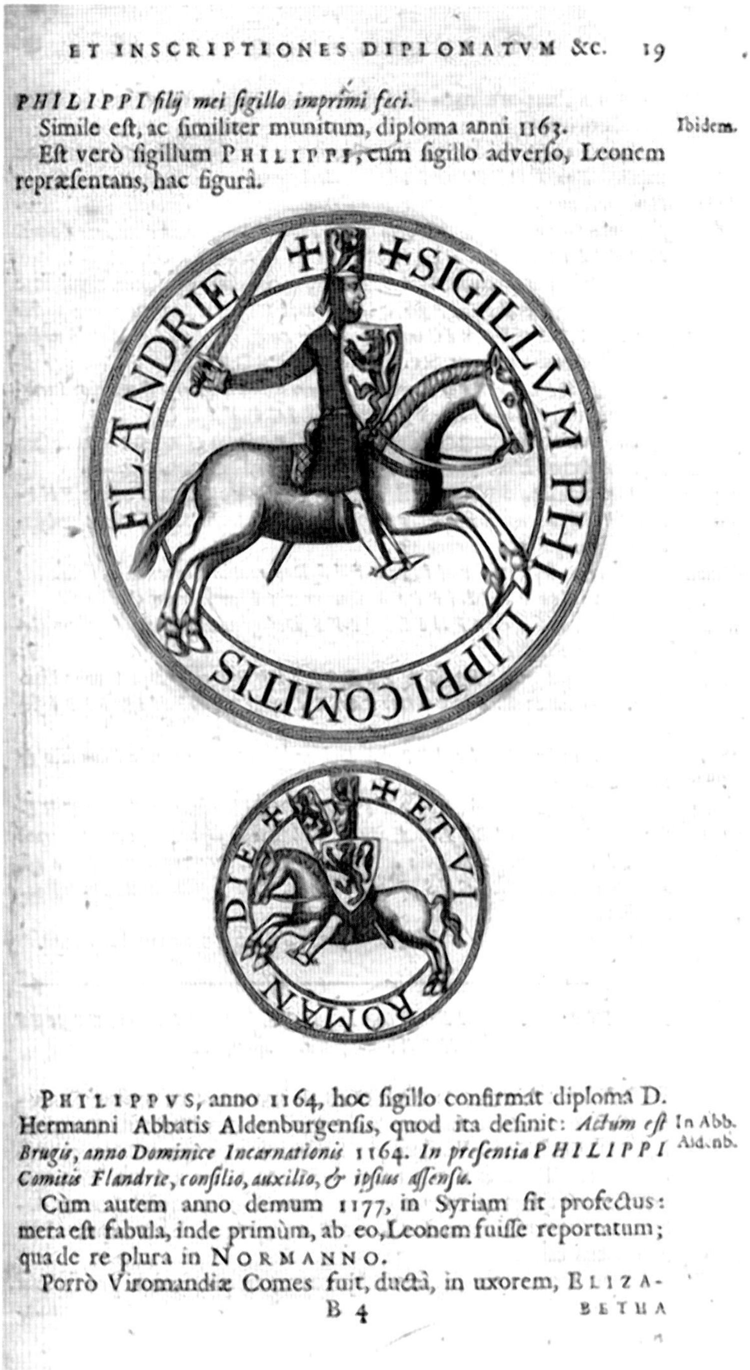
ET INSCRIPTIONES DIPLOMATVM &c. 19

PHILIPPI filij mei sigillo imprimi feci.

Simile est, ac similiter munitum, diploma anni 1163. Ibidem.

Est verò sigillum PHILIPPI, cum sigillo adverso, Leonem repræsentans, hac figurâ.

+ SIGILLVM PHILIPPI COMITIS FLANDRIE

+ ET VIROMANDIE

PHILIPPVS, anno 1164, hoc sigillo confirmat diploma D. Hermanni Abbatis Aldenburgensis, quod ita desinit: *Actum est Brugis, anno Dominice Incarnationis* 1164. *In presentia* PHILIPPI *Comitis Flandrie, consilio, auxilio, & ipsius assensu.* In Abb. Aldenb.

Cùm autem anno demum 1177, in Syriam sit profectus: mera est fabula, inde primùm, ab eo, Leonem fuisse reportatum; qua de re plura in NORMANNO.

Porrò Viromandiæ Comes fuit, ductâ, in uxorem, ELIZA-

B 4 BETHA

FIGURE 9. (*Left*): Seal and counter-seal of Marguerite, countess of Flanders (d. 1194), sister and heiress of Count Philip of Alsace, from Vredius; (*Right*): Seal and counter-seal of Philip of Alsace, count of Flanders and of Vermandois (d. 1191), from Vredius, *Sigilla comitum Flandriae* (1639).

engravings to put them under the eyes of all and everyone. In ancient Rome, the exhibition of wax portraits was meant to inspire the imitation of ancestral virtues. Similarly, the portraits of your majesty's ancestors will invite him to follow their examples. You will outshine your predecessors, and merit the name of 'Greatest.[16]

Flattery aside, this text is extraordinary, in its association of medieval seals with the practice of wax *imagines*, followed in antiquity by Roman patricians, who had funerary masks molded directly from the face of their dead relatives and thereafter proudly exhibited them in their gallery of ancestors. I will return later to this forceful association, which tests the nature of seal resemblance, since medieval seals, of the counts of Flanders and of others for that matter (Figs. 3, 5), were not physiognomic. For now, I wish to emphasize the many ways in which Vredius' comparison holds: seals and masks were both made of wax, resulted from an imprinting process, and produced resemblance by direct physical contact. Furthermore, both types of image had a legal dimension: the funerary mask legitimized the status of individuals within their families and in society; the seal authorized and legitimized written commitments. Both types of image involve encounters between matter, process of image production, identity, and law.[17] It is noteworthy that the treatment of seals by antiquarians in Northern Europe just described, though derived primarily from actual wax seal impressions affixed to documents, came to obscure this fundamental reality by conflating wax seals with other media and artifacts, by failing to distinguish between originals and copies, and by transposing seals to another medium (casts, drawings) so that contemplation of surface, that is, of the image, was fostered while the very stuff that made the seal an actual thing was rendered effectively invisible.

Turning now to sixteenth-century Italy, it appears that the interest in seals there took a different direction, focusing comprehensively on the seals themselves and on their use. In 1615 Giorgio Longo published his *De anulis signatoriis antiquorum sive de vario obsignandi ritu tractatus* in Milan.[18] The work is exhaustive in its consideration of seal terminology, usage, image, and inscription; in its description of sealing rituals; and in its attention to both seal matrices and the impressions issued from them. Longo's example was followed by the Tuscan, Domenico Maria Manni (1637–1712), who authored a volume entitled *Historical Observations on the Seals of the Middle Ages*. Given this rather encyclopedic approach, it comes as no surprise that the word "sigillography" first appeared in Italy, about 1680, to refer to the study of seals. The term itself was coined by Anton Stefano Cartari (1651–1685) whose ambition, curtailed by a short life, had been to write a universal sigillography.[19] Finally, it was also in Italy that the first systematic collections of seals were formed; thus Roman seal matrices were collected by Athanasius Kircher (1602–1680) and medieval matrices were gathered by Carlo Strozzi (1587–1671).[20] Significantly, these collections favored the metallic seal, the matrix or die (Fig. 1), the unique device from which imprints were produced. This mode of collecting thus privileged a manufactured object which, hand engraved rather than replicated, was seen as the result of conceptualization, originality, and creativity.[21]

The Rise of the Scientific Method: The Late Seventeenth Century

In humanist and antiquarian scholarship, seals were seen as having a history, and as historical witnesses. They were assigned testimonial authority, as first-hand evidence, on the grounds that they manifested a particular relationship with their owners. As such, seals were

16. Vredius, *Sigilla* (as in note 14), fol. 2^{r-v}.

17. G. Didi-Huberman, *Devant le temps: histoire de l'art et anachronisme des images* (Paris, 2000), 68, where he analyzes the meaning and agency of the Roman *imago*.

18. G. C. Bascapé, *Sigillografia; Il sigillo nella diplomatica, nel diritto, nella storia, nell'arte*. Vol. 1: *Sigillografia generale* (Milan, 1969), 36–37.

19. Bascapé, *Sigillografia* (as in note 18), 1, 42–44.

20. *Ibid.*

21. For the further development of sigillographic studies in seventeenth-century Italy, see Bascapé, *Sigillografia* (as in note 18), 1, 44–45, and B. Bedos-Rezak, "Les voies du savoir. Du sceau à la sigillographie (XVIe–XVIIIe siècle)," in *Genèse et constitution des sciences de l'histoire et de la philologie de la fin du Moyen Âge au coeur des Temps Modernes*, ed. F. Collard, B. Grunberg, and D. Marcotte (Librairie Droz, forthcoming).

understood and treated as vestigial portraits, giving a face to the past, even as their capacity for circulation, by permitting comparison and touch, allowed for the formation of an integrated and international connoisseurship in the present.

In the course of the seventeenth century, however, the quest for first-hand evidence took on a tone of apologia, since it was often associated with the assertion of national independence, the substantiation of rights, or the justification of particular traditions.[22] It was largely this attempt to establish proof in the service of (political) truth that led to the epistemological treatment that seals received when Jean Mabillon (1632–1707) published his *De Re Diplomatica Libri VI* (*Six Books On Diplomatics*) in 1681.[23] Mabillon's main goal was to create rules for establishing the *discrimen veri ac falsi*, for distinguishing truthful charters and diplomas from false ones. His method consisted in establishing a taxonomy of verifiable documentary features—material support, ink, handwriting, discursive formulae, linguistic forms, graphic signs and seals were all catalogued, categorized, and displayed in patterns of general regularity (Fig. 10). Thus, Mabillon's method established criteria of reliability as grids for judgment and verification that assumed a notion of self-validating autonomy. Such epistemology made a particular place for seals as trustworthy historical indicators (Fig. 6), for seals' medieval operations had been explicitly, if tortuously, described by medieval lawyers as providing documentary authenticity.[24] The medieval process of seal authentication, however, had been predicated upon the seal's embodiment of an authorizing presence, the authority and status of the seal's owner. In his construction of authenticity as an absolute and objective category, Mabillon crucially reversed this medieval dynamic: where authority, authorship, and presence had been the determinant of medieval authenticity, authority was now conceived as deriving from authenticity, that is, from documents judged to be scientifically true.[25] In the seventeenth-century discipline of diplomatics, the medieval fabric of seals was re-woven. The modality of their creation and being was no longer to be sought in the medieval sphere of their operation, but rather in their position within a reified sequence of types.[26]

22. The politics of erudition and the birth of scientific history in France of the Ancien Regime (17th–18th century) have been magisterially analyzed by B. Barret-Kriegel in a series of studies that appeared under the title: *Les Historiens et la monarchie.* Vol. 1: *Jean Mabillon*; vol. 2: *La Défaite de l'érudition*; vol. 3: *Les Académies de l'histoire*; vol. 4: *La République incertaine* (Paris, 1988). The particular treatment reserved to seals by the French scholars of the Ancien Regime is described in great detail by L. de Laborde, "Préface" (as in note 5), vol. 1, 9–16.

23. The bibliography on Jean Mabillon and his contribution to historical scholarship is vast. Recent and significant works include L. Levillain, "Le 'De Re Diplomatica,'" in *Mélanges et documents publiés à l'occasion du 2e centenaire de la mort de Mabillon* (Paris, 1908), 192–252; R. Aris, "Jean Mabillon (1623–1707)," in *Medieval Scholarship: Biographical Studies on the Formation of a Discipline.* Vol. 1: *History*, ed. H. Damico and J. Zavadil (New York, 1955), 15–32; Barret-Kriegel, *Mabillon* (as in note 22); "Jean Mabillon," with partial English translation of the *De Re Diplomatica* by R. Wertis, in *Historians at Work*, Vol. 2, ed. P. Gay and V. G. Wexler (New York, 1972), 161–98; L. Duranti, "Diplomatics: New Uses for an Old Science," *Archivaria* 28–33 (1989–92), at 28 (1989), 13, 17, 22; R. Starn, "Truths in the Archives," *Common Knowledge* 8: 2 (2002), 387–401, at 396–401.

24. For an analysis of medieval legal discourse on seals, see M. Welber, *I sigilli nella storia del diritto medievale italiano*, vol. 3 of *Sigillografia: Il sigillo nella diplomatica, nel diritto, nella storia, nell'arte* (Milan, 1984); B. Bedos-Rezak, "The Efficacy of Signs and the Matter of Authenticity in Canon Law," in *Zwischen Pragmatik und Performanz. Dimensionen mittelalter Schrifkultur*, Utrecht Studies in Medieval Literacy, 18, ed. Ch. Dartmann, Th. Scharff, and Ch. Weber (Turnhout, 2011), pp. 199–236. The medieval concept of authenticity is complex and continues to attract much scholarly attention: M.-D. Chenu, "Auctor, Actor, Autor," *Bulletin du Cange* 2 (1927), 81–86; Chenu, "Authentica et magistralia, deux lieux theologiques aux xii–xiii siècles," *Divus Thomas* 28 (1925), 257–85; B. Guenée, "Authentique et approuvé," in *La lexicographie du latin médiéval et ses rapports avec les recherches actuelles sur la civilisation du Moyen-Age* (Paris, 1981), 215–29; J. Ziolkowski, "Cultures of Authority in the Long Twelfth Century," *Journal of English and Germanic Philology* 108 (2009), 421–48.

25. Barret-Kriegel, *La Défaite de l'érudition* (as in note 22), 161–64, 145–75, fully unravels Mabillon's general re-organization of the concept of authenticity. Starn, "Truths in the Archives (as in note 23)," 398–99, building upon Barret-Kriegel's analysis considers the implications for historical knowledge of Mabillon's goal of and method for exposing false witnesses or ascertaining their sincerity. For a clear definition of the concept of authenticity in diplomatics, see Duranti, "Diplomatics" (as in note 23), 28 (1989), 17–19.

26. For this paper, I used the version of the *De Re Diplomatica*

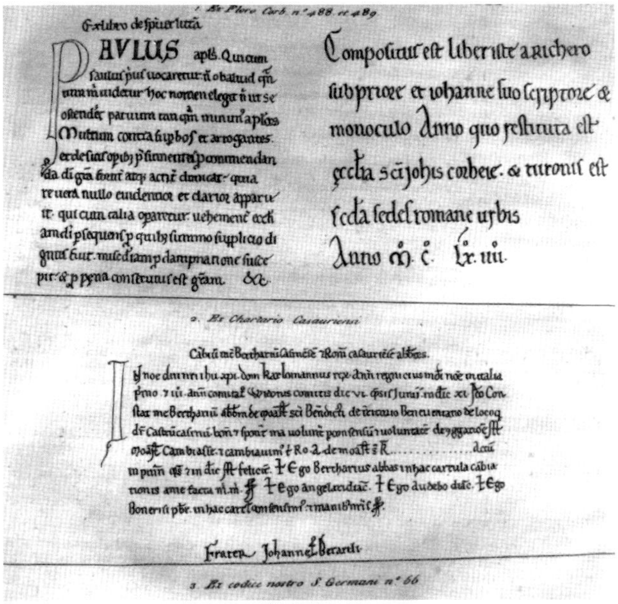

FIGURE 10. Facsimiles of handwriting from twelfth- and thirteenth-century books and cartularies, from Mabillon, *De Re Diplomatica* (1681).

Seals had become signposts, defined and categorized by their modes of being: styles of affixation, shape, matter, color, legends, and paleography, image and iconography. Such totalizing taxonomy promoted an understanding of seals as separate objects, not unlike coins and medals (Fig. 11).[27]

The Nineteenth Century

This "numismatization" of seals became an organizing principle of their study during the nineteenth century, and remains predominant to this day.[28] The impetus for this development derived in part from the tenets of positivist history, according to which a rigorous heuristic could lead directly and mimetically from truthful documents to the truth of the past. The written text, therefore, came to be particularly privileged, with a narrative and referential format that achieved a singular effect of reality.[29] Within newly created repositories of national and regional archives, intensive and extensive campaigns of cataloguing were undertaken to support and promote documentary research and the production of historical writing.[30] Eager for the written word, archivists soon confronted the hybrid nature of medieval charters, which contained both texts and images (Fig. 5). Although seals were an integral part of medieval documentary practice, they came to be institutionally re-situated within the world of images, their relevance remaining primarily a matter of interest for numismatists. In 1832, the creator of the French Mint Museum (Musée de la Monnaie royale), Collin de Sussy (1776–1837), decided to complement the chronological series of royal coins with seals, and received authorization to aftercast the royal seals appended to charters stored at the Royal Archives. At the same time, such medal engravers as John Doubleday and Alexis-Joseph Depaulis (1792–1867) requested permission to cast beautiful seals that had belonged to famous personages.[31] Sets of the casts resulting from all three projects were deposited at the Archives, where they provided the concrete kernel and inspired the conceptual framework for a radical re-invention of the medieval seal. In his advocacy (*c.* 1860) of the casting process that was to be systematically applied to seals from 1842 onward, Léon de Laborde, then director of

published in Naples in 1789 (as in note 5). Mabillon treated seals in vol. 2 (chapters X, XI, XIV–XIX). For a detailed examination of Mabillon's treatment of seals in the *De Re Diplomatica*, see my forthcoming essay "Les voies du savoir" (as in note 21).

27. The assimilation of seals to numismatics reinforced their integration to the group of such artifacts as tombs, stained glass, medals, see Bedos-Rezak, "Les voies du savoir" (as in note 21), and below, note 28.

28. de Laborde, "Préface" (as in note 5), vol. 1, 1–2, 14, 16, 26, compared seals to coins, considering coins to be vastly inferior to seals; yet he emphasized that the study of seals (sigillography) and of coins (numismatics) were sisters who had to be mutually helpful.

29. Among the many works devoted to the study of history during the nineteenth century, see H. White, *Metahistory: The Historical Imagination in Nineteenth-Century Europe* (Baltimore, 1973), 133–264; G. G. Iggers, *Historiography in the Twentieth Century: From Scientific Objectivity to the Postmodern Challenge* (Middletown, Conn., 1997), 23–20.

30. Randolph Starn's critical discussion of the modern "emergence of archives as primary locations of historical research" is accompanied by further bibliographical references on the subject, "Truths in the Archives" (as in note 23), 387–401 and at 395–96, on nineteenth-century European archives.

31. de Laborde, "Préface" (as in note 5), vol. 1, 25–27.

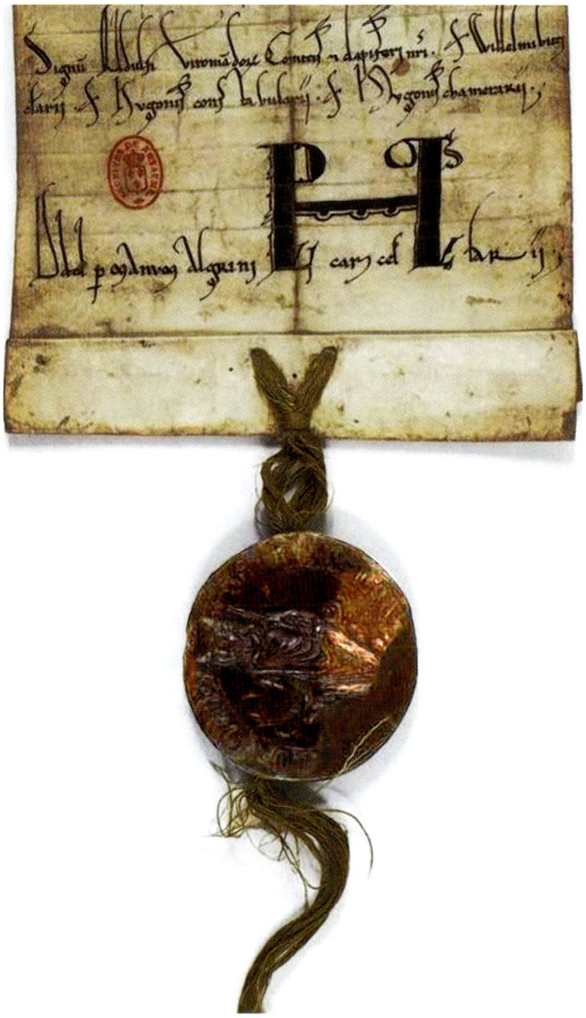

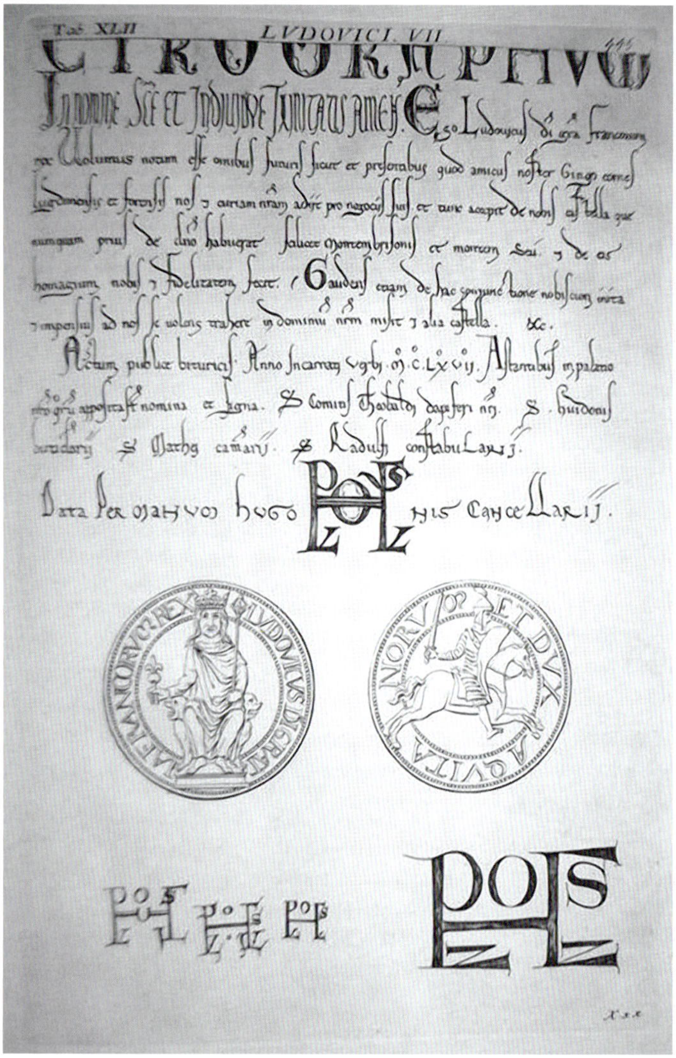

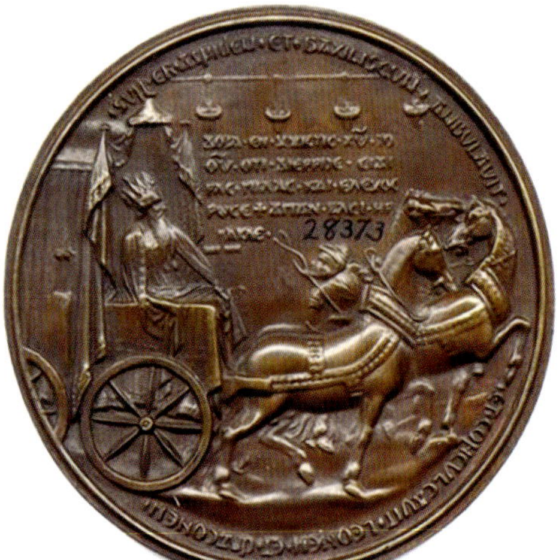

FIGURE 11. (*Top left*): Original sealed diploma issued by King Louis VII in 1137 (partial view), AE/II/147. (*Right*): Seal of Louis VII (obverse and reverse), from Mabillon, *De Re Diplomatica* (1681). (*Lower left*): Medal, Constantine the Great, *c.* 1400 (copy).

the French Imperial Archives, specifically mentioned the need for archived seals to gain the mobility of coins so that they could be brought together, classified, and compared.[32] He praised the emergence from the messy world of dusty, broken, imprinted waxes dangling from parchment documents (Fig. 2), of what was, in effect, an artificial and selective collection of pristine sulfur casts all made from plaster molds directly taken from single originals, the best impression of each given seal type. The process of metamorphosis began with the original sealed document and moved to an exclusive focus on the wax imprint, and to its final arrival in a tray as a separate cast. The seal catalogues that were then prepared typically described these casts, discounting information inherent in original seal impressions, and subsuming variants within a single archetype.[33]

This radical move to cast an archetypical individualization also signaled the official entry of seals into the world of art history. Depaulis' intention, in particular, had been to create a collection of seal-casts for the École des Beaux Arts, where it would complement the already existing museum of plasters. There, plaster molds were valued like originals, highly regarded for their reproductive and didactic qualities.[34] De Laborde's own rationale for the archival transformations of seals into casts had invoked antique, medieval,[35] and antiquarian traditions of casting, even citing the praise Vasari had bestowed upon Andrea Verrocchio as the first artist to mold from nature.[36] Prior to his functions as the head of the French archives, De Laborde had been a curator at the Louvre, in charge of the medieval and Renaissance collections, where he had developed his own sense of both the historical and artistic significance of casting.[37] Thus seals entered the world of art, as pedagogical devices, and also as objects of study in terms of their style, their attribution to workshops and, even in some rare cases, to artists. Seals were particularly prized as tools for localizing and dating stylistic variations—information derived from their host document turned ghost by the casting process. Apart from being a minor art, seals now entered the service of art history, to quote an expression that appears regularly in modern publications about seals.[38]

From Modern Outcast to Medieval Wax Imprint and Back

From this survey of 500 years of seal study, it is possible to identify a number of trends with important epistemological consequences. First, and perhaps foremost, is the virtually normative change in the medium of the preservation and of the study of seals from wax originals to aftercasts in various plastic materials, and to two-dimensional renderings in manuscript and in print (Figs. 6–10, 12). To be sure, casting as a duplicative technique imitates the seal's own imprinting process, and it has the virtue of maintaining the seal's relief, its three-dimensionality. Similarly, the use of casting

32. de Laborde, "Préface" (as in note 5), vol. 1, 19. De Laborde, however, denounced the practice followed in some contemporary archival repositories of cutting the seals from their documents so as to display them in showcases, remonstrating that seals were not medals (*ibid.*, 18) and advocating a process that would permit the reproduction of seals without altering them: i.e., by casting.

33. See, for instance, Douët d'Arc, *Collection de sceaux* (as in note 5): in this catalogue, which was to serve as the model for subsequent seal catalogues published by French archivists well into the late twentieth century, the author describes 11,840 casts made from seals (some with counterseals or reverses) attached to documents housed in the Archives nationales. Entries contain descriptions of seals' size, shape, image, and legend, and an analysis of the documents to which they are affixed; absent from such descriptions are wax color, modes of attachment, and mention of other imprints issued from a same matrix. As recently as 2003, the Royal Archives of Belgium published the catalogue of their seal-cast collections, R. Laurent, *Inventaire de la collection de moulages de sceaux des Archives générales du Royaume à Bruxelles*, 2 vols. (Brussels, 2003). In the same year, the French *Archives départementales* of the Aube released a CD-Rom: *Sceaux et usage des sceaux: Images de la Champagne médiévale*, a database of 300 images in which a majority of casts cohabit indiscriminately with original waxes photographed and cut from their documents.

34. M. Mekouar, "Étudier ou rêver l'antique. Félix Ravaisson et la reproduction de la statuaire antique," *Images Re-vues* 1 (2005), 2–14, at 6.

35. de Laborde, "Préface" (as in note 5), vol. 1, 21–22, and *idem*, *Notice des émaux, bijoux et objets divers exposés dans les galeries du Musée du Louvre*. IIe partie (Paris, 1853), 215, 259–60, 484.

36. de Laborde, "Préface" (as in note 5), vol. 1, 22.

37. L. de Laborde, *De l'union des arts et de l'industrie* (Paris, 1856), and above at note 35.

38. See for instance Pastoureau, *Les sceaux* (as in note 1), 62–63, 74–76.

and drawing is of course legitimate when deployed for preliminary research and analysis, and for conservation of general forms: casts made over the past two centuries have undoubtedly preserved the integrity of seals that have since then themselves deteriorated (Fig. 12). Nevertheless, the radical transfer and resulting negation of the original medium is unfortunate, on several accounts. Casts have fully commanded the attention of most twentieth-century scholars, who thus rarely have experienced seals through their actual physical presence.[39] This is particularly a problem, since aftercasting alters the locus of seals from intimate apposition and attachment to their documents, as well as undermines their status as signs by transmuting them into discrete entities of deracinated referentiality, removed from their original cultural sphere of discourse and practice.[40] Forgery aside, on the other hand, aftercasting does not seem to have afflicted the preservation and study of matrices, whose collections in museums and archives alike thus have respected their original metallic medium (Fig. 1).[41] The disregard for wax implicit in systematic aftercasting was and is particularly endemic within the communities of scholars in the humanities, and in the liberal arts more generally. Conservators, on the other hand, deal with wax: not only restoring it when necessary, as one would expect, but analyzing its chemical components and deriving information about past environmental settings; interesting biological work is currently being done on medieval wax seals.[42] Then too, it is ironical that seal matrices are preserved in their original medium, though in medieval times they were not supposed to survive their owners, but were either buried with them, defaced or destroyed by melting;[43] while, on the other hand, modern scholarship has effectively buried wax seals, which were intended not only to survive their seal owners but to attest their commitments in perpetuity. Indeed, it was wax seal impressions that primarily informed the medieval perception of seal agency and significance, as we shall soon see.

A second noteworthy trend in the survey briefly conducted here, again a consequence of the displacement of interest from wax originals, is the traditional indifference to the generation of medieval seal images as imprints, a process that amounted in fact to serial reproduction. There is now ample evidence that these aspects of seals and sealing processes were central to medieval thought and served to articulate specific concepts about the nature of resemblance, causation, and representation, all issues which resonated deeply within contemporary ontological concerns.[44]

These last remarks introduce the third important observation to emerge from the present survey: a striking lack of attention to recurrent use of the seal topos and of metaphors of sealing within diverse medieval discourses: legal, medical, mystical, philosophical, theological, magical, and metaphysical.[45] Within this pluri-disciplinary deployment, one cluster of interrelated themes was especially prominent. The issue,

39. As in note 33.

40. It was during the three years (1977–1980) I served as Curator-in charge of the Seal Department of the French National Archives that I began to experience the limitations seal casts impose on the understanding of medieval sealing practices: B. Bedos-Rezak, "Les politiques du service des sceaux des Archives nationales: bilan et perspectives," *La gazette des archives* 125–126 (1984), 156–64; Bedos-Rezak, "La sigillographie," in *Les archives de France, mémoire de l'histoire*, ed. F. Hildesheimer (Paris, 1997), 51–54; Bedos-Rezak, "Le sceau médiéval et son enjeu dans la diplomatique urbaine en France," in *La diplomatique urbaine en Europe au Moyen Âge: actes du congrès de la Commission internationale de diplomatique*, ed. W. Prevenier and Th. de Hemptinne (Louvain, 2000), 23–44 at 35.

41. Some examples of catalogued collections of seal matrices include A. B. Tonnochy, *Catalogue of British Seal-Dies in the British Museum* (London, 1952); C. Battenberg, *Die Sammlung der Siegelstempel im Kestner-Museum Hannover* (Hannover, 1985); F. Ménendez Pidal and E. Gómez Pérez, *Matrices de sellos españoles: Siglos XII al XVI* (Madrid, 1987); A. Muzzi, B. Tomasello, and A. Tori, *Sigilli nel Museo nazionale del Bargello—*I: *Ecclesiastici* (Florence, 1988); II (in 2 vols.): *Privati* (Florence, 1989); III: *Civili* (Florence, 1990); R. Laurent and C. Roelandt, *Inventaire des collections de matrices de sceaux des Archives générales du Royaume et de la Bibliothèque royale* (Brussels, 1997).

42. Fabre, *Sceau médiéval* (as in note 1), 279–84.

43. J. Cherry, "The Breaking of Seals," *Middelalderlige seglstamper i Norden*, ed. M. Andersen and G. Tegnér (Roskilde, 2002), 81–96; B. Bedos-Rezak, "L'au-delà du soi. Métamorphoses sigillaires en Europe médiévale," *Cahiers de civilisation médiévale* 49 (2006), 337–58.

44. The full argument is made in B. Bedos-Rezak, *When Ego was Imago: Signs of Identity in the Middle Ages* (Leiden, 2010).

45. Such is the concern of my book in progress, "Marked

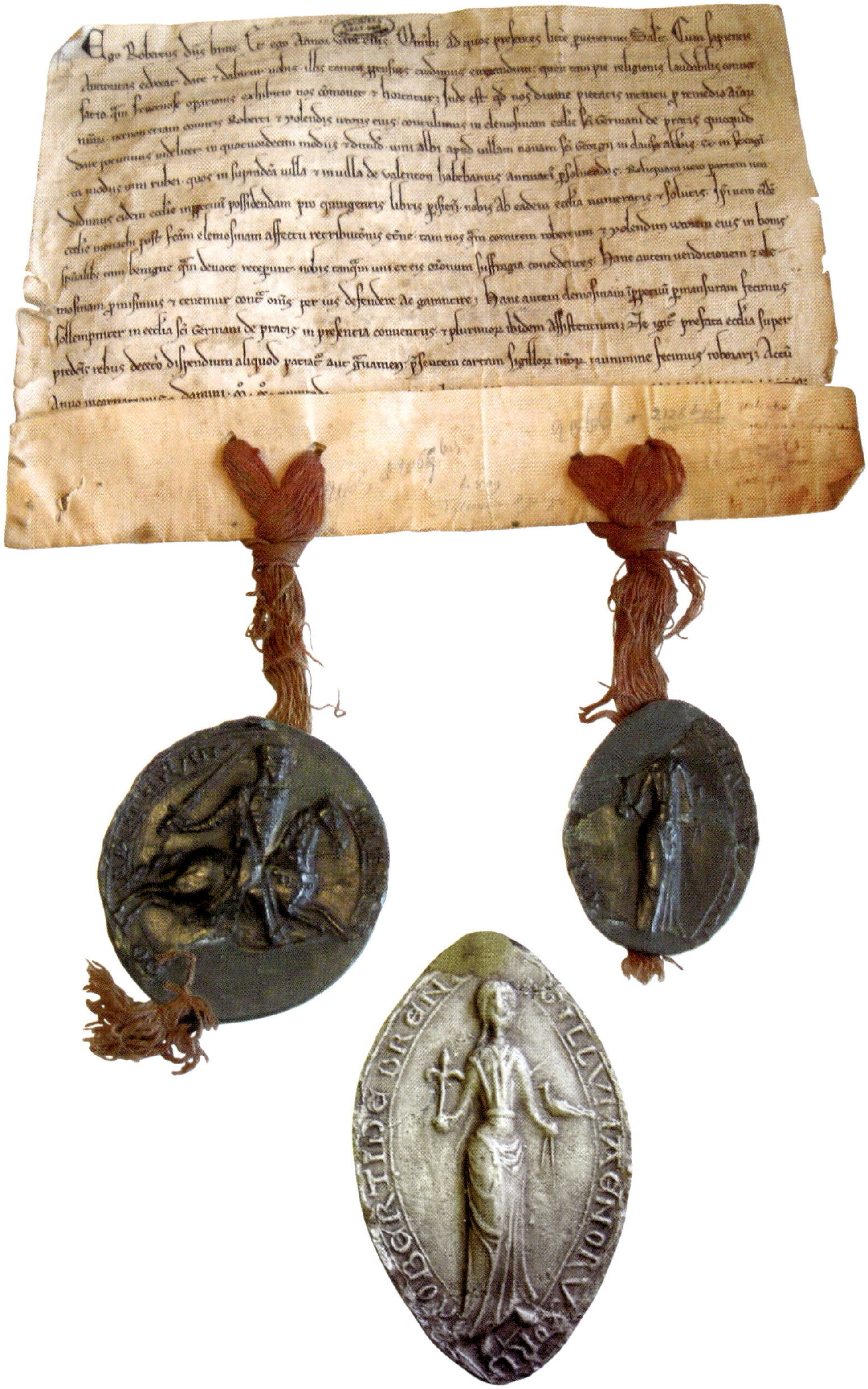

FIGURE 12. (*Top*): Charter given by Robert, count of Braine, and Aenor, his wife, in favor of the abbey of Saint-Germain-des-Prés, March 1215, Paris, Archives nationales, L 809 no. 34. (*Bottom middle*): Nineteenth-century cast of the now fragmentary seal of Aenor, wife of Robert of Braine, Paris, Archives nationales, Collection de sceaux, D 1548.

to generalize somewhat, was the extent to which any, indeed every created thing occurred according to the order of the material. The imprinted wax seal expressed, both tangibly and discursively, the principle that its waxen material participated in the creation of the image impressed upon and within it by physically and mechanically modulating its resemblance to its originating model. Physically (personally, as one may be tempted to write), for it was the warmth of a hand that rendered the wax sufficiently malleable to receive the imprint of the template; and mechanically, for resemblance to the template was automatic, imposed by matter upon matter, without the intervention of an idea.[46] The wax, thus, received the impression both of fingers, whether accidentally or intentionally, and of the matrix (Fig. 13). Emerging from such direct physical contacts, the produced image was understood to embody, to incorporate the presence of its originator.[47] As imprints, seals might actually be either formless, or formed, for resemblance was not a matter of optical imitation. Rather, resemblance was conceived as the result of an originating contact and, as such, was a quality believed to inhere within the material itself.[48] An image of substance, the seal was understood as analogous to the God-man and as expressing the relationship between God and man,[49] for the seal was also a touch-image, an image in process, contingent upon the plasticity of its medium, replicated but unstable, marked and figurative in its incorporation both of form and formlessness. As such, the seal image could and did stand for man as God's creation, man whose own malleable material had distorted the image of God within which he had been imprinted. Medieval texts of theological anthropology are replete with seal metaphors seeking to explicate the divine incarnation, as well as the human condition which involves both resemblance to and acquired dissimilarities from its divine creator.[50] Seals as wax imprints thus supported the notion that material process and qualities constituted a primary framework for conceptual reasoning about resemblance. In this discourse, external resemblance was less pertinent than the intrinsic and exemplary powers of materiality and material process.

Conclusion

Medieval seals cannot be said to have metamorphosed a minor into a major art.[51] However, to be other than minor is not to be the opposite of minor. Otherness is actually the crucial issue here. Medieval seals insistently

Matter: The Imprint and the Logic of Signs in Medieval Europe." The presence of seal metaphors in anthropological theology is discussed in Bedos-Rezak, *When Ego* (as in note 44), 140–50, 186–95. Some preliminary remarks on the broader presence of the seal *topos* in medieval discourse can be found in Bedos-Rezak, "Le sceau et l'art de penser au xiie siècle," in *Pourquoi le sceau? La sigillographie, nouvel enjeu de l'histoire de l'art*, ed. M. Gil and J.-L. Chassel (Lille, 2011), pp. 153–176.

46. G. Didi-Huberman, "Wax Flesh, Vicious Circles," in *Encyclopaedia Anatomica: A Complete Collection of Anatomical Waxes*, ed. M. von During and M. Poggesi (Cologne, 1999), 64–74; Didi-Huberman, "The Matter-Image: Dust, Garbage, Dirt, and Sculpture in the Sixteenth Century," *Common Knowledge* 6 (1997), 90; Bedos-Rezak, "L'empreinte: Trace et tracé d'une mediation," in *Matérialités et immatérialité de l'église au Moyen Âge*, ed. A. Oroveanu, M. Voicu, S. Daussy, C. Girbea, and B. Elena-Grigoriu, Actes du colloque de Bucarest, New Europe College, 22–23 octobre 2010 (Bucharest, forthcoming).

47. B. Bedos-Rezak, "In Search of a Semiotic Paradigm: The Matter of Sealing in Medieval Thought and Praxis (1050–1400)," in *Good Impressions: Image and Authority in Medieval Seals*, ed. J. Cherry and J. Robinson (London, 2008), 1–7 at 2; M. Pastoureau, "Le doigt dans la cire: Cent mille empreintes digitales médiévales," *The Human Skin/Le pelle umana. Micrologus* 13 (2005), 331–44.

48. G. Didi-Huberman, "Ex-voto, Image, Organ, Time," *L'esprit créateur* 47 (2007), 7–16 at 12–13.

49. On the Christic body as establishing a contractual, documentary bond with humankind, see E. Steiner, *Documentary Culture and the Making of Medieval English Literature* (Cambridge, 2003); in her "Cutting Edge: The Economy of Mediality in Twelfth-Century Chirographic writing,"—in *Modelle des Medialen im Mittelalter*, ed. Christian Kiening and Martina Stercken, special issue of *Das Mittelalter* 15 (2010), 134–161—Bedos-Rezak analyzes a twelfth-century sealed chirograph that was divided both through the word *chirographum* and the crucified figure of Christ with halo; it was cut in half so that each party could keep a record of the written transaction for eventual later verification.

50. B. Rezak-Rezak, *When Ego* (as in note 44), 140–50, 186–95, 225–30.

51. Recently, seals have occupied an enviable place in art exhibits and publications in medieval art history, even being the objects of solo exhibitions and conferences: R. Kahsnitz, "Siegel und Goldbullen," in *Die Zeit der Staufer: Geschichte, Kunst, Kultur: Ka-*

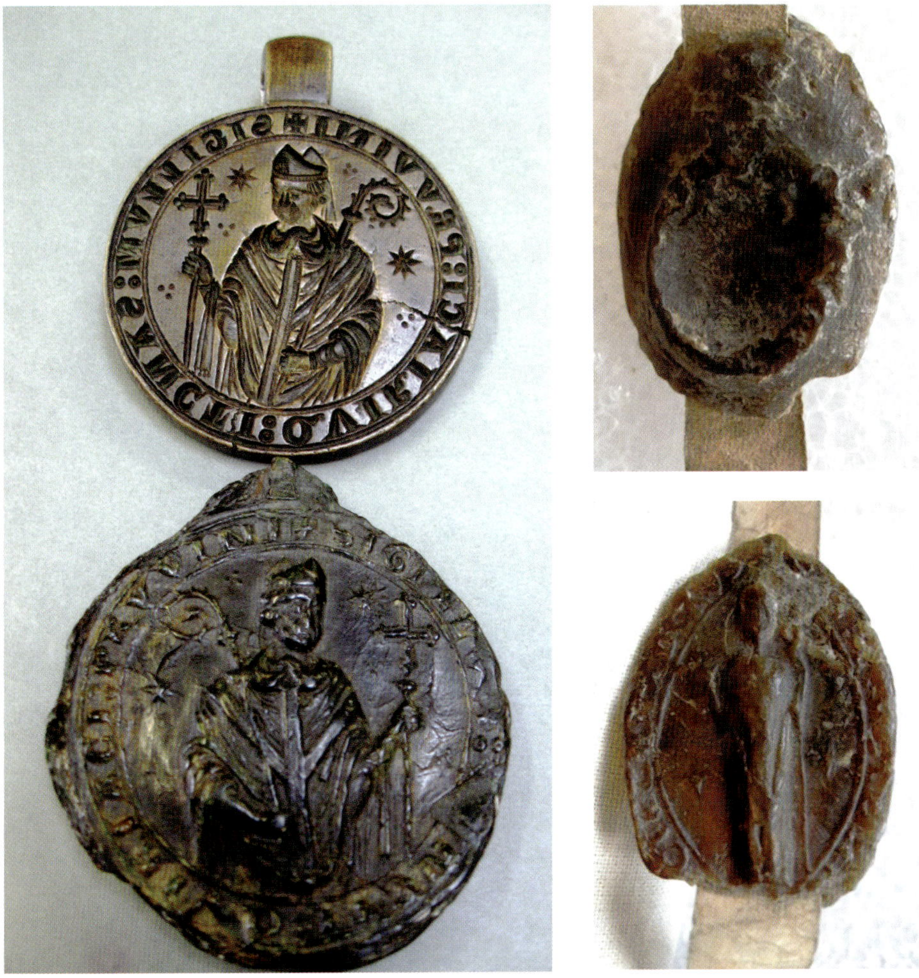

FIGURE 13. (*Left*): Detached wax seal impression (*below*), originally stamped from the seal-matrix of the collegial chapter of Saint-Quiriace of Provins (*above*), Paris, Archives nationales, Collection de sceaux, no. 18. (*Right*): Thumb impression (*reverse*) and imprinted image (*obverse*), Paris, Archives nationales, J 414B no. 418.

talog der Ausstellung Wurttembergisches Landesmuseum Stuttgart, 5 vols. (Stuttgart, 1977–1979), vol. 1: 17–107, figs. 11–92, vol. 3: figs. 1–30, 83–104; T. Diederich, "Siegelkunst," in *Die Parler und der Schöne Stil 1350–1400. Europäische Kunst unter den Luxemburgern* (Cologne, 1978), 151–163; T. A. Heslop, "Seals," in *1066: English Romanesque Art* (London, 1984), 298–320; Kahsnitz, "Imagines et signa. Romanische Siegel aus Köln," in *Ornamenta Ecclesiae. Kunst und Künstler der Romanik.* Katalog zur Ausstellung des Schnütgen-Museums in der Josef-Haubrich-Kunsthalle, ed. Anton Legner. 3 vols. (Cologne, 1985), vol. 2: 21–60; *Il sigillo nella storia della civiltà attraverso i documenti dell'Archivio segreto vaticano.* Mostra documentaria (Vatican, 1985); *Il sigillo nella storia e nella cultura.* Mostra documentaria societa' editoriale Jouvence, ed. S. Ricci (Rome, 1985); H. Collin, *Sceaux de l'histoire de Lorraine, Lotharingia* I (1988); T. A. Heslop, "English Seals in the Thirteenth and Fourteenth Centuries," and "Techniques for Making Seal Matrices and Impressions," in *Age of Chivalry: Art in Plantagenet England 1200–1400*, ed. J. Alexander and P. Binski (London, 1987), 114–17, 396–400; *Otto der Grosse: Magdeburg und Europa*, ed. M. Puhle (Mainz, 2001); H.-G. Boehm, *Das Marienbild auf Siegeln im Wandel der Zeiten* (Mergentheim, 2001); *Sceaux et usages de sceaux: images de la Champagne médiévale*, ed. J.-L. Chassel (Paris, 2003); *Colecção Esfragistica da Facultade de Letras da Universidade de Coimbra: Catálogo da Exposição* (Coimbra, 2003); *Empreintes et matrices: les sceaux du patrimoine historique et artistique du Nord, XIIe–XVIIIe siècle.* (Lille, 2008). A listing of recent conferences comprises: *Good Impressions: Image and Authority in Medieval Seals*, London, British Museum, February 2007, ed. N. Adams, J. Cherry, J. Robinson (London, 2008); *Pourquoi le sceau? La sigillographie, nouvel enjeu de l'histoire de l'art* (Lille, Université de Lille III, October 2008, *acta*, as in note 45); *Insculpta imago: Seal*

called attention to their material mode of production, that is, imprinting, being simultaneously effective signs of representation and eloquent tools of conceptualization. Until recently, most scholarship devoted to seals has ignored their medieval operations, concentrating rather upon their typological and surface aspects. Thus situated, access to seals' proper historical agency has been severely curtailed. In the light of modern scholarship,[52] however, it is fair to say that seals have now graduated from being representatives of a minor art and may be more properly recognized as significant historical actors.

Matrices and Seal Impressions in the Mediterranean, Kunsthistorisches Institute in Florence, Max-Planck-Institute, Florence, February 2011 (*acta* forthcoming, ed. Ruth Wolff). Some recent publications on seals and medieval art include J. Déer, "Die Siegel Kaiser Friedrichs I. Barbarossa und Heinrichs VI. in der Kunst und Politik ihrer Zeit," in *Festschrift Hans R. Hahnloser zum 60. Geburstag,* ed. E. Beer (Basel, 1961), 47102, reprinted in *Byzanz und das abendländische Herrschertum.* Ausgewählte Aufsätze (Sigmaringen, 1977); G. Brunel, *Images du Pouvoir royal: les chartes décorées des Archives nationales, XIIIe–XVe siècle* (Paris, 2005); M. Späth, "Mikroarchitektur zwischen Repräsentation und Identitätsstiftung: Die Siegelbilder englischer Klöster und Kathedralkapitel im 13. Jahrhundert," in *Mikroarchitektur im Mittelalter: ein gattungsübergreifendes Phänomen zwischen Realität und Imagination. Beiträge der gleichnamigen Tagung im Germanischen Nationalmuseum, Nürnberg vom 26. bis 29. Oktober 2005,* ed. Ch. Kratzke and U. Albrecht (Leipzig, 2008), 253–77.

52. In addition to the studies cited throughout this essay, good examples of the new attention given to seals as agentive images are M. Pastoureau, "Les sceaux et la fonction sociale des images," in *L'Image: fonctions et usages des images dans l'Occident médiéval,* ed. J. Baschet, J. C. Schmitt (Paris, 1996), 275–308; H. Keller, "Ottonische Herrschersiegel. Beobachtungen und Fragen zu Gestalt und Aussage und zur Funktion im historischen Kontext," in *Bild und Geschichte: Studien zur politischen Ikonographie. Festschrift für Hansmartin Schwarzmaier zum fünfundsechzigsten Geburtstag,* ed. K. Krimm (Sigmaringen, 1997), 3–51; P. Schmidt, "Materialität, Medialität und Autorität des vervielfältigten Bildes. Siegel und andere Bildmedien des Mittelalters in ihren Wechselwirkungen," in *Die Bildlichkeit korporativer Siegel im Mittelalte: Kunstgeschichte und Geschischte im Gespräch,* ed. M. Späth (Cologne, 2009), pp. 89–111.

JOHN CHERRY

Medieval Jewelry: From Collections to Consumerism

COMPARED with painting, sculpture, and architecture, jewelry is small in size. Its scale and value made it both easy to lose and hoardable in the Middle Ages, as well as collectable today. Collecting laid the foundation for analysis, and such collections have been examined not only for their beauty but also for their connections to amuletic protection, religious belief, the history of dress, and finally luxury and consumerism. In this essay, medieval jewelry is primarily looked at within an English historical perspective.[1]

Although the study of medieval jewelry lies in the collecting mania of the nineteenth century, such collecting began earlier. The collection in the British Museum comes from Sir Hans Sloane, a medical doctor, who practiced in the late seventeenth and eighteenth centuries, and his collection was itself created from earlier seventeenth-century collections. Given the source of his income, it is not surprising that objects and inscriptions thought to protect from disease and to produce good health are included.

Sir Augustus Wollaston Franks (Fig. 1) provided the main impetus for collecting jewelry for the British Museum in the nineteenth century. Here, the motives were different. Franks, influenced by the Oxford Movement and Augustus Welby Pugin's ideas of Gothic as a true Christian style, collected rings and jewelry as antiquities that would form a National Collection. Obviously, items of precious metal were collected at the expense of jewelry of lesser materials, and this has biased the study.[2]

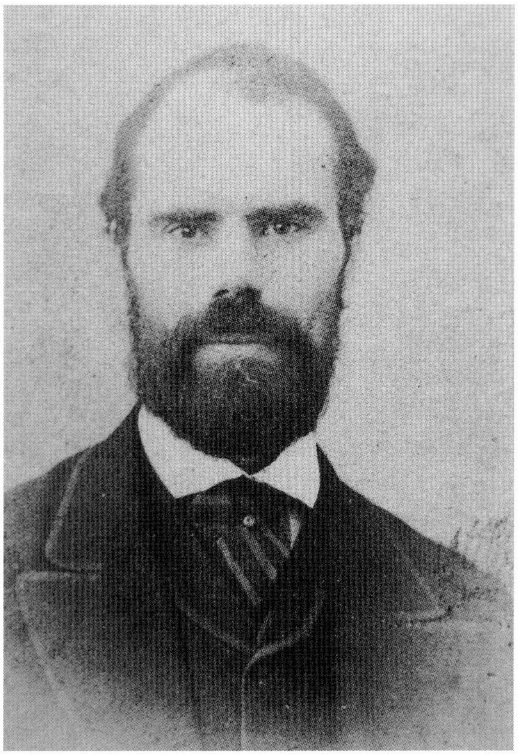

FIGURE 1. Sir Augustus Wollaston Franks (photo: Trustees of the British Museum).

Sometimes jewelry was not acquired by the British Museum because it was thought to be too Catholic or "Popish." In 1851, a gold reliquary found at Devizes was offered to the Museum. Since the Museum would have had to go the Treasury for a special grant, the proposal was declined, since it "would be beyond the courage of our present ministers and would frighten the ultra Protestants out of their senses. Some of them already begin to fancy they perceive popery lurking in the intricacies of medieval art."[3] We owe much to

1. I am most grateful to Colum Hourihane for the opportunity to give this paper at the very stimulating conference *From Major to Minor* held in March 2011.

2. *Sir Hans Sloane, Collector, Scientist, Antiquary: Founding Father of the British Museum*, ed. Arthur Macgregor (London: British Museum, 1994). For Franks, see *A. W. Franks: Nineteenth-Century Collecting and the British Museum*, ed. Marjorie Caygill and John Cherry (London: British Museum, 1997).

3. Edward Hawkins in a letter to an unknown recipient dated 13 Jan. 1851. British Museum Archives, SCAR Box 21, no. 181. For

those collectors, and the study of medieval jewelry is largely based on their collections. Some of the collections were published in catalogues providing detailed descriptions and measurements, though little in the way of an overall picture of development.[4] How did the study develop from their collections? Dame Joan Evans (Fig. 2) provides the link between collecting and analysis. Daughter of John Evans, the great prehistorian and half-brother of Arthur Evans, excavator of Knossos, she had a personal link with Franks, whom she knew as a girl. She collected and wore pre-Revolutionary French jewelry with distinction.[5] Her vision of art history encompassed the "understanding of the environment that produced works of art including geographical contexts, economic circumstances and historical circumstances: in other words art history and history should be the 'study of civilisation.'" Her books included *English Jewellery from the 5th Century BC to 1800*, published in 1921, and *A History of Jewellery, 1100–1870*, published in 1953. From their date range it is clear that she was taking the long view and she interpreted jewelry as an art confined to ornaments actually worn upon the person. Her feeling for the Gothic period is clear from the following quote:

> The early fourteenth century was a time of delicate lyricism in all the decorative arts. The love of romance that found expression in amatory inscriptions, the feeling for natural beauty that was expressed in every art from monumental sculpture to illumination and embroidery, the taste for a mannered elegance were all reflected in the style of jewels.

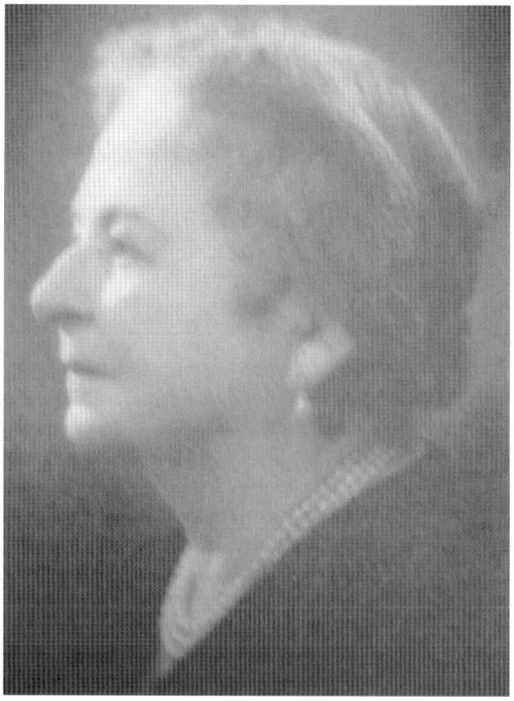

FIGURE 2. Joan Evans (photo: Society of Antiquaries).

In 1931 came her ground-breaking book entitled *Pattern: A Study of Ornament in Western Europe, 1180 to 1900*, which argued that pattern and ornament provided a bridge between the major and minor arts. As a historian of style in jewelry, her work provided the seeds for later approaches.[6]

One of Evans's focuses was belief in the ability of jewelry to protect from evil, illness, and misfortune. Two pioneering works were, in the first instance, on

---

nineteenth-century collecting in the Victoria and Albert Museum, which was perhaps less nervous about acquiring Continental art, see the articles by Clive Wainwright, "The Making of the South Kensington Museum, I–IV," *Journal of the History of Collections* 14, no. 1 (2002), 3–78. For Fortnum, see *C. D. E. Fortnum and the Collecting and Study of the Applied Arts and Sculpture in Victorian England*, ed. Ben Thomas and Timothy Wilson (Oxford, 1999). The Devizes pendant was eventually acquired by Sir Augustus Wollaston Franks and was bequeathed by him to the Museum in 1896.

4. M. Dalton Ormonde, *Franks Bequest: Catalogue of the Finger Rings: Early Christian, Byzantine, Teutonic, Medieval, and Later* (London: Trustees of the British Museum, 1912). O. M. Dalton, *Catalogue of Engraved Gems of the Post-classical Periods in the Department of British and Mediaeval Antiquities and Ethnography in the British Museum* (London: Trustees of the British Museum, 1915). Charles C. Oman, *Catalogue of Rings* (London, 1930).

5. H. G. M. Leighton, "Memoir," *Transactions of the Bristol and Gloucester Archaeological Society* 95 (1977), 123. Eventually the Ashmolean Museum, Oxford, Birmingham City Museums and Art Gallery, the British Museum and, above all, the Victoria and Albert Museum, were the beneficiaries of her generosity in giving away her collection.

6. The first quotation is an amalgam from *Nature in Design: A Study in Naturalism from the Bronze Age to the Renaissance* (Oxford, 1933) and *The History of the Society of Antiquaries* (London, 1954). The second is from *A History of Jewellery: 1100–1870* (London, 1953; 2nd ed., 1970), 53. Her first book was *English Jewellery from the 5th Century B.C. to 1800* (London, 1921). *Pattern: A Study of Orna-*

early medieval lapidaries, which were responsible for passing onto the medieval world the classical belief in amulets, and, most importantly, on magical jewels, and she showed that belief in their efficacy continued up to the eighteenth century.[7] Since Evans's death in 1977, there has been an increased interest in magic and amulets, as exemplified by the work of the social historian Sir Keith Thomas. His book, *Religion and the Decline of Magic*, which was published in 1971, began with an analysis of the religious magic of the medieval church, and proceeded to popular forms of magic and religion, astrology, witchcraft, and so to magic's decline.[8]

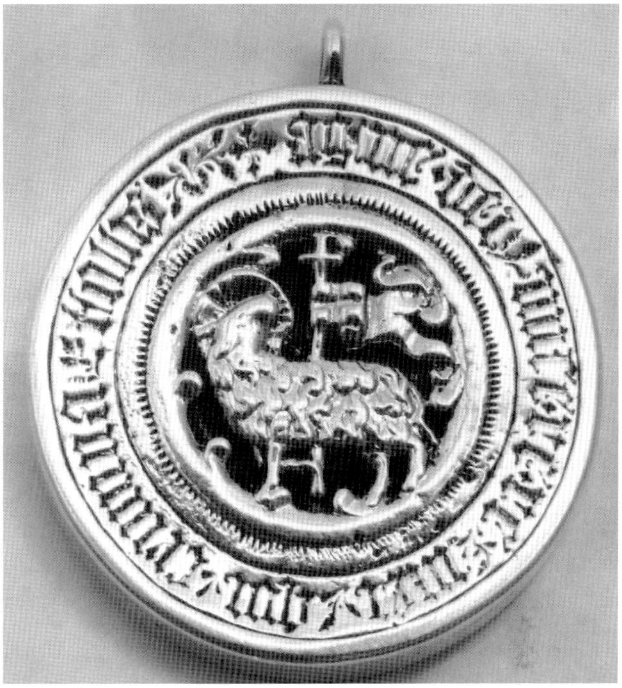

FIGURE 3. Silver *Agnus Dei* showing the Lamb and the standard of the Resurrection, private collection (photo: Trustees of the British Museum).

In Thomas's first chapter he refers to the devotion to the saints, *Agnus Dei* containers (Fig. 3), and relics worn as charms, which were—later in the sixteenth century—to attract the scorn and derision of the Protestants. Such containers as that found at Gleaston in Lancashire show a two-sided look at health and religion.[9] Thomas sets them in a sociological background and compares medieval Catholicism to newly converted African Christians.[10] But the magic of religion was approached from another direction, too. The eminent Catholic historian Eamon Duffy asserted the value of traditional beliefs in late medieval Catholic worship, including the amuletic potential of worship and the material manifestations of the faith. His *The Stripping of the Altars: Traditional Religion in England, 1400–1580* asserted the importance of late medieval piety by analyzing devotion to the saints and their prayers and charms. Two rings that combine religious and spiritual healing are the Coventry ring in the British Museum and the Thame ring in the Ashmolean Museum. The Coventry ring (Fig. 4) makes an appeal to the five wounds of Christ and their therapeutic effect, while the Thame ring, set with amethysts, provides spiritual help through the fragments of the True Cross, which would have been contained within its box-shaped bezel reliquary.[11] Jewelry provides new evidence for late medieval belief: the large number of rings found in England with bezels engraved with figures of saints and other iconographic scenes, such as the remarkable ring found at

ment in Western Europe, 1180 to 1900 (Oxford, 1931) followed later. For Joan Evans, see Nicola Coldstream, "Joan Evans 1893–1977: Art Historian and Antiquary," in *Women Medievalists and the Academy*, ed. Jane Chance (Madison, Wis.: University of Wisconsin Press, 2005), 399–422.

7. With Paul Studer, Marbode, Philippe de Thaon, and Joan Evans, *Anglo-Norman Lapidaries* (Paris: Champion, 1924). *Magical Jewels of the Middle Ages and Renaissance, Particularly with Reference to England* (Oxford: Clarendon Press, 1922).

8. Keith Thomas, *Religion and the Decline of Magic* (London, 1971).

9. For *Agnus Dei* pendants, see John Cherry, "Containers for Agnus Deis," in *Through a Glass Brightly*, ed. Chris Entwistle (Oxford: Oxbow, 2003), 171–183. Ronald W. Lightbown discusses *Agnus Dei* pendants in *Medieval European Jewellery* (London, 1992), 504–5 and pl. 80.

10. Thomas (as in note 8), 33–34. Max G. Marwick, *Sorcery in Its Social Setting: A Study of the Northern Rhodesia Cewa* (Manchester, 1965), 90.

11. Eamon Duffy, *The Stripping of the Altars: Traditional Religion in England 1400–1580* (Yale, 1992). See also Eamon Duffy, *Marking the Hours: English People and their Prayers 1240–1570* (London: Yale University Press, 2006). For the Coventry and Thame rings, see John Cherry, "Medieval Rings" in Anne Ward *et al.*, *The Ring from Antiquity to the Twentieth Century* (London, 1981), 82, no. 189, and 72, no. 152.

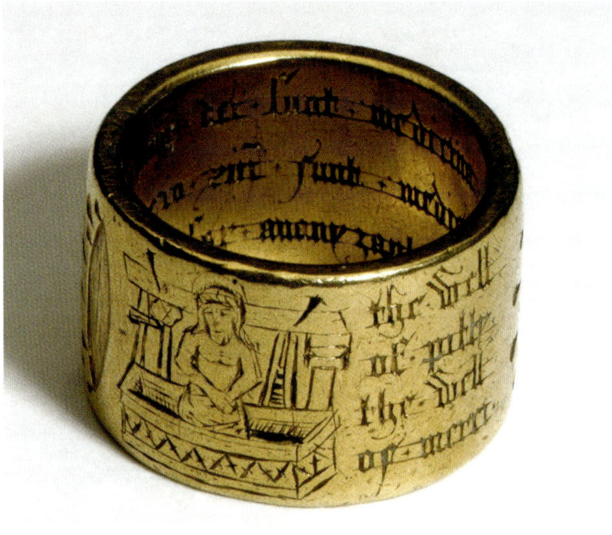

FIGURE 4. Gold ring, found at Coventry, known as the Coventry Ring, BM P&E AF 897 (photo: Trustees of the British Museum).

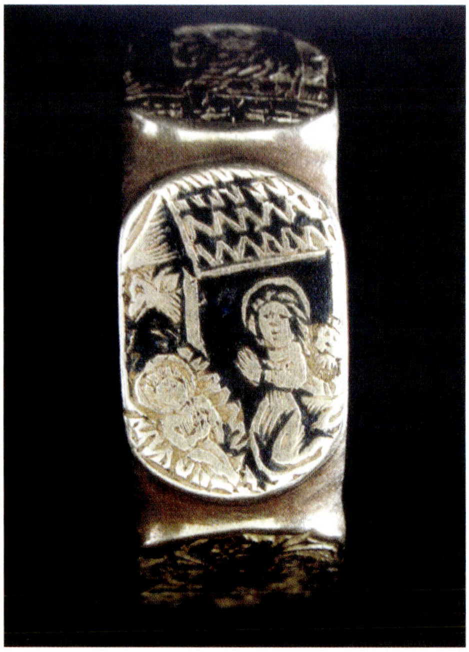

FIGURE 5. Gold ring found at Sleaford, Lincolnshire, BM P&E 2004,0202.1 (photo: Trustees of the British Museum).

Sleaford, Lincolnshire, and now in the British Museum (2004,0202.1) (Fig. 5), points to this fact.[12]

Some might not define pilgrim souvenirs as jewelry, but they are an interesting type of minor object, which is discussed elsewhere in this volume by Jos Koldeweij. Cheap, mass-produced items reflecting collective behavior, they attest to the operation of saints' cults and the commercial and devotional activities that they fostered. For instance, the lead *ampulla* from Trig Lane, London (Museum of London), of the mid-thirteenth century, shows St. Thomas and describes him as the best doctor: *Optimus egrorum medicus fit Toma bonorum* (St. Thomas is the best doctor of the worthy sick).[13]

Both religious and amuletic, *ampullae* contained Holy Water and were sometimes seen as an aid to agricultural fertility. A recent study of *ampullae* by William Anderson, entitled "Blessing the Fields," raises the question of whether they were used in some sort of crop-enhancing role, since they were not lost complete and intact but often have torn mouths. However, this does not necessarily mean that they were opened in the fields. Whatever one's view on this, the nature of the approach is interesting.[14] Similar approaches have been used by both Roberta Gilchrist (who has studied the bending and placing of coins in graves) and Henry Maguire.[15]

This combination of religious belief and medical value can be seen in the Middleham Jewel (Yorkshire

12. Every year medieval religious rings of varying quality are found in different parts of the country, and a complete survey would be an interesting project. For Sleaford, see James Robinson, Silke Ackermann *et al.*, *Masterpieces: Medieval Art* (London: British Museum, 2008), 142.

13. Brian Spencer, *Pilgrim Souvenirs and Secular Badges* (MOL, 1998), no. 9, 52–3. See also Ronald C. Finucane, *Miracles and Pilgrims: Popular Beliefs in Medieval England* (London, 1977).

14. William Anderson, "Blessing the Fields? A Study of Late Medieval *Ampullae* from England and Wales," *Medieval Archaeology* 54 (2010), 182–203. One wonders whether the use of ears of corn and fish in Finland have some food improving purpose, see Visa Immonen, *Golden Moments: Artefacts of Precious Metals as Products of Luxury Consumption in Finland, c. 1200–1600,* Archaeologia Medii Aevi Finlandiae, XVI (Turku, 2009), 191 and 194–7.

15. Roberta Gilchrist, "Magic for the Dead? The Archaeology of Magic in later Medieval Burials," *Medieval Archaeology* 32 (2008), 119–158. Henry Maguire, "Magic and Money in the Early Middle Ages," *Speculum* 72 (1997), 1037–54.

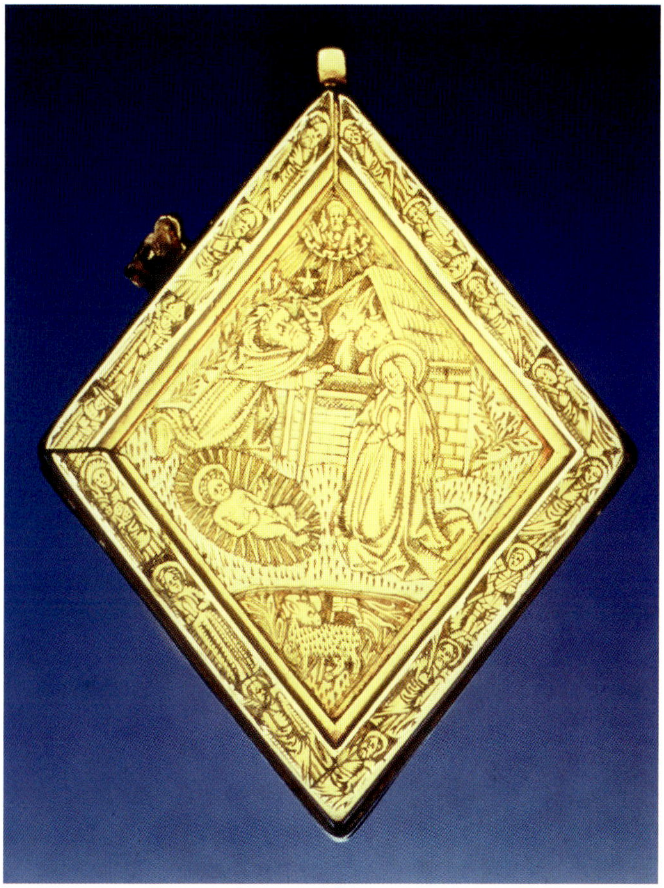

FIGURE 6. The Middleham Jewel, Yorkshire Museum, YORYM 1992.21 (photo: Trustees of the British Museum).

Museum) (Fig. 6), which was found in 1985 and combines the virtue of the sapphire and magical words with religious scenes of the birth of Christ and the Trinity, as well as in the more recently discovered Kilgetty Pendant, from Wales (National Museum of Wales, PAS NMGW-9E8024) (Fig. 7). The Kilgetty Pendant has an engraving on the back that shows the Passion of Christ, and dates to the early sixteenth century. The front opens and reveals a Trinity of haloed saints (St. John the Baptist, St. Catherine, and St. Mary Magdalene). Its form imitates the shape of the larger paxes that were kissed to celebrate the unity of the Church through the bond of charity. An item of personal adornment, it also had a physical function and was used for devotional meditation.[16]

Both pendants were worn as items of clothing. While Joan Evans contributed much to the study of jewelry, her only book solely devoted to dress, *Dress in Mediaeval France* (1952), excludes jewelry. Traditionally, dress historians had looked to funeral effigies for evidence of dress and adornment.[17] It was a new generation of younger female historians who, by analyzing a range of material from manuscripts, documentary sources, as well as the objects themselves, shed great light on dress in social history—particularly touching fashion, chivalry, and the important matter of gifts of both jewelry

16. John Cherry, *The Middleham Jewel and Ring* (York: Yorkshire Museum, 1994). For Kilgetty, see *Portable Antiquities and Treasure Annual Report* (London, 2007), no. 321.

17. Roy C. Strong, *Recreating the Past: British History and the Victorian Painter* (London, 1978), gives a good account of this attitude.

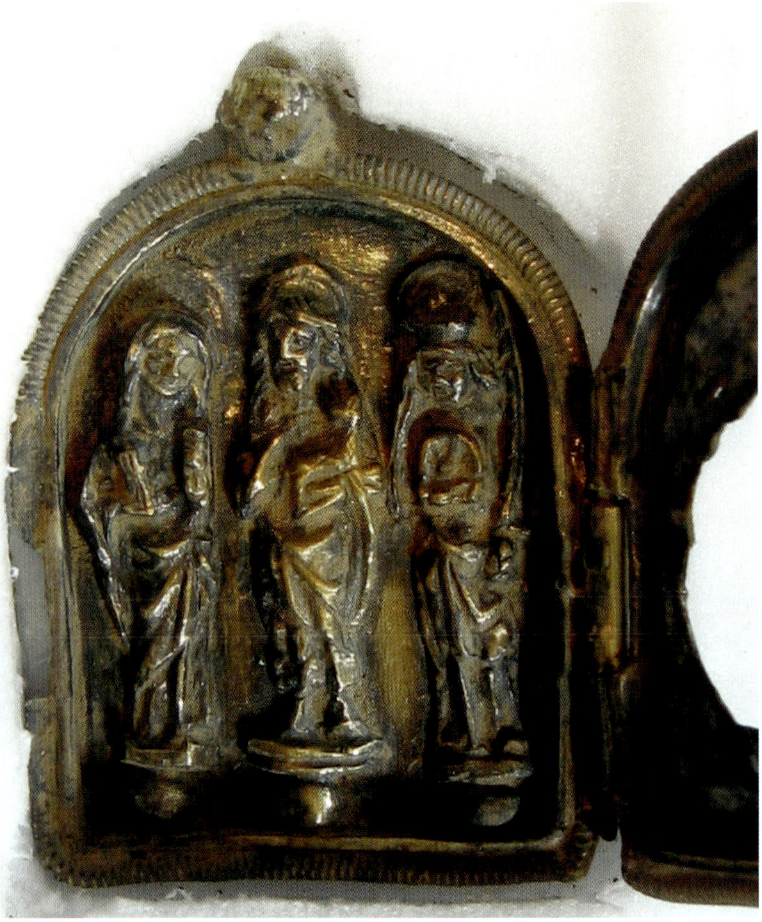

FIGURE 7. The Kilgetty Pendant, National Museum of Wales, Cardiff, PAS NMGW-9E8024 (photo: Trustees of the British Museum).

and clothing. Stella Mary Newton's *Fashion in the Age of the Black Prince: 1340–1365* (1980) was exemplary in this regard.[18]

The relationship between dress and jewelry at a higher social level is shown by exquisite objects such as the Dunstable Swan Jewel (Fig. 8), a masterpiece of Parisian white enamelling, which may be compared with a similar swan worn on the memorial brass of Jane Perient, a lady-in-waiting in the royal household of Kings Henry IV and V.[19] The latter jewel is an example of a livery badge and the study of jewelry in the fifteenth century has to take in the range of livery badges widely worn in both France and England, an example of which is the silver boar found at Chiddingly in East Sussex (Fig. 9). This was the livery badge of King Richard III (r. 1483–1485). A copper-alloy ver-

18. For recent work on medieval dress, see Stella N. Newton, *Fashion in the Age of the Black Prince: A Study of the Years 1340–1365* (Bury St. Edmunds: Boydell, 1980); Margaret Scott, *Late Gothic Europe, 1400–1500* (Atlantic Highlands, N.J., 1980); Jacqueline Herald, *Renaissance Dress in Italy, 1400–1500*, (London, 1987); Francoise Pipponier and Perrine Mane, *Dress in the Middle Ages* (Paris, 1997); Margaret Scott, *Medieval Dress and Fashion* (London: British Library, 2007); Lisa Monnas, *Merchants, Princes, and Painters: Silk Fabrics in Northern and Italian Paintings, 1300–1550* (London: Yale, 2008).

19. John Cherry, "The Dunstable Swan Jewel," *Journal of the British Archaeological Association* 32 (1969), 38–53.

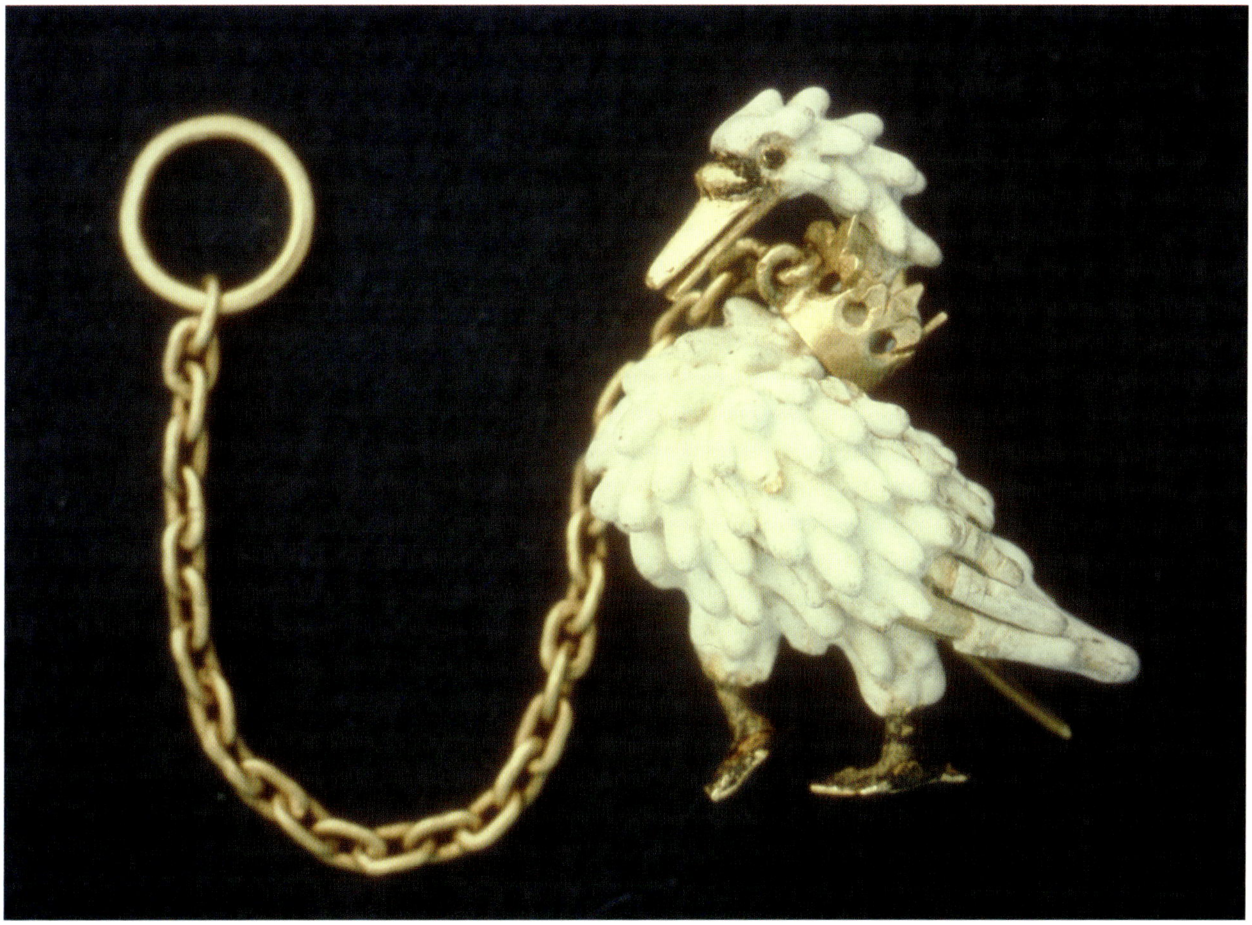

FIGURE 8. The Dunstable Swan Jewel, BM P&E 1966,0703.1 (photo: Trustees of the British Museum).

sion was found in the moat of Richard's hereditary home at Middleham Castle, North Yorkshire, and a pewter example was found in London. So it can be shown that a range of metals was used for these badges, which are clearly of different values.[20] There has also been much research undertaken on the dress of those who would never feature in effigies, paintings, or manuscripts. Archaeology has produced finds of textiles and also, on an increasing scale, of dress fittings, buckles, buttons, and pins. The system of reporting treasure in England and Wales has documented many silver dress hooks and pins, and there is much work to be done to produce an overall picture. A notable start was made by Geoff Egan with his *Dress Accessories* (1991).[21]

Dress protects the body and gems sometimes protect life itself. A type of jewelry that has recently received

20. *Treasure Annual Report 2000* (London, 2000), 83, no. 155. John Cherry, *The Middleham Jewel and Ring* (York: Yorkshire Museum, 1994), 38. Brian Spencer, *Pilgrim Souvenirs and Secular Badges: Medieval Finds from Excavations in London* (London, 1998), 289–290, cat. no. 281h.

21. Geoff Egan and Frances Pritchard, *Dress Accessories, c. 1150–c. 1450: Medieval Finds from Excavations in London* (London: HMSO, 1991). See also S. V. Smith, "Materializing Resistant Identities Among the Medieval Peasantry: An Examination of Dress Accessories from English Rural Sites," *Journal of Material Culture* 14 (2009), 309–32.

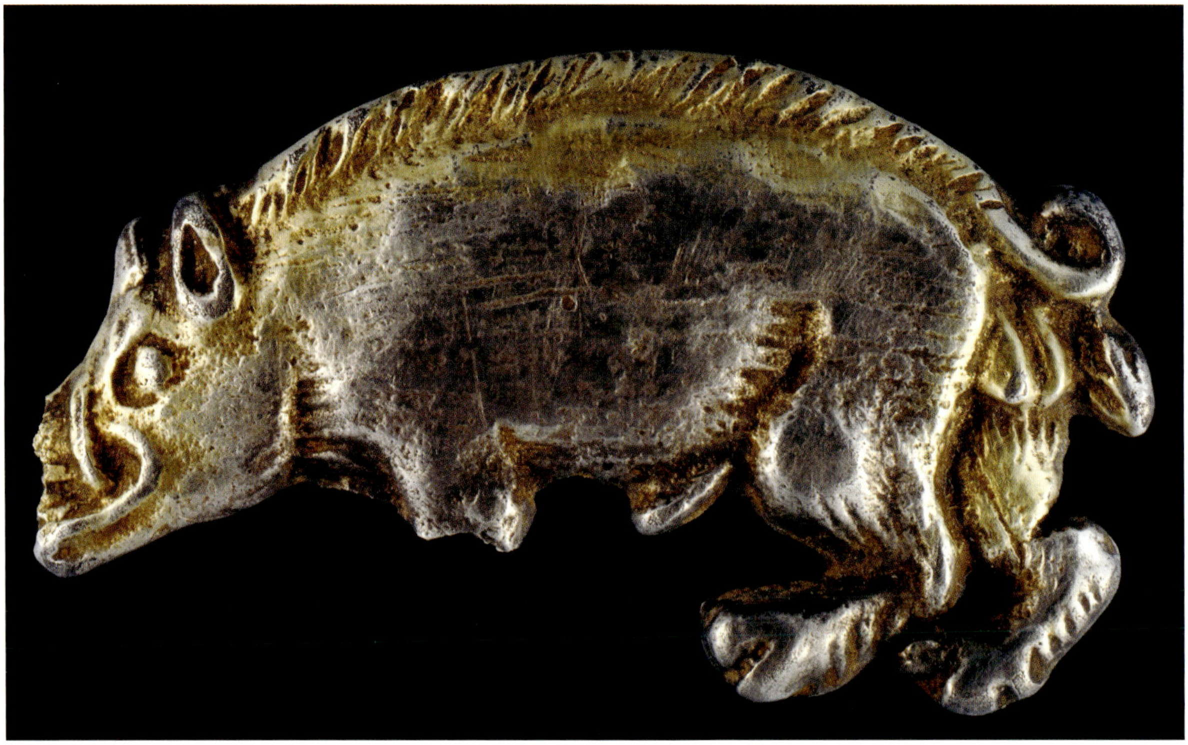

FIGURE 9. The Silver Boar Badge found at Chiddingley, East Sussex, BM P&E 2003,0505.1 (photo: Trustees of the British Museum).

much attention is the reuse of classical gems and intaglios, as shown on the Cross of Lothar (Aachen Cathedral Treasury), which dates to *c.* 985. This work shows the mobility of the gem from the secular (image of Augustus) to the sacred, as well as the appropriation of the classical past into the Lotharingian present by the setting of Augustus in the center and Lothar below. Gems were copied in the Middle Ages and new gems and cameos were carved. Many had an amuletic purpose, but they also provide through their miniature scale an interesting link between the major and minor arts. Gem-set jewelry was socially distinctive. The highest social level is shown by the drawing of the St. Alban's Cameo that depicts Hercules, which was said to aid childbirth and was significant enough to be drawn in a St. Albans manuscript. The Oxwich Brooch (National Museum & Galleries of Wales, 76.39h) (Fig. 10) was found at an important castle site in Oxwich, Wales. These medieval cameos belonged to a person of importance, especially since they were carefully preserved from an earlier object and reused in this brooch.[22]

Literary studies have exerted considerable influence on the conception of jewelry. More recently, Valerie Gontaro's *Parures d'or et de gemmes* provides a very modern viewpoint on this.[23] The literary background plays a large part in Michael Camille's only venture into jewelry studies in his *The Medieval Art of Love*, published in 1998, where he examines Love's gifts, especially the girdle and the purse, the depiction of Love's places on jewelry, and the use of jewelry in the form of the locket to provide Love's signs.[24] The amount of jewelry found today—especially in England and Wales documented

22. John Lewis, "The Oxwich Brooch," *Jewellery Studies* 2 (1985), 23–28.

23. Valerie Gontaro, *Parures d'or et de gemmes: L'orfèverie dans les romans antiques du XIIe siècle* (University of Provence, 2002).

24. M. Camille, *The Medieval Art of Love* (New York, 1998). This theme is well illustrated by the gold heart-shaped pendant from Dorset. See John Cherry, "A Late Medieval Love Jewel," *Jewellery Studies* 1 (1983–4), 45–48.

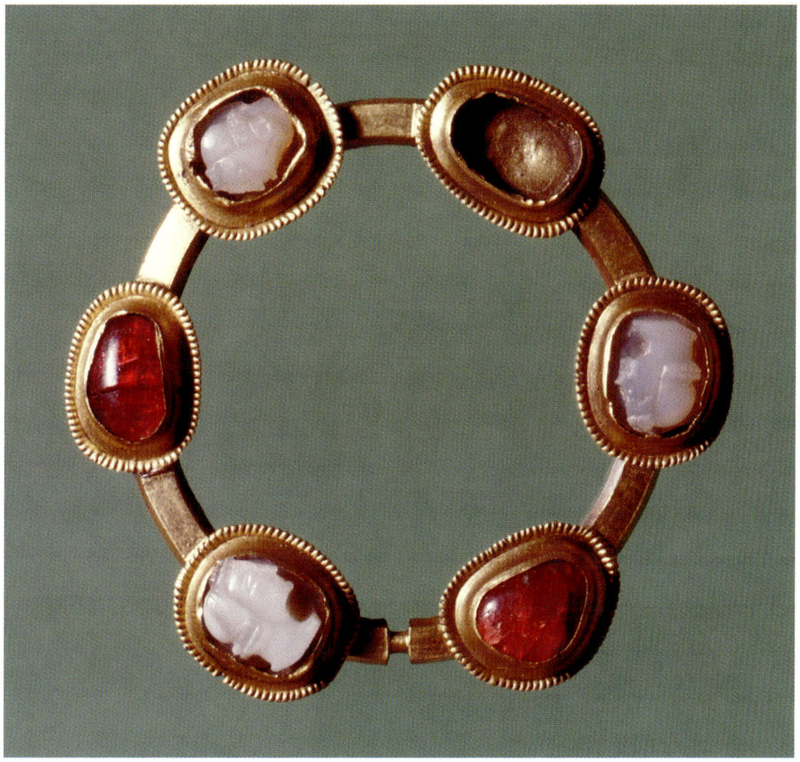

FIGURE 10. Gold brooch set with cameos found at Oxwich Castle, Wales, National Museum of Wales, Cardiff (photo: Trustees of the British Museum).

under the arrangement of the Treasure Act passed in 1997—constantly leads to changes and reassessment. Nowhere is this more evident than in the discovery of hoards of jewelry buried in times of uncertainty, which are often found with coins that provide valuable dating evidence.[25] The Fishpool Hoard, buried in 1464, provides an interesting example of a hoard entirely of gold that must have belonged to paymaster of the Yorkist or Lancastrian armies in the Wars of the Roses. The jewelry portion is insignificant when compared to the value of the whole.[26] There have also been major finds and studies of hoards on the Continent. Two major examples are the discovery of the Fuchenshof Hoard in Upper Austria in 1997, and the Erfurt Hoard found in Germany in 1998. Hoards found long ago have also been subjected to modern analysis, such as the Pritzwalk Hoard, Berlin.[27]

A remarkable series of medieval hoards, found on the Continent, belonged to Jews and were hidden at the time of the Black Death in 1348. They may show the nature of the jewelry owned and used in Jewish communities at that time, although it is arguable that some may have been pawned and so it does not necessarily present a true picture of the Jewish consumer. The hoard found at Colmar in the 1890s has long been in the Cluny Museum. It was studied in detail in the

25. The quantity of material is revealed by the Treasure Annual Reports, produced for England and Wales by the Department for Culture, Media, and Sport. They have been produced annually since 1997.

26. John Cherry, "Medieval Jewellery from the Fishpool Hoard, Nottinghamshire," *Archaeologia* civ (1973), 307–321.

27. Bernhardt Prokisch and Thomas Kühtreiber, eds., *Der Schatzfund von Fuchsenshof: Studien zur Kunstgeschichte von Oberösterreich*, Folge 15 (Linz, 2004). Stephan Krabath, Lothar Lambacher, and Bernd Kluge, *Der Pritzwalker Silberfund: Schmuck des späten Mittelalters* (Berlin: Kunstgewerbe Museum, 2006).

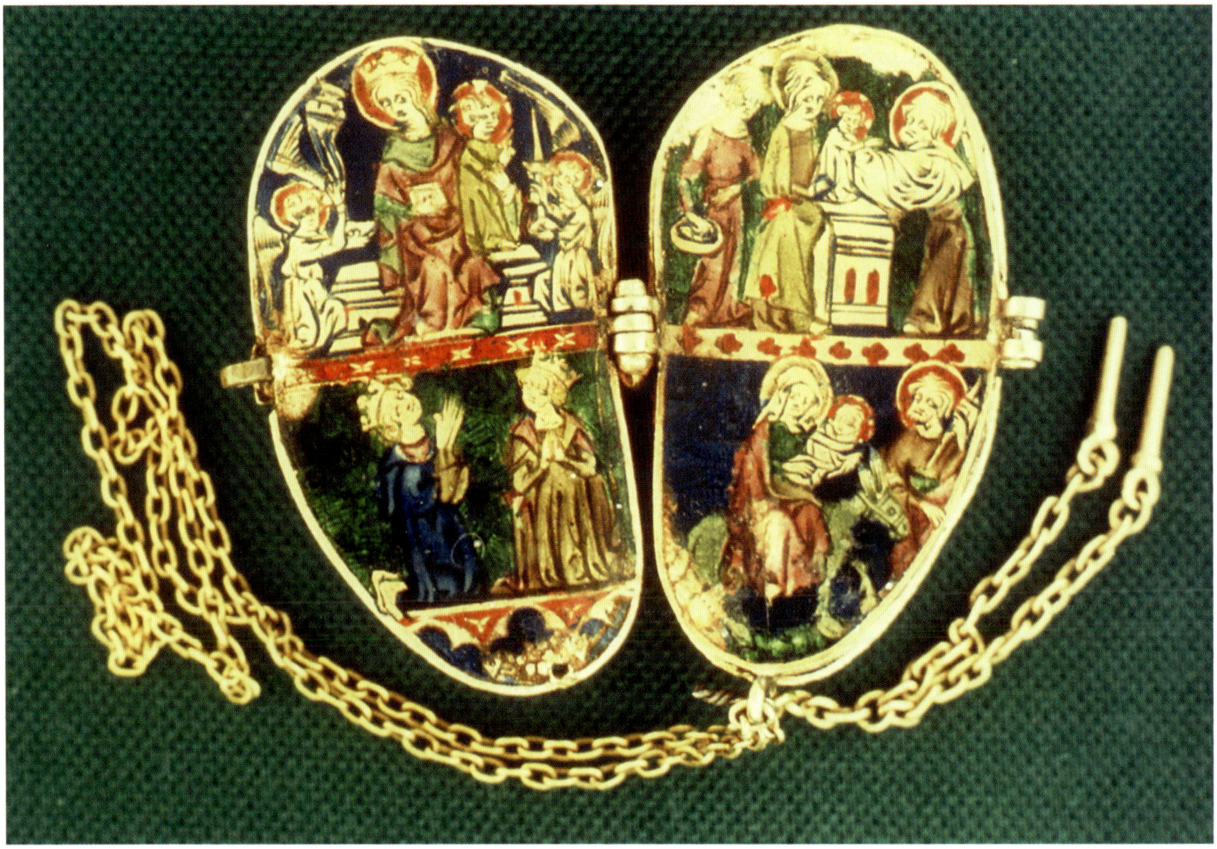

FIGURE 11. Reliquary containing a thorn from the Crown of Thorns, French, *c.* 1340, BM P&E 1902,0210.1 (photo: Trustees of the British Museum).

1990s by Elisabeth Taburet-Delahaye. The hoard at Erfurt was found in 1998 in the Jewish quarter (and published in 2009).[28] These had remarkable examples of Jewish marriage rings. The most noteworthy of these hoards was the Sroda Slaska Hoard found in the town of that name in Poland in the late 1980s and deposited in 1348.[29]

Medieval jewelry is now studied from a sociological perspective that Joan Evans would have found surprising. The way it is worn, who owned and wore it, and the ability of objects themselves have a life of their own are now the focus of attention. The work of Arjun Appadurai entitled *Social Life of Things: Commodities in Cultural Perspective* has influenced Visa Immonen's magisterial study of luxury of the use of gold and silver in Finland and neighboring countries.[30] Jewelry is now

28. The bibliography of these can be found in the catalogue of the exhibitions *Tresors de la peste noire: Erfurt and Colmar*, Musée National du Moyen Âge–Thermes et hotel de Cluny, ed. C. Descatoire *et al.* (Paris, 2007), and *Treasures of the Black Death*, ed. C. Descatoire (London: Wallace Collection, 2009). For the Erfurt hoard, see Maria Sturzebecher, "Der Schatzfund aus der Michaelistrasse in Erfurt," in *Die Mittelalterliche Jüdische Kultur, Band 1—Der Schatzfund: Archaeologie, Kunstgeschichte, Siedlungsgeschichte*, ed. Sven Ostritz (Erfurt, 2009).

29. Jerzy Pietrusinski and Jacek Witkowski, *Klejnoty Monarsze: Skarb Ze Środy Śląskeij* (Wroclaw, 1996).

30. Arjun Appadurai, *Social Life of Things: Commodities in Cultural Perspective* (Cambridge: Cambridge University Press,1986). B. Brown, "Thing Theory," *Critical Inquiry* 28:1 (Autumn, 2001), 7. P. Stallybrass and R. A. Jones, "Fetishizing the Glove in Renaissance Europe," *Critical Inquiry* 28:1 (Autumn, 2001), 14–32. The latter points out that detachable parts—rings, gloves, and jewels—have troubled the opposition of person and thing, even as

seen through the theory of design and even psychology. Marcia Pointon's book *Brilliant Effects* (2009), although dealing with a later period, presents as mainstream a minor detail in the history of luxury, which, within humanist and protestant culture, is a manifestation of frivolity. She uses portraiture to reveal the meaning that jewelry had for the wearers and also has for the viewers of pictures. It is the relationship between jewelry and the body that concerns her, and she uses pictures such as William Holman Hunt's *The Birthday* (1868) to illustrate this.[31] How far this approach can be projected back in time is an open question. However, it is noticeable that recent studies of small hand-held reliquaries, such as that of the Holy Thorn Reliquary (British Museum, WB 67) (Fig. 11), concentrate on the physical nature of the relationship between jewel and body. Both Ronald Lightbown in his wide-ranging study of *Medieval European Jewellery* and Marian Campbell and Diana Scarisbrick in their recent studies use portraits to illustrate the wearing of late medieval jewelry.[32] And more analysis is needed of the depiction of jewelry in religious paintings from the point of view of both the painter and the devotional audience. Medieval jewelry has been seen from a number of perspectives. It was at the same time amuletic, a worldly good, part of fashion, and an aid to devotion, reflecting the paradoxes of the late medieval world obsessed with the fear of mortality, death, and hell, but whose members enjoyed consumption at different levels and in different ways.

---

the concept of fetish was forged to formalize such an opposition. Visa Immonen, *Golden Moments: Artefacts of Precious Metals as Products of Luxury Consumption in Finland, c. 1200–1600* (Turku, 2009).

31. Marcia Pointon, *Brilliant Effects: A Cultural History of Gemstones and Jewellery* (Yale, 2009).

32. Ronald W. Lightbown, *Medieval European Jewellery* (London: Victoria and Albert Museum, 1992). Diana Scarisbrick, *Jewellery in Britain, 1066–1837: A Documentary, Social, Literary and Artistic Survey* (London, 1994). Marian Campbell, *Medieval Jewellery in Europe, 1100–1500* (London, 2009).

CYNTHIA HAHN

Production, Prestige, and Patronage of Medieval Enamels

AT THE STUDY DAY at the Walters Art Museum for the extraordinary exhibition of reliquaries, *Treasures of Heaven,* it was remarked—not without a certain envy—that curators are the "new priests." [1] Fortunate few, they have the privilege of access to the art historical holy of holies, the physical art object, and share with one another a *hands on* knowledge that is essential to understanding the so-called "minor arts." Indeed, to make a positive of what is in origin a pejorative label, the minor arts could be thought of as generally consisting of objects small enough to cherish and explore in the hand (an idea to which I will return at the end of this essay). It comes as no surprise, therefore, that modern study of enameled art works, exquisitely made and typically small, relies on the work of museum-based scholars who in books, catalogues, and investigative work in concert with conservators and scientists, have established a solid body of information about medieval enamel production.[2] Attempting to balance on the shoulders of such giants, I offer here some observations concerning technique, production, and patronage, ultimately seeking to answer two interlocked and very basic questions: First, why did enamelwork come to such prominence in the high and late Middle Ages? In particular, why is it so valued as a means of manufacture for church furnishings, *ornamenta ecclesiae*? And second, does its very success as a medium, especially as produced in enormous numbers by artisans of the city of Limoges, consign it to the category of minor arts as a mass-produced product?

1. The exhibition *Treasures of Heaven: Saints, Relics, and Devotion in Medieval Europe* was organized by the Cleveland Museum of Art, the Walters Art Museum, Baltimore, and the British Museum, London, and was held at the following venues: The Cleveland Museum of Art, 17 October 2010–17 January 2011; The Walters Art Museum, Baltimore, 13 February 2011–15 May 2011; The British Museum, London, 23 June 2011–9 October 2011

2. My inspiration for this essay, above all, derives from the work of Barbara Drake Boehm, a most valued friend and colleague. One must first consult her essays and catalogue entries along with those of other museum professionals in the catalogue (with comprehensive earlier bibliography): E. Taburet-Delahaye, B. D. Boehm, *et al., Enamels of Limoges, 1100–1350* (New York, 1996). See also: B. D. Boehm, "'A Brilliant Resurrection': Enamel Shrines for Relics in Limoges and Cologne, 1100–1230," In *Treasures of Heaven: Saints, Relics, and Devotion in Medieval Europe*, ed. M. Bagnoli, H. A. Klein, C. G. Mann, and J. Robinson (New Haven, 2010), 149–162; N. Stratford, *Catalogue of Medieval Enamels in the British Museum. Vol. II: Northern Romanesque Enamel* (London, 1993); P. Barnet, "Medieval Limoges Enamels in the Detroit Institute of Arts," *Bulletin of the Detroit Institute of Arts*, 63 (1988),16–25; M.-M. Gauthier, *Emaux méridionaux: Catalogue international de l'œuvre de Limoges. Vol. I: Époque romane* (Paris, 1987); *idem, Émaux limousins champlevés des XIIe, XIIIe et XIVe siècles* (Paris, 1950); *idem, Émaux du moyen-âge occidental* (Fribourg, 1972). For technical analyses, see I. Biron, P. Dandridge, and M. T. Wypyski, "Techniques and Materials in Limoges Enamels," in *Enamels of Limoges*, 48–62; L. Martinot, G. Weber, B. Gilbert, and J. Guillaume, "PIXE Analysis of Medieval Enamels: Preliminary Analytical Results Concerning Five Samples of Mosan Enamels from the Four Gable-reliquaries of Maestricht, Musée royaux d'art et d'histoire, inv. 1036–1039," *Bulletin des Musées royaux d'art et d'histoire*, 70 (1999), 199–205; P. Dandridge, "Reconsidering a Romanesque Reliquary Cross," *Met Objectives*, 4 (2002): 5–7, http://www.metmuseum.org/Works_of_Art/objects_conservation/fall_2002/cross.asp?printFlag=1; and P. Dandridge and M. T. Wypyski, "Preliminary Technical Study of Medieval Limoges Enamels," In *Materials Issues in Art and Archaeology III: Symposium Held 27 April–1 May 1992, San Francisco*, Materials Research Society Symposium Proceedings, 267 (Pittsburgh, Pa., 1992), 817–826. Other recent bibliography of interest includes: O. Meyer, N. Meyer, and M. Wyss, "Un atelier d'orfèvre-émailler récemment découvert à Saint-Denis," *Cahiers Archeologique* 38 (1990), 81–94; S. La Niece, S. Röhrs, and B. McLeod, eds., *The Heritage of 'Maître Alpais': An International and Interdisciplinary Examination of Medieval Limoges Enamel and Associated Objects*, British Museum Research Publications, 182 (London, 2010).

Indeed, why enamels at all? The question might seem more appropriate when pressed in regard to printmaking, a new art form that emerged in the late Middle Ages; or might also be asked of the rise of stained glass, an expensive and labor-intensive medium that experienced a tremendous surge in popularity after 1140. But, similar to the rapid emergence of those new, and newly exploited, techniques of art manufacture, we might ask why enamel came so quickly to prominence between the tenth and twelfth centuries? Although occurring widely on small objects such as brooches in the Roman world (with a peak of popularity in the second century A.D., Fig. 1),[3] and passed on from Roman soldiers to the "barbarians" as a popular decorative technique on jewelry, enameling was still a relatively rare medium in the early Middle Ages. However, through the twelfth and thirteenth centuries, its production quickly became a growth industry, consistently used on ever larger and more prestigious objects. In the later Middle Ages, it might be fair to say that its use became again more common on smaller objects and that may serve as justification for focusing on developments up to the thirteenth century.

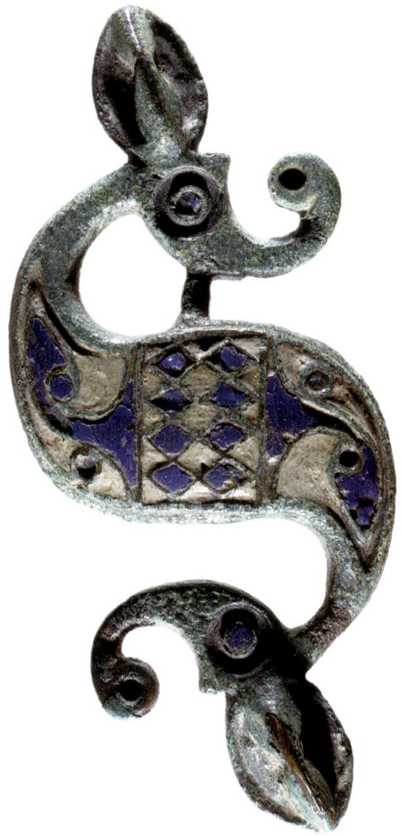

FIGURE 1. London, British Museum, Roman Dragonesque Brooch, first or second century A.D., P&EE POA 201 (photo: © The Trustees of the British Museum).

A comparison comes to mind. Computers existed before the late 1970s. Nevertheless, it was the advent of the Personal Computer that really opened up the production and use of the thing. Similarly, there was some cloisonné enamel in the Carolingian, Ottonian (Fig. 2), and of course, the Byzantine world,[4] but only with the advent of commonly produced champlevé enamel does enameling become a medium in demand in all the churches and courts of the world. Examples are far flung and significant: a Limoges panel is embedded in the door of the Church of Saint Catherine's on the Sinai peninsula (perhaps the gift of a crusader); the sacred confessio of Saint Peter's in Rome was once remodeled with Limoges enamel by Pope Innocent III; and Limoges artisans supplied secular enamel basins that were reminiscent of earlier courtly Islamic examples to wealthy patrons.[5] To take the analogy

3. F. McIntosh, "A Study into Romano-British Enamelling—With a Particular Focus on Brooches," *The School of Historical Studies Postgraduate Forum E-Journal Edition* 6 (2009), http://www.societies.ncl.ac.uk/shspgf/Ed_6/McIntosh.pdf (accessed 19 April 2011); C. Johns, *The Jewellery of Roman Britain* (London and Ann Arbor, Mich., 1996).

4. R. Kahsnitz, "Ottonische Emails: Zum Stand der Forschung" *Zeitschrift des Deutschen Vereins fur Kunstwissenschaft* 52/53 (1998/1999), 114–50. David Buckton argues that cloisonné enameling was developed by the Carolingians and passed to Byzantium after Iconoclasm: "Enamelling on Gold: A Historical Perspective," *Gold Bulletin* 15 (1982), 101–109; and *idem*, "Byzantine Enamel and The West," in *Byzantium and the West, c. 850–c. 1200. Proceedings of the XVIII Spring Symposium of Byzantine Studies*, Byzantinische Forschungen 13, ed. J. D. Howard-Johnston (Amsterdam, 1988), 235–244. I thank Chuck Little for sharing this bibliography with me.

5. For the Sinai example: J. Folda, *Crusader Art in the Holy Land: From the Third Crusade to the Fall of Acre, 1187–1291* (Cambridge, 2005), 1, 93. For the confession: B. D. Boehm, "*Opus Lemovicense*: The Taste for and Diffusion of Limousin Enamels," in *Enamels of Limoges* (as in note 2), 40–47, and see fig. 17 for a photograph

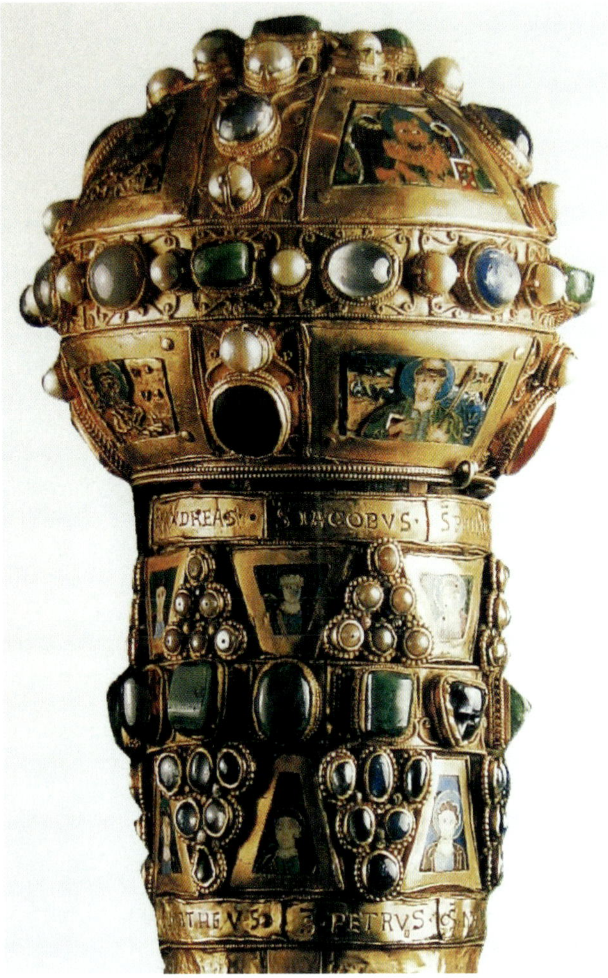

FIGURE 2. Limburg an der Lahn, Cathedral Treasury, Reliquary Staff of Saint Peter (gold, enamel, gems), *c.* 980 (photo: Wikimedia Commons, public domain).

still further: the elegance of the Macintosh computer and other Apple products might dominate design in personal computing, but the sheer proliferation of the IBM clones spread computing far and wide. Similarly, although Mosan and German artists were renowned, perhaps were more frequently cited by name, and, as in the case of Nicholas of Verdun and the Klosterneuberg altarpiece, produced exquisite work at incomparable levels of craftsmanship and artistry,[6] French Limoges artists substantially outproduced them.[7] The abundance of surviving Limoges enamels speaks to their popularity in the Middle Ages and warrants attention to the circumstances of their creation. Just as it has always been a matter of prestige to own the latest technology, it would seem to have been prestige that drove production. And, of course, in the Middle Ages, it was patrons who sought that prestige and turned enamel into the medium of the moment.

There is clear evidence that enamelwork generated a particular frisson for patrons throughout the Middle Ages. In the late Roman and early medieval period, enamel remains a limited element of the decorative surface, added almost as what seems to be a novelty item, and very much equivalent to gems as a means of embellishment (Fig. 2). Scholars trace its origins in Britain to the use of glass substituted for red coral.[8] A rough equivalence can also be posited between early medieval cloisonné involving the insertion of such gems as garnets (Fig. 3), and the later use in cloisonné designs of the fused glass of enameling. Medieval texts, in comparing gems and glass, indeed consistently find them to be equal, and metalworkers use the same sorts of settings to secure both gems and enamels.[9] As a particularly spectacular gem-like inset, Roman *millefiori* glass, often also called enamel, had obvious status value (Fig. 3).

Furthermore, such *millefiori* work and more typical enamelwork may, in the Middle Ages, have shared the added attraction of a status as valuable *spolia*. It has been suggested that *millefiori* checkerboard-pattern in-

---

of the Sinai plaque. For the "gemellions" or basins, see H. Buchthal, "A Note on Islamic Enameled Metalwork and Its Influence on the Latin West," *Ars Islamica* 11/12 (1946), 195–198.

6. H. Buschhausen, *Der Verduner Altar: das Emailwerk des Nikolaus von Verdun im Stift Klosterneuburg* (Vienna, 1980); and *idem*, "The Klosterneuburg Altar of Nicholas of Verdun: Art, Theology, and Politics," *Journal of the Warburg and Courtauld Institutes* 37 (1974), 1–32.

7. And some pieces were signed as well. For example, the Frassinora Candlestick signed by Constantine of Limoges and the Ciborium signed by Alpais in the Louvre (Fig. 6): Boehm, "*Opus Lemovicense*" (as in note 5), 43, and *Enamels of Limoges*, no. 69 (as in note 2), 246–249.

8. McIntosh, "Romano-British Enamelling" (as in note 3).

9. Boehm, "*Opus Lemovicense*" (as in note 5), 40.

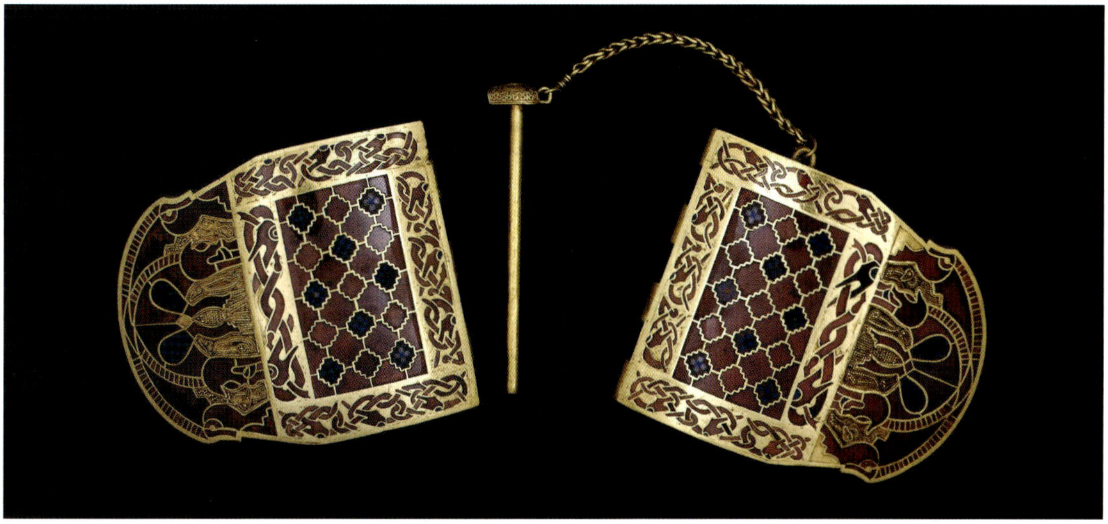

FIGURE 3. London, British Museum, Shoulder Clasp from the Ship-burial at Sutton Hoo (detail showing garnet cloisonné decoration), early seventh century, M&ME 1939,10-10,4; M&ME 1939,10-10,5 (photo: © The Trustees of the British Museum).

sets in the Sutton Hoo objects are Roman in origin.[10] In his twelfth-century treatise and artist's handbook *De diversus artibus*, Theophilus comments on the reuse of ancient glass tesserae in a much later period:

> Different kinds of glass, namely, white, black, green, yellow, and blue, red, and purple, are found in mosaic work in ancient pagan buildings. These are not transparent but are opaque like marble, like little square stones, and enamel work is made from them on gold, silver, and copper.... There are also found various small vessels in the same colors, which are collected by the French, who are most skilled in this work. They even melt the blue in their furnaces ... [making blue, purple and green glass for windows]. The Byzantines ... make ... goblets ... of the same blue stones.[11]

Theophilus's emphasis on blue is of particular interest, given the "rise" of the color blue in the twelfth century, especially in enamels and stained glass.[12] Contrasted with rich greens and deep reds, it dominates the color palette of the "new" media.

Moreover, Theophilus clearly conceives of enamel as a high-status material, in at least two instances in discussion of ornament for metalwork, he classes together "stones and enamels and pearls."[13] At times other medieval observers even seem to elide the relative status of such valued materials: although made of copper and enamel, the funerary plaque of Geoffrey Plantagenet was described in a chronicle as made of "gold and gems."[14] Finally, one more equivalence of gems and enamels might derive from their significance: if gems had virtuous, healing, and mystical qualities, often discussed in medieval medical and theological sources, enameling carried the virtue of having been manufactured and purified in fire, creating divine and virtuous associations as well.[15]

Like gems, moreover, enameling almost always

10. R. Bruce-Mitford, *The Sutton Hoo Ship Burial* (London, 1975–1983), III, 936.

11. Theophilus, *On Divers Arts*, trans. J. G. Hawthorne and C. S. Smith (New York, 1963), 59. The antique origin of the glass seems likely, given technical qualities, documentation of reused tesserae in mosaics, and the discovery of antique tesserae at Scandinavian bead-making sites: Buckton, "Enamelling on Gold" (as in note 4), 103.

12. M. Pastoureau, *Blue: The History of a Color* (Princeton, N.J., 2001), 49–55; and J. Gage, "Gothic Glass: Two Aspects of a Dionysian Aesthetic," *Art History* 5 (1982), 36–58.

13. Theophilus, *Divers Arts* (as in note 11), 120–21, 157.

14. *Enamels of Limoges*, no. 15 (as in note 2), 98.

15. C. Meier, *Gemma spiritalis: Methode und Gebrauch der Edelsteinallegorese vom frühen Christentum bis ins 18. Jahrhundert* (Munich, 1977); and B. Buettner, "From Bones to Stones: Reflections on

occurred in symbiosis with metalwork—perhaps the most prestigious medium or material of the Middle Ages, certainly the medium with which the greatest numbers of names of artists and patrons is associated. Examples include Archbishop Egbert of Trier in the late tenth century, and Abbot Begon III at Conques *c.* 1100, who both founded metalworking shops in order to produce beautiful objects for their churches. Enameling was notably part of their efforts. Begon is said to have "enshrined numerous relics in reliquaries of gold and silver." The workshop he founded persisted into at least the next abbacy.[16] A contemporary praises Egbert for his "grand and celebrated ingenuity" in the use of enamels and the employment of superior artists, and notes that the resulting "admirable form" pleased both "eye and spirit" (Fig. 2).[17] Wibald, Abbot of Stavelot, wrote in encouragement and appreciation to the artist "G" who was working for him, and Stavelot is renowned for its spectacular works in metal with champlevé.[18] These patrons were praised for the beauty of the objects with which they furnished their churches, and other churchmen begged to have such artisans produce things for their own institutions. Although gold and silver is almost always mentioned in such praise as it was for Begon, clearly using new media was also considered part of the accomplishment of these patrons and workshops.

With a turn to patrons we begin to address achievements but also, implicitly, motivations. It would seem undeniable that the social and cultural ambitions of patrons are a major component of the rise in the production of enamels. Just as getting the newest and smartest computer gives the owner status today, recognizing the value of enamels in the Middle Ages seems to have won a certain prestige for the patron. Barbara Boehm recounts an anecdote that demonstrates how this might work. Richard, prior at Saint Victor in Paris, is reminded in a letter by John of Saint-Satyre that he had shown him a book cover of Limoges work, and considered sending it to an abbot in England (1167–1169). One would have loved to overhear such a conversation: did they discuss its new technique, its iconography, its beauty? At any rate, we do know they were able to identify its distinctive and presumably prestigious place of manufacture: "Limoges work" (*opus Lemovicense*) is a common phrase of identification in medieval texts (*nota bene*, there is no equivalent medieval descriptive term for the less widely traded Mosan or Rhenish work).

So a first motivation for patrons might be early adoption of a recognizable luxury product, coming in tandem with a certain sense of being in the know, demonstrated in the case of enameling through the recognition of the artist's skill in using the medium. Of course, there can be only so many early adopters before something becomes a trend, but the recognition of skill and the self-congratulation of one's own aesthetic appreciation of such skill can be continued endlessly through the advent of technical innovations, large and small. One can be the early adopter of the next generation iPad or move from commissioning champlevé enamels to translucent enamel (Fig. 4) or, eventually, *émail en ronde bosse*, although in these techniques of the later Middle Ages, Limoges is surpassed by Paris as a center of production. Or within Limoges production, one could move from early vermiculé, that is, scroll or vine-like decoration (Fig. 5), to later use of relief (Fig. 6), to unusual patterns and colors, to exotic details such as pseudo-kufic lettering (Fig. 6).

It seems clear that innovative qualities of enamel and metalwork were appreciated in tandem with the mastery of fine points of execution. And indeed, unlike a medium like oil painting in which command of

---

Jeweled Reliquiaries" in *Reliquiare im Mittelalter*, ed. B. Reudenbach and G. Toussaint (Berlin, 2005), 43–59; Theophilus discusses the multiple firings of enamel, creating a polished and gleaming surface, *Divers Arts* (as in note 11), 125–127.

16. E. Taburet-Delehaye, "Beginnings and Evolution of the *Oeuvre de Limoges*," in *Enamels of Limoges* (as in note 2), 33–39, 33.

17. Exiguam materian nostram magnum ac celebre ingenium vestrum nobilitabit, cum adjectione vitri, tum compositione artificis elegantis; … destinato operi designatas mittimus species … admirabilem formam et quae mentem et oculos pascat frater efficiat frati: J. Havet, ed. *Lettres de Gerbert* (*983–997*) (Paris, 1889), 104, 97: as cited by E. Lesne, *L'inventaire de la propriété. Églises et trésors des églises du commencement du VIIIᵉ à la fin du XIᵉ siècle*, Vol. 3 of *Histoire de la propriété ecclésiastique en France* (Lille, 1936), 183.

18. S. Wittekind, *Altar–Reliquiar–Retabel: Kunst und Liturgie bei Wibald von Stablo* (Cologne, 2003), with complete bibliography.

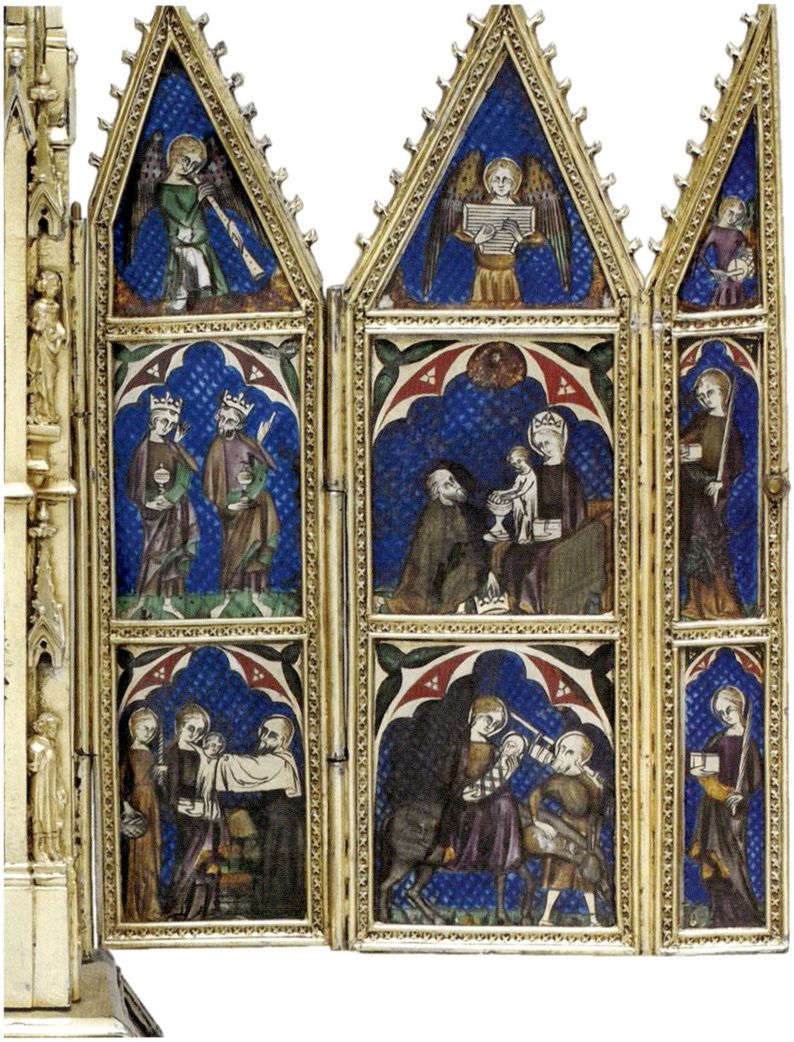

FIGURE 4. New York, Metropolitan Museum of Art, Reliquary Shrine (detail of right wing). Attributed to Jean de Touyl, French (d. 1349), gilt silver and translucent enamel (photo: © The Metropolitan Museum of Art / IAP).

the material represents the exquisite ability and momentary touch of the hand of the artist, the mastery and production of this demanding medium required a highly technical, almost mechanized skill; one presumes it was the product of teamwork rather than the exclusive output of an individual. In his description of the processes of making cloisonné enamel, Theophilus does not describe a momentary and inspired flourish, but a long complex process with the repeated and meticulous application of glass powder with a fine quill, multiple firings, and finally and literally much "spit" and polish.[19] The glow and beauty of enamel represents not a quick artistic gesture but the highly technical and superbly perfected achievement of a team of

19. Theophilus, *Divers Arts* (as in note 11), 125–127. Theophilus is not the first to mention the technique. It is somewhat inaccurately described already in an eleventh-century treatise: J. Wolters, "On the Noble and Illustrious Art of the Goldsmith: An 11th-Century Text," *Historical Metallurgy* 40 (2006), 72. Again, thanks to Chuck Little for this reference.

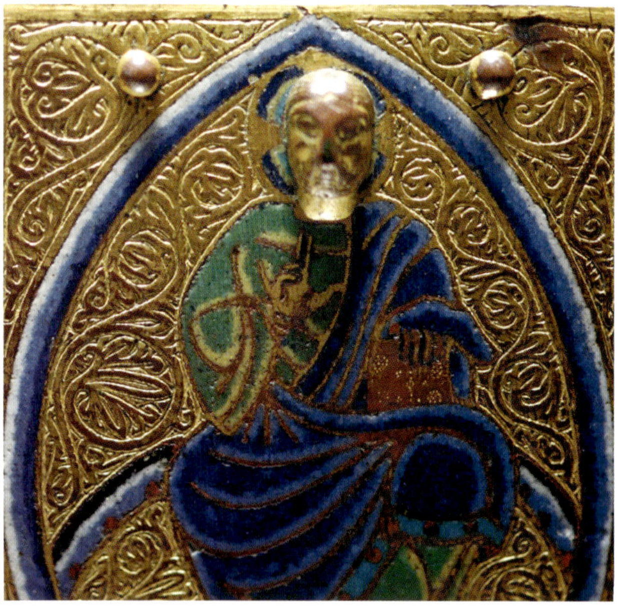

FIGURE 5. Paris, Louvre Museum, Chasse with *Majestas*, late twelfth century (detail of Fig. 12), vermiculé enamel, OA 5892 (photo: Wikimedia Commons, public domain).

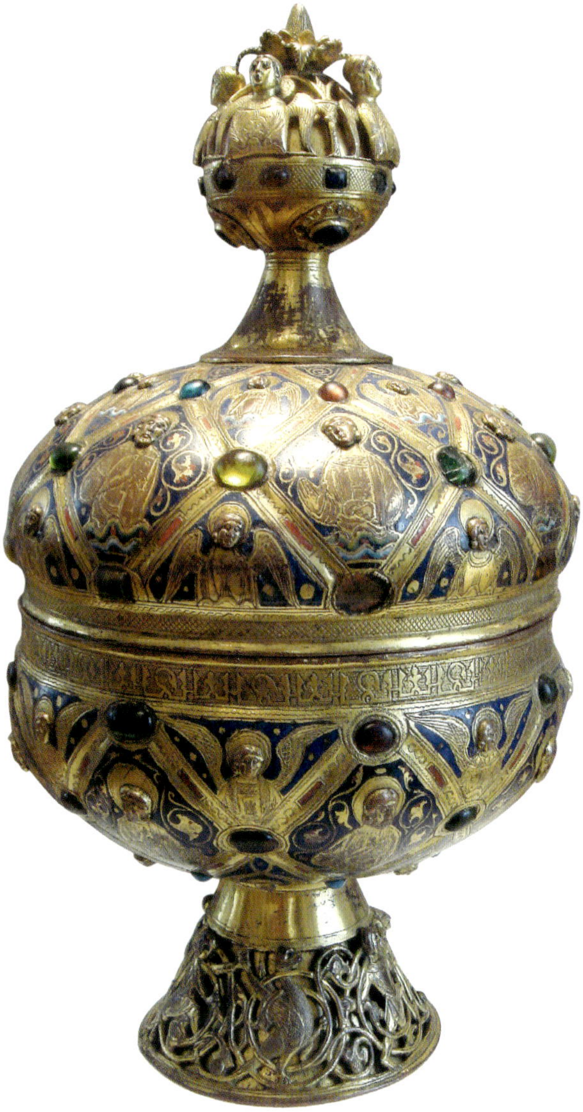

FIGURE 6. Paris, Louvre Museum, Limoges Enamel Ciborium, *c.* 1200, signed by "Master Alpais," MRR 98 (photo: Wikimedia Commons, Gnu license).

artisans—only if such group work becomes hackneyed and repetitious could it ever deserve the somewhat negative epithet, "minor" art.

But it might be argued, as we look more closely at specifically Limoges enamel production, and the veritable flood of objects issuing from its workshops by the thirteenth century, precisely such specters of "mass production" and rote repetition seem to threaten. We might profitably ask, what effect did the popularity of the medium have on production? We have already seen innovation, is there mindless repetition as well?

By the thirteenth century most certainly, additional motivations for choosing enamel come to the fore among patrons. Indeed, one of the primary reasons for commissioning enamelwork must surely have been its relative value for money. Instead of the expense of gold and gems, the patron was investing in craftsmanship (which given the economy of the Middle Ages came a great deal more cheaply). After Henry the Younger "borrowed" from the treasures of Saint-Martial of Limoges and Grandmont and then fell ill, from his deathbed he begged his father Henry II to replace what he had taken. Saint-Martial had no luck in this matter, as Henry II was hostile towards it, but Grandmont received substantial subsequent donations from the Plantagenet king. Grandmont, indeed, was one of the most spectacular ensembles of Limoges works, including some of the largest works made in the enameled technique, many of which also had exquisite detailing as in a surviving plaque representing Saint Matthew (Fig. 7). The results were surely impressive, but must have also represented an impressive savings for the king.[20]

Although German and Mosan metalworkers created ensembles even larger and more magnificent than that at Grandmont, as for example at Klosterneuburg and Stavelot,[21] other sorts of ambitious projects carried out in Limoges would have been unlikely if not impossible for German and Mosan craftsmen and may represent savings through an economy of scale. Between 1195 and 1220, more than fifty reliquary chasses celebrating the martyrdom of Thomas Becket were produced in Limoges and distributed throughout Europe, perhaps as fundraising for the shrine at Canterbury (Figs. 8–10).[22] Similarly, more than twenty chasses dedicated to the virgin martyr Valerie were made and disseminated throughout the Limousin region.[23] In each case, there were important political reasons to promote these martyr cults and disseminate the relics. The beautiful shining chasses allowed the smallest relics or even a pinch of dust to be fully realized as a cult object.[24] If Thomas was one of the saints most quickly canonized after his death (he died in 1170, and was canonized in 1174), could the unequalled production of reliquaries have had some part in the post-canonization campaign of spreading his cult? Or were these objects made "on spec" for the relics of the very popular saint in recognition of a new and emerging market? Either way, in these examples we see these workshops operating in an unprecedented manner.

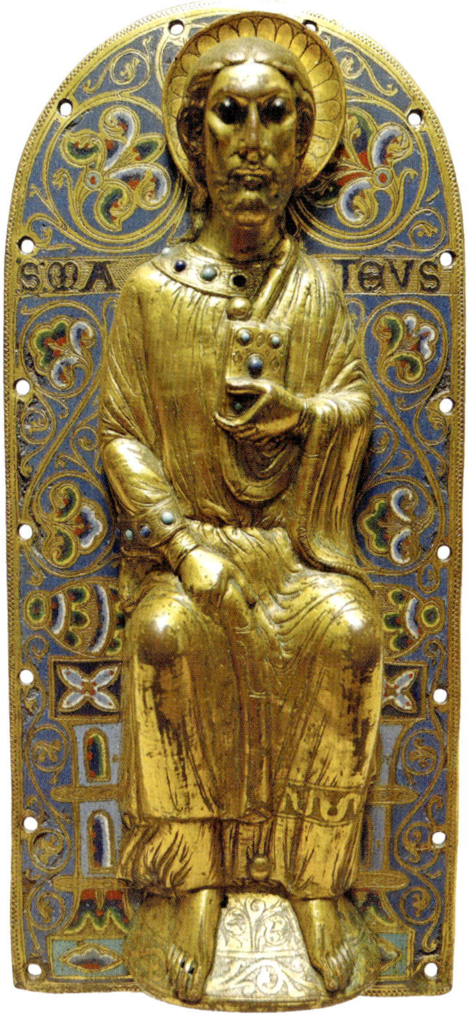

FIGURE 7. Paris, Louvre Museum, Grandmont Enamel Plaque of Matthew, 1220–1230, MR 2650 (photo: Wikimedia Commons, public domain).

20. B. Barrière, "The Limousin and Limoges in the Twelfth and Thirteenth Centuries," in *Enamels of Limoges* (as in note 2), 28.

21. See notes 6 and 18.

22. See S. Caudron, "Les Châsses de Thomas Becket en émail de Limoges," *Thomas Becket, Actes du Colloque international de Sédières, 19-24 aout 1973*, ed. R. Foreville (Paris, 1975), 233–241; M.-M. Gauthier, "La Meurtre dans la cathédrale, theme iconographique médiéval," *ibid.*, 247–253; R. Foreville, "La Diffusion de la culte de Thomas Becket dans la France de l'ouest avant la fin du XIIe siècle," *Cahiers de civilisation médiévale* 19 (1976), 363–64; S. Caudron, in M. M. Gauthier and G. François, eds., *Emaux méridionaux* (as in note 2), II (Paris, forthcoming); *Limoges Enamels*, no. 39 (as in note 2), 162–164; T. P. F, Hoving, "A Newly Discovered Reliquary of St. Thomas Becket," *Gesta* 4 (1965), 28–29. Caudron and Gauthier have suggested that the chasses may have been intended to raise funds for the new shrine of the saint begun in 1185 and completed 1220.

23. Gauthier and François, *Émaux méridionaux* (as in note 2), no. 91.

24. Valerie's relics were only known in the form of "dust." See C. Hahn, "Valerie's Gift: A Narrative Enamel Chasse from Limoges," in *Reading Medieval Images: The Art Historian and the Object*, ed. E. Sears, and T. K. Thomas (Ann Arbor, Mich., 2002), 187–200; and *idem*, "Interpictoriality in the Limoges Chasses of Stephen, Martial, and Valerie," in *Image and Belief: Studies in Celebration of the Eightieth Anniversary of the Index of Christian Art*, ed. C. Hourihane (Princeton, N.J., 1999), 109–124.

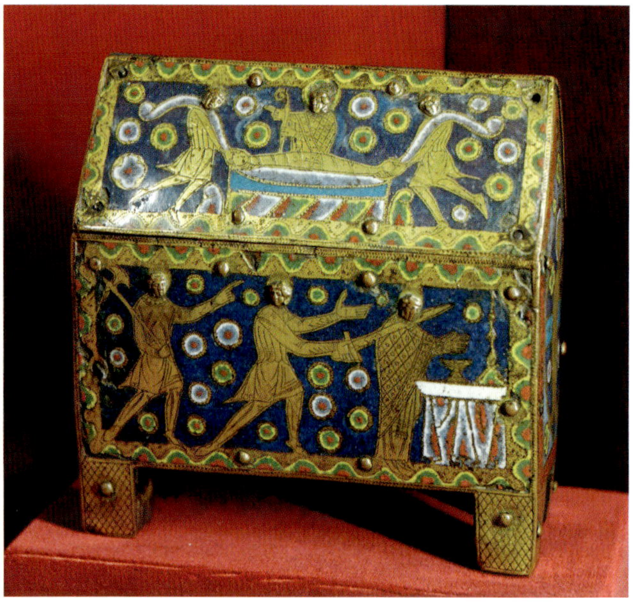

FIGURE 8. Paris, Musée National du Moyen Âge, Limoges Enamel Chasse with Thomas Becket, twelfth century, Cl. 22596 (photo: Wikimedia Commons, public domain).

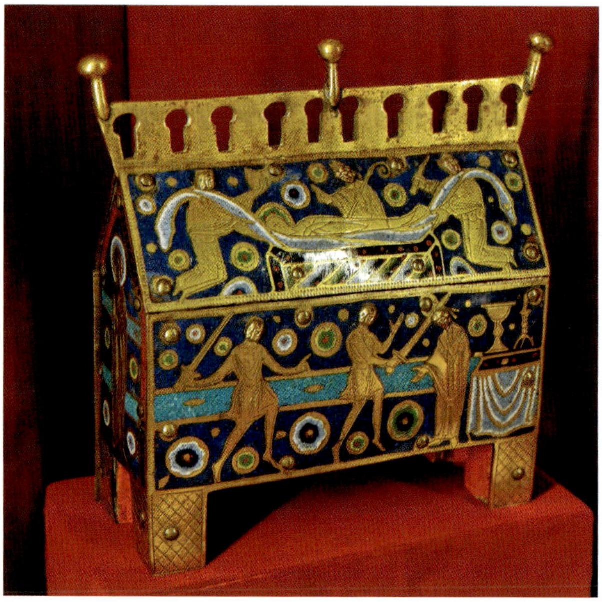

FIGURE 10. London, British Museum (on loan from the Society of Antiquaries, London), Limoges Enamel Chasse with Thomas Becket, *c.* 1180 (photo: Wikimedia Commons, public domain).

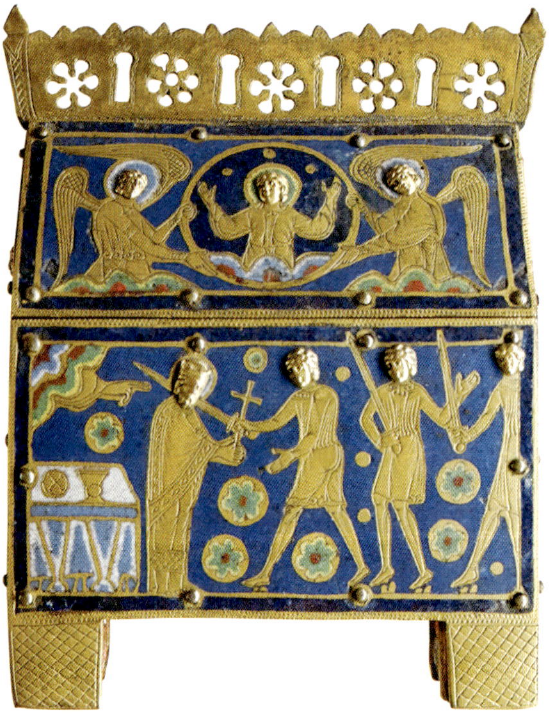

FIGURE 9. Lyon, Museum of Fine Arts, Limoges Enamel Chasse with Thomas Becket, *c.* 1210, D 411 (photo: © Marie-Lan Nguyen / Wikimedia Commons).

But, interestingly enough, such precise imagery is not the typical approach in Limoges reliquary production. More common is the depiction of subjects that are more general and unspecific as to the contents of a given chasse. Perhaps the two most common images on Limoges chasses include *Christ in Majesty*, with or without Apostles, and the *Three Magi* bringing gifts to the Christ Child (Figs. 11 and 12).[25] Many scholars and viewers today assume that the decoration of the surface of a reliquary reflects its contents, an idea seemingly supported by examples such as the Thomas Becket reliquaries. But if exterior revealed interior, one might also be justified in expecting a significant and sizable relic inside these boxes, most of which exceed six inches, with some as big as twelve or more. Instead, the relic likely consisted of a small packet of cloth containing a bit of blood, brains, or dust. In contrast to the Thomas reliquaries, in most cases, Limoges chasses give no clue as to their contents and today are empty. Very few are even inscribed, and, as above, imagery tends to be

25. *Treasures of Heaven* (as in note 2), no. 94, 184; Gauthier and François, *Émaux méridionaux* (as in note 2), 68–69, 70.

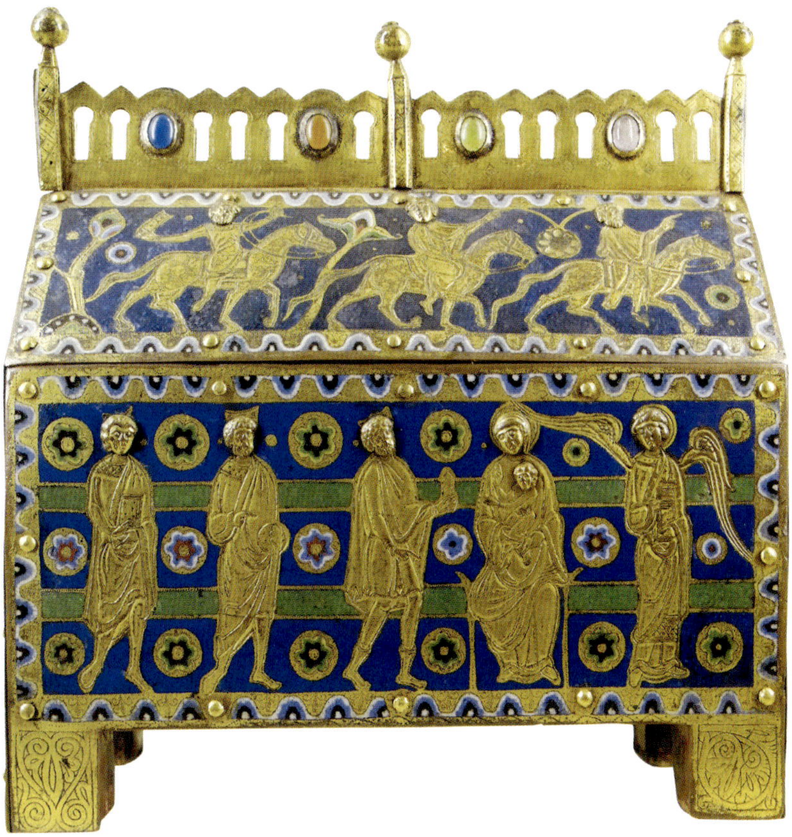

FIGURE 11. Paris, Musée National du Moyen Âge, Limoges Enamel Chasse with Three Magi, *c.* 1200, Cl. 23822 (photo: © Marie-Lan Nguyen / Wikimedia Commons).

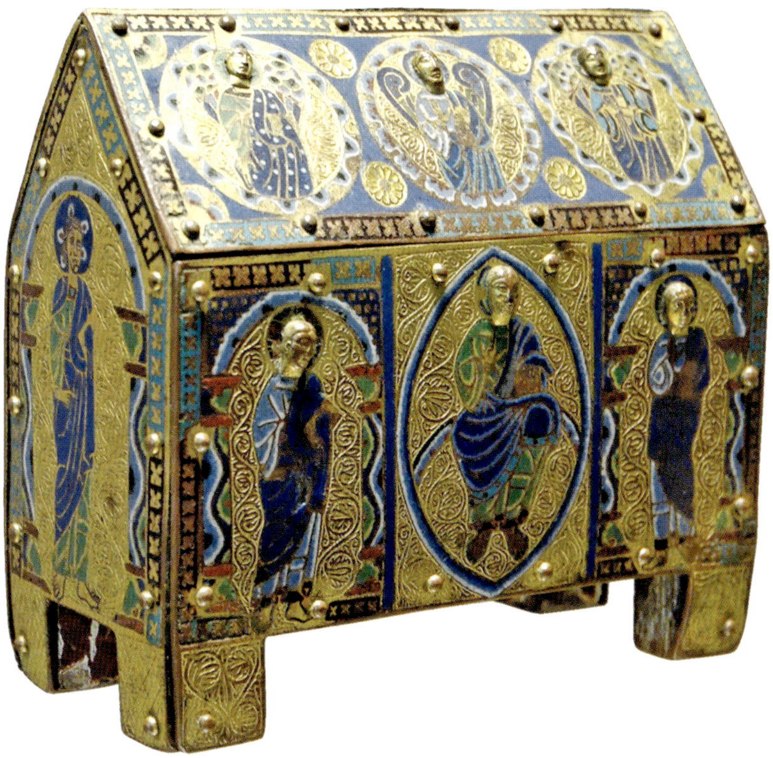

FIGURE 12. Paris, Louvre Museum, Limoges Enamel Chasse with *Majestas*, late twelfth century, OA 5892 (photo: courtesy of Wikimedia, public domain).

general rather than specific. The interiors, if wood, were painted white or red and a contrasting red or white cross was painted inside (see the traces of white paint visible on the legs of Fig. 12). These signs speak to a generally sacred imagery created in the production of the reliquaries, but are not an indication of specific contents. The solution could be that the chasses were produced in advance of any particular patron's request and that the imagery served a generic holy function without specific meaning. Again, we seem to be heading toward a situation that indicates mass production.

So, were the chasse reliquaries of Limoges mass produced? Again, some evidence shows that they were assembled in great numbers in workshops (Fig. 13). A few show markings on the interior that would have assisted in the proper assemblage and ordering of parts, a feature only necessary if there was the possibility of confusion created by multiple projects underway at any one time.[26] Furthermore, it is easy to see that the small relief heads that begin to be attached to the chasses in the thirteenth century are repeated (with just a few variants—bearded or not, looking left or right), and conservators have shown that the heads, were hammered into matrices and therefore precisely replicated (Figs. 6, 8–12).[27] However, these observations are not surprising given what we have already concluded, arguing that the technical mastery of the medium would have been impossible without workshop organization and production.

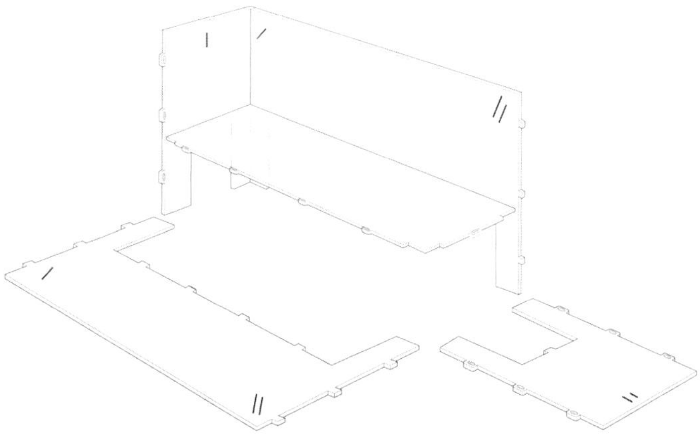

FIGURE 13. Diagram of interior markings on Paris, Musée National du Moyen Âge, Chasse, Cl. 4505, from Stohlman, *ArtBul*, 1935.

What remains surprising, nonetheless, is that no other evidence beyond sheer numbers and these few shortcuts confirms mass production. Most significantly, so far as I have been able to find, designs are never repeated exactly. (On the contrary, If a design is repeated, this seems to be good evidence of a fake.) Among the Thomas reliquaries, there are innumerable variations—two, three, or four knights; the murderers strike the saint on his neck or on his "crown;" Thomas celebrates Mass or turns toward his attackers; the altar is at the left or the right; Thomas is accompanied by one or two monk witnesses or no one; in the upper register, he is buried or rises to heaven as a saint (Figs. 8–10). Most assuredly, similar compositions occur, but true mass production would have been more mindless and exact in its repetition and would have sought economies that could be achieved through the precise reuse of designs. The only case in which a design is clearly reused (without, however, line-for-line exactitude), concerns, not small objects created rapidly, but two of the finest of Limoges chasses—the two largest of the series made to honor Valerie (now in London and St. Petersburg). I have argued elsewhere that the repetition of Valerie's story was not an artisanal shortcut, but involved the production of a purposeful copy meant to transfer the prestige of the original.[28]

Although the repetitions within the series of the Thomas and Valerie chasses can thus be explained, the repetitive use of the *Christ in Majesty* and *Three Magi* iconographies on Limoges reliquaries remains to be explored—should one assume it to be the outcome of a lack of artistic imagination? Once more I would argue—quite the contrary. Again, many small variations occur in the designs, and indeed, the artists may have simply been fulfilling their patron's requests in repeating the iconography. Prelates from all over Eu-

26. W. F, Stohlman, "Production of Limoges Champleve Enamels," *Art Bulletin* 17 (1935), 390–394.
27. Biron *et al.*, "Techniques and Materials" (as in note 2), 52–53.
28. Hahn as in note 24.

rope were ordering metalwork for their churches from Limoges.[29] Many pieces were produced but it was the rare case when a local patron (as in the example of the Valerie chasse) could specify the details of his commission. The two iconographies in question, along with the most obvious choice, the Crucifixion, were the images that surely satisfied the largest number of patrons.

If we think of episcopal patronage in its most general terms, the repetition of these two themes becomes an obvious solution to this problem of imagery choice. As Eric Palazzo has argued, bishops as patrons envisioned their actions as ideally following the example of Solomon and his building of the Temple of Jerusalem.[30] Their intention was to make a gift to the Church. To furnish it worthily and beautifully: "Lord I have loved the beauty of thy house…" Ps. 26:8; and to create a symmetry in the production of a beautiful church and a pure and beautiful congregation or "Church." In this way, pontiffs accomplish both meanings of the episcopal goal of *edificare*, edification through both building *and* teaching.[31] Ivo of Chartres supplies a fitting example. Having received a gift of a luxurious liturgical comb, the bishop justified his acceptance of the precious object by arguing that the comb had a symbolic and didactic meaning—its use could be said to represent the ordering of the soul which could be compared to the smoothing and ordering of the hair that is the work of a comb.[32]

In much the same way, all the objects in a treasury, as well as the liturgical objects created for a church must do the job of reflecting the worth of a saint and the church.[33] Even the smallest chapel had to have liturgical objects and it was the bishop's specific obligation to make certain that every church in his diocese had a liturgical sufficiency. That would have included, of course, a chalice, a paten, candlesticks, crosses, liturgical books and cloths (for example as represented on the altar in Figs. 8–10, or the Eucharistic dove of Fig. 14).[34] So we must understand that bishops were in the business of furnishing church after church. In some sense, they were the interior decorators of the Middle Ages and although they wanted the best and the most beautiful, economies must have appealed.

What better parallel to these bishops than the Wise Men of the Gospel story who gave gifts of recognition to the Christ Child? The *Majestas* imagery could be said to be more generic, but perhaps no less satisfying to the donor. The image of Christ in Majesty represents Jesus surrounded by the Evangelical Beasts in a depiction of Ezechial 1:5, usually along with Apostles. A tenth-century text by Arnaud concerning Bishop Stephen II of Clermont-Ferrand makes connections, subtle and not so subtle, between the bishop's donation and the Celestial Jerusalem as figured by this imagery.[35] Such imagery undeniably represents the glorious "Church" to which the bishop is contributing.

Such are indeed the most general and universal meanings available to our medieval patron, but also *and always* the most significant. The reliquary itself becomes an image of the donor's aspirations and evokes the perfection, if in miniature, of the image the bishop wants to create and to emulate. This goal of heavenly perfection is much more important than any specific identification of a relic. Thus, no matter how "generic," this imagery is perfect and sufficient for any reliquary. Furthermore, even the most common color on Limoges chasses—the rich celestial azure—further reinforces the significance of this heavenly reference.[36]

29. Boehm argues that the location of Limoges on the pilgrimage road and at the intersection of major trade routes also helped promote its wares: "*Opus Lemovicense*" (as in note 5).

30. E. Palazzo, *L'évêque et son image: l'illustration du pontifical au Moyen Âge* (Turnhout, 1999), 60.

31. C. Hahn, *Portrayed on the Heart: Narrative Effect in Pictorial Lives of Saints from the Tenth through the Thirteenth Century* (Berkeley, 2001), 34–38.

32. Palazzo, *L'évêque et son image* (as in note 30), 56.

33. C. Hahn, "The Meaning of Early Medieval Treasuries," in *Reliquiare im Mittelalter* (as in note 15), 1–20.

34. J. Le Maho, "Le trésor de la cathédrale de Rouen de l'époque mérovingienne aux premières années du XIIIe siècle," in *Les Trésors de sanctuaires, de l'Antiquité à l'époque romane: communications présentées au Centre de recherches sur l'Antiquité tardive et le haut Moyen Âge de l'Université de Paris X-Nanterre, 1993–1995*, ed. J.-P. Caillet, and P. Bazin (Paris, 1996), 125.

35. Palazzo, *L'évêque et son image* (as in note 30), 60.

36. Boehm, "*Opus Lemovicense*" (as in note 5), 41. For the use of imagery on reliquaries more generally, see C. Hahn, *Strange Beauty: Issues in the Making and Meaning of Reliquaries from the Fourth Century to circa 1204* (State College, Pa., 2012).

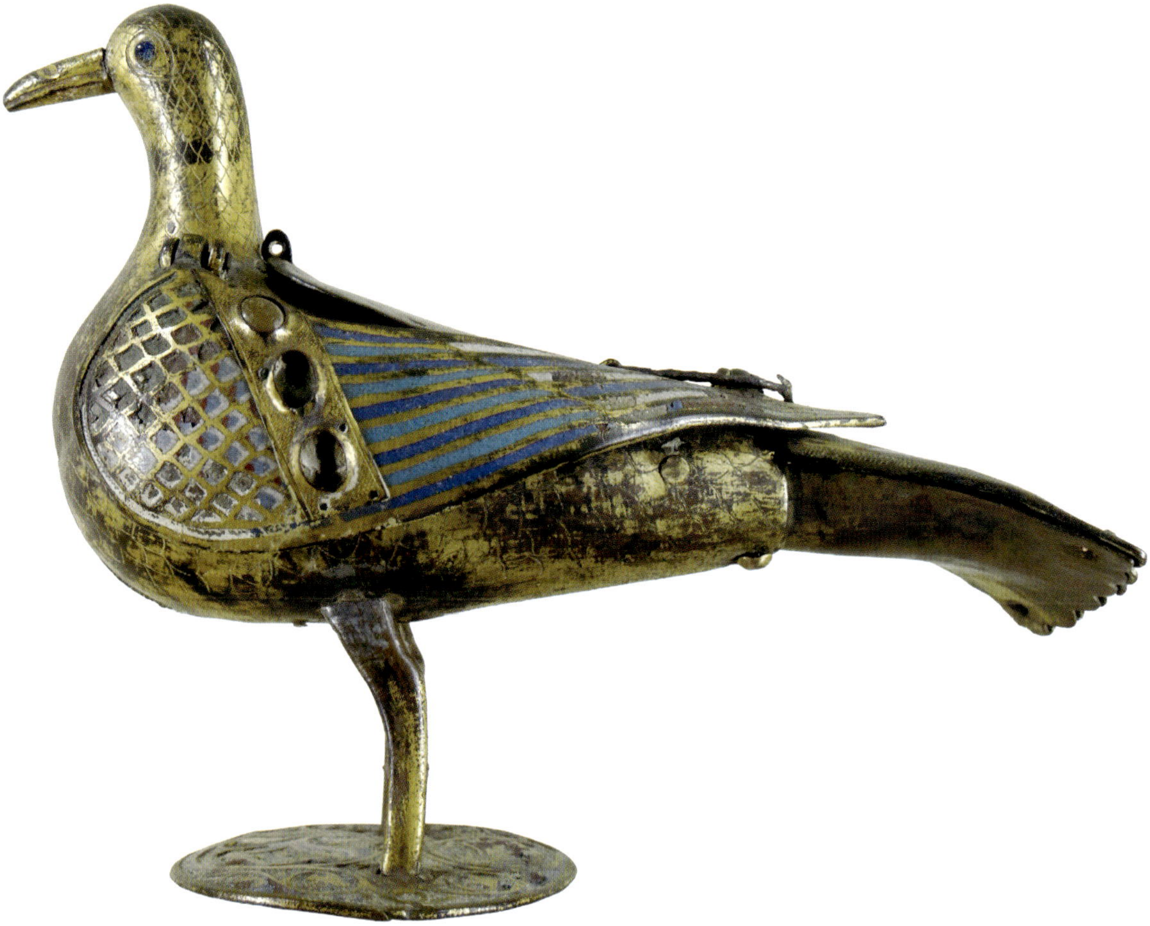

FIGURE 14. Paris, Musée National du Moyen Âge, Limoges Enamel Eucharistic Dove, mid-thirteenth century, Cl. 1957 (photo: © Marie-Lan Nguyen / Wikimedia Commons).

In sum, there were many good and sufficient reasons for Limoges enamelwork to be the medium of choice for the bishop furnishing his church, and there was also, perhaps above all, practicality. Not only was Limoges work less expensive, but its value, in the workmanship rather than the materials, made it precious but less likely to be melted down. Virtually no trace of the many shrines made by the Merovingian goldsmith Saint Eligius survives because the shrines were ravaged by the Vikings. In post-Viking Europe, Limoges objects obviate any temptation. They are also sturdier than objects made of gold and silver, and less likely to tarnish or be damaged by use. One technical innovation occurs in recognition of that fact—early chasses had wooden cores in imitation of gold and silver prototypes, but later ones forego this element. Finally, enamel is very stable and long-lived at normal temperatures (although fires would destroy them). In sum, not only was enamel less expensive, but it was also more likely to last. Before their gilt surfaces suffered the scratches and wear of long use, the objects presented an even more beautiful aspect than they do now. No one could argue that the result is not exquisite as well as practical. Finally we must ask, are these Major arts or Minor?

Practical, affordable, beautiful, and available; no wonder the fame of "Limoges work" spread far and wide, even garnering a note in the canons of the Fourth Lateran Council of 1215, declaring that churches must have two Eucharistic pyxides, and that one could be Limoges work.[37] It must be admitted that this notice is not altogether straightforward. It seems a very clear indication that, when it came to specifications (operational since Carolingian legal pronouncements) that the Eucharistic elements deserved only the finest materials, Limoges work was acceptable, but perhaps not recognized as the best. Nevertheless, given the unprecedented number of churches built and furnished in the period that Limoges enamelwork is produced, it was judged a viable and even elegant solution.

Finally, and for many reasons: because we must argue that mass production did not mean the same thing in the Middle Ages that it means now; that Limoges enamel amply exhibits signs of artistic invention; that it was much admired and sought after; and that it was often classed with the finest materials and even judged by the Church to be equal in worth to them; we can conclude that enamel work was a minor art of major aspirations and achievement. In some sense it is minor passing as major, although of course, these terms are modern and ultimately mean little in a medieval context. I would like, in these last pages, to think about action and more importantly interaction as a quality important to these objects and their significance to medieval viewers.

I began this essay by mentioning that today's curators are something like the equivalent to yesterday's priests or bishops. Let us work a bit with that metaphor. Does it make a difference to the perception of the thing if one gets to come into close contact with the object? Were our medieval patrons experiencing these objects differently than museum visitors do today, perhaps more in the way that a curator is privileged to do? Does that make the difference between minor and major?

The question of how we have arrived at our current definition of the minor arts bears examination. According to Aristotle, all art-making produced by any sort of physical effort was labor, (separate and distinct from the liberal arts).[38] Unfortunately, the corollary was that laborers did not have the "leisure" to develop higher virtues like civic consciousness. Artists were condemned by the philosopher to a lower class of citizenry and the arts were deemed craft. On the other side of the Middle Ages, as Renaissance artists of certain types aspired to join the practitioners of the liberal arts, a category like "minor arts" as opposed to fine arts appeared in texts like *De architectura* by Brunelleschi. Similar divisions persisting throughout the history of art are: Fine versus Applied arts, or fine arts versus mechanical arts, craft, or manual work. The division of art into two categories with its implied judgment of superior and inferior status, creative versus manual persists today. It must be said that the division is especially inappropriate when applied to the Middle Ages, for in the medieval world all artists were in some sense artisans working with the materials supplied by nature, that is, by God.[39] We have already argued that enamel technique, although intensely technical and requiring a high level of manual skill does not lower the worth of enamel work in the eyes of medieval viewers.

Let us quickly dispose of other "minor art" stigmas that continue to circle in our literature but are irrelevant in the medieval and also contemporary spheres, constructs of the Renaissance or Enlightenment valuation of art. First, such objects were made by anonymous artisans—well, actually we probably have the names of more of the metalworkers than almost any other type of artist of the Middle Ages. Second, they are mixed media—here modern art has revised our ideas with the practice of collage and assemblage. Third, they were frequently restored or remade, destroying their "artistic integrity" and obscuring their date and provenance—again, assemblage helps us deal with such ideas without relegating complex metalwork objects to the ash-heap of aesthetic trash. Fourth, they were works of craft following types and patterns, not works of the imagination—we have already discussed this and found it mostly irrelevant in practice. But we still have not come to the end of our rapid list of classificatory denigrations.

One last aspect of medieval metalwork pushes it in

37. Boehm, "*Opus Lemovicense*" (as in note 5), 44.
38. U. Eco, *Art and Beauty in the Middle Ages* (New Haven, Conn., 2002), 97.
39. Eco, *Art and Beauty* (as in note 38), 95–6

the direction of "minor arts" or craft and tends to hold it there. This has to do with the viewer's experience of the object, or more particularly, the art historian or even *connoisseur or curator's* experience. Let me quote Thomas Hoving, the infamous former director of the Met, in his praise of one of his famous contemporaries:

> Hanns Swarzenski (medieval curator of the Boston MFA) was blessed with an uncanny sensitivity for objets d'arts and preferred them by far to paintings or large-scale sculptures. He had a special affinity through "vision, touch, and taste," as a competitor phrased it, with the physical and even the inner spirituality of the minor arts. He realized that inherent power could possess more monumentality than size alone.[40]

This description from 1981 introduces a number of difficult issues expressed in a rather intuitive fashion but, nonetheless, essential.

Hoving cites Swarzenki's "affinity" for an inherent physical power and "inner spirituality" of what he prefers to call *objets d'art.* Hoving is not alone. Other sources about the German scholar repeat these ideas, arguing that, rather than take the more typical art-historical approach of the era—iconographic analysis—Swarzenski was a connoisseur and his *Monuments of Romanesque Art* remains a characteristic work. It lacks extensive comment on the objects in favor of allowing the works to "speak for themselves."[41] Hoving himself goes on to describe Swarzenski as "magically wedded" to the artifact and "inarticulate" about it. These ideas about connoisseurship repeat those that Edgar Wind skewers so effectively in his important article on the subject of Morelli and connoisseurship—somehow the object "speaks" to the connoisseur, perhaps communicating its power or spirituality directly, without mediation.[42] The connoisseur spiritually opens the object, penetrates its nature and makes a pronouncement but, in general, despairs of communicating his perceptions in words. He is indeed purposely inarticulate. Surely great connoisseurs work within an almost exclusively sensory realm, but does that mean that their subjects are out of the bounds of scholarly study?

Richard Neer in his recent article in *Critical Inquiry* mounts a vigorous defense of connoisseurship's importance to modern art history,[43] and if we might return to Hoving's description of Swarzenski, we see that perhaps some of the qualities of *objets d'art* that particularly excite the feelings of the connoisseur are, in the end, not the weaknesses but the strengths of enamels and metalwork. Hoving notes that "inherent power could possess more monumentality than size alone" implying that small size was a detriment, but one that could be overcome.

A second aspect—that these objects communicate through "vision, touch and taste"—may show the particular strength of the diminutive in its possibility of making a direct appeal to the senses. In implicitly disparaging the small and preferring the large, Hoving may have been following human nature as recently argued by the experimental sciences, or, more likely, he is parroting standard aesthetic judgment prevailing from ancient times: large is better. This is, remarkably, the crux of the matter for the minor arts.

In addressing the issue, can we turn to medieval aesthetics? The power of "aesthetics" in the Middle Ages lay in the possibilities of sensory knowledge; things that were not verbal or logical but were perceived by means of the senses. There is some help here in imagining where the value of beauty might lie. Although Umberto Eco maintains that there is no systematic theory of art in the Middle Ages, he nonetheless notes John of Salisbury's willingness to allow that art encourages the "mind's genius" through the perception of things, and further emphasizes Aquinas' understanding of beauty as perceptible to the delectation of sight.[44] However, for Aquinas, just as the human intellect is "discursive"

40. T. Hoving, *King of the Confessors* (New York, 1981), 49.

41. "Swarzenski, Hanns [Peter]" *Dictionary of Art Historians*, ed. L. Sorenson, (website) http://www.dictionaryofarthistorians.org/swarzenskih.htm.

42. E. Wind, "A Critique of Connoisseurship," *Art and Anarchy* (London, 1963), 30–46.

43. R. Neer, "Connoisseurship and the Stakes of Style," *Critical Inquiry* 32 (2005), 1–26.

44. Eco, *Art and Beauty* (as in note 38), 94.

so is the "aesthetic *visio*," it is a complex, composite act of looking involving knowledge and judgment.[45] Of even greater interest, another scholastic thinker, Witelo in his *De Perspectiva* of 1270 (a text of great interest to Renaissance artists such as Ghiberti) elaborates some of these ideas about aesthetic looking. In that treatise, Witelo emphasizes that, in the artistic product, size may matter (the large is intrinsically beautiful) but that interrelations are all important. He remarks that sometimes small may be "looked at from close up" showing "subtle intentions," "beautiful ordering" of parts and "decorum" of line or design. In fact, his discussion of the play of distance and nearness, and possibilities of the axis of vision (direct or oblique) all show that, for Witelo, the position of the viewer is essential to the discovery of the beauty of an object.[46]

I would argue that as we think of near and far and shifting points of view, especially for a small object, we are automatically considering handling the object. Holding it, manipulating it, feeling its weight is one of the great pleasures of encountering an art object and one that, it must be noted, gives a sense of "power" to the holder/beholder. In one sense one begins to feel ownership and to make a connection with all the "owners" of the past, those who have handled the object before. This sense should be understood as indexical, an aspect of meaning that flourishes through presence and contact—a sense of the sharing of "touch." Hoving himself feels and weighs the artwork, dragging his eyes over every millimeter, as if "my eyes could touch the surface."

If metalwork constitutes some of the most important and valued objects of their era, can we assess them in this fashion? Is there any historical validity to such an approach? Of course, often their *beauty* is unmistakable. But can we link this to medieval experience?

Paulinus of Nola is one of the first to discuss handling a reliquary. He speaks of his precious relic of the true cross and also the shrine he builds for his patron saint, Felix. About the reliquary he writes that he becomes

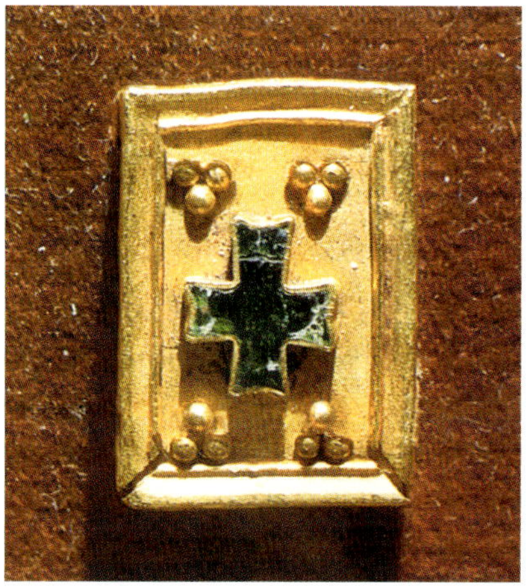

FIGURE 15. Grado, S. Eufemia, Gold Reliquary Box with enamel detail, fourth to fifth century, Grado Cathedral Treasury (photo: © Bruno Fachin Editore).

lost in contemplation of the "invulnerable sign," that is, the cross. The sort of reliquary that Paulinus was handling survives in a number of examples. They tend to be small and made of gold, as was that of Paulinus, perhaps with gems or enamels (Fig. 15). Most have a sliding lid which would have allowed the owner to open it in order to look upon the relic and focus his or her meditation. One imagines the caress that Paulinus applied to his tiny reliquary, containing the relic that he had purposefully saved out of the relics in the altar in order to indulge himself with looking at it in "times of need." Paulinus, indeed, wrote to a friend about this sort of experience, "Let not your faith shrink because the eyes of the body behold evidence so small; let it look with the inner eye on the whole power of the cross in this tiny segment..."[47] Two ideas are important here—that of the importance of sight with the inner eye, and the that of the very small size of the relic.

Peter Brown writes eloquently about the potential meaning of the very small in regard to relics which were often tiny fragments:

> how better to express the paradox of the linking of Heaven and Earth than by an effect of "inverted mag-

45. Eco, *Ibid.*, 73. 46. Eco, *Ibid.*, 69.

47. *The Poems of St. Paulinus of Nola*, translated and annotated by P. G. Walsh (New York, 1975), 291, and 152–154; and *idem*, *Letters of St. Paulinus of Nola* (New York, 1967), 36.

nitudes," by which the object around which boundless associations cluster should be tiny and compact?[48]

Indeed, the literary theorist Susan Stewart also observes that the miniature can be particularly effective in its promise that it might "open itself to reveal a secret life indeed to reveal a set of actions and hence a narrativity and history outside the given field of perception," Of course the narratives that were revealed for the relic were the legends of the saints or the story of the Bible. Stewart further remarks that, when one examines a tiny object, scientific studies document a "compressed time of interiority," a remarkable change in the experience of time.[49] Gaston Bachelard links the small to the poetics of space and sites of "grandeur" through the concentration of essence[50] and, finally, Richard Etlin links it to imagined life: "the small seems to concentrate a limitless power through its miniaturization and through a natural process of animism whereby we invest matter with spirit."[51]

Many of these observations seem to revert to a sense of indexicality; a linking of essences, a mystical connection, something that prompts the desire to touch and be part of that connection. Again, Peter Brown argues that the fragment and its associations rise above normal place and time, and quotes the fourth-century sermon of Victricius of Rouen, "here are bodies where every fragment is 'linked by a bond to the whole stretch of eternity.'"[52] Such observations precisely match Paulinus' experience of meditating on a relic of the True Cross in its tiny golden capsule, he writes: "the whole power of the cross [is] in this tiny segment."

In sum, we must conclude that the small is not necessarily minor and that such classification has little or no meaning for the Middle Ages. If instead of minor, the small can be particularly powerful, perhaps the beauty and life of small objects should be considered as even more important than the power of large ones. The key, I would argue is in the contingent nature of the medieval object. It is made to be touched and to be handled, to be gazed upon with reverence. Admittedly, perhaps only the priestly class ever had this opportunity but surely every viewer had the desire to touch and to hold such precious things. Furthermore, is it not this very desire that parallels in spiritual significance the reverence with which gloved curators handle art works today? Is it not that very desire that gives these small objects their outsize qualities of beauty and preciousness?

48. P. Brown, *The Cult of the Saints: Its Rise and Function in Latin Christianity* (Chicago, Ill., 1981), 78.

49. S. Stewart, *On Longing: Narratives of the Miniature, the Gigantic, the Souvenir, the Collection* (Baltimore, 1984), 54 and 66.

50. G. Bachelard, *La Poetique de l'espace* (Paris, 1957), 146.

51. R. A. Etlin, "Space, Stone, and Spirit: The Meaning of Place," in *The Eight Technologies of Otherness*, S. Golding, author-editor (London, 1997), 318.

52. Brown, *Cult of the Saints* (as in note 48), 78.

ALICIA WALKER

'The Art That Does Not Think': Byzantine 'Decorative Arts'—History and Limits of a Concept

THE TERM "decorative arts" is not often applied in a direct fashion to the arts of Byzantium. Yet many Byzantine objects—such as ivory boxes, silver vessels, silk hangings, enamel plaques, golden necklaces, and even ceramic bowls—can be classified in this category.[1] Since at least the early twentieth century, medieval art historians have questioned the appropriateness of the labels "decorative" and "minor" arts, although they rarely explain the insufficiency of these concepts in a sustained fashion.[2] The following comments are proposed as something of an account for why the designation "decorative arts" is no longer considered a useful rubric and how it came to be that the field moved beyond it. I briefly trace the history of the term as well as its demise and then survey a number of alternative approaches to the study of so-called decorative or minor objects that have emerged in Byzantine art history over the last thirty years.

Rather than simply rejecting the labels "decorative" or "minor," I suggest that the field has benefitted from embracing the very aspects of the decorative arts that previously led to their marginalization. In particular, the ornamental, functional, and material aspects that originally set the decorative arts apart from and below the so-called fine arts can be understood as the roots for a number of profitable innovations in medieval art-historical interpretation. I posit that earlier scholars perceived Byzantine objects as unable to "think" like works of fine art—especially painting—and therefore relegated them to subordinate status in the artistic hierarchy.[3] In contrast, recent scholarship engages with Byzantine visual and material culture on its own terms, recognizing value in the different cognitive processes

1. Regarding the early historiography of Byzantine decorative arts, see the exhibition at Dumbarton Oaks, "Before the Blisses," 15 April–31 July 2011: http://library.doaks.org/exhibitions/before_the_blisses/ (accessed 1 March 2012). For general introductions to and recent discussions of the state of research on individual media of Byzantine "decorative arts," see the relevant essays in E. Jeffrey, J. Haldon, and R. Cormack, eds., *The Oxford Handbook of Byzantine Studies* (Oxford, 2008); A. Laiou, ed., *The Economic History of Byzantium from the Seventh through the Fifteenth Century* (Washington, D.C., 2002).

2. Notable exceptions include M. M. Fulghum, "Under Wraps: Byzantine Textiles as Major and Minor Arts," *Studies in the Decorative Arts* 9.1 (2001–2002): 13–33. In an early passing critique of the "minor" status of Byzantine decorative arts, O. M. Dalton states: "The artistic influence of the Byzantine Empire is due in no small degree to those minor arts of which the very name has a certain depreciatory sense. Few peoples have done more than those composing that empire to correct the error thus implied. The effect of these lesser arts on the development of culture is often of a high significance; and as there is truth in the saying that the ballads of a nation may contain the key to its history, in like manner it might be maintained that from what remains of its minor arts it is possible to divine its achievement in the most diverse fields of action," although he subsequently claims that Byzantium's greatest artistic contributions are found in architecture. O. M. Dalton, *Byzantine Art and Archaeology* (Oxford, 1911), 35–36 at 35.

3. A receptive attitude toward the different thought processes of the "decorative arts" and the way in which their logic can open new avenues of interpretation is found in the recent study Jonathan Hay, *Sensuous Surfaces: The Decorative Object in Early Modern China* (Honolulu, 2010). Hay posits that "decorative objects" "have the capacity for *thinking* materially.... Luxury objects *think with us* materially in order to create pleasure in the beholder that will allow them to fulfill their most fundamental function as decoration.... To connect us visually and physically to the world around us, to weave us into our environment in ways that banish the arbitrary and recreate a sense of meaningful order" (italics his), *ibid.*, 13.

at play in Byzantine works of art. These interpretive currents are apparent in a number of post-decorative art rubrics—including material culture studies,[4] visual culture studies,[5] thing theory,[6] the biography or social life of objects,[7] and portability[8]—which embrace the properties of functionality, ornamentation, materiality, and production that distinguish the decorative arts from their fine art cousins.[9]

The "Decorative Arts": History and Definition of the Term

Within the broader field of art history, much ink has been spilt in efforts to define precisely what the decorative arts are, although this body of literature is noteworthy above all for its engaging diversity of opinion.[10] Still throughout these writings a set of four characteristics consistently comes to the fore: the decorative arts are distinguished by functionality, materiality, ornamentation, and conditions of production.[11] As is well known, the concept of the decorative arts is a by-product of a historical "fine art" hierarchy that places architecture, painting, and sculpture (along with music and poetry) in the highest echelons.[12] The remaining arts have been known by a variety of more or less interchangeable labels, including the applied arts, minor arts, ornamental arts, industrial arts, and of course, the decorative arts. All of these terms encode a sense of lesser value in relation to the fine arts.[13]

This hierarchical system has its origins in the Italian Renaissance, when architecture, painting, and sculpture were excerpted from the western medieval category of the "mechanical arts" and distinguished as the three "arts of design."[14] The resulting notion of the "fine arts" was further refined in the eighteenth century, at which point the aesthetic prerogative of the category was firmly articulated, thereby removing the "fine arts" from the need to fulfill the functional requirements imposed on all the other arts.[15] These other arts, which occupied the lingering category of the "mechanical arts," were generally defined by their exclusion from the "fine arts" rather than by any common, intrinsic characteristics.

Toward the end of the eighteenth century, interest in these "other" arts was spurred by the growth in industrial manufacturing, which resulted in the burgeoning production of non-fine-art goods and an increasing need to understand them in relation to the fine arts.[16] It was in the eighteenth and nineteenth centuries that the key features of the decorative arts as utility, production, materiality, and decoration came to be defined. An effort was also made to inter-relate these qualities and to synthesize an understanding of the decorative arts as a whole.[17] These theories and definitions followed distinct trajectories in different national schools of thought, but the four factors of functionality, materiality, ornamentation, and conditions of production consistently circulate throughout all discussions, and

4. See n. 58, below, and M. Grünbart and D. Stathakopoulos, "Sticks and Stones: Byzantine Material Culture," *Byzantine and Modern Greek Studies* 26 (2002), 297–327. Also see "The Bibliography on Byzantine Material Culture and Everyday Life," http://www.univie.ac.at/byzantine/ (accessed 1 March 2012).

5. R. Nelson, ed., *Visuality Before and Beyond the Renaissance: Seeing as Others Saw* (Cambridge, 2000).

6. Bill Brown, "Thing Theory," *Critical Inquiry* 28 (2001), 1–22; L. E. Saurma-Jeltsch and A. Eisenbeiss, eds., *The Power of Things and the Flow of Cultural Transformations* (Munich, 2010).

7. A. Appadurai, *The Social Life of Things: Commodities in Cultural Perspective* (Cambridge, 1986); C. J. Hilsdale, "The Social Life of the Byzantine Gift: the Royal Crown of Hungary Re-invented," *Art History* 31.5 (2008), 602–31.

8. E. Hoffman, "Pathways of Portability: Islamic and Christian Interchange from the Tenth to the Twelfth Century," *Art History* 24.1 (2001), 17–50.

9. The following discussion is not intended as a definitive statement but rather as an overview of discernible trends and new directions of interpretation. Likewise the citations offered are not exhaustive but instead represent some—although certainly not all—noteworthy work in the field.

10. See, for instance, the collected primary sources in I. Frank, ed., *The Theory of Decorative Art: An Anthology of European and American Writings, 1750–1940* (New Haven, Conn., 2000).

11. I. Frank, "Introduction: The History of the Theory of Decorative Art," in *The Theory of Decorative Art* (as in note 10), 1–2.

12. P. O. Kristeller, "The Modern System of the Arts: A Study in the History of Aesthetics (II)," *Journal of the History of Ideas* 13.1 (1952), 17–46.

13. Frank, "Introduction" (as in note 11), xi and 1.

14. Frank, "Introduction" (as in note 11), 3–4.

15. *Ibid.*, 4.

16. *Ibid.*, 4–5.

17. *Ibid.*, 5–10.

the material culture of the medieval world sometimes factored into these new ideas.[18] For instance, in the writings of William Morris—the founder of the British Arts and Crafts movement, whose philosophies greatly influenced American design theory in the early twentieth century—medieval models found particular pride of place in relation to the theme of production. Morris' anti-industrialist discourse idealized the medieval guild system as an exemplar of cooperative artistic production in which design and manufacture were unified in the creative work of the artisan.[19]

During the nineteenth century, debates over the decorative arts also expanded beyond the written word, playing out in the physical form of international exhibitions of applied arts. Perhaps most famously, the Great Exhibition of the Industry of All Nations was held in London in 1851 and offered a venue for the display of manufactured goods from around the world as well as modern renditions of historical design models, which included installations representing Byzantium.[20] Byzantine forms subsequently entered into modern design vocabularies produced in the wake of these exhibitions, including the famous *Grammar of Ornament* of 1856 by Owen Jones (Fig. 1).[21]

These nineteenth- and early twentieth-century expositions not only spurred debate about contemporary arts production but also served as the impetus for establishing permanent exhibitions of modern and historical decorative arts. For instance, the Great Exhibition and its subsequent incarnation as the "Crystal Palace" at Sydenham in 1854 laid the foundation for the founding of the South Kensington Museum in London in 1857 (renamed the Victoria and Albert Museum in 1899).[22] The nineteenth century was also an important period for the private collecting of Byzantine ivories, jewelry, enamels, textiles, and other so-called decorative arts. In some cases these personal assemblages were later sold or gifted to museums, forming the basis of many of the premier public museums of today including the Hermitage, the Victoria and Albert Museum, and the Metropolitan Museum, to name only a few. Furthermore, the cataloging of these public and private collections established some of the earliest scholarship on the decorative arts of Byzantium.[23] Through display and publication, these collections introduced Byzantine objects to a wider audience. Growing institutional and private collections and the publicity of world fairs and expositions led to the incorporation of Byzantine models in the work of popular designers of the period, for example Louis Comfort Tiffany.[24]

Needless to say, the categories of the fine and decorative arts that were defined from the Renaissance to the nineteenth century have no historical basis in the

18. On these differences, see for example S. Muthesius, "Handwerk/Kunsthandwerk," *Journal of Design History* 11.1 (1998), 85–95.

19. Frank, "Introduction" (as in note 11), 8–10.

20. The Great Exhibition is perhaps better known through its more permanent form as the Crystal Palace Exhibition, which opened in 1854. See M. Digby Wyatt and J. B. Waring, *The Byzantine and Romanesque Court in the Crystal Palace* (London, 1854). Regarding Victorian-era attitudes towards and conceptions of Byzantine architecture, see M. Crinson, "Oriental Byzantium: Interpreting Byzantine Architecture, 1840–70," in *Empire Building: Orientalism and Victorian Architecture* (New York, 1996), 72–92.

21. J. B. Waring, "Chapter VII. Byzantine Ornament," in O. Jones, *The Grammar of Ornament* (London, 1856), 49–54, pls. XXVIII–XXX; Frank, "Introduction" (as in note 11), 8. The criteria for the designation "Byzantine" in *The Grammar of Ornament* do not align, however, with modern definitions. Indeed several of the objects are of Western medieval origin. Furthermore, plate XXX, which depicts architectural details, draws from monuments located exclusively on Italian soil, which were the Byzantine (and in some cases Byzantinizing) architectural works best known and most accessible to Western Europeans in this period. On the factors effecting the Western European definition of "Byzantine" at this time, see Crinson, "Oriental Byzantium," 72–89.

22. It is worth noting that Jones played a pivotal role in the mounting of both the Great Exhibition and the Crystal Palace exhibition as well as the foundation of the South Kensington Museum. Regarding the formation and early ideologies of the Victoria and Albert Museum, see A. Arieff, "Reading the Victoria and Albert Museum," *Victorian Poetry* 33.3/4 (1995), 403–24.

23. Dumbarton Oaks Research Library and Collection, "Collectors," in "Before the Blisses," http://library.doaks.org/exhibitions/before_the_blisses/exhibits/show/collectors (accessed 1 March 2012).

24. J. B. Bullen, "Louis Comfort Tiffany and Romano-Byzantine Design," *The Burlington Magazine* 147 (2005), 390–98. Regarding European and American revivals of Byzantium in the modern era, see *idem*, *Byzantium Rediscovered* (London, 2003);

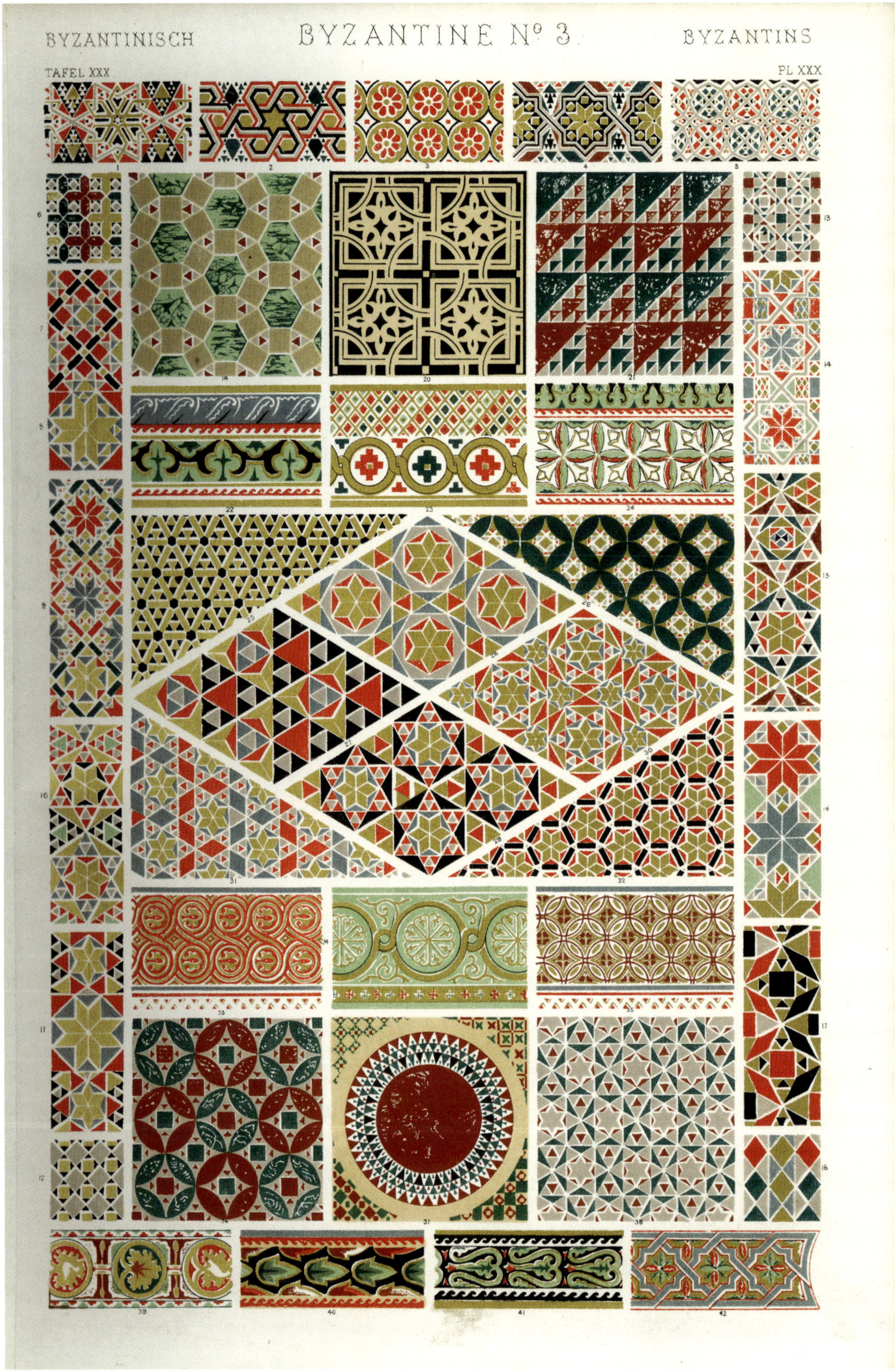

FIGURE 1. "Byzantine Ornament. Byzantine No. 3," in Owen Jones, *The Grammar of Ornament* (London, 1856), pl. XXX (image in the public domain).

Byzantine tradition.[25] Nonetheless they affected the way Byzantine art has been studied and interpreted during the modern era.[26] In world exhibitions and the practices of design and display that they engendered, Byzantium emerged as one among a multitude of sources for aesthetic models.[27] Yet the process of recording these ornamental typologies often resulted in the decoupling of decorative elements from their original contexts, a phenomenon particularly evident in *The Grammar of Ornament*, which excised patterns from Byzantine works of art and architecture, reducing them to anonymous ciphers of essential formal properties (see Fig. 1). Similar strategies were applied in the cataloging of actual fragments of Byzantine works of art, such as textiles, by collectors and curators.[28] In these instances, the nature of the Byzantine objects and monuments on which these motifs had appeared—as well as their original function and meaning—was lost. As such they became mere storehouses of ornamental elements for modern inspiration and analysis.

The close affiliation of the decorative arts with ornament might have eventually disadvantaged Byzantine works of art in the polemical discourse of early twentieth-century functionalism. Epitomized in the strident essay by Adolf Loos "Ornament and Crime" of 1912, progenitors of European and American modernism rejected the decorative flourishes found in nineteenth- and early twentieth-century design on ethical as much as aesthetic grounds. Their position resulted in the increasingly low estimation of decidedly ornate artistic traditions like the "decorative arts" of Byzantium.[29]

Decorative Arts as Ornament in the Early Twentieth Century: Riegl and "The Art that Does Not Think"

Whether presented as a virtue or a vice, "ornament" has been commonly understood to operate in the domain of sensual, affective experience that is exclusive of rational, intellectual processes.[30] The title of this essay, "The Art that Does Not Think," reflects this position and comes from an article by Christopher Wood in which he relates a Frankish brooch (Fig. 2) and the concept of *mache* ("making" or "fabrication") to Alois Riegl's treatment of late antique jewelry in *Die spätrömische Kunst-Industrie*, Volumes One (published in 1901) and Two (published posthumously in 1923).[31] Riegl was, of course, one of the foremost nineteenth-century theorists of the decorative arts and was particularly interested in the late antique and medieval traditions as well as the status of ornament in art history. He was intimately associated with the establishment of modern

---

R. S. Nelson, *Hagia Sophia, 1850–1950: Holy Wisdom Modern Monument* (Chicago, 2004).

25. To my knowledge, there is no equivalent term in medieval Greek for a category of objects like the "decorative arts," although this question—and the larger issue of Byzantine artistic typologies—is worthy of further research. For some preliminary comments of relevance to this topic, see A. Cutler, "Uses of Luxury: On the Function of Consumption and Symbolic Capital in Byzantine Culture," in A. Guillou and J. Durand, eds, *Byzance et les images* (Paris, 1994), 287–327; *idem*, "The Industries of Art," in Laiou, *The Economic History of Byzantium* (as in note 1), 555–87.

26. A remnant of this system is evident, for example, in the housing of medieval metalwork and enamel in the "Decorative Arts" Department of the National Gallery in Washington, D.C., where it remains to this day.

27. On the universalist and synthetic impulses underlying the work of, for instance, Jones, see S. Sloboda, "*The Grammar of Ornament*: Cosmopolitanism and Reform in British Design," *Journal of Design History* 21.3 (2008), 223–36.

28. Regarding the early twentieth-century practice of mounting textile fragments on boards in collage format for study and storage, see T. K. Thomas, "From Curiosities to Objects of Art: Modern Reception of Late Antique Egyptian Textiles as Reflected in Dikran Kelekian's Textile Album of ca. 1910," J. D. Alchermes, H. C. Evans, and T. K. Thomas, eds., *Anathemata eortika: Studies in Honor of Thomas F. Mathews* (Mainz, 2009), 305–17, esp. 306–11.

29. On Loos' critique of ornament—and the suggestion that the modernist movement simplified and misrepresented his position—see M. Gusevich, "Decoration and Decorum, Adolf Loos's Critique of Kitsch," *New German Critique* 43 (1988), 97–123. For a brief discussion of the Modernist attitude toward the decorative arts, see Frank, "Introduction" (as in note 11), 13–15.

30. The affiliation of ornament and pleasure continues to feature prominently in current (and relatively current) scholarship. See O. Grabar, *The Mediation of Ornament* (Princeton, N.J., 1992), esp. 37; Hay, *Sensuous Surfaces* (as in note 3), 8–15.

31. C. Wood, "Riegl's *mache*," *Res* 46 (2004), 155–72 at 155; A. Riegl, *Die spätrömische Kunst-Industrie, nach den Funden in Österreich-Ungarn*, vol. 1 (Vienna, 1901) and vol. 2 (Vienna, 1923).

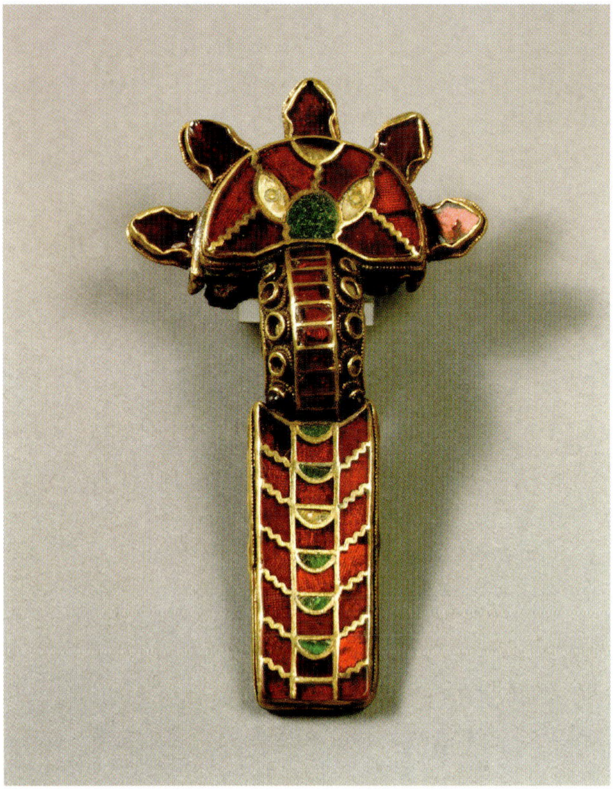

FIGURE 2. Fibula of Picquigny, Frankish, sixth century, Museo Nazionale del Bargello, Florence (photo: Scala / Art Resource, N.Y.).

European museums, serving as the curator of textiles (*c.* 1886–1896) at the Österreichisches Museum für Kunst und Industrie (opened in 1864; today the Museum für angewandte Kunst) in Vienna, which itself was inspired by the founding of the South Kensington Museum in London. Riegl's theories on ornament and its historical development were articulated in his seminal study *Stilfragen* of 1893, a volume in which Byzantium is denied status as one of "the truly creative artistic styles" because of its purported lack of innovation or originality.[32]

In an argument that could be applied equally to Byzantine items of jewelry (for example, Fig. 3), Wood expounds on the late nineteenth-century Symbolist poet Stefan George's use of the word *mache* in the interpretation of medieval jewelry as "not redeemed by a concept," as objects that do not serve as "vehicles for an idea."[33] In other words, they are not objects that "think." Instead they insist on their physical nature as raw material transformed through making. It is this "capacity of the fabricated thing to put in place its own reality" and to deny movement beyond itself that captured Riegl's interest.[34] Because the object does not readily gesture to some symbolic, narrative, or social meaning, it "is in no danger of being discarded once the idea is conveyed."[35] By refusing to "think" in the same way as works of fine art—like painting and sculpture—objects like the fibula (and earring) stake an insistent claim to their own materiality and presence.

Wood identifies this absence of thought as a climactic end point to Riegl's theory of ornament in the decorative arts as well as the epitome of Riegl's new way of understanding art as an "optical" phenomenon, but one in which the haptic properties of the object serve as the departure point for engagement. According to his approach, all works of art—painting as much as an earring or a brooch—operate through properties of line, color, and form, although objects like the brooch do so in a pure fashion. In this respect, the decorative arts can be understood as a stepping stone toward Riegl's conception of a universal history of art that approached objects and monuments from all eras and of all aesthetic traditions on equal terms, as participants in a common lineage of formal development.[36] His notion of the relationship between haptic and optic embraces the distinct characteristics of the ornamental arts and casts this innovative perspective back onto art history as a whole. To the extent that Riegl positioned

32. A. Riegl, *Stilfragen: Grundlegungen zu einer Geschichte der Ornamentik* (Berlin, 1893), translated as *Problems of Style: Foundations for a History of Ornament*, by D. Castriota (Princeton, N.J., 1992), see esp. "Tendril Ornament in Byzantine Art," 240–66 at 241.

33. Wood, "Riegl's *mache*" (as in note 31), 155 and 158-9. For the current state of research on Byzantine jewelry, see C. Entwistle and N. Adams, eds., *Intelligible Beauty: Recent Research on Byzantine Jewellery* (London, 2010), the title of which neatly challenges the notion of this material as an "art that does not think."

34. Wood, "Riegl's *mache*" (as in note 31), 155.

35. *Ibid.*, 155.

36. *Ibid.*, 158–9 and 168; Frank, "Introduction" (as in note 11), 11–13, esp. 12.

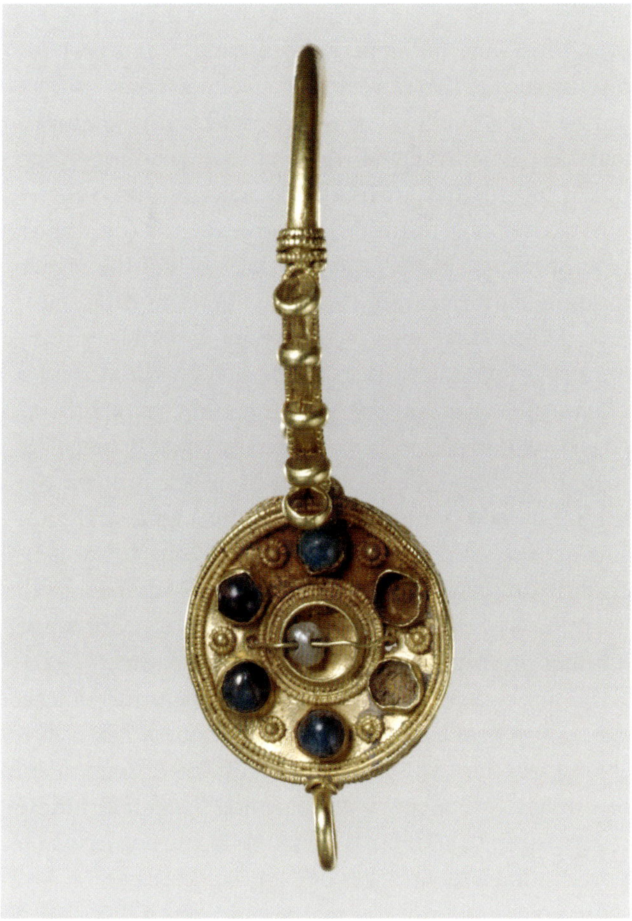

FIGURE 3. Earring, Byzantine or Langobardic(?), sixth to seventh century, gold, glass, and pearls, 4.5 × 1.5 × 2.6 cm, Metropolitan Museum of Art, N.Y., purchase, 1895 (95.15.124).

the decorative arts as leading the way toward a new method for interpreting art more broadly, we might say that in his argument the decorative arts found a moment of quiet triumph.

The hyper-formalist crescendo in Riegl's theory illustrates one instance of an exhaustion of the notion of a "decorative" art, resulting in a breaking down of the division between the major and minor arts. By reducing the objects to their made-ness and form, Riegl created a more democratic mode for engaging with all works of art, whether painting, sculpture, jewelry, or a tin cup. Yet as Wood observes, the focus on the ornamental and the formal, on surfaces and materiality comes at the expense of repressing other key aspects of the fibula, including its medieval function and meaning. Riegl's valorization of form simultaneously occludes the historical "object-quality" of the fibula, that is to say, its presence in an original context of reception and use.[37]

We might understand these items of jewelry as a sort of ideal zero point within theories of the decorative arts because of the way they cooperate with the notion of the absence of meaning or thought. The excessive privileging of the formal qualities of the made-thing ultimately fails to satisfy, however, because it denies engagement with other aspects of the object, in particular its social-historical value and functionality. Indeed, few works of Byzantine decorative art are as conveniently devoid of extra-formal features as the brooch and the earring. Rather, they commonly include narrative and symbolic iconography that equip them to "think" in the same terms as works of fine art, like painting and sculpture. At the same time, their media and formats tether them to the category of the decorative arts, and they evince functional features in a manner that cannot be obscured or deferred as easily as in the cases of brooches and earrings.

Decorative Arts as Fine Arts: Byzantine "Painting" in the Mid-Twentieth Century

Early to mid-twentieth-century interpretations of Byzantine decorative arts often take an approach different from that of Riegl, perhaps in part because they were not aiming to establish a universal method for interpreting ornament but rather to understand medieval art on its own terms.[38] Yet unlike Riegl, these interpretations tend not to question the hierarchical system that

37. Wood, "Riegl's *mache*" (as in note 31), 159–63.

38. A pan-cultural, pan-historical approach continues to characterize many art historical investigations of ornament. See E. H. Gombrich, *The Sense of Order: A Study in the Psychology of Decorative Art* (Ithaca, N.Y., 1979); J. Trilling, *The Language of Ornament* (New York, 2001); *idem*, *Ornament: A Modern Perspective* (Seattle, 2003). Universal ambitions are claimed even by discussions that focus on specific artistic traditions, for example Grabar, *The Mediation of Ornament*, 6. Important exceptions to these patterns include J. Trilling, *The Medallion Style: A Study in the Origins of Byzantine Taste* (New

privileges the fine arts. Instead they attempt to redeem the decorative arts by claiming status for them on par with their fine art cousins.

For example, André Grabar's *Byzantine Painting* of 1953 (reprinted in 1979) is most noteworthy for its relative lack of actual paintings.[39] The majority of works illustrated are wall mosaics (as on the cover of the 1979 edition, Fig. 4), with manuscript painting and fresco together composing almost all of the remaining documentation. The book ends with a short section on icons, however, only one of the five illustrations depicts a panel painting: three of the images of icon "paintings" show enamels and one a micro-mosaic.[40] Grabar does not address this disconnect between title and content in an immediate or direct fashion, but over the course of the text an explanation emerges: since actual paintings of sufficient quality to be considered of true Byzantine (that is to say Constantinopolitan) production are in relatively short supply for the period considered, mosaics and enamels are taken as the surrogate for that lost tradition.[41] An implicit attitude can be detected here by which painting is understood as the medium most qualified as "art," and the value of other media (such as enamels and mosaics) comes from their pictorial properties, that is to say, from the degree to which they are "like painting" and allow us to recuperate a sense of this superior medium.

To be fair, the volume was part of a Rizzoli/Skira series for which the publisher's note begins with something of an apology for even including Byzantine art in their line-up: "We of the twentieth century have learnt to appreciate beauty under all its many aspects; not only those complying with the rules of Greek art formulated in the age of Pericles, but also those of other, sometimes very different, civilizations."[42] It is perhaps not surprising, therefore, that the volume contorts Byzantine art to fulfill criteria generated from systems of artistic convention that are not its own. Indeed the publishers further justify the presence of this "other," non-classicizing tradition by appealing to the notion that "modern art has prepared the way" for the reader to appreciate Byzantine works, which are diplomatically claimed to possess "a strikingly contemporary appeal."[43] Although the specific qualities that render Byzantine art as "other" (and, therefore, implicitly inferior) are not enumerated, we can reasonably speculate that the publisher was attempting to account for the tradition's non-naturalistic conventions. Indeed Byzantine art might have been perceived by the European-American "period eye" of the 1950s to resonate with "primitive" art of the non-Western world, which was another prominent artistic "other" of the time.[44] In the Rizzoli/Skira volume, Byzantine art, including objects that could be classified as so-called decorative arts, is shoe-horned into a system that required it to conform to the fine art category of "painting" and that judges it according to standards dictated by Eurocentric and post-medieval definitions of "art."

Indeed, in the work of many mid-twentieth-century scholars there is a tendency to treat decorative arts like paintings by focusing on their iconographic elements and equating these symbolic and narrative features across media without paying sustained attention to the unique properties of the objects on which these motifs appear.[45] Such pictorializing of essentially non-pictorial works of art is further enacted through the

York, 1985); E. Swift, *Style and Function in Roman Decoration: Living with Objects and Interiors* (Aldershot, 2009); Hay, *Sensuous Surfaces*.

39. A. Grabar, *Byzantine Painting: Historical and Critical Study* (Geneva, 1953; rpr. New York, 1979).

40. *Ibid.*, 186–92. 41. *Ibid.*, *passim*. 42. *Ibid.*, 5.

43. "Thus after our books on Etruscan and Roman Painting, we follow up with a volume dealing with Byzantine Painting, for whose full enjoyment modern art has prepared the way and whose beauties of form and style have indeed a strikingly contemporary appeal." Grabar, *Byzantine Painting* (as in note 39), 5.

44. The early to mid-twentieth-century modernist perspective on Byzantium as a source of authentic artistic expression and pure formal power is an attitude similar to that projected onto works of non-Western art at that time. This connection awaits full exploration; preliminary work on the issue includes: D. Lewis, "Matisse and Byzantium, or Mechanization Takes Command," *Modernism/Modernity* 16.1 (2009), 51–59; Glenn Peers, "Utopia and Heterotopia: Byzantine Modernisms in America," *Studies in Medievalisms* 19 (2010), 77–113, with additional bibliography of note. An upcoming symposium promises to shed additional light on this question: "Byzantium/Modernism: Art, Cultural Heritage, and the Avant Gardes," 20–22 April 2012, Yale University, New Haven, Conn.

45. See, for example, K. Weitzmann, *Greek Mythology in Byzantine*

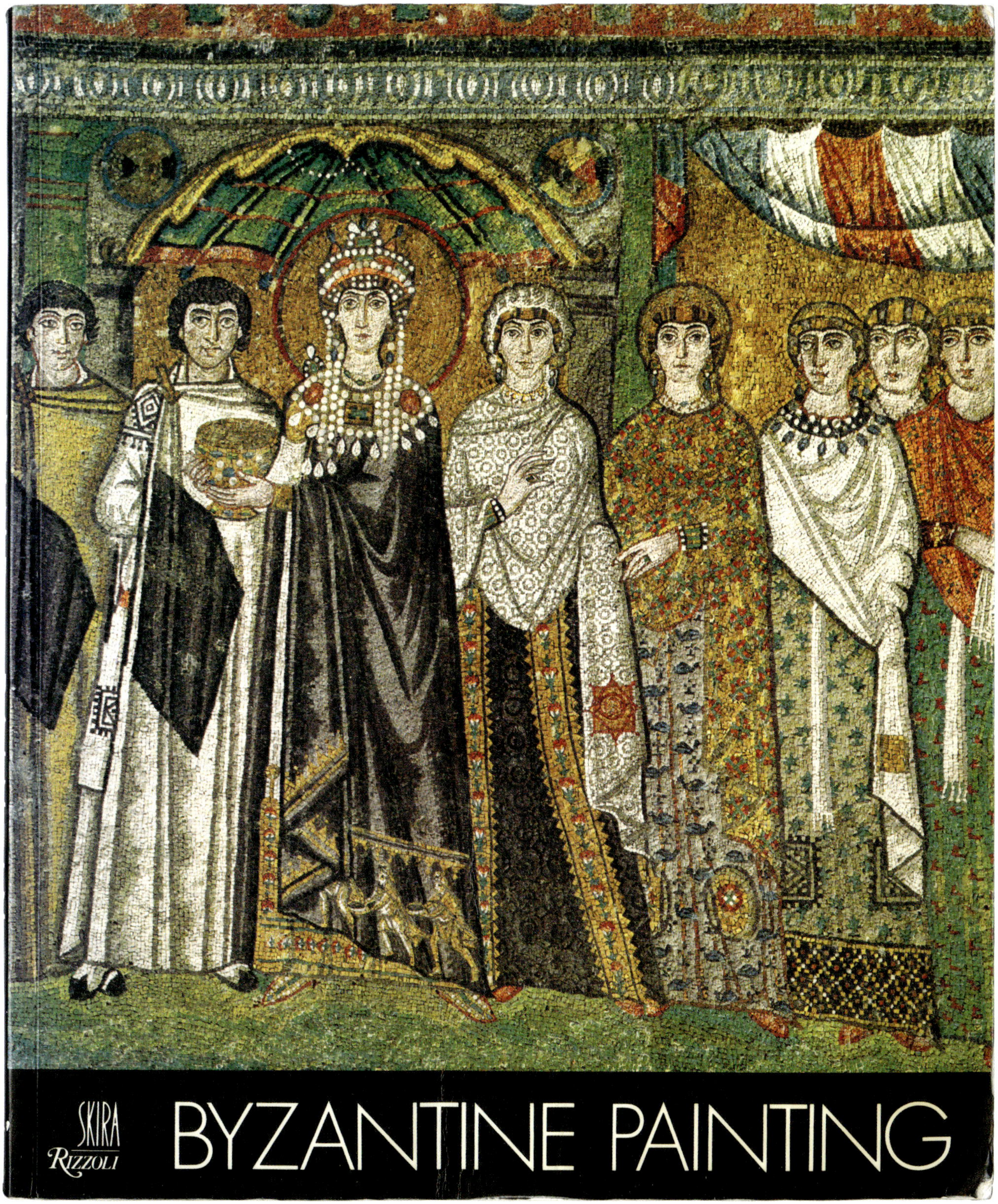

FIGURE 4. Cover of André Grabar, Byzantine Painting (New York, 1979).

selective cropping of the photographs that illustrate these objects such that the iconographic features are framed to appear like paintings, thereby obscuring evidence of their ornament, function, and materiality. As a result, Byzantine decorative art objects are claimed to "think" like fine art objects.

Challenging the "Minor" Status of Medieval "Decorative Arts"

One of the earliest direct and sustained challenges to the category of medieval decorative arts is found in William Wixom's 1970 essay "The Greatness of the So-Called Minor Arts," in which he extols the ivory, gold, silver, bronze, enamel, and gem-work of the Middle Ages, and suggests that a better term for characterizing these works would be "the art of church treasures."[46] The concept of the "sumptuous arts" or "luxury arts" also appears as a common alternative term to the "decorative arts" in museum catalogues and exhibitions of the mid- and late twentieth century, perhaps because it accomplishes the gesture of elevating the works in question to a separate but equal status *vis-à-vis* the fine arts.[47]

Wixom argues for an equivalent station for the decorative arts on the basis of the precious materials from which they were crafted as well as their associations with elite individuals and institutions of medieval society, whose appreciation of and value for these objects is demonstrated by their monetary investments in them. He also cites evidence for named craftsmen and their relationships to specific works of art, perhaps to preempt claims that the anonymous production of medieval decorative art objects indicates their lower prestige.[48] These propositions challenge the authority of the fine arts to the extent that they allow the decorative arts to participate in systems of value established by painting, sculpture, and architecture. Yet the approach remains complicit in a fine art model by leaving the undergirding hierarchy of that system in place.

Recuperating Function and Context in the Late Twentieth Century

Real movement away from the major/minor and fine/decorative arts hierarchies came only in the 1980s, appearing in the wake of an institutional critique of museums that focused on the problematic representation of non-Western artistic traditions and the legacy of cultural and political colonialism from which these practices of display grew.[49] This literature informed a new perspective on the categorization and display of medieval works of art, drawing attention to how the conceptual taxonomies and physical environments of the museum are at odds with the functional, often ritual

---

Art (Princeton, N.J., 1951), which explores the enduring presence of classical iconographic and stylistic features in Byzantine art, but does so in a manner that disassociates such imagery from the objects on which it appeared. This aspect of Weitzmann's approach is highlighted by comparison with recent scholarship on the role of the classical—and Christian—tradition in early Byzantine silver, which focuses on the cultural dimensions of the medium, exploring the iconography of objects in relation to their materiality and function. See R. Leader-Newby, *Silver and Society in Late Antiquity: Functions and Meanings of Silver Plate in the Fourth to Seventh Centuries* (Aldershot, 2004); Swift, *Style and Function in Roman Decoration* (as in note 38), 105–38.

46. W. D. Wixom, "The Greatness of the So-Called Minor Arts," in F. Deuchler, ed., *The Year 1200: A Background Survey* (New York, 1970), 93–99 at 93.

47. The term appears already in the first quarter of the twentieth-century: see J. Ebersolt, *Les Arts Somptuaires de Byzance* (Paris, 1923); it reappears more recently, for example, in I. Kalavrezou, "Luxury Objects," in H. C. Evans and W. D. Wixom, eds., *The Glory of Byzantium: Art and Culture of the Middle Byzantine Era, A.D. 843–1261* (New York, 1997), 218–23. For a useful reflection on the social dimension of Byzantine consumption of luxury goods, see Cutler, "Uses of Luxury" (as in note 25), 287–327.

48. Wixom, "The Greatness of the So-Called Minor Arts" (as in note 46), 93–99.

49. See, for example, I. Karp and S. D. Lavine, eds., *Exhibiting Cultures: The Poetics and Politics of Museum Display* (Washington, D.C., 1991), which was based on a symposium held in 1988. The roots of the tradition embodied in museums of applied arts like the Victoria and Albert—and the exhibitions that preceded them—have also been seen as entangled in the ideologies and agendas of modern European colonialism. See T. Barringer, "The South Kensington Museum and the Colonial Project," in T. Barringer and T. Flynn, eds., *Colonialism and the Object: Empire, Material Culture and the Museum* (London, 1998), 11–27; J. M. Ganim, "Medievalism and Orientalism at the World's Fairs," *Studia Anglica Posnaniensia* 38 (2002), 179–90.

nature of medieval objects.[50] Scholarship on Byzantine art that directly addresses the question of function versus display in the museum setting emphasizes that when pinned to walls and clipped to stands, Byzantine objects become as lifeless as butterflies inventoried in an entomologist's cabinet. At a time when galleries of African art were reinstalled to show masks rejoined with their full costumes of raffia alongside videos that depicted the ritual performance in which they were used, historians of Byzantine art were drawing attention to the fact that clay lamps, ivory boxes, enamel reliquaries, and even icon paintings were not created for display on the walls and in the vitrines of museums, but were instead part of the daily life of Byzantine homes or the architectural environments of churches and palaces as well as the ceremonies that took place within and around them.[51]

This new self-consciousness is apparent in collection catalogues of the era, including those that do not fully embrace new museological principles. For instance, the catalogue of the medieval objects in the Victoria and Albert Museum, published in 1986 to mark the reinstallation of the collection (and reprinted ten years later) begins: "At first sight, it might appear that the displaying of medieval works of art in a museum gallery was an act which, in separating the objects from their original context and intended function, would render them as no more than expensively wrought and precious trinkets."[52] Yet the author, Paul Williamson, goes on to defend the installation of medieval objects in modern museums by arguing that in their original liturgical contexts, they not only functioned as integral parts of church rituals but were also objects of display, viewed "in the sacristy or in secure treasury areas."[53] He extends the parallel between medieval cathedrals and modern museums by comparing "the pious and generous donors who donated relics of the saints" to the late nineteenth- and early twentieth-century benefactors like J. P. Morgan and Henry Walters, while the twelfth-century Abbot Suger is likened to a contemporary museum director.[54] Finally, he posits that the market for decorative arts in the Middle Ages was spurred in part by the cult of relics, which he characterizes as a "burgeoning industry surrounding the cathedral treasuries."[55] In the latter comment rings a faint but fascinating echo of the explanation for the expansion in eighteenth- and nineteenth-century decorative arts production to be the result of the industrial revolution.[56]

Regardless of whether we endorse Williamson's intriguing defense for the display of medieval art objects, the point remains that his justification is a sign of the times. When reinstalling the Victoria and Albert's collection in the 1980s, he was forced to account for the decorative art characteristics of functionality, materiality, ornament, and production, properties that demanded a response outside the traditional hierarchies and interpretative practices of the fine arts system.

Studies of Byzantine art since the late 1980s have increasingly removed objects, at least conceptually, from the museum environment in order to recuperate some aspect of their original context of use, a call heard clearly in Robert Nelson's important article of 1989, "The Discourse of Icons Then and Now."[57] As a result, the utility of Byzantine works of art emerges as an intrinsic aspect of their value. This shift to a contextual and functional approach was a first real step away from the limitations that the concept of the "decorative arts" had imposed, but it is essential to note that it was the recognition and redemption of their defining attribute of utility—a feature that had earlier resulted in their second-tier status—that offered an alternative to the fine arts hierarchy that long insisted on their inferior

50. Indeed, since the late 1980s, it has become increasingly common to draw attention to the way in which the museum environment obscures access to the Byzantine experience and understanding of works of art. See R. Nelson, "The Discourse of Icons Then and Now," *Art History* 12:2 (1989), 144–57.

51. For instances, see E. Maguire, H. Maguire, and M. Duncan-Flowers, *Art and Holy Power in the Early Christian House* (Urbana, Ill., 1989); Nelson, "The Discourse of Icons" (as in note 50).

52. P. Williamson, "Introduction," *The Medieval Treasury: The Art of the Middle Ages in the Victoria and Albert Museum* (London, 1986), 5.

53. *Ibid.*, 5.

54. *Ibid.*, 6.

55. *Ibid.*

56. See note 16 above.

57. Nelson, "The Discourse of Icons" (as in note 50), esp. 145.

position. Indeed, the manner in which the meaning of Byzantine objects is generated through their functionality might be understood as one of the most important ways in which they "think."

The resulting new methodologies for understanding Byzantine works of art can perhaps best be labeled as anthropological and archaeological in nature. In their wake, art historians have become increasingly committed to recuperating a sense of the use and meaning of works of art in their original contexts, attending not only to the spaces and rituals in which they were employed, but also to visual documentation of objects in action. Such approaches fundamentally reject any lingering opinion that asserts the aesthetic and conceptual inferiority of Byzantine art by rejecting the fine arts system altogether and allowing Byzantine objects to be explained on their own terms, in relation to their own aims.

The first firm steps outside the "decorative arts" shadow focused on religious objects, perhaps because their ritual contexts could be more readily and consistently identified. But similar methods for interpreting more "secular" arts have also emerged, often under the rubric of "material culture" studies. For example, in a recent expansive study, Maria Parani catalogs and analyzes the depiction of objects such as table implements, furnishings, and clothing represented in Byzantine sacred icons and religious narrative imagery in order to compose a picture of the realia of everyday life.[58] While material culture studies often trace a path within the disciplinary boundaries of anthropology, archaeology, or economic history they can also overlap extensively with the concerns of art history.[59]

In his foundational study, *The Hand of the Master*, published in 1994, Anthony Cutler examines ivory carving in terms of both modern and Byzantine perception, attending not only to its "technique and function," but "to the place that ivories held in Byzantine culture."[60] His contextualized approach implicitly refuses to endorse the interpretative practices of the fine arts model or the hierarchy it constructs. He does not confine his survey to the "best" examples of the corpus but instead defends opening consideration to the full range of high and low quality works still extant. He also engages questions of production and function with a keen eye toward materiality, exercising unprecedented care in meticulously surveying the topography of the ivories' carved surfaces to record the traces of the craftsman's tool in elephant tusk and animal bone, and cataloging these indexes of the "master's hand" to establish patterns in the handling and treatment of raw material.

In addressing function, he explores the use of ivory panels in action, as tools for personal prayer that withstood the very haptic manner in which Byzantine users engaged with these objects, caressing, cradling, and kissing them.[61] He also considers the reception of these objects not only in terms of the user's dynamic, physical interaction with them, but also the way that environmental factors such as lighting could transform the most basic material properties of color and thereby animate the ivory object in dramatic and compelling ways (Fig. 5).[62] Finally he explores how the exotic origins of ivory imbued the material with social value and meaning.[63] In his study, materiality is no longer the domain of only production and technique, nor a blunt statement of the luxury and economic value of an

58. M. Parani, *Reconstructing the Reality of Images: Byzantine Material Culture and Religious Iconography (11th–15th Centuries)* (Leiden, 2003). Also see B. Pitarakis, "Daily Life in Byzantine Constantinople," in K. Durak, ed., *From Byzantion to Istanbul—8000 Years of a Capital* (Istanbul, 2010), 144–55. The term "material culture" is increasingly apparent in Byzantine studies publications. See, for example, note 4 above, and Michael Grünbart, ed., *Material Culture and Well-being in Byzantium (400–1453): Proceedings of the International Conference*, Cambridge, 8–10 September 2001 (Vienna, 2007). Also see the research project at the University of Amsterdam, *Material Culture, Consumption and Social Change: New Approaches to Understanding the Eastern Mediterranean during Byzantine and Ottoman Times*, http://www.hum.uva.nl/byzottarch/ (accessed 1 March 2012).

59. For example, see D. Jacoby, "Silk Economics and Cross-Cultural Artistic Interaction: Byzantium, the Muslim World, and the Christian West," *Dumbarton Oaks Papers* 58 (2004), 197–240.

60. A. Cutler, *The Hand of the Master: Craftsmanship, Ivory, and Society in Byzantium (9th–11th Centuries)* (Princeton, N.J., 1994), 1.

61. *Ibid.*, 22–27.

62. *Ibid.*, 249–50, pl. v, which shows the same relief as fig. 5 (referenced above) but lit from behind as might have happened when the plaque passed in front of a candle.

63. *Ibid.*, 29–30 and 56–59.

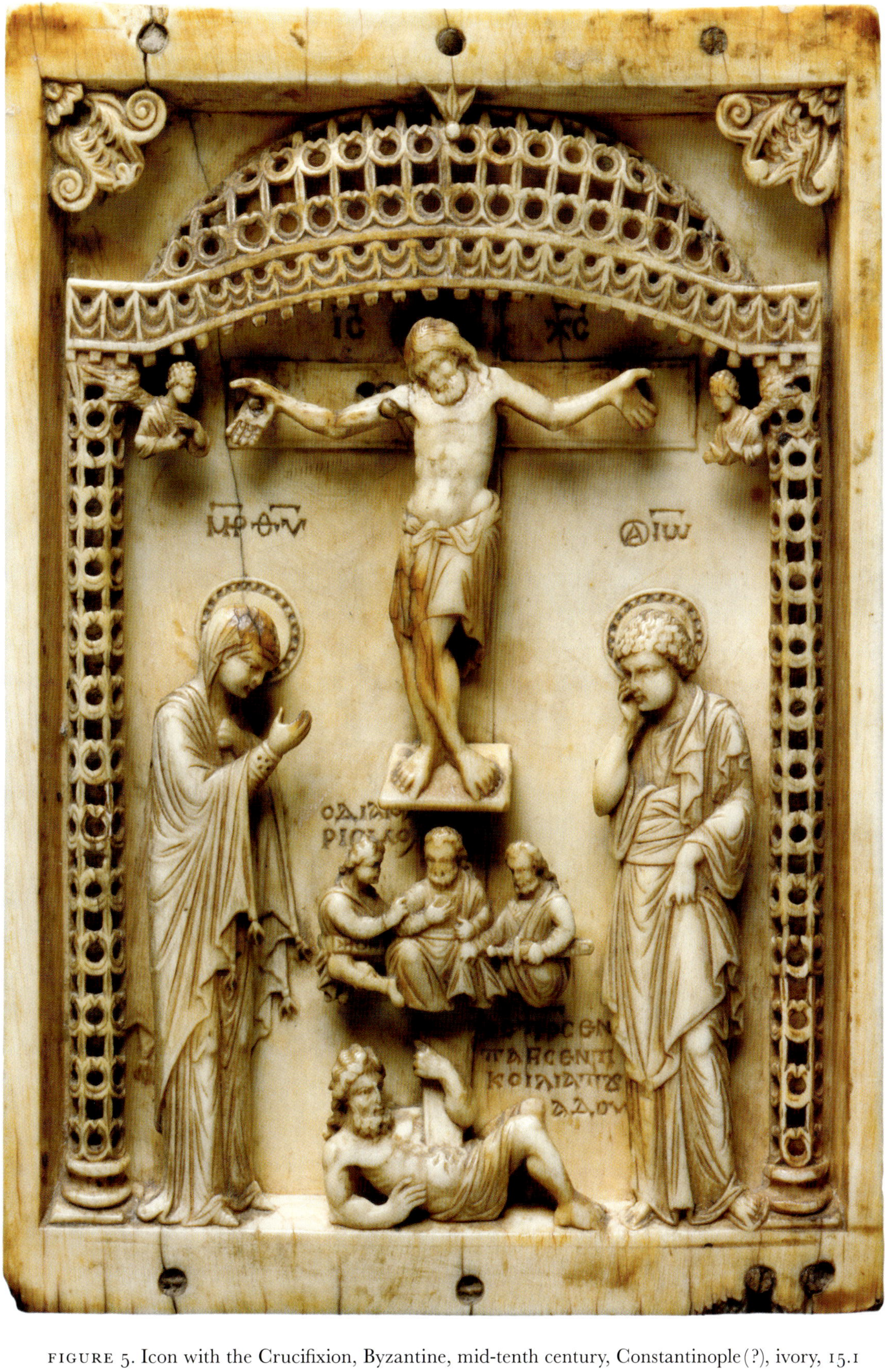

FIGURE 5. Icon with the Crucifixion, Byzantine, mid-tenth century, Constantinople(?), ivory, 15.1 × 8.9 x 0.8 cm, Metropolitan Museum of Art, N.Y., gift of J. Pierpont Morgan, 1917 (17.190.44) (photo: © The Metropolitan Museum of Art).

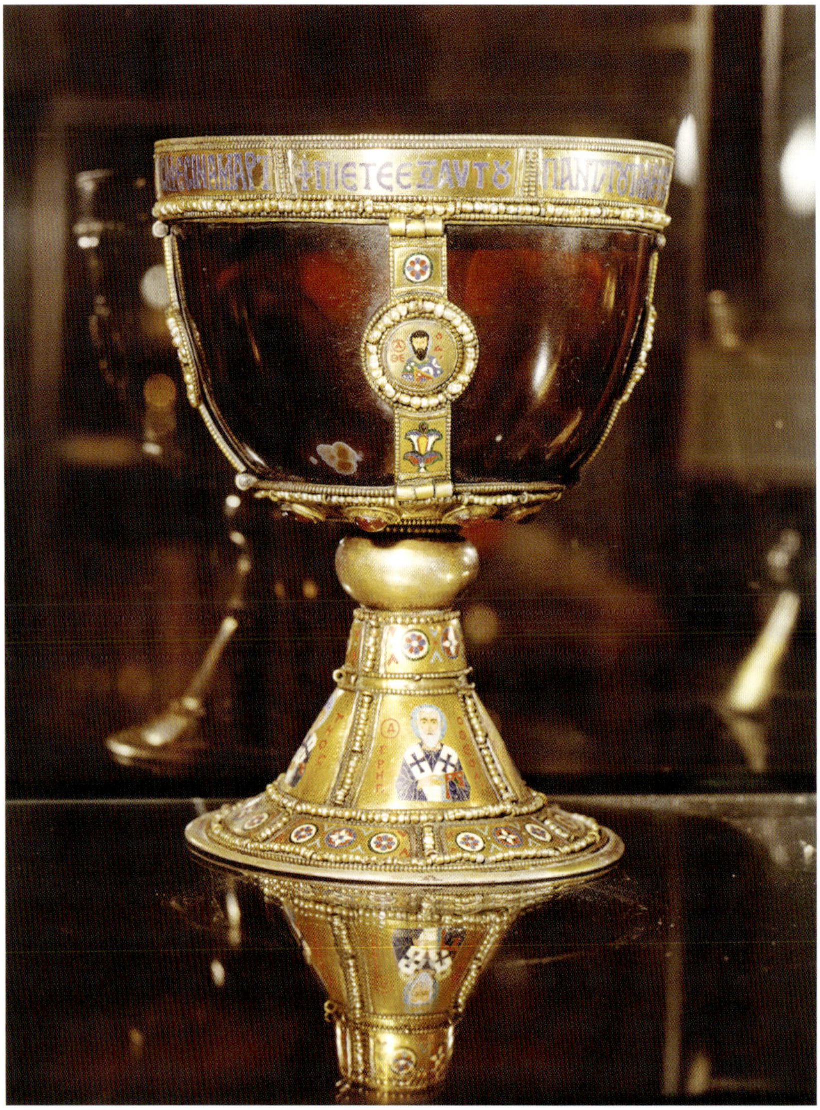

FIGURE 6. Chalice of the Patriarchs, Byzantine, tenth century, sardonyx, gold, enamel, *c.* 22 × 17 cm, Tesoro, S. Marco, Venice (photo: Art Resource, N.Y.).

object. It becomes instead part of the object's meaning. Materiality, then, marks another way in which Byzantine objects "think."[64]

These dynamic properties are of course not unique to ivory. As Bissera Pentcheva observes, the capacity of the sardonyx bowl of a tenth-century Byzantine chalice to change colors as it is filled with and drained of Eucharistic wine animated both the object and the ritual of which it was a part (Fig. 6). She argues that the inscription around the rim—which reads "Drink ye all of it, for this is my blood of the New Testament, which is shed for many for the remission of sins" (Matt. 26:27–28)—and the very specific function of the object in the liturgical feast collaborate with its transformative

64. The theme of materiality in relation to Byzantine art will receive unprecedented attention in an exhibition organized by Glenn Peers at the de Menil Collection, Houston, and scheduled for fall 2013. The topic is also shaping scholarship in medieval art history more broadly, as indicated by a stimulating session sponsored by the International Center for Medieval Art at the

material to stage in dramatic terms the mystical conversion of transubstantiation.[65] From these examples, we can appreciate how the very "stuff" of a Byzantine work of art could be as carefully selected and orchestrated as the motifs in an iconographic program so as to convey the meaning and, more importantly, fulfill the function of the object. Related interpretations can be found in the work of Liz James, Rico Franses, and Glenn Peers, each of whom in a different way attends to the meaningfulness of materiality and ornament in Byzantine art.[66]

In another important shift away from the lingering authority of fine arts hierarchies in the study of Byzantine objects, Pentcheva proposes that it is not the familiar painting of encaustic or tempera on wood panel that best embodies the Byzantine notion of an icon but rather metal reliefs enlivened with colorful enamel and radiant jewels—decorative art objects par excellence—that best satisfy the requirements of Byzantium's particularly tactile vision and sensorially saturated devotion (Fig. 7).[67] These various studies together embody another quiet triumph of Byzantine decorative arts, in which their defining characteristics of functionality, materiality, and ornament garner them due status at the top of a complex system defined by practices, beliefs, and values specific to Byzantine culture. In this new outlook, however, the meaning of, for example, an icon is realized not only through its function—an aspect that is consistent regardless of medium—but also through its particular substance. Furthermore, comprehension of this meaning is achieved not by transcending the object's substance through allegorical and spiritual reflection, but by remaining with the material, bearing witness to and participating in its performance of divine presence.

With regards to their status as decorative arts, textiles have received especially interesting treatment.[68] As is well known, the majority of extant late antique textiles come from burials, particularly from funerary deposits in the dry sands of Egypt. Many of the garments and shrouds retrieved from these sites show signs of corrosion and decomposition. But in the hands of nineteenth- and twentieth-century dealers and collectors, they were snipped and trimmed to remove evidence of their messy histories. This process effectively transformed the medallions and bands of garments and hangings into pictures. Framed like paintings, these decontextualized iconographic and ornamental elements were primarily appreciated for their narrative references or as design elements (Fig. 8).[69] It is only by reconstituting the original composition of these elements within garments and hangings, and in turn by considering the function of the garments and hangings in Byzantine society that a deeper appreciation of the objects emerges (compare Figs. 8 and 9). Rather than rejecting the corporeal associations of these textiles, scholars have more recently embraced their role in protecting and adorning bodies and the spaces through which these bodies moved.[70] In addition, the metaphors associated with textiles in Christian thought have come to imbue the medium itself with richer, culturally specific value.[71] It is, again, by embracing aspects of

---

2012 College Art Association, Los Angeles, "*Res et significatio*: The Material Sense of Things in the Middle Ages."

65. B. Pentcheva, "The Performative Icon," *The Art Bulletin* 88.4 (2006), 631–55, at 644–46 and 649–50.

66. R. Franses, "When All that is Gold Does not Glitter: On the Strange History of Looking at Byzantine Art," in A. Eastmond and L. James, eds., *Icon and Word: The Power of Images in Byzantium. Studies Presented to Robin Cormack* (Aldershot, 2003), 13–23; L. James, "Senses and Sensibility in Byzantium," *Art History* 27.4 (2004), 522–37; G. Peers, *Sacred Shock. Framing Visual Experience in Byzantium* (University Park, Pa., 2004).

67. Pentcheva, "The Performative Icon" (as in note 65), 631; B. Pentcheva, *The Sensual Icon: Space, Ritual, and the Senses in Byzantium* (University Park, Pa., 2010).

68. Their historiography is usefully outlined and highlighted in the important essay by Fulghum, "Under Wraps" (as in note 2).

69. Thomas, "From Curiosities to Objects of Art" (as in note 28), 306–309.

70. H. Maguire, "Garments Pleasing to God: The Significance of Domestic Textile Designs in the Early Byzantine Period," *Dumbarton Oaks Papers* 44 (1990), 215–24; Fulghum, "Under Wraps" (as in note 2), 18–27; V. Marinis, "Wearing the Bible: An Early Christian Tunic with New Testament Scenes," *Journal of Coptic Studies* 9 (2007), 95–109; W. T. Woodfin, *The Embodied Icon. Liturgical Vestments and Sacramental Power in Byzantium* (Oxford, 2012).

71. N. Constans, "Weaving the Body of God: Proclus of Constantinople, the Theotokos, and the Loom of the Flesh," *Journal of*

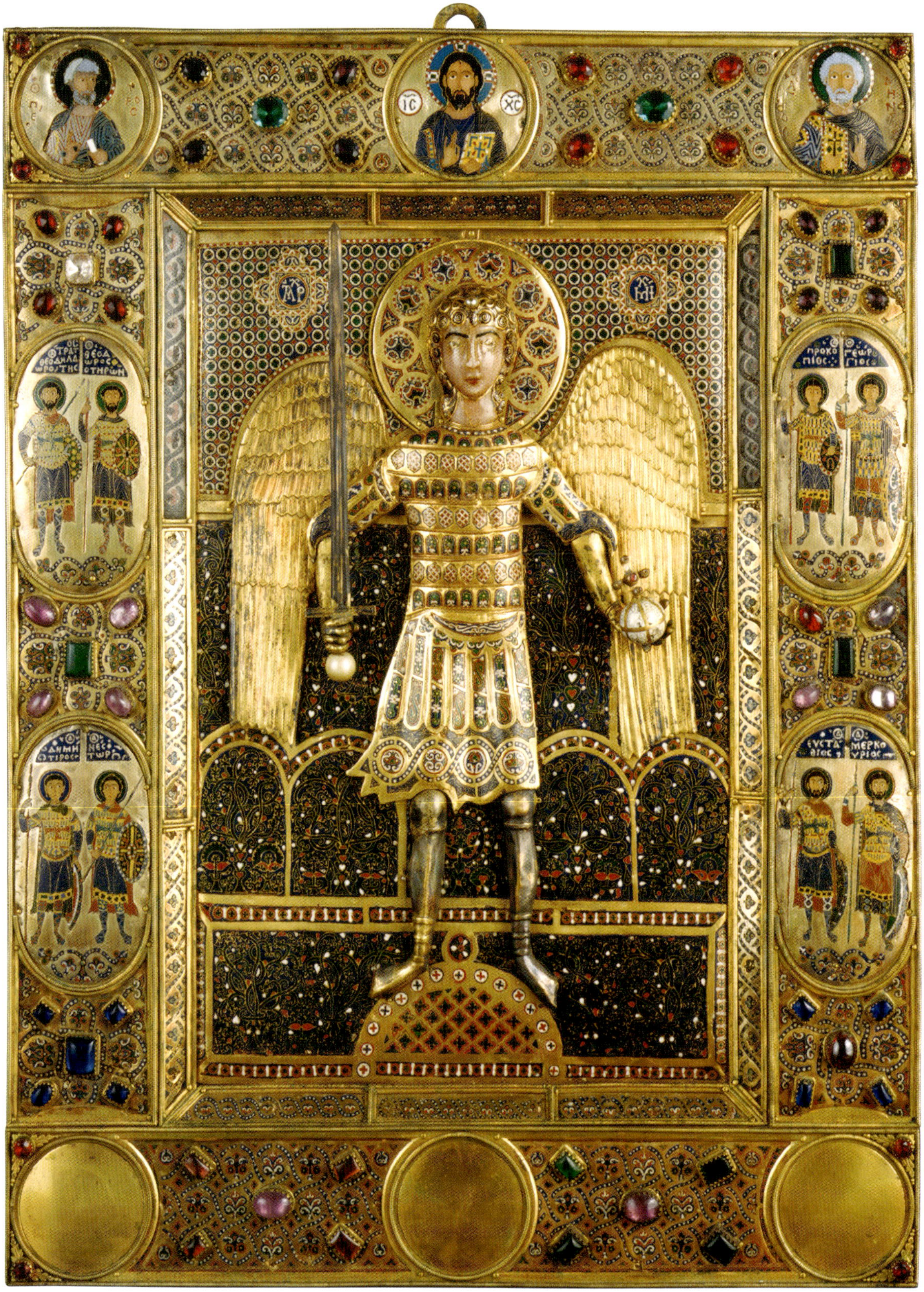

FIGURE 7. Archangel Saint Michael with sword, Byzantine, late eleventh to twelfth century, Constantinople (?), gold, enamel, and precious stone, *c.* 22 × 18.5 cm, Tesoro, S. Marco, Venice (photo: Cameraphoto Arte, Venice / Art Resource, N.Y.).

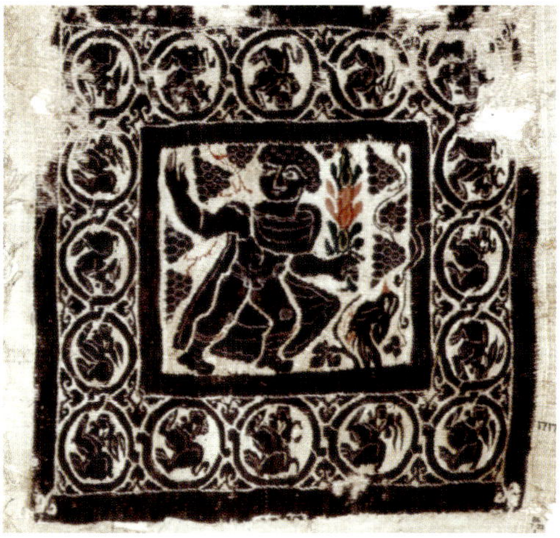

FIGURE 8 (*left*). Tapestry square panel, early Byzantine (Coptic), fourth to sixth century(?), undyed and purple linen, 66.5 × 37.5 cm, British Museum, London (1886,0723.1) (photo: © Trustees of the British Museum).

FIGURE 9 (*below*). Tunic, early Byzantine, fifth century, probably from Panopolis (Ahkmim), Egypt, undyed linen and purple wool, design in tapestry weave, 183 × 135 cm, Metropolitan Museum of Art, N.Y., gift of Edward S. Harkness, 1926 (26.9.8) (photo: © The Metropolitan Museum of Art).

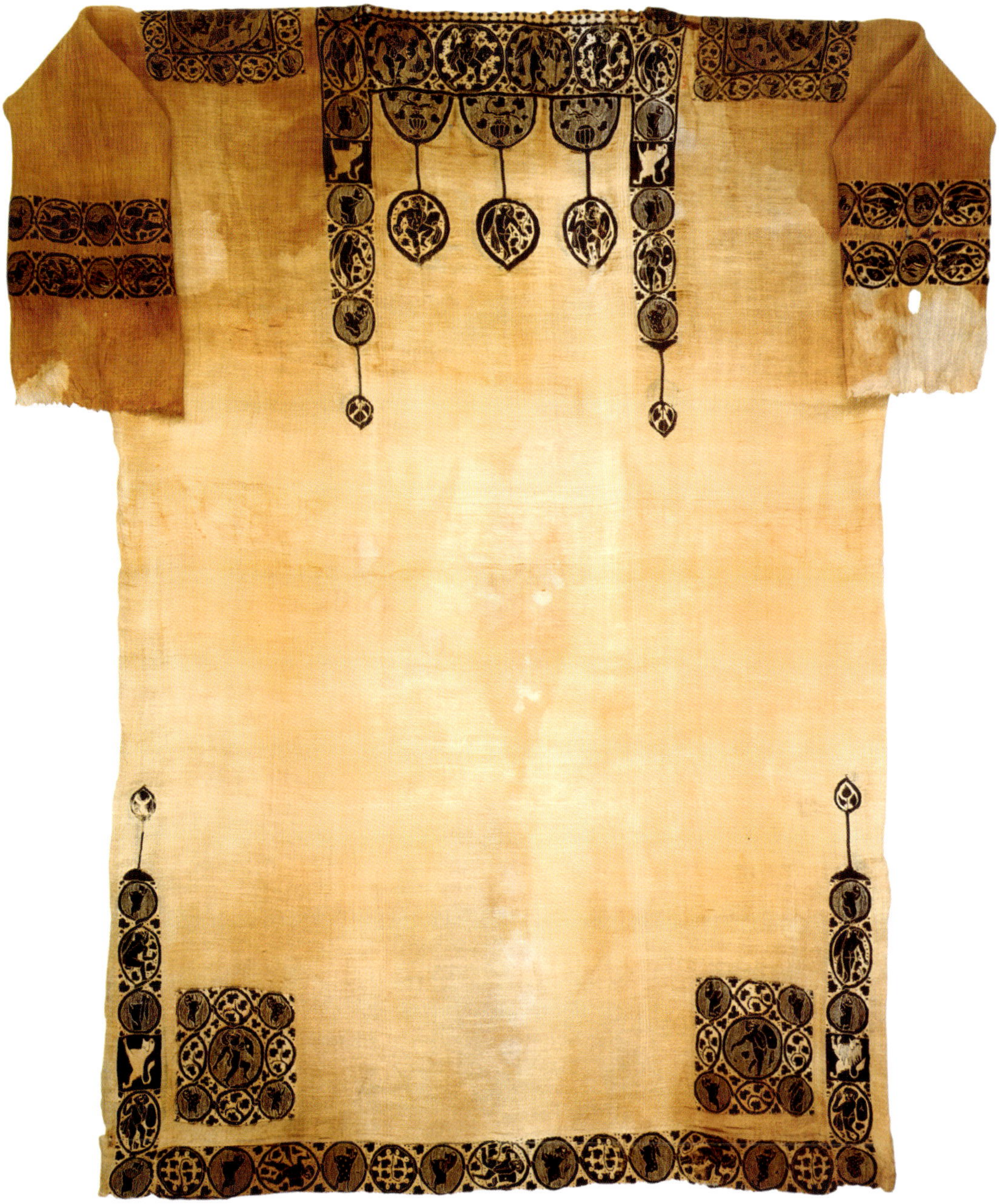

function and materiality that a more accurate understanding of the object's original significance is grasped and the limitations of the "decorative arts" concept is fully revealed.

My argument may raise objection that a focus on the "thingness" of medieval works of art is merely a contemporary scholarly imposition. But in some instances medieval objects draw attention to their own function and context in surprisingly direct ways. For instance, the so-called Projecta casket, a well-known fourth-century silver gilt container for the accoutrement of the late Roman woman's bath, is often illustrated to depict an almost architectonic view of the two front panels or the picture-like portrait of the owner and her spouse found on the lid (Fig. 10). All of these iconographically rich images allow the casket to "think" like a painting or sculpture, directing our attention beyond the container to the woman who owned it or to the goddess Aphrodite to whom she is explicitly paralleled.[72] Yet on the reverse, the casket illustrates the procession to the bath, and in this scene one of Projecta's attendants carries a box, the distinct shape and scale of which leave little doubt that it is, or at least is very much like, the box itself (Fig. 11). Through this self-reference, the casket insists on its functionality as a container for holding articles of the bath and perhaps as an object for displaying social status and wealth.[73] It does not, in the end, pretend to be a painting or a building, rather it insists on its own utility and on the particular meanings that derive from its function.

The larger move to seek the meanings of objects in their functions has led to interest in medieval "performance," which addresses the experience of works of art during ephemeral events such as the church liturgy or imperial ceremony.[74] Objects associated with Byzantine dining culture, such as metal and ceramic vessels, have undergone especially interesting reappraisal in light of their role in the performance of cultural and social status.[75] Scholarship on medieval performance also highlights the consideration of works of art in relation to the architectural environments in which they were used, challenging another hierarchy inherent in the fine arts system that artificially separates the study of monuments and objects.[76]

Another way that scholars of Byzantine material and visual culture have reshaped our understanding of the decorative arts is by introducing the possibility that objects possessed agency. Rather than being passive sites where ornament and luxury accumulate, they exercised power and acted in the world. This idea was conveyed in an elegant and persuasive manner by the important exhibition of 1989 *Art and Holy Powers in the Early Christian House*, curated by Eunice Maguire, Henry Maguire, and Maggie Duncan-Flowers.[77]

Early Christian Studies 3 (1995), 180–83; Fulghum, "Under Wraps" (as in note 2), 27–31; M. Evangelatou, "The Purple Thread of the Flesh: the Theological Connotations of a Narrative Iconographic Element in Byzantine Images of the Annunciation," A. Eastmond and L. James, eds., *Icon and Word: The Power of Images in Byzantium. Studies Presented to Robin Cormack* (Aldershot, 2003), 261–79.

72. J. Elsner, "Visualising Women in Late Antique Rome: The Projecta Casket," in C. Entwhistle, ed., *Through a Glass Brightly: Festschrift for David Buckton* (Oxford, 2003), 22–36. As Cecily Hilsdale rightly observes, in theorizing medieval art and attending to the socio-historical contexts of Byzantine objects, we must be vigilant against "looking through things" and neglecting their material particularities. Hilsdale, "The Social Life of the Byzantine Gift" (as in note 7), 4.

73. Swift, *Style and Function in Roman Decoration* (as in note 38), 125–28.

74. On the value of the performative approach to medieval art, see R. Nelson, "Empathic Vision: Looking at and with a Performative Byzantine Miniature," *Art History* 30.4 (2007), 489–502; E. Gertsman, *Visualizing Medieval Performance: Perspectives, Histories, Contexts* (Aldershot, 2008).

75. Leader-Newby, *Silver and Society* (as in note 45); Swift, "Vessels: Articles for Dining and Toiletry," in *Style and Function in Roman Decoration* (as in note 38), 105–38; E. D. Maguire and H. Maguire, "The Marvels of the Court," *Other Icons. Art and Power in Byzantine Secular Culture* (Princeton, N.J., 2007), 29–57.

76. This point has been particularly emphasized in scholarship on textiles, which merged with architectural environments when used as wall hangings or curtains and echoed monumental programs when the bodies on which they hung moved through space. Fulghum, "Under Wraps" (as in note 2), 19–22; Woodfin, *The Embodied Icon* (as in note 70). For an important comparative study of textiles in the field of Islamic art, see L. Golombek, "The Draped Universe of Islam," in P. P. Soucek, ed., *Content and Context of Visual Arts in the Islamic World* (University Park, Pa., 1988), 25–38.

77. Maguire, Maguire, and Duncan-Flowers, *Art and Holy Power in the Early Christian House* (as in note 51).

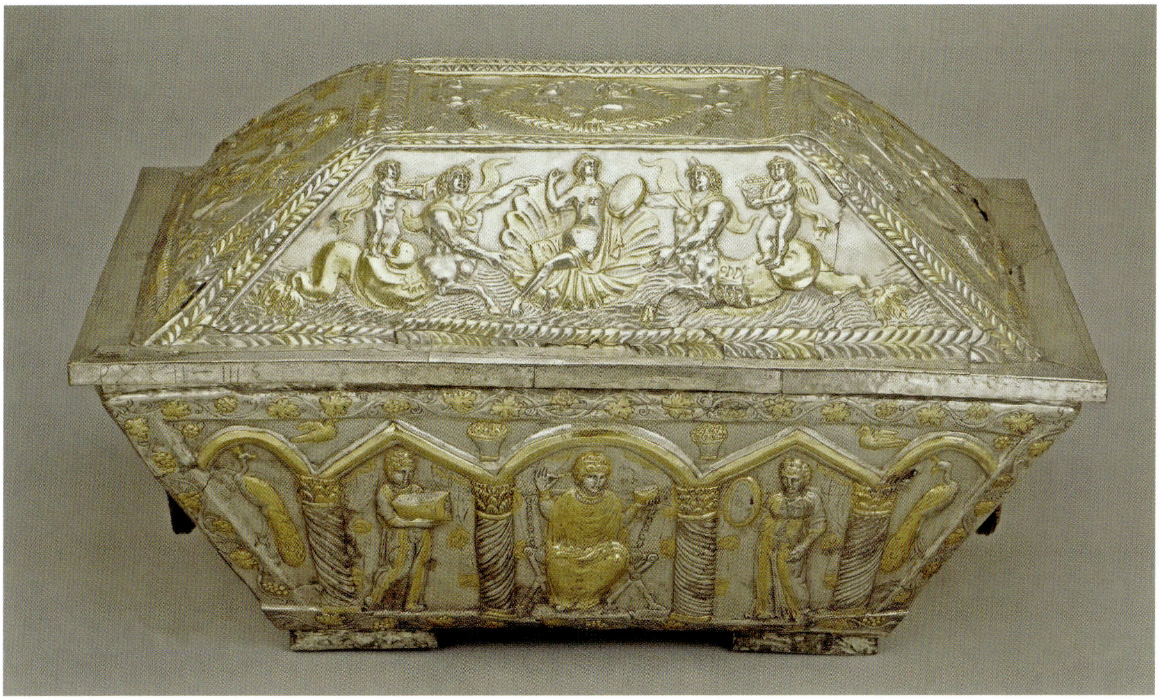

FIGURE 10. Projecta casket, early Christian, Rome, *c.* 380, gilded silver, 28.6 × 55.9 × 43.2 cm, British Museum, London, (1866, 1229.1) (photo: © Trustees of the British Museum).

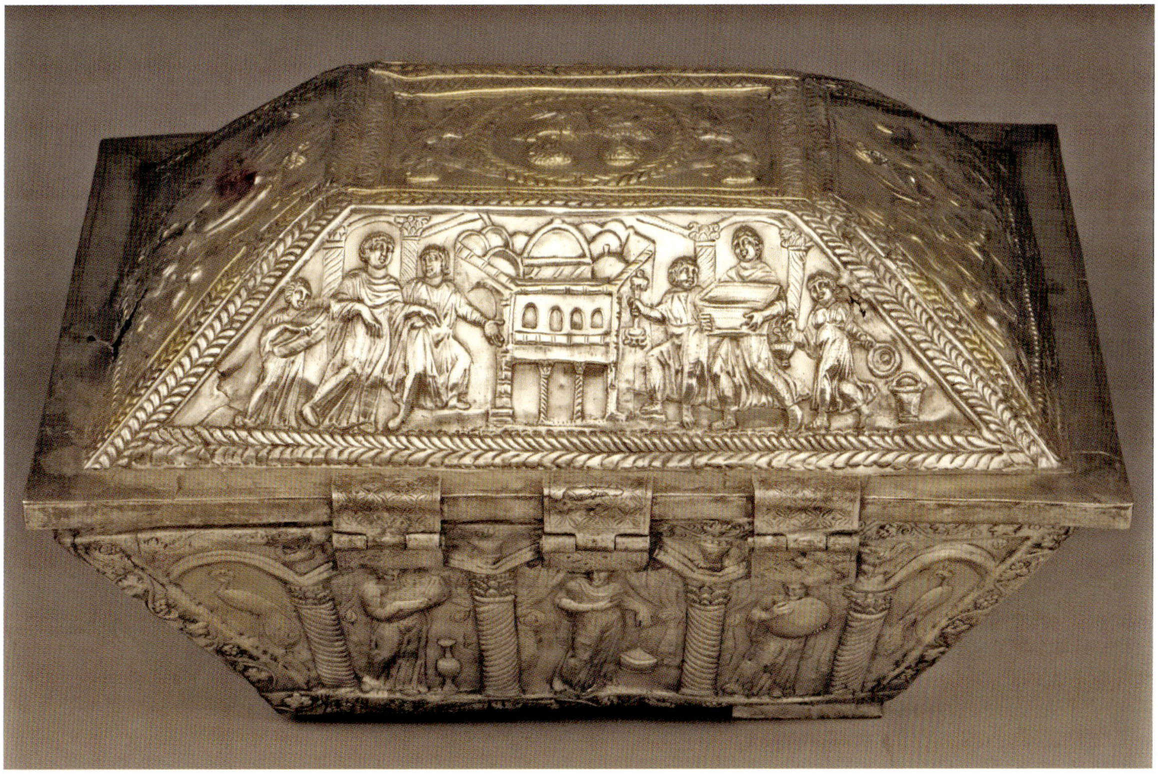

FIGURE 11. Projecta casket, view of back panel of the lid, early Christian, Rome, *c.* 380, gilded silver, 28.6 × 55.9 × 43.2 cm, British Museum, London (1866, 1229.1) (photo: © Trustees of the British Museum).

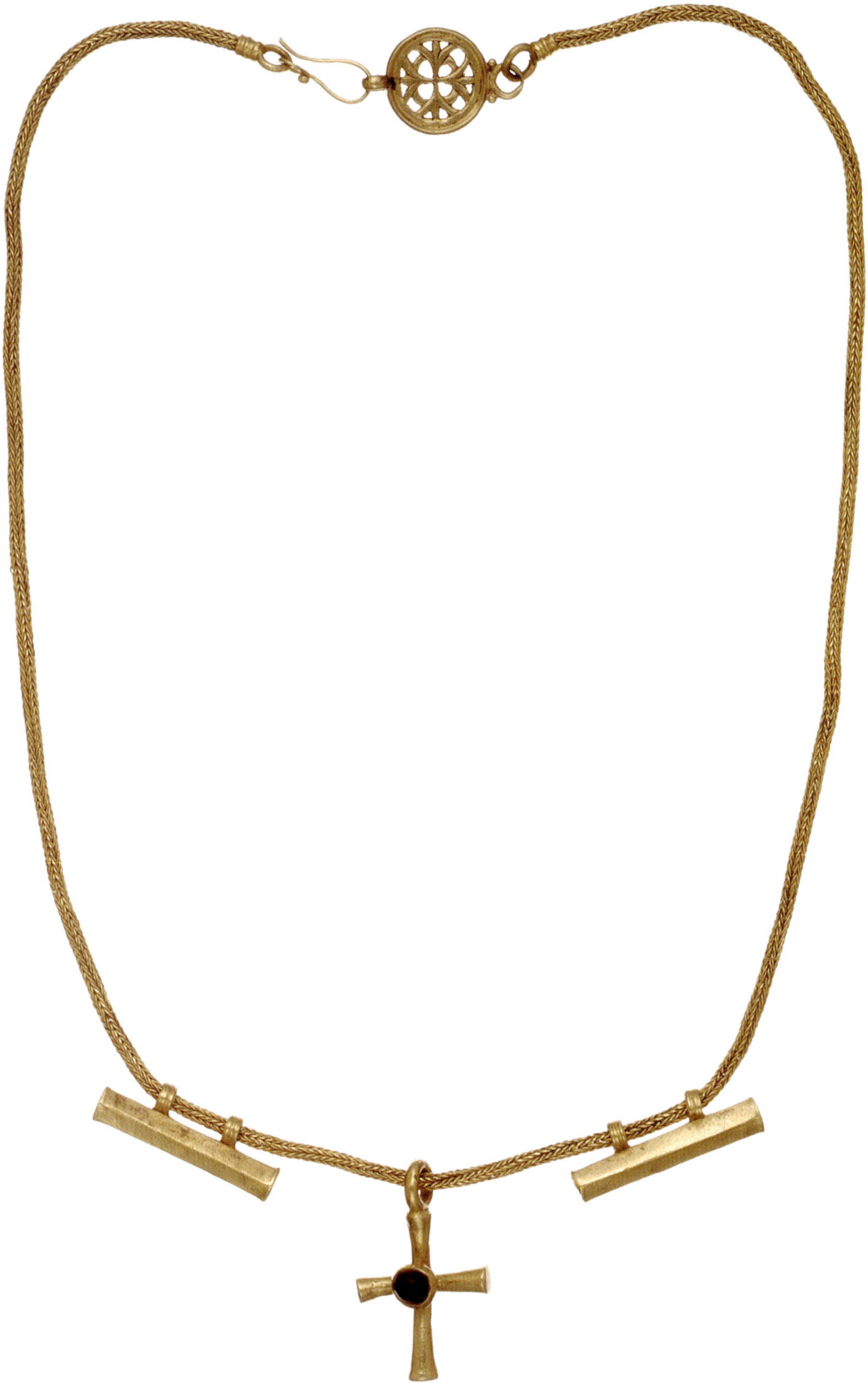

FIGURE 12. Necklace with Cross Pendant and Amulet Cases, Byzantine, fifth to sixth century C.E., gold and glass, chain: 54.3 cm, cross: 3.3 cm, phylacteries: 3.0 cm, Burton Y. Berry Collection, Indiana University Art Museum (70.56.11) (photo: Michael Cavanagh and Kevin Montague).

A good example of this different way of looking at the decorative arts is illustrated by a necklace, composed of a golden chain with a pendant cross flanked by two phylacteries (Fig. 12). Despite its eye-engrossing golden surfaces, delightfully elegant lines, and luscious ruby-like embellishment, the necklace demands attention beyond a Rieglian formal analysis or a focus solely on materiality because of the cross. Consideration of this symbolic feature calls for contextualization of the object, perhaps leading to an anthropological approach, viewing the necklace as a tool of devotion, an advertisement of religious affiliation, or a luxury item that projected the owner's economic status. Yet these pathways of interpretation may ultimately direct us away from the object, seeing it merely as a vehicle for a sign or an index of the user's social identity.

An alternative is found in scholarship that attends to utility, but in a way that remains intimately connected with materiality and presence. The necklace plays a distinctly talismanic function indicated by the presence of phylacteries. Within these containers were inserted gold tablets inscribed with protective charms and prayers (as illustrated in an unrolled comparative example, Fig. 13). From this perspective, the cross becomes much more than an iconographic sign. As Jacqueline Tuerk explains, such apotropaic devices assume a performative role through their inscriptions and images.[78] Rather than serving as passive ornament or transitive iconography, the cross and phylacteries are active agents of supernatural protection, defending the wearer by engaging in an ongoing confrontation with malevolent forces. To paraphrase J. L. Austen, talismans possess an autonomous and animate presence because through their inscriptions and images they "do something in the world."[79] Indeed, in Byzantium this agency can extend more deeply, such that the very material of the object is understood to be empowered, as is the case with hematite amulets in which the stone was believed to staunch the flow of blood and the amulet

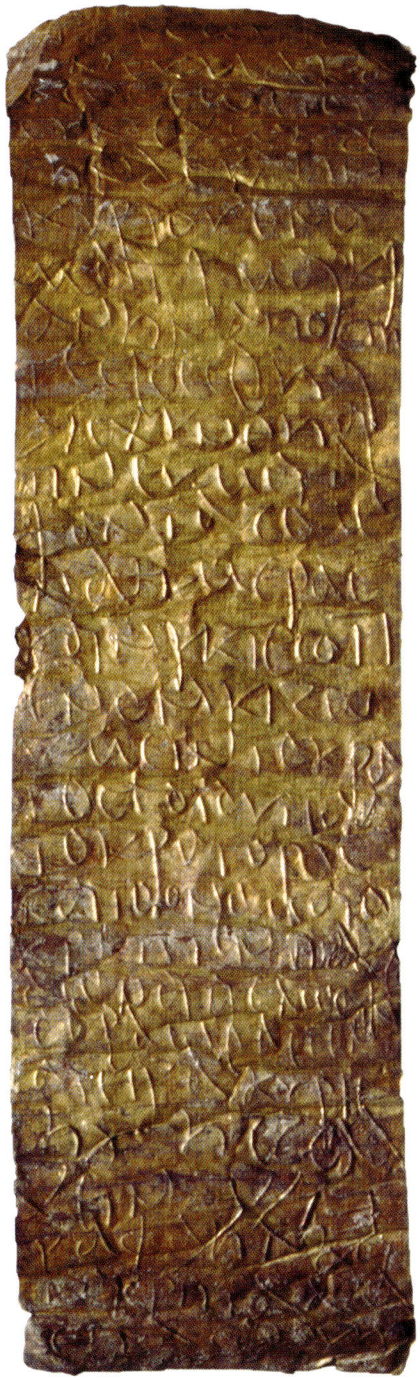

FIGURE 13. Foil Tablet with Spell in Greek Script, Late Roman, 200–300 C.E., glyptic, gold, 7.6 × 2.1 × 0.03 cm, Burton Y. Berry Collection, Indiana University Art Museum (71.22.125) (photo: Michael Cavanagh and Kevin Montague).

78. J. Tuerk, "How to Do Things with Words and Images in Late Antiquity and the Early Middle Ages" (Ph.D. Diss., University of Chicago, 2002).

79. J. L. Austin, *How to Do Things with Words* (Oxford, 1962), 6.

therefore realized a curative function through inscriptions, imagery, and the very medium of the device.[80] In the case of talismanic jewelry, we can see how attention to function, one of the key aspects of their designation as decorative art, can lead to a deeper understanding of the very different manner that objects "think" in the Byzantine world, of how they act in ways outside the more limited notions of object-hood encompassed by the traditional hierarchy of the fine and decorative arts. Of course, the pathway to this understanding begins by embracing the previously maligned nature of the object as overtly material and explicitly functional.

Approaches such as these—that attend to the anthropology of objects and their functions in social practices and beliefs of the Byzantine world—have also informed new perspectives on the treatment of ornament. While scholars continue to pursue interpretations of ornament that privilege formal concerns (i.e., exploring the ways in which it orders and gives visual logic to works of art), they also consider its particularly medieval role in empowering objects and the spaces and people with whom they were associated. Ornament can also be understood as an index of identity, equipping works of art to serve as surrogates for their owners or users.[81]

"Decorative Arts" as "Portable Arts"

In our engagement with the so-called decorative arts, Byzantinists can gain much from the perspectives of colleagues in related fields, in particular from scholars of Islamic art. For instance, Eva Hoffman has drawn attention to how the portability of so-called decorative objects has facilitated their extensive movement throughout the medieval world and up until the present day. Dislocated from their contexts of production, they often defy efforts to identify their provenience. A disciplinary inclination to secure the sources for works of art has resulted in marginalizing or over-interpreting objects of uncertain origin, like a well-known medieval Islamic bronze sculpture, the so-called Pisa Griffin. It employs stylistic and iconographic features that were used in multiple locations and across broad periods of time, thereby defying its localization.[82] Similar ambiguity characterizes some works of Byzantine "decorative art," whose relative anonymity of production and lack of secure provenience have left them at the periphery of scholarly attention, or mired in a literature that endlessly endeavors upon a fruitless attempt to fix them in time and space, or languishing in an interpretive dead end as curios that fascinate through their material richness but cannot participate in a history of art that is defined by sources and origins.

In response, Hoffman recognizes the limitations of a provenience-focused approach proposing instead a method that embraces the "portability" of these objects, valorizing the rich lives that small scale, iconographically and stylistically ecumenical works of art experienced because of their easy movement and lack of cultural specificity. She perceives meaning to be generated not only from original intentions and contexts, but also, and just as importantly, from interactions with the diverse and changing environments through which portable objects traveled. Hoffman proposes that rather than perceiving these objects as decorative or minor, we can see them as major players in an intercultural visual and material culture, and can explore the fascinating "biographies" and enviably active "social lives" that inform the meaning of these things just as much if not more than their origins.[83] Attention to portability has also invigorated the study of ornament, which

80. J. Tuerk, "An Early Byzantine Inscribed Amulet and Its Narratives," *Byzantine and Modern Greek Studies* 23 (1999), 25–42.

81. For example, see Maguire, Maguire, and Duncan-Flowers, *Art and Holy Powers in the Early Christian House* (as in note 51); Swift, *Style and Function in Roman Decoration* (as in note 38). Such interpretations have been extensively developed in other subfields of material and visual culture, which can serve as useful comparative studies. For instance, see M. Snodin and M. Howard, *Ornament: A Social History since 1450* (New Haven, Conn., 1996); M. J. Powers, *Pattern and Person: Ornament, Society, and Self in Classical China* (Cambridge, Mass., 2006).

82. Hoffman, "Pathways of Portability" (as in note 8), 18–19.

83. *Ibid.*, 17–42. Regarding the "biography" of objects and the "social life of things," see Appadurai, *The Social Life of Things* (as in note 7); Saurma-Jeltsch and Eisenbeiss, *The Power of Things* (as in note 6); Hilsdale, "The Social Life of the Byzantine Gift" (as in note 7), esp. 605.

is increasingly viewed in cross-cultural and diachronic terms as a vehicle of visual expression that transcended geographic, chronological, and social divisions of the medieval and early modern worlds.[84]

Production

The question of production—another perennial theme in scholarship on the decorative arts—has perhaps received less critical attention or innovative treatment in Byzantine art-historical literature as compared to function, materiality, and ornament.[85] Unlike earlier interpretations that tended to argue for a status of medieval craftsmen on par with artists and architects, recent discussions posit the more open term "makers" for this productive role, and perceive the process of making as a potentially collaborative effort between patrons, designers, and craftsmen.[86] This configuration engages with the more complex process of creation that seems to have obtained in the medieval era.

It is, of course, also likely that different modes of production obtained depending on the nature of a given work of art. For example, manufacture of the so-called rosette caskets seems to have been characterized by a modular approach, whereby the individual plaques affixed to the sides of a box could be essentially "mass produced" and configured in an *ad hoc* fashion along thematic lines (Fig. 14).[87] The connection among the individual scenes is generic and would not have demanded the involvement of a designer or patron. Furthermore, as Anthony Cutler has demonstrated, many of these boxes are made predominantly of the low-end material of bone, although cut and polished to resemble ivory.[88] These characteristics suggest that at least some of these objects could have been produced for an open market.[89]

Yet select members of the rosette group, like the famed Veroli Casket, are more specific in their iconographic references and imply a more fixed, even programmatic message (Fig. 15). Unlike the generic ivory boxes of piecemeal production, the Veroli Casket likely required a special commission and more intense collaboration between patrons and/or designers and craftsmen. Its extensive use of substantial ivory panels (which were usually reserved for devotional ivories) to depict mythological scenes further substantiates a claim that the Veroli Casket is the result of a different production process than objects of generic decoration and less valuable materials. Here we might benefit from retaining some consciousness of different levels of production and quality that the fine versus decorative arts hierarchy can be argued to have illuminated, although these distinctions can now be drawn in a more nuanced fashion, with closer attention paid to how they intersect with other concerns relating to materiality, function, and meaning.

Conclusion

This brief survey of the history and shortcomings of the "decorative arts" and their legacy in Byzantine art history has aimed to shed light not only on the good reasons for the demise of the term, but also on how the very characteristics that previously closed the door to

84. This direction of research is illustrated by a recent conference, *Ornament as Portable Culture: Between Globalism and Localism*, Harvard University, 12–14 April 2012, which included new work on the nature of ornament in Byzantium and other medieval traditions.

85. Important exceptions include, Cutler, *The Hand of the Master* (as in note 60); *idem*, "A Christian Ewer with Islamic Imagery and the Question of Arab *Gastarbeiter* in Byzantium," in R. Favreau and M. H. Debies, eds., *Iconographica: mélanges offerts à Piotr Skubiszewski* (Poitiers, 1999), 63–69; *idem*, "The Industries of Art" (as in note 25). I exclude here the robust literature that documents or seeks to identify named painters of late Byzantine icons, an effort that in some cases reflects a "cult of the artist" that derives from values of the historical fine-arts system.

86. A. Cutler, "Makers and Users," in L. James, ed., *A Companion to Byzantium* (Chichester, 2010), 301–12.

87. A. Cutler, "On Byzantine Boxes," *The Journal of the Walters Art Gallery* 42/43 (1984–85), 32–47.

88. A. Cutler, *The Craft of Ivory: Sources, Techniques, and Uses in the Mediterranean World, A.D. 200–1400* (Washington, D.C., 1985).

89. A similar distinction between mass-produced and commissioned objects in other Byzantine media—such as metalwork—might be drawn based on whether the inscriptions are individualized or refer to a generic "wearer."

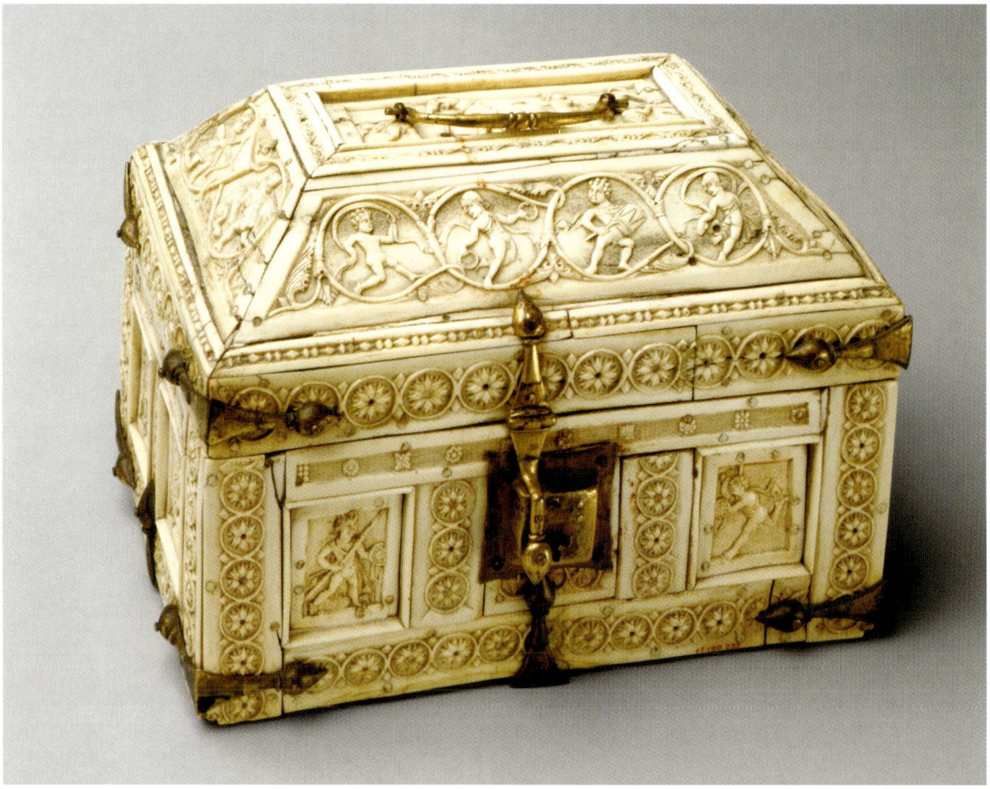

FIGURE 14. Casket with Warriors and Dancers, Middle Byzantine, eleventh century, Constantinople(?), ivory and bone, gilded copper mounts, 20.3 × 28.9 × 19.1 cm, Metropolitan Museum of Art, gift of J. Pierpont Morgan, 1917 (17.190.239).

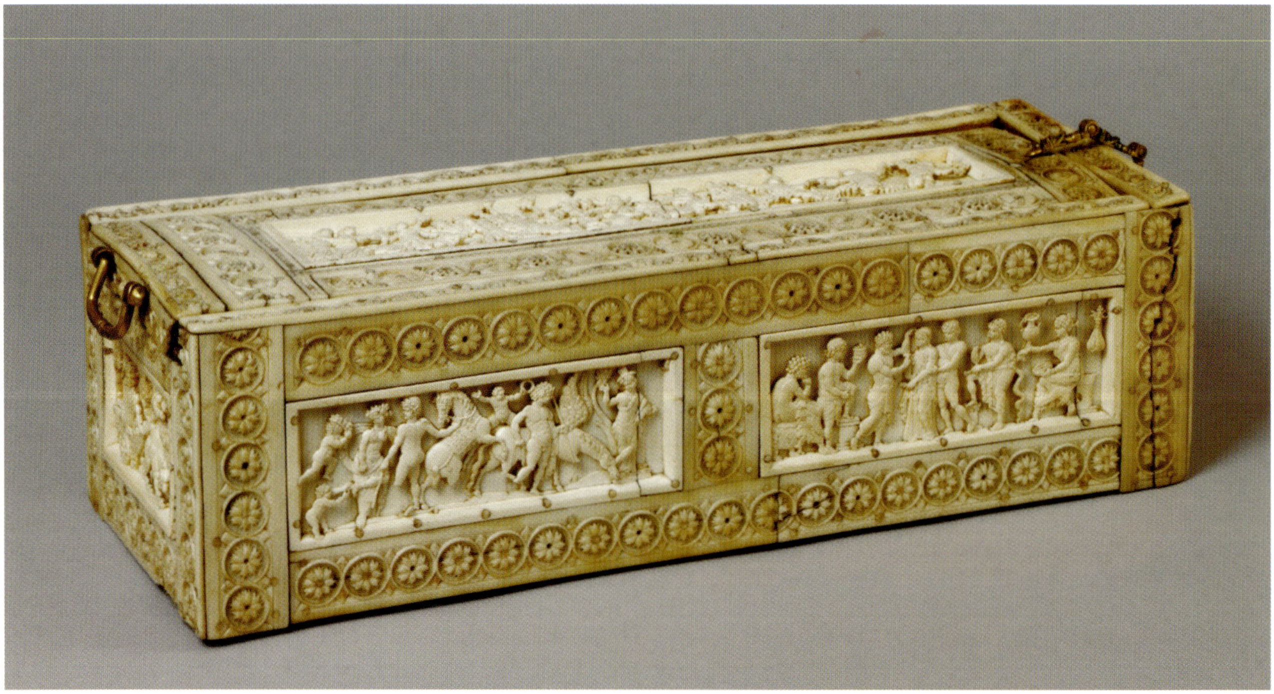

FIGURE 15. Veroli Casket, Middle Byzantine, second half of the tenth century(?), ivory, bone, and wood, 11.5 × 40.3 × 15.5–16 cm, Victoria and Albert Museum, London (216-1865) (photo: © Victoria and Albert Museum, London).

some objects' membership in the category of the fine arts have slowly opened different vantages on these works of art that reveal the practices, beliefs, and values of Byzantine society. Contrary to common assumptions about the decorative arts of the Middle Ages, the ivory boxes, enamel reliefs, woven garments, and metal containers of the Byzantine world are works of art that did "think" and communicate, however they convey meaning and hold value in a manner sometimes similar to the "fine arts" but also in a host of other ways, the diverse potential of which we are only just coming to see, feel, and know.

JOS KOLDEWEIJ

Notes on the Historiography and Iconography of Pilgrim Souvenirs and Secular Badges

CANON EDMOND REUSENS (1831–1903), librarian, historian, and Christian archaeologist at the University of Louvain, included in his *Manuel d'Archeologie Chrétienne* (Louvain 1886), and in his two volume *Éléments d'Archéologie Chrétienne* (Paris 1890), a lemma devoted to "Enseignes et médailles de pèlerinage." [1] He was, as a nineteenth-century antiquarian, not against paying attention to these at the time rather cheap and common trinkets, which must be considered examples of early mass-production. Reusens followed in the footsteps of such great French antiquarians as Victor Gay and A.-N. Didron. In between all other aspects of Christian medieval art, from architecture to applied arts and from early Christian to late Gothic, these scholars paid attention to the pilgrim badges and devotional medals on a serious level. Less interest was paid to other badges and folk jewelry, never mind the more sexual or erotic pins and amulets. After a slight increase in interest in the second half of the nineteenth century, attention declined until the later twentieth century, as a result of new discoveries that came out of the introduction of the metal detector.

Late medieval religious and secular badges as well as the historiography of badges together with "minor" and "major" arts will be the subject of this essay. I am interested in examining how cheap, mass-produced trinkets are related to, and how this material interacts with, expensive jewelry as well as the other arts. Consequently, this essay will refer to "high" and "low" in late medieval and early modern cultures.

The oldest publications on medieval pilgrim badges and secular badges of all kinds—from livery badges to erotic amulets and decorative trinkets—appeared when the most spectacular archaeological finds in this field came to light, and this happened in England from about the middle of the nineteenth century onwards. It occurred in France once the many finds from the Seine, especially those from Paris, became known. This happened mainly in the 1860s, although even before that medieval pilgrim badges were known.

Badges of All Kinds

Quentin Durward, the main Scottish character in the novel of the same name by Sir Walter Scott (1771–1832) from 1823,[2] meets two enigmatic figures in the environs of the town and castle of Tours in France at the very start of the story: [3] "The eldest and most remarkable of these men in dress and appearance, resembled the merchant or shopkeeper of the period. His jerkin, hose, and cloak were of a dark uniform colour, but worn so threadbare that the acute young Scot conceived that the wearer must be either very rich or very poor, probably the former." And as a remarkable detail Scott describes his head cap: "His cap, in particular, in which all men of any quality displayed either a brooch of gold or of silver, was ornamented with a paltry image of the Virgin, in lead, such as the poorer sort of pilgrims bring from Loretto (Chap. 2)." As an individual of high rank this man should have worn an ensign of precious metal.

Later in the novel Quentin Durward meets king Louis XI of France. The second time he sees the king,

1. E. Reusens, *Manuel d'archeologie chrétienne* (Louvain, 1885–86), 489–491; E. Reusens, *Éléments d'archéologie chrétienne* (Paris, 1890), vol. II, 450–53.

2. W. Scott, *Quentin Durward* (Edinburgh and London, 1823). Quotes from: W. Scott, *Quentin Durward, with the Author's Last Notes and Additions* (Paris, 1832).

3. Scott, *Quentin Durward, with the Author's Last Notes* (as in note 2), 14–15.

Scott describes the monarch as wearing:[4] "an old dark blue hunting dress.... And instead of his cap with a single [more precious] image, he now wore a hat, the band of which was garnished with at least a dozen of little paltry figures of saints stamped in lead" (Chap. 8). And three times more Scott emphasizes that the devout, sanctimonious king didn't wear precious ensigns but on the contrary cheap and rather common pilgrim badges. In Chapter 9 during a hunting party, the king kneels down suddenly to pray:[5] "... then took off his hunting cap, hung it on a bush, and devoutly made his orisons to the little leaden images which it contained...," in Chapter 26: "... doffed, as usual, his hat, selected from the figures with which it was garnished that which represented his favourite image of the Virgin, placed it on the table, and, kneeling down, repeated reverently the vow he had made," and in Chapter 12 the king has a reason to pray to a special saint:[6] "doffed his hat, and selecting from the numerous little leaden figures with which the hat band was garnished that which represented Saint Julian, he placed it on the table, as was often his wont when some peculiar feeling of hope, or perhaps of remorse, happened to thrill across his mind, and, kneeling down before it, muttered, with an appearance of profound devotion, "*Sancte Juliane, adsis precibus nostris! Ora, ora, pro nobis!* [St. Julian, give heed to our prayers. Pray, pray for us!]."

The main historical source for Walter Scott's novel was the chronicle of Philippe de Commynes, *Mémoire des faits du feu roy Louis onziesme.* There is no doubt but that he got his information on the lead pilgrim badge worn by King Louis from this source. Among many details, De Commynes describes how Louis XI was dressed when he met the Spanish king Enrico IV of Castile in 1468 (Livre 2, Chapitre 8).[7] The Spaniards didn't understand his devout simplicity and scoffed at his drab attire and the peculiarly shabby hat which sported a lead badge:

> Nostre roy s'habilloit fort court, et si mal que pis ne pouvoit, et assez mauvais drap portoit aucunes fois, et un mauvais chapeau, différent des autres, et une image de plomb dessus. Las Castillans s'en moquoient, et disoient que c'estoit par chicheté.

In 1620 a lead badge of the Virgin Mary in the collection of *curiosa* at Fontainebleau was believed to be one of the badges worn by King Louis XI. In the *Trésor des merveilles de Fontainebleau* it is described as "... une petite image de plomb représentant la Vierge, que l'on tenoit estre la mesme que Louis XI portoit ordinairement à son chapeau." This badge has been missing since that description was written but it was remembered as being about the length of one finger.[8]

In the known portraits of King Louis XI he is naturally shown wearing precious badges and even on his deathbed his hat seems to have been ornamented with a golden badge. No matter how devotional his intentions were, it was unseemly for a monarch to wear cheap commonplace trinkets.

The nobleman pretending to be of a lower rank who met the poor Quentin Durward in Chapter 2 had a lead Loreto badge pinned on his hat. This would have been seen as an indication of his low social status and poverty, and therefore it functioned as part of his disguise. Etiquette brooked no infringement: *enseignes* were quite literally signs of social status too.

In studying badges, trinkets, pins, and popular jewelry, this aspect of the meaning of badges frequently comes to the fore. One of the very few extant late-medieval specimens of the Loreto badge (Fig. 1) has been found in the Zeeland delta (Netherlands) and dates from the first half of the fifteenth century.[10]

4. *Ibid.*, 99. 5. *Ibid.*, 122. 6. *Ibid.*, 161.

7. R. W. Lightbown, *Mediaeval European Jewellery: With a Catalogue of the Collection in the Victoria & Albert Museum* (London, 1992), 195; J. Koldeweij, *Geloof & Geluk: Sieraad en Devotie in Middeleeuws Vlaanderen*, Exhib. Cat., Bruges, Gruuthusemuseum (Arnhem, 2006), 30.

8. P. Dan, *Trésor des merveilles de la maison royale de Fontainebleau* (1642): from L. de Laborde, *Glossaire français du moyen âge, à l'usage de l'archéologue et de l'amateur des arts, précédé de l'inventaire des bijoux de Louis, duc d'Anjou, dressé vers 1360* (Paris, 1872), 262–63.

9. Portrait of Louis XI (1423–1483), oil on panel, French School, 17th Century copy, State Collection France; The death of Louis XI (r. 1461–1483), miniature painting in *The Memoires of Philippe de Commines*, vellum, French School, 15th Century, Musée Dobrée, Nantes.

10. H. J. E. van Beuningen and A. M. Koldeweij, *Heilig &*

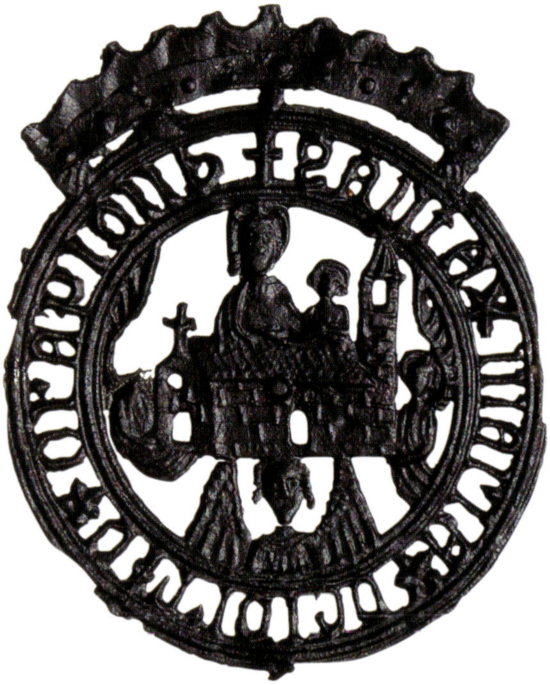

FIGURE 1. Pilgrim Badge from Loreto, Italy, Mary and Child above the Santa Casa carried by three angels. Legend: SANTA MARIA DE LORETO—ORA PRO N[O]B[IS], lead-tin, height 51 mm, *c.* 1400–1450. Found in Nieuwlande (Neth.). Langbroek, Van Beuningen Family Collection.

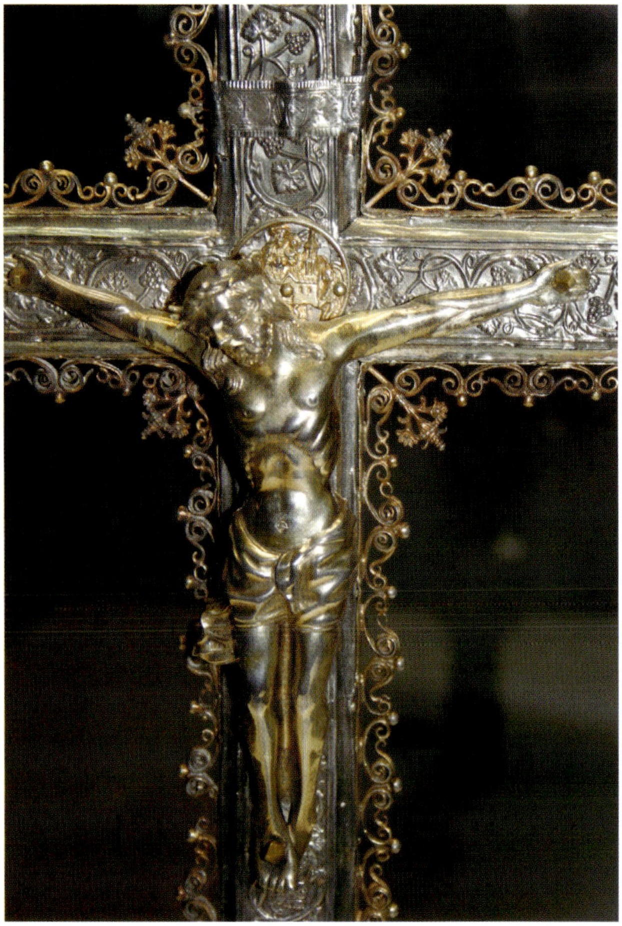

FIGURE 2. Processional Cross, Douai, France, 1541, silver and gilded silver (detail). Pilgrim Badge from Loreto, Italy, Mary and Child above the Santa Casa carried by three angels, gilded silver. Arras Cathedral Treasury.

Another one is found on a silver gilt processional cross (Douai 1541), which is now in the church treasury in Arras (Fig. 2).[11] The halo behind the head of Christ is a gilt silver badge from Loreto. Its circular shape was surely the main reason why it was reused on this cross. Similarly, its value as a precious object—it is from a sacred place referring to the birth of Christ and is made of costly metals—added to its suitability in this position. The nobleman in Walter Scott's novel should have worn a Loreto badge like this one. In both the novel and on the cross, it is of great importance that the badge originated in Loreto, a city that had the sanctuary of the Virgin Mary, called the Santa Casa, reputedly brought there by angels from Nazareth.

A well-known portrait of Charles V (a copy of the original by Bernard van Orley, from around 1515) (Fig. 3) shows Charles wearing the collar of the Order of the Golden Fleece. Several smaller golden brooches and an enamelled *enseigne* with an image of the Virgin and Child in an aureole and surrounded by the prayer (*o mater dei—memento mei* [o mother of God, remember me]) are shown on his hat.[12] Higher and lower nobility followed his example and wore similar badges. This

Profaan: Vol. 1. 1000 laatmiddeleeuwse insignes, Rotterdam Papers 8 (Cothen, 1993), 226, nr. 468; Koldeweij, *Geloof & Geluk* (as in note 7), 229.

11. N. Cartier, *Les Orfèvres de Douai: Dictionnaire des poinçons de l'orfèvrerie française*, Exhib. Cat., Musée de Douai 1995–96 (Douai, 1995), 190–91; Koldeweij, *Geloof & Geluk* (as in note 7), 229.

12. Koldeweij, *Geloof & Geluk* (as in note 7), 52–53.

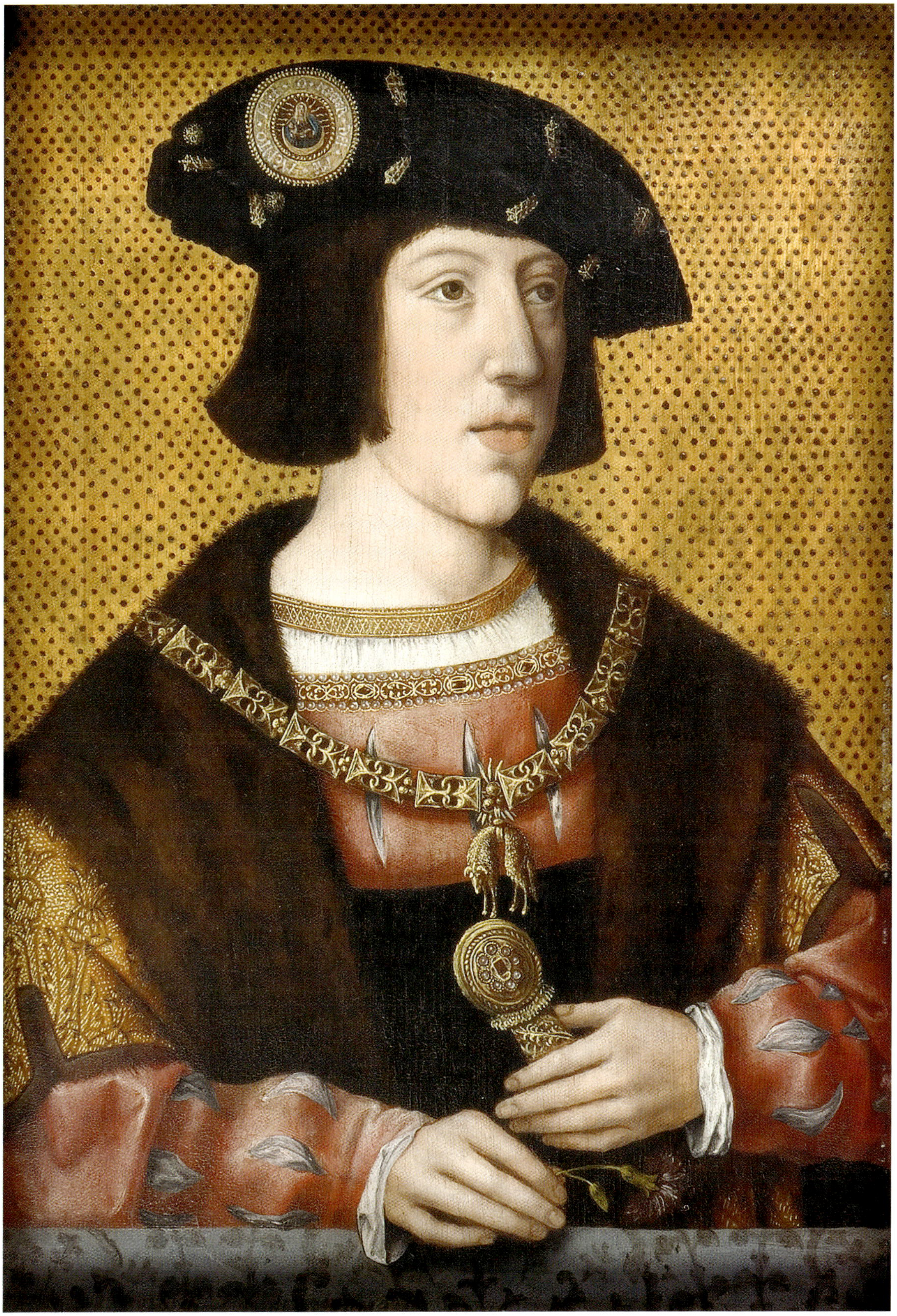

FIGURE 3. Bernard van Orley (*c.* 1480–1541), Portrait of Charles V, copy, oak panel, 41 × 29 cm, *c.* 1515. Ensign: Mary and Child, legend: O MATER DEI MEMENTO MEI. Bruges, Cathedral S. Salvator, Treasury.

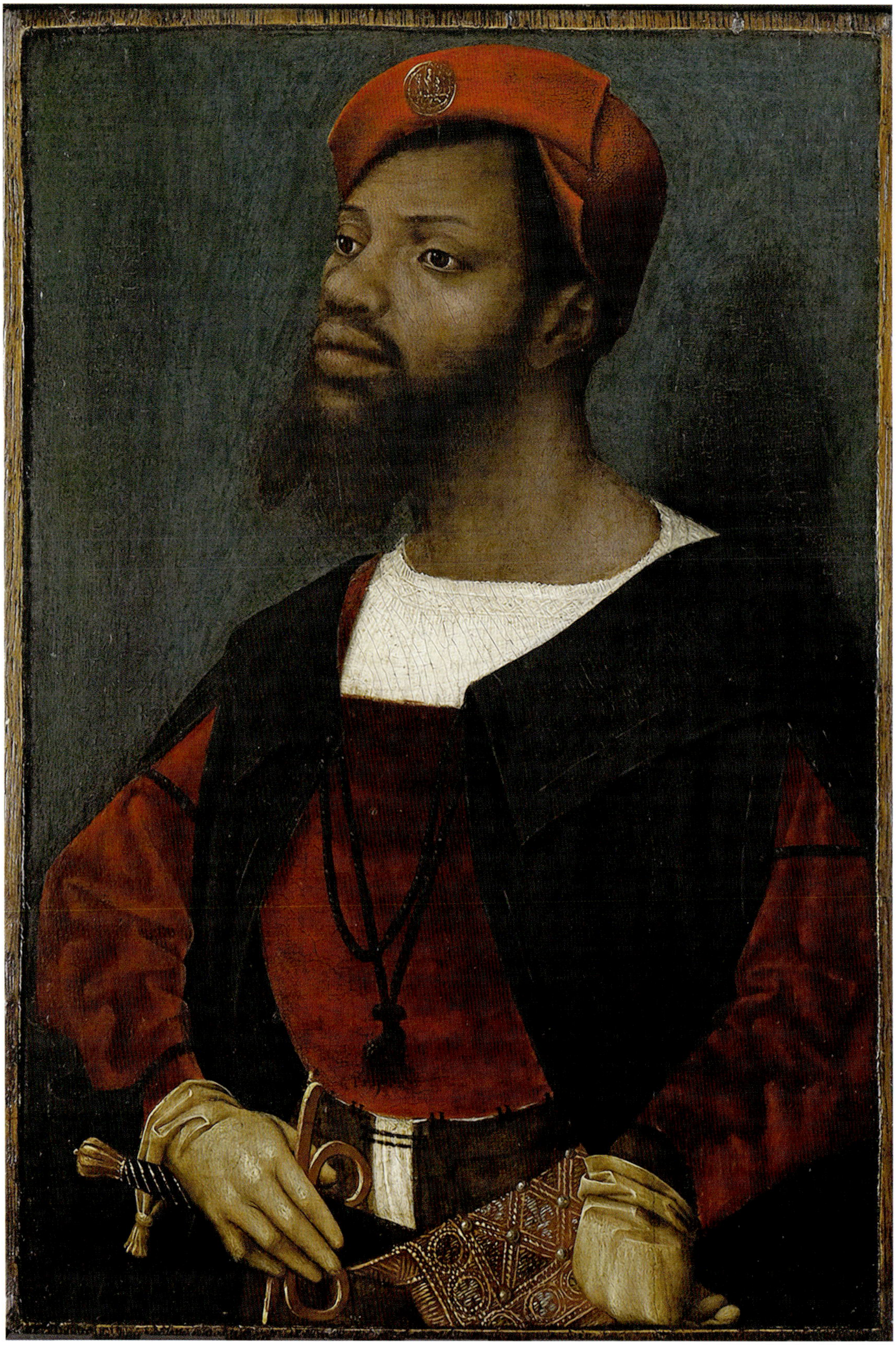

FIGURE 4. Jan Mostaert (*c.* 1474–1552/53), Portrait of Christoph le Mohr(?), oak panel, 30.8 × 21.2 cm. Pilgrim Badge: Mary and Child between two angels. Amsterdam, Rijksmuseum.

FIGURE 4 (detail).

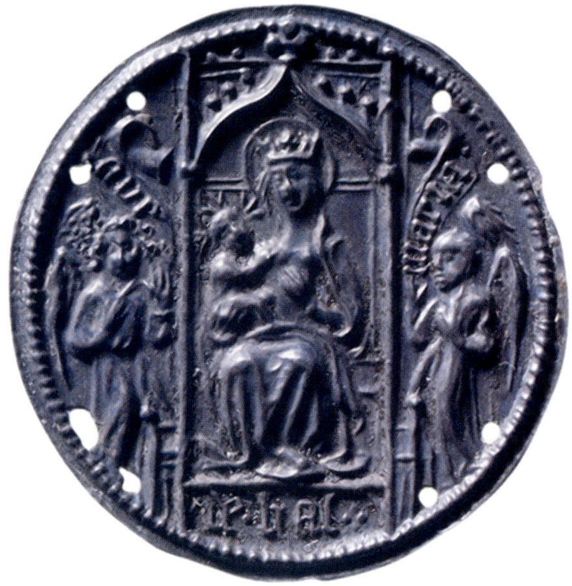

FIGURE 5. Pilgrim Badge from Halle, southern Netherlands, Mary and Child between two angels. Legend: "de hal" and "ave Maria," silver, diameter 35 mm, *c.* 1474–1525. Nuremberg, Germanisches Nationalmuseum.

ensign of the Virgin Mary and Child in all probability refers to the veneration of the Holy Virgin at Aachen, the city in which Charles would be crowned King and Emperor of the Holy Roman Empire in 1521. As soon as Charles heard the news in 1519 that he was to be crowned King, he went with his brother Ferdinand on a pilgrimage to Our Lady of Halle, a sanctuary not far south of Brussels. Charles had been there before and had bought badges of silver and gold for himself and his close retinue, as well as pewter or lead ones for the lower ranks.[13] One of his personal guards, a certain Christoph le Mohr, got such a badge of precious metal (Figs. 4, 5).[14] The black man is represented in this portrait with his status as guard: he is not only proud of his badge but also of his clothing and purse, and, above all, his self-confident, almost ducal, attitude bespeak how far he climbed the social ladder.

In contrast, the adolescent Cosimo de' Medici was lowering himself in social rank when he had himself painted by Pontormo circa 1535 (Fig. 6).[15] The Florentine nobleman wished to associate himself with the German and Swiss mercenaries who were marching through Northern Italy under the command of the Emperor Charles V. In this image, once again, etiquette has been broken. Cosimo wished to dress this way in the years 1532–1533, when he was traveling with the court of his uncle Duke Alessandro de' Medici in the train of the Habsburg Emperor. It was reported to Pope Clement VII (Giulio de' Medici) that Cosimo "went about clad like a cavalier and seeming such in his actions." Papal orders were sent to Alessandro forbidding Cosimo from wearing such "foreign dress" (*quelle uzanze forestiere*) and instructing him instead to wear the Florentine *lucco*, the traditional long robe. During the ten days when he was forced to wear the *lucco* Cosimo hardly ever appeared in public. Alessandro relented and allowed Cosimo to return to his customary dress as a mercenary amongst mercenaries. It should be noted,

13. H. van der Velden, "Karel de Stoute op bedevaart: de aanschaf van pelgrimstekens door de graaf van Charolais," in H. J. E. van Beuningen, A. M. Koldeweij, D. Kicken, *Heilig & Profaan: Vol 2. Laatmiddeleeuwse insignes uit openbare en particuliere collecties*, Rotterdam Papers 12 (Cothen, 2001), 234–40; Koldeweij, *Geloof & Geluk* (as in note 7), 56.

14. J. P. Filedt Kok and M. de Winkel, "Een portret van een zwarte Afrikaanse man door Jan Mostaert," *Bulletin van het Rijksmuseum*, 53 (2005), 380–411; E. van den Boogaart, "Christoph le More, lijfwacht van Karel V?" *Bulletin van het Rijksmuseum*, 53 (2005), 412–33; Koldeweij, *Geloof & Geluk* (as in note 7), 47, 54–55.

15. *An Important Painting by Pontormo from The Collection of Chauncey D. Stillman* (New York, 1989) (Christie's, New York: Wednesday, 31 May 1989, lot 55); Koldeweij, *Geloof & Geluk* (as in note 7), 55.

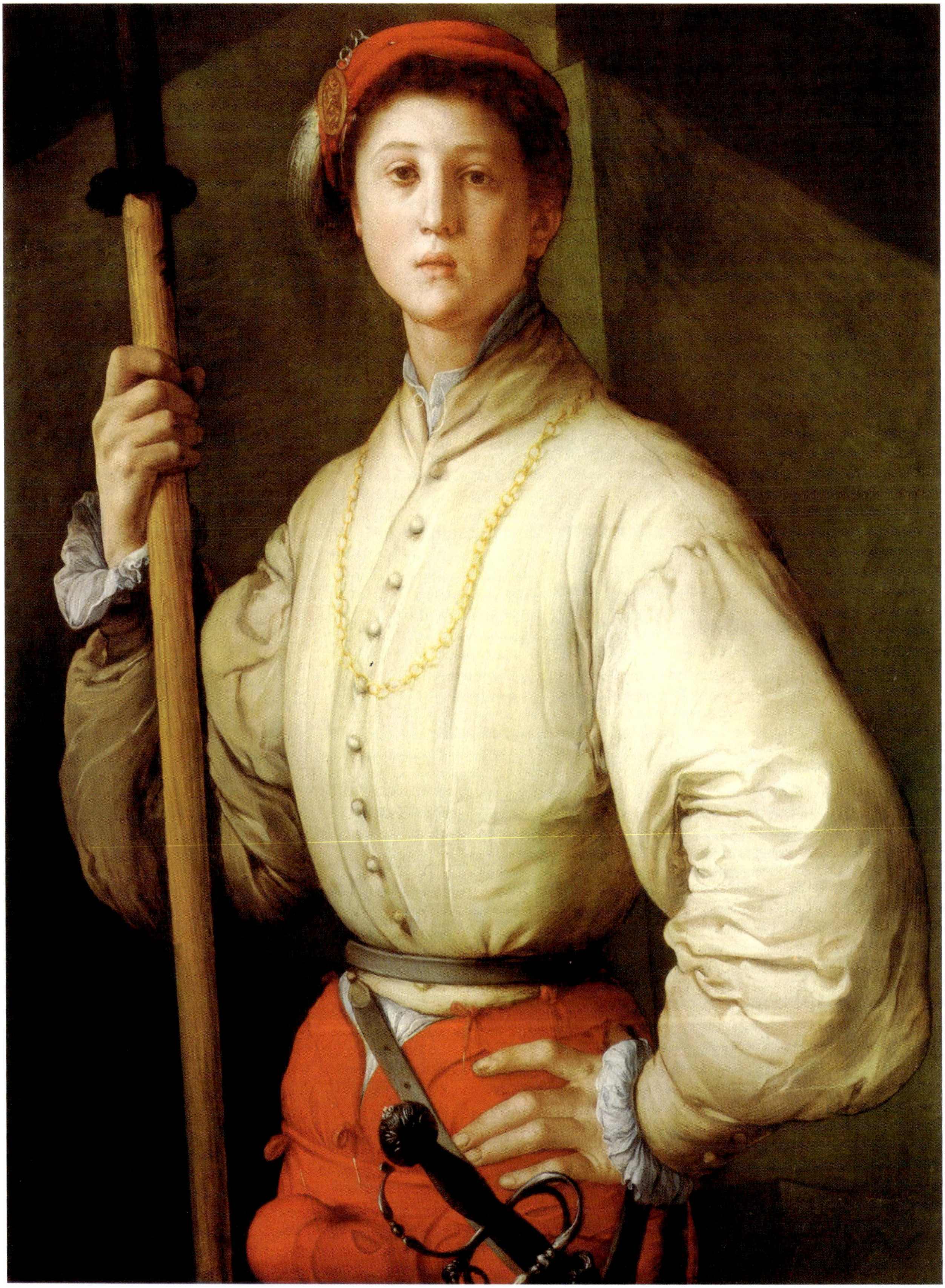

FIGURE 6. Pontormo (1494–1556), Portrait of Duke Cosimo I de' Medici in a mercenary's costume, Florence, *c.* 1530–1535. Golden ensign showing Hercules and Antaeus. Los Angeles, The J. Paul Getty Museum.

however, that Cosimo is shown wearing a golden medallion pinned with a silver pin and chain on his red cap. This precious medallion with its representations of Hercules and Antaeus, as well as his hat worn flat on the head, demonstrate that Cosimo is not actually a mercenary soldier. He is not a *Landsknecht* and is not dressed literally—down to the last detail—as one, but it is clear that he is only posing as one.

Common people, of course, imitated the fashion, dress, and jewelry of higher ranks. Wealthy men and women wore ornamented golden and silver brooches with precious stones or pearls. Those who could not afford these, bought themselves trinkets of cheaper material, like the ones from Bruges and Ypres, which were not made of silver but cast in pewter and garnished with colored glass instead of precious stones (Figs. 7, 8). Pock, who was Maximilian's court jester, however, and who has been identified in one of the woodcuts from the famous Triumphal Procession of the Emperor Maximilian by Albrecht Dürer, Hans Burgkmair, and others, is shown wearing a damaged jewel (Fig. 9). The small Latin cross of amaldine red garnets should have four black pearls but the uppermost one is missing.[16] The jester purposely wears a broken jewel, which of course a courtier never would do.

Another type of brooch also highlights the difference between rich and poor, high and low. If wealthy enough, it was possible to use gold and silver coins literally as jewelry. Wearing them was an indicator of status and wealth and this is shown in a painting of an unknown adolescent from Bruges, painted around 1515. Here he possibly wears a French gold coin as *enseigne* (Fig. 10)[17] and this is similar to some excavated brooches that were also made from real coins. Examples include two silver ring-brooches, dating from the fourteenth century and found in Scandinavian treasure

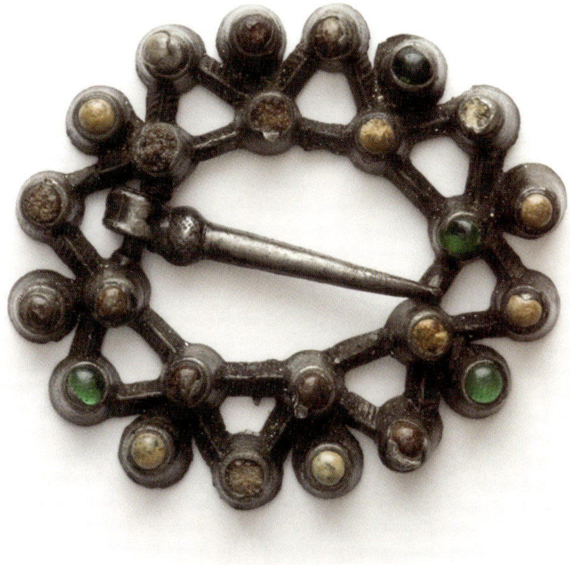

FIGURE 7. Brooch, lead-tin and colored glass, height 35 mm, *c.* 1275–1325. Found in Bruges, Flanders. Bruges, Brugge-museum Archeology.

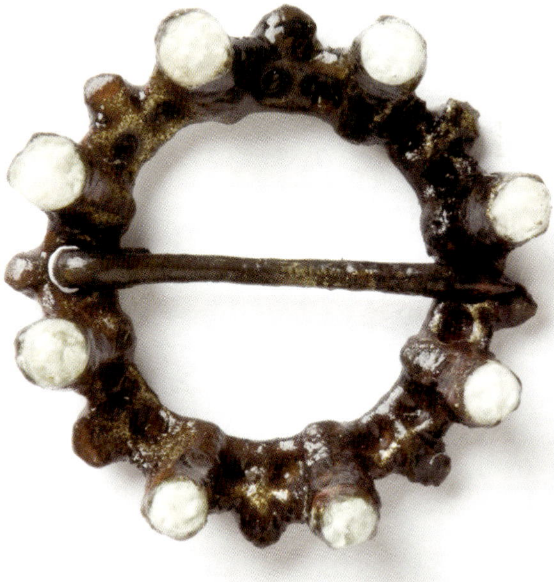

FIGURE 8. Brooch, sliver and white stones, height 43 mm, *c.* 1300–1350. Found in Ypres. Ypres, Stedelijke Musea.

16. Y. Hackenbroch, *Enseignes: Renaissance Hat Jewels* (Florence, 1996), 210–11; A. Schneckenburger-Broschek, *Altdeutsche Malerei. Die Tafelbilder und Altäre des 14. bis 16. Jahrhunderts in der Gemäldegalerie Alte Meister und im Hessischen Landesmuseum Kassel* (Kassel, 1997), 262–68; Koldeweij, *Geloof & Geluk* (as in note 7), 56–57.

17. Hackenbroch, *Enseignes* (as in note 16), 223–25; B. P. J. Broos, A. van Suchtelen, *et al.*, *Portraits in the Mauritshuis: 1430–1790* (The Hague/Zwolle, 2004), 153–57, nr. 34; Koldeweij, *Geloof & Geluk* (as in note 7), 152–53.

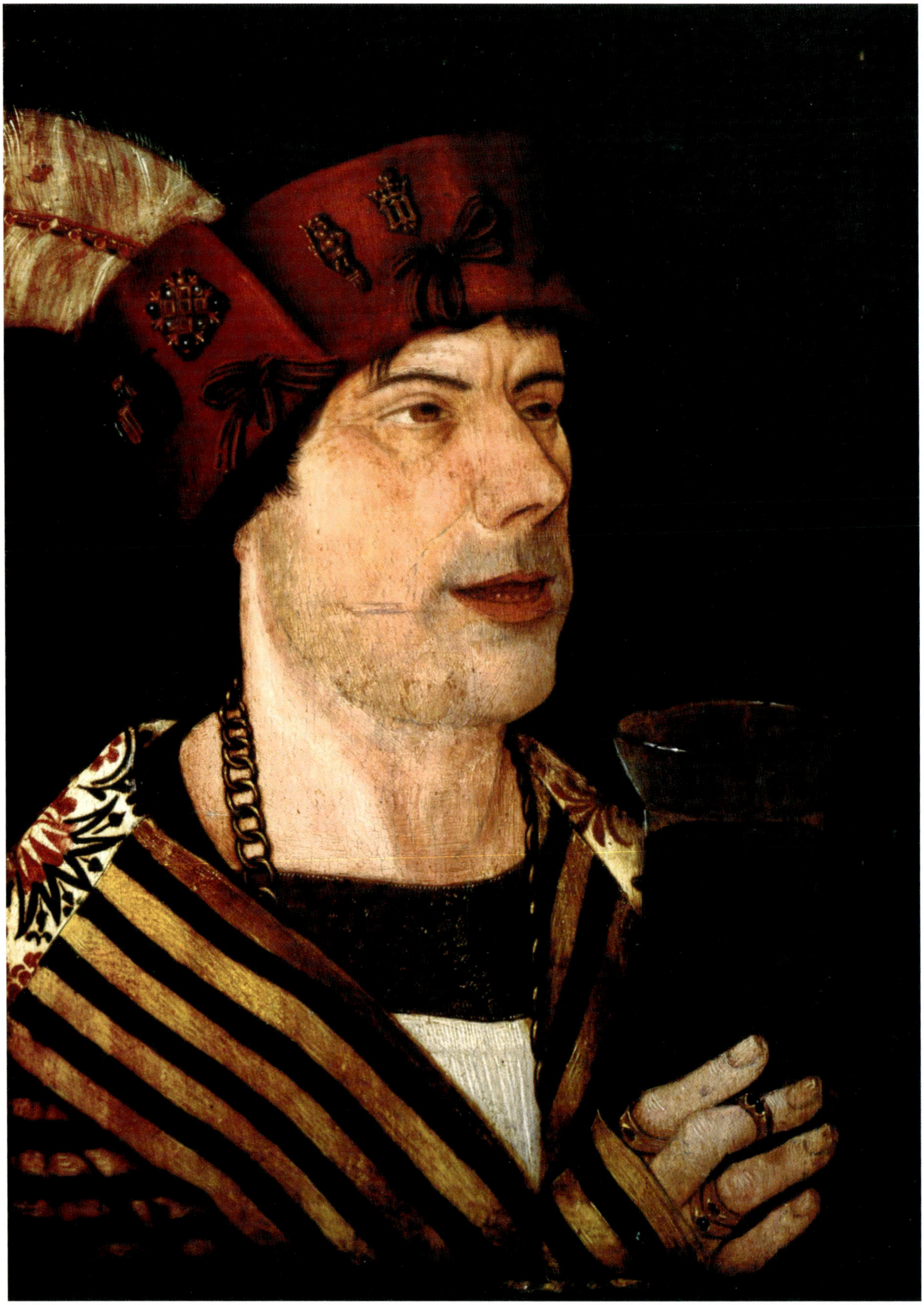

FIGURE 9. Anonymous, School of Bernhard Strigel (*c.* 1480–1528), Portrait of Pock, court jester to the Emperor Maximilian of Austria, oak panel, 31 × 32 cm, *c.* 1517–1519. Various insignia: crowned M (here for Maximilian); St. Christopher; a weapon; and a damaged jewel in the form of a cross with black pearls. Private collection.

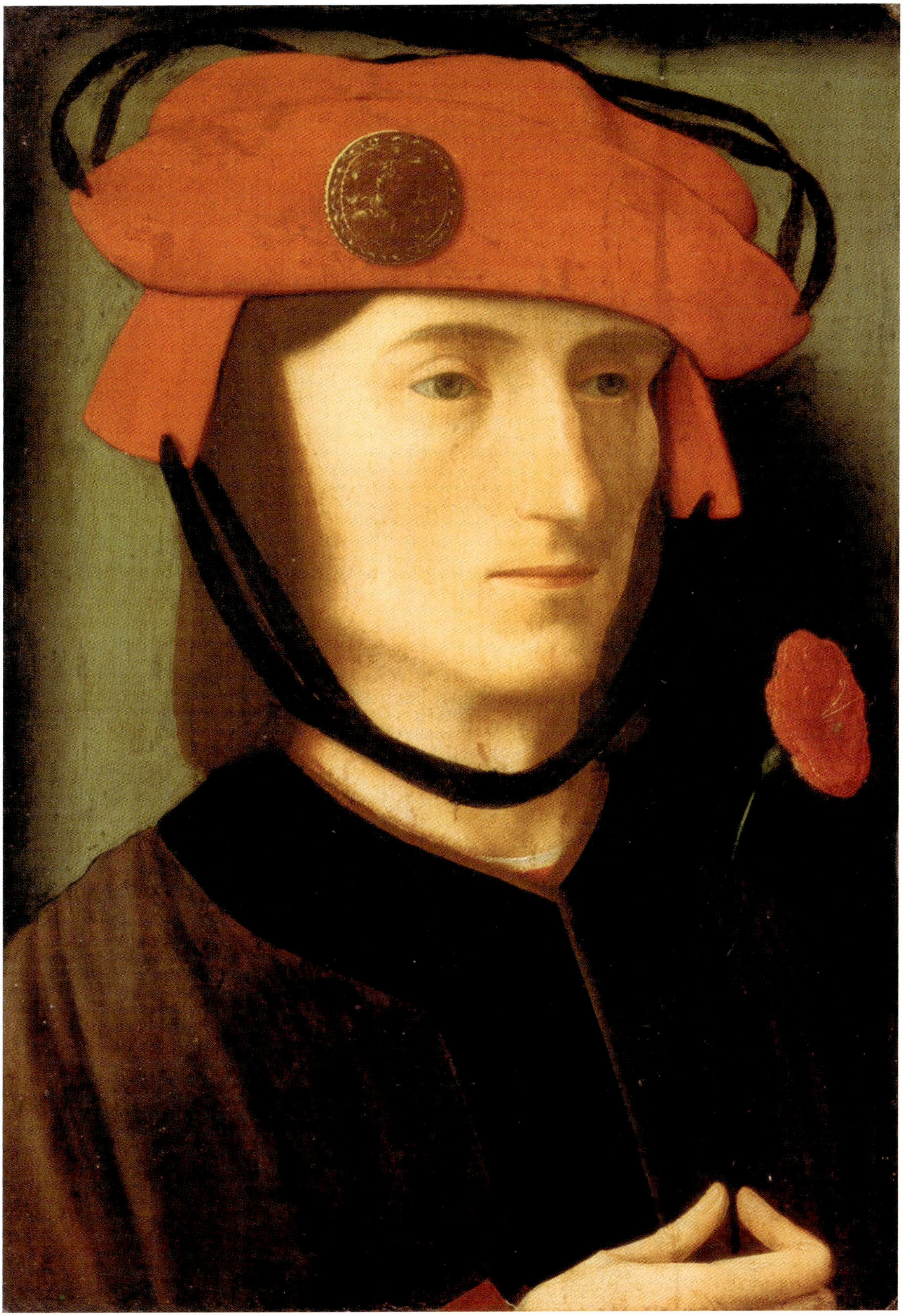

FIGURE 10. Master of the Brandon Portrait, Portrait of a young man, oak panel, 33.8 × 24.4 cm, *c.* 1515. Ensign: golden medal with Samson fighting the lion. The Hague, Koninklijk Kabinet van Schilderijen Mauritshuis.

finds (Figs. 11–12),[18] a sixteenth-century copper coin reused as a brooch or as a button (Fig. 13),[19] as well as a pewter badge made in imitation of a fourteenth-century coin (Fig. 14).[20]

A sixteenth-century painting by Jan Massys of a merry company, and now in private ownership in Scotland, also shows coins being used as jewelry (Fig. 15).[21] The musician to the left has two small silver coins pinned to his hat. A similar trinket of a low alloy silver coin with a bent copper pin was recently acquired by the Mint and Money Museum in Utrecht (Fig. 16). The copper *enseigne* of the rather vulgar bagpipe player refers to Job, who was venerated in the Brabantine village of Wezemael as patron saint of the musicians. Its depiction is significant and shows how Massys invested serious consideration and thought in all details. The fact that this badge was so invested in meaning highlights the need to look into the other details in the picture: the Raeren jug with three ears, for example, without any doubt refers to the relationship of the woman who holds it, and to the two men holding her.

Jan Massys painted these lower-class scenes for the upper classes. The lower class naturally did not have paintings of their own. Instead they had cheap, mass-produced badges and it is these that inform us about their visual culture. Their badges, cheap jewelry, and trinkets show us what their visual language was. The themes of this late medieval material are, as we have already seen, surprisingly varied and extend from the fervently religious to the fantastically erotic.

Some of the clearly profane imagery on the badges raise questions about the higher and lower class divisions. What did common people know—was there a common knowledge of stories and tales, an exchange between the higher and lower ranks, or were social circles hermetically separated from each other? The newly discovered visual corpus of these mass-produced badges clearly reveals the visual vocabulary of the lower and middle classes. There are, surprisingly enough, also many links to the visual culture of the elite, some of which are quite literal, while others are more on an associative or thematic level. A spectacular example of this kind of visual language is the erotic procession of three phallic animals on a badge found in Bruges, which can be compared to the religious processions organized by church, town, and state (Figs. 17, 18).[22] The visual similarity is obvious, but the question remains as to how the erotic procession should be interpreted: a simple explanation of seeing it as a persiflage or raillery on the religious event is not sufficient.

In principle two distinct types of badges are known that show that the same stories were current in the upper classes as well as in the lower strata: the courtly love story of La Chatelaine de Vergi (Fig. 19) and the woman's story of Aristotle and Phyllis (Fig. 20). Both were known in higher and lower strata, but told in a different language—courtly and polite in elite circles and rather rude and straightforward in that of the common people. Two specimens have been found up to now of a pewter badge illustrating the story of the Chatelaine de Vergi and her lover. The first of these, excavated in Bruges, is fragmentary, while the other is well preserved and was found in Dordrecht.[23] These two badges (and only a few others that are known) show the crucial episode of the story where the lord observes the Chatelaine and her lover after the lady's lapdog had signalled that the coast was clear. As already emphasized, these trinkets must have been cheap, as is proven by the techniques of manufacture, slipshod workmanship, and base material, and they must have been produced in large quantities. Their popularity is also proven by the fact that these two brooches, which are different in design, are also mirror images of each other: new dies were evidently cut after the example of actual brooches resulting in inverted left-to-right images. The Chatelaine de Vergi brooches prove that this story was not

18. L. Jørgensen and P. Vang Petersen, *Guld, Magt og Tro: Danske skattefund fra oldtid og middelalder* (*Gold, Power, and Belief: Danish Gold Treasures from Prehistory and the Middle Ages*) (Copenhagen, 1998), 323–24; Koldeweij, *Geloof & Geluk* (as in note 7), 154–55.

19. Koldeweij, *Geloof & Geluk* (as in note 7), 155–56.

20. *Ibid.*, 155.

21. L. Buynsters-Smets, *Jan Massys: Een Antwerps schilder uit de zestiende eeuw* (Zwolle, 1995); Koldeweij *Geloof & Geluk* (as in note 7), 60–62.

22. Van Beuningen, Koldeweij, *Heilig & Profaan: Vol. 1* (as in note 10), 262, nr. 652; Koldeweij, *Geloof & Geluk* (as in note 7), 115.

23. Koldeweij, *Geloof & Geluk* (as in note 7), 23, 119, 160–61.

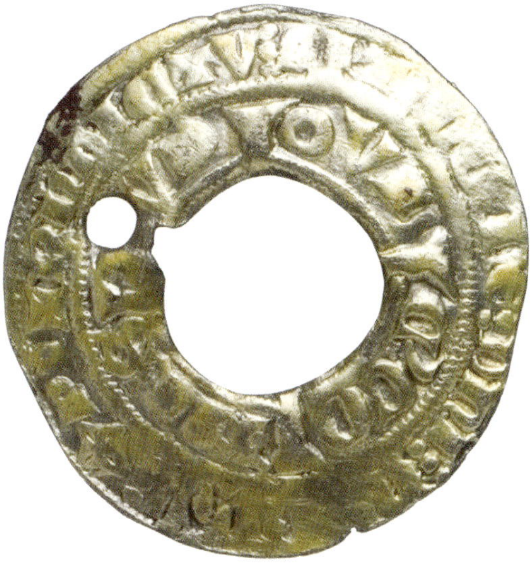

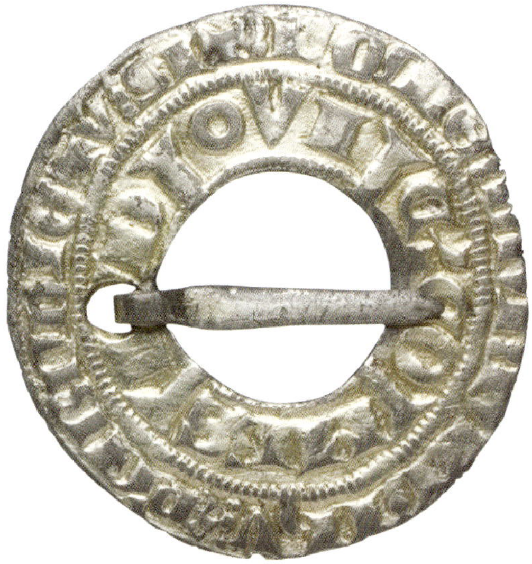

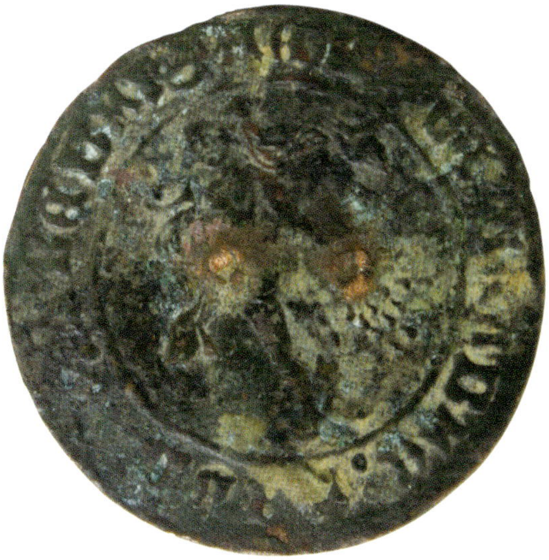

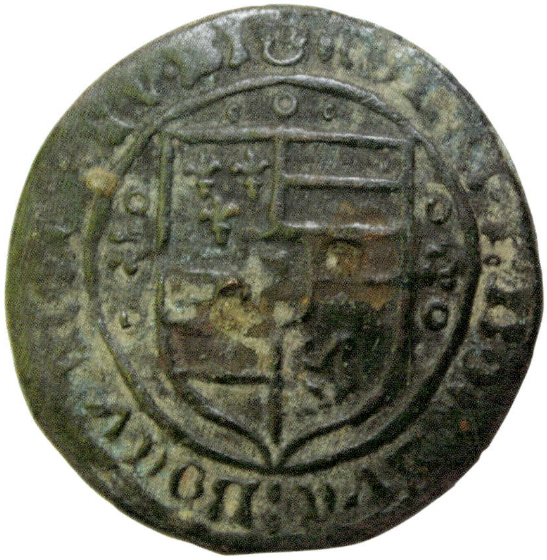

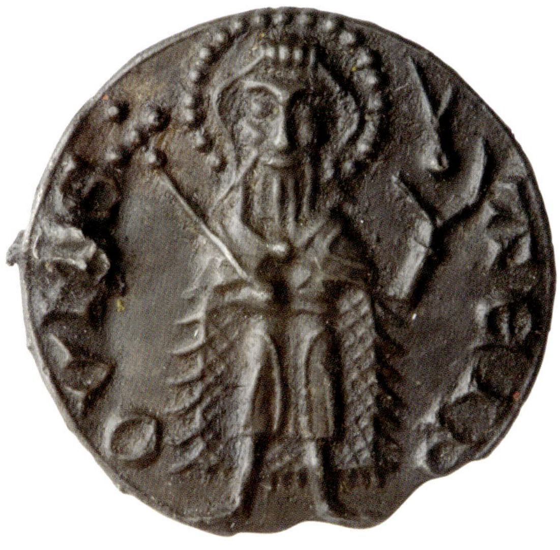

FIGURES 11–12 (*top*). Two ring-brooches, mid-fourteenth century, made from Flemish coins. (*Left*): a "Tournooise groot," silver, diameter 26 mm, 1275–1325, treasure find Slagelseskatten, Slagelse (Sjaelland). (*Right*): a "leeuwengroot" of Louis of Male (1346–1384), silver, diameter 26 mm, treasure find Gammelkøgegoard near Køge. Copenhagen, National Museum.

FIGURE 13 (*middle*). So-called "Venus token," reused as a button or badge, brass, diameter 33 mm, sixteenth century. Found in Damme, Flanders. Bruges, Bruggemuseum.

FIGURE 14 (*bottom*). Coin Badge, imitating a golden "fiorino" from Florence 1252–1533, St. John the Baptist and illegible legend, lead-tin, diameter 22 mm, 1300–1400. Found in Bruges. Bruges, Bruggemuseum.

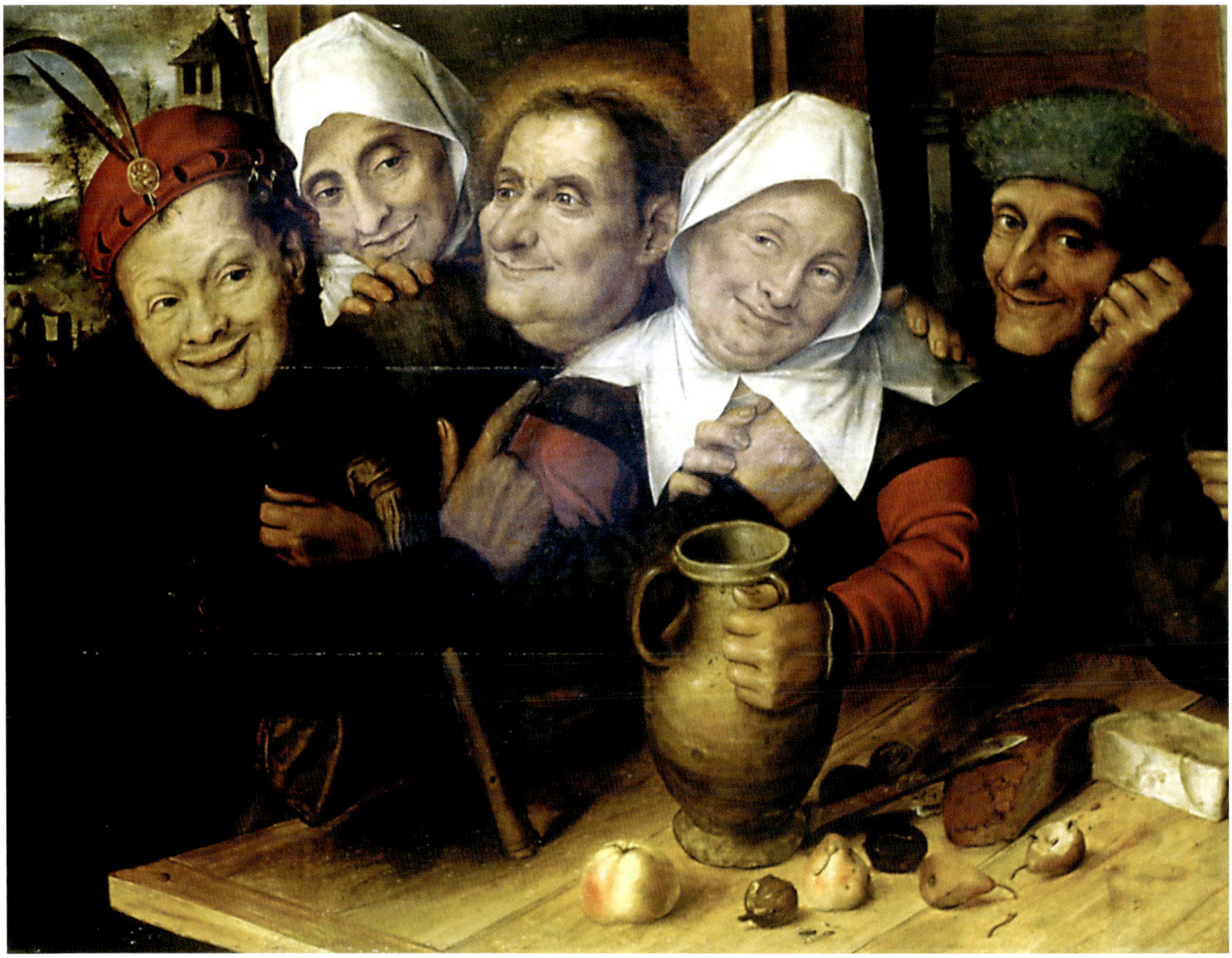

FIGURE 15. Jan Massys (*c.* 1509–1573), Merry Company, oak panel, 74.5 × 103.5 cm, 1557. Figure at the left: hat badge of St. Job from Wezemael (Brabant), and two coins. Scotland, Collection The Earl of Wemyss & March.

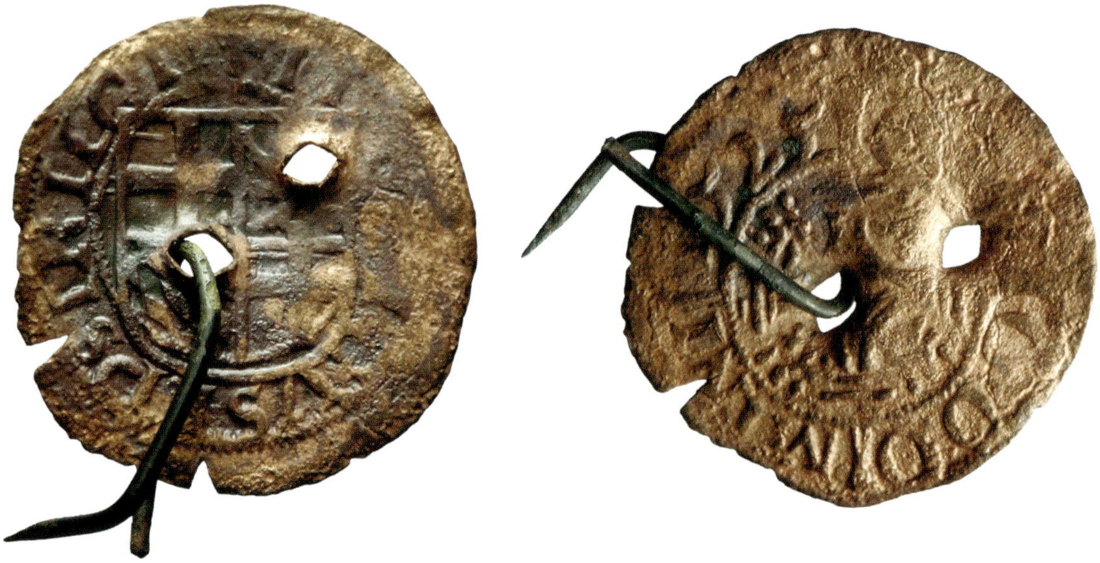

FIGURE 16a–b. Penny, 1525, reused as trinket, copper, 18 mm. Found in Dordrecht. Utrecht, Geldmuseum (MU-05553).

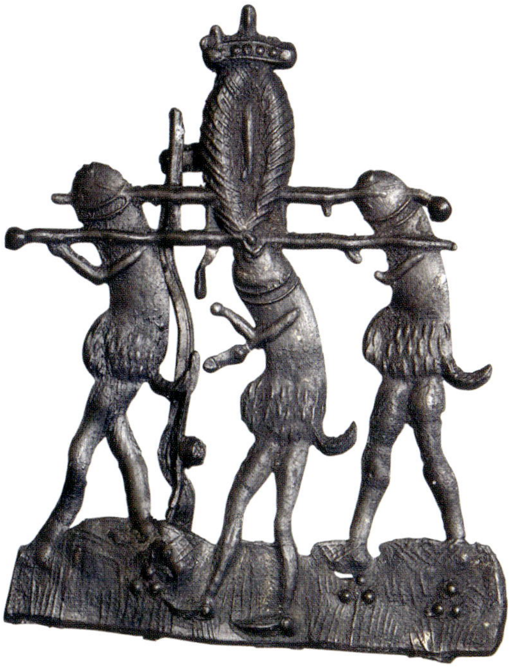

FIGURE 17. Secular badge, erotic procession: three phallic animals carrying a vulva, lead-tin, height 56 mm, 1375–1425. Found in Bruges. Langbroek, Van Beuningen Family Collection.

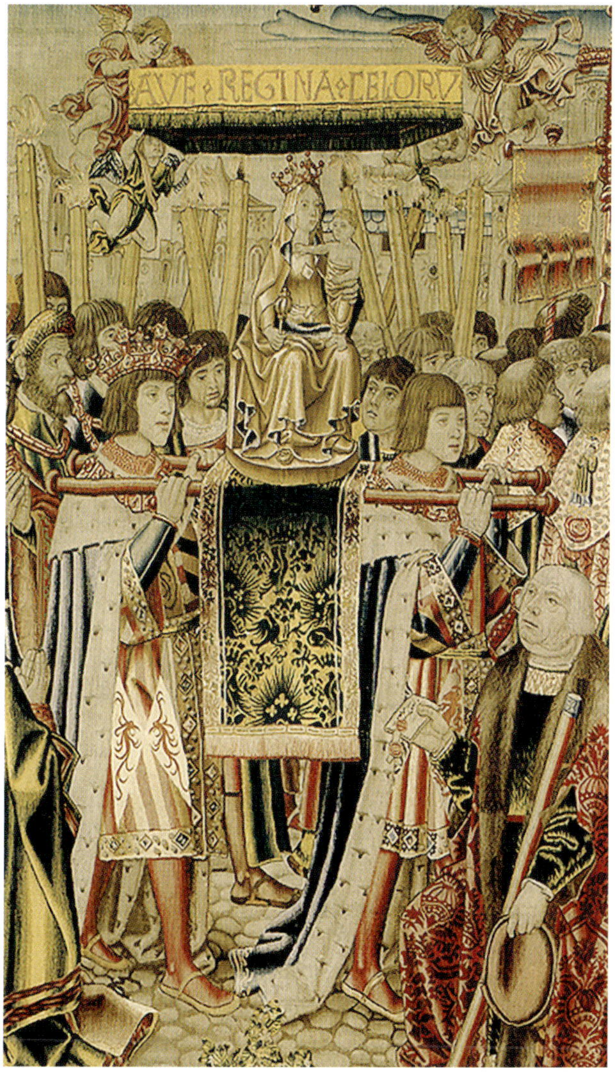

FIGURE 18. Tapestry with the Legend of Our Lady of the Sablon, Brussels, 1516–1518, 341 × 528 cm. Detail of the arrival of the miraculous statue in Brussels, carried by Charles V and his brother Ferdinand. Brussels, Koninklijke Musea voor Kunst en Geschiedenis.

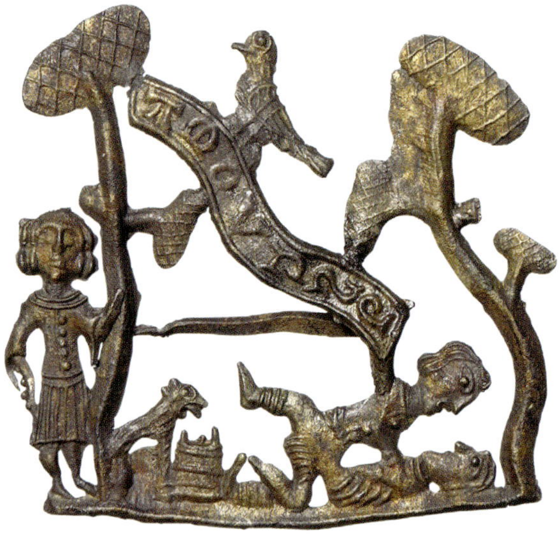

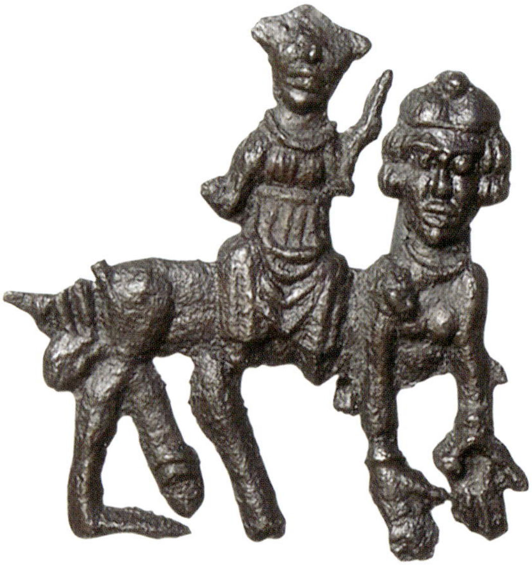

FIGURE 19 (*left*). Secular Badge, the orchard scene from the tale the Chatelaine Vergi, lead-tin, height 44 mm, 1375–1425. Found in Dordrecht. Langbroek, Van Beuningen Family Collection.

FIGURE 20 (*right*). Secular Badge, Aristotle and Phyllis, lead-tin, height 28 mm, 1325–1375. Found in Nieuwlande, Zeeland. Langbroek, Van Beuningen Family Collection.

confined to elite circles but that it gained considerable popularity in the late fourteenth and early fifteenth centuries, although we do not know exactly how this happened. It is also just as likely that the story existed earlier in a more popular, widespread version that has not survived. In that case it would have evolved from a now-lost oral tradition into the more courtly, elitist version that was handed down in writing, and later, in the sixteenth century, served as educational reading for the young and was used in schools. So we have to see the pewter badges as a source, the only one up to now, of a popular and more crude version of the story, from an earlier narrative tradition. All the other visual material pertaining to the Chatelaine de Vergi story belongs to the culture of the upper social stratum. Examples of this upper culture are found in illuminated manuscripts as well as on skillfully carved French ivory caskets that date to the same period.

The motif of Aristotle and Phyllis comes from one of the best known and most widely disseminated stories of the late Middle Ages and the subject is found throughout Western European art.[24] Once again the visual source material is associated mainly with an elite culture and reflects the popularity of this ancient story in aristocratic and upper-class circles, in manuscripts, in *aquamanilia*, in early prints, and so on. However, from literary and other sources it is also clear that the amusing tale gradually percolated through to broader social strata down to ordinary folk. One of the female wiles enacted on a wagon in a Shrovetide procession in Metz in 1510 showed Aristotle mounted by Phyllis, and in 1511 the frolicking couple appeared in the guise of snowmen in Brussels.[25] From an entry in thirteenth-century sermons it is clear that the traditional theme developed into a favorite courtly story and later on into the subject of fifteenth- and sixteenth-century

24. C. Herrmann, *Der gerittene Aristoteles: das Bildmotiv des "gerittenen Aristoteles" und seine Bedeutung für die Aufrechterhaltung der gesellschaftlichen Ordnung vom Beginn des 13. Jhs. Bis um 1500* (Pfaffenweiler, 1991); Koldeweij , *Geloof & Geluk* (as in note 7), 10–12.

25. H. Pleij, *De sneeuwpoppen van 1511: literatuur en stadscultuur tussen middeleeuwen en moderne tijd* (Amsterdam/Louvain, 1988), 86, 93, 267–268.

Shrovetide plays. As a scene in late medieval popular drama, "Aristotle ridden by Phyllis" is thus well documented. It is more than likely that the rather vulgar pewter badges (two different ones have been found) were sold at common holiday fêtes. Like the Chatelaine de Vergi brooches, the representation is highly erotic. None of the several hundreds of the extant late medieval depictions of Aristotle being ridden shows the philosopher in such an explicit state of sexual arousal. This crude depiction of the legend surely appealed to a broad and unsophisticated public—exactly the kind of audience that would be found at folk-drama. In one of the Nuremberg *Fastnachtspiele*, for instance, which relates how Aristotle was ridden by a female, we read that the text sought to convey the same effect.[26] Aristotle had to defend his ludicrous behavior and the King took the wise philosopher's part: for he who *sin rohr niht auf tet stan* when tempted by a female, *war kein rechter man* (he who didn't have an erection, when tempted, was not a proper man). At the end of such entertainment the audience was undoubtedly eager to buy badges, just as they purchased devotionalia after reliquary processions and other religious spectacles.

The meaning of all these badges was in principle positive. They were used to commemorate an event, to get protection from a saint, or to be identified as a pilgrim. Other badges were obligatory and worn as negative signs.[27] From the fifteenth century onwards demarcation of certain groups and individuals became more important in Western-European society. Beggars had to wear their beggars badge, some of which survive. Others, like Jews and whores had to wear signs as well, and in many towns special clothing or textile marks such as the color yellow was used as a negative sign.

In the right foreground of Jan Provoost's Crucifixion panel from the Jerusalem Chapel in Bruges, one of the gambling soldiers wears a striking yellow shirt and is depicted negatively. His bare feet, facial features, gestures, and dagger all characterize him as an evil figure.[28] One tiny detail emphasizes that above all else and that is a small rectangular plaster that covers a wound on his head (Fig. 21). This may not be a badge in proper sense, but it is surely a sign.

The Historiography of Pilgrim Badges

Research on the "minor" art of pilgrim badges and of secular badges as well, started around the middle of the nineteenth century. It is clear that, when he wrote, Walter Scott already knew how commonplace pilgrim badges were and he was aware of the discrepancy between cheap, mass-produced badges and elitist precious jewelry. The real breakthrough in research came between 1855–1865 with the canalization of the Seine in Paris and the renovation of the bridges on that river. Amongst the many finds that came to light were badges, ranging from the nowadays well-known pilgrim badges to amulets and livery badges.[29] Arthur Forgeais (1822–1878), an antiquarian and primarily a collector of seals and seal matrices, brought together his huge "Collection des plombs historiés trouvés dans la Seine," into one publication in ten volumes that he funded himself.[30] Other collectors and antiquarians also paid attention to badges, and these included

26. Herrmann, *Der gerittene Aristoteles*,(as in note 24), 63.

27. R. Mellinkoff, *Outcasts: Signs of Otherness in Northern European Art of the Late Middle Ages* (Berkeley, Calif., 1993), 44; F. Irsigler and A. Lassotta, *Bettler und Gaukler, Dirnen und Henkler. Aussenseiter in einer mittelalterlichen Stadt. Köln 1300–1600* (Cologne, 1984; reprint Munich, 2004), 196; Koldeweij *Geloof & Geluk* (as in note 7), 37–42.

28. R. Spronk, "The Reconstruction of a Triptych by Jan Provoost for the Jerusalem Chapel in Bruges," *Burlington Magazine* 147 (2005), 109–11. Reprinted in: R. Spronk, *Examining Materials and Techniques of Easel Paintings: Ten Technical Studies (1996–2005)* (Groningen, 2005), 255–57; Koldeweij, *Geloof & Geluk* (as in note 7), 190–92.

29. E. Grésy, "Notice sur quelques enseignes et médailles en plomb, trouvées dans la Seine," *Mémoires de la Société Imperiale des Antiquaires de France* 25 (III–5) (1862), 117–43.

30. A. Forgeais, *Notice sur des plombs historiés trouvés dans la Seine* (Paris, 1858); A. Forgeais, *Collection de plombs historiés trouvés dans la Seine* (Paris, 1862–1866), 5 vols., I: *Méreaux des corporations de métiers*, II: *Enseignes de pèlerinages*, III: *Variétés numismatiques*, IV: *Imagerie religieuse*, V: *Numismatique populaire*; A. Forgeais, *Numismatique des corporations parisiennes, métiers, etc., d'après les plombs historiés trouvés dans la Seine* (Paris, 1874); A. Forgeais, *Crayons, écritoires et ampoules du Moyen Âge d'après les plombs historiés trouvés dans la Seine* (Paris, 1875); A. Forgeais, *Blasons et chevaliers du Moyen Âge d'après les plombs historiés trouvés dans la Seine* (Paris, 1877).

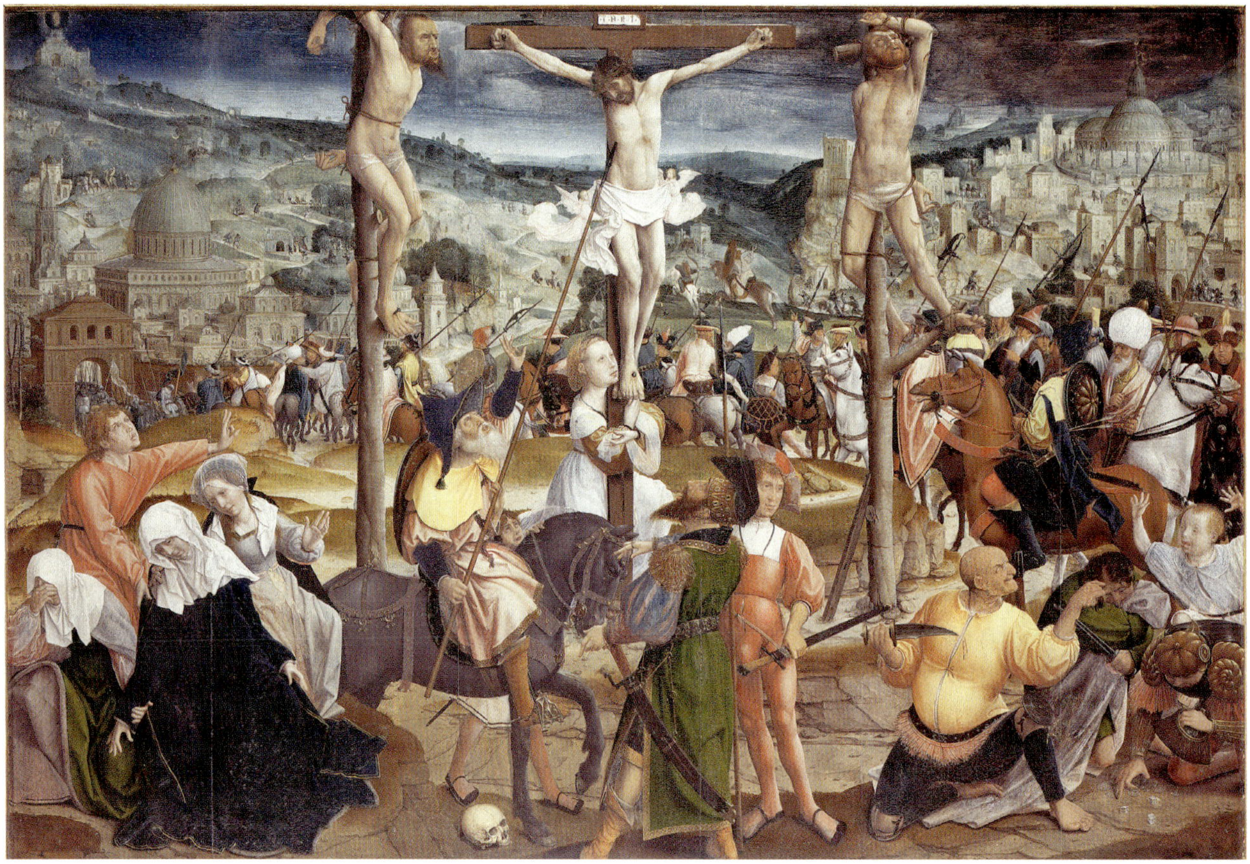

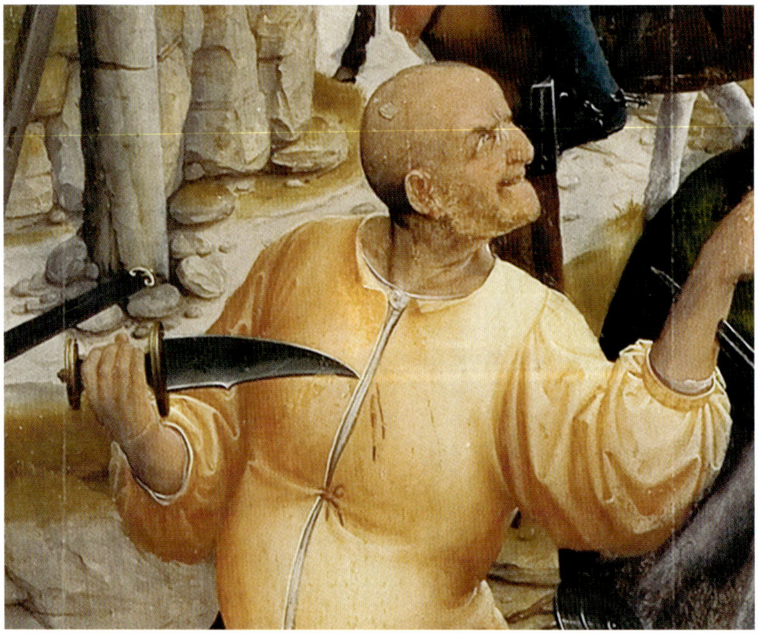

FIGURE 21. Jan Provoost (*c.* 1465–1529), Crucifixion, central panel of a triptych from the Jerusalem-Chapel in Bruges, oak panel, 117 × 172.5 cm, *c.* 1505. Bruges, Groeningemuseum.

Marcel-Jérôme Rigollot, Louis Dancoisne, F. E. Desnoyers, M.E. Hucher, Victor Gay, and A.-N. Didron.[31] More recent French studies on pilgrim badges have been undertaken by Colette Lamy-Lasalle[32] and Denis Bruna.[33] A spectacular group of badges recently found in the Northern French town of Valenciennes was published in a separate monograph.[34] From 1848 onwards Charles Roach Smith (1806–1890) published on pilgrim badges, brooches, and other archaeological items in England.[35] Brian Spencer (1928–2003) continued this tradition in the later twentieth century.[36] The research history in Germany, where not many badges have been found, is slightly different: from the early twentieth century onwards studies were published there on pilgrim badges that had been cast on church bells.[37] The finds from the river Weser near Worms, which were discovered in the 1920s, are an exception and were published almost immediately.[38] The church bells,

31. M.-J. Rigollot, *Monnaies inconnues des éveques des innocens, des fous, de quelques autres associations singulières du meme temps* (Paris, 1837); E. Hucher, "Des enseignes de pèlerinage," *Bulletin Monumental,* 2nd series 19 (1853), 505–36; L. Dancoisne, *Souvenirs métalliques du pèlerinage d'Ablain-Saint-Nazaire* (Arras, 1856); L. Dancoisne, *Numismatique Béthunoise: receuil historique de monnaies, méraux médailles et jetons de la ville et de l'arrondissement de Béthune* (Arras, 1859); A.-N. Didron, "Mélanges et nouvelles," *Annales Archéologiques,* 21 (1861), 368; L. Dancoisne, *Les Médailles religieuses du Pas-de-Calais* (Arras, 1880); F.-E. Desnoyers, "Nouveaux objets trouvés dans la Seine pendant les années 1872, 1873 et une partie de 1874," *Mémoires de la Société archéologiques et historique de l'Orleanais* 15 (1873), 283; V. Gay, *Glossaire archéologique du Moyen Âge et de la Renaissance,* I (Paris, 1887).

32. C. Lamy-Lassalle, "Recherches sur un ensemble de plombs trouvés dans la Seine, musée des antiquités de Rouen et collection Bossard de Lucerne," *Revue des sociétés savantes de Haute-Normandie* 49 (1968), 5–24; C. Lamy-Lassalle, "Une collection d'enseignes de pèlerinage au musée des Arts décoratifs de Lyon," *Bulletin de la Société nationale des Antiquaires de France* (1969), 264–70; C. Lamy-Lassalle, "Les enseignes de pèlerinage du Mont-Saint-Michel," in *Millénaire monastique du Mont-Saint-Michel,* vol. III: *Culte de saint Michel et pèlerinages au Mont,* ed. M. Baudot (Paris, 1971), 271–86; C. Lamy-Lassalle, "Les Représentations de saint Jean-Baptiste sur les enseignes de pèlerinage," *Bulletin trimestriel de la Société des Antiquaires de Picardie* (1973), 156–64; C. Lamy-Lassalle, "Les enseignes de pèlerinage de saint Mathurin de L'Archant," *Bulletin de la Société nationale des Antiquaires de France* (1988), 100–06.

33. D. Bruna, "Les enseignes de pèlerinage et les coquilles Saint-Jacques dans les sépultures du Moyen Âge en Europe occidentale," *Bulletin de la Société nationale des Antiquaires de France* (1991), 178–190; D. Bruna, "Un moule pour enseignes de pèlerinage à l'image de la 'Belle Vierge' de Ratisbonne," *Bulletin de la Société nationale des Antiquaires de France* (1992), 317–324; D. Bruna, "La marchande d'enseignes de pèlerinage des stalles de la cathédrale d'Amiens," *Bulletin de la Société nationale des Antiquaires de France* (1994), 199–206; D. Bruna, "La diffusion des enseignes de pèlerinage," in *Pèlerinages et croisades L. Pressouyre, ed.* (*actes du 118e congres national des sociétés historiques et scientifiques, section: Relations interculturelles au Moyen Âge, pèlerinages et croisades, Pau 25–29. Octobre 1993*) (Paris, 1995), 201–14; D. Bruna, *Enseignes de pèlerinages et enseignes profanes,* Exhib. Cat., Musée National de Moyen Âge / Thermes de Cluny (Paris, 1996); D. Bruna, "Quelques images de chefs-reliquaires à travers les enseignes de pèlerinage," in D. Kicken, A. M. Koldeweij, and J. R. ter Molen, eds., *Gevonden voorwerpen: opstellen over middeleeuwse archeologie voor H.J.E. van Beuningen* (*Lost and Found: Essays on Medieval Archaeology for H.J.E. van Beuningen*), Rotterdam Papers 11 (Rotterdam, 2000), 73–80; D. Bruna, "Enseignes de pèlerinage et identité du pelerin," in *Les pèlerinages à travers l'art et la société à l'époque préromane et romane, Les Cahiers de Saint-Michel de Cuxa* 31 (2000), 59–63; D. Bruna, *Enseignes de plomb et autres menues chosettes du Moyen Âge* (Paris, 2006); D. Bruna, *Saints et diables au chapeau: Bijoux oubliés du Moyen Âge* (Paris, 2007).

34. A. Tixador, *Enseignes sacrées et profanes médiévales découvertes à Valenciennes: Un peu plus d'un kilogramme d'histoire* (Valenciennes, 2004).

35. C. R. Smith, *Catalogue of the Museum of London Antiquities* (London, 1854), 134–45 (Pilgrim's and other signs); C. R. Smith, *Collectanea Antiqua, Etchings and Notices of Ancient Remains, Illustrative of the Habits, Customs, and History of Past Ages,* I (London, 1848), 81–91 (Religious signs or tokens of the Middle Age); IV (London, 1857) 108–12, 165–72; VI (London, 1868), 286.

36. B. W. Spencer, *Pilgrim Souvenirs and Secular Badges* (London, 1998; new ed., Woodbridge, 2010); B. W. Spencer, "Medieval Pilgrim Badges," in *A Contribution to Medieval Archaeology,* ed. J. G. N. Renaud, Rotterdam Papers I (Rotterdam, 1968), 137–53; B. W. Spencer, *Pilgrim Souvenirs and Secular Badges,* Salisbury Museum, Medieval Catalogue, Pt. 2 (Salisbury, 1990); a select list of Brian Spencer's publications by G. Egan in: *Beyond Pilgrim Souvenirs and Secular Badges: Essays in Honour of Brian Spencer,* S. Blick, ed. (Oxford, 2007), xi–xiii.

37. P. Liebeskind, "Pilger-oder Wallfahrtszeichen auf Glocken I," *Die Denkmalpflege* 6 (1904), nr. 7, 53–55; P. Liebeskind, "Pilger- und Wallfahrtszeichen auf Glocken II," *Die Denkmalpflege* 7 (1905), nr. 15, 117–120; P. Liebeskind, "Pilger- und Wallfahrtszeichen auf Glocken III," *Die Denkmalpflege* 7 (1905), nr. 16, 125–28; P. Liebeskind, "Pilgerzeichen," *Die Denkmalpflege* 9 (1907), nr. 8, 56; A. Petersen, "Das ältere Wilsnacker Pilgerzeichen," *Die Denkmalpflege* 9 (1907), nr. 16, 131.

38. E. Grohne, "Bremische Boden- und Baggerfunde," in *Jahresschrift des Focke-Museums Bremen 1929* (Bremen, 1929), 44–102.

which were seized during World War II, inspired Kurt Köster (1912–1986) to publish some fine research on pilgrim badges.[39] After the war Köster was responsible for the inspection, return, or replacement of the bells of the *Deutschen Glockenfriedhof* in Hamburg and for the documentation on melted bells. In 1957 he published his extensive study on the bell founder Tilman von Hachenburg (*c.* 1420–1479) in which he also paid attention to pilgrim badges.[40] A year before, in 1956, Köster presented his pioneering discovery on the manufacture of pilgrim badges in Aachen by Johannes Gutenberg (*c.* 1400–1468).[41] Many other contributions on pilgrim badges followed[42] and he bequeathed his huge *Pilgerzeichen-kartei* to the Germanische National-

39. W. Brückner, "Kurt Köster und die Pilgerzeichenforschung," in *Das Zeichen am Hut in Mittelalter: Europäische Reisemarkieriungen. Symposium in Memoriam Kurt Köster (1912–1986)* H. Kühne, L. Lampacher, and K. Vanja, eds. (Frankfurt am Main, New York, 2008), 19–29.

40. K. Köster, "Meister Tilman von Hachenburg. Studien zum Werk eines mittelrheinischen Glockengiessers des fünfzehnten Jahrhunderts. Mit besonderer Berücksichtigung der als Glockenzier verwendeten mittelalterlichen Pilger- und Wallfahrtszeichen," *Jahrbuch der Hessischen Kirchengeschichtlichen Vereinigung* 8 (1957), 1–206. Later additions in: K. Köster, "Neue Studien zu Meister Tilman von Hachenburg und seinen Glocken," *Jahrbuch der Hessischen Kirchengeschichtlichen Vereinigung* 10 (1959), 77–91; K. Köster and Tilman von Hachenburg, "Nachlese zum Werk eines mittelrheinischen Glockengießers im Spätmittelalter," *Jahrbuch der Hessischen Kirchengeschichtlichen Vereinigung* 31 (1981a), 1–28.

41. K. Köster, "Gutenbergs Aachener Heiltumsspiegel," in Fritz Hodeige, ed., *Das Werck der Bucher: Von der Wirksamkeit des Buches in Vergangenheit und Gegenwart. Ein Festschrift für Horst Kliemann zu seinem 60. Geburtstag* (Freiburg, 1956), 284–301; K. Köster, *Gutenberg in Straßburg: Das Aachenspiegel-Unternehmen und die unbekannte "afentur und kunst"* (Mainz, 1973); K. Köster, "Gutenbergs Straßburger Aachenspiegel-Unternehmen von 1438/40," *Gutenberg-Jahrbuch* 58 (1983), 24–44.

42. For a survey of Köster's publications, see L. von Freyberg, "Bibliographie der Veröffentlichungen von Kurt Köster," in *Bibliothek, Buch, Geschichte: Kurt Köster zum 65. Geburtstag,* G. Pflug, B. Eckert, H. Friesenhahn, eds. (Frankfurt am Main, 1977), 583–596; "Publizierte Arbeiten Kurt Kösters zu Pilgerzeichen und Glocken—chronologische Gesamtbibliographie," in *Das Zeichen am Hut in Mittelalter: Europäische Reisemarkierungen. Symposion in Memoriam Kurt Köster (1912–1986) und Katalog der Pilgerzeichen im Kunstgewerbemuseum und im Museum für Byzantinische Kunst der Staatlichen Museen zu Berlin.* H. Kühne, L. Lambacher, K. Vanja, eds. (Frankfurt am Main, 2008), 385–389. On pilgrim badges, see K. Köster, "Neusser Pilgerzeichen und Wallfahrtsmedaillen. Ein Beitrag zur Geschichte der Quirinius-Verehrung," *Neusser Jahrbuch* 1 (1956), 15–28; K. Köster, "Ein unbekanntes mittelalterliches Pilgerzeichen aus Eberhardsklausen," *Trierisches Jahrbuch* 9 (1958), 79–88; K. Köster, "St.-Quirinius-Wallfahrten und ihre Pilgerandenken. Neue Studien zur Kultgeschichte und Ikonographie des Neusser Heiligen," *Neusser Jahrbuch* 5 (1960), 8–26; K. Köster, "Gottsbüren, das 'hessische Wilsnack.' Geschichte und Kultgeschichte einer mittelalterlichen Heiligblut-Wallfahrt im Spiegel ihrer Pilgerzeichen," in V. Ekkehard Kaufmann, ed., *Festgabe für Paul Kirn zum 70. Geburtstag dargebracht von Freunden und Schülern* (Berlin, 1961), 198–222; K. Köster, "St.-Quirinius-Pilgerandenken. Ein unbekanntes Neusser Wallfahrtszeichen auf einer Altartafel Derick Baegerts," in *Neusser Jahrbuch* 7 (1962), 39–42; K. Köster, "Pilgerzeichen-Studien. Neue Beiträge zur Kenntnis eines mittelalterlichen Massenartikels und seiner Überlieferungsformen," in *Bibliotheca docet. Festgabe für Carl Wehmer* (Amsterdam, 1963), 77–100; K. Köster, "Eine neuerschlossene Quelle zur Geschichte der Blomberger Wallfahrt und ihrer Pilgerzeichen," in *Lippische Mitteilungenaus Geschichte und Landeskunde* 32 (1963), 5–15; K. Köster, "Religiöse Medaillen und Wallfahrtsdevotionalien in der flämischen Buchmalerei des 15. und frühen 16. Jahrhunderts. Zur Kenntnis gemalter und wirklicher Kollektionen in spätmittelalterlichen Gebetbuch-Handschriften," in *Buch und Welt. Gustav Hofmann zum 65. Geburtstag dargebracht* (Wiesbaden, 1965), 459–504; K. Köster, "Mittelalterliche Pilgerzeichen und Wallfahrtsdevotionalien," in *Rhein und Maas. Kunst und Kultur 800–1400*, Exhib. Cat. (Cologne, 1972), 146–160; K. Köster, "Wallfahrtszeichen und Pilgerdevotionalien aus der Frühzeit der Dürener Sankt-Anna-Wallfahrt," in E. Gatz, ed., *St. Anna in Düren* (Mönchengladbach, 1972), 191–209; K. Köster, "Pilgerzeichen und Wallfahrtsplaketten von St. Adrian in Geraardsbergen. Zu einer Darstellung auf einer flämischen Altartafel des 15. Jahrhunderts im Historischen Museum zu Frankfurt am Main," in *Städel-Jahrbuch* 4 (1973), 103–120; K. Köster, "Ein spätmittelalterliches Blomberger Pilgerzeichen. Zu einem Amsterdamer Bodenfund von 1973," *Lippische Mitteilungen aus Geschichte und Landeskunde* 43 (1974), 9–18; K. Köster, "Die Neusser Quirinius-Wallfahrt im Mittelalter und ihre Pilgerzeichen," *Almanach für das Erzbistum Köln. Jahrbuch 1974 und 1975* (Cologne, 1976), 185–193; K. Köster, "Ein rätselhafter 'Siegeldruck' des fünfzehnten Jahrhunderts aus Regensburg. Studien zur mittelalterlichen Wallfahrt nach St. Emmeram und ihren Pilgerzeichen," in P. Schweigler, ed., *Bibliothekswelt und Kulturgeschichte. Eine internationale Festgabe für Joachim Werner zum 65. Geburtstag, dargebracht von seinen Freunden* (Munich, 1977), 123–137; K. Köster, "Kollektionen metallener Wallfahrts-Devotionalien und kleiner Andachtsbilder, eingenäht in spätmittelalterliche Gebetbuch-Handschriften," in B. Haller and G. Liebers, eds., *Erlesenes aus der Welt des Buches: Gedanken-Betrachtungen—Forschungen* 1 (Wiesbaden, 1979), 77–129; K. Köster, "Pilgerzeichen und Pilgermuscheln," in *St. Elisabeth. Fürstin-Dienerin-Heilige Aufsätze, Dokumentation, Katalog*, Exhib. Cat. (Sigmaringen, 1981), 452–459; K. Köster, *Pilgerzeichen und Pilger-*

museum in Nuremberg, where the Deutsches Glockenarchiv is also found.[43] Jörg Poettgen[44] and Hartmut Kühne[45] continue research on pilgrim badges in Germany. Kühne and his students at the Theologische Fakultät of the Von Humboldt University in Berlin have a database devoted to pilgrim badges (Pilgerzeichen-Datenbank: www.pilgerzeichen.de), and this is currently managed by the Kunstgewerbemuseum der Staatlichen Museen in Berlin. Scandinavian church bells, which sometimes have pilgrim badges, have been

---

muscheln von mittelalterlichen Santiago-Straßen: St-Léonard, Rocamadour, St-Gilles, Santiago de Compostella (Neumünster, 1983) (*Ausgrabungen in Schleswig.* 2); K. Köster, "Mittelalterliche Pilgerzeichen" in L. Kriss-Rettenbeck and G. Möhler, eds., *Wallfahrt kennt keine Grenzen: Themen zu einer Ausstellung des Bayerischen Nationalmuseums und des Adalbert Stifter Vereins, München* (Munich, 1984), 203–223; K. Köster, "Pilgerzeichen und Ampullen. Zu neuen Braunschweiger Bodenfunden," in H. Rötting, ed., *Stadtarchäologie in Braunschweig. Forschungen zur Denkmalpflege in Niedersachsen* 3 (1985), 277–286; K. Köster, "Mittelalterliche Pilgerzeichen," in C. Meckseper, ed., *Stadt im Wandel: Kunst und Kultur des Bürgertums in Norddeutschland, 1150–1650,* 1. *Katalog der Objekte*, Exhib. Cat. (Stuttgart, 1985), 404–414; K. Köster, "Les coquilles et enseignes de pélerinage de Saint-Jacques de Compostelle et des routes de Saint-Jacques en occident," in *Santiago de Compostela: 1000 ans de pèlerinage européen*, Exhib. Cat. (Gent, 1985), 85–95.

43. J. Poettgen, "Europäische Pilgerzeichenforschung. Die zentrale Pilgerzeichenkartei (PKZ) Kurt Kösters (†1986), in Nürnberg und der Forschungsstand nach 1986," *Jahrbuch für Glockenkunde* 7–8 (1995–1996), 195–206.

44. J. Poettgen, "Magister Sifride. Ein Kölner Glockengießer des 14. Jahrhunderts?" *Jahrbuch des Kölnischen Geschichtsvereins* 58 (1987), 35–66; "Zwei unbekannte Medaillen der Dürener St.-Annen-Wallfahrt," *Dürener Geschichtsblätter e. V.* 77 (1988), 25–28; J. Poettgen, "Die Andernacher Glockengießerwerkstatt nach Tilman von Hachenburg: Ein Beitrag zur Glockenkunde im Kurfürstentum Trier von der Mitte des 15. bis zur Mitte des 16. Jahrhunderts," *Kurtrierisches Jahrbuch* 32 (1992), 21–43; J. Poettgen, "Trierer Glockengießer bis zum Ende des 16. Jahrhunderts: Studien zur Glockenkunde im Kurfürstentum Trier," *Kurtrierisches Jahrbuch* 33 (1993), 65–122; J. Poettgen, "Vorreformatorische Wallfahrtsdevotionalien aus dem Matthiaskloster zu Trier: Mittelalterliche Pilgerzeichen auf Glocken," *Kurtrierisches Jahrbuch* 34 (1994), 47–76; J. Poettgen, "Mittelalterliche Glocken an Glahn und Nahe: Eine unbekannte Gießerwerkstatt in Speyer zwischen 1340 und 1550," *Westricher Heimatblätter* 27 (1996), nr. 3, 3–44; J. Poettgen, "Kryptogramme und Pilgerzeichen auf spätmittelalterlichen Glocken im östlichen Thüringen: Studien zur Werkstatt des Meisters Herlin in Jena," *Jahrbuch für Glockenkunde* 9–10 (1997), 81–98; A. Haasis-Berner and J. Poettgen, "Pilgerzeichen als Zeugnisse der Wallfahrt zu den Heiligen Drei Königen—Neue Funde und Typologie," in *Ad Summum, 1248:—Der gotische Dom im Mittelalter. Ausstellung des historischen Archivs der Stadt Köln* (Cologne, 1998), 167–179; J. Poettgen, "Die mittelalterliche Wallfahrt zum Heiligenberg—ein bisher ungedeutetes Pilgerzeichen aus Höxter- Ovenhausen," *Jahrbuch für Glockenkunde,* 11–12 (1999–2000), 145–150; J. Poettgen, "Die Anfänge der Dürener St.-Anna-Wallfahrt im Zeugnis der Anna-Glocke von Vianden (1503)," *Dürener Geschichtsblätter. Mitteilungen des Dürener Geschichtsvereins e. V.* 85 (2001), 31–59; J. Poettgen, "Die Leidenswerkzeuge Jesu auf einer Glocke. Ein spätgotisches Pilgerzeichen aus Brauweiler?" *Pulheimer Beiträge zur Geschichte und Heimatkunde* 27 (2003), 36–40; J. Poettgen, "Der Beitrag der Glockenkunde zur Pilgerzeichenforschung von Kurt Köster bis heute," in *Das Zeichen am Hut im Mittelalter. Europäische Reisemarkierungen* (2008), 31–46; J. Poettgen, "Karl der Grosse auf Aachener Pilgerzeichen des Mittelalters. Mit einem Katalog der bisher bekannten Exemplare," *Zeitschrift des Aachener Geschichtsvereins* 110 (2008), 65–100.

45. H. Kühne, "Zwei Unbekannte in 'Sankt. Martin.' Ein Pilgerzeichenrätsel," in Th. T. Müller, ed., *Die St.-Martins-Kirche zu Heiligenstadt. 17 Beiträge zu ihrer Geschichte* (Heiligenstadt, 2003) (*Heiligenstädter Schriften* 2), 127–134; H. Kühne, "Pilgerzeichen—Spuren mittelalterlicher Wallfahrten auf märkischen Kirchenglocken," *Offene Kirchen…: Brandenburgische Dorfkirchen laden ein,* (Berlin, 2005), 14–17; H. Kühne, "Zu Millionen gegossen. Das Projekt 'Wallfahrt und Pilgerzeichen' an der Berliner Humboldt-Universität," *Der Dom. Kirchenzeitung des Erzbistums Paderborn*, nr. 18 (2008); H. Kühne, "Funde brachten Licht ins Dunkel. Das 'Pilgerzeichen'-Projekt der Humboldt-Universität und die Wallfahrt zum Jakobsberg bei Beverungen," *Der Dom. Kirchenzeitung des Erzbistums Paderborn*, nr. 20 (2008), 34; H. Kühne, "Der Pilgerzeichenfund am Kloster Seehausen und sein historischer Kontext. Mit einem Katalog des Seehausener Fundes von Carina Brumme," in D. Schumann, ed., *Sachkultur und religiöse Praxis* (Berlin, 2007) (*Studien zur Geschichte, Kunst und Kultur der Zisterzienser* 8), 406–457; H. Kühne, "Pilgerzeichen [der hl. Elisabeth]," in D. Blume and M. Werner, eds., *Elisabeth von Thüringen—eine europäische Heilige*, Exhib. Cat. (Petersberg, 2007), 215–219; H. Kühne, L. Lambacher, and Konrad Vanja, eds., *Das Zeichen am Hut im Mittelalter. Europäische Reisemarkierungen: Symposion in memoriam Kurt Köster (1912–1986) und Katalog der Pilgerzeichen im Kunstgewerbemuseum und im Museum für Byzantinische Kunst der Staatlichen Museen zu Berlin* (Frankfurt am Main, 2008) (*Europäische Wallfahrtsstudien* 4); H. Kühne, "Die Pilgerzeichenforschung in Deutschland seit dem Tod von Kurt Köster 1986," in *Das Zeichen am Hut im Mittelalter,* 153–160; H. Kühne, "Zur Bedeutung der Pilgerzeichensammlungen der Staatlichen Museen zu Berlin," in *Das Zeichen am Hut im Mittelalter*, 221–232; H. Kühne, C. Brumme, St. Krabath, and L. Lambacher, "Europäische Pilgerzeichen und verwandte Weißmetallgüsse des hohen und späten Mittelalters im Kunstgewerbemuseum und im Museum für Byzantinische Kunst der Staatlichen Museen zu Berlin [Katalog]," in *Das Zeichen am Hut*

studied by F. Uldall in the early twentieth century,[46] while Niels Knud Liebgott, Monica Rydbeck, and Lars Andersson took up pilgrim badge research for the most northern parts of Europe.[47]

In Belgium and the Netherlands a spectacular amount of late medieval religious and secular badges have been unearthed in the last fifty years. The majority of these are, as was the case in France and England, cast from pewter, lead, or a tin-lead alloy; some are made of bronze and, in a few exceptional cases, silver. Handmade and engraved badges, usually of bronze or brass, and occasionally of tin-lead or even silver have also been found. Badges stamped out of wafer-thin sheets of metal, mostly of soft brass, silver, or (rarely) pewter, and dating from the late fifteenth and the first half of the sixteenth century, have also survived. Most recently, attention has focused on an assortment of stamped badges mainly found in the town of Malines, in a distinctive and typically Flemish devotional context: the so-called "enclosed garden," which are small triptychs made for private devotion. The practice of displaying pilgrim badges and other small devotional objects in these "enclosed gardens" is described in the catalogue published in conjunction with the exhibition *Faith & Fortune* in the Gruuthuse Museum, Bruges (2006–2007).[48] Flemish Books of Hours are another non-archaeological *Fundgrube* for these thin and lightly stamped badges. Sometimes these have survived *in situ*, glued or sewn on the blank first or last folios of the manuscripts, but more frequently they are preserved as imprints on the parchment where the badges formerly were.[49]

The exhibition and its accompanying catalogue, *Geloof & Geluk: Sieraad en Devotie in middeleeuws Vlaanderen* (*Faith & Fortune. Ornament and Devotion in Medieval Flanders*, also available in French),[50] is the most recent and intensive study of late medieval badges within a cultural-historical context. Some five hundred badges originating from the County of Flanders or originating from Flemisch finds, were shown in connection with a broad spectrum of other thematically related objects.

At the time this exhibition catalogue was published, a research project in the same field at the Radboud University Nijmegen was also underway. The database devoted to pilgrim badges and known as Kunera (www.kunera.nl), was launched early in 1998 and was jointly funded by the Netherlandish Organization for Scientific Research (NWO) and the Radboud University. This extensive international database of both religious and secular badges currently contains some 15,500 badges. It is set up as a modern digital version of Kurt Köster's *Pilgerzeichenkartei*. In 2006–2007 all the badges catalogued by Kurt Köster were integrated in the Kunera database and are now available on-line. The database

---

im Mittelalter, 249–384; H. Kühne and J. Ansorge, "Barfuß und in Wolle gekleidet ... Pilger in Güstrow," in *Archäologie in Deutschland* 2 (2009), 46–47; H. Kühne, "'Wir sind noch da'—spätmittelalterliche Pilgerzeichen auf einer Glocke der St. Blasii-Kirche in Nordhausen," in *Beiträge zur Geschichte aus Stadt und Kreis Nordhausen* 34 (2009), 139–151; H. Kühne and C. Brumme, "Jenseits von Wilsnack und Sternberg: Pilgerzeichen spätmittelalterlicher Heilig—Blut—Wallfahrten," in *Varia campanologiae studia cyclica. 25 Jahre Deutsches Glockenmuseum auf Burg Greifenstein. Zugleich eine Festschrift für Jörg Poettgen zur Vollendung des 70. Lebensjahres* (Greifenstein, 2009) (*Schriften aus dem Deutschen Glockenmuseum* 6), 129–142; H. Kühne and J. Poettgen, "Mittelalterliche Pilgerzeichen aus der Diözese Trier: Kurzkatalog und Befunde," in Th. Frank, M. Matheus, and S. Reichert, eds., *Wege zum Heil. Pilger und heilige Orte an Mosel und Rhein* (Stuttgart, 2009) (*Geschichtliche Landeskunde* 67), 135–180.

46. F. Uldall, *Danmarks middelalderlige Kirkeklokker* (Copenhagen, 1906).

47. N.-K. Liebgott a.o., *Pilgerreisen im Mittelalter* (Odense, 2003) (*University of Southern Denmark Studies in History and Social Sciences* 267); Niels Knud Liebgott, "Afstobninger af pilgrimstegn pa danske middelalderlige kirkeklokker," *Aarboger for nordisk Oldkyndighed og historie* (1971), 196–240. M. Rydbeck, "Grav 301 vid dominikanerklostret i Hälsingborg," *Kring Kärnan* 6 (1955), 79–93; *idem*, "Pilgrimsmärket fran Fornasa," *Fornvännen* 51 (1956), 283–285; M. Rydbeck, "Thomas Beckets ampuller," in *Fornvännen* 59 (1964), 236–248. L. Andersson, *Pilgrimsmärken och vallfart: Medeltida Pilgrimskultur i Skandinavien* (Stockholm, 1989)

48. M. Kruip, "Het Besloten Hofje: een spirituele pelgrimage," in J. Koldeweij, *Geloof & Geluk* (as in note 7), 231–234.

49. H. van Asperen, *Pelgrimstekens op perkament. Originele en nageschilderde bedevaartsouvenirs in religieuze boeken* (*ca. 1450 – ca. 1530*) (Nijmegen, 2009); H. van Asperen, "Bedevaart en devotie: insignes in laatmiddeleeuwse manuscripten," in *Geloof & Geluk* (as in note 7), 234–245.

50. J. Koldeweij, *Foi & bonne fortune: Parure et dévotion en Flandre médiévale* (Arnhem, 2006) (trans. of *Geloof & Geluk*—as in note 7).

continues to grow as more examples and different types of badges are discovered by archaeologists and treasure hunters in the Netherlands and throughout Europe. Similarly, an ever increasing number of private and public collections have become accessible, while older publications from the mid-nineteenth and early twentieth century have yet to be reviewed in the light of modern studies and finds. The spectacular finds in the area of the Zeeland Delta from the seventies onwards were first highlighted in an exhibition in the Rijksmuseum Het Catharijneconvent in Utrecht in 1982,[51] presenting around one hundred and thirty badges together with other, more modern mass-produced devotional objects. A much wider range of medieval finds—mainly of metal and found in the East Scheldt river estuary, which included both religious and secular badges—was subsequently exhibited in *Schatten uit de Schelde* (*Treasures from the Scheldt*), at Bergen-op-Zoom in 1987. The lewd and erotic subject matter of some of the profane badges caused a commotion at the time, and triggered a revival of interest in this material, some of which had actually been published in France in the nineteenth century.[52] Stéphane Vandenberghe, curator at the municipal museums of Bruges, published several articles on badges in Belgium in the 1970s, and the priest and historian Antoon Viaene from Bruges, who has written numerous articles on pilgrimage in general, also undertook some research on badges. An inventory of all the religious badges found in the province of Zeeland was also compiled for a publication and exhibition in 1987/1988 entitled *Saints from the Mud*, which was shown at the Zeeuws Museum in Middelburg and the Museum for Religious Art in Uden.[53] Over a period of many years, the Dutch connoisseur and private collector H. J. E. Van Beuningen built up his own extensive and valuable documentation on Netherlandish and Flemish badges (from his and other collections), which has now been partly digitalized and made available online (Medieval Badges Foundation: www.medievalbadges.org). The best examples from the Van Beuningen collection and a first inventory of badges found in the Netherlands from other private and public collections was published in two volumes entitled "Heilig en Profaan" (Sacred and Secular), in 1993 and 2001, respectively, while a third volume with another 1,200 badges will be published in 2012.[54] The first volume of "Heilig en Profaan" (1993) provided the basis for an exhibition in the Boijmans Van Beuningen Museum in Rotterdam in which a selection from the 1,036 published badges of the Van Beuningen collection was displayed, while the second volume accompanied a selection of badges shown in the Hieronymus Bosch exhibition in Rotterdam in 2001.[55] Several essays on badges were included the Festschrift for Hendrik Jan van Beuningen, which was published to commemorate his eightieth birthday in 2000.[56]

Local or more regional groups of badges have been published as well, only some of which will be mentioned here. Excavation campaigns from 1992 onwards as well as metal detector hunting on the Belgium coast near Oostende resulted in an interesting collection of one hundred and ninety badges from the former fishing village of Raversyde,[57] and many more from the town of Ypres. Construction work for new developments in

51. *Vroomheid per dozijn*, Exhib. Cat. (Utrecht, 1982).

52. A. Forgeais, *Priapées* (probably Paris, 1865)—I am indebted to Dr. Denis Bruna for providing me with a photocopy of this extremely rare booklet; Thomas Wright, *The Worship of the Generative Powers During the Middle Ages of Western Europe* (London, 1865), reprinted in, *A History of Phallic Worship* (New York, 1992), 59–65, and pls. IX–X.

53. R. M. van Heeringen, A. M. Koldeweij, A. A. G. Gaalman, *Heiligen uit de modder. In Zeeland gevonden pelgrimstekens*, Clavis Kunsthistorische Monografieën 4 (Zutphen, 1987; reprinted 1988).

54. H. J. E. van Beuningen and A. M. Koldeweij, *Heilig & Profaan: Vol. 1* (as in note 10); H. J. E. van Beuningen, A. M. Koldeweij, and D. Kicken, *Heilig & Profaan*: *Vol. 2* (as in note 13); H. J. E. van Beuningen, A. M. Koldeweij, and D. Kicken, *Heilig & Profaan: Vol. 3. 1200 laatmiddeleeuwse insignes uit openbare en particuliere collecties*, Rotterdam Papers 13 (Langbroek, 2011).

55. J. Koldeweij, P. Vandenbroeck, B. Vermet, eds., *Hieronymus Bosch: The Complete Paintings and Drawings* (Gent, Rotterdam, New York: Ludion, 2001).

56. D. Kicken, A. M. Koldeweij, J. R. ter Molen, eds., *Gevonden Voorwerpen: opstellen over middeleeuwse archeologie voor H. J. E. van Beuningen / Lost and Found: Essays on Medieval Archaeology for H. J. E. van Beuningen*, Rotterdam Papers 11 (Rotterdam, 2000).

57. M. Pieters, E. Cools, J. Koldeweij, A. Mortier, "Middeleeuwse en latere insignes en devotionalia uit Raversijde (gemeente Middelkerke en stad Oostende, prov. West-Vlaanderen)," in *Archeologie in Vlaanderen* 6 (2002), 261–301.

the old city of 's-Hertogenbosch unexpectedly brought hundreds of badges along with other late medieval finds to the surface, and these were published in detail in 2007.[58] From a thematic point of view, badges and *ampullae* from Canterbury, but which have been found in the Netherlands, were published in a volume on Thomas Becket in Flanders.[59] Similarly, erotic badges were included in an exhibition catalogue on Carnival in England.[60] Various articles on pilgrim badges and the iconography of saints, and *ampullae* from Vendôme, as well as erotic badges as parodies of popular devotion, were published in the two volume *Art and Architecture of Late Medieval Pilgrimage in Northern Europe and the British Isles*, in 2005.[61] Badges cast on medieval bells from the duchy of Brabant were also studied in a doctoral dissertation, as were the badges of St. Job from Wezemaal (Flanders)[63] and a thesis on *ampullae* will be published shortly.[64] Badges are certainly receiving a higher profile than in the past and many examples which have been excavated in the Netherlands have also been shown in exhibitions all over Europe, as for example at Lisbon, Antwerp, Rome, and Frankfurt.[65] The size of these small objects bears no relationship to their importance and it is rewarding to see that they are now being incorporated into the mainstream of medieval research. They have the potential to offer significant insights into medieval life and culture and it is hoped that over time they will be considered a major art form.

58. H. L. Janssen, "Insignes, persoonlijke sieraden en kledingaccessoires," and A. M. Koldeweij, "Opgespeld Geloof & bijgeloof. Geloof & magie," in H. L. Janssen, ed., *'Tekens van Leven. Opgravingen en vondsten in het Tolbrugkwartier in 's-Hertogenbosch* (Utrecht, 2007), 110–146 and 147–189, respectively.

59. J. Koldeweij, "Te Sente Thomas van Cantelberghe, in Inghelant ... Pelgrimsinsignes en pelgrimstochten naar Thomas Becket," in *Thomas Becket in Vlaanderen. Waarheid of legende?* Exhib. Cat., Stedelijke Musea Kortrijk (Kortrijk, 2000), 49–72.

60. *Vastenavond, carnaval: feesten van de omgekeerde wereld*, Exhib. Cat. Noordbrabants Museum ('s-Hertogenbosch / Zwolle, 1992), 85; T. Hyman and R. Malbert, *Carnivalesque*, Exhib. Cat., Brighton Museum and Art Gallery; Castle Museum and Art Gallery, Nottingham; City Art Centre, Edinburgh (London, 2000).

61. M. de Kroon, "Medieval Pilgrim Badges and Their Iconographic Aspects"; K. Boertjes, "Pilgrim *Ampullae* from Vendôme: Souvenirs from a Pilgrimage to the Holy Tear of Christ"; J. Koldeweij, "'Shameless and Naked Images': Obscene Badges as Parodies of Popular Devotion," all in S. Blick and R. Tekippe, *Art and Architecture of Late Medieval Pilgrimage in Northern Europe and the British Isles* (Leiden / Boston, 2005), 385–404, 443–472, and 493–510, respectively.

62. E. van Loon–van de Moosdijk, *"Goet ende wael gheraect": Versieringsmotieven op luid- en speelklokken uit Middeleeuwen en Renaissance in het hertogdom Brabant (1300 tot 1559)* (Nijmegen, 2004).

63. B. Minnen, ed. (Averbode, 2011), especially: M. de Kroon and B. Minnen, "Pelgrimssouvenirs van Sint-Job uit Wezemaal," vol. 2, 11–40.

64. K. Boertjes, Radboud University, Nijmegen. See as well: K. Boertjes, "Pilgrim *Ampullae* of York Minster and the Healing Oil from the Shrine of St William," and J. Koldeweij, "A Pilgrim's Badge and *Ampullae* possibly from the Chartreuse of Champmol," in S. Blick, ed., *Beyond Pilgrim Souvenirs and Secular Badges: Essays in Honour of Brian Spencer* (Oxford, 2007), 48–63, 64–72, respectively. See also: W. Anderson, "Blessing the Fields? A Study of Late-medieval *Ampullae* from England and Wales," *Medieval Archaeology* 54 (2010), 182–203.

65. J. Koldeweij, "Insignia," in I. Kockelbergh, ed., *The Fascinating Faces of Flanders—Through Art and Society*, Exhib. Cat., Lissabon / Antwerpen (Antwerp, 1998), 162–166, 199–201; J. Koldeweij, "Insegna con le immagini di san Pietro e san Paolo; Insegna con l'immagine di San Pietro; Insegna con le immagini di san Pietro e san Paolo con la Vera Icona (Veronica); Insegna con le ciavi di san Pietro, la tiara e la Vera Icona (Veronica); Insegna con le chiavi di san Pietro, e la spada di san Paolo; Insegni con i santi Pietro e Paolo e santa Veronica con il sudario; Insegna con la Vera Icona (Veronica); Insegna di santa Maria Rotonda (Pantheon)," in M. D'Onofrio, ed., *Romei & Giubilei. Il pellegrinaggio medievale a San Pietro (350–1350)*, Exhib. Cat., Palazzo Venezia, Rome, 1999–2000 (Milan, 1999), 340–342, 345–347, cat. 101, 103–104, 110–112, 114–115; U. Schneider, "Straßen des Glaubens. Der Souvenir im Mittelalter," in *Der Souvenir. Erinnerung in Dingen von der Reliquie zum Andenken*, Exhib. Cat., Museum für Angewandte Kunst (Frankfurt, 2006), 60–78.

ALAN M. STAHL

Image and Art on Medieval Coinage

IN ITS PHYSICAL DIMENSION, no object of medieval material culture was more minor than coinage. The technical demands of die engraving, as well as the necessity of producing tens of thousands, even millions, of identical objects contributed to the formulaic nature of its appearance. As the value of a coin often rested on its recognition as the official issue of a respected minting authority, repetition of imagery was generally more important than variety in the production of a successful issue.

On the other hand, coinage constituted the most widely disseminated set of images throughout all levels of the populace and for most people represented the only visual representation of political authority they were likely to encounter on a regular basis. References in medieval literature to the appearance of widely circulating issues confirm the importance of this consistent coin imagery in popular culture. There is no question that coinage was a major part of the visual material world of the Middle Ages. Whether that qualifies it as a major art form, or an art form at all, begs the distinction between material culture and art, one that is at least as problematical as that between minor and major art forms.

The historiography of medieval coinage to a great extent mirrors the preoccupation of minters and users of medieval coinage in its stress on the functional rather than the aesthetic aspect of the appearance of the coins. The emphasis has always been, understandably, on establishing the mint attributions and chronology of issues, and then examining how the coins functioned in the monetary systems for which they were issued. Those coinages of the greatest monetary importance have received much of the attention, and these by the centrality of their economic role are least likely to display the kinds of innovations or experimentation that would make them of interest to art historians. I would like to take this opportunity to contrast examples of the formulaic common coinages of medieval Europe with some cases where it can be argued that a desire to present the viewer with images of beauty and variety rather than with comforting familiarity qualify them as objects for art-historical consideration and study.[1]

The coinage of ancient Athens offers a classical example of the phenomenon that those coinages with the greatest monetary importance were the least subject to change and visual innovation. In the two centuries of the city-state's greatest political and economic power, as well as artistic achievement in other art forms, the coinage of Athens retained a strong visual consistency.[2] This situation can be contrasted with coinages of much less monetary significance, such as those of Syracuse in Sicily, whose coinage reflected artistic developments in Greek art as a whole and where the artistry of coinage was so appreciated and encouraged that die engravers were permitted to sign their names on their productions.[3]

In early medieval Europe, most of the emerging

I am grateful to Julian Baker of the Heberden Coin Room, Ashmolean Museum, Oxford; Barrie Cook of the Department of Coins and Medals, British Museum; and Elena Stolyarik of the American Numismatic Society for images of and permissions to illustrate coins in those collections. The other coins are in the Princeton University Numismatic Collection, Department of Rare Books and Special Collections, Firestone Library.

1. For an overview of medieval coinage, see Philip Grierson, *The Coins of Medieval Europe* (London, 1991) and, more completely if not as well illustrated, Arthur Engel and R. Serrure, *Traité de Numismatique du Moyen Âge*, 3 vols. (Paris, 1891–1905).The best general introduction to the monetary aspects of medieval coinage is Peter Spufford, *Money and Its Use in Medieval Europe* (Cambridge, 1988). An annotated bibliography of the field is to be found in Alan M. Stahl, "Coins," *Oxford Bibliographies Online: Medieval Studies* (2010). http://www.oxfordbibliographiesonline.com.

2. Ian Carradice and Martin Price, *Coinage in the Greek World* (London, 1988), pl. 8, 108; 10, 137.

3. Carradice and Price, *Coinage*, pl. 5, 70; 6, 81.

states based their coinage on that of the late Roman and Byzantine Empire, especially on the gold tremissis of such emperors as Anastasius I, with its obverse imperial bust and its reverse figure of a winged victory, itself an anachronistic carry-over from the coinage of the pagan era (Fig. 1, Coin 1). The tremissis coinage of the Ostrogothic king Theoderic the Great bears the name of Anastasius rather than his own name, and can be distinguished from genuine products of the imperial mint only by a few details of its inscription and by its style, which is generally finer than that of Constantinople.[4] The Lombards continued the practice of immobilizing the name of a Byzantine ruler and maintained the general iconography of the earlier issues.[5] The style of their issues easily distinguishes their products from earlier ones, at least to the eyes of the modern numismatist. The earliest coinage of the Merovingians had garbled letters and distinctively blundered features. Again, the reference to the authority of the Byzantine coinage was more important in validating the issue than any recognition of the actual ruler.[6]

By the seventh century, the coinages of the successor states had moved away from the classical style of Constantinople but maintained the basic iconography as a validation of the monetary integrity of their issues. Eventually, these successor states of the Western Empire replaced the name of the Byzantine ruler with the identification of the actual issuer, but generally maintained the familiar iconography. By the time that coinage reached beyond the extreme limits of the former Western Empire, the forms had become greatly simplified and the fineness of the gold considerably debased. It was here, in the North Sea area, that the coinage began to depart from its imperial antecedents and new elements were added to the coinage, whose purpose was other than assuring the user of the ancient legitimacy of the issue.

Anglo-Saxon England began its minting with a coin based on the tremissis, called, at least by modern numismatists, a *thrymsa*; at first it continued the imperial imagery. In the seventh century, however, new elements were introduced onto this coinage, many ultimately deriving from Roman and Byzantine prototypes, but combined in a novel way, such as the sheltering of two imperial figures under the wings of the reverse Victory, which harkened back to a fourth-century issue of Rome (Fig. 1, Coin 2).[7] In the course of the century, the base gold alloy gave way to one of pure silver, and the coins come to be called *sceattas*, following a modern misuse of an Anglo-Saxon term for treasure.

Anna Gannon's 2003 monograph *The Iconography of Early Anglo-Saxon Coinage* makes this series unique among medieval coinages in having been the subject of a comprehensive art-historical treatment placing the coins in the context of other media of their day.[8] While earlier scholars considered the introduction of such elements as fanciful animals to the coinage to be the sign of an inherently Germanic influence on the visual arts, Gannon has adduced Mediterranean antecedents for the imagery and compared the iconography and style with such works as Insular manuscript illumination and standing stone crosses.

By the end of the seventh century, the sceatta coinage became common to both sides of the English Channel, with particular examples of disputed mint attribution. Elements were introduced to the iconography outside the range of standard numismatic imagery, such as a bird, whose configuration seems to derive from the obverse bust of earlier issuers (Fig. 1, Coins 3 and 4). As the coinage of the rising emporia of Frisia became widespread, the imagery on the coinage became simplified, and inscriptions disappeared entirely. Reliable attributions of the date and place of manufacture of these issues have been established only in the past two decades, and remain subject to revision. The most common issue is that known to numismatists as the "porcupine sceatta"; its imagery results from the total geometrical abstraction of that of the Byzantine tremissis

4. Philip Grierson and Mark Blackburn, *Medieval European Coinage*, Vol. 1 *The Early Middle Ages, 5th–10th Centuries* (Cambridge, 1986) (hereafter MEC), no. 114.

5. MEC 1.1, no. 298.

6. MEC 1.1, no. 349.

7. D. M. Metcalf, *Thrymsas and Sceattas in the Ashmolean Museum Oxford*, 3 vols. (London, 1993–4).

8. Anna Gannon, *The Iconography of Early Anglo-Saxon Coinage: Sixth to Eighth Centuries* (Oxford and New York, 1993).

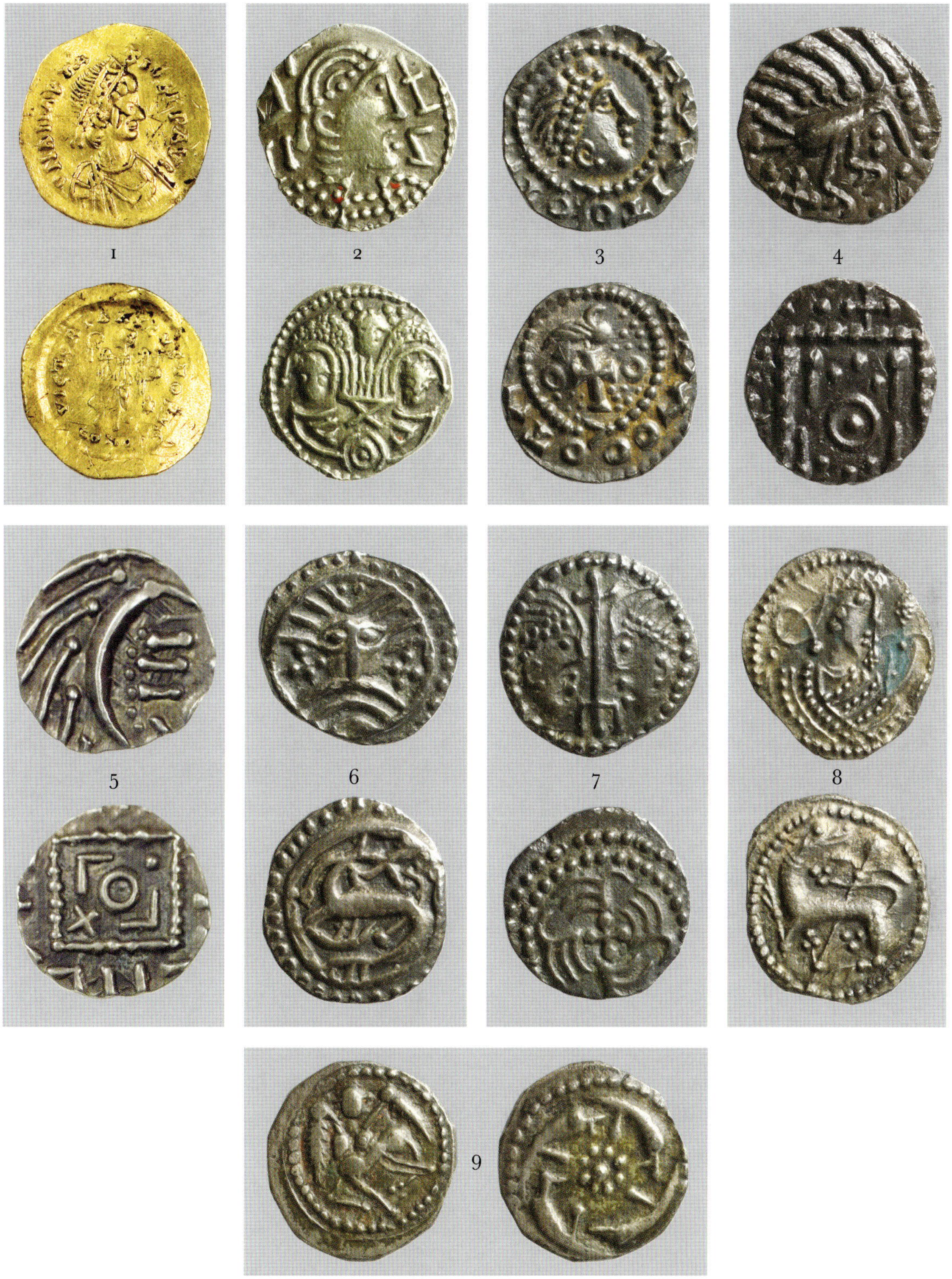

FIGURE 1. The Byzantine tremissis and North Sea coinages of the early Middle Ages derived from it.

1. Princeton 86, gold tremissis of Byzantium, Anastasius I, 491–518.
2. Oxford 79, pale gold thrymsa, Anglo-Saxon England, mid-7th century.
3. Oxford 104, silver sceatta, Anglo-Saxon England, late seventh to early 8th century.
4. Oxford 191, silver sceatta, Anglo-Saxon England, late 7th to early 8th century.
5. Princeton 7806, silver sceatta, Anglo-Saxon England or Frisia, late 7th to early 8th century.
6. Oxford 175, silver sceatta, Denmark, early 8th century.
7. Oxford 299, silver sceatta, Ango-Saxon Northumbria, early 8th century.
8. Oxford 311, silver sceatta, Anglo-Saxon England, early 8th century.
9. Oxford 441, silver sceatta, Anglo-Saxon England, early 8th century.

(Fig. 1, Coin 5). This issue itself became so basic to the developing trade on both sides of the English Channel that its distribution does not allow us to be certain on which side of it any given example was minted.

In some regions north of the European continent, however, new elements continued to be introduced onto the sceatta issues of the eighth century, reflecting an amalgamation of classical and northern motifs and styles common in other media. A Danish example is typical; formerly known as the "Woden, monster" series, it is now termed the "facing head, ithyphallic beast" issue (Fig. 1, Coin 6).

In Anglo-Saxon England, a refined style characterized the appearance of many of the issues of these tiny coins, which are significantly smaller in diameter than the United States dime. Humans, animals, vegetation, and decorative elements mingle in a manner that recalls the interlace motifs of manuscripts (Fig. 1, Coins 7 and 8). The winged female centaur and chain of beasts biting tails again reflect the amalgam of southern and northern influences (Fig. 1, Coin 9). As the heptarchy gave way to the unified Anglo-Saxon kingdom, many of the fanciful elements of the coinage iconography disappeared, though pennies of Offa contrast classicizing obverse bust imagery with inventive decorative elements on their reverse, a continuation of the motifs of earlier sceatta issues.[9] This reign, however, marked the end of the innovative period of Anglo-Saxon coinage, whose forms became more formulaic as the economic importance of the kingdom grew and Carolingian culture came to dominate the West.

On the Continent, the central Middle Ages was dominated by the silver denier, or penny, coinage established by Charlemagne, whose imagery was based entirely on simple and distinctive graphics, usually a simple cross on one side and a very simple image on the other.[10] However limited and evanescent some aspects of the Carolingian Empire may have been, the monetary reforms of Charlemagne succeeded in establishing his coinage as universal in Western Europe and set a visual pattern for coin issues that was to last for the entire central Middle Ages. The conservatism of this imagery is reflected in the denier of Charlemagne's successor four centuries later, Phillip II, whose coinage maintained the obverse cross and bore instead of the reverse monogram an emblematic image of a tower as a pun on the mint name of the city Tours (Fig. 2, Coin 10). This coinage in turn became the basis of issues as far away as Greece, introduced there by Philip's grandson Charles of Anjou and maintained by his Lusignan successors. The rigid, visually immobilized imagery of the Carolingian and Capetian coinages was eschewed in certain other parts of Europe, most notably in the Eastern parts of Germany, relatively recently annexed to the medieval European cultural and monetary world. It was here, outside the mainstream of the medieval monetary economy, that artistic innovation can be found in the coinage of the central Middle Ages, especially in the issues of the Bishops, Abbots, and Abbesses of Saxony, whose rights to coinage derived from the establishment of their institutions on the wilderness edges of the Ottonian world. The twelfth-century denars, or pennies, of the Saxon bishopric of Halberstadt began with an obverse image of the bishop and on the reverse a highly simplified representation of a church (Fig. 2, Coin 11).[11] Even this relatively conventional imagery was more complex than that of the various French royal and seigneurial issues of the day.

The size of Carolingian pennies and their successors, which were smaller than the diameter of a United States quarter, gave little space for artistic invention. An experiment by Bishop Rudolf of Halberstadt in broadening the blank on which the coin was struck, while maintaining its weight, resulted in a piece of metal so thin that the reverse cross ghosted through to the obverse and obliterated its image (Fig. 2, Coin 12).[12] A solution that allowed increased room for imagery was to strike the blank on only one face, resulting in a series of coins typical of twelfth and thirteenth century Saxony and Bohemia known to modern numismatists

9. MEC, I, nos. 1122–1129.

10. MEC, I, no. 735.

11. Hermann Dannenberg, *Die deutschen Münzen der sächsischen und fränkischen Kaiserzeit*, 4 vols. (Berlin, 1876–1905), Ill. 628.

12. Frank Berger, *Die mittelalterlichen Brakteaten im Kestner-Museum Hannover* (Hannover, 1993), Ill. 1255.

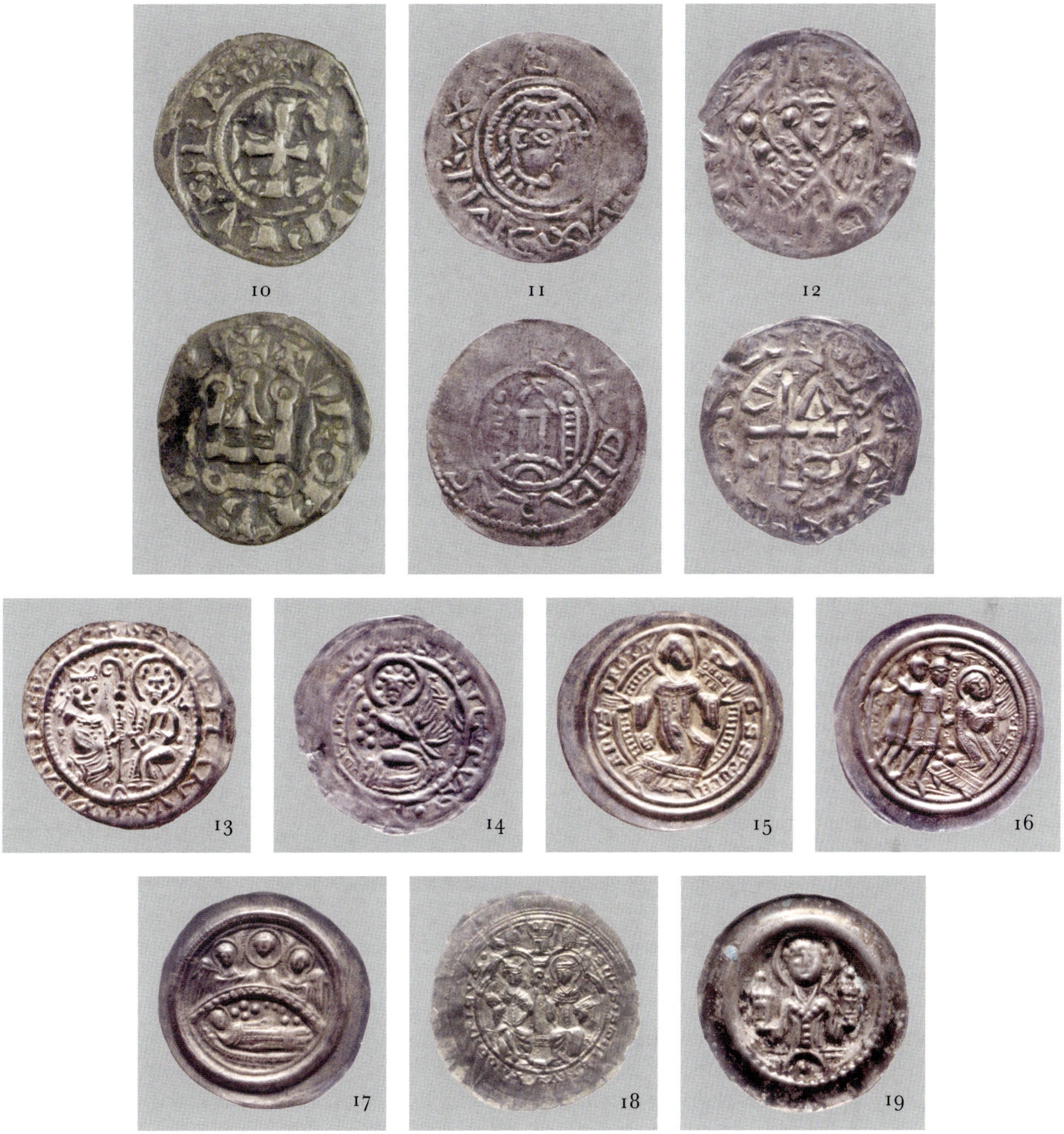

FIGURE 2. Silver pennies of the central Middle Ages and bracteates of Halberstadt.

10. Princeton 1829, silver denier tournois, France, Philip II, 1204–1223.
11. ANS 1960.111.108, silver denar, Halberstadt, Burchard, 1036–1059.
12. ANS 1992.2.7, silver half-bracteate, Halberstadt, Rudolf, 1136–1149.
13. ANS 1930.99.2, silver bracteate, Halberstadt, Ulrich I, 1149–1160.
14. ANS 1970.156.217, silver bracteate, Halberstadt, Ulrich I, 1149–1160.
15. ANS 1970.156.221, silver bracteate, Halberstadt, Ulrich I, 1149–1160.
16. ANS 1955.109.3, silver bracteate, Halberstadt, Ulrich I, 1149–1160.
17. ANS 000.999.17056, silver bracteate, Halberstadt, Gero, 1160–1177.
18. ANS 1955.108.66, silver bracteate, Halberstadt, Dietrich, 1180–1193.
19. ANS 1955.108.100, silver bracteate, Halberstadt, Frederic II, 1209–1236.

as *bracteates*. The resulting coins, at least double the diameter of French deniers, gave scope for more complicated and detailed scenes, such as one in which the bishop is portrayed kneeling before the patron saint Stephen, and one of the saint kneeling before the hand of God, with the stones that represent the instruments of his martyrdom depicted behind him (Fig. 2, Coins 13 and 14).[13]

The artistic ambitions of the Halberstadt bishops reached a height in a series of bracteates recounting the life of the Protomartyr Stephen, a rare case in numismatic history of a narrative sequence in coin issues. These dies show a consistency of style that has been attributed to the hand of a single die engraver, known as the Master of the Saint Stephen Bracteates, whose products can also be seen in the issues of surrounding mints. It is perhaps significant that the only identification provided by the inscriptions on these coins is of Stephen; their attribution to Halberstadt and to the bishoprics of Ulrich I and Gero is based on exterior criteria and is subject to challenge. The bracteate in the Halberstandt series illustrating the calling of Stephen is accompanied by an issue in which the Saint is seen kneeling to the right, while two Jews (identified as such by their distinctive caps) begin to cast stones at him. The final scene of the series depicts the saint in his tomb with the stones hovering above him, while his soul is borne skyward by two angels (Fig. 2, Coins 15, 16 and 17).[14]

In the reign of the next bishop, the coin blanks became even broader, although the extent of their surface struck by a die did not keep up (Fig. 2, Coin 18).[15] The monetary use of such thin objects, more than two inches in diameter and the consistency of aluminum foil, is attested by documentation as well as coin hoards in which they are found mixed with more conventional two-sided coins of the Rhineland. However, the bent and fragmentary nature of some of the bracteates found in such hoards attests to the impracticality of such a format, whose only justification appears to have been to allow more space for artistic expression. As the twelfth century gave way to the thirteenth, the bracteate coinages continued, but the technical and inventive quality of the die engraving declined. Forms became simplified and details were rarely struck fully into the blanks (Fig. 2, Coin 19).[16] Eventually, images on Saxon coins returned to a simplified iconography similar to that of other parts of Europe.

The later Middle Ages presents a third episode in the coinage of medieval Europe where the imagery of a marginal issuer reflected a greater sense of innovation and creativity than that of the major commercial and political centers. The standard gold coin of late medieval Europe was the florin of Florence, issued virtually unchanged for the final centuries of the Middle Ages. It was typically conservative in its imagery; a depiction of Saint John the Baptist on the obverse and a fleur-de-lis on the reverse representing a pun on the name of the city and denomination. Its weight and fineness were maintained in the face of frequent changes in Florentine silver coinage (Fig. 3, Coin 20).[17]

The florin was taken up in other parts of Europe, where the appearance was maintained, if not always the standards. The Aragonese florin was of less-fine gold than that of Florence, and became an Iberian standard in its own right. In the Rhineland and the realms to the East yet another standard of the florin became the basis of the gold circulation. In some places the saint on the obverse and the symbol on the reverse were changed to meet local circumstances, such as the florin of Hungary whose saint was identified as Ladislaus and whose reverse bore the Angevin arms of the ruling family. The style was updated, but the consistency of the basic iconography identified the coin as a florin and remained as a validation of its monetary identification.[18]

The French kings chose to tie their gold coinage into their silver monetary system, rather than keeping it fixed in standard and floating against the silver-based money of account as in Italy. They adopted imagery

13. Berger, *Brakteaten,* Ills. 1268, 1265.
14. Berger, *Brakteaten,* Ills. 1271, 1275, 1297.
15. Berger, *Brakteaten,* Ill. 1335.
16. Berger, *Brakteaten,* Ill, 1360v.
17. Mario Bernocchi, *Corpus nummorum Florentinorum,* 4 vols. (Florence, 1974–78), vol. 2, Corpus 218.
18. Spufford, *Money and Its Use,* pp. 267–88.

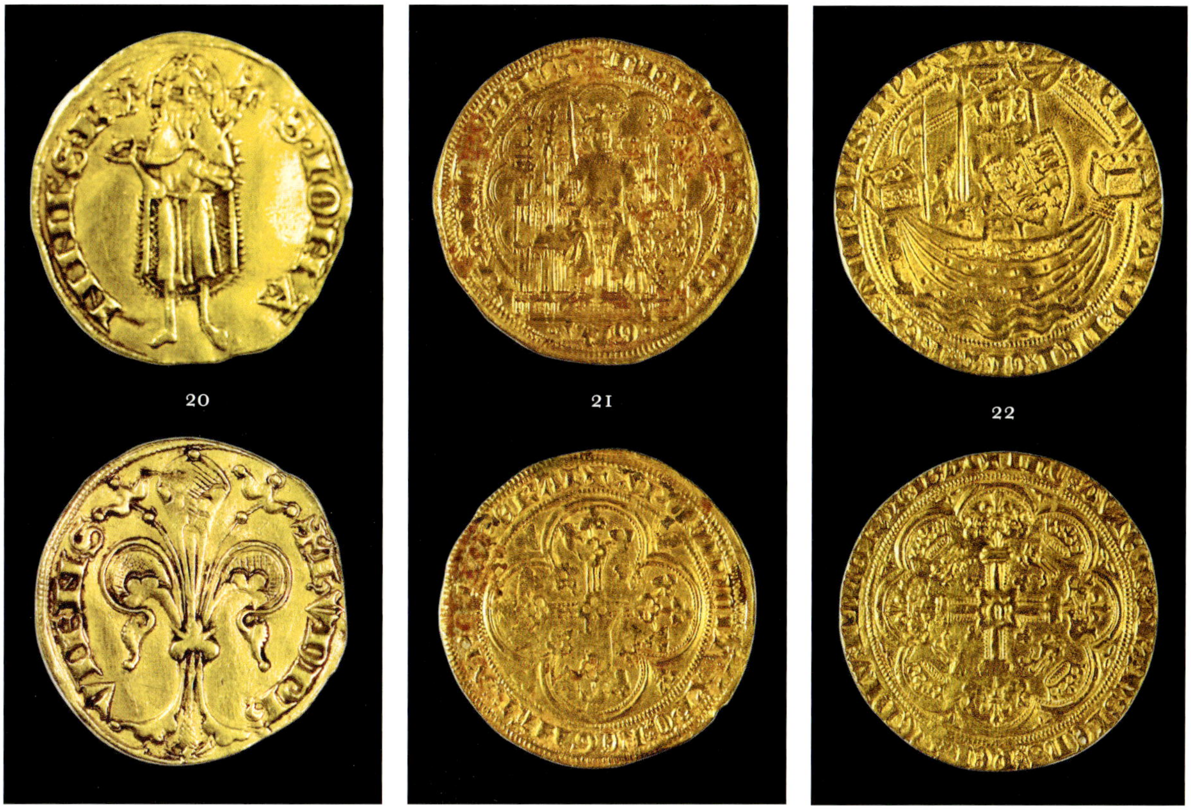

FIGURE 3. The standard European gold coins of the later Middle Ages.

20. Princeton 7804, gold florin, Florence, 1366.
21. Princeton 1118, gold écu, France, Philip VI, 1337–1349.
22. Princeton 7803, gold noble, England, Edward III, 1361–1369.

redolent of Gothic style for the coin called the écu in recognition of the shield in the ruler's hand (Fig. 3, Coin 21). The French silver coinage was frequently debased in the course of the fourteenth and fifteenth centuries, but for the most part the appearance of the écu was altered only by subtle changes in details of the inscription or the ornamentation. The monetary importance of the French gold écu is reflected by its imitation by the Counts of Flanders, in which only the ruler's name, titles, and shield depart from the French prototype.

England also chose to tie its gold coinage into its silver in the form of a coin called the noble on which the diminutive ship bearing the king recalls naval victories in the ongoing war against France (Fig. 3, Coin 22). Though English silver coinage was not debased as the French was, changes in the international ratio of value between gold and silver entailed frequent changes of the weight of the noble, but its appearance was maintained with only minor modifications. The economic relations between Britain and Flanders, based on the mutually beneficial wool trade, led to the introduction of a Flemish version of the noble, again differing from the prototype only in inscription and heraldry.

While the coinage of Flanders reflects its marginal position between the French and English powers through imitation of them both, the gold coinage issued by England for its possessions in Aquitaine, site of much of the actual fighting of the Hundred Years War, departed from that of both claimants and emerged as one of the most beautiful of late medieval series. This coinage has been much less studied than that of

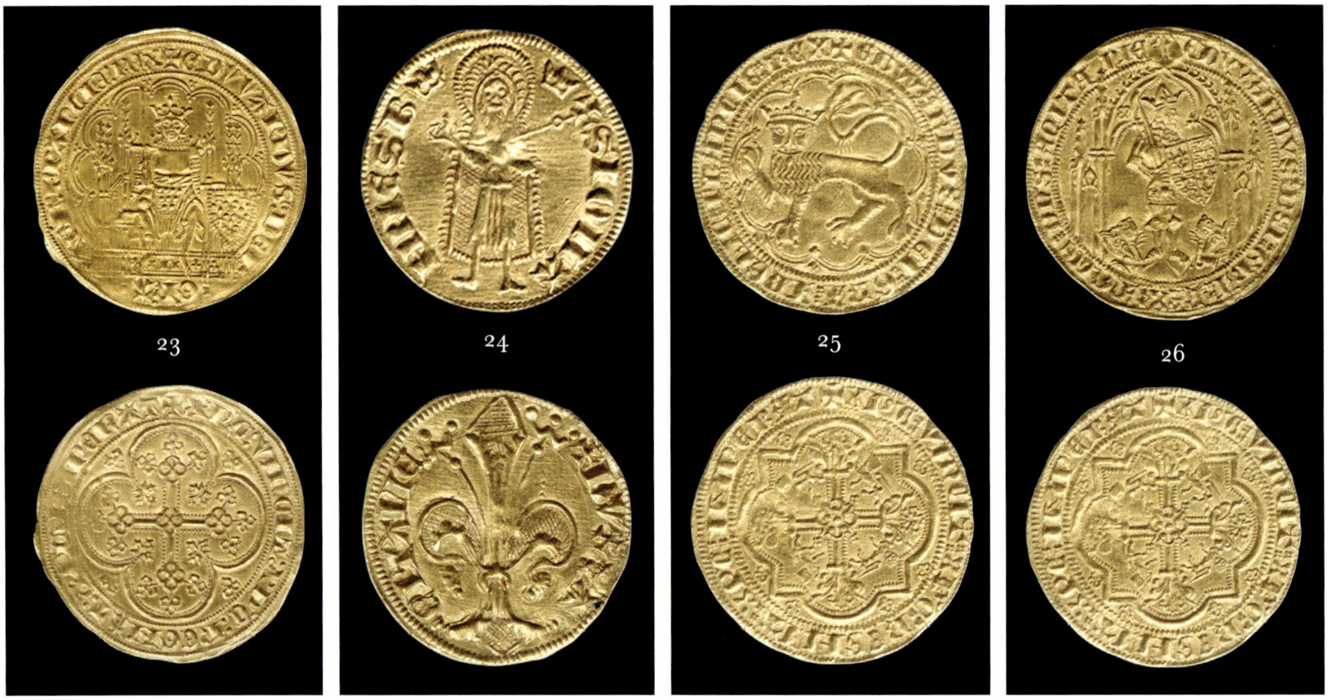

FIGURE 4. Gold coins of Edward III for his French possessions.

23. BM 1840,0403.116, gold écu, Anglo-Gallic, Edward III, 1348–1352.
24. BM 1840,0714.29, gold florin, Anglo-Gallic, Edward III, 1353–1354.
25. BM E3620, gold leopard, Anglo-Gallic, Edward III, 1355–1357.
26. BM 1922,1217.2, gold guyennois, Anglo-Gallic, Edward III, 1361–1362.

France or England, and many aspects of its chronology remain uncertain.[19] The first gold coin of Edward III for his continental possessions appears to have been an écu closely modeled after that of the French kings (Fig. 4, Coin 23).[20] The florin that Edward III issued as Duke of Aquitaine had been thought to be his earliest issue of gold, but is now placed after the écu issue (Fig. 4, Coin 24).[21] It represented a fleeting and ultimately unsuccessful attempt to tie the English continental coinage in with more universally circulating denominations.

The first coin of Edward with imagery specific to his continental holdings is the golden leopard, featuring the Plantagenet heraldic image in defiance of the French crown, which had recently issued its own gold coin with a lamb on the obverse (Fig. 4, Coin 25).[22] The dialogue between the French coinage and the Anglo-Gallic issues continued in Edward's final gold coin, the guyennois (Fig. 4, Coin 26).[23] This was likewise a response to a French issue, the franc à cheval, in which the French king John the Good was depicted on horseback. Edward appears on his Aquitainian issue as a fully-armored knight, advancing through a Gothic gate.

The English gold coinage for Aquitaine came into its own under the rule of Edward's son, the Black Prince, who ruled the region for a decade as his father's vassal. After issues resembling his father's leopard and guyen-

19. The best study of this series, produced mainly as a manual for collectors, is E. R. Duncan Elias, *The Anglo-Gallic Coins* (Paris and London, 1984).
20. Elias, *Anglo-Gallic Coins*, Ill. 33.
21. Elias, *Anglo-Gallic Coins*, Ill. 36.
22. Elias, *Anglo-Gallic Coins*, Ill. 38.
23. Elias, *Anglo-Gallic Coins*, Ill. 43.

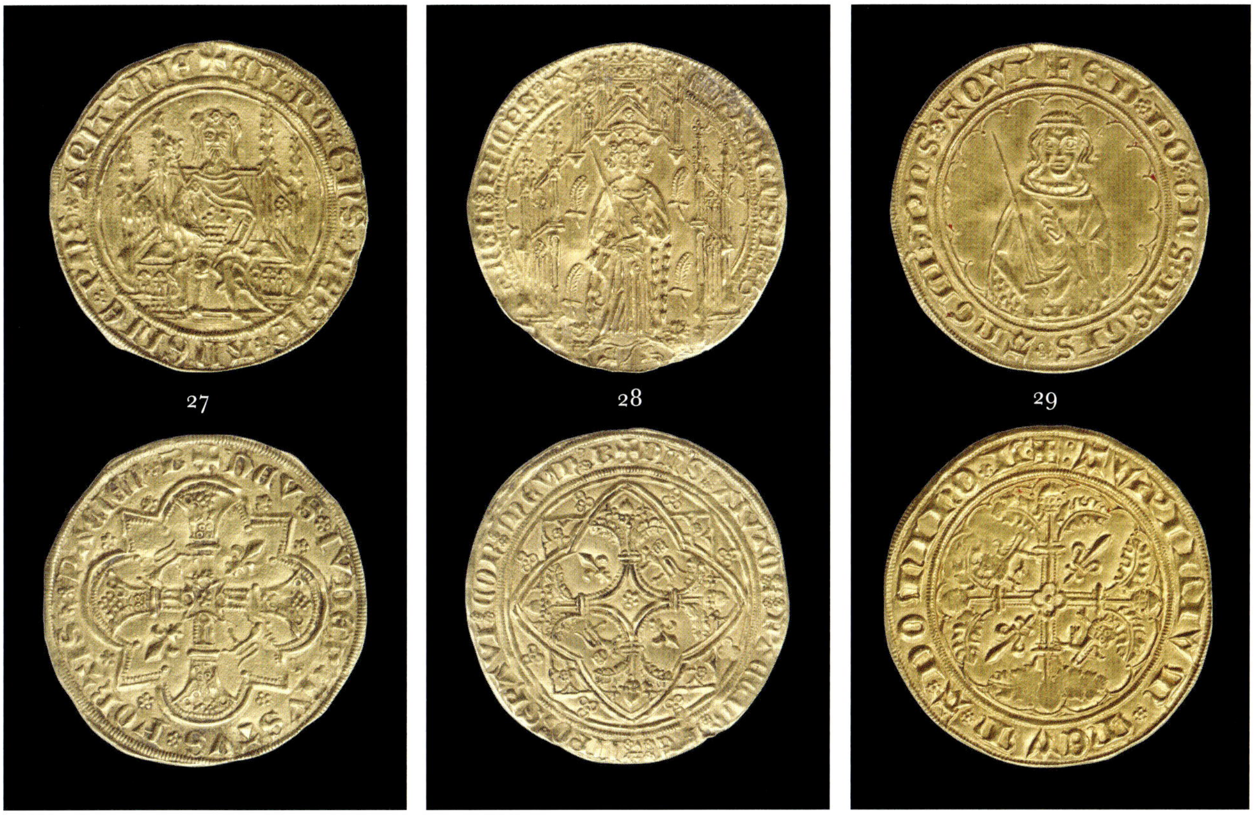

FIGURE 5. Gold coins of Edward the Black Prince for his French possessions.

27. BM E.3651, gold chaise, Anglo-Gallic, Edward the Black Prince, 1373–1372.
28. BM 1935, 0401.6560, gold pavillon, Anglo-Gallic, Edward the Black Prince, 1373–1372.
29. BM 1840,0714.42, gold hardi, Anglo-Gallic, Edward the Black Prince, 1373–1372.

nois, he minted a denomination known as a chaise, in which he is depicted on a large, platform throne, with no shield and, for the only time in his numismatic imagery, unarmed (Fig. 5, Coin 27).[24] On the coin known as the pavillon, the architectural frame was expanded and a sword replaced the scepter (Fig. 5, Coin 28).[25] The Black Prince's final gold issue, the hardi, lived up to its name in the boldness of its design, with the image of the ruler stripped of most of its regalian trappings as well as architectural setting, and his sword commanding the imagery (Fig. 5, Coin 29).[26] In the choice of reverse devotional inscriptions as well as in the obverse imagery, these successive issues differentiate Edward's coinage from those of England as well as France and can be seen as a manifesto of the Prince's independence from both.

At the death of the Black Prince, England lost most of its continental possessions, and did not mint a distinctive Gallic coinage until after the battle of Agincourt in 1415, in which Henry V gained a claim to the title of all of France. In his brief rule there, Henry issued coins following the French models, with the exception of his (exceedingly rare) salut d'or, a coin depicting the Annunciation, with the word "Ave," *salut* in French, above the quartered arms of England, flanked by the Angel Gabriel and the Virgin; a simple Latin cross

24. Elias, *Anglo-Gallic Coins,* Ill. 143.

25. Elias, *Anglo-Gallic Coins,* Ill. 149.

26. Elias, *Anglo-Gallic Coins,* Ill. 161.

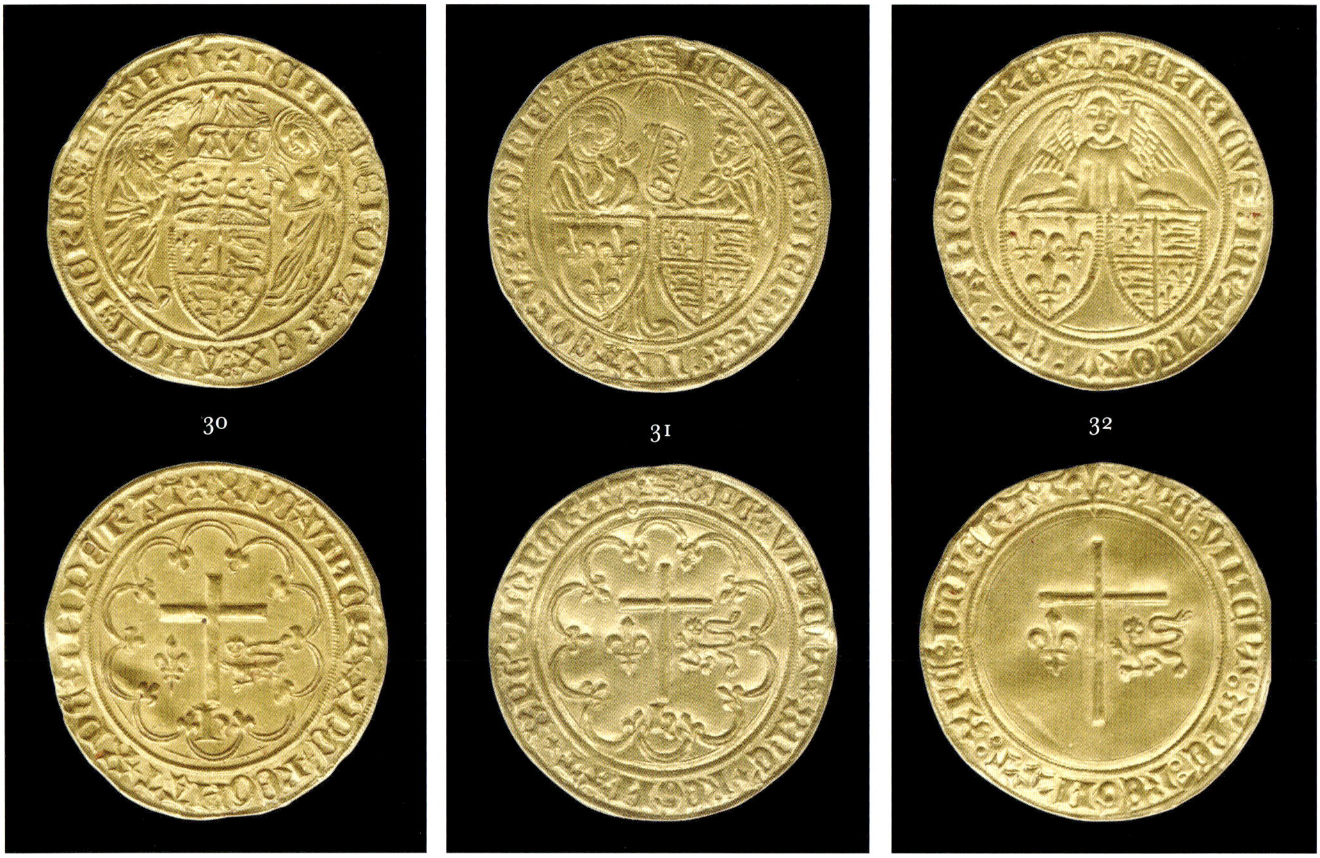

FIGURE 6. Gold coins of Henry V and Henry VI for their French possessions.

30. BM 1896,0604.5, gold salut, Anglo-Gallic, Henry V, 1421.
31. BM 1935,0401.6671, gold salut, Anglo-Gallic, Henry VI, 1423.
32. BM 1840,0714.64, gold angelot, Anglo-Gallic, Henry VI, 1427.

between the fleur-de-lis and the leopard dominates the reverse (Fig. 6, Coin 30).[27]

In 1422, at the death of his English father and French grandfather, the infant Henry VI became monarch of both kingdoms. The coins issued in his name as king of France, the salut and the angelot, are generally considered among the most beautiful of medieval coins. While Henry's English coinage retained the traditional types, in his French realm he issued a salut d'or differing from that of his father in that the Virgin and the Archangel appear above the arms of France and England, respectively, rather than flanking those of England alone (Fig. 6, Coin 31).[28] The question of agency behind this and other types is even more problematic than that behind most coinage issues; when the salut d'or was issued, Henry was a child and his realms were administered by his uncles John of Bedford and Henry of Gloucester.

In 1427, as his troops were massing that would encounter Joan of Arc at Orléans, a new gold coin was issued in the name of Henry, the angelot, in which the angel stands alone above the two shields, and the reverse cross shelters the symbols in eloquent simplicity (Fig. 6, Coin 32).[29] Again, these two distinctive issues can be seen as an attempt to signal a new polity, distinct from both England and France. These English

27. Elias, *Anglo-Gallic Coins,* Ill. 244.
28. Elias, *Anglo-Gallic Coins,* Ill. 264.
29. Elias, *Anglo-Gallic Coins,* Ill. 274.

experiments with innovative coin design were limited to the Gallic possessions and ended with their loss. The coinage of England itself retained its medieval formulaic types well into the Tudor period.

The contrast between the artistically stagnant imagery on the money of major economic powers and the inventive possibilities exploited by other issuers continues to the present day. It scarcely needs mention how little the United States dollar has changed in the century since it achieved its present appearance. Elsewhere, paper money has been a medium for artistic expression that kept up with the artistic styles of the period. The coming of the Euro has stifled the possibility of artistic innovation on more of the world's central currencies, leaving only the farthest periphery to explore the possibilities of numismatic art.[30]

The overriding function of numismatic design in all periods has been to establish the monetary legitimacy of the medium. To the extent to which art is defined as that part of an object which is not functional, art on medieval coinage is to be sought most on those coins whose monetary role was of relatively low importance. If, however, we define art by the efficacy of an image rather than in basically aesthetic terms, medieval coinage can be seen as one of the dominant art media of the era.

30. Alan M. Stahl, *Money on Paper: Bank Notes and Related Graphic Arts* (Princeton, 2010), pp. 63–78.

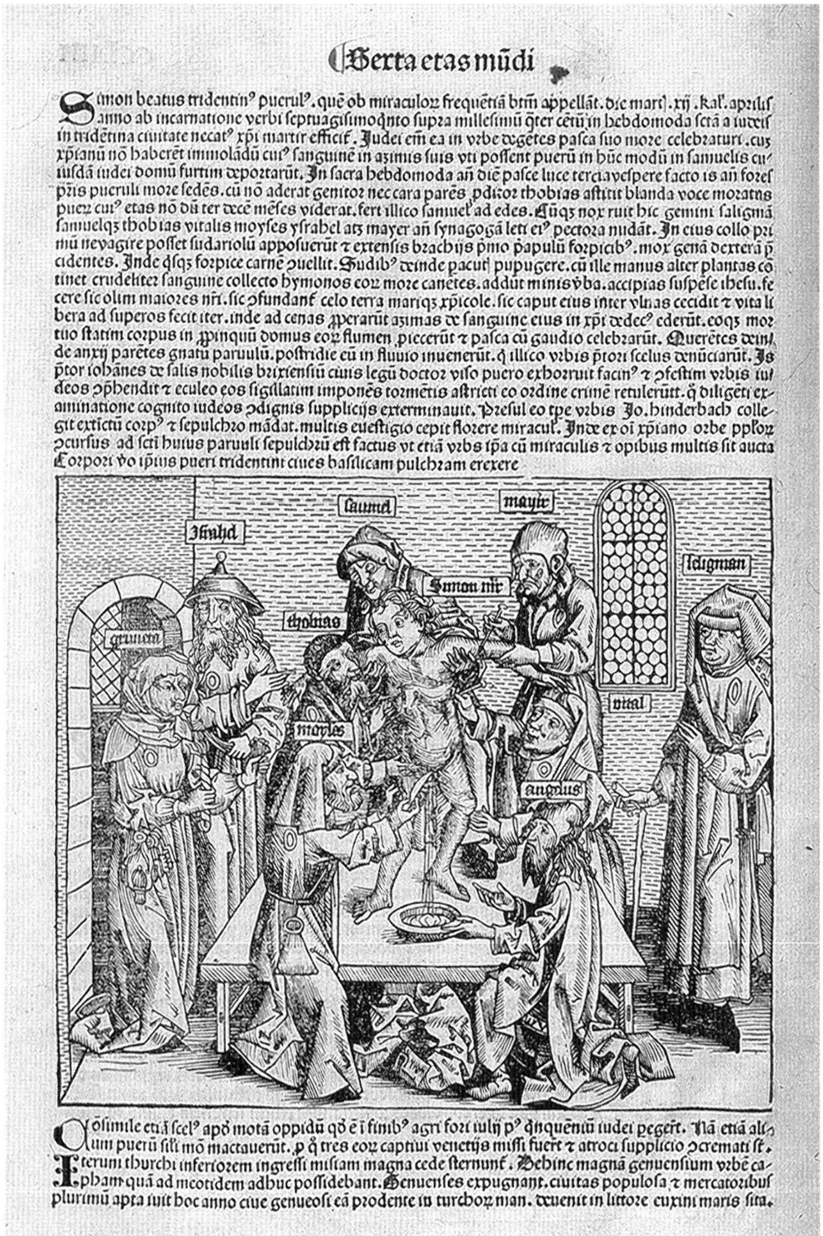

FIGURE 1. Martyrdom of Simon of Trent, woodcut, in Hartmann Schedel, *Liber chronicarum*, Latin edition (Nuremberg: Anton Koberger, 1493), fol. 254v. Munich, Bayerische Staatsbibliothek, Rar. 287.

DAVID S. AREFORD

Print Trouble: Notes on a Medium In Between

LATE MEDIEVAL PRINTS have made some unexpected recent appearances in popular culture, including at least two instances that serve as useful points of departure for thinking about the nature of artistic media and meaning. On 12 January 2011, the "NBC Nightly News" featured a report about former Alaska governor Sarah Palin's response to the mass shooting four days earlier of Congresswoman Gabrielle Giffords and eighteen others. In a video statement posted on her Facebook page, Palin complained that pundits and journalists were exploiting the tragic event for political reasons and were guilty of constructing a "blood libel." In order to explain Palin's inaccurate and seemingly inflammatory use of this term, reporter Andrea Mitchell defined it as a "central myth of anti-Semitism used in the Middle Ages to justify the massacre of Jews by falsely accusing them of using the blood of slain Christian children for rituals." This explanation was accompanied by a montage of images, including two close-up views of a page from the 1493 *Nuremberg Chronicle* featuring a woodcut of Simon of Trent, a little boy supposedly murdered by Jews in 1475 (Fig. 1).[1] This particular depiction was modeled after one of several single-sheet woodcuts produced in Italy and the southern Holy Roman Empire to promote Simon's cult and his miracle-working relics and to advance his canonization.[2] These prints were designed to take advantage of the medium's ability to communicate simultaneously to a wide audience and to the individual viewer, thus serving both documentary and devotional functions. For the producers of the nightly newscast, the use of a printed image served other purposes. It not only provided a vivid illustration of exactly what "blood libel" entailed but also quickly communicated a notion of a remote and primitive medieval past by equating ignorance, bigotry, and grotesque violence with the crude stylistic features of an early woodcut.

Another fifteenth-century print was featured in a more precise historical recreation in the Showtime television series "The Tudors," the docudrama of the life of Henry VIII. The 2009 season included the king's brutal crushing of the Pilgrimage of Grace, the religious rebellion that occurred in northern England in 1536. For the scenes of the rebels, production designers supplied the crowds with banners and badges that were evidently modeled after early prints of the Five Wounds of Christ. Although the iconographic theme is historically accurate, the visual sources might be considered somewhat anachronistic since they predate the events by several decades. Yet, the decidedly medieval choice of model perfectly fits the rebellion's goals of restoring traditional Catholic institutions and practices. The reliance on mass produced printed images also makes sense in terms of the need for a uniform insignia to inspire and outfit the rebellion's troops. Indeed, there is even a scene in which a stack of cloth badges, each apparently printed with the Five Wounds, are distributed to new recruits who affix them to their clothing. Less convincing is the translation of the woodcut models into large banners carried into battle. One prominently featured banner is clearly based on an English woodcut that survives inserted in a Carthusian devotional manuscript now in the British Library (Fig. 2).[3] In the process of copying the print, the prop designers retained all the material specifics of its original book context, in that the banner simply replicates on a much

1. Hartmann Schedel, *Liber chronicarum*, Latin and German editions (Nuremberg, 1493), fol. 254v.

2. David S. Areford, *The Viewer and the Printed Image in Late Medieval Europe* (Burlington, Vt., 2010), Ch. 4: "Little Simon's Body," 164–227 (187).

3. London, The British Library, Egerton 1821. For the manuscript, see *Catalogue of Additions to the Manuscripts in the British Museum in the Years MDCCCLIV–MDCCCLXXV*, vol. 2 (1877), 889; and F. A. Gasquet, "An English Rosary Book of the 15th Century," *The Downside Review* 12 (March, July, December, 1893):

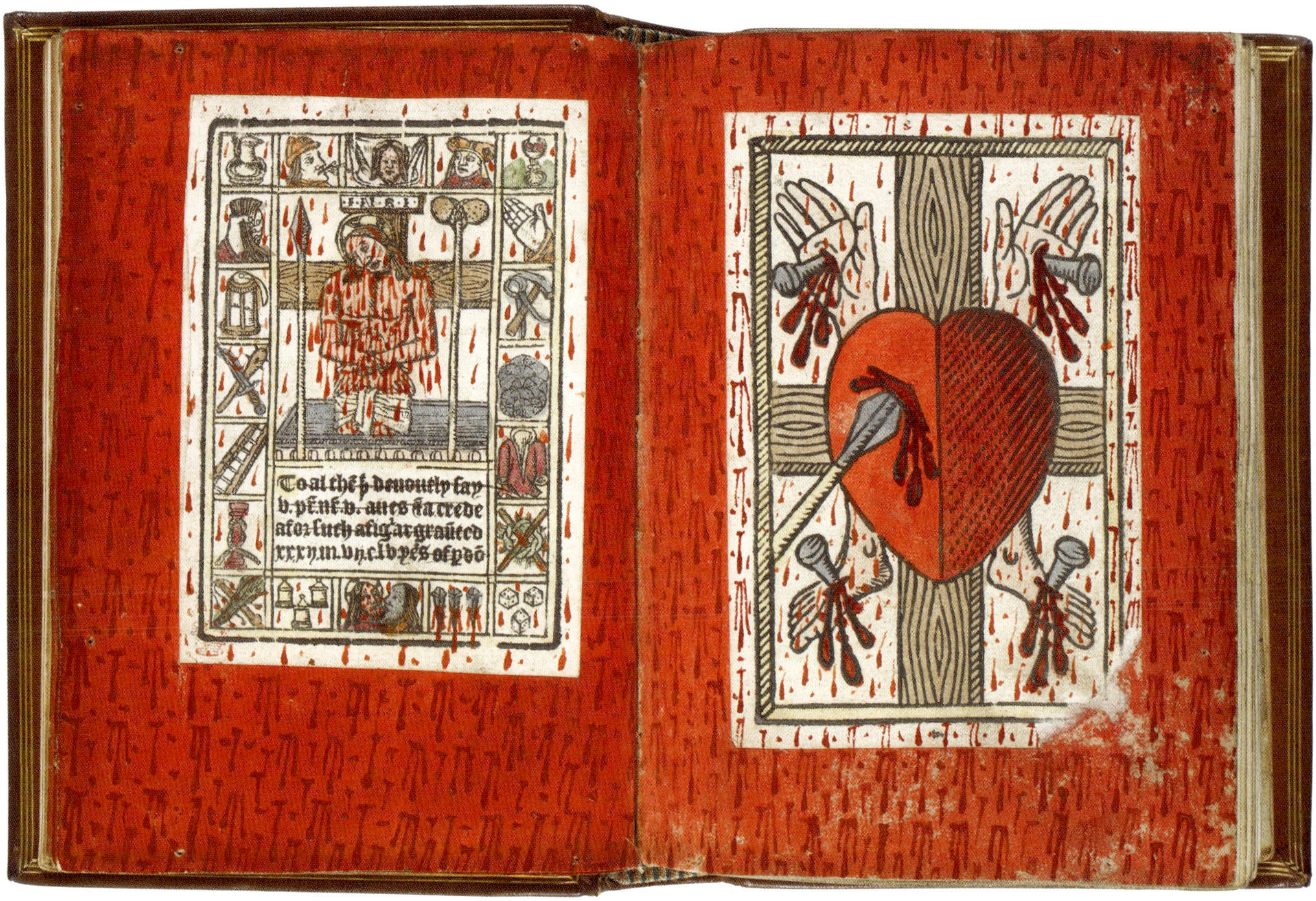

FIGURE 2. Man of Sorrows with the *arma Christi*, and Five Wounds of Christ, colored woodcuts, *c.* 1490 (image: 111 × 80 mm, sheet: 125 × 89 mm; image: 122 × 80 mm, sheet: 135 × 89 mm). London, British Library, Egerton 1821, fols. 8^{v} and 9^{r} (Schr. *868c and *1795h).

larger scale the hand colored woodcut on a sheet of paper glued to a page that has been painted to appear as if it were bleeding. Thus the print's transformation into a cloth-borne image fails to make sense historically or artistically; the result is a strange amalgam of painted and appliquéd elements united by a woodcut's bold graphic lines.

Both examples depend to some degree on the fact that the majority of television viewers are unfamiliar with the history of early printmaking. In the newscast, the woodcut is used primarily as a visual shorthand for a clichéd view of the Middle Ages as a period of irrational hatred and violence; although the particular image is from one of the masterworks of early printed

215–228. For the print, see Wilhelm L. Schreiber, *Handbuch der Holz- und Metallschnitte des XV. Jahrhunderts*, 8 vols. (Leipzig, 1926–1930), no. *1795h; Campbell Dodgson, *English Woodcuts of the Fifteenth Century*, vol. 88 of *Einblattdrucke des fünfzehnten Jahrhunderts*, ed. Paul Heitz (Strasbourg, 1936), 10, no. and pl. 21; Campbell Dodgson, "English Devotional Woodcuts of the Late Fifteenth Century, with Special Reference to Those in the Bodleian Library," *The Seventeenth Volume of the Walpole Society* (1928–1929): 95–108, plus figures (98); entry by David S. Areford, in Peter Parshall, and Rainer Schoch, *Origins of European Printmaking: Fifteenth-Century Woodcuts and Their Public* (Washington, D.C., 2005), 185–188, cat. 49; and Areford, *Viewer and Printed Image* (as in note 2), 77, pl. 12.

books, a key artistic and literary monument of the northern Renaissance. (Early prints often get stuck between conceptions of the medieval and the early modern, as I will explore later in this essay.) In the case of "The Tudors," the production designers can be confident that their audience is unaware of the woodcut model or any chronological disjunction. Furthermore, unlike art historians, most people are insensitive to the defining particularities of different artistic media. This is often the fate of art beyond the walls of university classrooms and galleries. Paintings, woodcuts, tapestries, reliefs, etc., often blur together in the visual imaginations of those unschooled in art history or the experience of the museum. This general uncertainty has been heightened by numerous films and television programs that present works of art out of their proper timeframe, at the wrong scale, or even in another medium. Every so often, I encounter students who are so distant from the material realities of art objects that they will mistakenly refer to a sculpture as a painting or a painting as a photograph, never quite engaging with the differences between media. Of course, this represents a broader and longstanding problem perpetuated by photographic reproductions. Today, the situation is exacerbated by digital images of art available on the Internet and mediated by computer screens. There are even kiosks in museum shops that allow visitors to order digital surrogates of artworks printed on their choice of paper or canvas, at various sizes, and with a selection of different frames.

In this essay, I want to expand on the notion of media confusion: first, by exploring the innate complexity and ambiguity characteristic of most fifteenth-century printmaking, specifically single-sheet relief prints of religious subjects; and second, through some observations concerning the reception and explication of these prints by art historians. As a medium, early printmaking was decidedly experimental and composite in its approach; and this state of instability has long been a source of trouble for the discipline of art history.[4] By accepting these printed images on their own terms—no matter how challenging their visual, material, and contextual contingencies—we are more likely to recapture the precise ways in which viewers engaged with late medieval images, as well as arrive at a richer understanding of an artistic medium that resists clear distinctions and definitions.

* * *

From their beginning, printed images were hybrid in nature, especially in terms of their materiality.[5] In part, this seems to have stemmed from a desire to imitate other media through borrowing material and visual aspects that result in a certain level of simulation. This is most evident in the relationship between early prints and textiles. In many accounts, the origin of printing on paper is closely linked to printing on fabric. The few surviving examples of printed textiles include large wall and lectern or altar hangings, as well as small-scale images produced for devotional purposes in a variety of settings.[6] Most fascinating are the varied techniques through which early single-sheet prints on paper simulate the appearance of woven, embroidered, or painted designs on cloth. The sophistication of such efforts is demonstrated by a woodcut of the Crucifixion pasted to the inside front cover of a manuscript from the Benedictine monastery at Altomünster (Fig. 3).[7] The image was created through several steps, starting with the layering of the paper with a gesso-like substance tinted brown. While still wet, the surface was

4. This notion of "trouble" (reiterated by this essay's title) in relation to the medium of early printmaking is meant to reference the conceptual framework of Judith Butler's now classic book *Gender Trouble: Feminism and the Subversion of Identity* (New York, 1990), which explores the instability of sexual and gender identities.

5. For more on the materiality of early prints, see Areford, *Viewer and Printed Image* (as in note 2), esp. 24–63 (ch. 1).

6. For the fourteenth-century *Sion Textile* and a fifteenth-century altar or lectern hanging, see the entries by Teresa K. Nevins and Richard Field, in Parshall and Schoch, *Origins of European Printmaking* (as in note 3), 62–68, cat. 2; and 118–121, cat. 24. Also, see Teresa K. Nevins, "Picturing Oedipus in the Sion Textile," in *The Woodcut in Fifteenth-Century Europe*, ed. Peter Parshall (Washington, D.C., 2009), 16–37. For a Crucifixion printed on a small piece of cloth and pasted in a manuscript, see Areford, *Viewer and Printed Image* (as in note 2), 28–29, fig. 7.

7. Munich, Bayerisches Staatsbibliothek, Clm. 2936. Schreiber, *Handbuch* (as in note 3), no. 371a; Georg Leidinger, *Einzel-Holzschnitte des fünfzehnten Jahrhunderts in der Kgl. Hof- und Staatsbibliothek München*, part 1, vol. 10 of *Einblattdrucke des fünfzehnten*

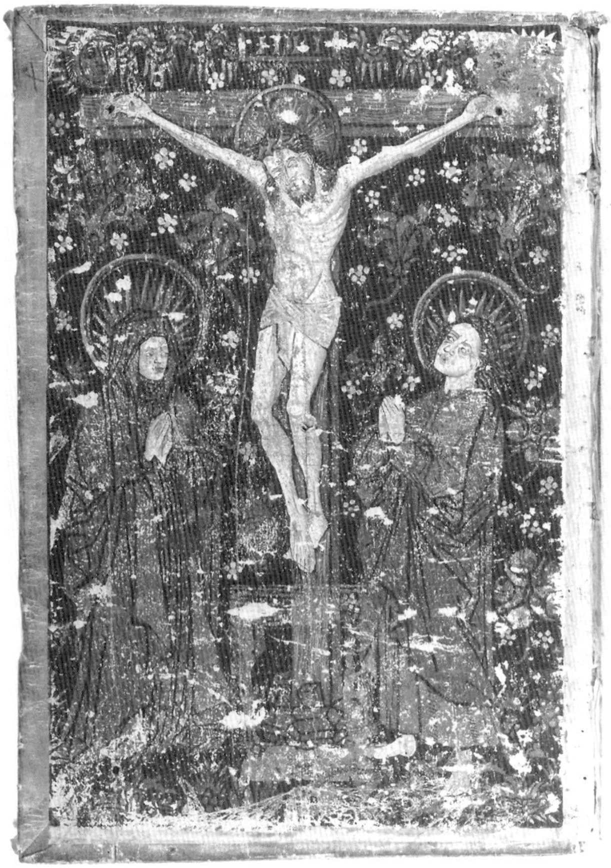

FIGURE 3. Crucifixion, colored woodcut, *c.* 1470 (image: 397 × 257 mm, sheet: 404 × 264 mm). Munich, Bayerische Staatsbibliothek, Clm 2936, inside front cover (Schr. 371a).

impressed with a piece of fabric to create the illusion of a warp and weft pattern, along with its texture. After drying, the image was printed in black ink and then the details of clothing, bodies, and blood were painted in touches of yellow, green, gray, white, and red. In parts of the image, such as Christ's body, the paint entirely obscures the printed lines; and adding to this overall layered quality is the dark background marked with large tapestry-like blossoms and tiny hand-stamped daisies in yellow and white. Experienced up close, the fabric texture creates the overall look and feel of a textile, resulting in a certain level of confusion that allows the pale body of Jesus to appear both painted in little strokes and woven entirely from white threads.

The connection to textiles can also be seen in the various woodcuts classified as tinsel prints.[8] These range from woodcuts that include discrete touches of gold glitter to those that combine gold glitter and quartz crystals in a thick layer glued to the image's surface. Of the very few surviving examples, the tinsel print of the Stigmatization of Saint Francis is especially striking (Fig. 4).[9] Once glued in a book from the Franciscan monastery in Meissen, the image still retains its vivid coloring of green, yellow, blue, and red against a black background, as well as a sparkling encrustation of quartz mixed with bits of gold that completely covers the saint's habit. Since this decorative layer obscures the printed details that define the clothing, these have been painted on top of the quartz and gold. Although not immediately apparent, the building up of the print's surface is meant to imitate the appearance and texture of textiles, specifically the shimmering surface of the colored silk and metallic threads used in embroidered and woven designs. Thus, similar to other tinsel prints, the encrusted layer is fittingly reserved for the figure's clothing. Furthermore, in this visionary scene of Francis receiving the stigmata, the glittering form of his body is an appropriate way to communicate the divine and transforming nature of his experience.

Jahrhunderts, ed. Paul Heitz (Strasbourg, 1907), 9–10, no. and pl. 5; Roland Damm and Alexandra Scheld, "Flock Prints and Paste Prints: A Technological Approach," in *Woodcut in Fifteenth-Century Europe* (as in note 6), 316–336 (322 and fig. 10); and Areford, *Viewer and Printed Image* (as in note 2), 29, 32, fig. 8. The manuscript dates to 1455–1460. For print production at Altomünster, see Richard S. Field, "Woodcuts from Altomünster," *Gutenberg Jahrbuch* (1969), 183–203, plus figures.

8. Areford, *Viewer and Printed Image* (as in note 2), 32–35, figs. 9, 10, and pl. 2.

9. Dresden, Kupferstichkabinett. Schreiber, *Handbuch* (as in note 3), no. 1425; Johann David Passavant, *Le peintre-graveur*, 6 vols. in 3 (Leipzig, 1860–1864), 1: 102–103; Max Geisberg, *Die Formschnitte des fünfzehnten Jahrhunderts im Kgl. Kupferstichkabinett zu Dresden*, vol. 22 of *Einblattdrucke des fünfzehnten Jahrhunderts*, ed. Paul Heitz (Strasbourg, 1911), no. and pl. 25; Max Geisberg, *Geschichte der deutschen Graphik vor Dürer* (Berlin, 1939), 39 and fig. 14; and Areford, *Viewer and Printed Image* (as in note 2), 32, 35, and pl. 3.

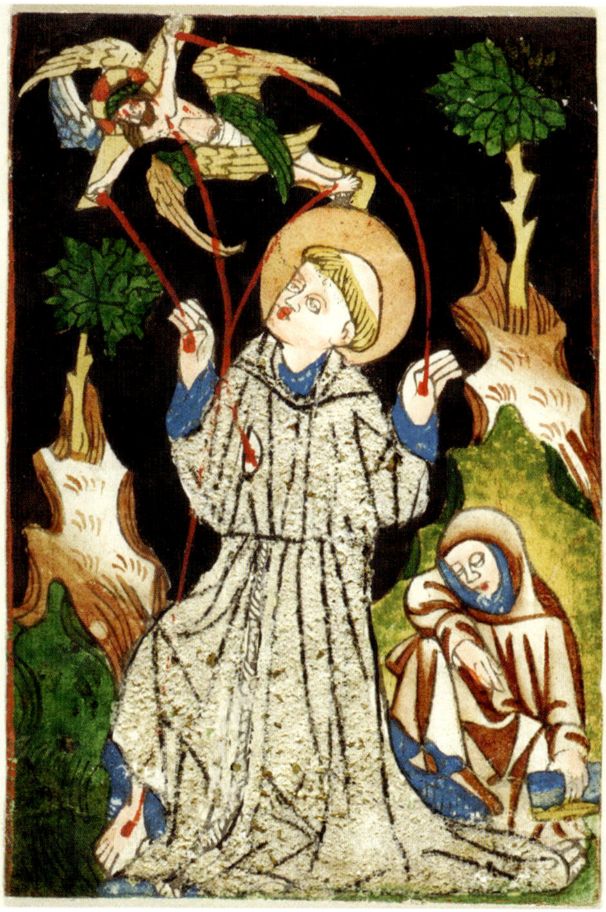

FIGURE 4. Stigmatization of St. Francis, colored tinsel print, *c.* 1440 (image and sheet: 198 × 135 mm). Dresden, Kupferstichkabinett, Staatliche Kunstsammlungen (Schr. 1425).

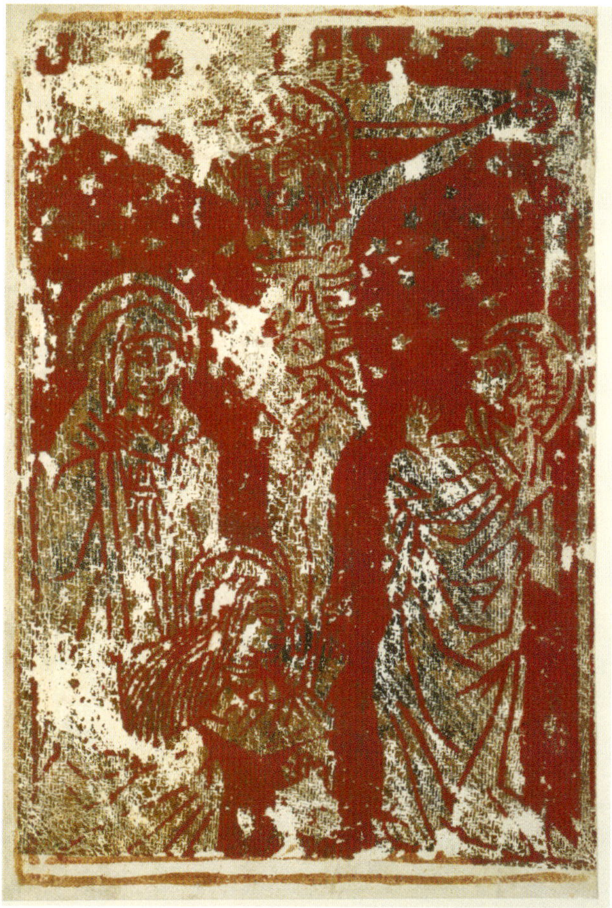

FIGURE 5. Crucifixion, flock print, *c.* 1470 (image: 265 × 188 mm, sheet: 285 × 195 mm). Oxford, Ashmolean Museum, WA1863.1872 (Schr. 2789x).

Among these experiments in imitation or simulation, perhaps the most successful was the so-called flock or velvet print. Like tinsel prints, these are extremely delicate and thus well-preserved examples are rare. Yet, a flock print of the Crucifixion, now in the Ashmolean Museum, remains a compelling image, due primarily to the monochromatic use of red to depict the scene of Mary and John flanking Christ with the Magdalen kneeling in front (Fig. 5).[10] However, most of the print's original visual effects have altered over time. As confirmed by the recent work of Roland Damm and Alexandra Scheld, the flock print of the Crucifixion began with a paper sheet layered with a metallic foil, made mainly of tin, affixed with an amber-colored binder.[11] Next, the sheet was impressed with a piece of fabric to simulate the texture of woven cloth and coated with an

10. Oxford, Ashmolean Museum, WA 1863.1872. Schreiber, *Handbuch* (as in note 3), no. 2789x; Campbell Dodgson, *Woodcuts of the Fifteenth Century in the Ashmolean Museum* (Oxford, 1929), 9–11, no. 1 and frontispiece; and Areford, *Viewer and Printed Image* (as in note 2), 34–36, and pl. 4. For the other known flock prints, see Arthur M. Hind, *An Introduction to a History of Woodcut*, 2 vols. (New York, 1935; reprint 1963), 172. One of the best-preserved flock prints is *St. George and the Dragon* (Schr. 2844); see Damm and Scheld, "Flock Prints and Paste Prints" (as in note 7), 316–322, and fig. 1; and entry by David S. Areford, in Parshall and Schoch, *Origins of European Printmaking* (as in note 3), 88–90, cat. 11.

11. Damm and Scheld, "Flock Prints and Paste Prints" (as in note 7), 318–322.

orange glaze that turned the foil from silver to gold. In the final two steps, the woodcut image was printed—not with ink but with an oil varnish mixed with red pigment—and then the wet lines were sprinkled with shavings of red-dyed wool. When the excess shavings were removed, the result was an image that simulated a velvet brocade, with the four figures seemingly made of gold threads against a red background dotted with bright stars. Similar to the tinsel print of Saint Francis, the flock print's raised design allows it to assert a material presence that goes well beyond the decorative. Imagined in its original state, the scene of execution and pain becomes a tactile experience, a perfect focus for the affective and sensual goals of late medieval piety, satisfying both ocular and haptic desires.

Beyond their material strata and its effects, early prints were complicated as well by the ease in which they could be adapted for various functions and in a range of contexts. Hand colored, single-sheet woodcuts were the perfect substitutes for illuminated images, and many were added to manuscripts to illustrate or expand the meanings of accompanying texts. The pairing of word and image could be fairly straightforward, as in the case of a woodcut of the Annunciation inserted in a book of German devotional texts, originally belonging to the abbey of Saints Ulrich and Afra in Augsburg (Fig. 6).[12] With its once golden touches of metal leaf on the halos, vase, and the angel's robe and scepter, the print is a fitting complement to the facing text of "the golden Ave Maria."[13] Long discounted, the book context is now at the center of early print scholarship, as championed by Peter Schmidt, Ursula Weekes, and David Areford and showcased in the 2005–2006 exhibition *Origins of European Printmaking: Fifteenth-Century Woodcuts and Their Public* and its catalogue.[14]

The many ways in which prints were integrated with texts reveal that they were appreciated as more than just practical, cheap substitutes for illuminations. Woodcuts, metalcuts, and engravings proved to be incredibly flexible; they could be edited and reconfigured or entirely reimagined. In a manuscript of hagiographic texts, compiled around 1513 at the monastery at Andechs, several fifteenth-century woodcuts of saints were inserted at appropriate points to correspond with the story of their lives.[15] In each case, the saint's standing figure was cut out of the print and pasted to a folio. The process was far from tidy, as demonstrated by the remains of a woodcut of Saint Benedict, his body roughly trimmed from the surrounding sheet (Fig. 7). Although the page layout is clumsy, the advance planning is evident in the way the lines of text wrap around the figure. Since the print predates the manuscript, its use here represents a recycling, the last of a series of functions. This kind of reuse of prints through the subtracting of certain elements could result in essentially new depictions as determined by their original viewers. A metalcut of the Crucifixion, now in the Metropolitan Museum of Art, has been so radically edited that only four fragments remain (Fig. 8).[16] At one time, the folio on which these were pasted was part of a manu-

12. Munich, Bayerische Staatsbibliothek, Cgm 4594, fol. 152v. Schreiber, *Handbuch* (as in note 3), no. 35b; Leidinger, *Einzel-Holzschnitte* (as in note 7), part 1, 8–9, no. and pl. 2; and Areford, *Viewer and Printed Image* (as in note 2), 75–76. For the manuscript, see Karin Schneider, *Die deutschen Handschriften der Bayerischen Staatsbibliothek München*, book 5, part 4 of *Catalogus codicum manu scriptorum Bibliothecae Monacensis* (Wiesbaden, 1978), 224–228.

13. See Kurt Ruh *et al.*, *Die deutsche Literatur des Mittelalters Verfasserlexikon* (Berlin and New York, 1981), 3: cols. 80–81.

14. Peter Schmidt, *Gedruckte Bilder in Handgeschriebenen Büchern: Zum Gebrauch von Druckgraphik im 15. Jahrhundert.* Pictura et Poesis 16. Interdisziplinäre Studien zum Verhältnis von Literatur und Kunst (Cologne, Weimar, and Vienna, 2003); Ursula Weekes, *Early Engravers and Their Public: The Master of the Berlin Passion and Manuscripts from Convents in the Rhine-Maas Region, ca. 1450–1500* (New York, 2004); Areford, *Viewer and Printed Image* (as in note 2); and Parshall and Schoch, *Origins of European Printmaking* (as in note 3).

15. Munich, Bayerisches Staatsbibliothek, Clm 3112d. *Catalogus codicum latinorum Bibliothecae Regiae Monacensis* (Munich, 1894), 76; and Areford, *Viewer and Printed Image* (as in note 2), 76. The woodcuts of Nicholas, Catherine, Blasius and Benedict are found, respectively, on fols. 18v, 105v, 211r, and 339r. For the first three of these, see Schreiber, *Handbuch* (as in note 3), nos. 1634b, 1320a, and 1282a.

16. New York, The Metropolitan Museum of Art, The Elisha Whittelsey Collection, The Elisha Whittelsey Fund, 60.703.26. See Richard S. Field, *Fifteenth-Century Woodcuts and Other Relief Prints* (New York, 1977), cat. 40; and Areford, *Viewer and Printed Image* (as in note 2), 73 and 75.

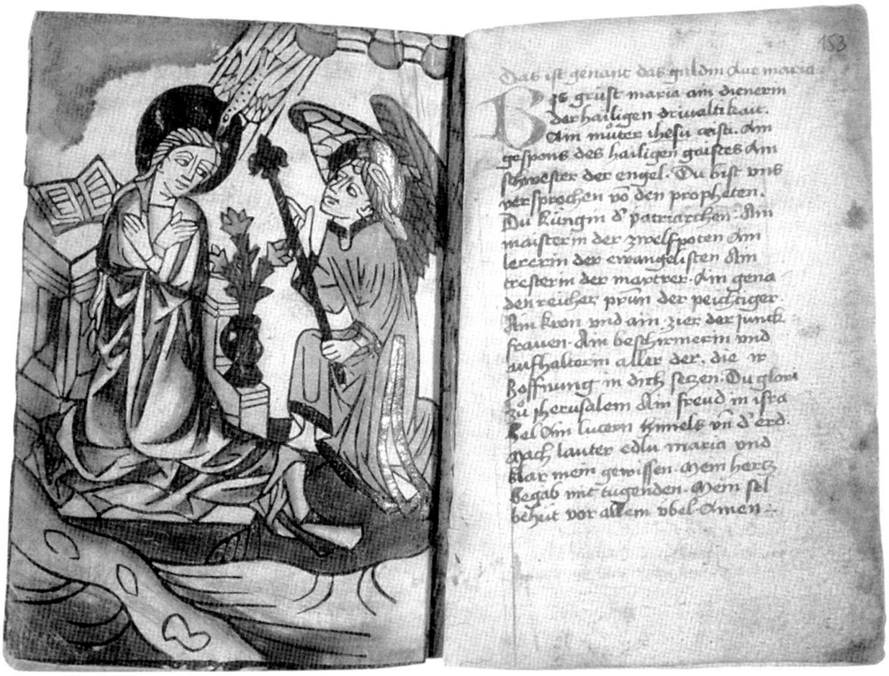

FIGURE 6 (*left*). Annunciation, colored woodcut, *c.* 1450 (image and sheet: 140 × 96 mm). Munich, Bayerische Staatsbibliothek, Cgm 4594, fols. 152ᵛ and 153ʳ (Schr. 35b).

FIGURE 7 (*below*). St. Benedict, colored woodcut fragment, late fifteenth century (111 × 31 mm). Munich, Bayerische Staatsbibliothek, Clm 3112d, fol. 339ʳ.

script owned by the Capuchin monastery at Lucerne, although the specific manuscript is unknown. Cut from what was probably a crowded scene, the three crucified bodies now float above the head and shoulders of a lone, veiled female figure, most likely the Virgin Mary, pasted in the lower left corner. Her marginal position seems an extreme choice, yet it is a fitting expression of physical and psychological suffering and isolation, an interpretation perhaps made explicit by the original textual setting.

The manipulation of prints by their fifteenth-century viewers provides intriguing evidence for a highly individual and creative engagement with the world of images, the specific dynamics of which can still be recovered in some cases. This is especially true of the prints once owned by Jacopo Rubieri, an undistinguished notary and lawyer who lived in Padua and Venice from the 1470s to around 1500.[17] Throughout his life, Rubieri collected various religious prints, mainly

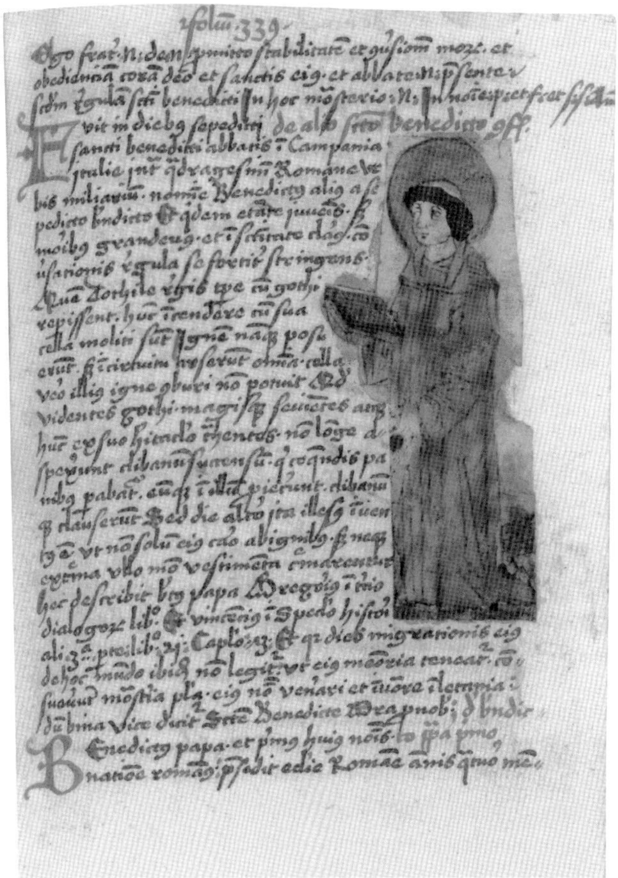

17. See Giancarlo Schizzerotto, *Le incisioni quattrocentesche della Classense* (Ravenna, 1971); Fiora Bellini and Evelina Borea, *Xilografie italiane del Quattrocento da Ravenna e da altri luoghi* (Ravenna, 1987); and Areford, *Viewer and Printed Image* (as in note 2), ch. 3: "The Ship and the Skeleton: The Prints of Jacopo Rubieri," 104–163; and 189–193.

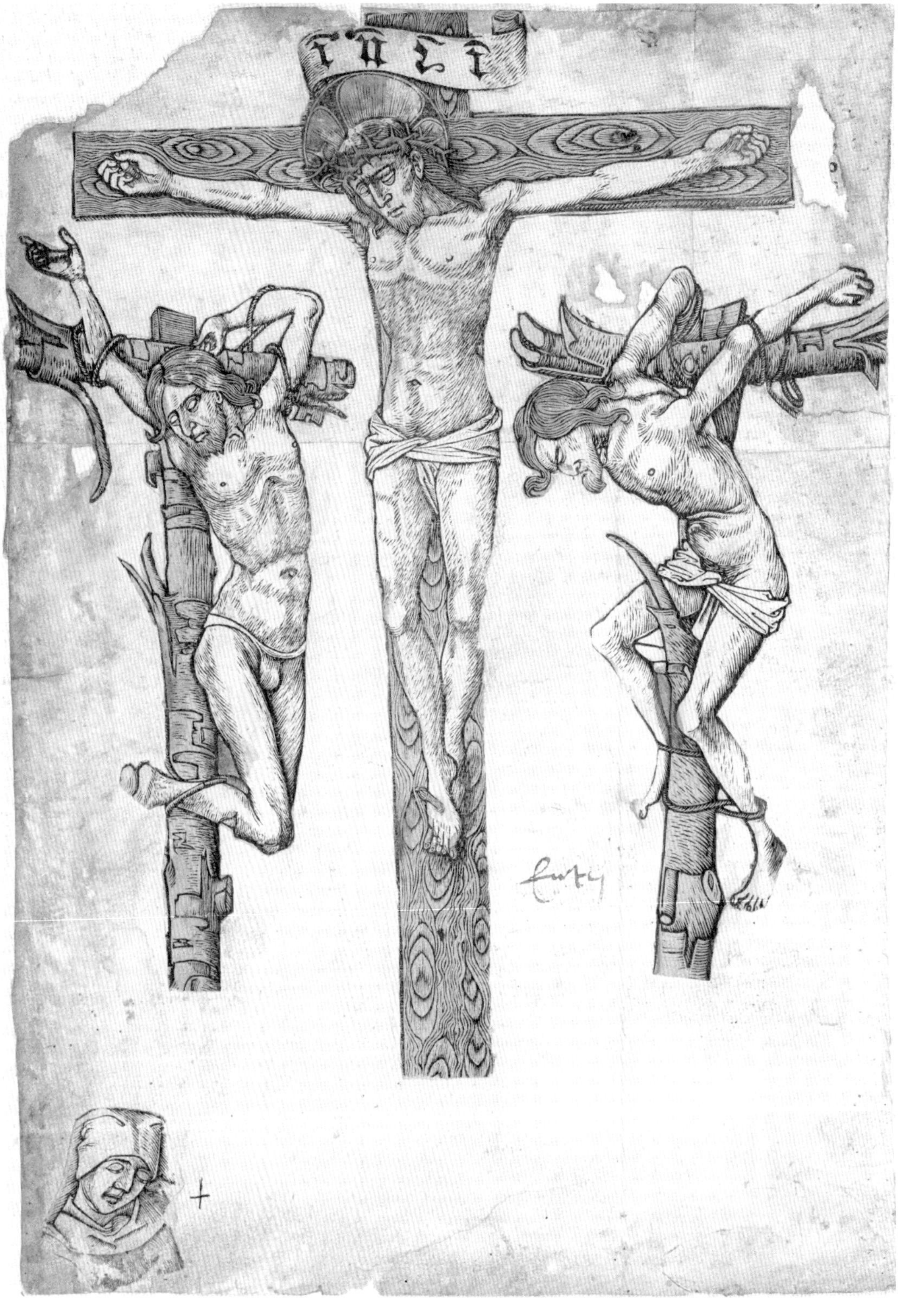

FIGURE 8. Crucifixion, colored metalcut fragments, *c.* 1460–1480 (central cross: 218 × 152 mm). New York, The Metropolitan Museum of Art, The Elisha Whittelsey Collection, The Elisha Whittelsey Fund, 60.703.26.

Italian woodcuts, which he eventually pasted into his legal manuscripts. For him, these simple images were important pious souvenirs of his travels to sacred sites and his devotion to favorite saints. Although the book context of the prints was mainly dismantled in the late nineteenth century, it can be partially reconstructed. In an ambitious two-volume compilation of judicial documents that he titled *Labor gravis*, Rubieri originally inserted forty-six prints, most serving as frontispieces that mark different sections of text.[18] The images were also meant as metaphoric and sacred counterpoints to the rather ordinary and tedious nature of the book's contents. Thus several prints of saints are positioned so that links can be made between the details of their life stories and the issues of the collected court cases, often involving property, inheritance, dowries, and marriage. Interpreted as a whole, *Labor gravis* represents a thoroughly personal integration of texts and images as an expression of one man's somewhat jaded journey through life.

Rubieri's use of prints was an extension of his piety, and he had no qualms about adapting the images in order to create more precise expressions of his particular religious and visual sensibilities. From 1937 to 1938, the restoration of the prints fully revealed the extent to which they were manipulated. Typically, each image was pasted against a dark background and identified by a handwritten label, as seen in a pre-restoration photograph of a woodcut of Saint Jerome (Fig. 9).[19] When removed from its page, the image was revealed to be a collage of three fragments: the saint and his hat, the church, and the crucifix. In other instances, as with a Venetian woodcut of the Martyrdom of Saint Sebastian, Rubieri left the print intact but covered the background, along with the border frame and xylographic text below, with black ink (Fig. 10).[20] He carefully painted around the contours of the saint and his attackers, as well as around every bow and arrow. In addition to his ruthless editing, whether with paint or scissors, the restoration brought to light even more surprising aspects of Rubieri's practice. Hidden beneath the awkward collage of Saint Jerome, a fragment of

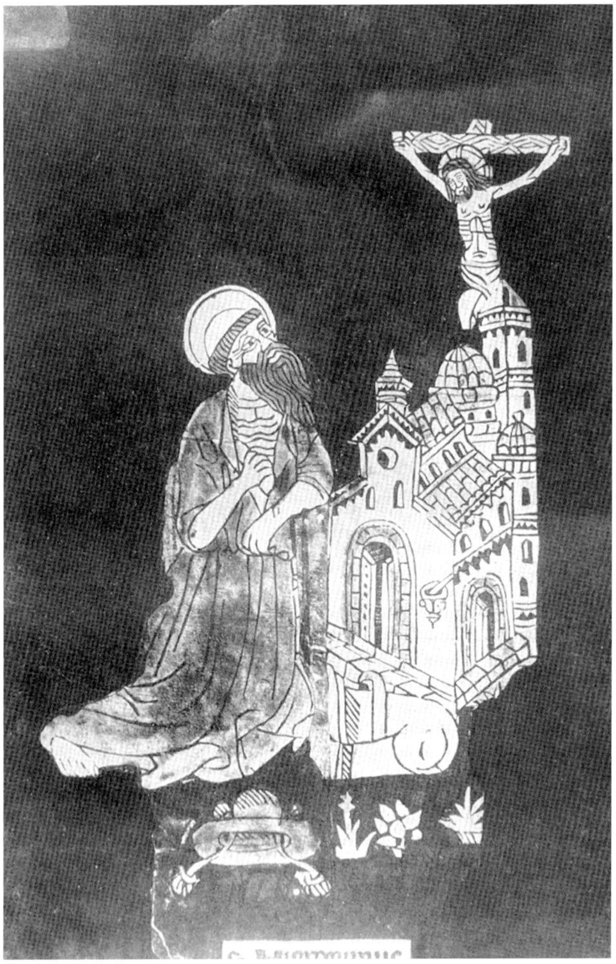

FIGURE 9. St. Jerome, colored woodcut fragments, *c.* 1440–1450 (saint: 173 × 80 mm; church: 175 × 80 mm; crucifix: 70 × 53 mm), pre-restoration photograph, 1929. Ravenna, Biblioteca Classense, 7 (Schr. 1542).

18. The manuscripts are in the collection of the Biblioteca Classense in Ravenna, Cod. 485 IV and V.

19. Ravenna, Biblioteca Classense, 7. Bellini and Borea, *Xilografie italiane* (as in note 17), 54–55, cat. 9; Schizzerotto, *Le incisioni quattrocentesche* (as in note 17), pl. 14, no. 7; Schreiber, *Handbuch* (as in note 3), no. 1542; and Wilhelm Schreiber, *Einzel-Formschnitte des fünfzehnten Jahrhunderts in der Biblioteca Classense Ravenna*, vol. 68 of *Einblattdrucke des fünfzehnten Jahrhunderts*, ed. Paul Heitz (Strasbourg, 1929), 11, no. 18.

20. Ravenna, Biblioteca Classense, 25. Bellini and Borea, *Xilografie italiane* (as in note 17), 46–47, cat. 5; Schizzerotto, *Le incisioni quattrocentesche* (as in note 17), pl. 22, no. 25; Schreiber, *Handbuch* (as in note 3), no. 1676; Schreiber, *Einzel-Formschnitte* (as in note 19), 13, no. 29.

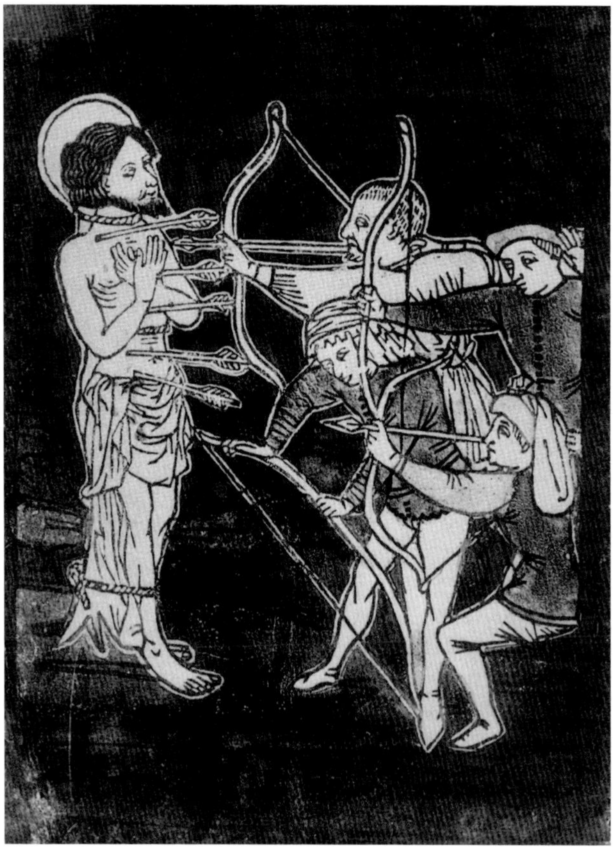

FIGURE 10. Martyrdom of Saint Sebastian, colored woodcut, *c.* 1480 (image: 272 × 200 mm, sheet: 280 × 200 mm), pre-restoration photograph, 1929. Ravenna, Biblioteca Classense, 25 (Schr. 1676).

another woodcut depicting Saint Stephen and Saint Lawrence was discovered.[21] Indeed, the presence of this image was always apparent, since it was only partially covered; in the pre-restoration photograph, the faint outline of Lawrence's torso and halo are revealed near the page's upper edge, although mainly obscured by paint (Fig. 9). Understood in the context of his overall project, these manipulations reveal Rubieri's disinterest in the visual subtleties of setting and space and the conceptual notion of the frame as a window for viewing. Instead, the goal was an iconic and otherworldly image of sainthood, heightened in its legibility and presence. In terms of Rubieri's image layers, we are confronted by a peculiar record of his shifting visual interests, but also proof of the general vulnerability of early prints as they were used and even destroyed in the process.

Rather than subtracting parts of prints, most viewers were prone to make additions, as vividly demonstrated by a woodcut of the Crucifixion now in Berlin (Fig. 11).[22] As with many early prints, hand coloring plays a crucial role here in completing the image in terms of its iconographic, symbolic, and expressive dimensions. In the tinsel print of Saint Francis, discussed above, the fluid red lines connecting the saint and the crucifix-seraph are an entirely painted element that clarifies the corporeal nature of the saint's visionary encounter (Fig. 4).[23] Of course, prints of Christ's Passion were especially dependent on color to activate the reality of physical suffering through the addition of painted streams and drops of blood. When originally produced, the Berlin woodcut was colored with a dark orange-red paint pouring from Jesus' five principal wounds. Later, probably after its insertion in a monastic manuscript, a scribe-viewer "finished" the image in a spectacular fashion by covering the entire body with innumerable slashes of red, careful not to overlap the pre-existing paint. He even added drops of blood to the Virgin's veil. This specifically painterly interaction remains today as a visual manifestation of the print's devotional efficacy. With each touch of red, the viewer implicated himself in Christ's suffering and death, not in terms of a distant event but an ongoing experience.

The addition of hand-painted blood is equally impressive in the case of a woodcut of the Man of Sorrows

21. Ravenna, Biblioteca Classense, 7 *bis*. Bellini and Borea, *Xilografie italiane* (as in note 17), 40–41, cat. 2; Schizzerotto, *Le incisioni quattrocentesche* (as in note 17), pl. 17, no. 7 *bis*. For a diagram showing the original positions of the prints, see Lamberto Donati, "Iter Iconographicum. Ravenna, Biblioteca Classense," *Maso Finiguerra* 2 (1937): 161–169 (164). For more image layers created by Rubieri, see Areford, *Viewer and Printed Image* (as in note 2), 133.

22. Berlin, Kupferstichkabinett, Staatliche Museen zu Berlin, Inv. 81–1. Schreiber, *Handbuch* (as in note 3), no. 480; Paul Kristeller, *Holzschnitte im Kupferstichkabinett zu Berlin* (Berlin, 1915), no. 60, pl. 26; and Areford, *Viewer and Printed Image* (as in note 2), 53–54, and pl. 11.

23. For the hand coloring of early prints, especially images of the Stigmatization of Saint Francis and the Passion of Christ, see Areford, *Viewer and Printed Image* (as in note 2), 36–54.

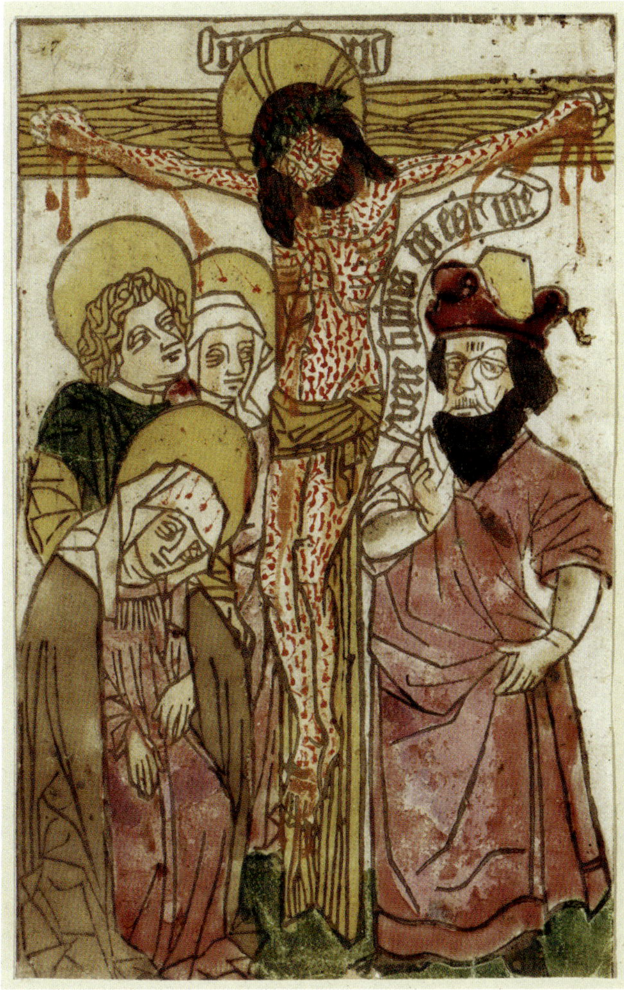

FIGURE 11. Crucifixion, colored woodcut, *c.* 1450 (image and sheet trimmed: 166 × 118 mm). Berlin, Kupferstichkabinett, Staatliche Museen zu Berlin, 81-1 (Schr. 480) (photo: Bildarchiv Preußischer Kulturbesitz / Art Resource, N.Y.).

framed by the *arma Christi* and paired with a woodcut of the Five Wounds, mentioned above (Fig. 2).[24] The prints are glued to facing pages that have been completely painted red and articulated by row after row of bloody wounds. This abundance of blood appears to rain down over the woodcuts so that their paper sheets are fully integrated with the manuscript's folios. Although the images clearly depict the blood's source in the form of Christ's wounded torso and his pierced hands, feet, and heart, the entire book seems to be made from his bleeding flesh. In this way, the prints and their surrounding pages literalize a popular medieval trope correlating Jesus' body and blood to vellum and ink. Later in the manuscript, a passage hints at such a figurative play between book and body specifically mediated by the pictorial: "Here, in place of a book, you shall have the image of Christ suffering and crucified."[25]

The most common additions made to early prints by their viewers were inscriptions.[26] These range from simple identifications of saints to more thoughtful interpretations of subject matter. In the late 1460s, a scribe at the monastery at Ebersberg decided to add two prints to a German/Latin dictionary he had just completed. On the inside front cover, he pasted a woodcut of the Entombment of Christ and on the inside back cover, a woodcut of the Crucifixion (Figs. 12 and 13).[27] Both prints include a Latin inscription in the scribe's distinctive handwriting. Along the upper border of the Entombment, he added one short line: *Omnis Christi am[or] est nostra instruccio* (Total love of Christ is our command), a fitting gloss on the Virgin Mary embracing her dead

24. For the print of the Man of Sorrows, see Schreiber, *Handbuch* (as in note 3), no. *868c; Dodgson, *English Woodcuts* (as in note 3), 5–6, 8, no. and pl. 8; Dodgson, "English Devotional Woodcuts" (as in note 3), 97–98; entry by David S. Areford, in Parshall and Schoch, *Origins of European Printmaking* (as in note 3), 185–188, cat. 49; and Areford, *Viewer and Printed Image* (as in note 2), 77 and pl. 12.

25. For this English translation of the Latin text, see Gasquet, "An English Rosary Book" (as in note 3), 220 and 223. (I have used modern English.) For more on the trope of Christ's body as a book, see the discussion and sources cited in Areford, *Viewer and Printed Image* (as in note 2), 79, notes 56–59.

26. See Peter Schmidt, "Beschriebene Bilder: Benutzernotizen als Zeugnisse frommer Bildpraxis im späten Mittelalter," in *Frömmigkeit im Mittelalter: Politisch-soziale Kontexte, visuelle Praxis, körperliche Ausdrucksformen*, ed. Klaus Schreiner (Munich, 2002), 347–384; and Areford, *Viewer and Printed Image* (as in note 2), 69–71.

27. Munich, Bayerische Staatsbibliothek, Cgm 673. For the manuscript, a German and Latin "Vocabularius ex quo," see Schneider, *Die deutschen Handschriften* (as in note 12), 384–386. For the prints of the Crucifixion and Entombment, see Schreiber, *Handbuch* (as in note 3), nos. 403a and 517b; Leidinger, *Einzel-Holzschnitte* (as in note 7), part 1, no. and pl. 6 and no. and pl. 9; and Areford, *Viewer and Printed Image* (as in note 2), 70–71, and fig. 24.

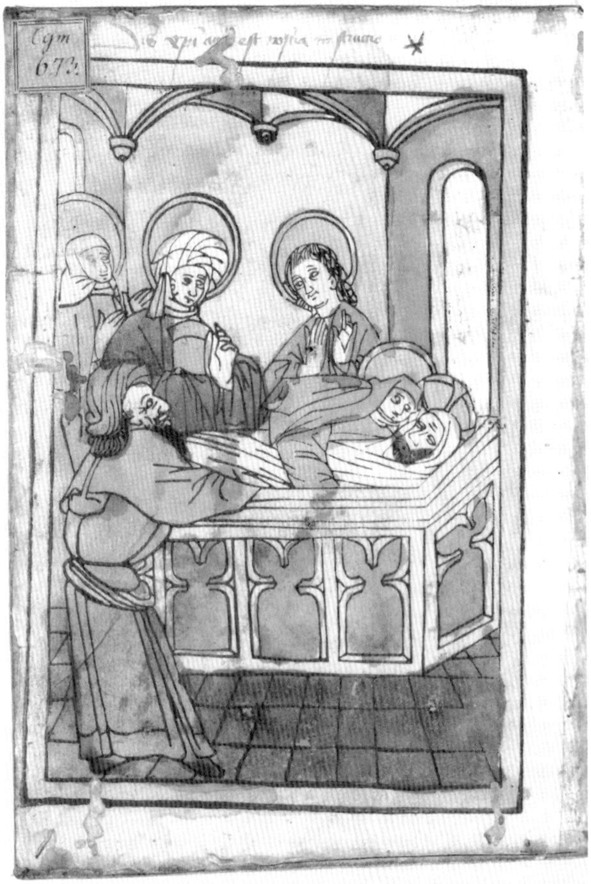

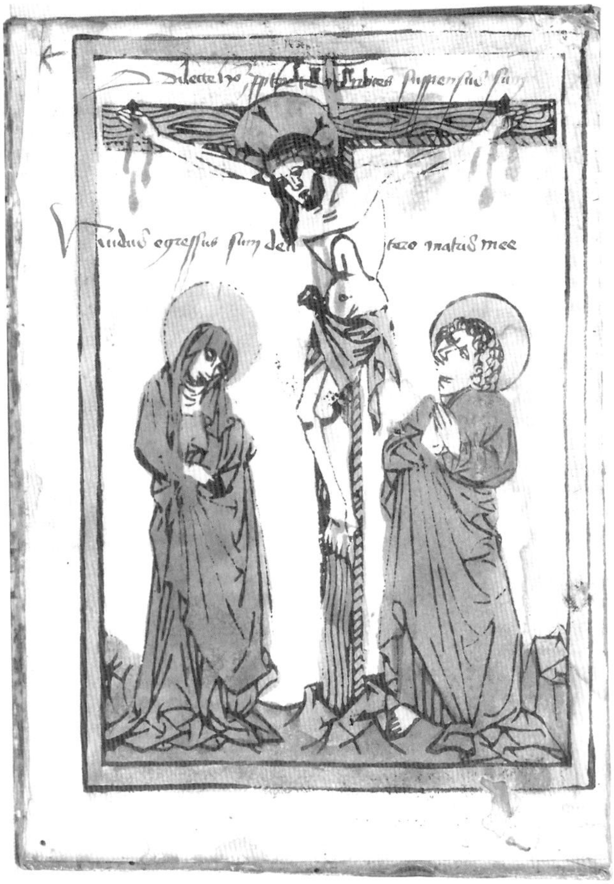

FIGURE 12. Entombment, colored woodcut, *c.* 1460–1470 (image: 190 × 130 mm, sheet: 216 × 152 mm). Munich, Bayerische Staatsbibliothek, Cgm 673, inside front cover (Schr. 517b).

FIGURE 13. Crucifixion, colored woodcut, *c.* 1460–1470 (image: 193 × 130 mm, sheet: 216 × 150 mm). Munich, Bayerische Staatsbibliothek, Cgm 673, inside back cover (Schr. 403a).

son in his tomb. The woodcut of the Crucifixion includes two lines of text. Above the cross-beam, the scribe has given voice to the crucified Jesus: *O dilecte homo propter te innocens suppensus sum* (O beloved man, on account of you, I am hanging [although] innocent). More intrusive is the second line of text, which overlaps the left border and is split on either side of Jesus' body: *Nudus egressus sum de utero matris mee* (Naked, I came out of my mother's womb). In relation to the scene, this is a blunt assertion of the truth of the Incarnation, as well as a touching recognition of Mary's maternal role in the salvation story. But ultimately, these words are a quotation from the long-suffering Job (1:21), the verse continuing: "And naked shall I return thither: the Lord gave, and the Lord hath taken away." Thus they serve as a typological interpretation of Christ's nakedness, suffering, and willing sacrifice. Furthermore, the positioning of the line is also meaningful, as the word *u* | *tero* (womb) is broken as the text seems to pass through the torso at the level of the side wound. This correlation of wound and womb is suggestive of the notion that Jesus gave birth to the church at the moment of his death.[28]

Although the book context has become a rich site for recent investigation, it was clearly only one of many

28. See Caroline Walker Bynum, "The Body of Christ in the Later Middle Ages: A Reply to Leo Steinberg," in Caroline Walker Bynum, *Fragmentation and Redemption: Essays on Gender and the Human Body in Medieval Religion* (New York, 1991), 79–117

possible settings for the use of prints. In recent years, attention has also been focused on prints that survive affixed to various boxes.[29] Most of these are late fifteenth-century French woodcuts glued inside the lids of so-called *coffrets de messagers*, leather and metal-clad wooden boxes complete with locks and metal loops on the sides for straps. Their functions, however, probably included more than just the transport of correspondence. Indeed, the surviving boxes exhibit a range of sizes that make them perfect for holding most books of standard dimensions (quarto, octavo, and smaller), as well as other objects.[30] Moreover, when propped open, the decorated lids provided an instant focus of devotion; and when closed, the contents potentially benefited from the apotropaic aura of the image.

A more complex, multimedia integration of a printed image and a box is found in a little-known example preserved in Berlin's Kupferstichkabinett.[31] In this case, the box is constructed of wood covered in dark reddish leather with a front lock and metal strips accenting the edges and sides. The outer lid consists of a leather panel embossed with the standing figure of Saint Albert of Trapani, clothed in a monastic habit and holding a book and lily in his left hand and a crucifix in his right (Fig. 14). One of the most revered Carmelite saints, Albert died in Messina, Sicily, in 1307.[32] Although his cult flourished from the time of his death, it was sanctioned by Pope Callixtus III only in 1454; and his official canonization was approved by Pope Sixtus IV in 1476. When opened, the box's inner lid reveals a second image: a painting of the saint in the same pose and with the same attributes but framed by seven miraculous episodes from his life (Fig. 15). Turning his head, as in the embossed image, Albert glances down at a kneeling monk, apparently meant to represent the owner of the box: a "brother Conrad" who asks the saint to pray for him (according to the inscribed banderole over his head). Also inside the box, there is yet another very similar depiction of Saint Albert: a single-sheet Italian woodcut glued to the bottom and framed by a scrolling vine motif against a red background (Fig. 16).[33] Despite being stained and abraded from use, a xylographic inscription at the print's upper edge is still legible: *Be[atus] Albertus de Tripanoving.*

Thus the Berlin box preserves an intriguing triple presentation of Saint Albert, each with almost the exact same features and pose but in different media: a highly tactile, monochromatic embossed image; a richly colored painting with sturdy three-dimensional figures posed against a gold background; and a bold and simply colored single-sheet woodcut. It is tempting to see these markedly contrasting visual modes as reflective of different periods in the promotion of the saint's cult over the course of the fifteenth century, from the development of his life story to the fixing of his official, iconic image. Both the embossed lid and the painting depict Albert with a full halo; and the painting's captions all refer to him as "saint." However, in the woodcut, which has been dated to around 1470, the figure is inscribed with the abbreviation for *beatus* and his head is surrounded by a scalloped halo marked by rays of light, often signifying someone who has yet to fully achieve sainthood.[34] As with other similar Italian prints, the woodcut may have been produced not only

---

(97). For another discussion of the print and its inscription, see Schmidt, "Beschriebene Bilder" (as in note 26), 361.

29. Entry by Peter Parshall, in Parshall and Schoch, *Origins of European Printmaking* (as in note 3), 171–173, cat. 42; and Suzanne Karr Schmidt, *Altered and Adorned: Using Renaissance Prints in Daily Life* (Chicago, Ill., 2011), 48, 57–59, figs. 38, 49, and 50. Also, see *Collection Marie-Thérèse et André Jammes: Coffrets de Messagers, Images du Moyen Âge et Traditions Populaires* (Paris, 2007), lots 11–32, 38–41; and Sandra Hindman, *Pen to Press, Paint to Print: Manuscript Illumination and Early Prints in the Age of Gutenberg* (Paris, 2009), 52–67, nos. 17–22.

30. See Schmidt, *Altered and Adorned* (as in note 29), 59.

31. Berlin, Kupferstichkabinett, Staatliche Museen zu Berlin, Inv. 43009.

32. On the saint's life and iconography, see *Acta sanctorum*, 58 vols. (Antwerp, 1643–1867), August II, 215–239; George Kaftal, *Iconography of the Saints in Tuscan Painting* (Florence, 1952), cols. 13–14; George Kaftal, *Iconography of the Saints in Central and South Italian Schools of Painting* (Florence, 1965), cols. 31–34; George Kaftal, *Iconography of the Saints in the Painting of North West Italy* (Florence, 1985), cols. 21–22; *Lexikon der Christlichen Ikonographie*, ed. Wolfgang Braunfels, 8 vols. (Rome, 1968–1976), 5: 75–76; and Louis Réau, *Iconographie de l'art chrétien*, 3 vols. in 6 (Paris, 1955–1959), 3:47.

33. Schreiber, *Handbuch* (as in note 3), no. 1184a; for another woodcut of Saint Albert of Trapani, see no. 1184.

34. André Vauchez, *La Sainteté en Occident aux derniers siècles du moyen âge* (Rome, 1981), 101–102.

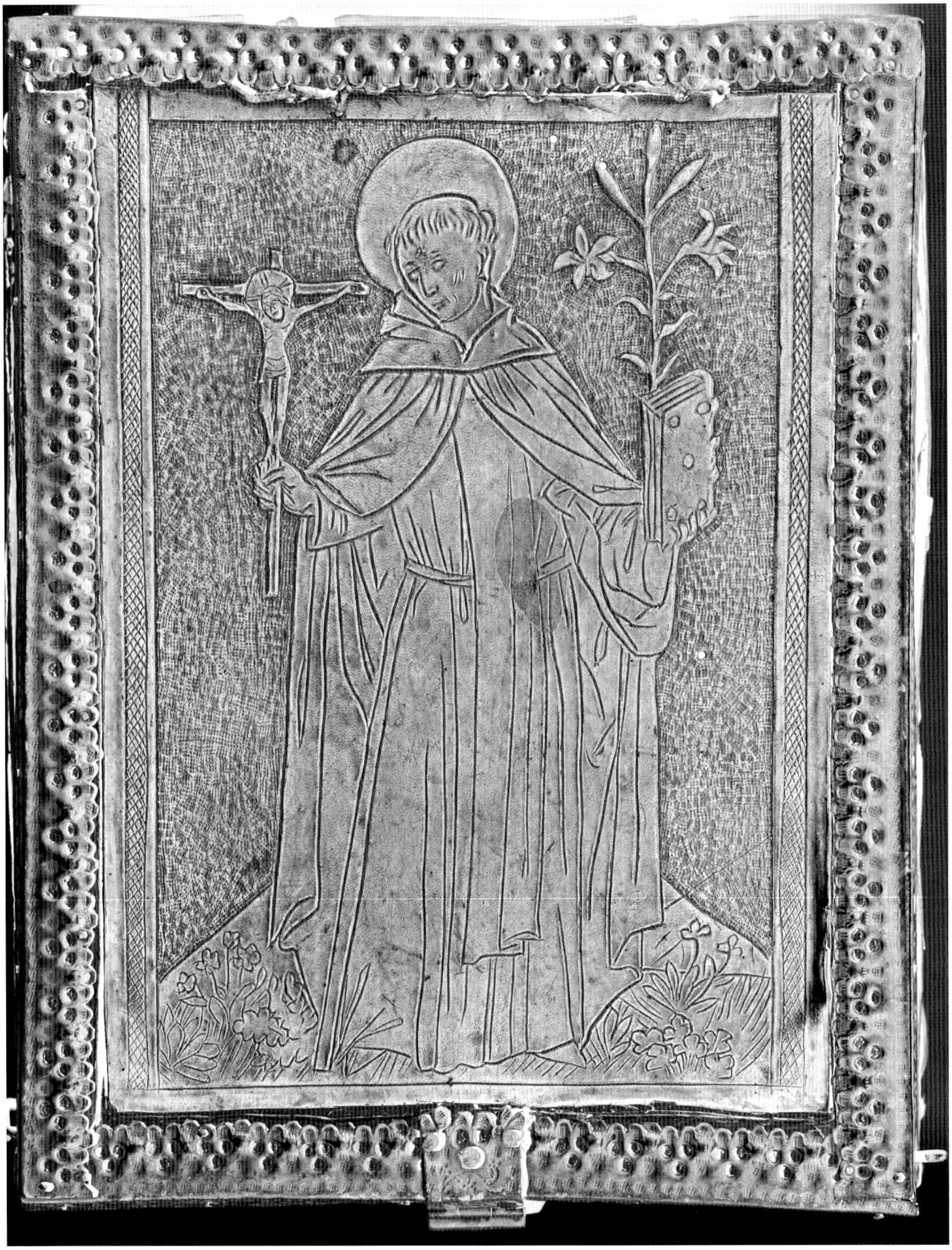

FIGURE 14. St. Albert of Trapani, embossed leather, late fifteenth century. Berlin, Kupferstichkabinett, Staatliche Museen zu Berlin, Inv. 43009 (leather and metal-clad wooden box, outer lid) (photo: Bildarchiv Preußischer Kulturbesitz / Art Resource, N.Y.).

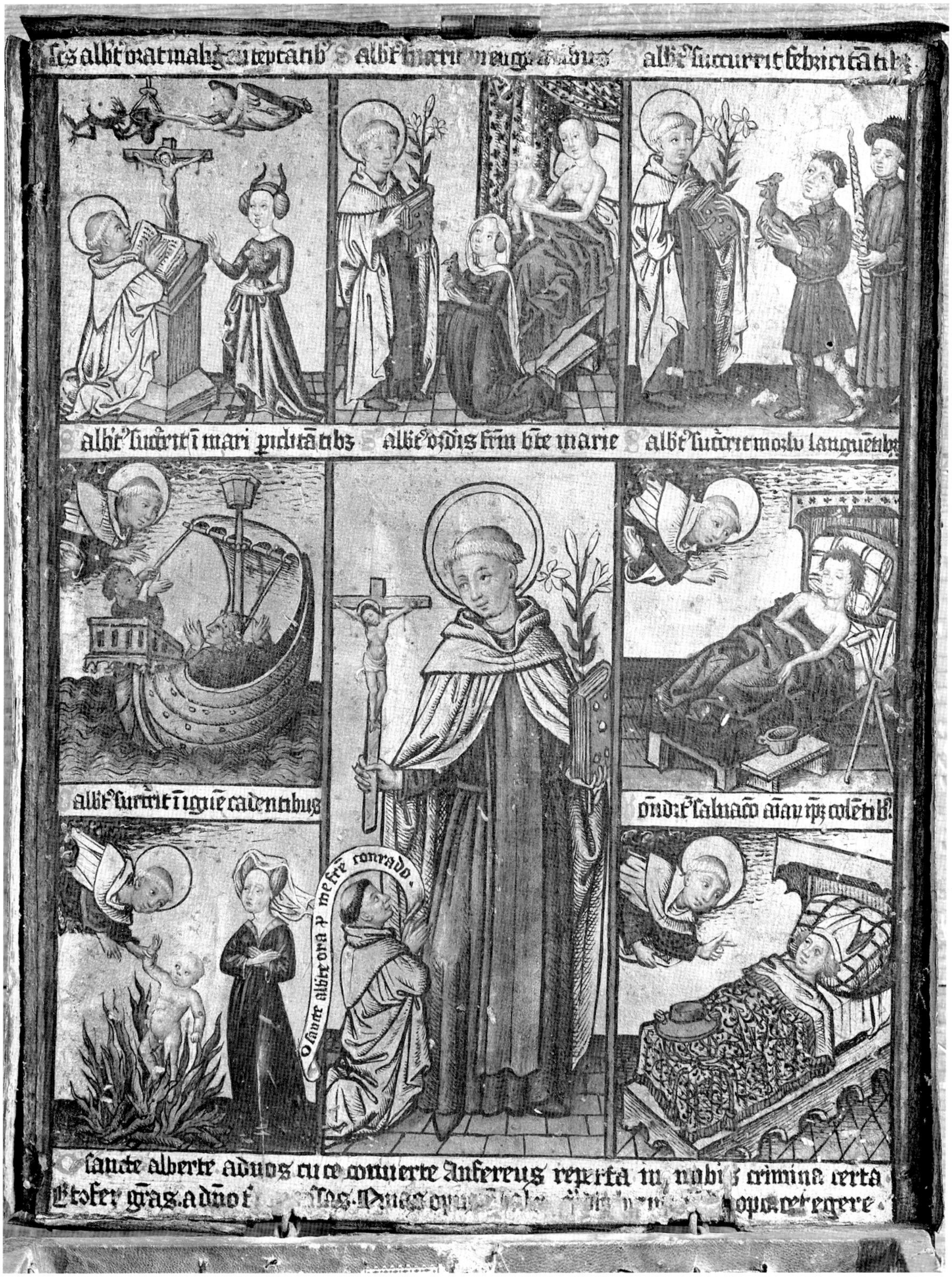

FIGURE 15. St. Albert of Trapani and scenes of his life, painting, late fifteenth century. Berlin, Kupferstichkabinett, Staatliche Museen zu Berlin, Inv. 43009 (leather and metal-clad wooden box, inner lid) (photo: Bildarchiv Preußischer Kulturbesitz / Art Resource, N.Y.).

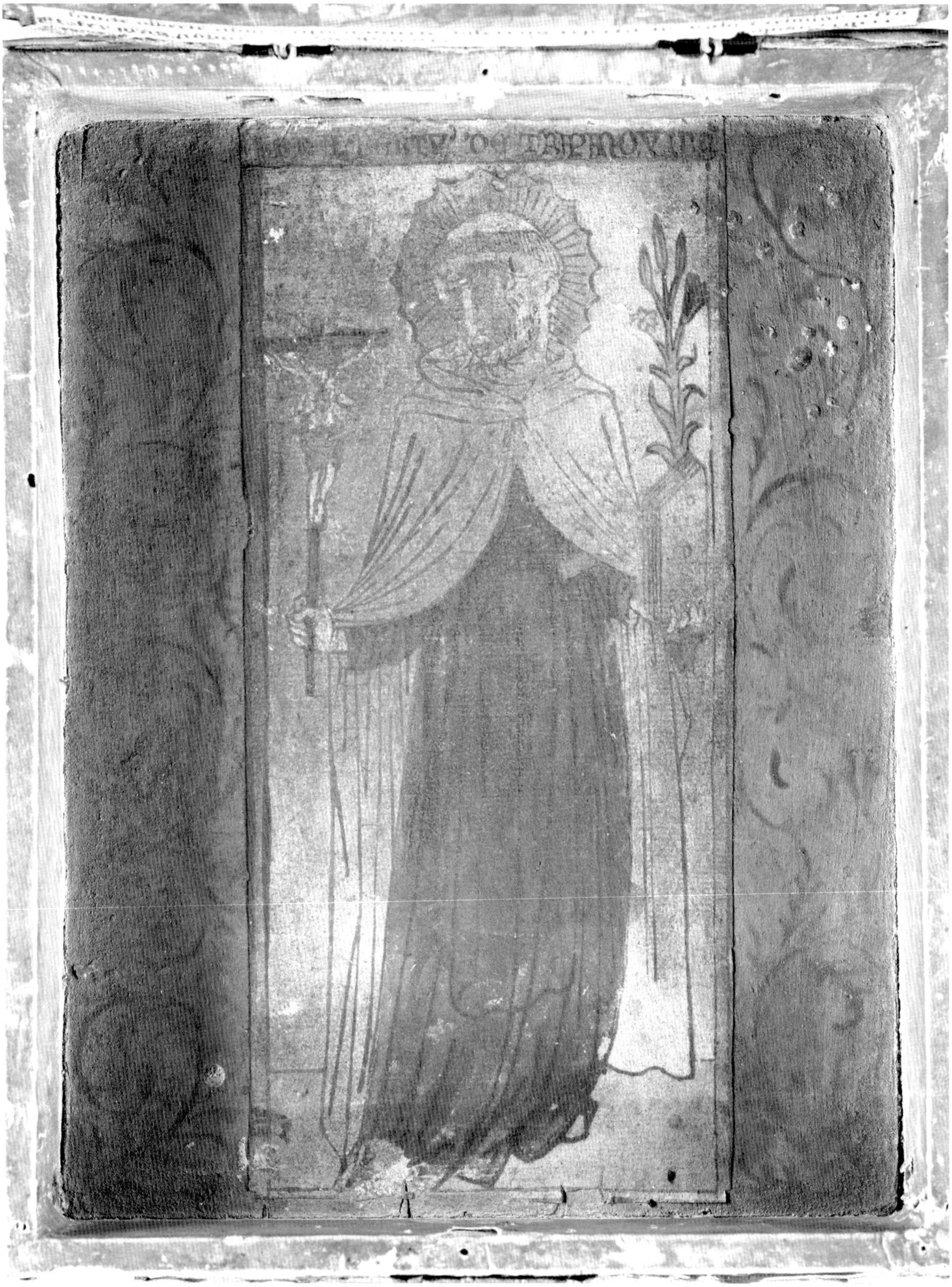

FIGURE 16. St. Albert of Trapani, colored woodcut, *c.* 1470 (image and sheet: 240 × 105 mm). Berlin, Kupferstichkabinett, Staatliche Museen zu Berlin, Inv. 43009 (leather and metal-clad wooden box, inner bottom; Schr. 1184a) (photo: Bildarchiv Preußischer Kulturbesitz / Art Resource, N.Y.).

to promote Albert's cult but to advance his eventual canonization.[35] Once existing in hundreds of impressions, it was perhaps distributed by a confraternity or monastery and even displayed in the street during various processions and promotions of the saint. Thus the print is preserved here as a souvenir of a slightly earlier moment than the painted and embossed images. Fixed in the private space of the box's interior, it potentially preserved memories of the more public spaces and communal activities of the saint's cult.

* * *

Confronted with this range of material and contextual complexity, the first scholars of fifteenth-century printmaking were definitely troubled by what they found. In terms of the traditional history of art, these objects remain thoroughly problematic. They challenge standard definitions of artistic media, since they are hybrid or multi-media. They also complicate ideas concerning originality, authorship, and style since they are mass produced, often endlessly copied, and mainly anonymous. In addition, early prints are unusually fragile and vulnerable to damage because of their paper support, as demonstrated by the tattered state of two woodcuts glued inside the back cover of a breviary written in 1431 at Schloss Altenburg (Fig. 17).[36] Since only a small fraction of impressions survive, early prints might be more properly categorized as *ephemera*. They certainly have much in common with other temporary and perishable images, decorations, and displays. Even today, the ramifications of this multiplicity and fragility have not been fully acknowledged and explored.

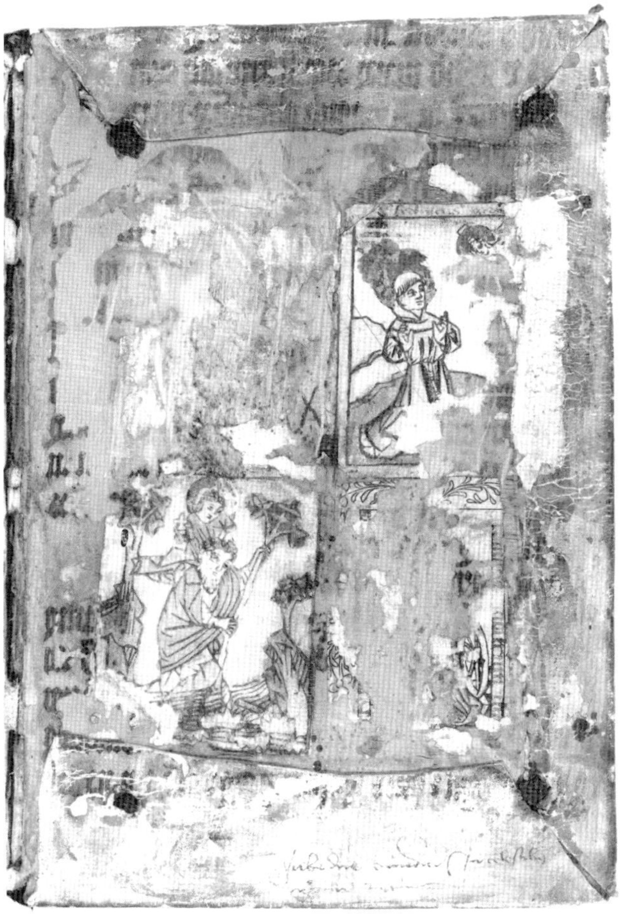

FIGURE 17. Stigmatization of St. Francis; St. Christopher, colored woodcuts, late 15th century (both fragmentary, 67 × 51 mm). Munich, Bayerische Staatsbibliothek, Clm 24888, inside back cover (Schr. 1752a and 1374a).

In the past, much effort was devoted to "rescuing" early prints from their original contexts of use and securing their survival as objects of art-historical study. Throughout the nineteenth century in Europe, thousands of fifteenth-century woodcuts, metalcuts, engravings, and etchings were taken from manuscripts and early printed books and transferred to collections of prints and drawings. Although scholars sometimes recorded the specifics of a print's original setting (since this information was often helpful to dating and localization), this was usually not the case. Indeed, often no set procedure was followed as evidenced by the signs of the reckless removal of prints, as in the case of the breviary from Schloss Altenburg (Fig. 17). Although some of the damage here can be attributed to age and use, it is obvious that someone once tried to peel and

35. See Roberto Cobianchi, "The Use of Woodcuts in Fifteenth-Century Italy," *Print Quarterly* 23, no. 1 (2006): 47–54; Henri D. Saffrey, "Les images populaires de saints dominicains à Venise au XVe siècle et l'édition par Alde Manuce des 'Epistole' de sainte Catherine de Sienne," *Italia Medioevale e Umanistica* 25 (1982): 241–312; and Mark J. Zucker, "Early Italian Engravings for Religious Orders," *Zeitschrift für Kunstgeschichte* 56 (1993): 366–84.

36. Munich, Bayerische Staatsbibliothek, Clm 24888, inside back cover.

scrape the prints from the cover, leaving only the fragmented woodcuts of Saint Francis and Saint Christopher behind.[37] On the lower right, a surviving bit of paper bearing the image of a wheel indicates that a print of Saint Catherine was once pasted there; and on the upper left, an array of gouges suggests the presence of an unknown fourth woodcut that was apparently removed in one piece.

The final step in the recovery of prints involved a certain level of restoration, as unruly material features were trimmed, cleaned, and repaired. Ripped and curling edges of paper sheets were flattened out and framed in cream-colored mat-boards designed to be stacked in archival boxes. Fortunately, for my scholarly project and that of others, there still remain many prints *in situ*. These tend to be the less beautiful and more clearly manipulated examples, like the woodcuts of Francis and Christopher (Fig. 17) and the Entombment and Crucifixion discussed earlier (Figs. 12 and 13), all preserved in manuscripts in Munich's Bayerische Staatsbibliothek. Unlike the hundreds of prints transferred from the library to the Staatliche Graphische Sammlung in the early nineteenth century, these were left in place. Thanks to the thorough research of the medium's pioneer scholars, the woodcuts were not forgotten, as most were eventually included in Georg Leidinger's 1907 and 1910 two-part catalogue of the library's woodcuts (part of a massive hundred-volume cataloguing project of international collections edited and published by Paul Heitz) and in Wilhelm Schreiber's foundational eight-volume handbook of fifteenth-century single-sheet relief prints.[38]

Leidinger's catalogue is notable not only for its detailed descriptions but also for its color plates of each print. In the early twentieth century, such reproductions were especially heralded as important scholarly contributions. They documented and made collections more accessible and were also seen as an attractive draw for book buyers. Their role in the critical and popular success of these publishing ventures is reflected at the end of the catalogue, where two pages feature excerpts from several positive reviews, many of which specifically praise the reproductions.[39] The catalogue's title page notes that each plate is a copy or replica (*Nachbildung*) in the form of a relief etching (which at the time was photo-based). Using this fairly exact technique, the plates are presented as if they are facsimiles. They are at the same scale as the originals with lines of a similar quality to woodcut and bright watercolors applied by hand; and they are even printed on loose sheets of paper that were then tipped into the catalogue. The desire for an accurate simulation—including the material support—is exemplified by the catalogue's first plate, which reproduces a textile print of the Crucifixion.[40] To match the original more exactly, a rectangular piece of cloth, instead of paper, has been used as the support. Thus the goal was to provide a kind of obsessive simulation, a substitute for the mainly inaccessible physical object; so much so that one might mistake these reproductions for the actual prints.

However, the seemingly exact reproductions represent a contradiction when compared to the real objects. In the entries for the woodcuts of the Entombment and the Crucifixion (Figs. 12 and 13), Leidinger is quite thorough in noting the manuscript in which the prints are inserted and the added inscriptions, which he even transcribes. Yet these inscriptions have been carefully edited from the hand-colored plates (Figs. 18 and 19). To be fair, Leidinger seems to acknowledge the problem. Parenthetically, he instructs the reader to compare his descriptions *not* to the reproductions tipped into the catalogue but to a set of photographs (not included in the book). The volume's preface mentions the existence of these photographs taken by a "Herr Hofphotograph

37. For the prints of Saint Francis and Saint Christopher, see Schreiber, *Handbuch* (as in note 3), nos. 1752a and 1374a.

38. Leidinger, *Einzel-Holzschnitte* (as in note 7) part 1; Georg Leidinger, *Einzel-Holzschnitte des fünfzehnten Jahrhunderts in der Kgl. Hof- und Staatsbibliothek München*, part 2, vol. 21 of *Einblattdrucke des fünfzehnten Jahrhunderts*, ed. Paul Heitz (Strasbourg, 1910); and Schreiber, *Handbuch* (as in note 3).

39. Leidinger, *Einzel-Holzschnitte* (as in note 38), part 2. These pages are found at the end of the catalogue and are labeled "Fachmännische Urteile" (Expert Judgments).

40. Leidinger, *Einzel-Holzschnitte* (as in note 7), part 1, 7–8, no. and pl. 1; Schreiber, *Handbuch* (as in note 3), no. 1b; and Areford, *Viewer and Printed Image* (as in note 2), 28–29, fig. 7.

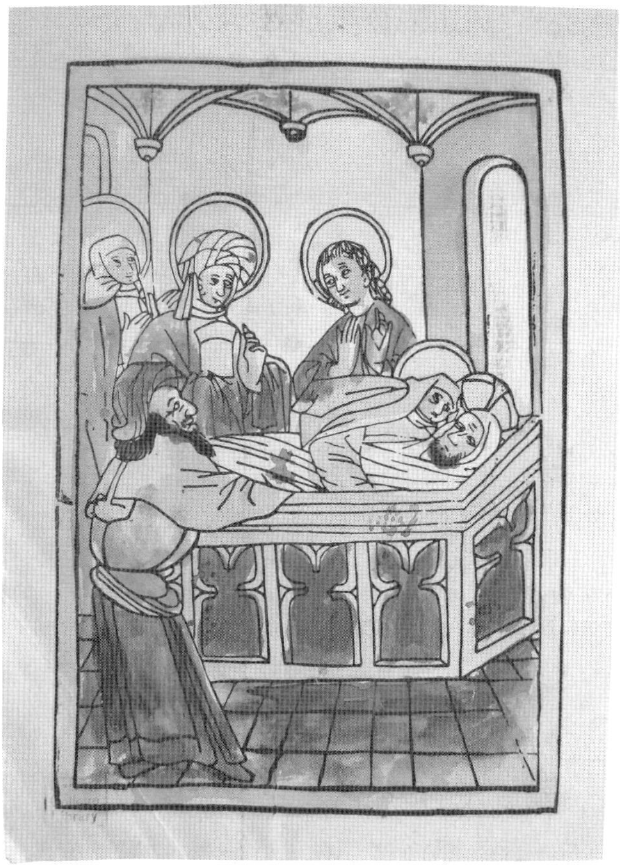

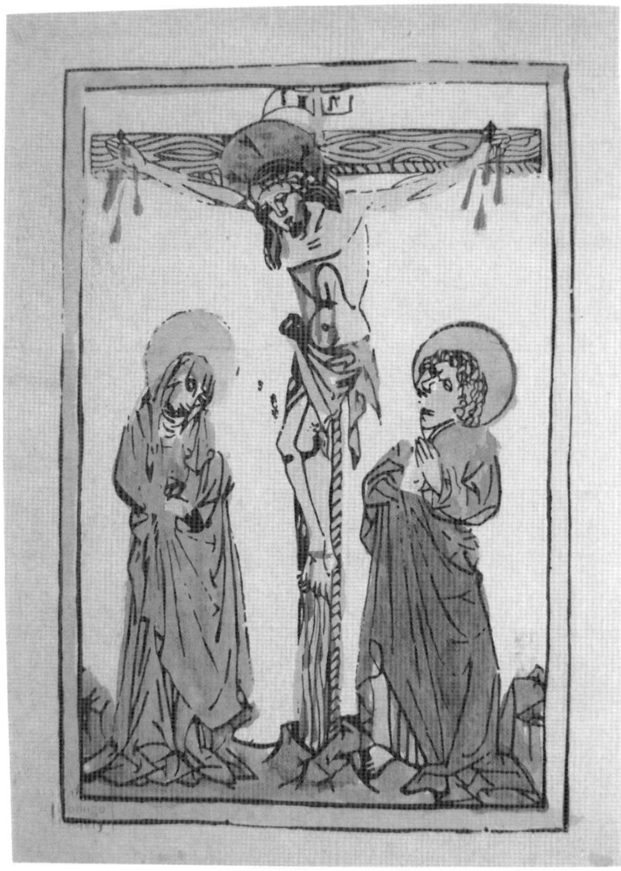

FIGURE 18. Reproduction of woodcut (Entombment), from G. Leidinger, *Einzel-Holzschnitte des fünfzehnten Jahrhunderts in der Kgl. Hof- und Staatsbibliothek München*, part 1, vol. 10 of *Einblattdrucke des fünfzehnten Jahrhunderts*, ed. Paul Heitz (Strasbourg, 1907), Pl. 9.

FIGURE 19. Reproduction of woodcut (Crucifixion), from G. Leidinger, *Einzel-Holzschnitte des fünfzehnten Jahrhunderts in der Kgl. Hof- und Staatsbibliothek München*, part 1, vol. 10 of *Einblattdrucke des fünfzehnten Jahrhunderts*, ed. Paul Heitz (Strasbourg, 1907), Pl. 6.

Teufel" and their availability for specialized research. To assist the reader, the Entombment and Crucifixion entries include numbers corresponding to this alternate set of reproductions.

Of course, the differences between the catalogue's reproductions of the two woodcuts and photographic reproductions (like those of Teufel or Figs. 12 and 13) is significant, as are the differences between the catalogue's reproductions and its entries. Notwithstanding Leidinger's careful inventory of the prints, their context, and the inscriptions, the contrast between his descriptions and the plates indicates an unarticulated theoretical and methodological tension in the early scholarship on fifteenth-century printmaking, one born primarily from the very different goals of connoisseurship versus codicology and palaeography.[41] For the connoisseur, the primary aim was to recover the print in some kind of pristine form and to elevate it as an

41. Wilhelm Schreiber's important catalogue of fifteenth-century relief prints also reveals this tension. Important details of the book context are often missing from his entries. In the case of the Munich woodcuts of the Crucifixion and the Entombment, he fails to mention the inscriptions. See Schreiber, *Handbuch* (as in note 3), nos. 403a and 517b.

art object worthy of study, with no ragged edges, water or dirt stains, or signs of an intervening context (textual or otherwise). Thus the catalogue's color plates serve as a virtual, ideal print collection. In surrogate form, each single-sheet woodcut has been freed from the book in which it was glued and affixed to a large black page like a little painting spotlighted in a dark gallery. Ultimately, however, the omission of the surrounding material setting of the book, along with any added inscriptions, highlights the project's conflicting aims. Even though motivated by a delight in the recovery of rare examples of early prints, the catalogue reveals a certain discomfort with the clear evidence of use and the involvement of viewers.

Although print experts have long struggled with the material and contextual peculiarities of early printmaking, scholarly resistance has been most explicitly articulated by the broader discipline of art history, which has generally excluded or marginalized these objects. As summarized in his 1989 study of Reformation prints, Keith Moxey blames the dismissive attitude on the application of "anachronistic aesthetic values." [42] In short, these mass-produced and often stylistically simplistic images do not qualify as works of art. Furthermore, the disciplinary resistance has resulted in certain stubborn historical and theoretical narratives concerning the role of early printmaking in communication and the promotion of knowledge. These narratives can be outlined using two ambitious texts written fifty-five years apart: William M. Ivins' *Prints and Visual Communication* (1953), still in print and often cited; and more recently, Christopher Wood's *Forgery, Replica, Fiction: Temporalities of German Renaissance Art* (2008).[43] Aimed at different audiences and contrasting in terms of their intellectual complexity, both books characterize the emergence of the printed image as a dramatic development that eventually generates a profound cultural shift from the medieval to the modern. Yet, in both cases, the majority of fifteenth-century prints—anonymous religious relief prints—are seen as tentative and deficient.

As his book's title suggests, Ivins is interested in the impact of prints on the spread of knowledge. In his introduction, he employs a metaphor of a road block to describe the medieval lack of a method for creating "exactly repeatable pictorial statements." [44] This block, standing in the "road of pictorial communication," is "broken" in the fifteenth century with the rise of printed images. More precisely, according to Ivins, the block is breached in 1467 when the "earliest set of datable prints was issued that purported to be pictures of precisely identifiable and locatable objects." [45] Interestingly, these were woodcuts included in Cardinal Torquemada's *Meditations on the Passion of Our Lord*, which the text notes were depictions of frescos commissioned by the cardinal for the church of Santa Maria sopra Minerva. Despite this seemingly fascinating instance of the use of prints as accurate pictorial links to other images (implicated in liturgical and devotional activities), this is not the kind of communication that interests Ivins. His narrative quickly shifts to early printed books, specifically scientific works that are finally able to communicate fully through their pairing of texts and increasingly precise printed illustrations. Thus the single-sheet print—the medium's most dominant format—is excluded from his narrative for reasons that, unfortunately, still command a large audience: "The subject matter of a print, like its purpose and the social group at which it is directed, has always had a great deal to do with how it is made... The single sheet woodcuts seem to have been made for very simple people." [46] For Ivins, these people "obviously looked to [prints] not for information but for the awakening of pious emotions," which were further tainted by "superstition." [47] As a result, these "crude and gaudy" devotional images failed to realize their inherent ability for spreading precise information. Thus Ivins' narrative is a variation of the aesthetic argument,

42. Keith Moxey, *Peasants, Warriors, and Wives: Popular Imagery in the Reformation* (Chicago, Ill., 1989), 1–9 (2).

43. William M. Ivins, Jr., *Prints and Visual Communication* (Cambridge, Mass., 1953; 1969); Christopher S. Wood, *Forgery, Replica, Fiction: Temporalities of German Renaissance Art* (Chicago, Ill., 2008).

44. Ivins, *Prints and Visual Communication* (as in note 43), 1–20 (2).

45. *Ibid.*, 31.

46. *Ibid.*, 28.

47. *Ibid.*, 28–29.

mentioned above, that casts fifteenth-century prints as feeble precursors to the artistic achievements of the Renaissance. In such a reductive view, early prints fail not only as "art" but also as "information."

Although more theoretically sophisticated and far-reaching in its implications, Wood's book also hinges on the communicative potential of printmaking. And while his conclusions are quite different from those of Ivins, the nature of his argument is strangely similar. In his exploration of concepts of time and history during the German Renaissance, Wood employs a theory of "substitution" in which a variety of objects, buildings, and devotional images were considered links in "substitutional" or "replica chains" that connected them to ancient originals.[48] In this way, a copy could be seen as a valid stand-in, one that was considered as important and powerful as the prototype. For Wood, the rise of the printed image during the period disrupts these chains of connection. As one case study, he discusses a woodcut of the Madonna and Child printed in Pforzheim in 1500 (Fig. 20).[49] The text surrounding the print indicates that it reproduces a well-known sacred image of the Virgin "as she was painted by the Evangelist Saint Luke."[50] This Lucan portrait had long been replicated through a "network of painted copies," each considered an identical substitute for the distant original. But the print, according to Wood, hinders the substitutional process, starting with its very different material makeup: the printed sheet of paper. In addition, it is framed by explanatory text that over-articulates the fact that the woodcut is a copy of another image. Furthermore, at the sheet's bottom, the printed city name and publication date anchor the copy to a specific contemporary place and time, making the viewer overly conscious of the mediating role of a printmaker and publisher. The woodcut, therefore, is incapable of serving as an effective devotional substitute. In Wood's analysis, "Metadata, the internally inscribed framing information, punctuated the transmission process, articulating the flow of meaning into a series of localizable relay stations"; and thus the print is hopelessly "apologetic," presenting a "divided message, pointing to more than one target at once… Substitution works only when the process of transmission is obscure or forgotten."[51]

Thus the arguments of Ivins and Wood present early printmaking as either an obstruction or a disruption; where Ivins perceives too little "information" in religious prints (blocking the advancement of knowledge), Wood sees "too much information" (replacing a rich devotional mystery with potential doubt).[52] Wood's theory is intellectually seductive, yet it is also overly predetermined by the demands of his overarching argument. And both scholars are too invested in seeing the medium of printmaking as a crucial and revolutionary technological phenomenon that must part ways with the past. Instead of treating prints as self-sufficient images, one must fully explore their material and contextual dimensions, from visual details and scale to physical proximity and touch.[53] In the end, the evidence of viewer reception suggests that the printed image could equally meet the demands of precise information and profound religious devotion.

The documentary and the devotional were often simultaneous goals when prints reproduced sacred objects or images, as can be demonstrated by printed depictions of a Byzantine icon and a Passion relic, both preserved in Santa Croce in Gerusalemme in Rome. Among this church's impressive collection of relics, one of the most treasured is the *titulus crucis*, the object believed to be the wooden panel ordered by Pilate and attached to the top of Christ's cross. During renovations

48. Wood, *Forgery, Replica, Fiction* (as in note 43), esp. 36–42.

49. Munich, Staatliche Graphische Sammlung, Inv. 118196D. See Schreiber, *Handbuch* (as in note 3), no. 1033; and Wood, *Forgery, Replica, Fiction* (as in note 43), 95–102, 224, and fig. 19.

50. Wood, *Forgery, Replica, Fiction* (as in note 43), 98.

51. *Ibid.*, 224–225.

52. *Ibid.*, 100 and 224.

53. For the ways in which early prints were linked to sacred images and objects, see Robert Maniura, "The Images and Miracles of Santa Maria delle Carceri," in *The Miraculous Image in the Late Middle Ages and Renaissance*, ed. Erik Thunø and Gerhard Wolf (Rome, 2004), 81–95; and David S. Areford, "Multiplying the Sacred: The Fifteenth-Century Woodcut as Reproduction, Surrogate, Simulation," in *The Woodcut in Fifteenth-Century Europe* (as in note 6), 118–153.

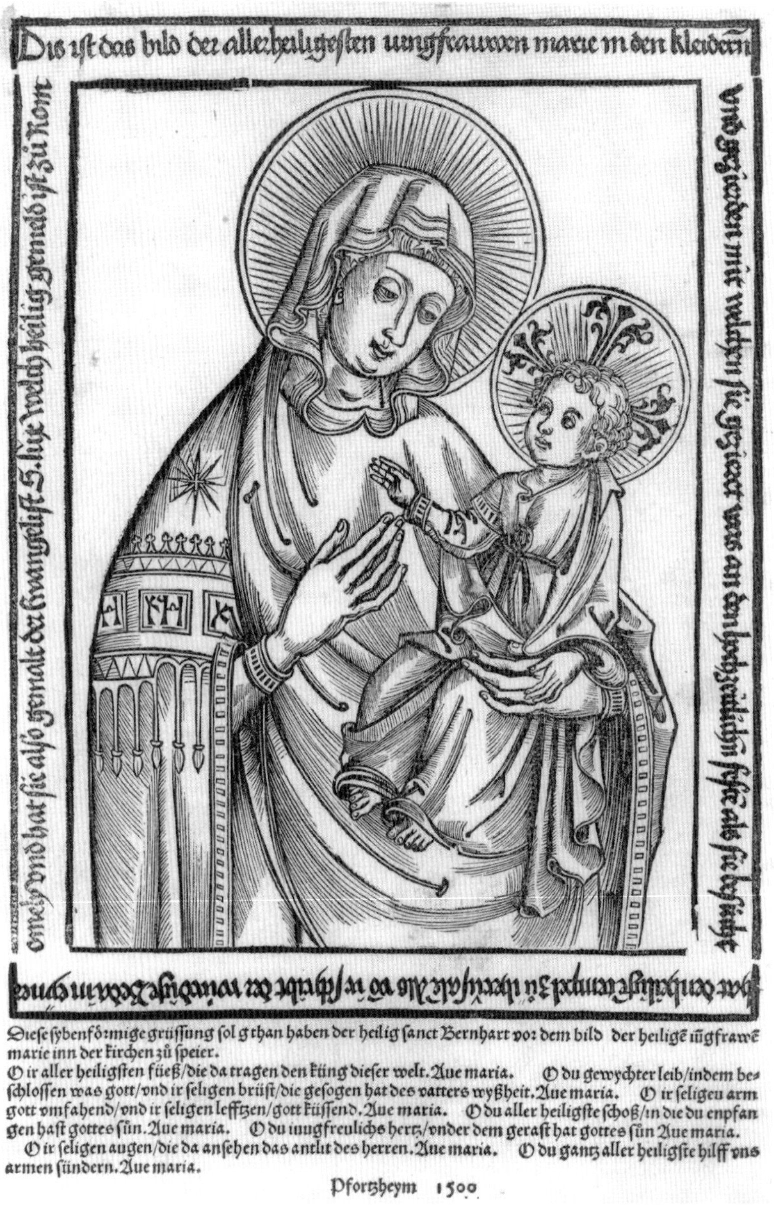

FIGURE 20. Madonna and Child, woodcut, 1500 (200 × 155 mm). Munich, Staatliche Graphische Sammlung, Inv. 118196D (Schr. 1033).

of Santa Croce in 1492, the relic was found hidden in a lead container within a wall. Although fragmentary, its Hebrew, Latin, and Greek inscriptions were still legible, identifying "Jesus of Nazareth, King of the Jews."[54] Not long after its discovery, several printed copies of the *titulus* were produced, including a woodcut once owned by Hartmann Schedel, the physician, scholar, and author of the *Nuremberg Chronicle* (Fig. 21.)[55]

54. Meredith J. Gill, "Antoniazzo Romano and the Recovery of Jerusalem in Late Fifteenth-Century Rome," *Storia dell'arte* 83 (1995): 28–47 (32–33); and Carsten Peter Thiede and Matthew d'Ancona, *The Quest for the True Cross* (London, 2000; reprinted New York, 2003).

55. Munich, Bayerische Staatsbibliothek, Rar. 287, fol. 334r.

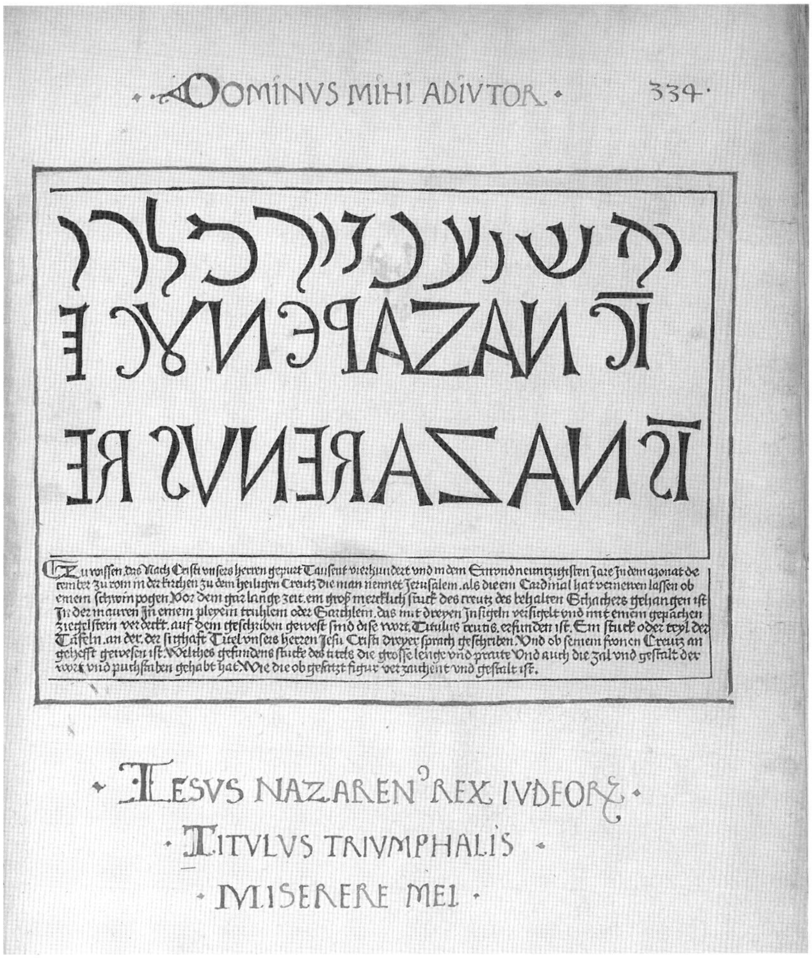

FIGURE 21. *Titulus crucis*, woodcut, *c.* 1492–1496. Munich, Bayerische Staatsbibliothek, Rar. 287, fol. 334^r.

The print survives because Schedel pasted it to a blank page of a personal copy of his famous book. With red ink, he added a simple border along the print's edges, as well as Latin inscriptions in red and blue above and below. The woodcut includes a xylographic German text that both recounts the relic's discovery in Rome and claims a high level of accuracy for the depiction above. The caption states that the print reproduces the exact form of the words of the *titulus* (matching its odd right to left orientation and reversed letters) and also the relic's precise "height, length, and width."[56] Thus, as argued by Christopher Wood, the print "offers itself as a completely authoritative indexical sign of the relic."[57] Indeed, the lifesize scale was an important claim of authenticity, one that depended on the viewer's spatial and bodily experience. For Schedel, it is clear

See Béatrice Hernad, *Die Graphiksammlung des Humanisten Hartmann Schedel* (Munich, 1990), 54, Abb. 25; and *Genie ohne Namen: Der Meister des Bartholomäus-Altars,* ed. Rainer Budde and Roland Krischel (Cologne, 2001), 410; and Areford, "Multiplying the Sacred" (as in note 53), 135–141, and fig. 14.

56. "Welches gefundens stucke des titels die grosse lenge und praite und auch die zal und gestalt der wort und puchstaben gehabt hat. Wie die ob gesatzt figur verzaichent und gestalt ist." The woodcut of the *titulus* is quite close to the dimensions of the actual relic, which according to Bella and Azzi, measures 26 cm by 14 cm (10.23 inches by 5.51 inches) and according to Thiede and d'Ancona measures 25.3 cm by 14 cm. See Francesco Bella and Carlo Azzi, "14C Dating of the 'Titulus Crucis,'" *Radiocarbon* 44, no. 3 (2002): 685–689; and Thiede and d'Ancona, *Quest for the True Cross* (as in note 54), 93.

57. Christopher S. Wood, "Notation of Visual Information in the Earliest Archeological Scholarship," *Word & Image* 17, nos. 1 and 2 (January–June, 2001): 94–118 (107).

that the woodcut served not only as a historical and archaeological record but also as a potent devotional focus, as reflected by his added inscriptions. Mimicking the relic's classicizing capitals, he wrote four short lines: *Dominus mihi adiutor* (Lord my helper) at the top; and *Iesus Nazarenus rex Iudeorum* | *Titulus triumphalis* | *Miserere mei* (Jesus of Nazareth, king of the Jews | Triumphal Title | Have mercy on me) below. With these words, Schedel frames the woodcut as much more than just visual information or documentation. For him, it was also a substitute for the relic in Rome and thus a focus for prayer.

In addition to the *titulus*, Santa Croce in Gerusalemme possesses a Byzantine icon of the *imago pietatis*, perhaps the most well-known example of a sacred image reproduced in printed form. The icon, which dates to the early fourteenth century and depicts the Man of Sorrows in micro-mosaic, was brought to Rome around 1380 from the monastery of Saint Catherine at Mount Sinai.[58] Surrounded by a silver frame, it is embedded in the middle of a triptych composed of more than two hundred compartments primarily holding saints' relics. Soon after its arrival, the icon was quickly associated with Pope Gregory (r. 540–604) and his miraculous vision of Christ's body while performing Mass. Between 1495 and 1500, the printmaker Israhel van Meckenem was employed by the Carthusians of Santa Croce to produce two engravings of the icon: a small and a large version (Fig. 22).[59] Both include similar Latin inscriptions that reference the icon, its location, and the link to Pope Gregory's visionary experience. Like the inscription included with the woodcut of the *titulus crucis*, the texts specifically assert the image's pictorial accuracy. The larger engraving's somewhat longer inscription declares that the print is "counterfeited (*contrefacta*) in the manner and likeness" of the image in Rome.[60] In addition to the inscription, the printmaker included his signature below the lower border.

Based on Wood's argument, as outlined above, every aspect of these printed versions of the sacred image inhibits their use as devotional substitutes—the paper support, the very different visual characteristics of engraving, and especially the inscriptions in which the print must explain itself and reveal the mediating process of its creation. Furthermore, the artistic agent responsible has inserted himself through his signature. For Wood, such an image is unable to act as an effective stand-in for its prototype. Yet, in addition to promoting the cult of the icon in Rome, the printed copies were obviously made to serve devotional purposes based on their ability to substitute for the original image.

A little-known later impression of Van Meckenem's smaller engraving of the *imago pietatis* survives with explicit evidence of the personal and pious ways in which viewers engaged with the image (Fig. 23).[61] In this case, the print was produced from the somewhat worn and reworked original engraved plate but without the inscription and artist's signature. Instead of paper, the image is printed in the middle of a roughly square sheet of parchment that—with its uneven surface and rippling edges—seems in a constant state of unfurling. Framed in the sheet's center, the depiction has been subtly hand-colored, with golden brown accenting Christ's hair, halo, and cross. Although faded, the wide surrounding border retains accents of red,

58. Rome, Basilica of Santa Croce in Gerusalemme. See *Byzantium: Faith and Power (1261–1557)*, ed. Helen C. Evans (New York, 2004), 221–223, cat. 131; and *Treasures of Heaven: Saints, Relics, and Devotion in Medieval Europe*, ed. Martina Bagnoli, Holger A. Klein, C. Griffith Mann, and James Robinson (Baltimore, Md., 2010), 201–202, cat. 116.

59. M. Lehrs, *Geschichte und Kritischer Katalog des deutschen, niederländischen und französischen Kupferstichs im XV. Jahrhundert* (Vienna, 1908-34), 9: 176–178, nos. 166–167; Fritz Koreny, *Hollstein's German Engravings, Etchings and Woodcuts 1400–1700* (Blaricum, 1986), 24: 74–75, nos. 166 and 167; Peter Parshall, "Imago Contrafacta: Images and Facts in the Northern Renaissance," *Art History* 16, no. 4 (December 1993): 554–579 (556–561); Henk van Os, *The Art of Devotion in the Late Middle Ages in Europe* (Princeton, N.J., 1994), 110–112, pl. 33 and fig. 54; and *Byzantium: Faith and Power* (as in note 58), 556, cat. 329, and fig. 329.1.

60. Parshall, "Imago Contrafacta" (as in note 59), 556.

61. Washington, D.C., Library of Congress, LC-USZC4-4525. See Edgar Breitenbach, "Israhel van Meckenem's Man of Sorrows," in *Graphic Sampler*, ed. Renata V. Shaw (Washington, D.C., 1979), 2–9; and Koreny, *Hollstein's German Engravings* (as in note 59), 74, no. 166. The Library of Congress impression is the only known example of a third state of the engraving.

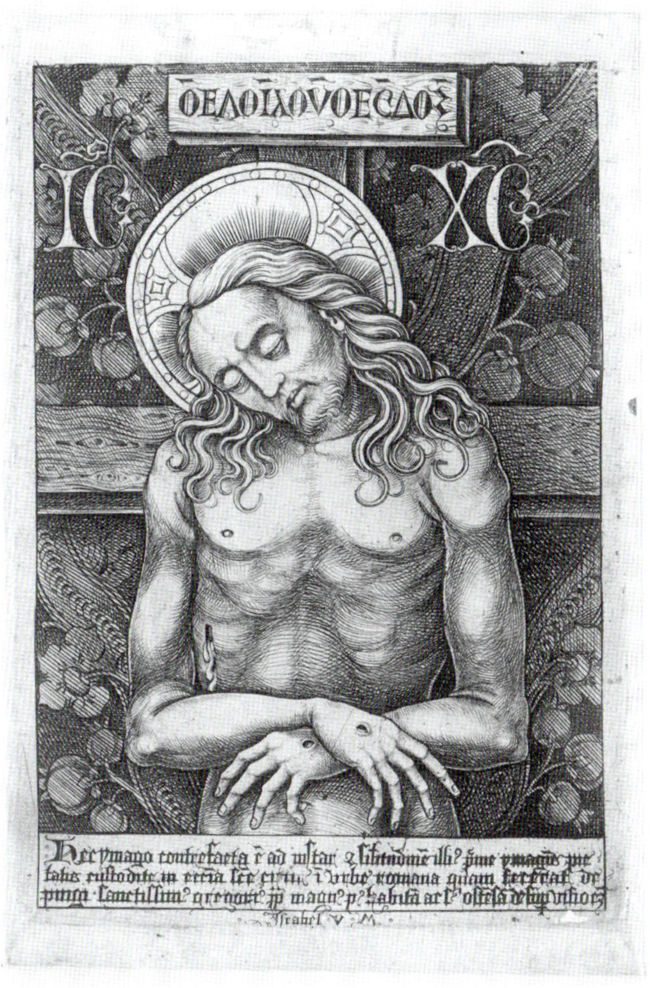

FIGURE 22. Israhel van Meckenem, *Imago pietatis*, engraving, *c.* 1495–1500 (image: 168 × 112 mm). Berlin, Kupferstichkabinett, Staatliche Museen zu Berlin, 943-1 (photo: Bildarchiv Preußischer Kulturbesitz / Art Resource, N.Y.).

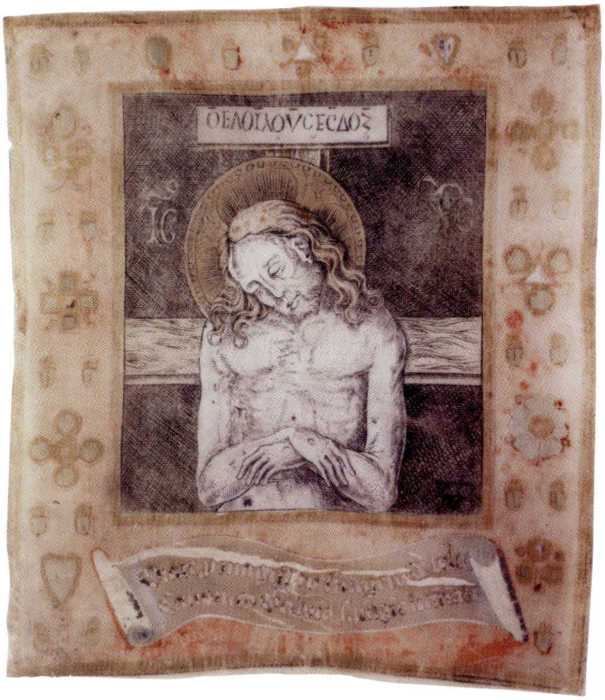

FIGURE 23. Israhel van Meckenem, *Imago pietatis*, engraving, *c.* 1495–1500 (image: 96 × 88 mm). Washington, D.C., Library of Congress, LC-USZC4-4525.

pink, and brown and is painted as if encrusted with gemstones and pearls. Through these additions, the print comes closer to the look of the actual icon with its elaborate silver frame (although the icon's frame is decorated with heraldic enamel panels and vegetal and animal motifs). In a banderole below, an inscription written in gold (much of which has flaked off) directs viewers: *Orate pro magistro Rutgero de Venlo | Canonico Gereonis, sacre pagine licentiate* (Pray for Magister Rutger de Venlo, canon of [Saint] Gereon, license in sacred scripture).[62] According to Edgar Breitenbach, Rutger de Venlo was a faculty member of Cologne University beginning in the mid-1490s, and the print was probably produced after his death in 1519. Significantly, this version of Van Meckenem's engraving is without the authenticating caption, as well as the artist's signature. In their place is the personalized handwritten inscription. Along with the visual elaboration of the parchment frame and the image's hand coloring, the inscribed banderole indicates that the printed image succeeds as a devotional stand-in for the Roman icon through a clear process of substitution and simulation. As a memorial image, the engraving focuses prayers for the benefit of De Venlo's soul, specifically inflecting them through the renowned sacred image in Rome. By the early sixteenth century, the icon had long been associated with the specific rewards of papal indulgences,

62. For the Latin inscription, see Breitenbach, "Israhel van Meckenem's Man of Sorrows" (as in note 61), 3.

available in person or through the use of image substitutes.[63] The English woodcut of the Man of Sorrows, mentioned above, is also based on the icon of the *imago pietatis* and retains an inscription that spells out the reward (although grossly inflated): "To all those who devoutly say five Paternosters, five Aves and a Creed before such a figure are granted 32,755 years of pardon" (Fig. 2).[64] Thus, far from failing as a link to the Roman icon, the engraving is framed and inscribed as if it were the icon itself; and although a print on parchment (a medium and material very different from that of micro-mosaic), it is nonetheless a convincing substitute with no need for "metadata" to explain or authenticate its connection.

Somewhere between conceptions of the medieval and the modern, fifteenth-century prints are best explored as they are: experimental, multimedia, and dirtied by the hands of viewers who activated the power and potential of each image for practical and religious goals. Based on the increasing acceptance of single-sheet relief prints in exhibitions and scholarly studies, one could argue that a "minor" art has become "major." Yet this is not because a "popular" medium is now appreciated as an important art form. That would simply mirror the aesthetic justifications typical of an outmoded connoisseurship. Instead, these long ignored objects are now more central because we are more interested in an expansive and inclusive visual culture, along with aspects of image production and visual experience that these prints so clearly reveal.

63. Breitenbach, "Israhel van Meckenem's Man of Sorrows" (as in note 61), 7.

64. London, British Library, Egerton 1821, fol. 8v. Schreiber, *Handbuch* (as in note 3), no. *868c; entry by David S. Areford, in Parshall and Schoch, *Origins of European Printmaking* (as in note 3), 185–188, cat. 49; and Areford, *Viewer and Printed Image* (as in note 2), 77, pl. 12.

MICHAEL W. COTHREN

Some Personal Reflections on American Modern and Postmodern Historiographies of Gothic Stained Glass

FOR MEREDITH PARSONS LILLICH

ALMOST EVERYONE loves stained glass, especially Gothic stained glass. There is the scintillating color, the consummate craft, the mysterious glow.[1] Most introductory art history survey courses in American colleges and universities must devote at least a few minutes to the subject when characterizing the "Gothic period," showing at least a few seductive images. But what do the art historians who teach these foundational, introductory classes to American undergraduates actually say about Gothic stained glass? What are the things that need to be conveyed from the outset about the significance of painted windows for the history of art? What did they actually mean for those who funded them, for those who made them, and for those who initially viewed them?

Recently, these have become especially compelling questions for me. Since becoming co-author of Marilyn Stokstad's introductory art history text book,[2] I have been reflecting on the Gothic passages in the text books of an earlier generation, associated with giant art historical forebears like Helen Gardner, H. W. Janson, and Frederick Hartt.[3] Stained glass is present in these venerable books, as well as in the more recent books that have followed them, but it does not figure large. For Gothic architectural arts, structure and sculpture occupy much more space and attention; for painting, the emphasis is on the small-scale, intimate art of the book. Little, if any attention is directed to the subject matter and meaning of stained-glass windows, aspects quite prominent in the discussion of Gothic portals and manuscripts.

Two themes predominate in the brief attention to stained glass: abstract symbolic meaning and multicolored atmospheric lighting. Here is an example of the broad claims for symbolism: "the formal qualities of light had been associated with Christ and divinity since the early Christian period"[4] or "to express the relationship between light and God's presence in a distinctive way."[5] Stained-glass windows are also credited with turning "solid architecture into a floating vision of

1. This personal reflection, based on almost four decades of research on French medieval stained glass, does not pretend to be a comprehensive state of the question on 20th- and 21st-century medieval stained-glass studies. For a more expansive sense of recent scholarship in the field, see the spectacular critical overview of B. Kurmann-Schwarz and C. Lautier, "Recherches récente sur le vitrail médiéval 1998–2009," *Kunstchronik* 63 (2010), 261–304, 313–356. Many colleagues and friends have advised and listened as I gathered these reflections, or have aided in finding published sources and publishable images. I owe special gratitude to Stacy Bomento, Painton Cowen, Colum Hourihane, Timothy Husband, Alyce Jordan, Meredith Lillich, Susan Lowry, Gordon Plumb, Helen Ronan, Stewart H. Rosenberg, Mary Shepard, Sarah Touborg, and Paul Williamson.

2. Marilyn Stokstad wrote this book during the 1990s for a new generation of students and with a passionate dedication to inclusiveness and reader engagement: *Art History* (New York, 1995). My association began with the most recent edition: M. Stokstad and M. W. Cothren, *Art History*, 4th edition (Saddle River, N.J., 2011).

3. H. Gardner (1878–1946), *Art Through the Ages: An Introduction to its History and Significance* (New York, 1926); H. W. Janson (1913–1982), with D. J. Janson, *History of Art: A Survey of the Major Visual Arts from the Dawn of History to the Present Day* (New York, 1962); F. Hartt (1914–1991), *Art: A History of Painting, Sculpture, and Architecture* (New York, 1976).

4. L. S. Adams, *A History of Western Art*, 5th ed. (New York, 2011), 198.

5. *Ibid.*

the celestial heavens."[6] In other words, the medium is the message. What is portrayed in these windows is incidental; their primary significance is as embodiments of traditional Christian light symbolism.[7]

The second theme in art history survey books is atmospheric architectural illumination. With stained-glass windows "Light and color were diffused throughout the interior of the cathedral"[8] or "The entire cathedral in the twelfth and thirteenth centuries became a framework to hold stained glass, which inevitably darkened the interior but had its own indescribable beauty of color and pattern."[9] This idea of darkness continues in another text that perceptively combines "the wonderfully warm and vibrant effect" of interior decoration with abstract symbolism: "In reality, the windows admit far less light than one might expect; they act mainly as huge, multicolored diffusing filters that change the *quality* of ordinary daylight, endowing it with the poetic and symbolic values so highly praised by Abbot Suger."[10]

This concentration on light-saturated Gothic spirituality may explain why so few stained-glass windows appear in these books, as well as why they are folded into discussions of architecture. In my own efforts to bring a few more windows into Marilyn Stokstad's book, I have been warned that there is an awful lot of stained glass in the Gothic chapter. But can we imagine a world where the Sistine Chapel in the Vatican would be discussed primarily as a work of architecture, its ceiling paintings characterized by the way they opened up the top of the building, projecting pictorial space illusionistically upward into a colorful, fictive world, with no discussion of Michelangelo's complex compendium of biblical narrative and theological juxtaposition? That is the sort of world in which survey discussions of Gothic stained glass seem to be stuck.

To put it another way, most survey text books—and I can only assume most of the courses that use them—still cling to a limited, Modernist approach to understanding Gothic stained glass, while the specialists who study this major medium of Gothic painting have progressed to a Postmodern, complex, and certainly more nuanced understanding of the significance as well as the meaning of these works. I will begin by exploring the context of this perhaps overly broad and generalized assessment.

Before the mid-twentieth century, the study of European stained glass—except for a few acknowledged "masterpieces," such as Chartres and the Sainte-Chapelle—was largely the domain of local antiquarians writing with great pride, and often with great sensitivity and insight, about the art treasures of their towns and their regions. World War II altered this landscape, and introduced the richness of Gothic and Renaissance stained glass into a broader art-historical enterprise. During the late 1930s across Europe, precious works of art from public and religious monuments, including many stained-glass windows, were taken out of their original buildings and hidden in storage to protect them from destruction. After the war, before they were returned to their buildings, many of these works were restored in consultation with art historians.

It is difficult to overemphasize the impact of this situation for stained-glass studies. Divorced from the architectural context that had kept them at an intimidating remove from those who would examine them, the now-isolated windows were available for close scrutiny. These proximate, out-of-context investigations focused quite naturally on the fine details of painting style and the process of production, aspects of this art that were difficult—often impossible—to evaluate when the windows were installed. In France, the postwar restoration of stained glass was complemented by a vast project to photograph every window, panel by panel, making them available to scholars in the future as well as the present.[11]

6. F. S. Kleiner, *Gardner's Art Through the Ages, A Global History*, 13th ed. (Boston, Mass., 2009), 471.

7. The "classic" discussion of Christian light symbolism in relation to medieval sainted glass is L. Grodecki, "Fonctions Spirituelles," in Marcel Aubert *et al.*, *Le vitrail français* (Paris, 1958), 39–45.

8. Adams, *History of Western Art* (as in note 4), 202.

9. Hartt, *Art* (as in note 3), 4th ed., 457.

10. Janson, *History of Art* (as in note 3), revised and enlarged edition (1969), 234.

11. International cooperation in this work eventually blossomed into the Corpus Vitrearum Medi Aevii project. See Kurmann-

From this situation, a whole new history of stained glass emerged, and since isolated looks emphasize certain things about works of art, the nature of this availability formed, to a certain extent, the art-historical project. Close access privileged iconographic study (that is, the identification of subject matter in individual windows) and formal assessments that revealed relationships among windows and provided evidence of the means of production. Stylistic study became the raw material to reconstruct the nature of medieval artistic workshops.

I will refer to this as the "Modernist approach" to the study of Gothic stained glass, and it was established and codified principally—especially for American specialists—by Louis Grodecki (1910–1982), a Polish, expatriot in France who established close ties to scholars in the United States, with whom he collaborated to create a new, scientifically rigorous form of stained-glass studies.[12] This mid-twentieth-century Modernist approach focused on four interpretive threads, two old and two new. Modernist Scholars continued two intertwined traditional assessments—still reified, as we have seen, in art history survey textbooks—by stressing first that the medium here was part of the message, that traditional Christian light symbolism was behind the popularity of stained glass,[13] and second that these windows functioned, at least in part, as interior decoration within the larger project of Gothic architecture.[14] In short, they transformed sunlight into a multicolored haze that dematerialized architecture and stressed its relationship to visions of the heavenly Jerusalem. But the closer examinations of individual windows guided Grodecki and his Modernist followers to supplement these chestnut generalizations with more specific interpretive projects. Two, I think, are most significant.

I would label the first "window as idea," and it generated from German trends in art-historical thought that were brought to the United States in the 1930s, most notably by Erwin Panofsky (1892–1968),[15] who was Grodecki's colleague at the Institute for Advanced Study, Princeton, during 1950–1951. After this experience, Grodecki moved beyond the identification of subject matter to probe its rationale, its relation to particular local and theological contexts. He focused this inquiry on the unusually learned and obtuse windows from Abbot Suger's reconstruction of the abbey church at Saint-Denis, especially a diptych in one choir chapel (Fig. 1) where in the window on our right, an "anagogical" method of Biblical interpretation, mined from the Pauline epistles, is symbolically outlined, while in the pendent window, on our left, this method is put into practice to find Christian meaning in a series of events from the life of Moses.[16]

But in this and other Modernist studies of individual windows, exquisitely crafted by Grodecki and his followers, little attention was given to the way these

---

Schwarz and Lautier, "Recherches récente" (as in note 1), 261–262; and the recent reflections of the late E. Frodl-Kraft, "Das Corpus Vitrearum Medii Aevi: ein Rückblick," in *Glas, Malerei, Forschung. Internationale Studien zu Ehren von Rüdiger Becksmann*, ed. Harmut Scholz, Ivo Rauch, and Daniel Hess (Berlin, 2004), 13–21.

12. Grodecki's foundational work, first summarized in two important essays—"Des origins à la fin du XIIe siècle," and "De 1200 à 1260," in *Le vitrail français* (as in note 7), 95–158—blossomed into two magisterial books written toward the end of his career—*Le vitrail roman* (Fribourg, 1977), and with C. Brisac, *Le vitrail gothique* (Fribourg, 1984). See also M. H. Caviness, "Louis Grodecki (1910–1982)," in *Medieval Scholarship: Biographical Studies on the Formation of a Discipline* 3, ed. H. Damico (New York, 2000), 307–321.

13. E.g., Grodecki, *Le vitrail gothique* (as in note 12), 22. More recently, however, our understanding of the complexity of light and color symbolism and meaning has been expanded: e.g., J. Gage, "Gothic Glass: Two Aspects of a Dionysian Aesthetic," *Art History* 5 (1982), 36–58; and M. P. Lillich, "Monastic Stained Glass: Patronage and Style," in *Monasticism and the Arts*, ed. Timothy G. Verdon (Syracuse, 1984), 207–254. See also the more recent studies cited in Kurmann-Schwarz and Lautier, "Recherches récente" (as in note 1), 326–327.

14. Grodecki's classic article set the stage here: "Le vitrail et l'architecture au XIIe et au XIIIe siècle," *Gazette des Beaux-Arts* 36 (1949), 5–24. See also Grodecki, *Le vitrail gothique* (as in note 12), 17–22. This remains a concern of contemporary stained-glass studies: Kurmann-Schwarz and Lautier, "Recherches récente" (as in note 1), 325–326.

15. The bibliography on this father-figure of modern American art history is vast and rich. See his entry in the online Dictionary of Art Historians: http://www.dictionaryofarthistorians.org/panofskye.htm.

16. Grodecki's fundamental work on the glazing of Saint-Denis is contained in two volumes of the French Corpus Vitrearum

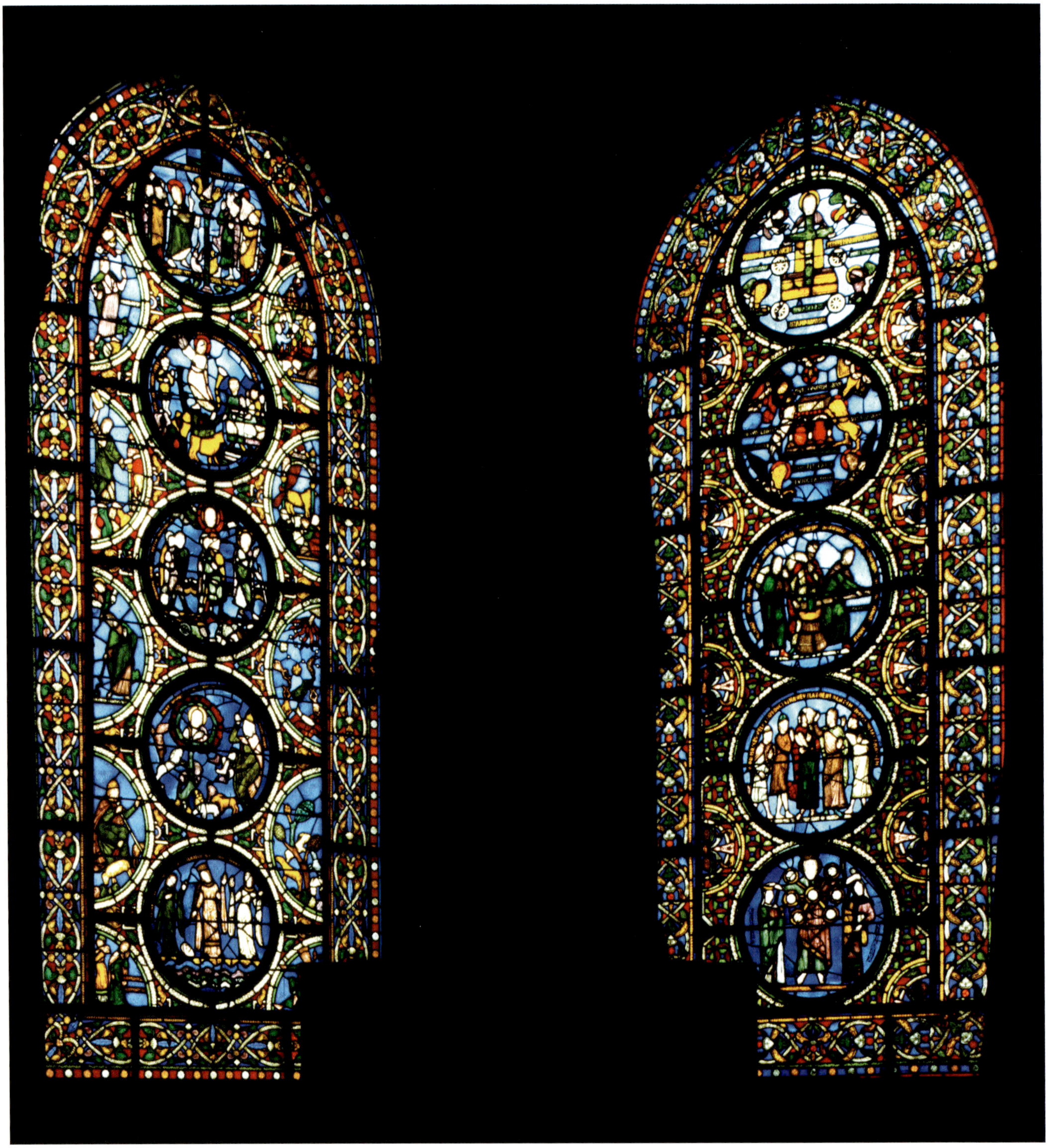

FIGURE 1. Saint-Denis, Abbey Church, diptych of windows in a choir chapel: Anagogical (or Allegories of Saint Paul) window on the right and Moses window on the left, early 1140s (photo: author).

windows were used by worshipers in buildings constructed for Christian liturgy, not scholarly research. Production of meaning rather than its reception was the focus, and the search was for the textual sources used by designers rather than the impact of this art on viewers—in other words, Panofskian iconography and iconology.[17] Gothic windows were seen as visualized ideas, rooted in an intellectual and theological culture of texts, not the rituals of religious life.

The second of the new trends that emerged from a close scrutiny of windows became more central to the work of Grodecki, his students, and his contemporaries. It could be called "production management," and used the scrutiny of style—both the minute details of painted execution and overall window design—to sort extant windows into workshops associated with regional tendencies.[18] As with iconography and iconology, the emphasis here was on evaluating works in relation to their production rather than their reception. In the process Gothic stained glass was confined to a relatively closed art world, dominated by the personal styles of masters and the regional trends of artistic formation—windows were products of influence, tradition, and innovation, operating within a situation similar to the Modern art world that was flourishing around these Modernist scholars. Like the emerging narrative about Modern art, this Modernist account of Gothic stained glass was rooted in the energy of artists more than the expectations of patrons or the experiences of a larger public, was more about facture than function.

Most current American specialists in Gothic stained glass, myself included, learned from Modernist practitioners, most of whom trace lineage to Grodecki through his own students.[19] And our work rests on an assumption that light-filled architecture carried theological meaning—that the medium may have delivered some of the message—although few of us would consign these works, even in part, to the realm of interior decoration, meant to dissolve the solidity of stone architecture with filtered light and essentially illegible in terms of subject matter or content.[20] Most of us still believe that windows were produced in inter-active

"Études" series: *Les vitraux de Saint-Denis: Étude sur le vitrail au XIIe siècle*, I (Paris, 1976); and *Études sur les vitraux de Suger à Saint-Denis (XIIe siècle)*, II (Paris, 1995). On these windows, see also K. Hoffmann, "Suger's 'Anagogisches Fenster' in Saint-Denis," *Wallraf Richartz Jahrbuch* 30 (1968), 57–88; J. A. Frank, "The Moses Window from the Abbey Church of Saint-Denis. Text and Image in Twelfth-Century Art," *Gazette des Beaux-Arts* 133 (1996), 179–194; *eadem*, "The *Quadrige Aminadab* Medallion in the 'Anagogical' Window at the Royal Abbey of Saint-Denis," *Gazette des Beaux-Arts* 141 (1999), 219–234.

17. E. Panofsky, "Iconography and Iconology," in *Studies in Iconology: Humanistic Themes in the Art of the Renaissance* (New York, 1939), 26–54.

18. Grodecki's influential method of determining workshop identification based on stylistic assessment was most clearly outlined in "A Stained Glass *Atelier* of the Thirteenth Century: A Study of the Windows in the Cathedrals of Bourges, Chartres, and Poitiers," *Journal of the Warburg and Courtauld Institutes* 11 (1948), 87–111.

19. I owe my own formation as a specialist in the study of stained glass to the generous and insistent guidance of Jane Hayward (1918–1994), Curator at The Cloisters and, during the 1970s and 1980s, adjunct professor at Columbia University, who was sent, soon after the end of World War II, by Sumner Crosby to work in France with Louis Grodecki on a stained-glass dissertation topic. See M. Stokstad, "Jane Hayward (1918–1994): *'Radiance and Reflection,'*" *Women Medievalists and the Academy*, ed. Jane Chance (Madison, Wis., 2005), 781–788.

20. The ultimate extension of this still-popular explanation of Gothic stained-glass as interior decoration is a lingering and widespread assumption that when installed in their architectural context, windows were unreadable, that the subjects, symbols, and stories represented within them could not be seen well enough by medieval viewers to be identified, much less understood. This is straightforwardly false. Even in a program as dizzyingly complex as the Parisian Sainte-Chapelle, where the individual scenes within narrative windows are relatively small, the artists who designed them took viewer vantage point into consideration in devising spare compositions populated by strongly silhouetted figures. Painted articulation is bold and forceful. Even in the tracery lights at the top, the identities and actions of the figures are clear, narratives are legible, and meaningful associations are discernible by viewers well-informed or well-directed enough to grasp them. Similarly, windows installed in the vast spaces of cathedrals such as Bourges and Chartres, were designed specifically to take their lofty locations in the high clerestory windows into account, specifically so that they could be seen and "read." Gothic stained glass was not an abstract art, even if some current viewers who find the subjects unfamiliar and the messages obtuse or unsavory choose to see it that way. We must keep in mind that we are not the intended audience for these windows.

artistic communities, within workshops, reflecting traditions and absorbing influences, and that stained-glass windows frequently embody ideas,[21] especially those aimed at learned audiences.

But most of us have moved beyond such Modernist concerns to explore now more nourishing Postmodern questions and broader Postmodern understandings. I am probably using this word "Postmodern" in a personal, perhaps Postmodern way. What I mean is that we are envisioning these works within a less tidy and more human-centered context of production, and most especially reception. Instead of confining them to an insular art world, we seek to conjure up how they functioned within Gothic social systems, ritual communities, and ideological frameworks. They are now allowed more than one context of meaning, as reflections of the deepest values and concerns of worshipers and patrons, rulers and bishops, women and men across the social order.

This humanizing and pluralizing Postmodern approach has revisited the production management concerns of Modernist interpreters, attempting to turn the artists within workshops or large cathedral projects into distinctive human beings, whose styles transcended regional or workshop definition. Meredith Parsons Lillich has been a pioneer here.[22] Assessing two artists who worked side by side in the glazing of the Norman Cathedral of Sées (*c.* 1270–1285),[23] she characterizes the Jean de Bernières Master's style in a representation of Saint Peter (Fig. 2a) through the "truncated, squirrel-like arms and hands, small knoblike heads on real necks; a torsion between the angled upper body and straight legs, and a careful silhouetting of the contained form against the ground." She contrasts the style of this painter with another, her Magdalen Master, who used the same design but gave it his own stamp (Fig. 2b). She says, "The Magdalen Master is an expressionist of flair and power, whose art, while related in its distortion to the Jean de Bernières Master, has thrown care to the winds." By allowing the painters of Gothic windows to have personalities—divergent and distinctive personalities—Postmodern interpreters like Lillich have brought Modernist production management concerns to a deeper level of human interest. Her work may seem speculative, but the rarified air needed freshening.

Other Postmodern explorers have gone elsewhere, opening up the possibility that style might not always be the personal marker of artist or workshop, suggesting it may have been tailor made to a certain extent from window to window, project to project, depending on the message that was being presented or the audience being addressed, sorted by modality not just rooted in individual artists' personality or training.[24] Others have attempted to personalize donors as well

21. For examples of impressive recent scholarship in the Panofskian mode of iconography and iconology, see Kurmann-Schwarz and Lautier, "Recherches récente" (as in note 1), 318–321.

22. These reflections began as a tribute to Meredith Parsons Lillich, presented as part of a symposium in November 2010—"Medieval Glass Illuminates What Art and Reason Reveal"—organized at the Corning Museum of Glass by Florian Knothe and Eric Ramírez-Weaver on the occasion of her retirement. This written version is affectionately dedicated to her as well, in acknowledgement of and in gratitude for her lasting impact on my life in art history. Meredith not only supported me—I am not sure I would have completed my dissertation without her—but challenged me to ever greater precision of thought and expression. For her own assessment of her life in art history, see "Ars Longa, Vita Brevis (1936–)," in *Women Medievalists* (as in note 19), 933–944.

23. Much as I admire Lillich's characterization of these artists' windows, and those of their colleagues, in her brilliant book, *The Armor of Light: Stained Glass in Western France, 1250–1325* (Berkeley, 1994), it was an earlier exploratory article that was most influential for me: "A Stained-Glass Apostle from Sées Cathedral (Normandy) in the Victoria and Albert Museum," *Burlington Magazine* 119 (1977), 496–501. Although Grodecki became the central figure in the formation of the Modernist school of stained-glass studies in France and its extension into the United States—because of his academic posts, his international contacts, and his forceful personality—it was his older contemporary, Jean Lafond (1888–1975), who stood behind this aspect of Lillich's scholarship, and thus prefigures this line of Postmodern inquiry. Lafond wrote poetically, perceptively, and profoundly of the art of the masters whose work captivated him—extraordinary artists like sixteenth-century master Engrand Le Prince, perhaps the greatest French painter of the Renaissance. See, e.g., J. Lafond, "La Renaissance," in *Le vitrail français* (as in note 7), 213–256. Lillich has walked proudly in Lafond's footsteps, and in doing so, inspired many of her own followers, including me, to probe the human dimensions of the staggering stylistic diversity among Gothic stained-glass windows.

24. I have explored this possible interpretation of stylistic diversity in the Virgin Chapel windows from the 1240s at Beauvais

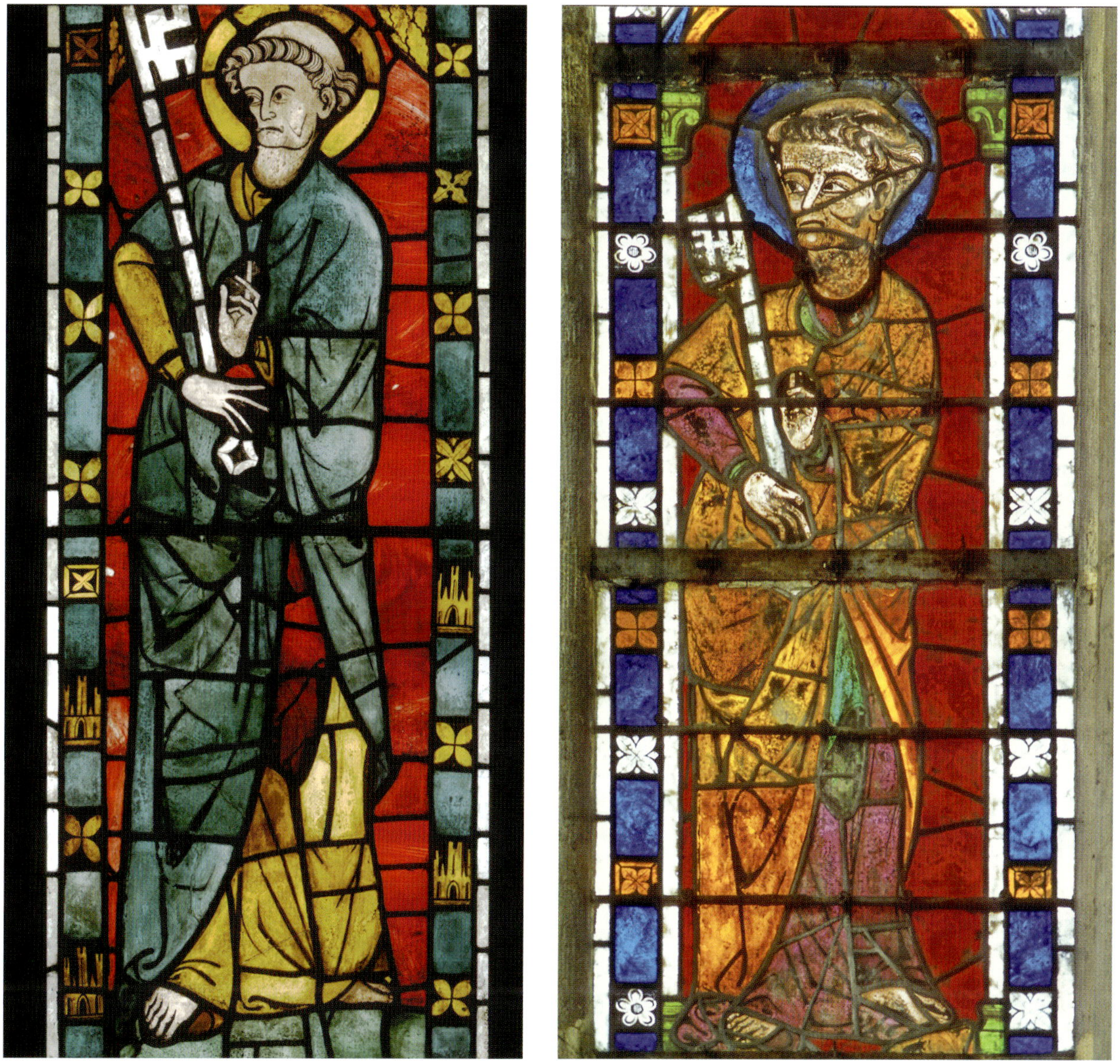

FIGURE 2. Cathedral of Sées, two figures from stained-glass windows (*c.* 1270–1285): (A) north transept figure of Saint Peter painted by Lillich's Jean de Bernières Master and now in London, Victoria and Albert Museum; and (B) axial chapel figure of Saint Peter painted by Lillich's Magdalene Master (photos: A: © London, Victoria and Albert Museum; B: Gordon Plumb).

as artists, exploring how stained glass windows could embody the individual concerns of wealthy nobles, or the ideology of rulers like French King Louis IX who built the Sainte-Chapelle to embody and proclaim the underpinnings of his right to rule, even situating himself, as Alyce Jordan has demonstrated, within a window that recounts his own life.[25]

Here, however, I want to focus on two other Post-

Cathedral: M. W. Cothren, *Picturing the Celestial City: The Medieval Stained Glass of Beauvais Cathedral* (Princeton, N.J., 2006), 98–99.

25. A. Jordan, *Visualizing Kingship in the Windows of the Sainte-Chapelle*, Publications of the International Center of Medieval Art 5 (Turnhout, 2002). For another instance of personalized donors, see M. P. Lillich, "The Choir Clerestory Windows of La Trinité at Vendôme: Dating and Patronage," *Journal of the Society of Architectural Historians* 34 (1975), 238–250.

modern concerns, involving reception more than production, the way thirteenth-century viewers encountered and interacted with these windows more than the way thirteenth-century artists and patrons created them.[26] First, I will stake a claim for some windows as visualized sermons, and then I will try to recreate the way others served as backdrops to set the stage for the performance of the liturgy.

Perhaps the most prevalent generalization about the interaction between stained-glass windows and their medieval audiences is a pervasive claim that these tableaux served as Bibles for the Illiterate, that folks who could not read words were able to gain access to scripture through works of visual art. Of course this is a ridiculous idea.[27] Medieval audiences learned their Bible stories by listening to them, part of a rich oral culture that we cannot recover and usually assume was equivalent to surviving texts. The observers of the stories in stained-glass windows already knew the plots, or they could depend on hearing the plots on site. Madeline Harrison Caviness was a pioneer here. Her powerful article of 1992 [28] argued convincingly for stained glass as an art of strategic story-telling, judicious juxtaposition, and multiple messages. Windows cast familiar stories in a special light, so to speak, interpreted them, used them to teach a focused lesson to a target audience. In this sense, they were similar to moralizing sermons. How the stories are told may be more important than the stories themselves.[29] Clear examples are the Theophilus windows that are common in thirteenth-century French cathedral glazing programs.[30]

The story of Theophilus the penitent may have been the most popular miracle of the Virgin Mary during this period because it was a powerful narrative evocation of her ability to intercede in the lives of repentant sinners and because it could be told in a way that would engage those who needed to know its lesson. Theophilus was a heinous sinner; he entered into an alliance with the Devil himself. But the power of the Virgin—most significantly, in the context of the institutional church and its leaders—was still capable of orchestrating his rescue.

What is particularly stunning about thirteenth-century Theophilus windows is the immediacy with which the story unfolds. Not only does it take place in the present—that is standard practice in thirteenth-century hagiographic and Biblical narrative—but many scenes are staged as contemporary social or political rituals that would have been familiar to mid-thirteenth-century observers. For example, Theophilus's pact with the devil is portrayed as a medieval ceremony in which fealty was signified through the grasping of hands (Fig. 3a).[31] One way the reinstated Theophilus displays power is through the ceremonial receipt of a fish, presented to the enthroned vidame by a kneeling suitor (Fig. 3b). Certain contemporary viewers would have recognized this as another feudal ritual: obligations were frequently paid in fish, and fish were popular good-will offerings from dependents to superiors.[32] In yet another scene—following his repentance and salvation—Theophilus is stripped to the waist, kneeling before his bishop for penitential scourging (Fig. 3c). Like

26. For a very thoughtful and perceptive overview of this trend toward exploring reception in the broader context of medieval art history, but with specific reference to stained-glass studies, see M. H. Caviness, "Reception of Images by Medieval Viewers," in *A Companion to Medieval Art: Romanesque and Gothic in Northern Europe*, ed. C. Rudolph (Oxford, 2006), 65–85.

27. On the critical history of this spurious notion, derived from comments made *c.* 600 by Pope Gregory the Great, see L. G. Duggan, "Was Art Really the 'Book of the Illiterate'?" *Word & Image* 5/3 (1989), 227–251; *idem*, "Reflections on 'Was Art Really the Book of the Illiterate?'" in *Reading Images and Texts: Medieval Images and Texts as Forms of Communication*. Third Utrecht Studies in Medieval Literacy (Turnhout, 2005), 109–120. See also H. L. Kessler, "Gregory the Great and Image Theory in Northern Europe during the Twelfth and Thirteenth Centuries," in *Companion to Medieval Art* (as in note 26), 151–172.

28. M. H. Caviness, "Bible Stories in Windows: Were They Bibles for the Poor?" in *The Bible in the Middle Ages: Its Influence on Literature and Art*, ed. B. S. Levy, Medieval and Renaissance Texts and Studies 89 (Binghamton, N.Y., 1992), 103–147.

29. On the way strategic story telling can frustrate the demands of Panofskian iconography, see M. W. Cothren, "Who Is the Bishop in the Virgin Chapel of Beauvais Cathedral?" *Gazette des Beaux-Arts* 125 (1995), 1–16.

30. M. W. Cothren, "The Iconography of Theophilus Windows in the First Half of the Thirteenth Century," *Speculum* 59 (1984), 308–341.

31. *Ibid.*, 324–325.

32. *Ibid.*, 325–327.

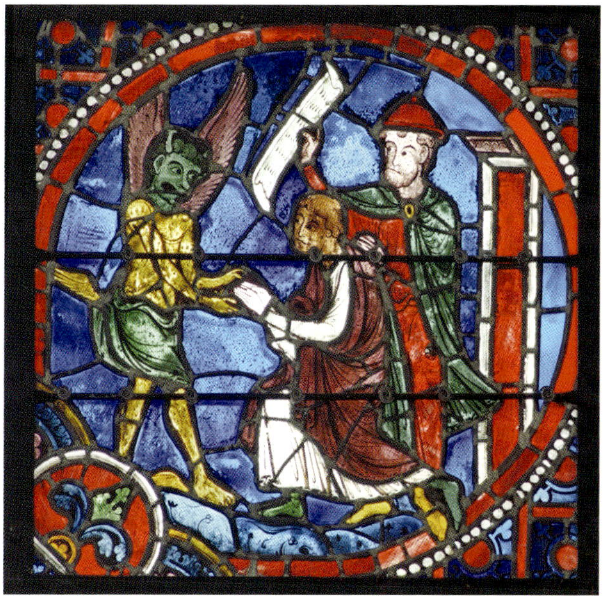

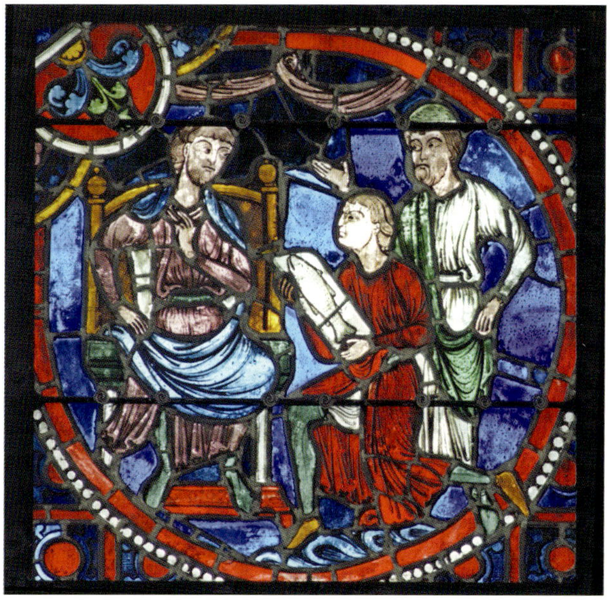

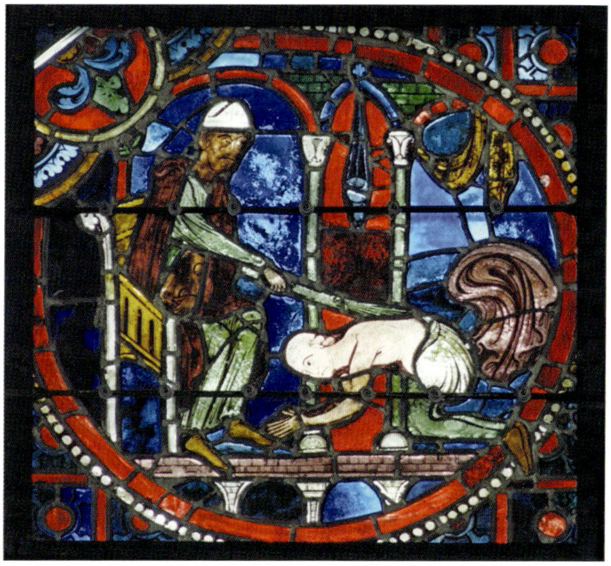

FIGURE 3. Cathedral of Laon, three scenes from the Theophilus window of the east wall, *c.* 1200: (A) Theophilus's Pact with the Devil; (B) Theophilus Receiving a Fish; (C) Theophilus's Penitential Scourging (photos: Stewart H. Rosenberg).

the sealing of the pact and the donation of the fish, this scene is rooted in actual thirteenth-century ceremony.[33]

The sense of immediacy gained through such references to the rituals of contemporary life, in the widely accessible monumental art of a stained-glass window, prominently located in a prominent building, capitalized on the ability of the Theophilus legend to teach its moral lesson in a direct manner to a particular class of thirteenth-century observers. Those who wielded power and amassed wealth were reminded that they were especially vulnerable to the temptations of earthly reward that led to Theophilus's downfall. But they were also assured that even if confused priorities had already compromised their position within the Christian order, repentance could mobilize a powerful ally, the Virgin Ecclesia, who would reroute their lives to the path of virtue. You can come home again.[34]

33. For example, Robert de Lisle, bailiff of Gerberoy in the diocese of Beauvais, was found guilty in 1247 of usurping power from the local church. His penitential sentence required him to walk from the marketplace to the church with bared feet and shoulders, carrying a switch in his hand. When he arrived he was directed to humble himself before the assembled clergy, promise never again to violate the rights of the church, and receive whatever punishment the clerics wished to inflict on him. After his performance in Gerberoy, he was to repeat the entire spectacle at the Cathedral of Beauvais, where the scene of penitential scourging in the Theophilus window of its Virgin Chapel had probably only recently been installed. *Ibid.*, 328–329.

34. For more recent examples of studies of narrative strategies that relate the stories in windows to contemporary or local concerns, see Kurmann-Schwarz and Lautier, "Recherches récente" (as in note 1), 316.

In her already cited, narratological study of the windows of the Sainte-Chapelle, Alyce Jordan has shown that the way stories are constructed in the royal chapel—both the scenes that are chosen and the way they are presented—is equally critical to their ability to "fuse biblical past and historical present in the figure of Louis IX."[35] Here the idea is not teaching a moral lesson but proclaiming an ideological manifesto. Jordan cites not only the well-known scenes of coronation, but also a conspicuous emphasis on the performance, in the lives of his sacred precursors, of royal duties such as fighting infidels and dispensing justice. She concludes, "Collectively, these themes compose a virtual essay on the topic of kingship that posits Old Testament leaders and exempla for Louis IX and, by implication, identifies Louis—the literal and metaphorical heir to the Crown of Christ—as the virtuous descendent of his biblical forebears."[36] Identifying the subject matter of these windows is not enough; we need to understand how the stories are told.

But not all Gothic windows used focused narrative strategies to preach sermons or embody political ideology. Some pictured theology. In the Virgin Chapel at the Cathedral of Beauvais—where a Theophilus window appears to the viewer's right—a central window combines three themes focusing on the relationship of Jesus and his Virgin Mother (Fig. 4). The left lancet contains a Jesse Tree, diagramming Jesus' descent, through his mother, from the kings of Judah. The flanking lancet on the right outlines Jesus' early life, celebrating the Virgin's role as vehicle of the Incarnation. Finally at the summit of the ensemble, in an iconic Crucifixion, the Virgin symbolizes the Church witnessing its institution, while underneath the cross, the original sinner Adam rises from his tomb to gather the blood of Christ's redemptive sacrifice.

I have argued that the position of this window at the center of the chapel ensemble, visible to worshipers in the main choir as well as within the chapel itself, is important (Fig. 5, lower arrow).[37] The top of the window hovers directly over the head of the celebrant while he re-enacts Christ's sacrifice by performing the Mass at the main, high altar, just as the whole window hovers above the priest when the same performance takes place within the more restricted space of the chapel itself. In the upper part of the lancets (Fig. 4), visible from the main choir, an enthroned Christ surrounded by doves at the top of the Jesse Tree sits as the culmination of a venerable, sacred, Jewish tradition, while the flanking Fall of the Idols at the top of the adjacent lancet signifies Christ's acceptance by gentiles, whose pagan deities tumble uselessly at the Holy Family's arrival in Egypt. Floating above these portrayals of Christ culminating one tradition and supplanting another, is a circular Crucifixion in which he institutes a third.

But such ensembles were not commentaries for scholars—either those who may have conceived them or those, like Panofsky and Grodecki, who labored to interpret their sources and significance. These were stage sets constructed for the performance of the Eucharist. The juxtaposition at Beauvais of this liturgical ceremony and a circular window that portrayed the event this ceremony is meant to commemorate had particular resonance toward the middle of the thirteenth century. At the climax of the Mass, when the celebrant elevated the conspicuously circular consecrated host, and with it the eyes of all present, these relationships—both symbolic and formal—would have been especially clear. After all, the sacramental significance of the Crucifixion is underlined in the window by the portrayal of Adam under the cross, whose elevation of the chalice makes a direct connection between Christ's sacrifice and the celebration of the Eucharist, both liturgically and gesturally. Full-page depictions of the Crucifixion incorporating Adam, often chalice in hand, at the foot of the cross, were common in thirteenth-century French Missals (Fig. 6), the books that outlined the liturgy of the Mass for priests, so the associations are documented concretely in service books.

For most who viewed the window in the context of thirteenth-century ceremony, however, books were not part of everyday life. The context was more visual than verbal. When these stained-glass windows were

35. Jordan, *Visualizing Kingship* (as in note 25), 73.
36. *Ibid.*, 28.
37. Cothren, *Picturing the Celestial City* (as in note 24), 17–24.

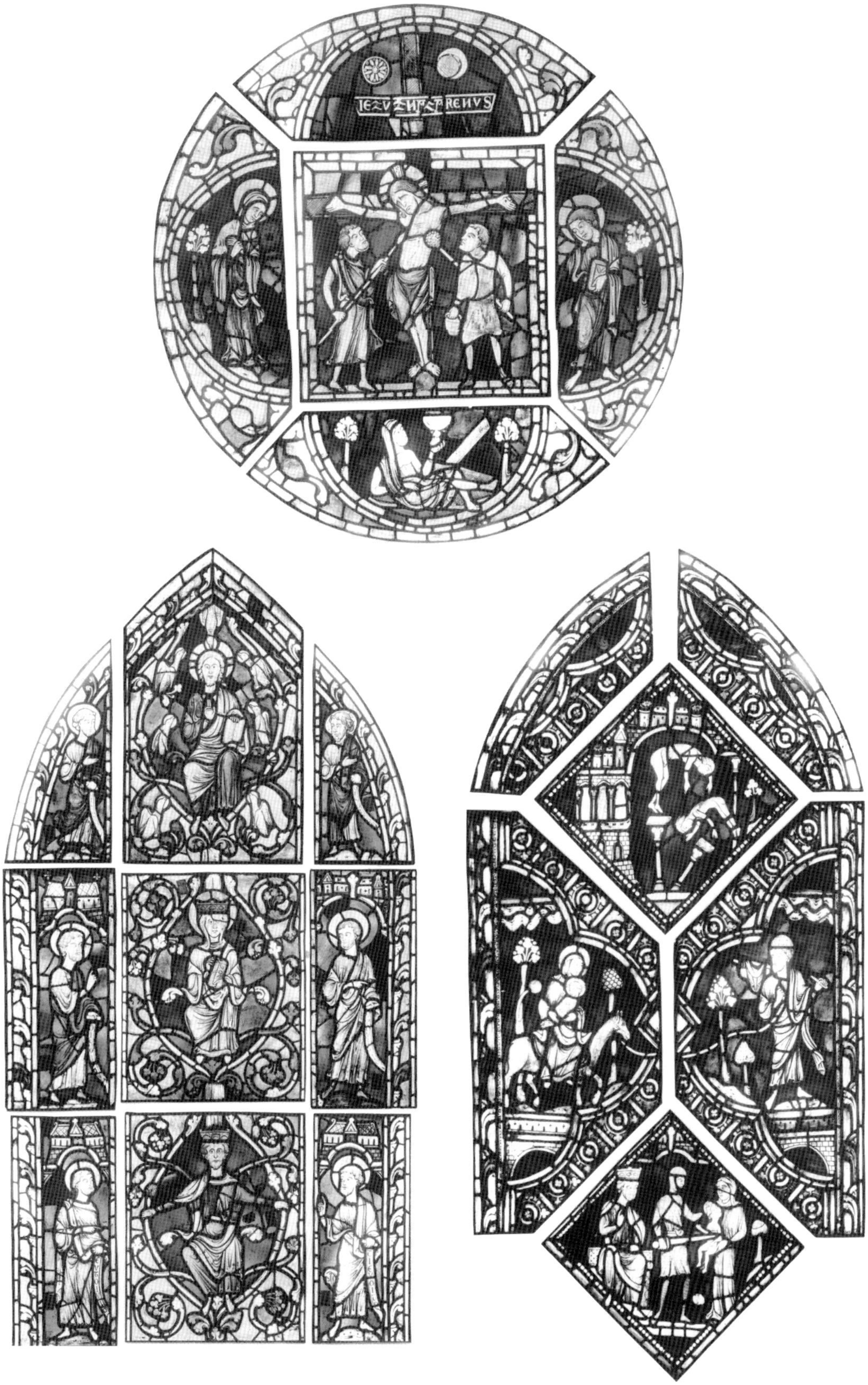

FIGURE 4. Cathedral of Beauvais, axial Virgin Chapel, upper registers and rose of axial Infancy and Jesse Tree window, 1240s (photomontage: author).

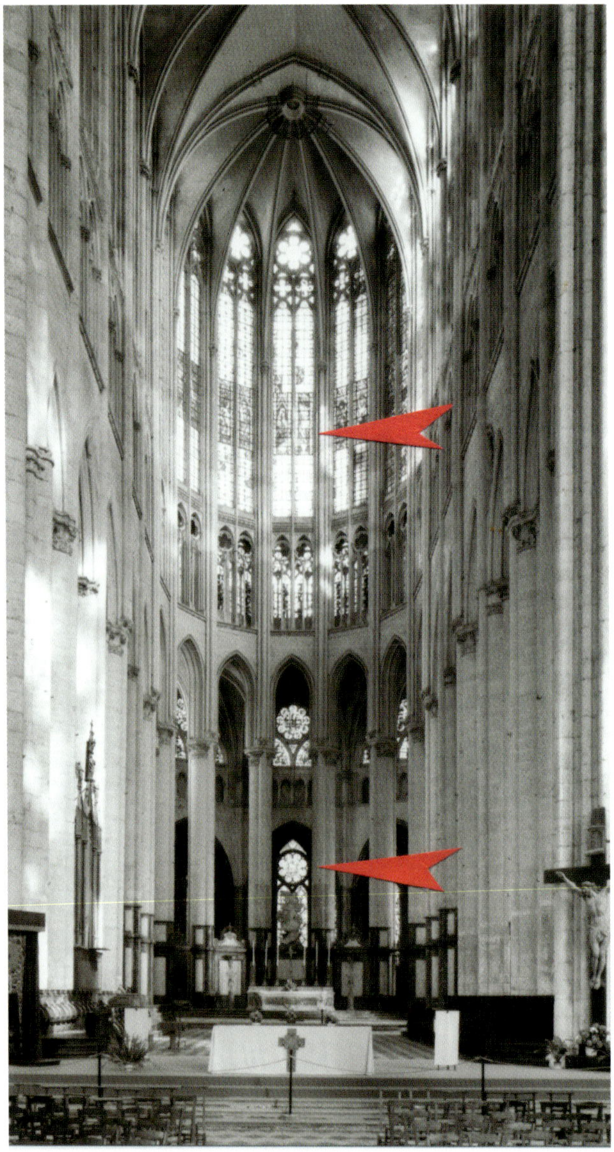

FIGURE 5. Cathedral of Beauvais, view into the choir with arrows indicating locations of Sacramental Crucifixions in the Virgin Chapel (*below*) and the hemicycle clerestory (*above*) (photomontage: author).

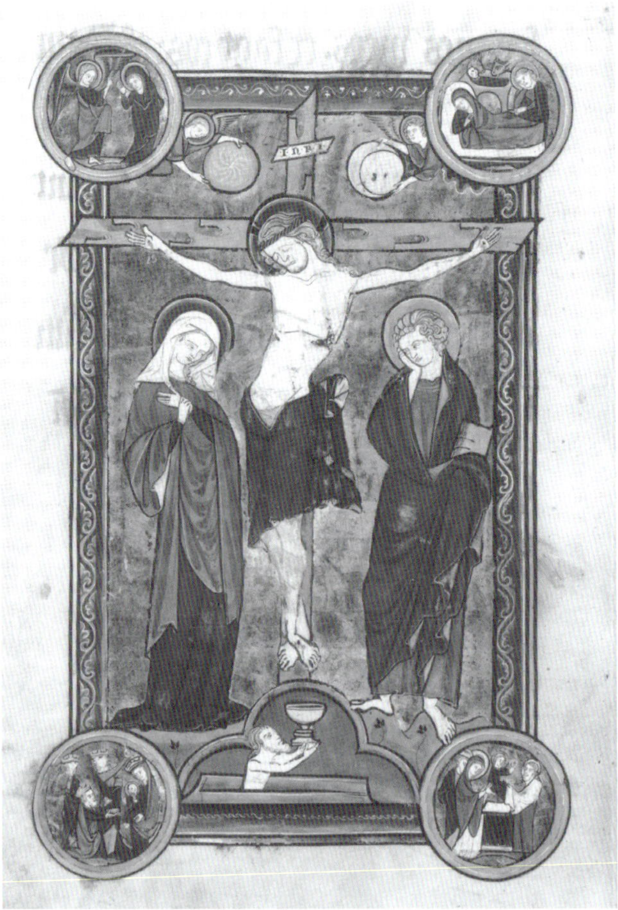

FIGURE 6. Sacramental Crucifixion with scenes from the Infancy of Christ, full-page miniature from a thirteenth-century Parisian missal (Paris, BNF, Ms. lat. 12054, fol. 148v) (photo: BNF).

installed in the Virgin Chapel during the 1240s, the elevation of Eucharistic bread during the Mass was a moment of real consequence. The proper gesture is outlined in the rubric of a Franciscan missal of 1243: as the priest recites the words *Hoc est corpus meum*—"This is my body"—he is given the following instructions: "as the Lord's body is adored, he raises it reverently with a moderate inclination so that all those surrounding can see it." [38] Such elevations of the host were accompanied by the ringing of bells to assure the attention of the faithful. Special provisions were made for illuminating the host to intensify its visibility. Indeed, *seeing* was a vital part of lay piety at Mass. Taking communion was mandated only once a year and generally recommended for the laity on no more than three occasions, but viewing the host at its elevation during the Mass

38. As cited in M. Rubin, *Corpus Christi: The Eucharist in Late Medieval Culture* (Cambridge, 1991), 56; see also p. 97.

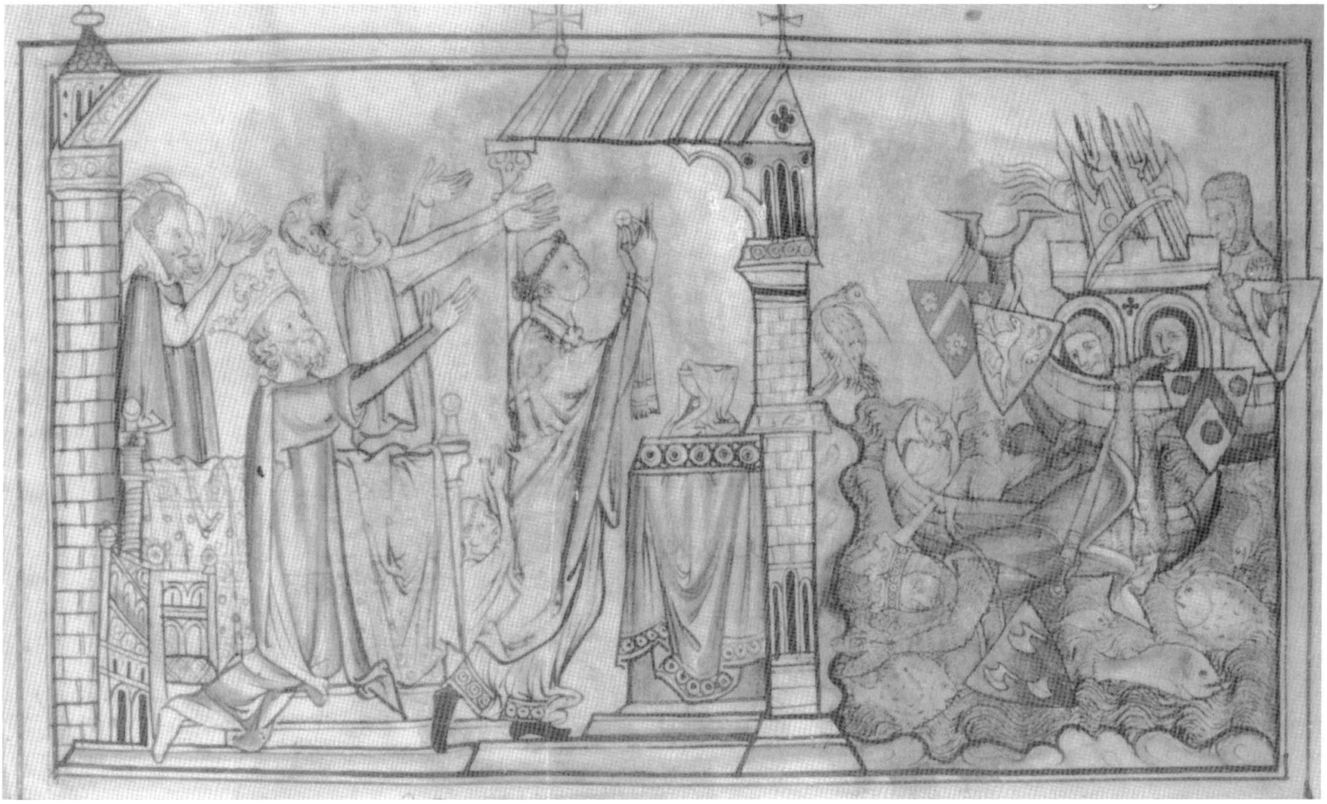

FIGURE 7. Saint Edward the Confessor's Vision at Mass of the drowning of the king of Denmark, from a thirteenth-century illustrated life of the saint (Cambridge, University Library, Ms. Ee.3.59, fol. 12) (photo: London, Conway Library, The Courtauld Institute of Art).

was a more frequent devotional experience. As Paul Binski has put it, "For the most part Mass was experienced not corporeally, by the consumption by the laity of the Body and Blood, but visually, by the ingestion of the elements of the Mass by the organs of sight ... the elevation of the Host after its consecration and transformation became the central moment of the Mass." [39] In thirteenth-century manuscripts—such as in the scene from the life of Edward the Confessor in Figure 7 [40]—this moment is often highlighted to represent Christian devotion and priestly activity, becoming a visual sign for the Mass itself. As is clear in this picture, visions were not uncommon at the sight of the elevated host.[41]

At Beauvais, it would seem, whether celebrated at the main choir altar or within the liturgical space of the Virgin Chapel, a vision at and of the elevation of the host was built into the glazing program, a circular illuminated apparition that perpetuated the moment of elevation. Representing the Eucharistic host by both shape and subject, the axial rose in the axial chapel was a continual reminder of the meaning of the Mass, a gargantuan blazing host, stamped with a vision of its roots in Christ's sacrifice on the cross.

This is not the end of the story as far as the Cathedral of Beauvais is concerned. The windows of the Virgin Chapel were installed sometime during the

39. P. Binski, *Westminster Abbey and the Plantagenets: Kingship and the Representation of Power, 1200–1400* (New Haven, Conn., 1995), 141; see also Rubin, *Corpus Christi* (as in note 38), 77.

40. For this and other visions of Edward the Confessor during Mass, see Binski, *Westminster Abbey* (as in note 39), 146 (and for the manuscript itself, 57–63).

41. Rubin, *Corpus Christi* (as in note 38), 108–129.

1240s, before the upper part of the choir had been constructed. That happened in the 1250s and 1260s, and the stained-glass windows installed there contain not stories, but rows of standing figures, more legible at such a lofty distance from viewers on the floor below.[42] The axial diptych window, situated above the Virgin Chapel, however, certainly evokes a story (Fig. 8). The Crucified Christ hangs from the cross in the right lancet, his arms bent and raised in order to fit this lateral subject into a vertical format, and his mother stands in the lancet next to him, adoring him and at the same time mourning his fate. Underneath the cross, a huge chalice, highlighted in white against the densely colored ground, collects Christ's blood in an obvious reference to the Mass. Therefore, on axis at Beauvais, in windows upstairs and downstairs, separated in date by several decades, the same theme appears, a theme that takes its meaning in relationship to the Mass celebrated below (Fig. 5). Clearly this is conceived as a setting for a sacred performance in a building that was much more like a theater than the art museum or sacred encyclopaedia that art historians so frequently make it.

I have concentrated here on Beauvais because it is the church whose windows I know best, but I suspect that using stained glass as a backdrop for the Mass was a widespread Gothic phenomenon. At the nearby Cathedral of Laon, there are no chapels surrounding the main altar, which is backed by an entire wall of windows—a gigantic wheel of a rose hovering over three tall lancets (Fig. 9). Consequently, as the priest stood at the main altar reciting the script of the liturgy, these windows appeared directly behind him (or, more strictly speaking, in front of him, since he would have faced them and the altar when saying Mass). In other words, they serve as a huge altarpiece backdrop. The program is not unlike that we have just examined in the Virgin Chapel at Beauvais.[43] The lancet to the viewers' right contains an account of the early life of Christ juxtaposed with scenes from the Hebrew Bible that prefigure them, functioning very much like the juxtaposition of Jesse Tree and early life in the central chapel window

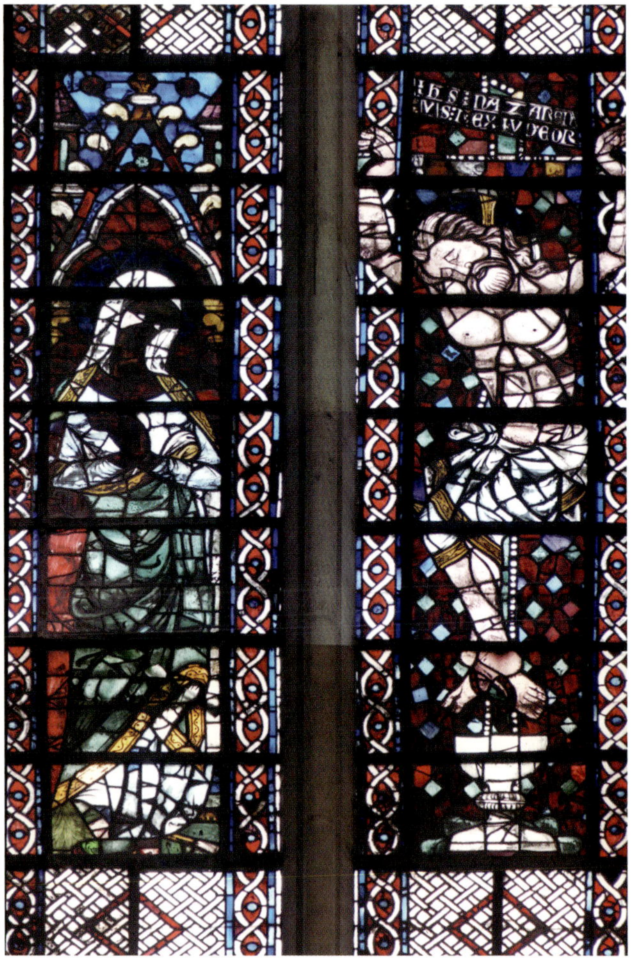

FIGURE 8. Cathedral of Beauvais, detail of axial choir clerestory window showing a sacramental Crucifixion, *c.* 1255–1265 (photo: Stewart H. Rosenberg).

at Beauvais, only here typology rather than genealogy pictures Christ's fulfillment of Jewish heritage. In the central lancet, the story of Christ's passion is told as a sequential narrative rather than condensed into the iconic Redemptive Crucifixion as at Beauvais, but the significance is the same in relation to the Mass, and the scenes are contained in forms that also recall the shape of the Eucharistic host that would be elevated in front of them. The window to the left is divided between the legend of Theophilus and the martyrdom of Saint

42. Cothren, *Picturing the Celestial City* (as in note 24), 100–123.

43. For a brilliant Panofskian analysis of the program in these windows, see C. Lautier, "Les vitraux du chevet de la cathédrale de Laon. Première approche," *Österreichische Zeitschrift für Kunst und Denkmalpflege* 54 (2000), 257–264.

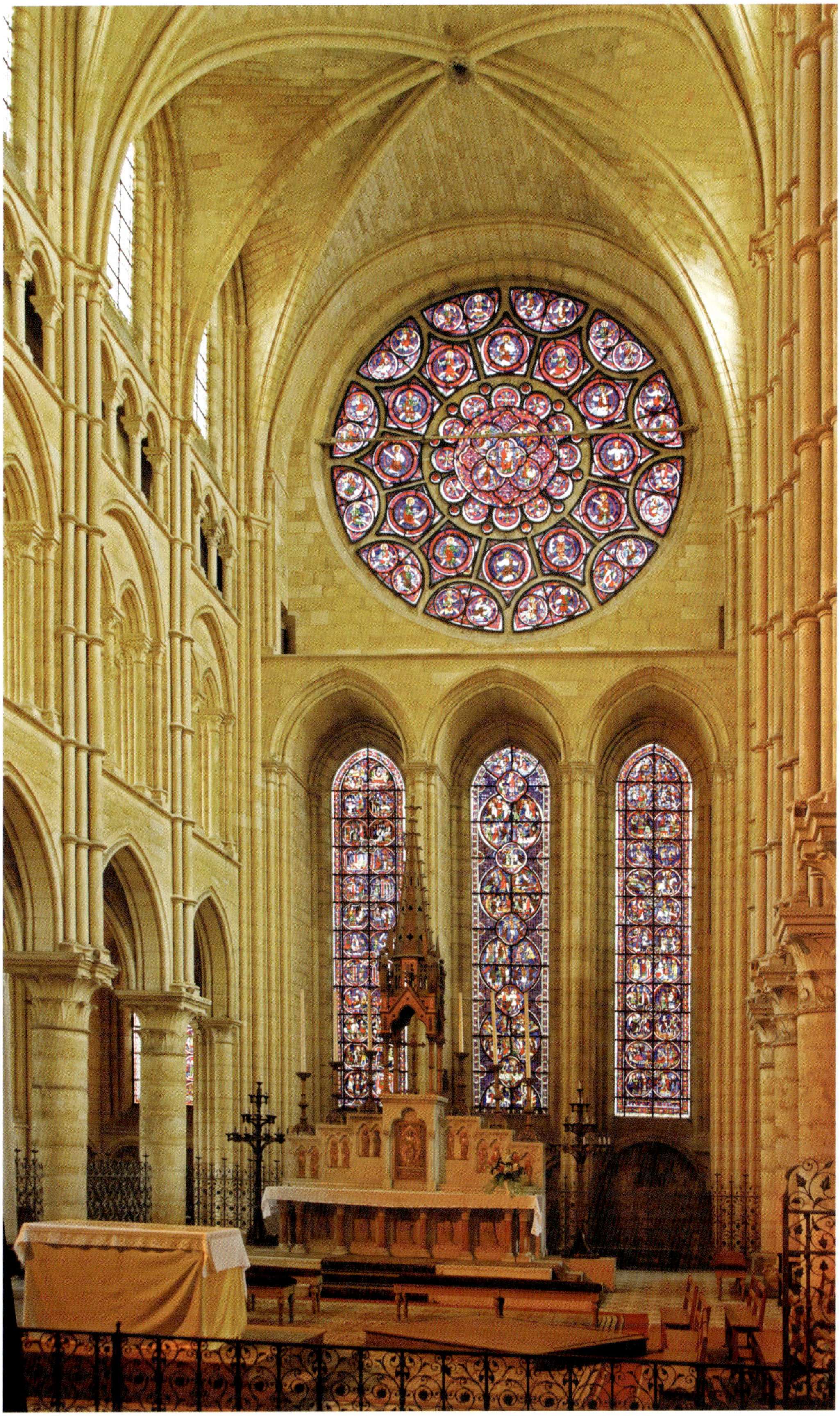

FIGURE 9. Cathedral of Laon, stained-glass ensemble in east wall, *c.* 1200 (photo: Painton Cowen).

Stephen, commentaries on sin, redemption, and sacrifice, all themes associated with the Mass. And at Laon the elevated host is evoked not in a small rose over paired lancets as at Beauvais, but in the monumental Apocalyptic glorification of the Virgin in the massive rose elevated above all three lancets. The program would have been completed only when the priest was under the windows saying Mass, and specifically when he was elevating the circular host, so it could resonate with the meanings, and also rhyme with the pervasive circular shapes, of the stained-glass ensemble.

As I hope to have shown, the foundational, Modernist, impersonal focus on abstract symbolism, architectural transformation, theological commentary, and production practice, has given way to—or at least been joined by—a new Postmodern attention to viewers as much as the newly humanized makers, to juxtaposed liturgical performance as much as to learned subject matter.[44] These new explorations deserve acknowledgement beyond the insular world of stained-glass studies, even beyond the somewhat broader world of medieval art history. The place to begin is with beginners. We must rewrite pertinent passages in our textbooks and rethink our lectures in art history surveys, making sure to acknowledge that this major medium of Gothic painting conveyed messages to diverse audiences, significant not only in moralizing and theological content, but centrally in relation to their performative context.[45]

44. Liturgical performance was not, of course, the only sort of ceremony or activity that took place surrounded by stained-glass windows in medieval churches. Relationships are emerging between windows and the local veneration of relics—e.g., C. Lautier, "Les vitraux de la cathédrale de Chartres: reliques et images," *Bulletin monumentale* 161 (2003), 3–96; *eadem*, "Le vitrail de Charlemagne à Chartres et les reliques du trésor de la cathédrale," in *Actes du colloque: Autour de Hugo d'Oignies* (Namur, 2004), 229–240; E. C. Pastan, "Charlemagne as Saint? Relics and the Choice of Window Subjects at Chartres Cathedral," in *The Legend of Charlemagne in the Middle Ages: Power, Faith, and Crusade*, ed. M. Gabriele and J. Stuckey (New York, 2008), 97–135; M. B. Shepard, "Power Windows: Relic Windows and the Context of Collective Remembering," in *Glasmalerei im Kontext: Bildprogramme und Raumfunktionen.* Akten des XXII. Internationalen Colloquiums des Corpus Vitrearum, ed. R. Becksmann, *Wissenschaftliche Beibände zum Anzeiger des Germanischen Nationalmuseums* 25 (Nuremberg, 2005), 75–88. Others are exploring the relationship with liturgical drama—e.g., A. F. Harris, "Saint Nicholas in Context: Stained Glass and Liturgical Drama in the Archbishopric of Sens," in *Glasmalerei im Kontext* (as above), 89–99; *eadem*, "The Performative Terms of Jewish Iconoclasm and Conversion in Two Saint Nicholas Windows at Chartres Cathedral," in *Beyond the Yellow Badge: Anti-Judaism and Antisemitism in Medieval and Early Modern Visual Culture*, ed. M. B. Merback (Leiden, 2007) 119–142. The breadth of approaches now actively pursued in stained-glass studies was clearly demonstrated in the extraordinarily wide-ranging papers presented in two sessions at the 46th International Congress on Medieval Studies in Kalamazoo in May 2011, organized for the International Center of Medieval Art by Elizabeth Pastan and Mary Shepard: "Glazing and Stained Glass: Collaborations, Analogies, and Investigations Involving Stained Glass and Other Disciplines."

45. I have moved in this direction in Stokstad and Cothren, *Art History*, 4th ed. (as in note 2), esp. 491, 503–505, 508–509.

WELLEDA MULLER

The Art of the Misericord: Neglected and Important

THE CARVED MISERICORDS of choir-stalls (folding benches against which a singer in a monastery or a cathedral might lean during the long chanted offices) are sometimes difficult to access in churches, even when they are not abandoned or damaged.[1] Frequently ignored by art historians, they have usually been considered as the work of carpenters (*huchiers*) who were often not necessarily skilled at woodcarving. The few twentieth-century art historians who were interested in choir-stalls first studied the large carved panels (*jouées*) at the sides and groups carved in high relief, such as those at Amiens (Fig. 1), whose

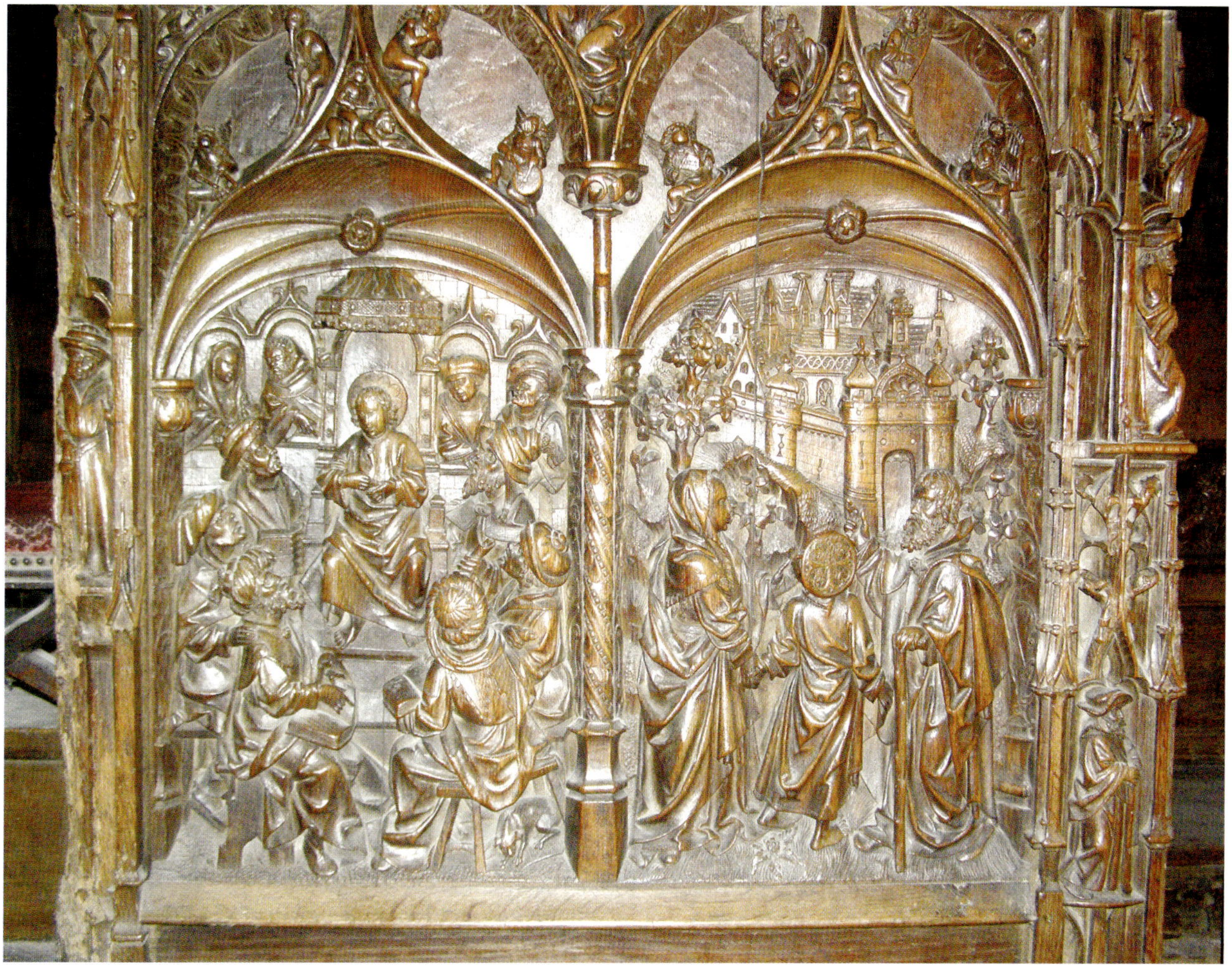

FIGURE 1. Amiens Cathedral, France, *Jouée*, 1508 (photo: author).

1. In France in particular, certain sets of stalls have been dismantled and stored in cellars, without any restoration or preservation.

dorsal panels and canopies are impressive. However, misericords have often been dismissed as an expression of the sometimes questionable fantasies of the *huchiers*, and were never thoroughly investigated until the last third of the twentieth century. Thus, the carved stalls, and especially the sculptures of the misericords, were seen by art historians as a minor form of art. But was this also true in the Middle Ages?

The thousands of photographs made available in the database of the Index of Christian Art reveal an art form much more subtle and sophisticated than has previously been recognized. The carvings are an important witness to daily medieval life, even more than the marginal iconography of manuscripts, which is often fabricated with fanciful non-realistic scenes. Furthermore, such insights into medieval society are even less represented in other media, such as altarpieces and stained glass, which depict essentially religious subjects.

Historiography

In the 1970s, Elaine C. Block, a professor at the City University of New York, hoping to teach the art of the Middle Ages to her students, began a systematic campaign to photograph misericords. She traveled across Europe to find groups of stalls and to study them for their anthropological and artistic potential. Prior to her work, there were very few studies on the subject, representative of which is the work of L. Maeterlinck on the misericords of Belgium (*Le genre satiriquee*), which was published in 1910.[2] Despite its value, Maeterlinck's work has many questionable iconographic interpretations, and moreover, he rarely references his sources. Following Elaine Block's pioneering work, other scholars became interested in misericords, including European philologists who founded the *International Reynard Society*.

In 1992, Elaine Block founded the association *Misericordia International* and attempted to make it as international as possible by involving academics from around the world (from the United States, France, England, Germany, Japan, etc.). Since 1997, *Misericordia International* has organized a conference every other year; it has its own journal, *Profane Arts of the Middle Ages*. The original interests of the group were both aesthetic and iconographic, and it is the latter that is now to the fore and the subject of all recent research.

Misericordia International has organized conferences dedicated to choir-stalls, and also supported colleagues in arranging seminars. The proceedings of two such conferences, those at Conques and Vendôme, were published in 1996[3] and 1999. Henry and Dorothy Kraus devoted a study to French misericords in 1986,[4] and Elaine Block began her *Corpus* series in 1990.[5] This latter publication was designed to publish her catalogue of all the choir-stalls in Europe, and to offer art historians basic information for their research. Each set of stalls was listed with a specific numbering and the iconography was identified in every case. She also developed a lexicon to describe the stalls, so that scholars could use the same vocabulary and the same numbering system. The lexicon has not yet been published and will be revised by members of *Misericordia International.*

Amongst the recent choir-stalls to be researched were the English examples in G. L. Remnant's 1969 catalogue of misericords in Great Britain.[6] This was prefaced by an iconographical essay by M. D. Anderson, and was followed by Remnant's catalogue of misericords in England, Scotland, Ireland, and Wales wherein he described each set of stalls and their iconography, and numbered them according to their position. Jan Verspaandonk undertook a systematic photographic coverage of misericords in Belgium and the Netherlands in the 1970s and 1980s and has published numerous articles and monographs on them.[7] More recently,

2. L. Maeterlinck, *Le genre satirique, fantastique et licencieux dans la sculpture flamand et wallonne: les miséricordes de stalles* (Paris, 1910).

3. *Le Miroir des Miséricordes XIIIe–XVIIe siècles: Les cahiers de Conques* 2 (March 1996).

4. H. & D. Kraus, *Le monde caché des miséricordes* (Paris, 1986).

5. E. C. Block, *Corpus of Medieval Misericords: France* (2003); *Iberia* (2005). (Turnhout: Brepols Publishers).

6. G. L. Remnant, *A Catalogue of Misericords in Great Britain* (Oxford, 1969).

7. For example, *Breda: de koorbanken van de Grote of Lieve Vrouwe Kerk* (Amsterdam, 1983).

Christa Grössinger has explored various iconographic themes in her articles and books (especially *The World Upside-Down*, and also *Humour and Folly*).[8] Since the late 1990s and early 2000s, a number of student theses have been undertaken on the stalls, all of which display an increasing interest in the study of this subject.[9]

The classification and the systematic development of a more comprehensive approach to the study of misericords throughout Europe is now being pursued by *Misericordia International*. Jos Koldeweij and Christel Theunissen at the University of Nijmegen in the Netherlands are working with Frédéric Billiet at the Sorbonne (who inherited Elaine Block's photographic collection), to create a documentary study that seeks to highlight the values of these carved works. The *Corpus* series of publications, although begun by Elaine Block, is being continued by members of *Misericordia International*. In her lifetime, Elaine Block published *France* (2003) and *Iberia* (2005); while Jos Koldeweij, Christel Theunissen, and Frédéric Billiet published the volume on the *Netherlands* in 2010.[10] Still remaining are those publications on Germany, Switzerland, and Northern Italy (in one volume) by Jos Koldeweij, Christel Theunissen, and Welleda Muller, and the corpus of Great Britain (England, Scotland, Ireland, Wales) under the direction of Paul Hardwick and Luuk Houwen.

The Internet has also revolutionized art-historical research, particularly on choir-stalls. Databases containing images of misericords and stalls have sprung up everywhere, providing researchers with valuable material. In Nijmegen (Radboud University), the database *Stalla* was created by Christel Theunissen to catalogue stalls across Europe, and it currently contains photos of stalls in the Netherlands, Belgium, part of Germany, and a few sets from France and Spain—through fully referenced pages including a detailed bibliography on each set. In Paris (Paris-Sorbonne University), *Musicastallis* was created by Frédéric Billiet and Xavier Fresquet, and lists images of musicians (including singers) and musical instruments in European stalls. This database is also the starting point of a larger project entitled *Musiconis*, which is envisaged as a web portal to access images of musicians or musical instruments in the Middle Ages in all media. The most comprehensive database to date is that in the Index of Christian Art, which hosts Elaine Block's entire photographic collection of choir-stalls.

Origin and Shape

Stalls existed from the early Christian period in the form of stone benches placed in the semi-circular apse of the choir, which were often fixed to the masonry. With the Gregorian reforms, the clergy used benches placed in front of the altar. Once these works were removed from their links to the masonry of the choir, wood came to be the preferred medium. Sitting was quite rare during the Mass and some theologians accused those who sat of "laziness," and saw standing as the only "valid" way to pray during divine service.[11] The invention of the misericord is more specific to the Middle Ages. The oldest preserved stalls today date from the early thirteenth century and it is even possible that an example now in the Museo Arqueologico Nacional of Madrid (mudéjars' choir-stalls without misericord) (Fig. 2) dates to the twelfth century. They are known to have existed from the eleventh century, since they are mentioned in the *Constitutiones* of the Monastery at Hirsau in Germany, which was founded in the eleventh century. In the monastic rules for this abbey the misericord is referred to by its correct name [12] and it

8. C. Grössinger, *The World Upside-Down: English Misericords* (London, 1997); *Humour and Folly in Secular and Profane Prints of Northern Europe, 1430–1540* (London, 2002).

9. For example, C. Charles, *Stalles sculptées du XVe siècle, Genève et le duché de Savoie* (Paris, 1999). K. Lemé-Hébuterne, *Les stalles d'Amiens* (Paris, 2008). W. Muller, *L'art des Huchiers restreint au mobilier liturgique des chœurs en pays bourguignon, flamand et rhéno-mosan aux XVe et XVIe siècles* (Dijon, 2009).

10. F. Billiet, J. Koldeweij, C. Theunissen, *Corpus of Medieval Misericords: Belgium and the Netherlands* (Turnhout: Brepols Publishers, 2010).

11. According to Peter Damian (988–1072) and Eudes Rigaud, Archbishop of Rouen from 1248 to 1269, quoted by Kraus, *Le monde caché des miséricordes* (as in note 4), 13.

12. *Constitutiones of Hirsau's monastery*, chap. XXIX.

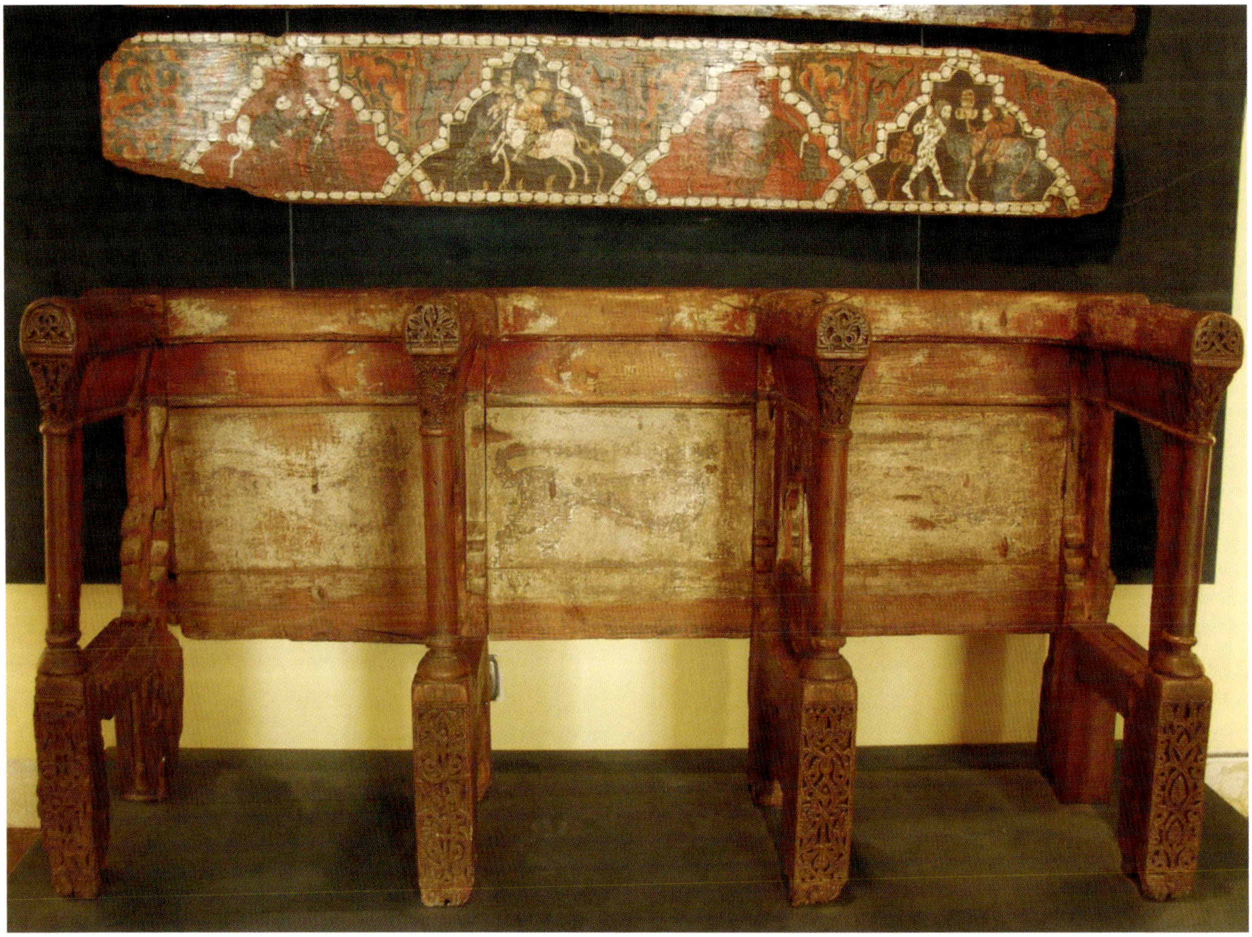

FIGURE 2. Museo Arqueologico Nacional, Madrid, Spain, Choir-stalls, twelfth century (photo: Elaine C. Block).

was reserved for the elderly or infirm monks who were to make use of it as discreetly as possible.

The use of a misericord to sit while seeming to stand, moreover, was strongly criticized in the eleventh century, notably by Peter Damian (d. 1072).[13] Ascetics saw it as a "depravity" on the part of monks whose only acceptable position during church services was to stand. Misericords therefore took several centuries to be adopted. By the thirteenth, fourteenth, and fifteenth centuries, stalls and misericords had become so indispensable to the clergy, that it seems that there was a real symbiosis between clerics and their stalls.[14] Every cleric had his own stall, and efforts to change seats, sometimes gave rise to quarrels. It happened in the case of canons that their stalls might be bequeathed.[15] Thus we may better understand the importance of stalls in the lives of the monks and canons.

The structure of misericords varied from region to region, and they had different shapes. Each group of misericords has a particular shape that may be considered a sort of a "signature" of the workshop of a single set of stalls. There are many different shapes from one

13. Especially in a letter to the Archbishop of Besançon cited by Kraus, *Le monde caché des miséricordes* (as in note 4), 13, 237.

14. Kraus, *Le monde caché des miséricordes* (as in note 4), 15.

15. The first case of a choir-stall being bequeathed dates to the 12th century: in the cathedral of Le Mans in 1137, when a canon donated his stall *Inventaire Sommaire* of Le Mans, série G, 21.

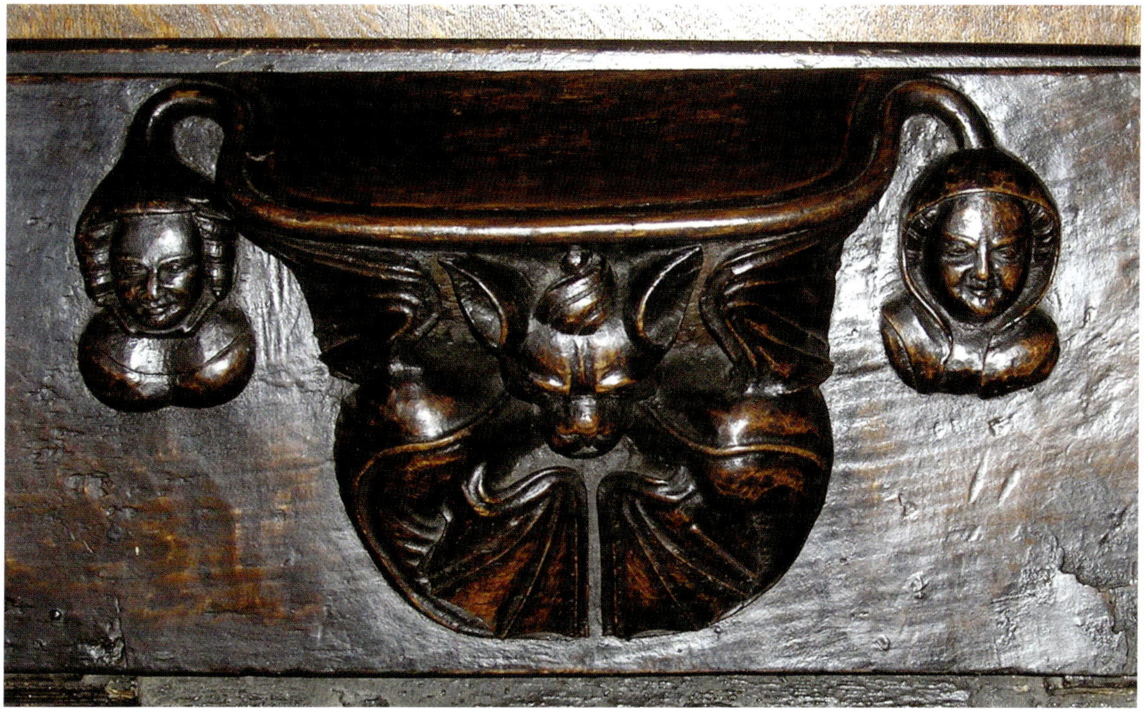

FIGURE 3. Chichester Hospital, Sussex, Great Britain, Misericord, 1290 (photo: Elaine C. Block).

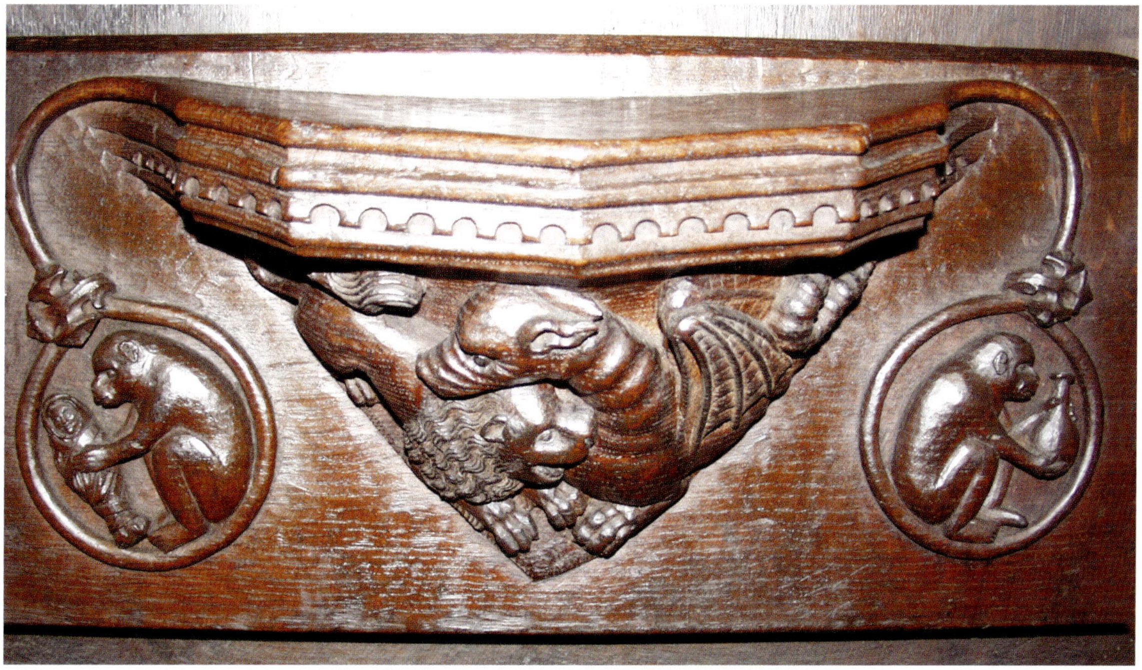

FIGURE 4. Beverley Minster, Yorkshire, Great Britain, Misericord, 1520 (photo: Elaine C. Block).

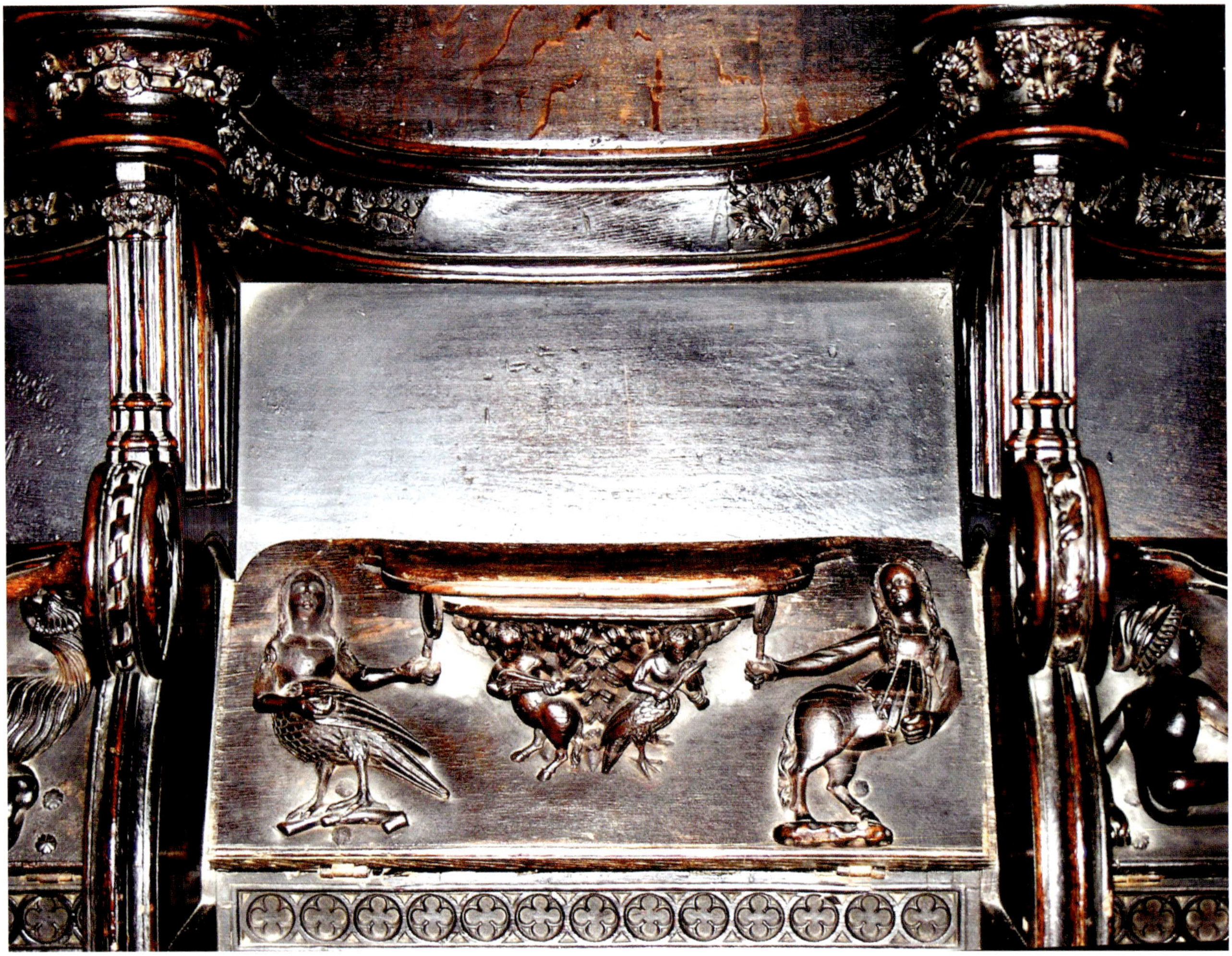

FIGURE 5. Barcelona Cathedral, Spain, Misericord, 1394–1399 (photo: Elaine C. Block).

century and from one country to another, as well as similarities, mainly among those made within the same local area. A unique style, with two sculptures on either side of the misericord's ledge, is associated with England (Figs. 3–4). Some English misericords have no sculptures,[16] but the vast majority of those from Great Britain (including Wales, Scotland, and Ireland), from the thirteenth to the sixteenth centuries, have two of these carvings on the ledge. One example found elsewhere is from the stalls of the cathedral in Barcelona (Fig. 5), which date from 1394 to 8 March 1399. We know that this set was made by two Flemish or Rhenish *huchiers*, Michael Lochner and Frederick Kassel, who were helped by "*Pere ça Anglada*" (Peter the English).[17] It is possible to deduce that they brought this structural and iconographic tradition from Great Britain.

The shapes of misericords are generally less elaborate in the thirteenth and fourteenth centuries. An early and original shape is found at the Abbey of Maigrauge in Fribourg (Fig. 6), which is curved and which

16. For example, Old Malton in the Yorkshire dated from the late 15th century and Ottery St. Mary in the Devonshire dated from 1342.

17. Elaine Block has several references to information about these three carvers in her *Corpus of Medieval Misericords, Iberia* (Turnhout, 2004), 17–22. See also T. Terés, "Pere ça Anglada Maestro del coro de la Catedral de Barcelona," *Lambard: Estudis d'art medieval*, vol. VII (1993–1994), 129–138.

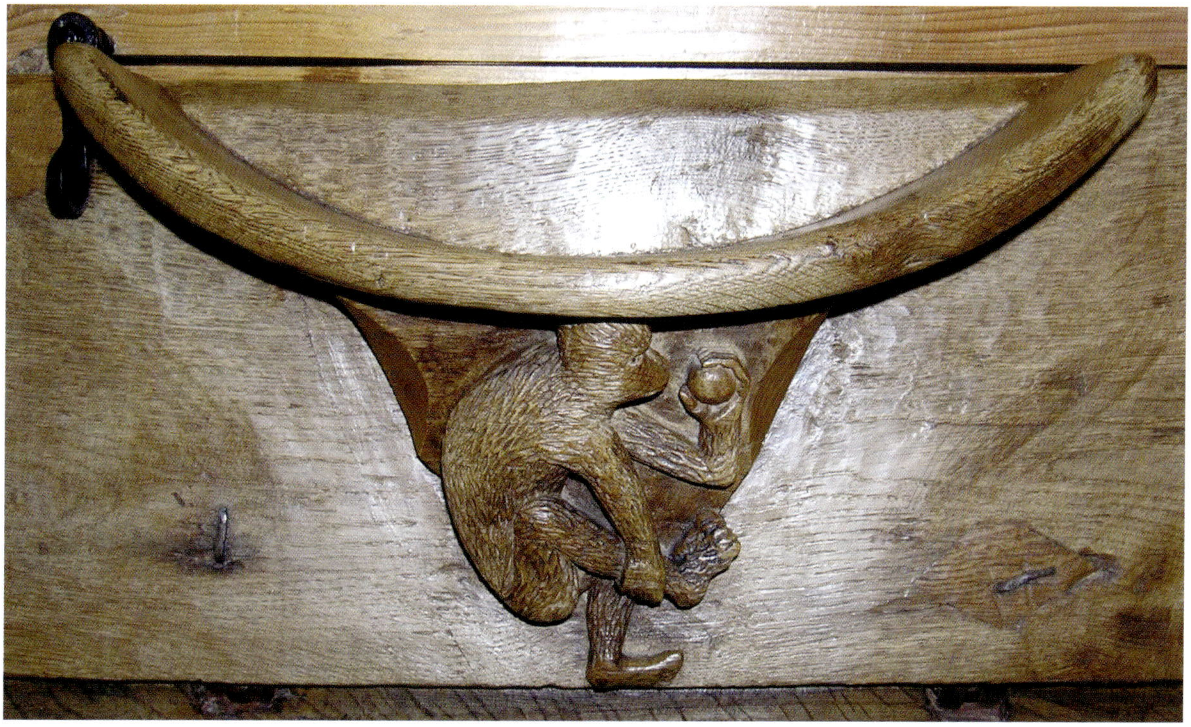

FIGURE 6. Maigrauge Abbey, Fribourg, Switzerland, Misericord, 1380 (photo: Elaine C. Block).

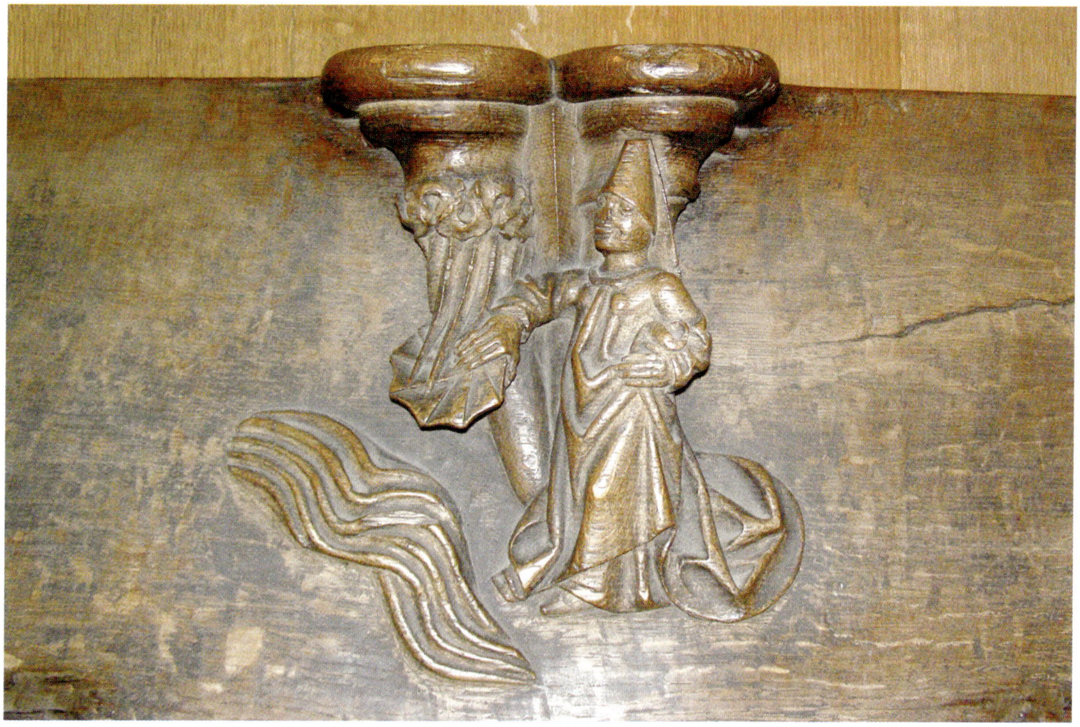

FIGURE 7. Church of St. Martin, Emmerich am Rhein, Nordrhein-Westfalen, Germany, Misericord, 1486 (photo: author).

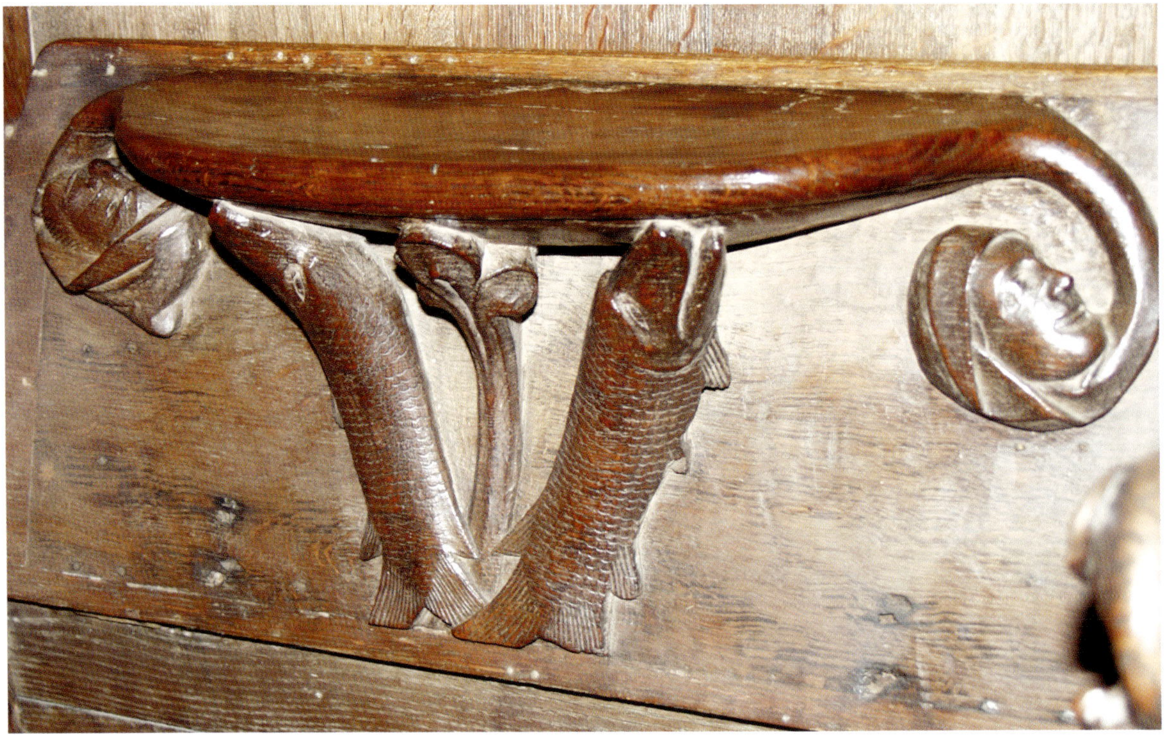

FIGURE 8. Exeter Cathedral, Devonshire, Great Britain, Misericord, 1238–1244 (photo: Elaine C. Block).

was certainly more comfortable than the flat examples found elsewhere. There is also a distinctive shape to some of the German stalls. In Nordrhein-Westfalen, several sets of misericords are carved in a form similar to two inverted cones (Fig. 7). This particular shape is also found in Cappenberg (Castel's chapel, late fifteenth century), Kleve (Minoriten Church, from 1474), Emmerich (St. Martin Church, from 1486, and made by the master of Cappenberg's choir-stall), Kempen (St. Mary Church, from 1487–1493), and Kalkar (St. Nicolas Church, from 1505–1508). Given these close dates, it appears that this was a style restricted to *huchiers* workshops in the region of Nordrhein-Westfalen. Unlike Great Britain, this shape is not found in other regions and did not appear to last very long.

Specific Iconography

Even though there are some sets of stalls in which certain episodes are taken from the Bible or from the lives of saints, by and large the iconography of misericords is almost exclusively profane. There is also considerable iconographical variety.

In the thirteenth and fourteenth centuries, however, the range of iconographic types was relatively limited. The subjects were mainly based on animals, literary characters, and monsters, and these occupied the whole misericord, without any secondary elaboration. There are Christological symbols, such as the fish (Fig. 8) or the Pelican, or even the *chrism*, but there are also other more exotic animals like the lion, the monkey (Fig. 6), or the elephant. These appear more frequently than the animals that were relatively "common" and known in western Europe, such as rabbits and chickens. Monsters and hybrids were also numerous, the most frequent being the mermaid, centaur, dragon or griffin. Many hybrid monsters consisting of completely fanciful and often unique combinations of human and animal forms (Fig. 5), similar to Hieronymus Bosch's *grylles*, are also found. Throughout the fourteenth and fifteenth centuries, the iconography displayed more imagination than realism and even the most common

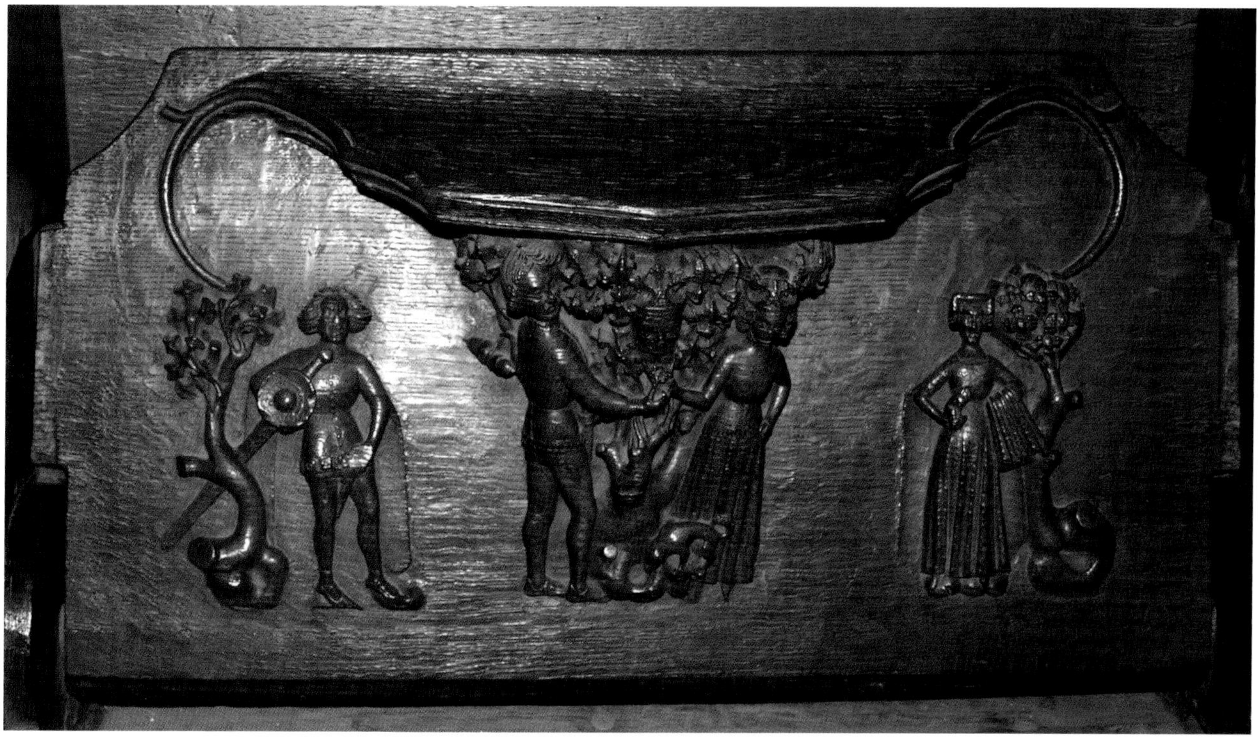

FIGURE 9. Chester Cathedral, Cheshire, Great Britain, Misericord, 1390 (photo: Elaine C. Block).

animals, such as deer and pigs, were not realistically represented. It is possible that it was the imagination that prevailed for sculptors, rather than objective reporting of the material world.

In fifteenth-century France—but from the fourteenth century in Great Britain—misericords became historiated, and figures and animals were linked. It was also at this time that fables and courtly romances were carved, especially in Great Britain, where the *Roman de Renart* and the story of Tristan and Isolde (Fig. 9) are found on several misericords. In the late fifteenth century and at the beginning of the sixteenth century, proverbs were illustrated on misericords (Fig. 10). This specific iconography appears to have started in Flanders, and spread from one end of Europe to another—from Portugal to Sweden.[18] Crafts and trades were also depicted. The *huchiers* who carved the stalls were of course shown, but depictions also included carpenters, blacksmiths, and cobblers (Fig. 11), as well as many other trades. In some places, as in Rouen for example, it is known that these trades were grouped into guilds or brotherhoods, and it is possible that they might have commissioned the stalls or offered financial assistance for their construction.[19] The scenes carved on misericords offer unrivalled insights into life and manners of the Middle Ages, making them important objects for material cultural studies in an anthropological context.

From the fifteenth century onwards and certainly into the sixteenth, carved scenes were much more realistic, and it is here that the subject matter was taken from nature. Examples include forest hunting scenes or urban settings showing small buildings. The quality

18. Elaine Block investigated the subject of proverbs in the stalls and highlighted their distribution in Europe, while establishing a connection between Flemish proverbs, the painting by Brueghel the Elder, and the proverbs that were depicted in groups of Belgian and Dutch stalls. See E. Block, "Proverbes flamands et miséricordes médiévales," *Le Miroir des Miséricordes* (as in note 3), 121–136.

19. E. Block and F. Billiet, *Les stalles de la cathédrale de Rouen, histoire et iconographie* (Rouen, 2001).

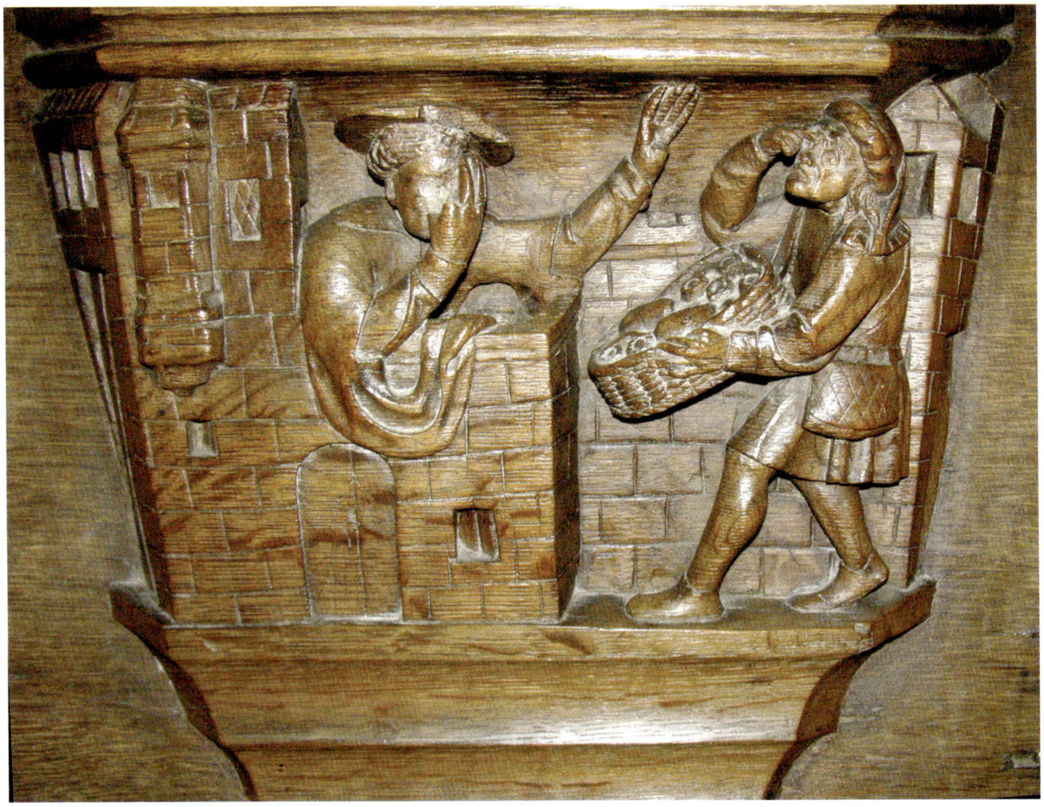

FIGURE 10. Church of St. Catherine, Hoogstraeten, Belgium, Misericord, 1532–1548 (photo: author).

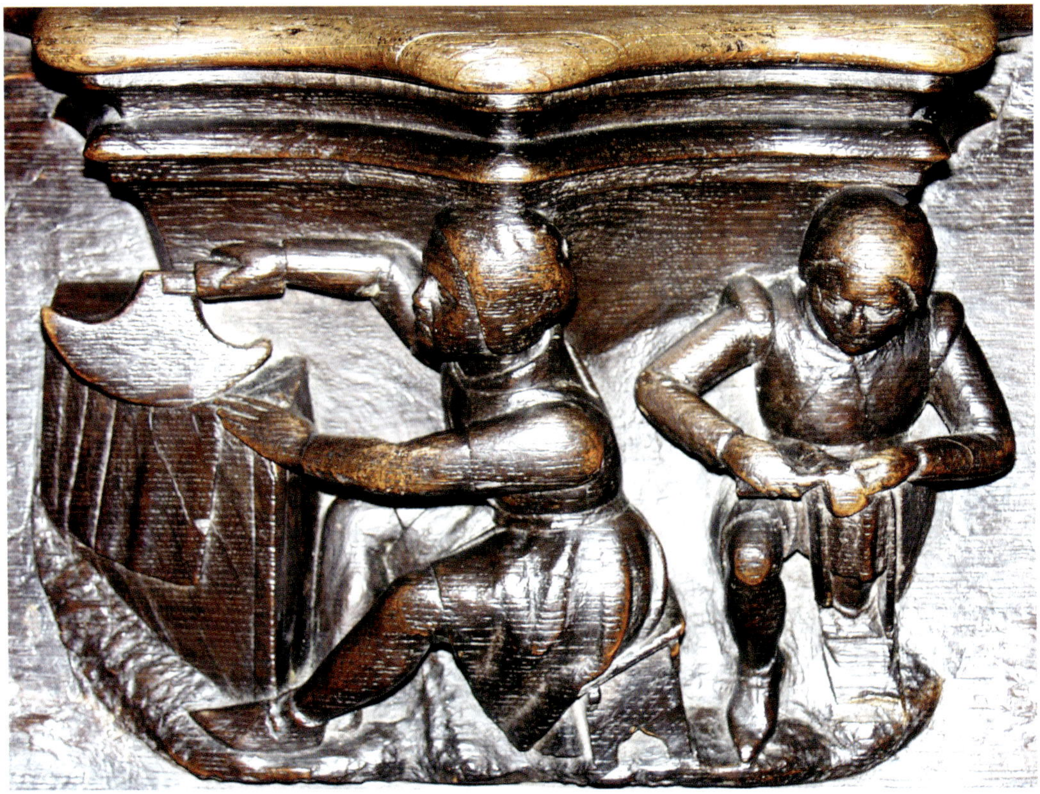

FIGURE 11. Rouen Cathedral, France, Misericord, 1457–1470 (photo: Elaine C. Block).

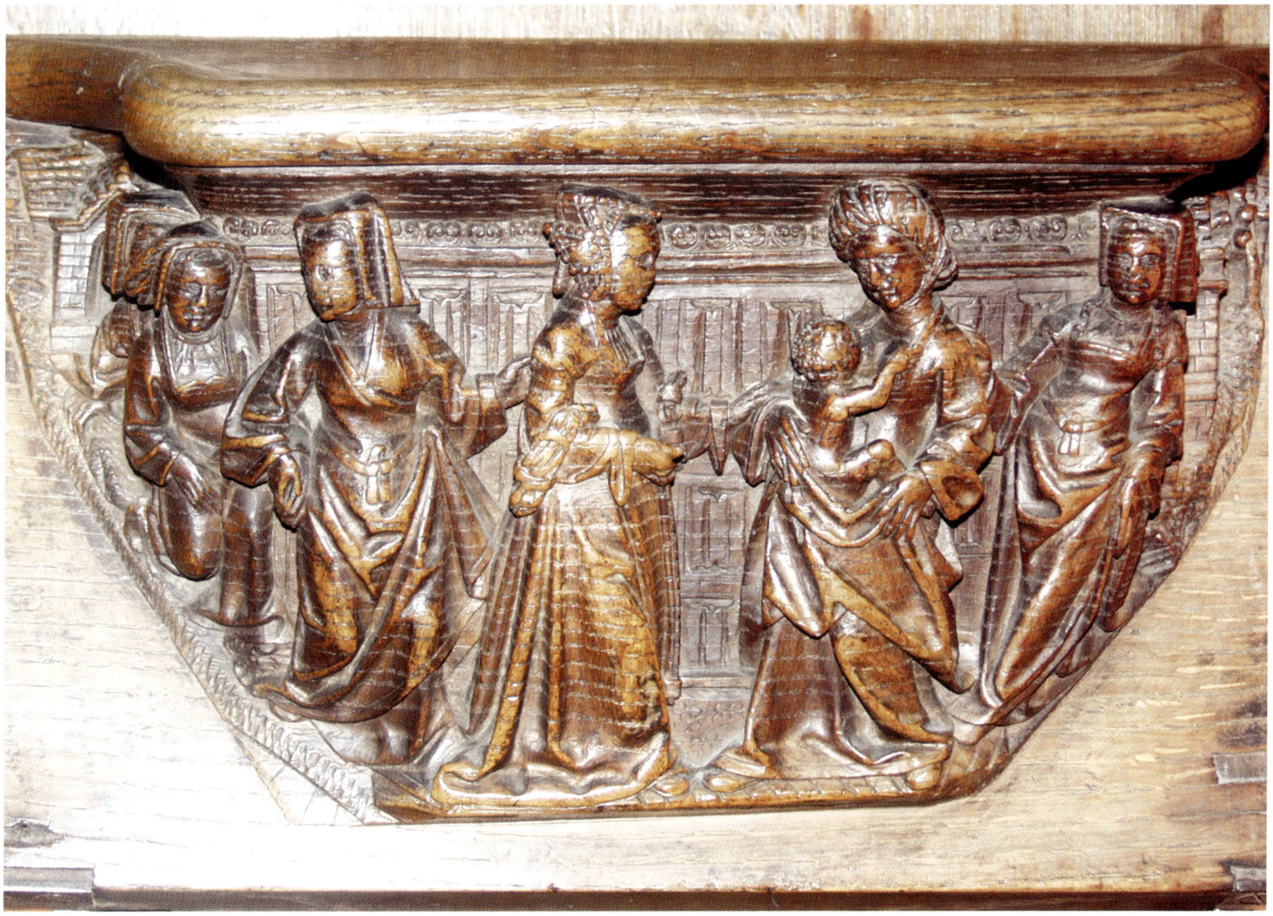

FIGURE 12. Amiens Cathedral, France, Misericord, 1508 (photo: Elaine C. Block).

of the sculpture also improved, although in some rare cases it looks like the work on the misericords and armrests might have been left to the apprentices, while the master was in charge of larger groups of figures in high relief, and in the most prominent *jouées.*[20] The quality varies from one set to another but there are some sculptural gems (Fig. 12), and it is clear from the detail of many that they were considered important works.

The iconography of misericords is varied, but it is also clear that certain themes predominate. This is certainly true of the many musicians that are depicted on misericords and that are described by Frédéric Billiet elsewhere in this volume.[21]

"Profane" Iconography and the Importance of Misericords

Satirical scenes are found repeatedly on these works. There are also numerous carvings throughout Europe of exhibitionists and figures defecating (Figs. 13–14). In addition, many scenes deride and mock the clergy and include, for example, a fox preaching to geese or

20. This was probably the case for stalls in Flavigny-sur-Ozerain (Côte d'Or, Burgundy, dating from the end of the 15th century).

21. Frédéric Billiet has written several articles on music and musical instruments in the mediaeval stalls. See, for example, "La représentation de la musique dans les stalles médiévales européennes," *Musiques et arts plastiques, quels rapports?* (Paris, 2000), 9–20.

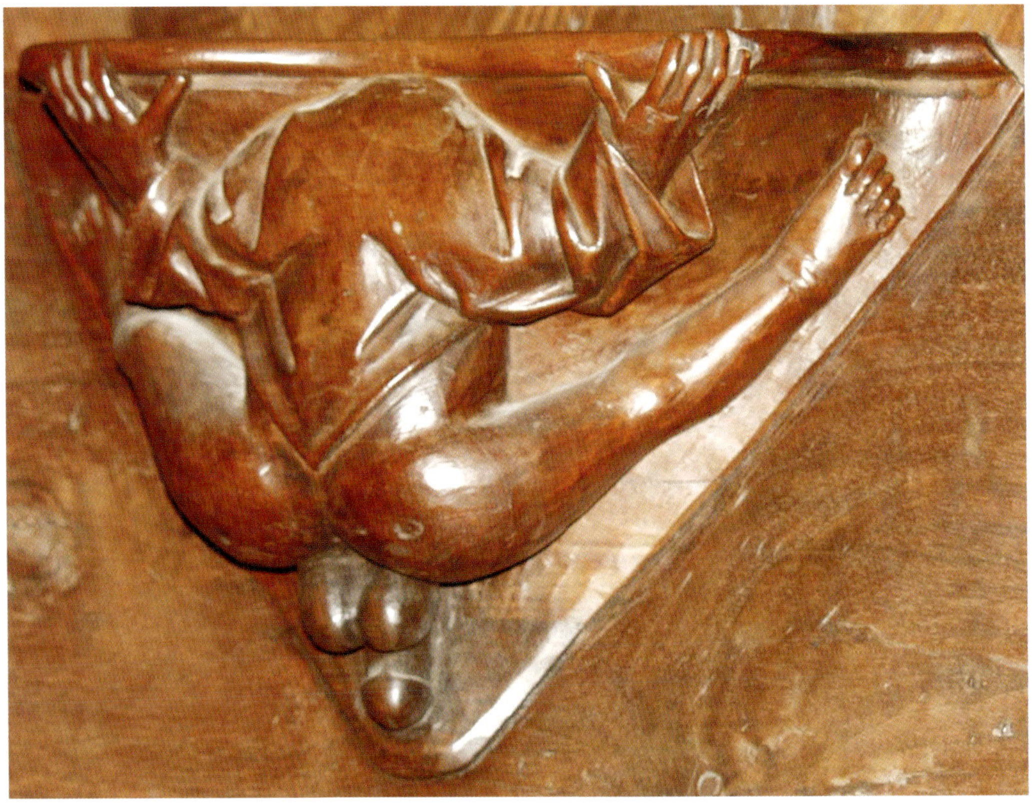

FIGURE 13. Najera Abbey, Spain, Misericord, 1493–1495 (photo: Elaine C. Block).

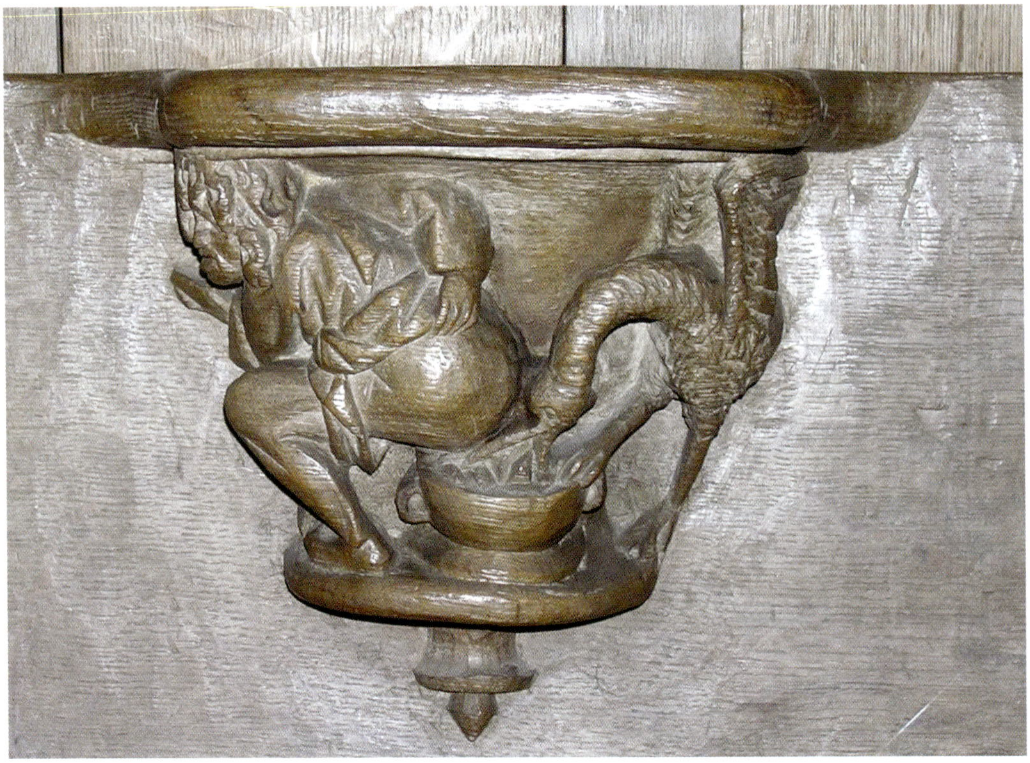

FIGURE 14. Church of St. Materne, Walcourt, Belgium, Misericord, 1510–1520 (photo: Elaine C. Block).

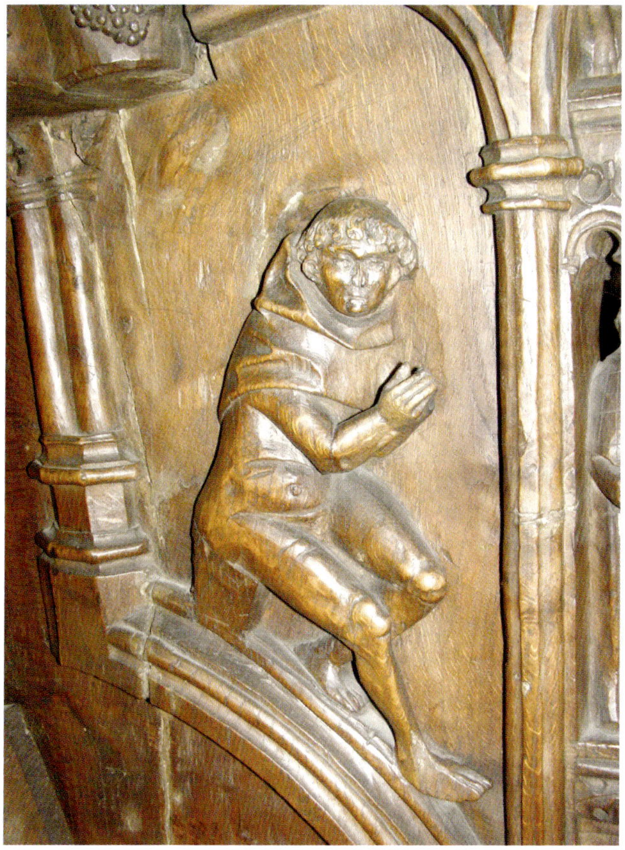

FIGURE 15. Church of St. Mary, Aarschot, Belgium, Armrest, 1500 (photo: author).

chickens;[22] there are also defrocked or naked monks (Fig. 15), monkeys dressed as monks,[23] and priests seducing women.[24] The question arises as to why this kind of scene was allowed in such a sacred place as the choir, which was closed and forbidden to the laity in the Middle Ages until the Council of Trent in 1562.[25] How were scatological scenes and the mockery of religion allowed to co-exist in a space that was devoted to the clergy, and was located in such an important place as the apse, with the altar nearby?

Several art historians have addressed this problem. H. and D. Kraus have suggested that the more trivial scenes were explained by their location under the buttocks of the monks or canons, and asserted, without stating why, that religious scenes were banned from the misericords. In fact, there are religious scenes on misericords (more numerous in the sixteenth century than earlier). Profane scenes are not always trivial or vulgar and they may represent crafts, proverbs, or scenes from popular tales and fables. It is clear however that ridiculing the religious was not simply the work of anticlerical carvers, but may instead have reflected antagonisms between various monastic orders, particularly the hostility between the "old" orders, such as the Benedictines, and the more recently established mendicant orders whose "success" was particularly important in the thirteenth and fourteenth centuries.[26] For example, relations between the Benedictines and the mendicant orders were particularly strained in Flanders in the late fifteenth and early sixteenth centuries. This perhaps explains the many monkey-like monks and the other monks ridiculed in the Flemish stalls.

Michael Camille suggested that the profane iconography of misericords is explained by the fact that only the clergy had access to the choir: in effect, it was mostly confined so that the laity could not see it. Through the doors of the rood screen, they could see groups in high relief, and *jouées* (panels in low relief) facing the nave. Also, according to Camille, profane scenes that developed on the misericords were popularized among the clergy by their physical location of being placed literally "under" the monks or canons who sat on them. This iconography was thus the result of a process of "belittling." The popular scenes, crafts, and illustrations of fables were belittled beneath the buttocks of the clergy. As Camille points out, the few religious scenes represented are not primarily

22. Fox preaching to geese is a classic iconography of the stalls; it is found in almost every country in Europe.

23. Especially in the Burgundian Netherlands.

24. This last example seems to be specifically Spanish and Portuguese, because no other examples are found.

25. Bernard Chedozeau has shown that the choirs of almost all religious buildings (except chapels and in little parish churches) were closed in the Middle Ages, but the decisions taken at the Council of Trent led to an opening of the choir and thus the destruction of many rood screens. *Chœur clos, chœur ouvert, de l'église médiévale à l'église tridentine* (Paris, 1998).

26. Relations with the mendicant orders were particularly strained in Flanders in the late 15th and early 16th century. This perhaps explains the many monkey-monks and the other monk figures ridiculed in the Flemish's stalls.

Christological, but episodes from the Old Testament that would have been be ranked lower than the New Testament. Of course this is not a hard and fast rule and at Auxerre (Burgundy) and St. Gertrude of Louvain (Belgium), to name just two examples, scenes from the New Testament are found in such a context.[27]

According to the authors of *Image et Transgression au Moyen Âge*, images of sex in medieval art had an apotropaic function. This may explain the many images of genitals, sometimes anthropomorphic, that are often found on pilgrim badges.[28] Choir-stalls may be different, because the relationship between sacred space and profane iconography is stronger, as in the marginalia of religious manuscripts.

Without contradicting the ideas outlined above, I believe that the profane iconography found on misericords also places a strong emphasis on the human body. Indeed, the body is presented in all its states from work to recreation and including its bodily functions of defecating. In fact, the main function of the misericord was precisely to relieve the body. In this context, the concept of the body as an entity entirely devoted to prayer and worship, in which humans seek to elevate their minds to the divine and to save their souls, would be entirely logical. This would have been perfectly logical in the Middle Ages, at which time many theologians, such as Maximus the Confessor and Nicolas of Cusa, asserted the importance of balancing the three "planes": the body, mind, and soul. Further research is needed on the religious iconography, but it is clear that the Annunciation is a recurring theme,[29] and this can possibly be interpreted as an indication of the carvers' interest in the incarnation of Christ's body, and as such a new expression of ideas about the body.

Bakhtin emphasized that the human body in medieval thought is related to the cosmic and universal world. Accordingly, the body, including its most "grotesque" aspects, has a privileged relationship with the subtle universe.[30] In this context, the images of defecators and exhibitionists in the choir stalls are less surprising and may be related to this vision of the "universal" body. This universal vision of the body seems to be as characteristic of the Middle Ages as it was in the sixteenth century, when Bakhtin noted that the idea of the body entered into the private sphere and into individual psychology.[31] It was Montaigne who regretted that it was no longer possible to speak of the body in its most trivial aspects.[32] Indeed, "secular" images of the human body disappear from the iconography of choir-stall after the second half of the sixteenth century.

Thus, misericords and especially the iconography that appears upon them are significant for a better understanding of the medieval world. It may have been easier for the monks and canons to see and accept their bodies through the imagery of the misericords, all the while raising their minds to the divine altarpieces shown above. The carved stalls are, therefore, certainly important from an anthropological point of view in understanding the Middle Ages. The iconography of misericords may have been left to the initiative of the carvers,[33] but it was nonetheless of fundamental importance in the context of medieval Christianity, whose devotees sought to live their lives in perfect harmony between body, soul, and mind.

Through their aesthetic value and iconographic richness, choir-stalls play an important role in church space. They deserve equal consideration with other "major" examples of medieval sculpture, and should not be simply dismissed. Their older reputation needs to be reconsidered. They offer valuable visual evidence for medieval life and thought and it still has to be remembered that the stalls are a fundamentally important piece of liturgical furniture. This is not only true from a functional perspective, but also from the more complex range and significance of their "symbolic" language.

27. Note that these two sets have only a dogmatic iconography, from armrest to dorsals (in St. Gertrude of Louvain, because in Auxerre there remain only misericords).

28. G. Bartoleyns, P.-O. Dittmar, and V. Jolivet, *Image et Transgression au Moyen Âge* (Paris, 2008), 108–125.

29. In the Auxerre and Bruges' misericords, for example.

30. M. Bakhtin, *L'Œuvre de François Rabelais et la culture populaire au Moyen Âge et sous la Renaissance* (Paris, 1970), 316.

31. M. Bakhtin, *L'Œuvre de François Rabelais* (as in note 30), 319.

32. Montaigne, *Œuvres complètes* (Paris, 1962), 825.

33. In the rare contracts recovered, the commissioner has almost never mentioned iconographic requirements for misericords. It is sometimes said that these materials will include the usual "grotesque" images on this kind of support.

FRÉDÉRIC BILLIET

Choir-Stall Carvings: A Major Source for the Study of Medieval Musical Iconography

Introduction

THANKS to the unrivalled photographic archive of images of choir-stalls amassed by Elaine C. Block, it has been possible to identify approximately one thousand scenes in which musical subjects are shown.[1] These medieval images, dating from the beginning of the fourteenth to the middle of the sixteenth centuries, have been catalogued and analyzed in the *Musicastallis* database.[2] This paper hopes to show the value of such small works as these choir-stalls in the study of medieval music and to draw attention to the ways in which major finds can come from what have traditionally been considered as "minor" works.

From 1330 to 1550, musical instruments were always represented with somebody playing them, be they human, animal, or hybrid characters. After the Council of Trent, they were mostly carved without human figures, as emblematic objects without realistic organological details. This represents an important division in musical iconography. The corpus of musical scenes carved on the choir-stalls is, therefore, highly important when it comes to iconographical research. But a distinction has to be made when looking at the quality of the carving. In some instances the quality is very poor, as for example on the Stendal Choir-stall (Fig. 1) where the fiddle is sketched without any visible strings. By and large, however, the quality of misericords depicting musical subjects is good and the carvers have gone to considerable care to reproduce a realistic image of the way in which the musical instrument produces sound, as on the example from Saumur (Fig. 2).

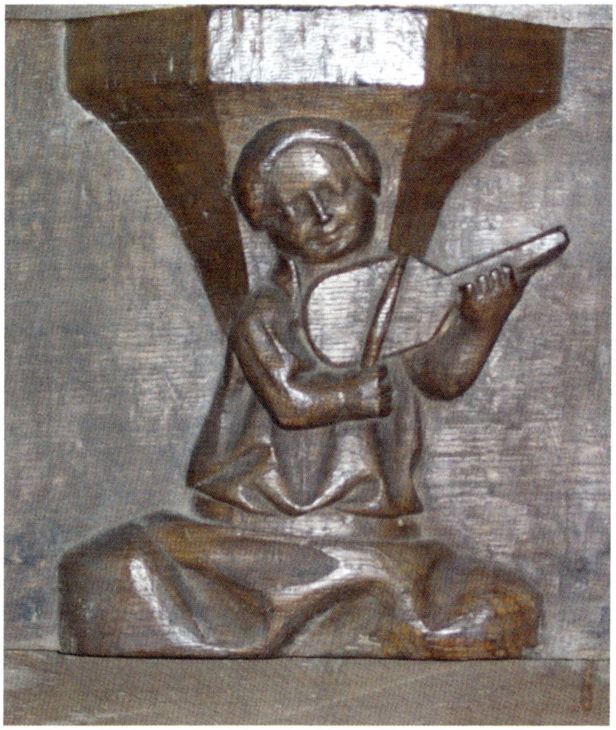

FIGURE 1. Man playing fiddle, Stendal, Dom, Germany, Misericord, 1431 (photo: Elaine C. Block).

Despite this level of detail, however, it is still not sufficient to reconstruct these lost instruments. The hurdy-gurdy played by a monkey on a misericord in Saint-Martin-aux-bois (Fig. 3) appears accurate enough (good proportions, significant details), but it is not sufficient to make a reconstruction of the instrument. The type of wood, thickness of the various parts, type of string, as well as the internal parts of the soundbox, all

1. The Elaine C. Block Database of Medieval Misericords, has been catalogued and digitized by The Index of Christian Art in Princeton University, http://ica.princeton.edu/misericordia/index.php.

2. The *Musicastallis* database is based at the Université Paris-Sorbonne, http://www.plm.paris-sorbonne.fr/musicastallis.

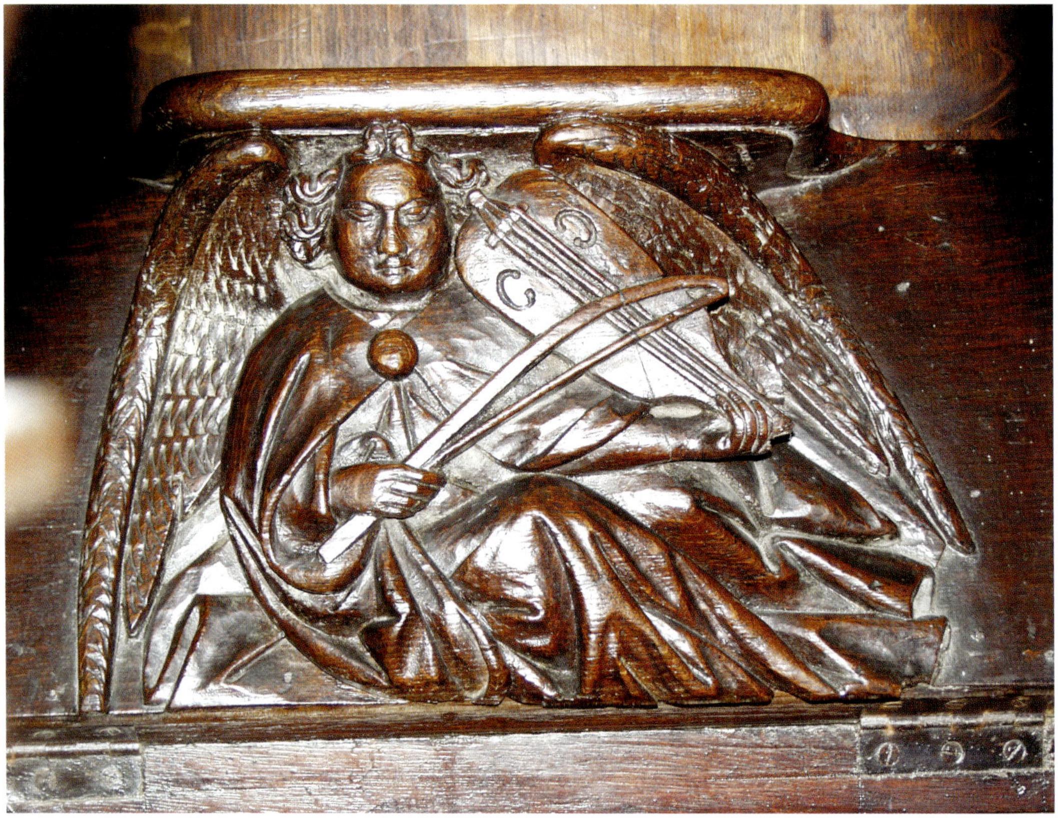

FIGURE 2. Angel playing fiddle, Saumur, Eglise Saint-Pierre, France, Misericord, *c.* 1475 (photo: author).

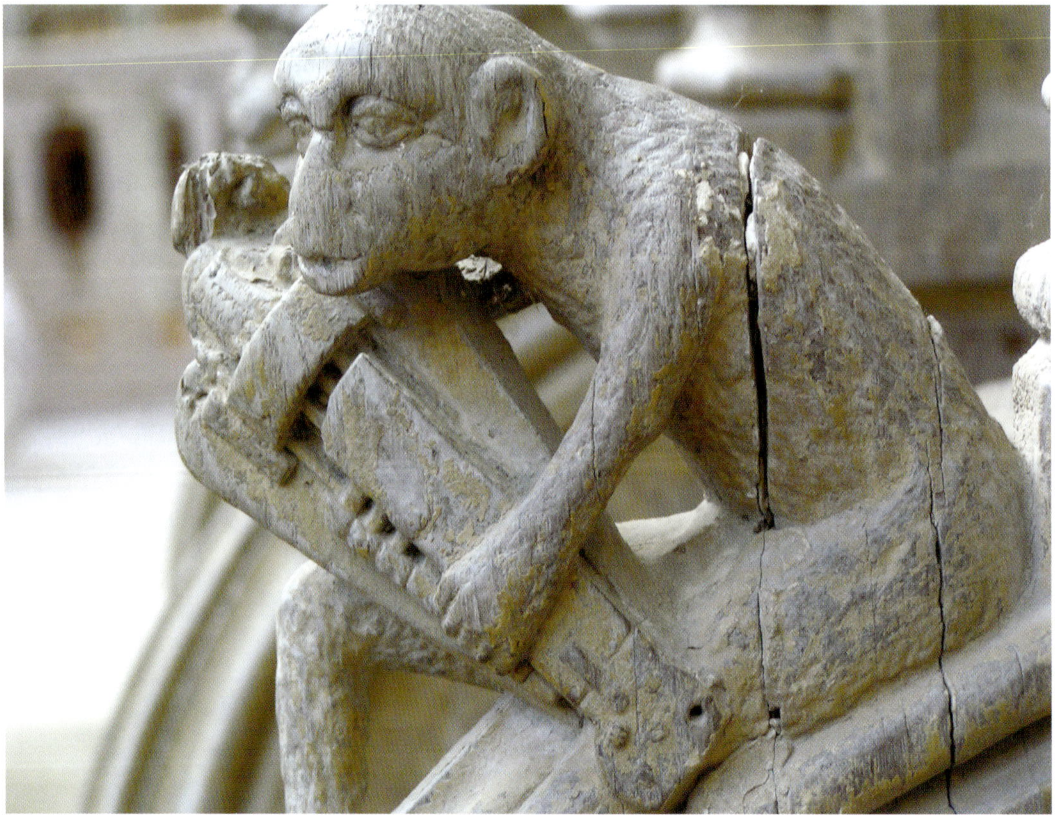

FIGURE 3. Monkey with hurdy-gurdy, Saint-Martin-aux-Bois, Abbatiale, France, Armrest, *c.* 1492–1500 (photo: author).

are subject to experimentation in the reconstruction of stringed instruments (Figs. 3 and 4).

Many of the details on these works are engaging because they give the modern scholar an idea of the sound of the medieval instruments, and such is the case with the triangle fitted with jangling rings on the example from Breda (Fig. 5). Another example is the Gothic harp shown with pegs between the soundbox and the strings. These are called "harpions" and they make the harp strings sound *nasarder* (nasal), in order to amplify and enrich the basic sound of the strings (Figs. 6 and 7).

These details, along with the representation of the musician in a dynamic posture with an instrument ready to play, show that the intention of the carvers was to give to the viewer the illusion of listening to music.

These few preliminary remarks explain why the art of choir-stall carving is important for the musicologist, especially on five levels of research, which I would now like to enumerate.

1. *Choir-Stalls as Musical Space*

Choir-stalls, which are iconographically similar to the illustrated margins of sacred chant books, were built for singing. Although they were conceived as simple, folding seats for the performance of psalmody, they became part of an enclosed musical space in the choir that was used to keep the chanting isolated from the noise of pilgrims and other clerical activities. The dorsal panels of these chairs act as walls and, along with the dais, serve as *abat-sons*, or sound louvers, which are very useful to help control the sound of the singing voices within the wider church (Fig. 8).[3]

The choir-stalls in effect acted as a soundbox for the chanting and it is, therefore, interesting to observe the positions of the singers within this configuration: psalmodic intonation sounded from the high stalls while singers of the *schola* gathered in the middle of the choir-stalls around the lectern with their voices directed toward the altar. This distribution within the

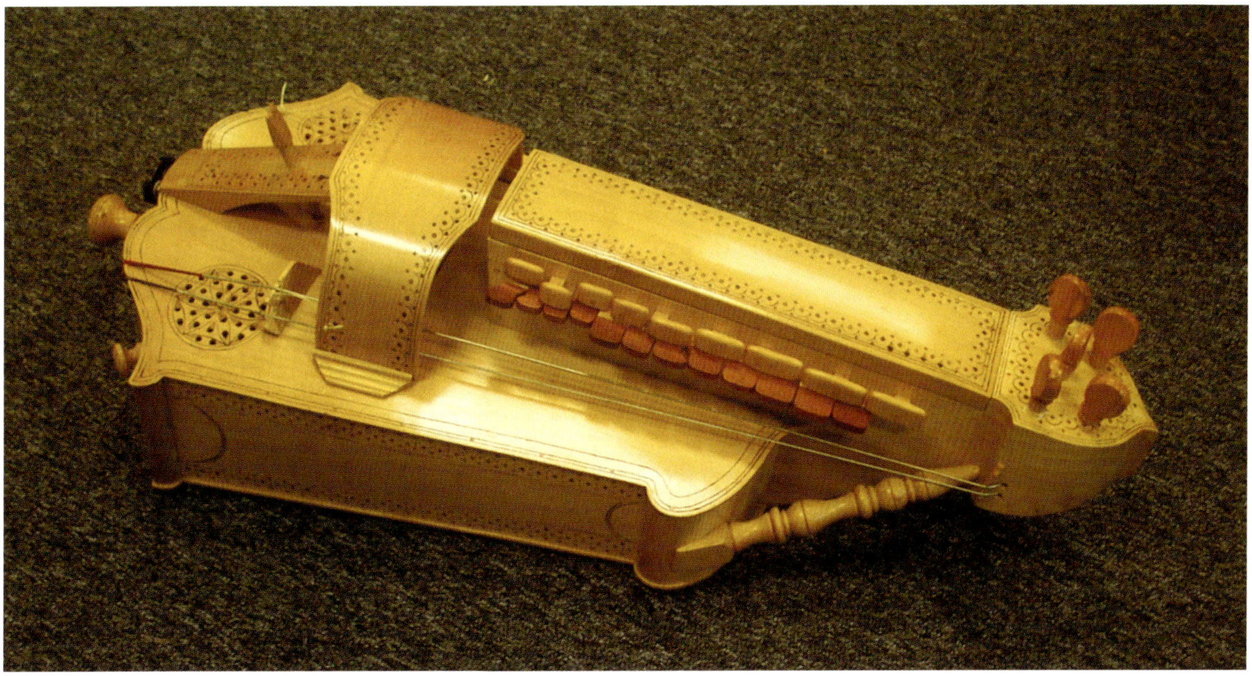

FIGURE 4. Hurdy-gurdy built by the luthier Jean Carton, 1985, private collection (photo: author).

3. Frédéric Billiet, "Un mobilier pour le chant: la vie musicale dans les stalles de la cathédrale d'Amiens," in *Actes du colloque de l'Université d'Amiens et de Rouen* (Amiens: Encrage, 2002).

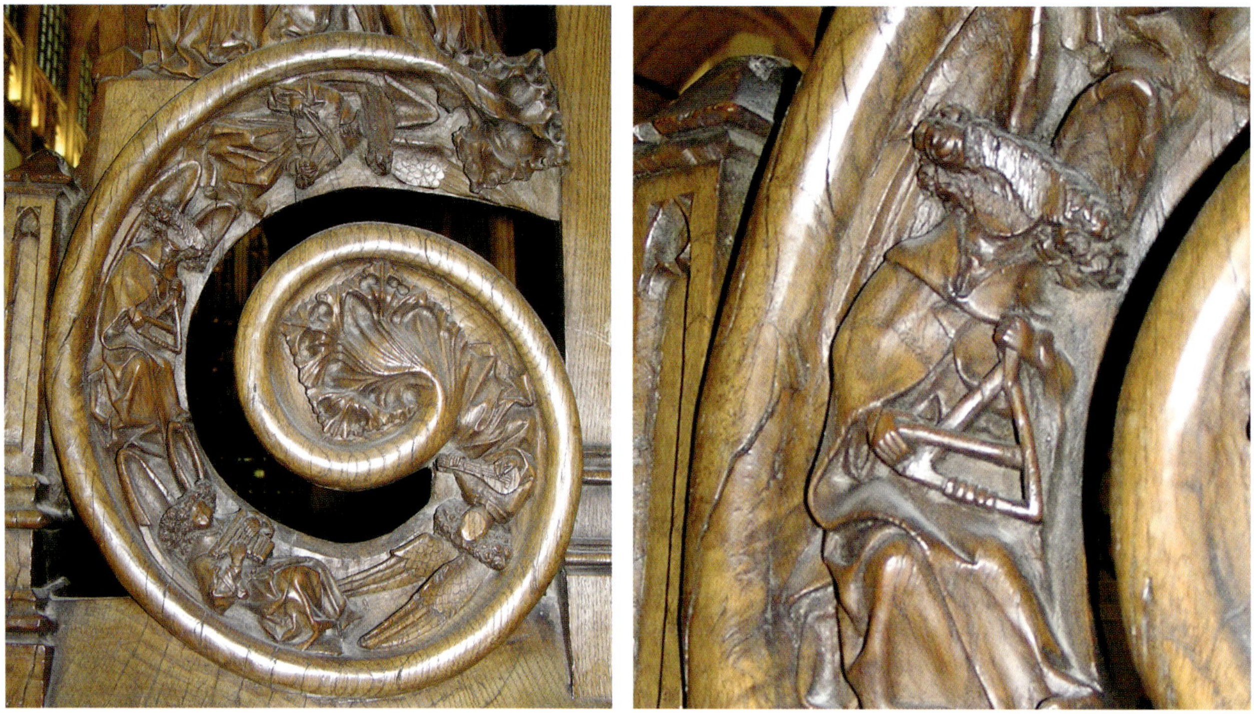

FIGURE 5. Angel with triangle, Breda Cathedral, Netherlands, *Jouée*, *c.* 1440–1460 (photo: author).

ensemble can be verified, in some cases, by the names of singers or instrumentalists engraved on the dorsals of the seats.[4] An exhaustive list of these names would of course help to complete the biographies of singers or composers, and to trace their movement throughout Europe from one church to another, but such a work has yet to be undertaken.

2. *Choir-Stall Carvings as Sources of Information on Medieval Instruments*

Musicologists can easily discover all the organological details that help in the reconstruction of lost instruments in these choir-stalls. However, these observations have to be combined with information from other sources, such as descriptions from treatises and other archival material. Such research is of considerable importance for performers of medieval music, who need to recreate the instruments on which to play early music.

3. *Choir-Stall Carvings as a Source of Information for Medieval Performance*

Not only can these small carvings provide us with details of the actual instruments or where they were played, but they also show how pieces were performed. One such carving, on a seat in a stall in Burgos Cathedral (Spain, *c.* 1550), shows a group of singers and is especially detailed. Here, the music master puts his hand on one of the three children's heads, as he points with his baguette to the musical notes that are represented on a manuscript resting on a large lectern. Three adults seem to lend their voices to this musical performance and it is clear that what we have here is an image of how singing was undertaken in the *schola* (Fig. 9).

Some scenes clearly depict, as in manuscripts, the improvisation called *cantus super librum*, which involved three or four singers gathered around a lectern. One of them makes the others feel the *tactus* or beat by

4. Frédéric Billiet, "Témoignages insolites dans le choeur des églises européennes (XVe–XVIe)," in *Histoire, humanisme et hymnologie* (Presses universitaires de Paris-Sorbonne, 1998), 47–56.

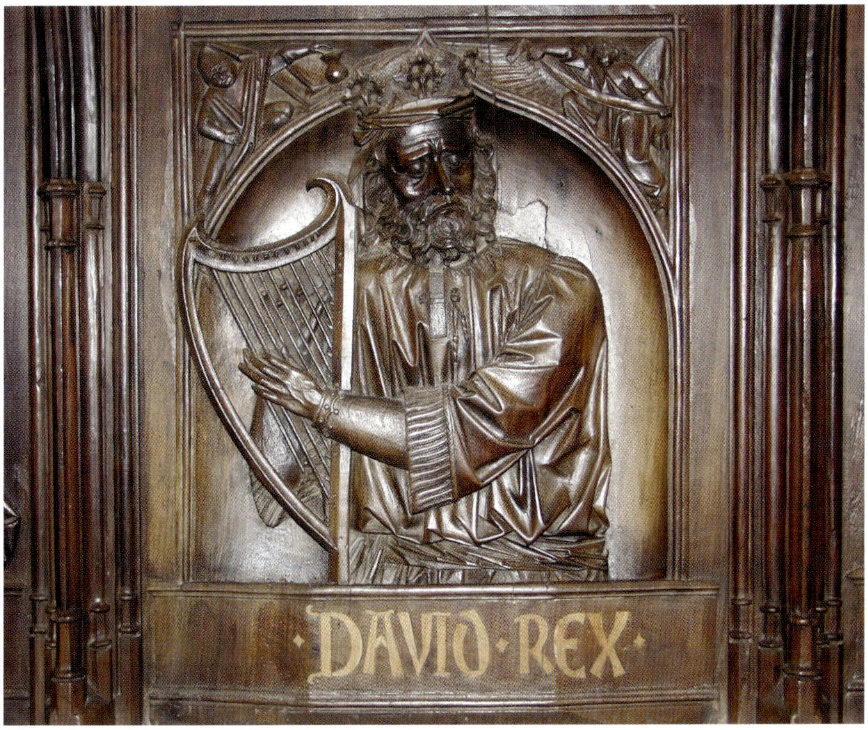

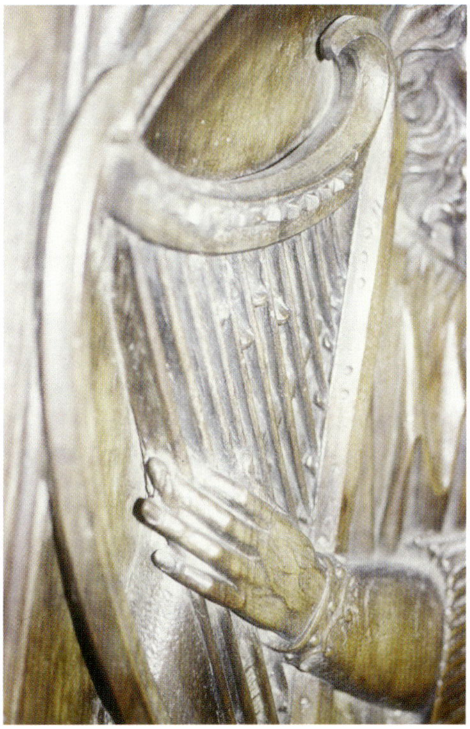

FIGURES 6–7. David Rex and detail, Leon Cathedral, Spain, Dorsal, 1461–1481, (photo: author).

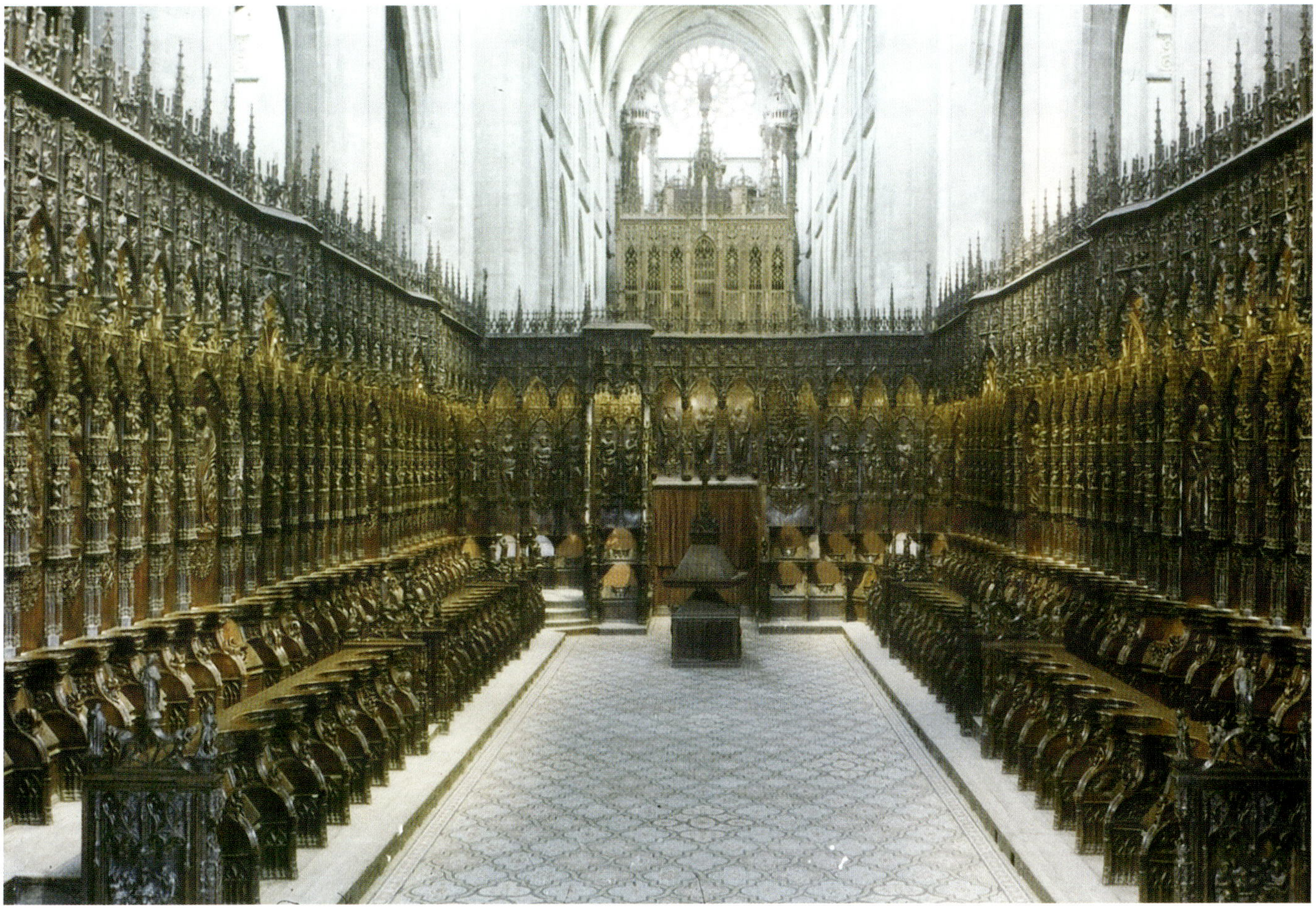

FIGURE 8. Auch Cathedral, France, Choir-stalls, 1540–1559 (photo: Elaine C. Block).

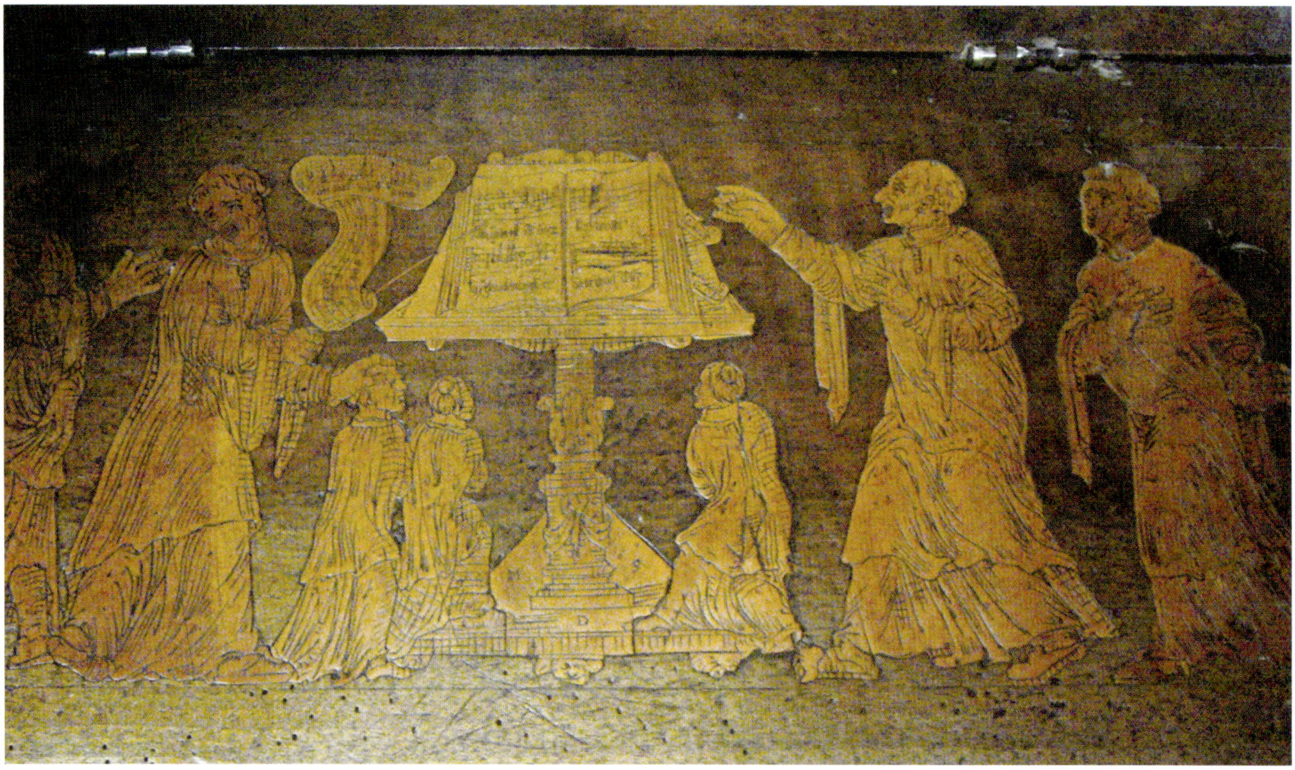

FIGURE 9. Marquetry, Burgos Cathedral, Spain, Misericord, sixteenth century (photo: author).

tapping on his neighbor's shoulder with his hand, so as to make all sing in polyphony from a book in which only one voice is notated (Fig. 10). This way of singing is similar to the traditional Corsican polyphonic method that was recorded by ethnomusicologists in 1977 in the small village of Rusiu.[5]

Cathedral choir singers, however, did not always use their voices in a way that was completely devoted to God, and some scenes show unruly behavior, thereby warning singers against possible excesses that need to be fought on a daily basis. Bishops frequently condemned the lifestyles of the clerical singers. Some misericords acted as warnings to clerics who spent too much time in taverns in much the same way that Veronese set his elaborate feast of the *Wedding at Cana* in a monastic refectory in order to highlight the sin of gluttony.[6] Another particularly colorful example is found in Spain on a misericord in the cathedral at Ciudad Rodrigo, which was carved by Rodrigo Aleman in 1498. It shows three singers gathered around a wine skin, singing from a manuscript with *vino puro* clearly visible in Figure 11.

4. *Choir-Stall Carvings as a Source of Information for Musical Repertoire*

With very few exceptions—such as the choir-stalls at Beverley Minster in England[7] or in Burgos Cathedral in Spain—it is nearly impossible to find representations of musical notation. Nevertheless, by observing musical gestures, it is still possible to discern from choir-stalls whether the figures represented are shown playing aca-

5. Corsica, *Religious Music of Oral Tradition from Rusiu* (CD-Audivis Unesco, 1977).

6. The piece was commissioned in 1562 by the Benedictine monastery of San Giorgio Maggiore in Venice, Italy.

7. Frédéric Billiet, "Le Magnificat dans les Stalles de Beverley," in *Grant risee? The Medieval Comic Presence / La Présence comique médiévale: Essays in Memory of Brian J. Levy* (Turnhout: Brepols, 2006), 347–356.

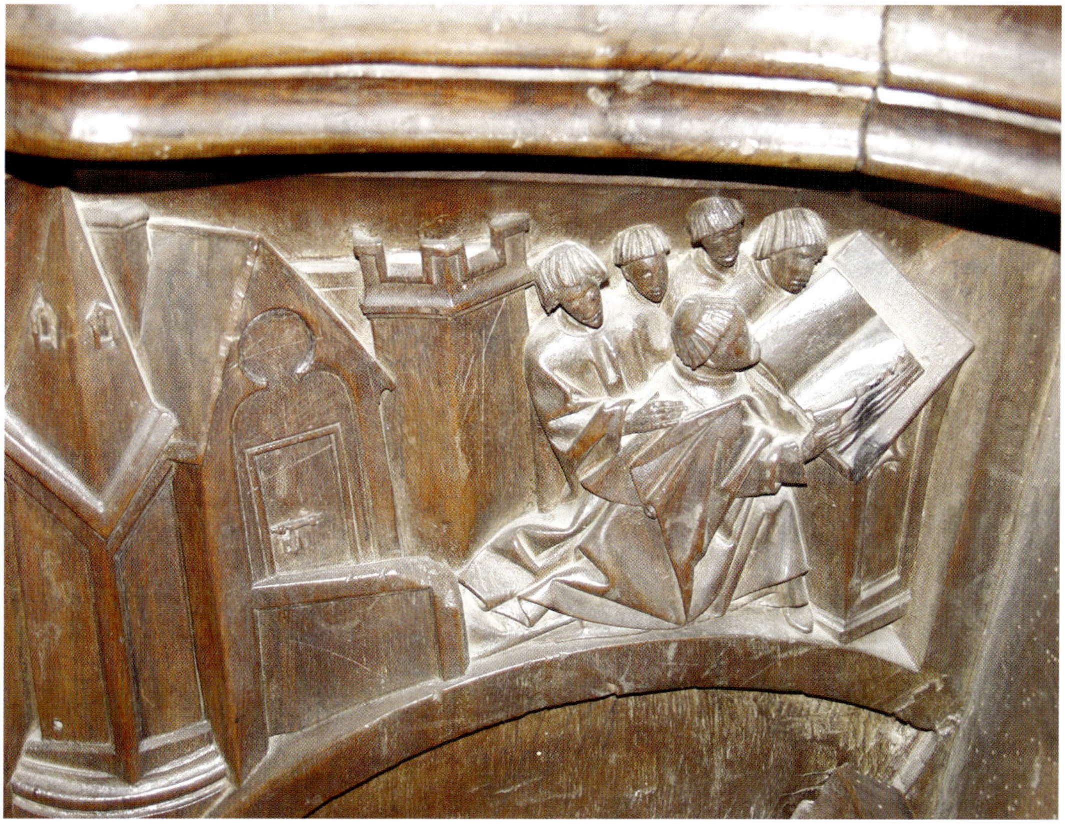

FIGURE 10. *Cantus super librum*, Leon Cathedral, Spain, *Jouée*, 1461–1481 (photo: author).

demic or traditional music. Such an analysis is now possible thanks to recent ethnomusicological studies. Jean During, for instance, has shown in his study "Hand Made" that the type of music played depends on the way the instrument is held.[8] When music was difficult to play, the best solution seems to have been to carry the instrument on the shoulder; by contrast, when it was easier to play, the instrument was held at a lower level with the fretboard toward the ground.

Ideas such as this have to be considered when looking at examples from the *Musicastallis* database. In looking at how the lute was played, it is important to see the different postures of the players. When played with a plectrum, it is usually popular music, whereas from the beginning of the sixteenth century, plucking a lute with all the fingers is usually indicative of academic music,

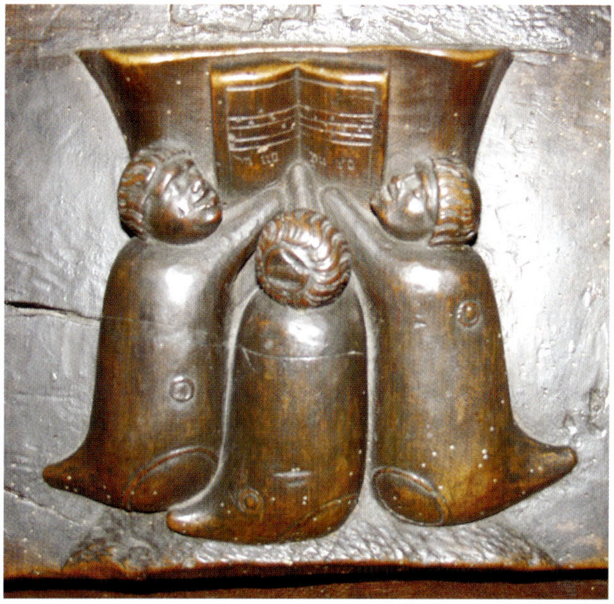

FIGURE 11. *Vino puro*, Ciudad Rodrigo Cathedral, Spain, *Jouée*, 1498, (photo: author).

8. Jean During, "Hand Made. Pour une anthropologie du geste musical," *Cahiers de musiques traditionnelles* (Geneva, 2001), no. 14, 39–68.

for which specific notations called tablatures still exist. These and many other such details on choir-stalls can help scholars discover in greater depth the music that was played at various events.

5. *Choir-Stall Carvings as an Important Aid to Iconological Analysis*

Despite their small scale and pejorative classification as a "minor" art, it is clear that choir-stall carvings are a treasure-house of information for various fields of research. When confronted with any of these choir-stall images, it is important to ask a number of questions. What is the meaning of this image? What did this image tell the canons about music? Are such images scientifically accurate, or are they simply warnings, caricatures, parts of a proverb, or symbolic of an upside-down world where animals played music instead of humans? These questions reveal a great deal about a misericord in the choir-stall of Château-Gaillon, which was part of a set carved for Cardinal Georges d'Amboise at the start of the sixteenth century.[9] This example seems to represent a concert of *menestriers* (wandering minstrels) with "bas-" or chamber-instruments. This interpretation would be anachronistic because we know that the "concert," as a social organization with music as its focus, was in reality founded in Paris in 1570, so this work, carved in 1520, shows five or six musicians represented for another purpose (Fig. 12).

On the left, there is a man playing a small lute with

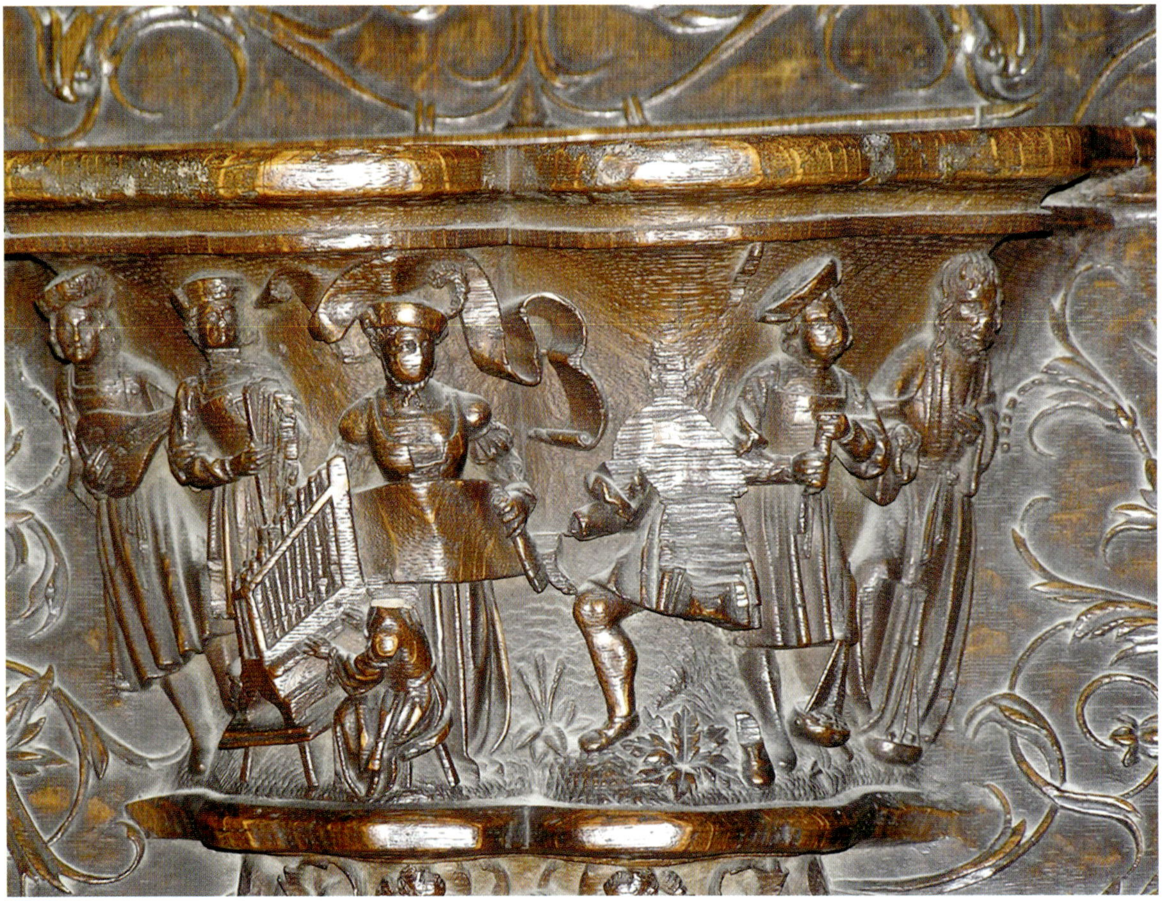

FIGURE 12. *Musica*, Basilica of Saint-Denis, France, Misericord, sixteenth century (photo: author).

9. These Choirstalls of Château-Gaillon are now at Saint-Denis to the north of Paris.

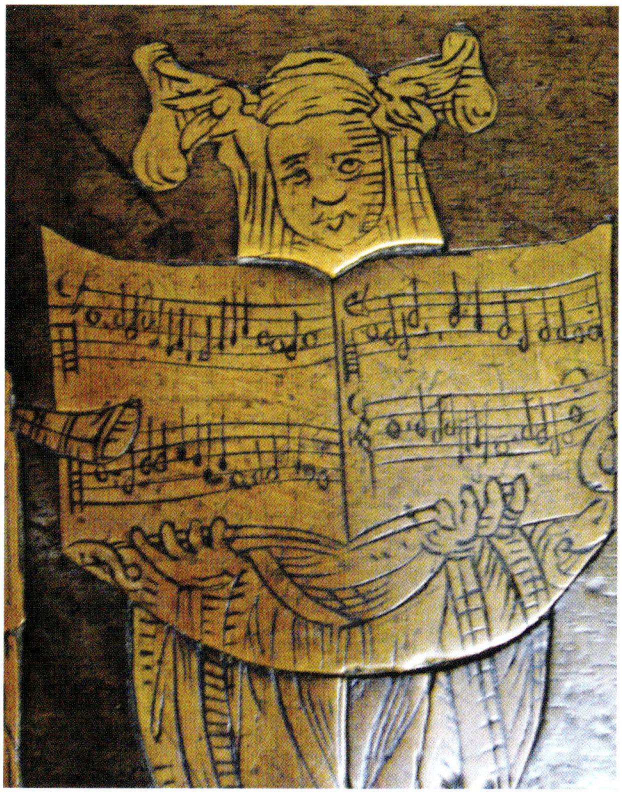

FIGURE 13. Singers, Burgos Cathedral, Spain, Misericord, sixteenth century (photo: author).

four strings. Next to him, there is another instrumentalist playing a harp (now damaged). While the next character, whose head has been lost, plays on a small positive organ of sixteen pipes, although no one is shown operating the bellows. Curiously, the bass pipes are situated on the right side of the instrument, an unusual arrangement that is also found on misericords at Saint-Chamant (France) and Tavalera (Spain). The next figure, a woman holding a scroll that may originally have been painted with musical notation, offers the musical score to the musicians, as in the example at Burgos (Fig. 13). The next figure is too damaged to identify whether it represents a musician or a dancer. On the right is shown a woodwind instrumentalist. The instrument is damaged, but the player's cheeks are inflated and his fingers are on the pipe's holes. At the far right of the misericord, another man is visible.

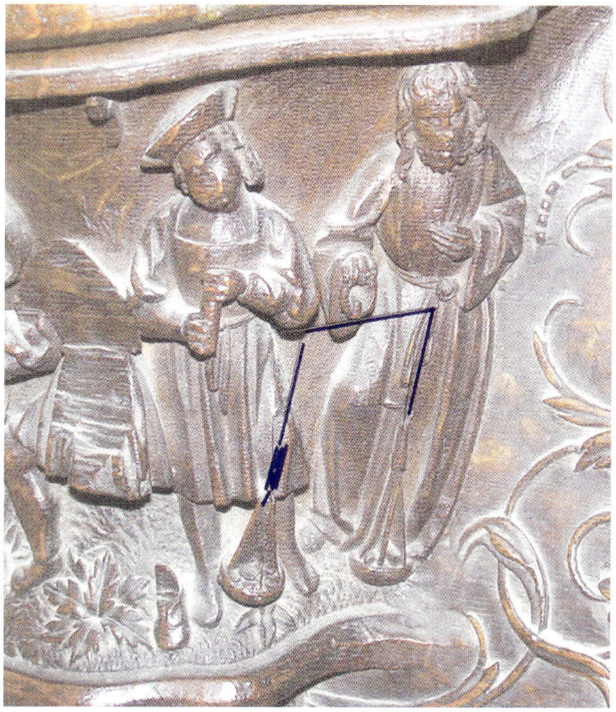

FIGURE 14. *Musica*, Basilica of Saint-Denis, France, Misericord (detail), sixteenth century (photo: author).

He is not playing music but instead holds a balance that is outlined in Figure 14. This figure is the key to understanding the scene depicted.

In fact, this is not a concert of "bas-instruments" of the type that could have been heard in Château-Gaillon, but rather an allegory of *Musica* as one of the arts of the *Quadrivium*. Music as the art of measure and proportion is symbolized here by the scales and instrumentalists. The Cardinal Georges d'Ambroise may probably have asked for this musical allegory to be represented here, as it is described in a book from his private library, Gregor Reisch's *Margarita philosphica*, published in Strasbourg in 1504, some four years before he commissioned the choir-stall.

This small carving must also be considered within the broader worldview prevalent at the end of the Middle Ages. Here, music is represented as one of the Liberal Arts, whereas in many other choir-stalls it is usually symbolic of Heaven or Hell.[10] To understand fully

10. Frédéric Billiet, "Diabolus in musica dans les stalles médiévales: significations du désordre musical," *Profane Images in Marginal Arts of the Middle Ages* (Turnhout: Brepols, 2009), PAMA no. 2, 315–338.

these small carvings, it is of course also necessary to integrate their study in the broader picture of medieval studies. We can only fully understand their value when they are compared and contrasted to such images as are found in medieval treatises, poetry, stained glass, sculpture, metalwork, etc. To this end, scholars at Paris-Sorbonne University and at the Centre de Civilisation Médiévale in Poitiers have launched a project for a digital portal called *Musiconis*, which will hopefully enable such a dialogue between databases dedicated to medieval iconography with a particular focus on the study of early music.

In this general overview, I hope that I have shown how the art of carving on choir-stalls is particularly interesting for understanding the world of musical iconography, and how it can reveal significant details about the instruments and the way music was played and performed.

INDEX

INDEX

(*Italic numbers indicate text illustrations*)

F

G

H

I

PRINTED AND BOUND

BY

TIEN WAH PRESS, LTD., SINGAPORE

DESIGNED AND COMPOSED BY

MARK AND

SOPHIE ARGETSINGER

ROCHESTER

NEW YORK

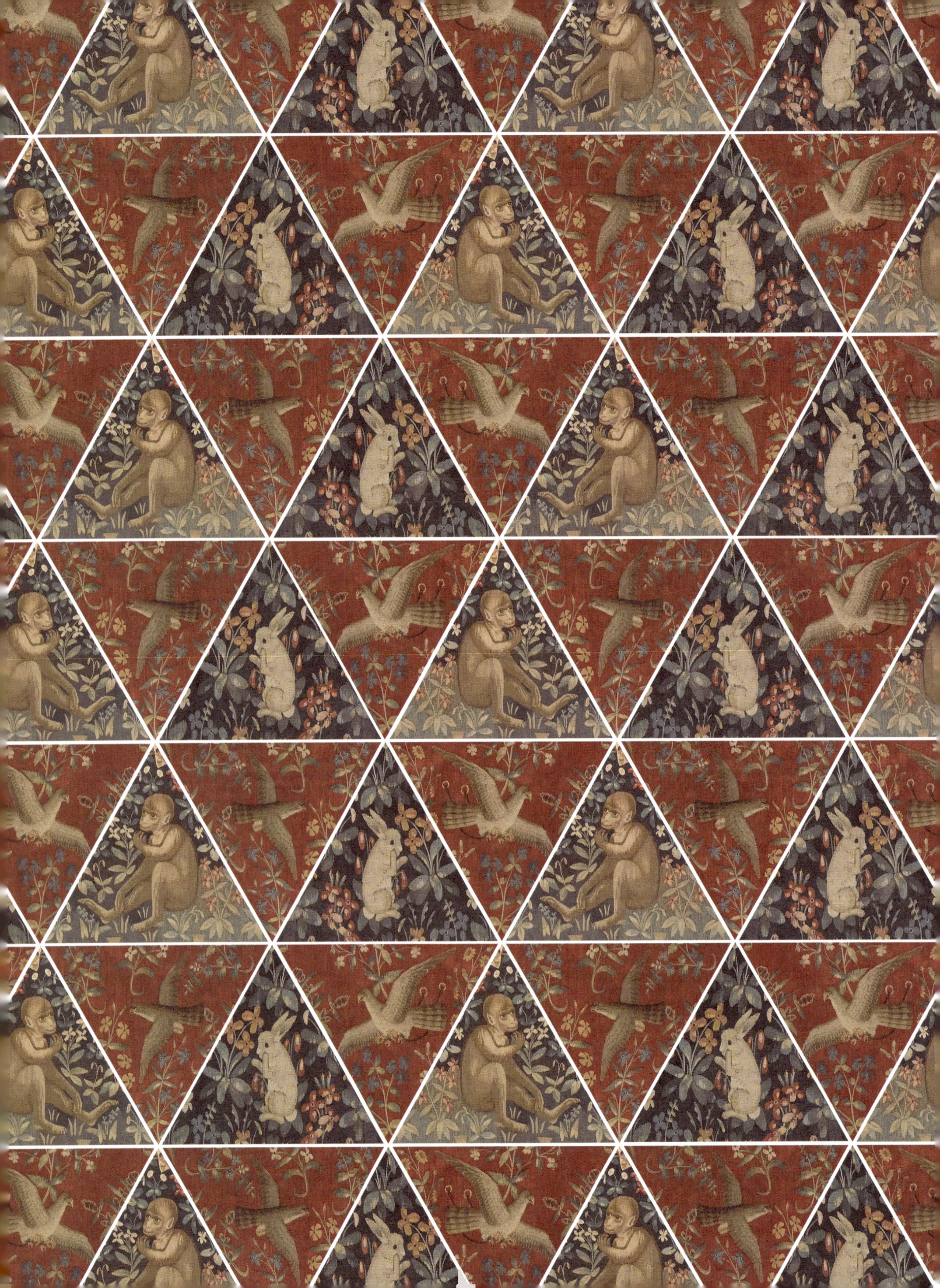